CALLIMACHUS
HECALE

CALLIMACHUS
HECALE

EDITED WITH
INTRODUCTION AND COMMENTARY
BY
A. S. HOLLIS

CLARENDON PRESS · OXFORD

Oxford University Press, Great Clarendon Street, Oxford OX2 6DP
Oxford New York
Athens Auckland Bangkok Bogota Bombay
Buenos Aires Calcutta Cape Town Dar es Salaam
Delhi Florence Hong Kong Istanbul Karachi
Kuala Lumpur Madras Madrid Melbourne
Mexico City Nairobi Paris Singapore
Taipei Tokyo Toronto Warsaw
and associated companies in
Berlin Ibadan

Oxford is a trade mark of Oxford University Press

Published in the United States by
Oxford University Press Inc., New York

British Library Cataloguing in Publication Data
Data available

Library of Congress Cataloging in Publication Data
Callimachus : Hecale / edited with introduction and commentary by
A. S. Hollis
Bibliography. Includes indexes.
1. Theseus (Greek mythology)—Poetry. I. Hollis, A. S.
(Adrian Swayne) II. Title. III. Title: Hecale.
PA3945.A5 1989 881'.01—dc20 89–16041
ISBN 0–19–814044–4

1 3 5 7 9 10 8 6 4 2

Printed in Great Britain
on acid-free paper by
Bookcraft (Bath) Ltd.,
Midsomer Norton

To
SPENCER BARRETT

for his seventy-fifth birthday

PREFACE

Two previous works have been devoted entirely to Callimachus' *Hecale*, by A. F. Naeke (*Callimachi Hecale*, 1845) and Ida Kapp (*Callimachi Hecalae Fragmenta*, 1915). The other most important landmarks for study of this poem in modern times are A. Hecker's *Commentationes Callimacheae* (1842), O. Schneider's *Callimachea* (vol. ii, *Fragmenta*, 1873), the great edition of Callimachus by R. Pfeiffer (vol. i, *Fragmenta*, 1949), and, for post-Pfeiffer discoveries, *Supplementum Hellenisticum* (edd. Lloyd-Jones and Parsons, 1983). Each successive editor was able to add at least a few fragments culled from ancient or Byzantine grammarians and lexicographers. In 1877–8 help began to come from a different quarter with the discovery in Egypt of a wooden board (the 'Vienna Tablet') containing four columns of our poem; now augmented by later papyri, this remains the most substantial source for the *Hecale*. Kapp, Pfeiffer and *S. H.* were able to use further papyri, including the one found at Tebtunis in 1934 which gave us the poem's first line and a brief prose summary (or *Diegesis*) of the plot.

As far as is known, the remaining unpublished Oxyrhynchus papyri contain no more of the *Hecale*, although some tiny fragment may have escaped notice there or in another collection. So this seems an appropriate time to offer a fairly detailed account of our present state of knowledge concerning the poem, together with the evidence (e.g. apparent imitations in later Greek and Roman poets) which may perhaps facilitate future progress. Although I have not been able to use any new papyri, fresh consideration of old ones has yielded some results. It seems to me that quite a number of plausible new suggestions can be made about the context and linking of individual fragments, but I have generally confined such conjectures to the apparatus criticus and the Commentary. I hope that I have distinguished clearly enough (though one wearies of the word 'perhaps') between established fact and speculation, and not impeded advances by others. It is reasonable to hope for continuing small accretions from some fuller manuscript of a grammatical treatise, lexicon or scholiast on another work; there may be yet more of the *Hecale* in Suidas (see below, Appendix V), and, if we had a complete text of the poem, I am sure that we should recognize more allusions in Hesychius too. But, for substantial progress, we need new papyri of the *Hecale* itself; as well as Egypt, perhaps one day Herculaneum will reveal its secrets.

This book, the product of some seven years' work, was almost complete by the end of 1986 (secondary literature which I read thereafter will be represented only briefly if at all). My involvement with the *Hecale* (the subject of my first article, in *CR* 1965) goes back to a 1962–4 Oxford B.Phil. thesis which included Ovid's *Baucis and Philemon*. Many colleagues and friends have been extraordinarily generous with their help and encouragement; of course, I am entirely responsible for mistakes in the final version. Dr M. Campbell, Professor M. L. West and Mrs S. R. West read a draft of almost the whole Commentary (and bits of the Introduction and Appendices), Dr G. O. Hutchinson and Professor Hugh Lloyd-Jones the Commentary on the Vienna Tablet. My Keble colleague Mr W. S. Barrett made a deep and detailed investigation of the papyrus scholia on Thucydides which quote *Hec.* fr. 85, and also contributed penetrating ideas on a number of other problems. Mr P. J. Parsons patiently answered questions about spaces and traces in the papyri; my Christ Church Greek History tutor, Professor D. M. Lewis, corresponded about Attic demes and inscriptions. Professor K. Alpers supplied information on some readings of *Et. Gen.* cod. B. Other scholars who have kindly answered questions are Drs W. E. H. Cockle and J. R. Rea (papyri), Professor A. M. Davies (Old Persian), Dr. J. Nimmo Smith (scholia to Gregory of Nazianzus), Dr C. Sourvinou-Inwood (mythology and art), and Mr N. G. Wilson (Byzantine matters). Professor L. Lehnus is preparing an Italian edition of the *Hecale* (as well as a complete bibliography of Callimachus since 1489); we have corresponded amicably, but have not seen each other's work.

I owe a special debt to Miss R. E. Woodrow, who typed the manuscript. It was a great relief to be able to entrust such intricate work to an expert typist who also had a postgraduate degree in Classics. Corporately, I must thank the Delegates and Staff of the Oxford University Press for undertaking publication, my colleges, Keble and Pembroke, for two terms' sabbatical leave in 1986, the Craven Committee for a grant to visit Athens, and the British School whose hospitality enabled me to taste the olives of Ekáli.

A.S.H.

Keble College, Oxford
September 1987

CONTENTS

Contents

ABBREVIATIONS

This list contains details of books that are regularly referred to in the following pages by surname, title-initials, or surname and title-initials; details of books referred to by surname and short-title will be found in section III of the Select Bibliography at the end of this book.

I.   Books including Fragments of the *Hecale*

Hecker	A. Hecker, *Commentationes Callimacheae* (1842)
Kapp	Ida Kapp, *Callimachi Hecalae Fragmenta* (1915)
Naeke	A. F. Naeke, *Opuscula*, ii (1845): *Callimachi Hecale*
Pfeiffer	R. Pfeiffer, *Callimachus*, i: *Fragmenta* (1949)
Schneider	O. Schneider, *Callimachea*, ii: *Fragmenta* (1873)
SH	H. Lloyd-Jones and P. J. Parsons (eds.), *Supplementum Hellenisticum* (1983)

II.   Other Books

Bulloch, *FH*	A. W. Bulloch, *Callimachus, The Fifth Hymn* (1985)
Hopkinson, *HD*	N. Hopkinson, *Callimachus, Hymn to Demeter* (1984)
Maas, *GM*	P. Maas, *Greek Metre*, tr. H. Lloyd-Jones (1962)
McLennan, *HZ*	G. R. McLennan, *Callimachus, Hymn to Zeus* (1977)
Mineur, *HD*	W. H. Mineur, *Callimachus, Hymn to Delos* (1984)
West, *GM*	M. L. West, *Greek Metre* (1982)
Williams, *HA*	F. Williams, *Callimachus, Hymn to Apollo* (1978)

INTRODUCTION

INTRODUCTION

I. COMPOSITION OF THE *HECALE*

Only one ancient authority, a scholiast on *H*. 2. 106 (= below, Test. 1), speaks about the genesis of our poem:

ἐγκαλεῖ διὰ τούτων τοὺς cκώπτοντας αὐτὸν μὴ δύναcθαι ποιῆcαι μέγα ποίημα, ὅθεν ἠναγκάcθη ποιῆcαι τὴν Ἑκάλην.

How much trust can we place in this? ἠναγκάcθη may suggest a degree of *naïveté* in the writer, and one could adopt a sceptical attitude towards almost everything in the scholion. As Mary Lefkowitz says,[1] ancient commentators characteristically sought out particular incidents to 'explain' what poets deliberately left general and metaphorical. The old notion[2] that the *Hecale* started with a polemical prologue has been refuted by discovery of the first line (fr. 1). Perhaps indeed the scholiast is trying to concoct an explanation for the poem's origin from the single objective fact—to which we shall return in Appendix II—that it was a μέγα ποίημα, allied to his knowledge (? from the *Aetia* prologue as well as the *Hymn to Apollo*) that Callimachus was involved in controversy over the length of poems.

If, however, anything more can be extracted from the scholion, one might deduce that *Hecale* was not Callimachus' first poem, but written at a time (? the 270s BC) when his literary principles and practice had already been established by published work, and had become well enough known to attract opposition. It would not be surprising if such criticism had been provoked by the early *Aetia*.[3] Then the *Hecale* could be both a response to criticism and a

---

[1] *The Lives of the Greek Poets* (1981), p. 122; cf. p. 120. I share her scepticism (pp. 119 ff.) about the alleged quarrel between Call. and Apollonius Rhodius (cf. Gregory Hutchinson, *Hellenistic Poetry* (1988), pp. 86–7).

[2] See on frs. 103, 113.

[3] Following the brilliant paper of P. J. Parsons (*ZPE* 25 (1977), 1–50), it is now widely accepted (cf. Lloyd-Jones, *SIFC* 77 (1984), 56) that originally the *Aetia* contained only bks. 1–2. Both A. W. Bulloch (*CQ*, NS 20 (1970), 269–76) and Annette Harder (*ZPE* 67 (1987), 21–30) have found evidence of literary polemic in *SH* 239, perhaps linked to *SH* 253 and, in Dr Harder's view, from the end of *Aet*. 2.

positive manifesto,[4] showing how a smart modern poet should
handle traditional epic subject-matter (one of the Labours of
Theseus) in the traditional epic metre. Certainly there is no sign of
Callimachus compromising his principles, let alone capitulating
to opponents; but, if one can draw any lesson from the longest
and best-preserved passages (frs. 69, 74), the *Hecale*, for all its
subtlety and learning, may have been the most immediately
approachable and enjoyable of Callimachus' major works.[5]

We can be reasonably confident, if not absolutely certain, that
the *Hecale* predates Callimachus' fourth *Iambus* (fr. 194 Pf.). This
latter poem tells of a dispute between the laurel and the olive; line
77 (= below, Test. 2), from an enumeration of the olive's virtues,
surely alludes to the meal offered by Hecale to Theseus (cf. fr. 36.
3–5 on various types of olive):

ἐν [δ' ἡ κολ]υμβὰς ἦν ἔπωνε χὠ Θησεύς.

Nor is that the only link with *Hecale*. In the olive's branches sit
two talkative birds (61–3), one of them a crow (82), recalling the
crow in the *Hecale* who perches on a tree (fr. 74. 11) and talks to
another bird. Both poems mention the struggle for Attica
between Athena and Poseidon, although in the *Hecale* (fr. 70. 11)
Cecrops is a witness, in the *Iambus* a judge (fr. 194. 67 Pf.). Finally,
the glare with which the laurel fixes an intrusive bramble at the
end of the *Iambus* (101–2 ὑποδράξ ... | ἔβλεψε) reminds one of
Hec. fr. 72, perhaps describing the fury of Pallas when the crow
tells her that Ericthonius has been revealed.

If Callimachus hoped that the *Hecale* would end hostile criti-
cism, he was apparently disappointed. Most scholars[6] incline to
accept the word of the scholiast on *H.* 2. 26 that 'my king' is
Ptolemy III Euergetes rather than II Philadelphus, in which case
the conclusion to that hymn shows Callimachus as vulnerable and
sensitive to criticism even near the end of his life. Certainly in the
Aetia prologue, a product of his old age, the Telchines still
complain (fr. 1. 3–5 Pf. with plausible supplements):

---

[4] P. M. Fraser (*Ptolemaic Alexandria* (1972), ii. 905 n. 203) commends the
opinion of Couat (*Alexandrian Poetry* (ET, 1931), p. 408) that the *Hecale* was a
manifesto rather than a defence, but the two purposes need not exclude each
other.

[5] Cf. Lloyd-Jones, *SIFC* 77 (1984), 67.

[6] e.g. Pfeiffer, ii, pp. xxxviii–xxxix. F. Williams (*HA*) suspends judgement.

εἵνεκεν οὐχ ἓν ἄεισμα διηνεκὲς ἢ βασιλ[ήων
πρήξι]ας ἐν πολλαῖς ἤνυσα χιλιάσιν
ἢ προτέρ]ους ἥρωας . . .

Eulogistic epics on contemporary kings were definitely not in Callimachus' line—his court poetry was much more subtle.[7] But might he not have pointed to the *Hecale*, which told the exploits of an 'ancient hero', and was, at least to later Greeks and Romans (e.g. Crinagoras and Petronius (= below, Test. 4, 7)), one of Callimachus' greatest triumphs? The answer probably lies in πολλαῖς . . . χιλιάσιν. *Hecale* must have been a substantial poem (see below, App. II), but was not likely to satisfy those looking for a full-blown *Theseid*.

II. SUBJECT-MATTER AND SOURCES

One could summarize the basic contents of the *Hecale* in such a way as to make it sound like a traditional epic: the hero's growth to manhood, his perilous journey from Troezen to Athens (in the course of which he overcame several bandits), escape from his stepmother's plot, victorious combat with the Marathonian bull, and triumphant homecoming. There was indeed at least one archaic *Theseid*, but we know little about it.[1] Up to the last decades of the sixth century BC Theseus is not very prominent in Attic art.[2] If we can draw any inference from the subsequent explosion of scenes involving Theseus, a patriotic Athenian *Theseid* perhaps appeared about 510 BC.[3] Whether Callimachus made any use of such work(s) is quite uncertain; Shefton's account[4] of Theseus dragging the captive bull, as typically

---

[7] Cf. Stephanie West, *CQ*, NS 35 (1985), 66.

[1] Kinkel (*Epicorum Graecorum Fragmenta* (1877), pp. 217–18) has four references but no verbatim quotation. Arist., *Po.* 8 ὅσοι τῶν ποιητῶν Ἡρακληίδα καὶ Θησηίδα καὶ τὰ τοιαῦτα ποιήματα πεποιήκασιν may allow for the possibility of several such poems. M. L. West (*IEG* ii. 61–2) argues that Δίφιλος ὁ τὴν Θησηίδα ποιήσας (schol. P. *Ol.* 10. 83b) composed a comic *Theseid* in choliambics. See further G. L. Huxley, *Greek Epic Poetry from Eumelos to Panyassis* (1969), 116 ff.

[2] Though his struggle with the Marathonian bull may be portrayed on a black-figure vase from a little before 550 BC (B. B. Shefton, *Hesperia*, 31 (1962), 347).

[3] Some would attribute it to the Pisistratid court, others to enemies of the Pisistratids. See Christiane Sourvinou-Inwood, *JHS* 91 (1971), 98–9.

[4] *Hesperia*, 31 (1962), 348, quoted on my fr. 68.

portrayed by vase-painters, sounds distinctly like *Hecale* frs. 68 and 69. 1, but our poet may rather have had Sophocles in mind (fr. 25 Radt, Pearson). Both Sophocles and Euripides composed an *Aegeus*; although it seems doubtful whether Callimachus followed the plot of either tragedy, he may have taken the occasional hint from each of them.[5] The bandits Sciron and Cercyon,[6] overcome by Theseus, were also thought fit subjects for satyr plays and comedies.

While much of the above material would be at home in an epic poem, Callimachus' very title shows that he is adopting an untraditional stance. He began from Hecale (fr. 1), and almost certainly ended with her funeral and posthumous honours (*Dieg.* xi. 4–7; cf. frs. 79–83) rather than Theseus' victorious return. One of the most striking features of the work must have been the poignant contrast between the two principal characters (brought together by something as mundane as a rainstorm)—Theseus at the outset of his heroic career, the old woman once rich (fr. 41) but robbed of all those closest to her by a series of disasters (frs. 47 ff.) and reduced to living alone in a desolate place (fr. 40. 5). We could say that Hecale represents a conflation of Eumaeus and Eurycleia from the *Odyssey*, but neither of these plays a leading part. G. Zanker believes that Callimachus was deliberately infringing the doctrine of Aristotle's *Poetics* in making the main character of his epos a person of lower social standing.[7]

Hecale, who entertained Theseus before he fought the Marathonian bull, is mentioned first by the Atthidographer Philochorus;[8]

---

[5] See my introductory note on frs. 3–7, and, for possible links with Euripides, on frs. 69. 1 and 165 inc. auct.

[6] See on fr. 49. 8 ff. and frs. 59–62.

[7] *Antichthon*, 11 (1977), 72. We should remember that Hecale, like Eumaeus, came from a prosperous family.

[8] *FGH* 328 F 109, from Plut., *Thes.* 14 (= below, Test. 9). We do not know in which work—presumably either *Atthis* or *Tetrapolis* (the Marathonian Tetrapolis comprised Marathon, Oenoe, Probalinthus, and Tricorynthus). Kapp (p. 10) doubted whether Call. could have used Philochorus 'propter temporum rationes', but there is no difficulty even if the *Hecale* belonged to Call.'s early period and if the poet drew from the *Atthis*, since the *Atthis* probably began to be published in the 290s and most, if not all, of the specialist works are earlier (*FGH* iiib, Suppl. i, 435; ibid. Suppl. ii., 340 n. 11). Call.'s habitual reliance on local chronicles is abundantly clear from the *Aetia*, where more than once he actually mentions his source (fr. 75. 54 ff. Pf., Xenomedes of Ceos; fr. 92. 2–3 Λε]ανδρίδες εἴ τι παλαιαί | φθ[έγγ]ονται ... ἱστορίαι). For use of the Ἀργολικά by Agias and Dercylus in the *Aetia* and (perhaps) the fifth *Hymn*, see Bulloch, *FH*, pp. 16–17.

our poet probably invented her sad and complex life-history,[9] of which frs. 41 ff. give only tantalizing glimpses. She is the eponym of the Attic deme Ἑκάλη.[10] Plutarch (*Thes.* 14, from Philochorus = below, Test. 9) writes ἡ δὲ Ἑκάλη καὶ τὸ περὶ αὐτὴν μυθολόγημα τοῦ ξενισμοῦ καὶ τῆς ὑποδοχῆς ἔοικε μὴ πάσης ἀμοιρεῖν ἀληθείας. ἔθυον γὰρ Ἑκαλῆσιν οἱ πέριξ δῆμοι[11] cυνιόντες Ἑκαλείωι Διὶ καὶ τὴν Ἑκάλην ἐτίμων κτλ. We have no evidence unconnected with Philochorus or Callimachus for the cult of Zeus Ἑκάλειος (or, in one variant, Ἕκαλος); some think that it may be more primitive than the story of Hecale herself.[12] Another Atthidographer, the mysterious 'Amelesagoras' (*FGH* 330), was plainly the source of a substantial digression (more than 80 lines long) in which a crow tells how she lost the favour of Athena and was banished from the Acropolis for ever (frs. 70 ff.).

[9] My Test. Dub. 17 purports to name a son of Hecale.

[10] As yet no ancient epigraphic evidence fixes with certainty the location of Hecale's deme. From Call.'s poem we may note that she lived 'in the hill country of Erectheus' (fr. 1), whence Theseus must 'go down' to Marathon (fr. 40. 1); fr. 169 inc. sed. may describe the τέμενος of Zeus Ἑκάλειος 'bordering on the flanks of Brilessus' (Pentelicus). Hecale's cottage at least made a convenient resting place for Theseus on his journey from Athens to Marathon. Attention has been directed to two sites near the modern Stamata: (*a*) Koukounari, the favourite (championed most recently by Robin Osborne, *Demos, the Discovery of Classical Attika* (1985), pp. 192–3), where in the 1890s American archaeologists found the sacrificial calendar (*IG* ii², 1358) of the Marathonian Tetrapolis—which did not, however, include Hecale. See R. B. Richardson, *AJA* 10 (1895), 209–26 with pl. xvi. (*b*) A fragment of a deme inscription, built into the remains of an early Christian church, was discovered at nearby Amygdaleza (E. Tsophopoulou-Gkini, *Ἀρχ. Ἐφ*: 1980, 94–5). The editor gave this to Hecale (cf. J. S. Traill, *Hesperia*, Suppl. 14 (1975), 46), but David Whitehead (*The Demes of Attica* (1986), 386–7) prefers Plotheia. D. M. Lewis (*Historia*, 12 (1963), 31–2), regarding Koukounari as merely a cult-spot on a hill, saw no reason to deny that Hecale was at or near the present village (by 1986 it would have to be called a dormitory suburb) of the name, south-west of Koukounari. But the modern application of Ekáli is hardly decisive, since it is a recent revival which I have not traced before 1900. D. Sourmelis (*Ἀττικά* (1854)) saw a trace of the ancient name in modern Kalénzi (see on fr. 47. 18): μέχρι τοῦ νῦν Καλένζι καλεῖται ἡ Ἑκάλη· ... κεῖται δὲ πρὸς τὰ ὅρια τοῦ Μαραθῶνος, καὶ κατοικεῖται ὑπ᾽ ὀλίγων. A nice fancy, but the name, according to Professor Trypanis, is of Albanian origin, and in any case Kalénzi lies too far north. I have not been able to take into account an article on the topography of the *Hecale* by N. A. Nikolaou in *Dodone* 14 (1985), 131–9, reported in *Année Philologique* 57 (1986), item 924.

[11] We cannot be sure to which demes Philochorus was referring.

[12] Jacoby, *FGH* iiib, Suppl. ii. 341 n. 17. Inscribed sacred calendars from Attica have produced many local titles of Zeus (Whitehead, *Demes of Attica*, pp. 191, 206)—perhaps one day we shall find Ἑκάλειος.

This leads us to the general subject of Attic geography, antiquities, and religion, which clearly fascinated Callimachus, like other learned Hellenistic poets.[13] Perhaps the *Hecale* deserves more explicit attention than it has received from modern scholars who write on such matters.[14] For example, those who mark 'Trinemeia' on a deme map of Attica[15] do not often mention that the one literary authority for this form of the name (otherwise Τρινεμεῖc) is Stephanus Byzantius quoting the *Hecale* (fr. 88). Fr. 52 provides one of just two witnesses for the form Δεκελειόθεν. Fr. 51 supports the existence of a deme called Colonae,[16] and fr. 83 is interesting for the cult of an eponym.[17] It is noticeable that our fragments mention several demes which lay close to Hecale's home: Aphidnae (fr. 42. 2), Colonae (fr. 51. 1), Decelea (fr. 52), Trinemea (fr. 88)—Semachidae might be added to the list (see on fr. 47. 18). Fr. 91 gives an old name for the island of Salamis; the authenticity of this fragment had been impugned, but has largely been vindicated by the discovery on Salamis of a fourth-century inscription which displays the name Κόλουρις (note that Philochorus' voluminous works included a Caλαμῖνος Κτίσις (*FGH* 328 T 1)).

There are also many allusions to local religious cults and special divine titles:[18] as well as Zeus Ἑκάλειος and the honours for Hecale in her new deme (frs. 81–3: cf. *Dieg.* xi. 5–7), we find Aphrodite Κωλιάς (fr. 92), Apollo Λύκειος (fr. 71. 2–3), and Dionysus Μελάναιγις and Λιμναῖος (fr. 85. 1–2). The story of Ericthonius and the daughters of Cecrops (frs. 70–2) may contain a number of religious references still obscure to us because of the

---

[13] e.g. Eratosthenes in the *Erigone*, and Euphorion, *SH* 418. 15–26, where several Attic demes are mentioned in a brief space.

[14] Though Jacoby, for example, was interested in our poem, it is not mentioned in C. Scherling's *Quibus Rebus Singulorum Atticae Pagorum Incolae Operam Dederint* (1897).

[15] e.g. Whitehead, *Demes of Attica*, p. xxiii (from J. S. Traill, *Hesperia*, Suppl. 14 (1975)).

[16] Not, in my opinion, for 2, even though D. M. Lewis (*BSA* 50 (1955), 12–17) is surely right in arguing for 2 Colonae. Modern scholars writing on this problem have, for the most part, shown themselves aware of the Callimachus fragment, but may not have interpreted the very difficult text correctly. (See on fr. 51.)

[17] See Whitehead, *Demes of Attica*, pp. 208–11, for cults of the eponymous hero in other demes.

[18] See generally ibid. ch. 7.

fragmentary state of the text; perhaps in the course of his commentary on this part of the poem Salustius spoke of the ἀρρηφορία (fr. 179 inc. auct.). Fr. 156 inc. sed. mentions the untilled plain or ὀργάς on the boundary between Attica and the Megarid, which was devoted to Demeter and Persephone.[19]

Another source of Attic colour and vocabulary in the *Hecale* was Comedy—not the New Comedy being written during Callimachus' lifetime by Menander and others, but the masters of Old Comedy, Eupolis, Cratinus, and Aristophanes. When Hecale makes Theseus welcome in her cottage, she sits him on an ἀσκάντης (fr. 29), a word which Callimachus almost certainly took from Ar. *Nub.* 633. Several other words in the *Hecale* are said by later Greek writers to be particularly at home in Comedy, e.g. ϲιπύη 'bread-bin' (fr. 35. 1) and μετάκερας 'warm water' (fr. 34, ingeniously accommodated to the hexameter by tmesis). A more complicated case is fr. 74. 25 ἀείδει καί πού τις ἀνὴρ ὑδατηγὸς ἱμαῖον. The 'well-song' (ἱμαῖος) may derive ultimately from Ar. *Ran.* 1297 ἱμονιοστρόφου μέλη, but, since ἱμαῖος does not occur there, Callimachus must have consulted some intermediary work, whether a commentary on the *Frogs* or a specialist monograph on Attic expressions (see ad. loc.). The 'avenging stork' of fr. 76 might perhaps be explained by something in a lost comedy, unless it is a folk-tale element.[20]

Many different authors and types of poetry have contributed to the *Hecale*. We can trace the theme of a hero received hospitably in a poor country cottage back to the entertainment of Odysseus by the swineherd Eumaeus in Homer, and find at least a hint of the same pattern in Euripides' *Electra*.[21] One might discern a Hesiodic air in those fragments (52 ff.) which describe toil, injustice, and poverty; fr. 54 νυκτὶ δ' ὅληι βαϲιλῆας ἐλέγχομεν recalls the βαϲιλῆας | δωροφάγουϲ of *Op.* 38–9, and Hecale lives in a καλιή (fr. 80. 4, a word common in *Works and Days*).[22] Traditional epic, local chronicles, Old Comedy, and Hesiod—the

---

[19] Moving outside Attica, note the cluster of allusions to Argive places and cults (frs. 95–6, 98–101, 174–5 inc. sed.); their precise relevance to the *Hecale* is not yet clear.

[20] For folk-tale motifs in the stories of the crow and the raven, see below, p. 232.

[21] See below, App. III.

[22] Usually = 'granary', but in *Op.* 503 = 'hut'. The general debt of Call. to Hesiod is discussed in H. Reinsch-Werner, *Callimachus Hesiodicus* (1976).

mixture is very rich, and I suspect that this diversity, as well as the poem's high calibre, may have moved Crinagoras (= below, Test. 4) to write of the *Hecale* δὴ γὰρ ἐπ' αὐτῶι | ὠνὴρ τοὺς Μουςέων πάντας ἔςειςε κάλως.

III. STYLE AND LANGUAGE

First, a few thoughts on the poem's overall impression, in so far as we are able to judge from the surviving fragments. The *Hecale* seems to have encompassed a variety of tone as wide as the range of literary genres (see sect. II above) from which Callimachus drew. We can distinguish the epic directness of fr. 69, where Theseus drags the captive bull before the eyes of the country people, from the 'weird beauty'[1] and folk-tale atmosphere of the raven's transformation from white to black (fr. 74. 15 ff.). The papyrus fragments (47 ff.) in which Hecale tells her life-story are miserably tattered, but enough remains to show with what intense emotion she bewails the two children's death (fr. 49. 2–3) and curses Cercyon (ibid. 13–15). Several other fragments express violent anger, sometimes in vividly colloquial language.[2] On the other hand, the artificial phrase ἀμαζόνες ἄνδρες (fr. 162 inc. sed.), not male Amazons but 'men who have no barley-cake' (μᾶζα), suggests ironical detachment.

A feature commonly ascribed to our poet is recondite learning. Certainly we can find some of this. Hecale herself was hardly well known—nor was the crow's part in the tale of Ericthonius (frs. 70 ff.). Callimachus clearly delights in the outlandish name of the Thracian mountain Hypsizorus (fr. 71. 1).[3] Was the place granted remission of Charon's ferry dues in fr. 99 really a certain Αἰγιαλός rather than Hermione? What can we make of fr. 103 on Apollo/ Helios and Persephone/Artemis? Why should Callimachus have found it necessary to remark that the earliest Athenians celebrated the Anthesteria to Dionysus of the Marshes rather than Dionysus Eleuthereus (fr. 85)? But even if we add the rare words to the rare myths and geography, it seems that the *Hecale* would have been

---

[1] Gregory Hutchinson's phrase (cf. his *Hellenistic Poetry* (1988), p. 61).
[2] Fr. 72 (?Athena), fr. 126 (??Medea), fr. 133 (?cf. fr. 530 Pf. in App. I).
[3] Fr. 18. 15 mentions another obscure Thracian mountain, Merisus.

far less impenetrable than a poem by, for example, Euphorion.[4]

Coming down to more specific details, we should always remember that most of the surviving *Hecale* fragments are quoted by grammarians or lexicographers precisely because they illustrate something unusual. So, for a fairer sample, let us consider the longest and best-preserved passages, from the wooden board known as the Vienna tablet. Fr. 69 (including col. i) consists of 14½ lines. These contain just two striking novelties, οἰόκερως, 'single horned' (l. 1) and—if the *Hecale* is earlier than Lycophron's *Alexandra*—cτόρνη, 'girdle' (15). Also unprecedented are θαρcήειc in line 5 (Callimachus greatly favours adjectives in -ήειc and -όειc) and the form νεύμενοc (6). ἀπηλοίηce (1) shows the Alexandrian predilection for Homeric *hapax legomena* (cf. *Il.* 4. 522), while both μέcφ' ὅτε and the Doric pronoun φιν (4) appear as variants in our text of Homer, and perhaps were adopted by Callimachus because of their controversial status. We may note parentheses (1, 7) and refined word order (ἐμῶι δέ τιc Αἰγέϊ πατρί, 5). Several lines (2, 9, 10, 14) have an appreciable sense-break at the bucolic diaeresis, and line 12 a monosyllabic ending (φυλλοχόοc μείc, borrowed from pseudo-Hesiod). Negatively, not one of the 14 hexameters has a spondaic fifth foot—a mannerism of the Hellenistic poets, but perhaps commoner in the generation after Callimachus. Homeric reminiscence abounds: e.g. when the young hero says of himself Θηcεὺc οὐχ ἑκὰc οὗτοc (8), he recalls Telemachus' οὐχ ἑκὰc οὗτοc ἀνήρ (*Od.* 2. 40). Parts of the passage can be described as highly traditional (though never lacking in elegance), e.g. lines 2–3 ὡc ἴδον, ὡc ἅμα πάντεc ὑπέτρεcαν, οὐδέ τιc ἔτλη | ἄνδρα μέγαν καὶ θῆρα πελώριον ἄντα ἰδέcθαι.

In fr. 74. 10 ff. two papyri coincide with col. iv of the Vienna tablet to give 18 consecutive lines in an almost perfect state of preservation. Here the style and language are generally more colourful and complex. We start (10 ff.) with a splendid prophetic utterance from the crow, involving parenthesis and aposiopesis, which had defied various attempts at restoration until all the papyri were in place. As Barrett writes,[5] 'The sentiment "time has not yet come to an end" is first inserted parenthetically between the oaths, and then [12–13] repeated more elaborately, only this

---

[4] To whom one might more appropriately apply the words of the *SH* editors 'integrum aegre intellexeris textum' (p. x).

[5] *Gnomon*, 33 (1961), 691.

time not in parenthesis but as part of the main statement, with the
substantive part added to it adversatively':

> ναὶ μὰ τόν—οὐ γάρ πω πάντ' ἤματα—ναὶ μὰ τὸ ῥικνόν
> cῦφαρ ἐμόν, ναὶ τοῦτο τὸ δένδρεον αὖον ἐόν περ—
> οὐκ ἤδη ῥυμόν τε καὶ ἄξονα κανάξαντες
> ἠέλιοι δυcμέων εἴcω πόδα πάντες ἔχουcι,
> δείελος ἀλλ' ἢ νὺξ ἢ ἔνδιος ἢ ἔcετ' ἠώc κτλ.

This string of oaths, with their somewhat exaggerated vehem-
ence, perhaps suggests the style of Comedy, while the custom of
swearing elliptically (ναὶ μὰ τόν without adding the name of the
god) is said to be Attic. We may be surprised that the prediction
of the time when the raven will be changed from white to black
(14) is so obviously modelled upon Achilles' prophecy of his own
death in *Il.* 21. 111 ἔccεται ἢ ἠὼc ἢ δείλη ἢ μέcον ἦμαρ. In these and
the subsequent lines, rare words and forms include ῥικνόc 'shriv-
elled', cῦφαρ 'hide' (Sicilian in origin), κανάξαντες (Aeolic—note
the cπονδειάζων), γάλακι (as if from the nominative γάλαξ),
ἄγχαυροc 'predawn' (Cyprian), ὑδατηγόc 'water-drawer', and
ἱμαῖοc 'well-song'. Line 22 contains a phenomenon unique in
Callimachus, indicating that his *Hecale* approaches Homer much
more closely than do the hexameter *Hymns*:[6] he has employed a
Homeric hexameter as far as the bucolic diaeresis, καδδραθέτην δ'
οὐ πολλὸν ἐπὶ χρόνον (= *Od.* 15. 494). Hellenistic poets often
embroiled themselves in the controversies of Homeric scholar-
ship, and in line 17 we find φή = 'as', which is associated with
Callimachus' contemporary Zenodotus, though in this case it is
by no means certain that Callimachus took the form especially
from Zenodotus.[7] The same line foretells that one day the raven
will have a πτερὸν οὐλοόν, black as pitch. What is the meaning of
οὐλοόc here? Is it equivalent to ὀλοόc, or to οὖλοc, the various
Homeric senses of which Callimachus carefully reproduces else-
where in his own poetry? The problem remains obscure—
perhaps our poet intended it to be so.

---

[6] The same conclusion might be drawn from a number of smaller linguistic
indications, e.g. the apparent greater frequency of 'epic τε' in the *Hecale* (see on
fr. 117), or the unique occurrence of pleonastic δέ τε in fr. 113. 2.

[7] Other connections exist between Call. and Zenodotus' text of Homer (see
Pfeiffer on *Aet.* fr. 12. 6 and id., *History of Classical Scholarship*, i. 139). καιτάεντοc
in *Hecale* fr. 47. 6 is also a Zenodotean form. On Zenodotus see further Stephanie
West in Heubeck, West, and Hainsworth, *A Commentary on Homer's Odyssey*, i
(1988), 41 ff.

Throughout the poem we shall encounter Homeric rarities and *hapax legomena*; the fact that a particular word or formation was rare or even of disputed status in Homer makes it all the more likely to attract the attention of learned Hellenistic poets. Sometimes analogy with Homer leads to a new formation, e.g. the unique epithet πολυπτώξ 'of many hares' applied to Melaenae in fr. 84. This pretty clearly derives from *Il.* 2. 502 πολυτρήρωνά τε Θίϲβην 'Thisbe of many doves'—the two epithets share the notions of 'cowering' (πτώξ) and 'trembling' (τρήρων). Similarly the unparalleled πολύκριμνοϲ 'rich in barley' (fr. 96. 3) owes something to Homer's πολύπυροϲ. Another principle is that of filling gaps in Homer. Consider fr. 18. 2 τόφρα δ' ἔην ὑάλοιο φαάντεροϲ οὐρανὸϲ ἦνοψ. The expression ὑάλοιο φαάντεροϲ is new; likewise the comparative φαάντεροϲ (Homer has only the superlative) and the nominative[8] ἦνοψ (Homer has only a dative). Under this heading one can add e.g. the masculine ἐλαχύϲ (fr. 26) and an indicative οἶϲε (fr. 36. 3).

Some of Callimachus' linguistic experiments have the air of deliberate provocation. e.g. the adjective ἀπούατοϲ (fr. 122) 'bringing bad news'. Although this had a background in Homeric controversy, I find it hard to believe that Callimachus' tongue was not in his cheek: the same spirit may be recognized in γηφάγοι (fr. 55) and ἀμαζόνεϲ ἄνδρεϲ (fr. 162 inc. sed.), or in artificial forms such as νήχυτοϲ (fr. 11)[9] and ἀϲταγέϲ (fr. 124) 'flowing abundantly', both of which rest on the view that in certain Homeric epithets the prefixes νη- and ἀ- can have an intensifying rather than a privative force.

Quite apart from the relationship to Homer, there are many other points of interest in the *Hecale*'s language. We have touched on the poem's debt to Old Comedy,[10] which brings with it words such as ἀϲκάντηϲ, μετάκεραϲ, and ϲιπύη. Callimachus is receptive to influences from all over the Greek world; ancient sources tell us that ἄλλιξ (a type of cloak, fr. 42. 5) comes from Thessaly, γέντα (flesh or entrails, fr. 127) from Thrace, εὖφαρ (a wrinkled skin, fr. 74. 11) from Sicily, δρόμοϲ (in the sense of a gymnasium, fr. 71. 3) from Crete, and ἄγχαυροϲ (fr. 74. 23, the time just before dawn) from Cyprus. A small number of his borrowings seem to be of non-Greek, Eastern origin: perhaps (again) ἀϲκάντηϲ, a couch (fr.

---

[8] Not content with this, Call. adds an acc. ἤνοπα in fr. 102. 2.

[9] Perhaps borrowed from Philet. fr. 21 Powell.

[10] Above, p. 9.

29), γεργέριμος, a type of olive (fr. 36. 4), κατακᾶσα 'prostitute' (fr. 90. 1), κοκύαι 'ancestors' (fr. 137), and probably δανάκης, a Persian coin (see on fr. 99). Callimachus was also an innovator in his own right, coining, for example, new epithets in -ήεις and -όεις (θαρσήεις, στιβήεις, θυμόεις, perhaps πυρόεις) and nouns in -τειρα (δαμάτειρα, καθηγήτειρα, ὀπτήτειρα) and in -τύς (ἀσπαστύς, ἀφραστύς). Here is a further sample[11] of words not attested before the *Hecale*: ἀείπλανος, ἀλυκρός, ἀμνάμων, ἀρπίς, βιοπλανής, βωνίτης, εἰδυλίς, ἔλλερος, ἐννότιος, κατάϊξ, κνηκίς, κολουραῖος, μύρσος, παλαιφάμενος, περίθριξ, πολύθρονος, σελαγίζω, σιπαλός, ὑπόκρηνος, χοροστάς. Most of these no doubt occurred in earlier Greek literature now lost to us, but I would be surprised if some were not Callimachus' own invention; while a few (e.g. κατάϊξ, σελαγίζω) became, through his example, popular in later Greek poetry, a larger number remain in splendid isolation, noticed only by grammarians and lexicographers.

A marked feature of Callimachus' poetic style is dislocation of the expected word order;[12] surely it was from him that Ovid developed a taste for similar audacities. Nothing extravagant has survived from the *Hecale*. But we may note a liking for insertions between preposition and noun—not that this is by any means unusual in other writers—as frs. 1 ἔν ποτε γουνῶι, 9. 1 ἐν γάρ μιν Τροιζῆνι, 35. 1 ἐκ δ' ἄρτους σιπύηθεν, and 51. 1 ἔκ με Κολωνάων. Also worth mentioning are the appositional pattern ἐμῶι δέ τις Αἰγέϊ πατρί (fr. 69. 5) and the ingenious fr. 167 inc. sed. ἀλλὰ θεῆς ἥτις με διάκτορον ἔλλαχε Παλλάς, where Παλλάς is attracted into the case of the antecedent relative.

In Callimachus' *Hymns* we seldom encounter full scale epic similes; only *H.* 4. 141–7, 228–32 are of Homeric dimensions.[13] Our very fragmentary evidence suggests that similes may have played a greater part in the *Hecale*. Fr. 18. 13 ff. appears to contain a simile of some length on the very traditional theme of battling winds, though enlivened at least by the rare word κατάϊξ and the recondite Thracian mountain Merisus (l. 15). In fr. 48. 7 ff. the

---

[11] Lapp, *De Callimachi Cyrenaei Tropis et Figuris* (diss. 1965), has full, if not quite complete, information covering all Call.'s poems.

[12] My favourite examples are *Aet.* fr. 1. 33 ff. Pf. ἁ πάντως, ἵνα γῆρας ἵνα δρόσον ἣν μὲν ἀείδω | πρώκιον ἐκ δίης ἠέρος εἶδαρ ἔδων,| αὖθι τὸ δ' ἐκδύοιμι, and *Victoria Sosibii*, fr. 384. 31–2 Pf. (the Nile speaking) ὃν οὐδ' ὅθεν οἶδεν ὁδεύω | θνητὸς ἀνήρ. See Lapp, *Tropis et Figuris*, pp. 35–9.

[13] Cf. Lapp, pp. 88 ff., 151.

two boys whom Hecale brought up are likened to aspens by a watercourse, recalling Thetis' words in the *Iliad* (18. 56, 437) on her son Achilles, likewise destined to die young. When Theseus returns victorious with the bull, the countrymen pelt him with leaves more thickly than when the winds bring down foliage in autumn (fr. 69. 11 ff.). We can add a number of briefer comparisons, the most striking in fr. 18. 2 where the sky is 'more brilliant than glass' (ὑάλοιο φαάντεροϲ).

IV. METRE[1]

M. L. West writes of Hellenistic hexameter verse: 'In many respects Callimachus represents the peak of refinement attained in this period.'[2] A grasp of Callimachus' metrical likes and dislikes is particularly important when one is dealing with a fragmentary poem. More than a hundred years ago Otto Schneider (whose *Callimachea*, ii (1873) none the less contained much of value)[3] freely supplemented incomplete lines in a way that would now be considered irresponsible, and it was pure coincidence if in the process he did not violate any of the Callimachean restrictions.[4] Even in this century reputable scholars have proposed or commended supplements (whether of papyri or of pieces preserved by ancient grammarians) which are implausible or, in some cases, impossible for reasons of metre. At this point I will give just two examples to show the part played by metrical factors. If Grenfell and Hunt were right in taking the first legible letter of *P. Oxy.* 853, col. x. 9 to be a doubtful eta, then, as Pfeiffer saw, the Thucydides commentator cannot be quoting two complete lines of the *Hecale*, because Callimachus does not allow a word-break after a fourth-foot spondee.[5] But a re-examination of the papyrus by Dr Walter Cockle, showing that the supposed *H* may be remnants of *ΔI*, nullifies this metrical objection (see on fr. 85). By contrast, we shall find in note 14 to sect. VI below that an

---

[1] The most useful accounts are Maas. *GM* and West, *GM*. See also the introductory pages on metre in Mineur, *HD* and Hopkinson, *HD*.

[2] *GM*, p. 153.

[3] See the judgement of Pfeiffer which I quote on p. 44 below.

[4] In this respect he represented a step backwards from Naeke.

[5] See below, p. 20 on Naeke's Law.

anonymous hexameter fragment,[6] which some would ascribe to the *Hecale*, contains so many metrical irregularities (from a Callimachean point of view) that it cannot have been written by our poet.

I have tried as far as possible to illustrate Callimachus' practices from the *Hecale* fragments, including, for this purpose, the Fragmenta Incerta.[7] Even when a line is incomplete, we may be able to tell whether it had a masculine or feminine caesura, a spondaic fifth foot, or a bucolic diaeresis.[8] Thus the single word πολύθρονον (fr. 3) suffices to establish a hexameter with feminine caesura and bucolic diaeresis, because Callimachus never violates Hermann's Bridge, nor would he start a line with –‿ πολύθρονον (Giseke's Law). Maas[9] prints the opening of *Il.* 1 to mark infringements of the Callimachean (and Nonnian) rules. I add some parallels from other Hellenistic poets; fine craftsmen that they are, none is as strict as Callimachus.[10] We shall see that even for Callimachus by no means all the 'rules' are invariable. His preferences were probably instinctive rather than consciously formulated and followed.

It is customary to give overall statistics for Callimachus' hexameters, but these sometimes conceal differences between individual poems (or groups of poems) which may not be fortuitous.[11] *H.* 1 boasts 14 cπονδειάζοντες in 95 lines (15%), *H.* 4 only 10 in 326 lines (3%); *H.* 6 has few cπονδειάζοντες (5 in 138 = 4%), but much the largest proportion of masculine caesurae (59 in 138 = 43%, contrasting with 46 in 326 = 14% in *H.* 4). As far as we can judge from the surviving *Hecale* fragments (and this is not very far), they contain a higher proportion of cπονδειάζοντες (29 in 222 = 13%) than any of the *Hymns* except for 1 and a lower proportion of masculine caesurae (56 in

---

[6] *P. Oxy.* 1794 = epic. adesp. 4 Powell (*CA*, pp. 78–9).

[7] But not, of course, those in App. I. I have disregarded cases where the text is too uncertain.

[8] I retain this familiar term. West calls it a 'modern pedantry' (*GM*, p. 192; cf. *CQ*, NS 32 (1982), 292) and prefers 'bucolic caesura'.

[9] *GM*, para. 100.

[10] It is fair to say that they show at least some feeling for Call.'s personal predilections.

[11] Whether they help to determine the relative date of poems is doubtful. The *Sixth Hymn* yields the largest crop of metrical oddities.

249 = 22%) than any *Hymn* apart from 4. Incidence of bucolic diaeresis (155 in 224 = 69%) is marginally above average.[12]

1. *Dactyls and Spondees*

West[13] remarks that Callimachus has less contraction of bicipitia (i.e. fewer spondees) than Homer, except in the second foot. This may be illustrated by the striking fact that we know only one Callimachean hexameter with a spondee in both the third and the fourth foot: *H.* 6. 72 οὔτε νιν εἰc ἐράνωc οὔτε ξυνδείπνια πέμπον.[14] There are about 20 such lines in *Il.* 1 alone. Although this scheme would require a masculine caesura but no bucolic diaeresis, thus reducing the candidates to little more than 5% of Callimachus' hexameters,[15] it is still surprising that Callimachus so firmly rejected endings like Arat. *Phaen.* 137 ὤμων εἱλίccεται ἀcτήρ.[16] Callimachus' favourite patterns for the first four feet are DSDD and DDDD. The former predominates in the *Hecale* (46 = 35% as against 32 = 25%), *H.* 2 and 3 (narrowly), *H.* 4 (by a wide margin), the latter in *H.* 1 and 6 (in *H.* 6 DSDD is markedly less popular than usual). Other sequences which Callimachus favours to a lesser extent are SSDD and SDDD. By contrast SSSS (unsurprisingly) does not occur in Callimachus,[17] and SSSD no more than a handful of times (never in the *Hecale*). SSDS (with feminine caesura) crops up some 8 times in the *Hecale*, and 18 times in the hexameter *Hymns*.

2. *Spondaic Fifth Foot*

In Homer some 5% of hexameters have a spondaic fifth foot.[18]

---

[12] West's overall figure for Call. is 63%.

[13] *GM*, p. 154.

[14] Doubly odd because of the spondaic word following the masculine caesura but without bucolic diaeresis—this is palliated by the repetition of οὔτε, as in *H.* 6. 47 by the repetition of τέκνον.

[15] M. L. Clarke (*CR*, NS 5 (1955), 18) gives 5.2% for Call.'s *Hymns*. I find 4 examples in the *Hecale*.

[16] At least 8 more examples in Aratus, a fair number in e.g. Apollonius Rhodius and Nicander.

[17] In Apollonius Rhodius I have noted only 2. 13, 4. 922.

[18] West, *GM*, p. 37, with n. 13 observing that, if one excludes instances arising from vowel contraction, the proportion falls to 2%.

Callimachus' overall proportion is 7% (West), well below that of his predecessor Antimachus (22%) and fellow third-century poets Aratus and Euphorion (both 17%) and Eratosthenes (24%).[19] Perhaps Callimachus favoured the cπονδειάζων rather more in the *Hecale* (29 in 222 = 13%), but I suspect that Roman neoteric poets derived their taste for it[20] more from someone like Euphorion. The following points arise in connection with Callimachus' cπονδειάζοντεc :

(a) The final word is nearly always of four syllables (as in fr. 2. 2 ἔχε γὰρ τέγος ἀκλήιστον), occasionally of six syllables[21] (e.g. *H*. 1. 46 προcεπηχύναντο and probably *Hec*. fr. 148 περιπηχύναντεc). Two instances of a trisyllabic ending are known: *H*. 1. 41 Λυκαονίης ἄρκτοιο, and παλαιφαμένης ἄγνοιο which may belong to the *Hecale* (fr. 166 inc. auct.).[22]

(b) The fourth foot must be a dactyl. This does not hold good for e.g. Philetas (fr. 7. 3 Powell ἀνῖαι τετρήχαcιν), Aratus (e.g. 811 ἀλωαὶ κυκλώcωνται), or Apollonius (e.g. 1. 186 ἀγανοῦ Μιλήτοιο). Since most of Callimachus' final words are tetrasyllabic (above), this requirement is connected with the ban on word-break after a spondaic fourth foot (Naeke's Law, see p. 20 below). It is interesting, however, that Euphorion, Eratosthenes, and Nicander seem to follow Callimachus in demanding a fourth-foot dactyl before spondaic fifth foot, though none of them (see below) is bound by Naeke's Law.

(c) A hexameter with spondaic fifth foot is significantly more likely to have a masculine caesura. In cπονδειάζοντεc from the *Hymns* masculine caesurae actually predominate (34 in 64 = 53%); the corresponding figure for the *Hecale* is 4 in

---

[19] All these figures from West, *GM*, p. 154. The learned second-century poet Nicander has a surprisingly low percentage in the *Theriaca* and *Alexipharmaca* (West gives 2.6% for Nicander), but 9% (13 in 146) in what survives of the *Georgica* (3 consecutive cπονδειάζοντεc in fr. 74. 64–6).

[20] Cf. R. O. A. M. Lyne's edition of the pseudo-Virgilian *Ciris* (1978), pp. 15–16.

[21] This category omitted hy Hopkinson (*HD*, p. 55). The concluding word will then be a compound verb (in *H*. 3. 237 ἐπιθυμήτειραι, a noun derived from a compound verb). Other poets may employ a compound epithet in this position (e.g. *Il*. 18. 382 λιπαροκρήδεμνος).

[22] Euphorion seems fonder than Call. of trisyllabic line-endings in his cπονδειάζοντεc (fr. 94. 2, fr. 130, *SH* 413. 10, 14). Euphorion's monosyllabic ending in *SH* 418. 17 βουφόντης λίς so far has no Callimachean parallel.

12 = 33%. In the hexameters of the *Aetia*, however, there is still no certain example of spondaic fifth foot coupled with masculine caesura.[23]

(*d*) Hopkinson[24] quotes Prahl to the effect that in most cases four dactyls precede. This is indeed the commonest pattern in the *Hymns*, but accounts for only 30% in *Hymns* and *Hecale* combined (as against 28% for DSDD), and applies to only 4 of the 15 complete cπονδειάζοντεc in the *Hecale*.

3. Main Caesura

(*a*) Every line has a masculine or feminine caesura in the third foot—no Callimachean hexameter postpones the caesura to the fourth foot, an option still found occasionally in some other Hellenistic poets, especially Aratus.[25]

(*b*) The feminine caesura predominates over the masculine to a greater extent than in Homer.[26] West's overall figure for Callimachus is 74%, mine for the *Hecale* alone 78%.[27] In more than 90% of cases a masculine caesura will be coupled with a bucolic diaeresis;[28] it should not be followed by a spondaic word unless there is also a bucolic diaeresis[29] (this point will come into play when we consider the text of fr. 17. 11).

4. Word-end in Other Positions

(*a*) Words of shape × – ∪ hardly ever end in the second foot (Meyer's First Law).[30] It is clear enough that e.g. fr. 1 Ἀκταίη τιc ἔναιεν does not count as an exception (see ad loc.), even though τιc

---

[23] Pfeiffer on his fr. 303, quoting fr. 80. 8 as possible.

[24] *HD*, p. 55.

[25] West, *GM*, p. 153.

[26] For whom West (*GM*, p. 36) gives a proportion of 4:3 feminine:masculine.

[27] See West, *GM*, p. 153 for other Hellenistic poets; but I find a very small majority (52%) of feminine caesurae in Aratus.

[28] Cf. above, n. 15.

[29] But see above, n. 14. On 3 occasions (*H*. 2. 99, 3. 111, 4. 39) a part of the adjective χρύcεοc stands in this position, unaccompanied by bucolic diaeresis. In these cases I would scan it as an anapaest (thus Pfeiffer on fr. 780, McLennan (*HZ*) on *H*. 1. 48) rather than as a spondee with synizesis (so Mineur, *HD*, p. 36 n. 5).

[30] West, *GM*, p. 38.

is postpositive, going with Ἀκταίη. We are left with just two violations, *H.* 2. 41 πρῶκες ἔραζε πέcωcιν (? a special effect) and *H.* 6. 91 ὡc δὲ Μίμαντι χιών, ὡc ἀελίωι ἔνι πλαγγών (where the repeated ὡc to some extent diverts attention from the irregularity).

(*b*) Words of shape × – ∪ ∪ never end with the second foot (Giseke's Law).[31] So Callimachus could not have written e.g. Ap. Rh. 1. 1346 μέλλεν ἐπώνυμον ἄcτυ.[32]

(*c*) There is very seldom word-break after a spondaic second foot (Hilberg's Law).[33] Occasionally, however, Callimachus allows a monosyllable in this position, particularly if another monosyllable precedes (e.g. *H.* 4. 113 ὦ πάτερ οὐ μὴν ἵππον;[34] *Aet.* fr. 115. 13 Pf. Ὄννης μὲν νῦν ἠχ[ ).[35] Thus in *Hec.* fr. 113. 1 ἡνίκα μὲν γὰρ ταὐτά would be a metrically possible restoration (though dubious on other grounds—see ad loc.).

(*d*) Iambic words rarely stand before the masculine caesura (Meyer's Second 'Law').[36] But there are enough exceptions,[37] e.g. *Hec.* fr. 70. 9 τουτάκι δ' ἡ μὲν ἑῆc, to make this 'law' no more than a general preference.

(*e*) Spondaic words should not stand immediately after the masculine caesura unless there is also a word-break at the bucolic diaeresis (as e.g. fr. 74. 13 εἴcω πόδα, 21 ὕπνοc λάβε). See subsection 3 above and n. 29 there.

(*f*) There is never word-break after the fourth trochee (Hermann's Bridge).[38] Of course patterns like fr. 18. 6 ἄγουcι δὲ χεῖραc ἀπ' ἔργου do not violate the rule, because δέ is postpositive.

(*g*) Word-break should not follow a spondaic fourth foot (Naeke's Law).[39] Callimachus alone among Hellenistic poets

---

[31] Maas, *GM*, para. 94; West, *GM*, p. 155.

[32] Note in passing that Call. likes, for occasional variety, hexameters in which two dactylic words form the first two feet, e.g. fr. 4. 2 τοὔνεκεν Αἰγέος.

[33] Maas, *GM*, para. 92; West, *GM*, p. 155.

[34] Cf. Mineur, *HD*, p. 38.

[35] In *epigr.* 34 Pf. = 22 G.–P. = *AP* 6. 351. 1, λεοντάγχ' ὦνα should surely be considered a single unit. For infringements with disyllabic words in other poets cf. Arat. 111, 345, etc.; Ap. Rh. 1. 69, 255, etc.; Euph. fr. 13; Nic. *Ther.* 97, 618, etc.

[36] West, *GM*, p. 155.

[37] A. Wifstrand, *Von Kallimachos zu Nonnos* (1933), p. 65.

[38] Maas, *GM*, para. 91; West, *GM*, p. 155.

[39] Maas, *GM*, para. 92; West, *GM*, pp. 154–5.

observed this rule; contrast e.g. Arat. 259. Ap. Rh. 1. 271, Euph.
fr. 59, Erat. fr. 9, Nic. *Ther.* 457.[40] See also subsection 2*b* above. It
must he said that Callimachus' manuscripts present an exception
at *H.* 4. 226 ἀμύνειν πότνια δούλοιϲ. Most scholars have followed
the celebrated Mass–Crönert emendation,[41] reading ἀμύνεο ...
δούλουϲ | ὑμετέρουϲ in 226–7 and ἐφετμήν for ἐφετμῆι at the end of
227. W. H. Mineur, however,[42] keeps the MSS reading.[43]

(*h*) Words of shape — — and ∪ ∪ - seldom end in the fifth
princeps.[44]

(*i*) A monosyllable at the line-ending (probably less common
in Callimachus than in some other Hellenistic poets) is always
preceded by a bucolic diaeresis.[45]

(*j*) It is still possible to discover new things about the
Callimachean hexameter. A. W. Bulloch has observed[46] that a
word-break after the third foot is accompanied not only by the
regular main caesura, masculine or feminine, but also by (i) a
bucolic diaeresis and (ii) a syntactical colon—sufficient to require,
or at least to suggest, punctuation—*either* at the main caesura *or* at
the bucolic diaeresis *or* at both. This rule necessitates careful
consideration whether a word is 'appositive', i.e. cohering closely
with its neighbour, in which case the scheme may not apply.[47]
That being said, Bulloch's rule covers a handful of lines in the
Hecale, raising one or two points of interest for corrupt or
incomplete hexameters. Thus in fr. 42. 3 οἵ τ' εἶεν Διὸϲ υἱέε[ϲ, since
there is no sense-break at the masculine caesura, we look for one
at the bucolic diaeresis, which Pfeiffer's υἱέε[ϲ, ἢ θεῶι αὐτῶι
would provide.

[40] καὶ λοξὸν ὑποδρὰξ ὄμμαϲι λεύϲϲων, curious because it combines remi-
niscence of the *Hecale* (fr. 72. 1) with un-Callimachean metre. The only other
violation of Naeke's Law in Nicander is fr. 83. 3.

[41] Maas, *Textual Criticism* (1958), para. 30; id., *GM*, para. 92.

[42] *HD*, p. 38 and ad loc.

[43] His description (p. 38) of the metrical point as 'not at all a serious objection'
seems cavalier.

[44] West, *GM*, p. 155, cites *H.* 4. 311 as the most blatant exception.

[45] Maas, *GM*, para. 96; West, *GM*, p. 156.

[46] 'A Callimachean Refinement to the Greek Hexameter', *CQ*, NS 20 (1970),
258–68.

[47] Bulloch, *FH*, p. 260.

5. Sense-pause

West[48] notes that sense-pauses seldom occur except in the following positions:

$$-\cup\cup\,|-|\cup\cup-|\cup|\cup-\cup\cup\,|-\cup\cup--|$$

So e.g. one would expect for fr. 64 ὡς ἔμαθεν κἀκεῖνον ἀνιστάμε-νον a line-ending such as Pfeiffer's κλισίηθεν, which does not involve a sense-pause after ἀνιστάμενον.

6. Hiatus

Hiatus after the princeps normally occurs only when the foot is a dactyl,[49] as in frs. 9. 1 κολουραίηι ὑπὸ πέτρηι[50] and 45. 2 ἐλιχρύσωι ἐναλίγκιος. The only other types of hiatus in the *Hecale* involve ἤ,[51] as in fr. 74. 14 ἤ ἔνδιος.[52] Sometimes 'hiatus' is allowed before words which originally began with digamma, e.g. frs. 16 ἔλλερα ἔργα,[53] 2.1 δέ ἑ, 57 δέ οἱ.[54]

7. Correption[55]

This occurs most often with -αι and -οι. Much the commonest type is when καί stands after the feminine caesura (e.g. fr. 72. 1 καὶ ὄμμασι λοξὸν ὑποδράξ); there are 20 such instances in the *Hecale* (including the Incerta). Pfeiffer notes on his fr. 284 that correption in the *second* syllable of a dactyl (e.g. κἀκείνωι ἐπέτρεχεν and ἄνθεϊ ἐλιχρύσωι in fr. 45) is acceptable in our poem (8 instances) and in the *Hymns*, but not, apparently, in the *Aetia*. As usual with Callimachus, there are subtleties to be observed. For example,

---

[48] *GM*, p. 153; cf. Maas, *GM*, para. 98.
[49] *H*. 4. 30 ἤ ὡς is a borrowing from early epic (*H. Hom. Ap.* 25*, 214*).
[50] Cf. fr. 40. 5 ἐρημαίηι ἔνι ναίεις, West, *GM*, p. 136.
[51] Cf. West, *GM*, pp. 15, 156.
[52] Whether Bentley's emendation ἤ ὕστατον could be right in fr. 77 is a greatly disputed point.
[53] Contrast fr. 111 ὄμπνιον ἔργον.
[54] For the treatment of ἑ and οἱ see further on fr. 2. 1; also Pfeiffer on *Aet.* fr. 2. 3, Maas, *GM*, para. 133, Mineur, *HD*, p. 43.
[55] See Maas, *GM*, para. 129; West, *GM*, pp. 11–13; Mineur, *HD*, p. 42; Clapp, *CP* 1 (1906), 239–52. Apollonius Rhodius' practice is studied in detail by Campbell, *R. Ph.* 47 (1973), 83 ff.

correption of -η or -ηι[56] in the *second* syllable of a dactyl seems confined to the first foot[57] of the hexameter (frs. 99. 2 μούνηι ἐνί, 119. 3 πέτρη ἔην;[58] probably αὐτὴ [ἐγώ at fr. 49. 14), but in the *third* syllable of a dactyl, -ῆ is free to wander (fr. 137 καθημένη ἀρχαίηιϲι).[59]

8. *Elision*[60]

This tends to be avoided in nouns and adjectives.[61] Fr. 113. 2 provides a rare example of elision at the masculine caesura (αὐτοὶ μὲν φιλέουϲ').[62]

V. *HECALE* AND THE HELLENISTIC EPYLLION[1]

It is well known that ancient critics do not employ the term ἐπύλλιον in the sense popularized by modern scholars; to the ancients a poem like Callimachus' *Hecale* would be simply ἔποϲ (as in Crinagoras (= below, Test. 4)). Some scholars have gone so far as to deny the existence of the epyllion as a literary category. Formidable problems admittedly arise when one addresses the Greek material. In the first place, which poems should we include?[2] As conventionally defined, the Hellenistic epyllion embraces poems quite disparate in size, from Callimachus' *Hecale*

---

[56] ῆ can behave differently (*H.* 6. 86 ῆ ἐν Ὀθρυί).

[57] Contrast - ῶι in the 2nd syllable of the 3rd foot (fr. 45. 1) and of the 5th foot (fr. 74. 16).

[58] A small point in favour of this fragment, the authenticity of which has been impugned.

[59] *H.* 4. 220 (1st foot), 209, 275 (4th foot), 156 (5th foot).

[60] See Mineur, *HD*, pp. 44–5.

[61] McLennan (*HZ*) on *H.* 1. 93 challenges the statement of Maas (*GM*, para. 121) that the elision of verb-endings in Call. is rare. Examples from the *Hecale* occur in frs. 34, 74. 14, 113. 2.

[62] Also *H.* 6. 65, *epigr.* 42 Pf. = 8 G.–P. = *AP* 12. 118. 1, 3.

[1] I do not wish to enter into lengthy discussion of this vexed topic. The latest treatment, Kathryn J. Gutzwiller, *Studies in the Hellenistic Epyllion* (1981), contains earlier bibliography. For the study of Latin epyllia there is much value in the Introduction to R. O. A. M. Lyne's edition of the pseudo-Virgilian *Ciris* (1978); in my view Lyne underestimates the direct influence on the *Ciris* of Hellenistic poetry.

[2] Some scholars even apply the term 'epyllion' to elegiac poems!

(hardly shorter than 1,000 lines and perhaps appreciably longer)[3] down to the mere 75 lines of Theocritus' *Idyll* 13 ('Hylas').[4] *P. Oxy.* 3000 reveals that the *Hermes* of Callimachus' pupil Eratosthenes was, in all probability, even longer than the *Hecale*, containing between 1,540 and 1,670 lines.[5] Many works which may have been important are little more than titles for us, e.g. two by elder contemporaries of Callimachus, Philetas' *Hermes*[6] and the *Fisherman* by Alexander Aetolus;[7] Euphorion composed many poems in hexameters, but, even though several papyri have accrued to him, it remains very hard to imagine what a complete poem by Euphorion might have been like.[8] And the works under consideration may vary as much in tone as in length. The keynote is usually taken to be 'genial wit and child-like charm', 'a charming or humorous effect'.[9] That fits well enough Theocritus' 'Heracliscus' (*Id.* 24), or Moschus' *Europa*, but scarcely does justice to the greater range of Callimachus' *Hecale*, while the fragments of Euphorion often seem sombre and melancholy in atmosphere.

For these reasons it is not easy to list the determining character-

---

[3] See below, App. II.

[4] I very much doubt whether 'Hylas' should be considered an epyllion. One can argue about other poems in the Theocritean corpus. For our purposes, perhaps the most relevant and interesting is 'Heracles the Lion-slayer' (*Id.* 25). Although external support is very weak, I would not rule out Theocritean authorship; the noticeable difference of style from Theocritus' undoubted works may be partly due to difference of genres (we have observed some similar points when comparing Call.'s *Hecale* with his *Hymns*). I agree with Gow (*A Commentary on Theocritus* (1950), ii. 440) in his high estimate of *Id.* 25's quality, and confess to sympathy for the unfashionable view that the piece, as we have it, may not be complete.

[5] See Parsons on *P. Oxy.* 3000 and *SH* 397.

[6] Frs. 5–9 Powell. Parth. *Narr.* 2 summarizes a story involving Odysseus which occurred in the poem. We cannot be sure that this was the main theme (though frs. 6–7 would suit Odysseus), and it does not explain why the poem was entitled *Hermes*.

[7] Fr. 1 Powell. The subject was apparently the fisherman Glaucus, who became a sea-god. Suidas credits Call. with a *Glaucus* (not even the metre is known), and the same title was used by Catullus' friend Cornificius (fr. 2 Buechner).

[8] For an attempt to say something worth while about the *Dionysus* (frs. 13–18 Powell and perhaps *SH* 418—but the editors are cautious) see A. Barigazzi in L. Ferrero *et al.* (eds), *Miscellanea di studi alessandrini in memoria di Augusto Rostagni* (1963), 416–54.

[9] Gutzwiller, *Hellenistic Epyllion*, pp. 5, 49 (the latter phrase is a comment on the *Hecale*).

istics of a Hellenistic epyllion, and an attempt to do so may run into the objection that they are not found in every example, and in any case are shared by other literary types.[10] Even so, I do believe that the category is a genuine one. Roman poets who composed such works as Catul. 64 or the pseudo-Virgilian *Ciris*—not to mention lost poems like Cinna's *Zmyrna* or Calvus' *Io*—must surely have believed that they were using a recognizable form inherited from the Greeks; and the traces of Callimachus' *Hecale* which may be found in both these works, as well as in several episodes of Ovid's *Metamorphoses*,[11] suggest that our poem was given an honoured place in the evolution of the genre. When Parthenius collected myths for his friend Cornelius Gallus to use εἰc ἔπη καὶ ἐλεγείαc (*Narr. Amat.*, praef.), he surely envisaged Gallus treating them in what we call 'epyllia' rather than in full-blown epics.

If we need to look for prototypes of the epyllion in pre-Hellenistic times, these may be sought in such works as the pseudo-Hesiodic *Shield of Heracles* (480 lines, of which 181 describe the shield itself) and certain of the *Homeric Hymns*, e.g. *Demeter* (2) and *Aphrodite* (5). Consideration of Callimachus' *Hecale* suggests a number of features which could have influenced later poems and may be typical of the genre. Several epyllia are named after a female character, and her emotions (usually, but not in our case, love) are explored in depth. The primary myth is obscure; other myths may be introduced more briefly, sometimes with a parade of learning or in a polemical tone. Digressions are often said to be a distinguishing mark of the epyllion, even if they do not occur in every specimen.[12] We may note the substantial digression on Ericthonius and the daughters of Cecrops, in the mouth of the crow (frs. 70–3). The narrative does not progress in an even and straightforward manner; sometimes important events may be dismissed in a few lines,[13] while elsewhere the poet will linger lovingly over the minutest details (e.g. in Hecale's cottage.

[10] Walter Allen, jun., *TAPA* 71 (1940), 1–26, discussed by Gutzwiller, *Hellenistic Epyllion*, pp. 2–3.

[11] See below, sect. VI.

[12] Lyne, in his edition of the *Ciris* (p. 35), does not consider the passage on Britomartis (294–309) to be a 'formal digression'.

[13] We have some slight reason for thinking that Theseus' combat with the bull was not treated at great length (see on fr. 69. 1).

frs. 28 ff.). The technique of 'flashback' may be employed for past
events,[14] and of prophecy for those in the future;[15] sometimes the
poet concentrates on vivid scenes (e.g. the country people con-
gratulating Theseus in fr. 69). Direct speech is of considerable
importance, as in Hecale's account of her previous life (frs. 41 ff.)
or the crow's narrative (frs. 70–4). There were almost certainly
other substantial speeches in our poem—by Aegeus trying to
deter his son from going against the Marathonian bull, and by
Theseus at Hecale's funeral.[16]

VI. INFLUENCE AND SURVIVAL

A great part of *Hecale*'s influence lies in the subsequent history of
the hospitality theme, which seems sufficiently interesting to
deserve separate treatment in Appendix III below. Even apart
from that, we can see how strong an impact the *Hecale* made on
later Greek and Roman poets from the frequency with which
they borrowed its words and motifs. As far as poets more or less
contemporary with Callimachus are concerned, we can seldom be
dogmatic about either their absolute or relative dates; nor do we
know at what point in Callimachus' long career the *Hecale* should
be placed.[1] I have, when quoting parallels in the Commentary,
arranged them in the belief that *Hecale* post-dates Aratus' *Phaeno-
mena*,[2] but pre-dates all four books of Apollonius' *Argonautica*,
Theocritus' *Idylls*, the *Alexandra* of Lycophron,[3] Philicus' *Hymn to
Demeter*, and Rhianus;[4] in several cases the chronological relation-
ship could be reversed by further argument or new evidence.

[14] e.g. perhaps with regard to Theseus' youth in Troezen (frs. 9 ff.).
[15] For the story of Coronis and the raven in fr. 74. 14 ff.
[16] I fully recognize that because of the fragmentary condition of the *Hecale*
many of the above points cannot be asserted with confidence.
[1] See above, sect. I.
[2] Call. referred respectfully to Aratus not only in the famous epigram (27
Pf. = 56 G.–P. = *AP* 9. 507), but also in his prose work *Against Praxiphanes* (fr.
460 Pf.). Ancient sources differ about the relative age of Aratus and Call. (K. O.
Brink, *CQ* 40 (1946), 12–14)—a matter which, even if it were settled, would not
necessarily determine the relative dating of particular poems.
[3] Though I would be prepared to accept a 3rd-cent. date for at least the great
part of that work.
[4] *FGH* 265 T 1 calls Rhianus a contemporary of Eratosthenes. Jacoby placed
him before Call., but, even though Rhianus' version of the Admetus myth (fr. 10
Powell) may predate Call. *H.* 2. 48 ff., the latter poem (at least according to the
scholiast on l. 26) belongs to the reign of Ptolemy III Euergetes.

Resemblances between the *Hecale* and Apollonius Rhodius are not as numerous as with the *Aetia*, but there are parallels (from every book of the *Argonautica* except 2) which are striking enough not to be due to chance: Ap. Rh. 1. 1203 θοὴ ἀνέμοιο κατάϊξ, cf. *Hec.* fr. 18. 15 θοὴ βορέαο κατάϊξ;[5] 3. 277 ὅν τε μύωπα βοῶν κλείουσι νομῆες, cf. fr. 117 ὅν τε μύωπα βοῶν καλέουσιν ἀμορβοί; 4. 111 ἄγχαυρον (adjective), cf. fr. 74. 23 ἄγχαυρος (noun). More generally, it is hard to believe that the talking crows in *Arg.* 3. 927 ff. and *Hec.* frs. 70 ff. are not somehow connected.[6] Callimachus and Lycophron have in common the similarity of *Alex.* 866–7 κακοξένους | πάλης κονίστρας to *Hec.* fr. 62. 1–2 κονίστραι | ἄξεινοι, and the picture of Diomedes' companions, transformed into birds, being fed on κρίμνα (*Alex.* 607) reminds one of the voracious crow in *Hec.* fr. 74. 5. It is worth dwelling a little longer on *Alex.* 793–4:

> εὖφαρ θανεῖται πόντιον φυγὼν σκέπας
> κόραξ σὺν ὅπλοις Νηρίτων δρυμῶν πέλας.

The aged Odysseus is described as a wrinkled skin (εὖφαρ) and a long-lived bird (κόραξ). In the *Hecale* too an old bird speaks of her εὖφαρ (fr. 74. 11, a very rare word); although a κορώνη rather than a κόραξ, she goes on to prophesy about a κόραξ four lines later (fr. 74. 15). I suspect that Lycophron has picked up the associations of εὖφαρ in the *Hecale* passage. If so, this is an indication that Callimachus wrote first, but there would be no need to deny at least the bulk of the *Alexandra* to its traditional author, the member of the tragic Pleiad in the first half of the third century — like Callimachus, Lycophron may have had a long literary career.

In Philicus' *Hymn to Demeter*, country people pelt the goddess with leaves (*SH* 680. 53), as happens to Theseus in *Hec.* fr. 69. 11 ff., and the old Attic woman Iambe (*SH* 680. 54 ff.) faintly resembles the heroine of our poem.[7] I think it more probable that Rhian. fr. 20 Powell πολυδρύμους ⟨τε⟩ Μελαινάς reflects *Hec.* fr. 84 πολυπτῶκές τε Μελαιναί than vice versa.[8]

---

[5] See below on fr. 18. 15 for Webster's attempt to prove Apollonius Rhodius' priority.

[6] The only verbal reminiscence is ἐπιπνείουσι(ν)* in *Arg.* 3. 937 and *Hec.* fr. 74. 9.

[7] Cf. A. Körte, *Hermes*, 66 (1931), 448–9; C. Previtali, *SIFC*, NS 41 (1969), 13–18.

[8] See above, n. 4; Pfeiffer on fr. 266; id., *History*, 122 n. 3.

Moving to the next generation of Hellenistic poets, I shall discuss Eratosthenes' *Erigone* in Appendix III below. Euph. fr. 9 Powell comes from a curse poem, perhaps the Ἀραὶ ἢ Ποτηριο-κλέπτης (cf. fr. 8 Powell), in which the writer attacks his enemy with a series of imprecations: 'may he (she) suffer the fate of A, B, and C etc.' This kind of work became largely a vehicle for mythological erudition; we imagine that Callimachus' lost *Ibis* (frs. 381–2 Pf.) was of such a nature. In lines 3–9 Euphorion seems to be using the *Hecale* (as Ovid's *Ibis* uses the *Aetia*) as a quarry for gruesome fates:

>]θι κάππεσε λύχνου
>]α κατὰ Γλαυκώπιον Ἕρςη⁹
> 5 οὕνεκ' Ἀθ]ηναίης ἱερὴν ἀνελύςατο κίςτην
> δεςποίν]ης. ἢ ὅςςον ὁδοιπόροι ἐρρήςςοντο
> Σκε]ίρων ἔνθα πόδεςςιν ἀεικέα μήδετο χύτλα
> ο]ὐκ ἐπὶ δήν· Αἴθρης γὰρ ἀλοιηθεὶς ὑπὸ παιδί
> νωιτέρης χέλυος πύματος ἐλιπήνατο λαιμόν.

The lamp (l. 3) recurs several times in Nonnus, perhaps from the *Hecale*,[10] and the sin of the daughters of Cecrops who opened the basket to look at Ericthonius was certainly recounted by the crow in Callimachus, (fr. 70. 5 ff.). Problems arise over line 4. If van Groningen (see above, n. 9) was right in taking Ἕρςη as nominative, subject of κάππεσε as well as ἀνελύςατο, it seems that Euphorion singles out for blame and punishment Herse, who in Callimachus' main source ('Amelesagoras') was apparently the only sister to be guiltless. Was it Callimachus himself or Euphorion who modified the Atthidographer's version? Γλαυκώπιον (4) shows Euphorion borrowing a learned allusion from elsewhere in the *Hecale* (fr. 17. 11). Lines 6–9 concern Sciron, whose death may have been described by Theseus to Hecale (see on frs. 59–60). I suspect that Euphorion's πόδεςςιν ... χύτλα(7) may give us the context of *Hec.* fr. 60 φράςον δέ μοι, εἰς ὅ τι τεῦχος | χεύωμαι ποςὶ χύτλα καὶ ὁππόθεν—not the foot-washing in Hecale's cottage (see fr. 34), as older scholars thought, but Theseus addressing Sciron and playing for time. ἀλοιηθείς (8) might recall ἀπηλοίηςε in *Hec.* fr. 69. 1 (the combat with the bull), or perhaps Callimachus used

---

⁹ I follow B. A. van Groningen (fr. 11 in his 1977 edition) in reading Ἕρςη, nom. with κάππεςε, rather than Ἕρςηι dat.; cf. Lloyd-Jones, *CR*, NS 29 (1979), 15.

¹⁰ See below, p. 228.

the same verb in connection with Sciron. Finally, Pfeiffer remarked (on his fr. 296) that ἐλιπήνατο λαιμόν (9) 'Callimachum sapit'. Other fragments of Euphorion indebted to the *Hecale* include fr. 144 Powell (the very rare noun ἄλλιξ, cf. *Hec.* fr. 42. 5), and *SH* 415, col. ii. 16–17 ἐκ [δὲ τ]ρίχα χρυσέην κόρςης ὤλοψε Κομαιθώ | πα[τρ]ὸς ἑοῦ, where Euphorion probably alludes to the parallel myth in *Hec.* fr. 90 Ϲκύλλα γυνὴ κατακᾶϲα καὶ οὐ ψύθος οὔνομ' ἔχουϲα | πορφυρέην ἤμηϲε κρέκα, but the father's lock is golden rather than purple, and 'wrenched'[11] rather than 'reaped'. The elegant verbal structure of *Hec.* fr. 113. 2–3, with repetition and antithesis, may well have inspired *SH* 443. 8–9 (likewise astronomical).

   P. Oxy. 1794 (= Powell, *CA* pp. 78–9, epic. adesp. 4) preserves an anonymous hexameter fragment which is generally considered to be of some quality,[12] and dated third- or second-century BC. In it an elderly woman, once rich but now impoverished, addresses a younger person as 'child' (1) and laments that she is reduced to the status of a vagabond (20–1). I quote lines 9–21:

> ἄλλοτε γὰρ ἄλλοις ὄλβου λάχος ἀνθρώποιϲιν·
> 10 οἵη τοι πεϲϲοῖο δίκη, τοίηδε καὶ ὄλβου·
> πεϲϲὸς ἀμειβόμενός ποτε μὲν τοῖς, ἄλλοτε τοῖϲιν
> εἰς ἀγαθὸν πίπτει καὶ ἀφνεὸν αἶψα τίθηϲι
> πρόϲθεν ἀνολβείοντ', εὐηφενέοντα δ' ἄνολβον·
> τοῖος διητῆϲι περιϲτρέφεται πτερύγεϲϲιν
> 15 ὄλβος ἐπ' ἀνθρώπους, ἄλλον δ' ἐξ ἄλλου ὀφέλλει.
> ἡ δ' αὐτὴ πολέεϲϲι ποτὸν καὶ ϲῖτον ὄρεξα
> τὴν ὁράας, ἐπεὶ οὔτι λιπερνῆτις πάρος ἦα,
> ἔϲκε δέ μοι νειὸς βαθυλήϊος, ἔϲκεν ἀλωή,
> πολλὰ δέ μοι μῆλ' ἔϲκε, τὰ μὲν διὰ πάντα κέδαϲϲεν
> 20 ἥδ' ὀλοὴ βούβρωϲτις, ἐγὼ δ' ἀκόμιϲτος ἀλῆτις
> ὧδέ ποθι πλήθουϲαν ἀνὰ πτόλιν ε[. . . ἕ]ρπω.

The resemblance to Callimachus' *Hecale* consists of the general situation and the wording of lines 17–18 (cf. frs. 41, 42. 1). A few scholars[13] have thought that this might actually be a piece of the *Hecale*. In my opinion the passage is not distinguished enough for Callimachus. Leaving aside subjective appreciation, (*a*) I find it

---

[11] Cf. the fate of the Cyclops in Call. *H.* 3. 77.

[12] 'Facili stilo sed citra artem exquisitam' (Powell), 'a good composition' (Page, *GLP*, p. 501).

[13] Most recently Hopkinson (*HD*) on *hymn* 6. 102.

hard to believe that Callimachus would make his heroine say both
οὐδ' ἀπὸ πάππων | εἰμὶ λιπερνῆτις (fr. 41. 1–2) and ἐπεὶ οὔτι
λιπερνῆτις πάρος ἦα (l. 17 of the anonymous piece); (b) the urban
setting (21) does not suit what we know of the *Hecale*; and, most
seriously, (c) there are many metrical features uncharacteristic of
Callimachus,[14] a few of which might be tolerated individually,
but, taken together, and in such a small number of lines, tell
decisively against Callimachean authorship. So this is an interest-
ing example of the *Hecale*'s influence, but not an addition to the
text of our poem.[15]

In the second century BC the *Hecale* seems to have been
Nicander's favourite reading, to judge from the number of his
imitations.[16] Gow and Scholfield, commenting on *Alex.* 463
τινθαλέοιcιν ἐπαιονάαcθε λοετροῖc consider (but reject) the possi-
bility that an anonymous citation in Suidas, τινθαλέοιcι κατικμή-
ναιντο λοετροῖc, might reflect a variant κατικμήναιο in Nicander.
A papyrus has since proved that the words in Suidas belong to the
Hecale (fr. 48. 5). Many other Nicandrean imitations are close: e.g.
Hec. fr. 72. 1–2 καὶ ὄμμαcι λοξὸν ὑποδράξ | ὀccομένη becomes καὶ
λοξὸν ὑποδρὰξ ὄμμαcι λεύccων (*Ther.* 457).[17] The first-century BC

[14] Compare the following points with my account of the Callimachean
hexameter (above, sect. IV). We could put up with the elision at the masculine
caesura ἀνολβείοντ' (13; cf. *Hec.* fr. 113. 2), perhaps with ἄλλοτε γὰρ ἄλλοιc (9; cf.
Mineur, *HD*, p. 42, but correct Powell's reference to Call.—he means *H. Hom.
Dem.* 57) and even with the infringement of Hilberg's Law πολλὰ δέ μοι μῆλ'|
ἔcκε (19). Harder to forgive are ll. 7 ..], ἐλπωραὶ δ' ἐάγηcαν (violation of
Bulloch's Law), 11 ποτὲ μὲν τοῖc,| ἄλλοτε τοῖcιν (violation of Naeke's Law), 12
καὶ ἀφνεόν (un-Callimachean, though found in some other poets, cf. Richardson
on *H. Hom. Dem.* 424), 15 ἄλλον δ' ἐξ ἄλλου ὀφέλλει (spondaic word after
masculine caesura, without bucolic diaeresis; 3rd and 4th feet both spondaic).

[15] The style of the anonymous piece is generally straightforward, and in places
strongly reminiscent of Homer (compare l. 10 with the structure of *Il.* 6. 146),
but incorporates several rare or even unparalleled locutions of a more Hellenistic
cast (e.g. l. 13). Another link with Call. is noted by Pfeiffer on his fr. 559; ὀλοὴ
βούβρωcτιc (20) occurs also in Nic. *Ther.* 409*. Supposing that the poet were
someone whose name we knew, I might wonder about Rhianus (for Rhianus
and the *Hecale* see on fr. 84). Both the style and the moralizing tone (with stress
on extremes of fortune) seem to me not unlike those of Rhian. fr. 1, our only
extended specimen of his work. In connection with εὐηφενέοντα (13), note
Rhianus' attested preference for εὐηφενέων in *Il.* 23. 81 (cf. Pfeiffer, *History*, i.
149).

[16] See below, Index of Allusions and Imitations.

[17] For the metrical oddity see above, sect. IV n. 40.

poet Parthenius perhaps borrowed from Callimachus (*Hec.* fr. 49. 3) the expression 'to rend one's clothes over' somebody, i.e. to mourn for them (*SH* 646. 5–6 ταὶ δ' ἐπ' ἐκείνηι | βεύδεα παρθενικαὶ Μιλησίδες ἐρρήξαντο).

Parthenius of Nicaea came to Rome as a prisoner in the Mithridatic Wars,[18] and we can be sure that, whether or not through his influence, contemporary Roman writers were familiar with the *Hecale*. The case of Lucretius is particularly instructive, because it used to be held that as an admirer of Ennius and old Roman poetry, he had little time for the Alexandrians. That view was rightly challenged by E. J. Kenney,[19] but he failed to quote the most striking allusion to learned Hellenistic poetry (Lucr. 6. 749 ff.; cf. below, Test. 3):

> est et Athenaeis in montibus, arcis in ipso
> vertice, Palladis ad templum Tritonidis almae,
> quo numquam pennis appellunt corpora raucae
> cornices, non cum fumant altaria donis.
> usque adeo fugitant non iras Palladis acris
> pervigili causa, *Graium ut cecinere poetae*,
> sed natura loci opus efficit ipsa suapte.

As we shall see, the mythological explanation of why crows avoid the Acropolis was not something Lucretius could have picked up from any old Greek poet. The only pre-Callimachean author whom we know to have mentioned this legend is an obscure Atthidographer 'Amelesagoras', who wrote in prose. That Lucretius does indeed refer to Callimachus is put beyond reasonable doubt by 'iras Palladis acris' (753), which echoes *Hec.* fr. 73. 12 βαρὺς χόλος αἰὲν Ἀθήνης.[20]

Knowledge of the *Hecale* can be claimed for Cicero from three diverse pieces of evidence. In his own poetry, fr. 6. 73 Buechner 'nitidoque Lyceo' may glance at *Hec.* fr. 71. 2–3 Λυκείου | καλὸν ἀεὶ λιπόωντα κατὰ δρόμον Ἀπόλλωνος. *Tusc.* 4. 50 'an etiam Theseus Marathonii tauri cornua comprehendit iratus?' probably alludes to the *Hecale*, and in particular to fr. 67 θηρὸς ἐρωήσας ὀλοὸν κέρας. This somewhat strengthens the case for ascribing to our poem fr. 165 inc. auct. πολλὰ μάτην κεράεσσιν ἐς ἠέρα

---

[18] Cf. Clausen, *GRBS* 5 (1964), 181–96.

[19] 'Doctus Lucretius', *Mnemosyne*, 23 (1970), 366–92. The allusion to the *Hecale* is picked up by R. D. Brown in *Illinois Classical Studies*, 7 (1982), 88–9.

[20] See also fr. 72, and perhaps fr. 73. 7.

θυμήναντα, which Cicero quotes anonymously (*Att.* 8. 5. 1) in the clear expectation that Atticus would be familiar with the line.[21]

For Roman poets the *Hecale* may have had a special position as one of the earliest, finest, and most substantial specimens of the epyllion.[22] If that were so, we need not be surprised to find traces of our poem in Catul. 64,[23] the pseudo-Virgilian *Ciris*, and Ovid's *Metamorphoses*. The anonymous line quoted by Cicero (fr. 165 inc. auct. above) was undoubtedly the model for Catullus 64. 111 'nequiquam vanis iactantem cornua ventis'. More generally, the speech of Aegeus to his son in Catul. 64. 215 ff. would be almost entirely appropriate to the *Hecale* if we substituted the Marathonian bull for the Minotaur. There must have been such a speech in Callimachus,[24] though we have only part of Theseus' plea to be allowed to go against the monster (see on fr. 17). The pseudo-Virgilian *Ciris*, whatever its date, contains several echoes and themes in common with the *Hecale*. Most strikingly, *Ciris* 351–2 reproduces the structure of fr. 113. The old woman Carme, who has lost one dear child, and fears losing another, recalls Hecale's position in fr. 49; *Ciris* 316 'cum premeret Natura,[25] mori me velle negavi' is suggestively similar to fr. 49. 2 ἠρνεόμην θανάτοιο πάλαι καλέοντος ἀκοῦσαι. Nisus' purple lock (e.g. *Ciris* 320) first comes in the *Hecale* (fr. 90), and in the *Ciris* we find Sciron with his tortoise (465–7; cf. *Hec.* frs. 59–60). *Ciris* 102 'Actaeos . . . colles' may reflect the opening line of Callimachus' epyllion.

The entertainment of Aeneas by old Evander in *Aen.* 8 belongs with examples of the hospitality theme (see below, App. III): no verbal similarities to the *Hecale* fragments are apparent. Otherwise the only Virgilian parallels I can offer are *Ecl.* 2. 24 'Actaeo', the earliest occurrence of this epithet in Latin (cf. *Hec.* fr. 1), and

---

[21] One might even see a link between the last two references—the bull was in a passion (θυμήναντα), but Theseus remained calm (was not 'iratus').

[22] See above, sect. V.

[23] See also below on *Hec.* fr. 113 for the conceit about the morning and evening star, which is taken up by Catullus (62), Helvius Cinna (*Zmyrna*), and the *Ciris*.

[24] I have speculated that fr. 122 might belong to it.

[25] Dr Lyne (in his 1978 edition *ad loc.*) wonders about these words. I would have thought the meaning is 'when Nature pressed me hard' (like e.g. an insistent creditor demanding repayment), with a subsidiary allusion to Lucr. 3. 931 ff. where Nature abuses the person reluctant to face death.

Aen. 9. 569, 10. 698 'ingenti fragmine montis', perhaps from the picturesque description of Athena carrying 'a great chunk of Hypsizorus' (μέγα τρύφος Ὑψιζώρου) in *Hec.* fr. 71. 1. Of Horace one can only say that he admired Callimachus' ὑάλοιο φαάντερος (fr. 18. 2; cf. *Carm.* 3. 13. 1 'o fons Bandusiae splendidior vitro'). The elegists Tibullus and Propertius, well-versed though they were in Hellenistic poets generally and Callimachus in particular, do not betray any specific connection with the *Hecale*.[26]

With regard to Ovid the position is very different. Our poem is a main source for two episodes in the *Metamorphoses* (2. 534 ff., 8. 626 ff.), and has probably contributed to a third (7. 404 ff.). In book 8, the tale of Baucis and Philemon is not just one more example of the hospitality theme (cf. below, App. III); many details follow Callimachus almost to the point of translation. The episode of the daughters of Cecrops, the crow, and the raven (2. 534 ff.) is especially interesting, because it is linked to the Vienna Tablet of the *Hecale*. If we remember that Ovid's method of adaptation is always ingenious and never slavish, it may be possible to pick up one or two hints on reconstruction of the fragmentary Greek model. A few allusions to the *Hecale* can also be found in Ovid's elegiac poems.[27] His one mention of Callimachus' heroine by name has caused much trouble (*Rem.* 747–8 (= below, Test. 5)):

> cur nemo est Hecalen, nulla est quae ceperit Iron?
> nempe quod alter egens, altera pauper erat.

Older scholars deduced with complete confidence from these words that in Callimachus Hecale never married. Recent papyri, however, have thrown more light on a passage (frs. 47–9) wherein a woman, probably Hecale herself, seems to lament the death of two boys whom she had brought up, and also of another male person. While it is quite conceivable that Hecale nursed two children for someone else, one would most naturally take the boys to be her own sons, and the man her husband. Perhaps, therefore, Ovid speaks only of Hecale's impoverished state, leaving aside her earlier, more prosperous period: if *Rem.* 747–8 glance at anything specific in Callimachus' text, perhaps 'pauper'

---

[26] Independent evidence of our poem in early Augustan Rome is provided by the Greek epigrammatist Crinagoras (*AP* 9. 545 = 11 G.-P. = below, Test. 4).

[27] See below, Index of Allusions and Imitations.

picks up λιπερνῆτις in fr. 41. 2, and the sentiment that no one would have her relates to Theseus' enquiry why she lives in such miserable solitude (fr. 40. 5).

The spirit of Ovid's Baucis and Philemon, which lingers like a Dutch painting over every detail of life in a country cottage, is also apparent in the pseudo-Virgilian *Moretum* (? of Tiberian date). This kind of scene appealed to Romans, no doubt because it harmonized with their own nostalgic feelings about the hardy peasants from whom they boasted their descent. Kenney, in his useful edition of the *Moretum*[28] suspects that the poet may specifically have Callimachus in mind; one could compare *Mor.* 49–50 with *Hec.* fr. 35. 2.[29]

Statius was the one Silver Latin poet on whom the *Hecale* made a deep impression: we should remember that Callimachus was a favourite author of his schoolmaster father (*Silv.* 5. 3. 156–7). Our heroine is the 'anus hospita' of *Theb.* 12. 582,[30] and Statius seems to have drawn on Callimachus for a number of Attic and Argive place-names.[31] Allusions in Petronius[32] and Apuleius[33] show that the *Hecale* was well known to other post-Augustan writers; and if Dr Lyne were correct in dating the pseudo-Virgilian *Ciris* after Statius,[34] that would be more evidence for the later period. On general grounds it would be surprising if Claudian did not know the *Hecale*, but I am aware of only one passage which can plausibly be interpreted as a verbal echo.[35]

The influence of Callimachus' epyllion on Greek poets of the Roman imperial age is very great indeed. To mention only more substantial figures, we shall often have cause in the Commentary to cite Dionysius Periegetes (time of Hadrian), the two Oppians (early third century), Triphiodorus, and Quintus of Smyrna (fourth century). Christian writers were as familiar with our

[28] Bristol Classical Press (1984), pp. xxx–xxxiv.

[29] Among Hellenistic descriptions of the simple country life in general, Kenney (op. cit. pp. xxx–xxxi) cites the pseudo-Theocritean 'Fishermen' (*Id.* 21) and two epigrams by Leonidas of Tarentum (*AP* 7. 736 = 33 G.–P., *AP* 6. 302 = 37 G/–P.).

[30] Below, Test. 8 (see on fr. 57).

[31] See below, Index of Allusions and Imitations.

[32] 135. 8. 15 ff. (= below, Test. 7).

[33] *Met.* 1. 23 (= below, Test. 10).

[34] pp. 48 ff. of his 1978 edn. My own feeling is for an earlier date.

[35] *Eutrop.* 1. 348–9; cf. *Hec.* fr. 74. 15–17.

poem as pagans; this may be due in part to the attraction of the
hospitality theme (see below, App. III), but in general, as we shall
see from the evidence of papyri, grammarians, and commentators
(below), Callimachus was more famous than any Greek poet
except Homer, and knowledge of his work was common to
pagans and Christians of any education. Among the latter group,
note especially St Gregory of Nazianzus (late fourth century,
Patriarch of Constantinople), who often imitates the *Hecale*, and
sometimes borrows phrases verbatim.[36] Callimachean echoes may
turn up in some unexpected places, e.g. the hexameter paraphrase
(?mid-fifth century) of the Psalms which has survived under the
name of the heresiarch Apollinarius, or the similar paraphrase of
St John's Gospel by Nonnus.[37] One small but telling indication of
common authorship for the St John paraphrase and the extraordi-
nary 48-book *Dionysiaca* is the way in which the same pieces of
learned Hellenistic poetry are echoed in the two works. Consider
Hec. fr. 85. 2 Λιμναίωι δὲ χοροστάδας ἦγον ἑορτάς, with its rare
cult title of Bacchus, and even rarer epithet χοροστάς. This is
reflected in both *Dionysiaca* (27. 307 Λιμναῖον μετὰ Βάκχον) and
Paraphrase (7. 140 χοροστάδος ἦμαρ ἑορτῆς). Parallels from Non-
nus can be of help in elucidating the fragmentary text of the
Hecale, though, as always, caution is necessary. For example,
Dion. 17. 210 ταυρείην ... ἀπηλοίησε κεραίην is one of several
supports for reading οἰόκερως· ἕτερον γὰρ ἀπηλοίησε κορύνη in the
first line of the Vienna tablet (fr. 69. 1), and a number of hints in
Dion. 27. 301–7 encourage me to think that the reconstruction of
Hec. fr. 85 may be along the right lines.

VII. ANCIENT COMMENTATORS, COPYISTS AND GRAMMARIANS

Further evidence for the high repute of the *Hecale* in ancient times

---

[36] A habit which leaves us in doubt whether Suidas cites καὶ ἄγριον οἶδμα
θαλάσσης from the *Hecale* (fr. 160 inc. auct.) or from Gregory of Nazianzus, who
uses the words twice.

[37] Cf. Alan Cameron, *YCS* 27 (1982), 235–9. I am confident that the
paraphraser of St John is identical with the poet of the *Dionysiaca*. It is not a
question merely of this being the style of the day; so close are the parallels that
the only alternative would be to consider the paraphrase a deliberate forgery by
someone pretending to be the composer of the *Dionysiaca*.

can be gleaned from the number of commentators and grammarians who turned their attention to the poem, together with the papyrus texts of which fragments have survived. We shall see (below, pp. 48–50) that for Oxyrhynchus alone[1] the remains (mostly very small) of nine copies of the *Hecale* have been found, dating from the second to perhaps the seventh century AD. I doubt whether this number of copies owes very much, if anything, to the fact that Callimachus was a 'local' poet, who had lived and worked in Egypt for almost all his career. Grammarians from the time of Aristophanes of Byzantium (*c.*255–180 BC) quote Callimachus more often than any other Greek poet apart from Homer;[2] the Lille papyrus of Callimachus' *Victoria Berenices* (*Aet.* 3), with interspersed commentary, dates from within a generation of the poet's death.[3]

Among the ancient commentators on Callimachus whose names have come down to us, three are of interest for the *Hecale*—Theon son of Artemidorus, Epaphroditus, and Salustius—but only the last-named certainly wrote a full commentary on our poem. Theon, much the most celebrated, belongs to the Augustan age;[4] he definitely composed a ὑπόμνημα on *Aet.* 1 (fr. 42 Pf.) and on *Aet.* 2, in the course of the latter quoting *Hec.* fr. 71. 1–2.[5] That he wrote also on the *Hecale* must remain a conjecture.[6] The date of Epaphroditus is unclear, but perhaps the second half of the first century AD; he is credited with a commentary on *Aet.* 2 (frs. 52–3 Pf.). Probably before AD 100, an unknown scholar compiled summaries of Callimachus' poems, to which he added explanatory material from a learned commentary. His work may

---

[1] 'Urbe ... litterarum humanarum studiosissima inde ab Augusti aetate' (Pfeiffer, ii, p. xxvi n. 2).

[2] Pfeiffer, ii, pp. xxvi, xxx ff.

[3] P. J. Parsons, *ZPE* 25 (1977), 4.

[4] Theon busied himself with many other Hellenistic poets too; the wealth of Callimachean quotations in the surviving scholia to Lycophron, Apollonius, Theocritus, and Nicander probably owes something to Theon's influence (Pfeiffer, ii, p. xxx). See also E. Diehl, *Hypomnema* (1937), 320 ff.

[5] Somewhere he also cited *Hec.* fr. 45. 1, arguing that ἁρμοῖ = 'recently' should have a smooth breathing. Since we now know that the other Callimachean quotation adduced by *Et. Gen.* at the same time (fr. 383. 4 Pf.) in fact belongs to *Aet.* 3 (*SH* 254. 4, *Victoria Berenices*), it seems possible that this is a remnant of Theon's commentary on *Aet.* 3.

[6] Pfeiffer, ii, p. xxix.

be reflected in the more detailed papyrus scholia on *Aet.* 1,[7] and the briefer *Diegeses*, including that on the *Hecale*.[8] All in all, Pfeiffer deduces that from the end of the first century BC up to the beginning of the second century AD a considerable number of scholars must have written on the poems of Callimachus.

The one ancient commentator who beyond question explained the *Hecale* may have lived several centuries later.[9] He was called Salustius, and is probably identical with the Salustius who wrote on Sophocles;[10] his name is mentioned by the *Etymologicum Genuinum* in connection with frs. 9 (οὕτω Cαλούcτιοc), 29 (οὕτω Cαλούcτιοc εἰς τὴν Ἑκάλην Καλλιμάχου), and 179 inc. auct. (οὕτω Cαλούcτιοc). Pfeiffer[11] allowed that the rich scholia in the sixth–seventh-century *P. Oxy.* 2258 (= below, pap. 2) may derive from Salustius. His commentary on the *Hecale* was also probably the one used by Suidas; we shall return later[12] to this question, which is of great significance for the *Hecale* because so many of the fragments ascribed to our poem depend on anonymous citations in the Byzantine lexicon.

VIII. THE *HECALE* IN BYZANTINE TIMES

As we have seen, imitations in Gregory of Nazianzus, pseudo-Apollinarius, and Nonnus make it plain that the *Hecale* was well known in the fourth and fifth centuries. In the reign of Anastasius (491–518) Marianus of Eleutheropolis summarized Callimachus' *Hecale*, *Hymns*, *Aetia*, and *epigrams* in 6,810 lines (= below, Test. 12);[1] our latest Egyptian papyrus to contain the *Hecale* (*P. Oxy.*

---

[7] *PSI* 1219, *P. Oxy.* 2263, both 2nd–3rd cent. AD.

[8] *P. Med.* 18 (= below, pap. 1).

[9] Wilamowitz thought of the fourth or fifth century AD. For more on Salustius see R. Reitzenstein, 'Inedita Poetarum Graecorum Fragmenta', *Index Lectionum in Acad. Rostochiensi* (1890/1), 14 ff.

[10] Pfeiffer (ii, p. xxix) notes that the Sophoclean scholia derived from Salustius often quote Call. It is a reasonable conjecture from Steph. Byz. s.v. Ἄζιλιc (οἱ . . . περὶ Cαλούcτιον) that Salustius also wrote on the *Hymns* (cf. 2. 89).

[11] *Callimachus*, ii, p. xxix; see further T. Ciresola, *RIL* 92 (1958), 283–5.

[12] See below, sect. IX.

[1] Cf. below, App. II; Alan Cameron, *Historia*, 14 (1965), 482; id., *CQ*, NS 20 (1970), 120–1; Averil Cameron, *Byzantion*, 37 (1967), 15 n. 6. An anonymous iambic epigram which summarizes the *Hecale* (= below, Test. 13) together with other poems by Call. may be sixth century or later (Pfeiffer, ii, p. lv; cf. Bulloch, *FH*, p. 80 n. 1).

2258) may have been written about 600, though the style of handwriting is a stereotyped one, and any date between *c.*500 and *c.*700 is possible. I myself doubt the opinion of I. Cazzaniga[2] that the life of St Philaretus of Amnia in Paphlagonia (702–92) by Nicetas[3] need be influenced by the *Hecale*, although it does indeed illustrate the continuing appeal of the hospitality theme among the Byzantines (see below, App. III). Arethas (born *c.*850) provides one piece of information not otherwise known—that Callimachus used an old name for the island of Salamis. This can almost certainly be trusted, even though Arethas seems to get the form of the name slightly wrong (see below on fr. 91); whether he had access to a complete text of the *Hecale* or drew the reference from an earlier secondary source cannot now be determined. The commentary of Salustius (see above) was used in the second half of the ninth century for the *Etymologicum Genuinum*, and probably survived until at least the middle of the tenth century, when numerous extracts were transcribed into the lexicon conventionally known as Suidas.[4]

Grave suspicions must surround the claim of John Tzetzes in the twelfth century to give the context of fr. 113. 3; experts whom I have consulted seem to disagree as to whether it would be characteristic of Tzetzes simply to invent a context. None the less, complete copies of the *Hecale* were almost certainly still extant in this period, and we may even be able to identify the owner of the very last one. Michael Choniates (Acominatos) from Chonae in Phrygia (St Paul's Colossae), was Archbishop of Athens for some twenty or thirty years up to the Frankish conquest of AD 1205.[5] He had brought with him from Constantinople a library which seems to have included the *Aetia* and *Hecale*. Although Athenian life disappointed his first high hopes, Michael drew a parallel between the welcome which the city, once great

---

[2] *Parola del Passato*, 23 (1968), 224–7.

[3] Text in M.-H. Fourmy and M. Leroy, *Byzantion*, 9 (1934), 85–170.

[4] I use this form (rather than 'the Suda') without, however, believing that Suidas was the name of the compiler; see Maas, *Kleine Schriften* (1973), pp. 494–5. N. G. Wilson (*Scholars of Byzantium* (1983), p. 145) judges disputes about the name and etymology to be unprofitable.

[5] See S. P. Lambros, *Athenaion*, 6 (1877), 354 ff.; K. M. Sutton, 'Athens in the later twelfth century', *Speculum*, 19 (1944), 179–207; Wilson, *Scholars*, 204–6.

but now decrepit, could provide, and the modest entertainment offered by old Hecale to Theseus:[6]

νῦν δὲ χρόνωι γεγηρακυῖα καὶ πρὸς γῆν καταρρεύcαca, προcτιθεμένη δ' ὅμως προθύμως ἦν ἔχει λόγου τράπεζαν ἄκομψον (cf. *Hec.* fr. 82) καὶ ὡς ἐξὸν ἐπιδεικνυμένη τὰ τῆς παλαιᾶc φιλοξενίαc (cf. fr. 2) καὶ φιλοφροcύνηc γνωρίcματα . . .

πέπειcμαι δ' ὅτι μᾶλλον ἂν χαίροιc πενιχρῶc οὕτω φιλοφρονούμενοc παρὰ τῆc coφῆc ποτε πόλεωc ἢ παρὰ τῆc πρώτηc τῶν ἄλλων φιλοτίμωc καὶ περιττῶc δεξιούμενοc, ὅτε καὶ Θηcεὺc ὡc ὁ λόγοc ἀρχόμενοc ἀνεβάλετο, τὸ πτωχικὸν καὶ ⟨πρεcβυτικὸν⟩ φιλοξένημα τῆc Ἑκάληc τῆc Ἀττικῆc ἥδιcτον ἐλογίcατο (cf. fr. 82).

Michael often alludes to the *Hecale* (cf. below, Test. 14, 15), both in his prose and his verse; for the most part these allusions are well signposted by their context, although one or two are slipped in unobtrusively, e.g. ii. 353. 24 ἀποικία Cκυθική, ἣ τοῖc Ἀcιανοῖc κακὴ παρενάccατο γείτων (cf. *Hec.* fr. 49. 10 κακὸc παρενάccατο γείτων of Cercyon). A typical specimen of his paraphrase might be i. 157. 9 ff. (from Test. 15a, on Hecale) ξενοδόχωι δ' ἄλλωc ἀγαθῆι καὶ τοῖc παροδεύουcιν ἄκλειcτον ἀεὶ προβαλλομένηι τὸ οἴκημα, which represents fr. 2 τίον δέ ἑ πάντεc ὁδῖται | ἦρα φιλοξενίηc· ἔχε γὰρ τέγοc ἀκλήιcτον. Recently doubts have been raised whether Michael had access to more than a summary of Callimachus,[7] which seems unnecessarily sceptical. True, he never mentions Callimachus by name, but the lack of a reference to an actual manuscript is not suspicious.[8] The suggested alternative, that the *Hecale* 'might have been known in the form of a Byzantine digest which preserved some of the Callimachean vocabulary' appears to me not wholly adequate. One could argue that Michael's description of Theseus breaking the bull's horn with his club (κορύνηι θάτερον κεράτων ἡλόηcεν, ii. 345. 10–11 (= below, Test. 15b)) derived from a mere summary of fr. 69. 1 οἰόκερωc· ἕτερον γὰρ ἀπηλοίηcε κορύνη, but for the fact that Michael uses the very rare compound οἰόκερωc elsewhere in his

---

[6] Mich. Chon. i. 158. 2 ff., 159. 5 ff. Lambros (addressed to an imperial official).

[7] A. W. Bulloch, *FH*, p. 82 n. 1, quoting Margaret Howatson.

[8] Michael's references to books often concern those recovered after 1205 (N. G. Wilson).

own verse.[9] Clearly, therefore, in this instance he knew the actual text of Callimachus.

Michael's copy may well have been kept on the Athenian Acropolis (then the Orthodox cathedral and archbishop's residence) and have perished when the Franks of the Fourth Crusade under Boniface, Marquis of Montferrat, sacked the city in 1205;[10] thereafter Michael fled to the island of Ceos, and attempted to recover the remnants of his library. So it seems possible that our poem, after surviving for nearly a millennium and a half, was lost in the city whose mythical history it celebrated. On this subject Wilamowitz[11] did not spare his words:

Constat igitur Callimachi carmina impio illo barbarorum cruce signatorum latrocinio perisse, quod etiam Constantinopoli vastata gravius bonis litteris damnum intulit quam omnes Arabum Turcorumque invasiones.

IX. THE GATHERING AND ASCRIPTION OF FRAGMENTS

If AD 1205 marked the destruction of the last complete copy of the *Hecale*, the slow and painful process of recovery may be dated from 1489, when Politian[1] included some testimonia and fragments in his *Miscellanea*.[2] The advances made by subsequent scholars before the nineteenth century are described by Pfeiffer;[3] of outstanding value (both in the gathering of further fragments quoted by ancient authors and in their elucidation) and lasting influence was the contribution of Bentley to Graevius' 1697 edition. Callimachus himself seems to have been involved in acrimonious literary disputes throughout his career, and it is ironical that Bentley's work on Callimachus led to him being

---

[9] Εἰς τὸν Μονόκερων 6 (ii. 393 Lambros).

[10] If any text remained in Constantinople, that too may have perished to the Crusaders in 1204.

[11] *Callimachi Hymni et Epigrammata*³ (1907), pp. 6–7 n. 3; cf. Wilson, *Scholars*, p. 218.

[1] On whom see Pfeiffer, *History*, ii (1976), 42–6. At the ninth Congresso Internazionale di Studi Umanistici (Sassoferrato, June 1988) Dr Annette Harder read a paper entitled 'Politian and the Fragments of Callimachus', now published in *Studi Umanistici Piceni* 9 (1989) = *Res Publica Litterarum* 12 (1989), 77–83.

[2] Vol. i, ch. 24.

[3] ii, pp. xliii ff.; see also *History*, ii. Index s.v. Callimachus.

accused by malicious critics—without any doubt falsely[4]—of
having plagiarized unpublished notes by Thomas Stanley.

Three nineteenth-century scholars deserved particularly well of
the *Hecale*. First came A. F. Naeke,[5] whose treatment is learned
and wide-ranging; his textual comments show for the most part
an appreciation of Callimachus' style and metre. We can now see
that some of his attempts to find a context for fragments,
following the outlines of the story as given in Plutarch's *Theseus*,
were wide of the mark. Also his idea of Callimachus' narrative
technique[6] was much too simple and straightforward, making no
allowance for the twists and turns which characterize our poet.

'Ingeniosissimum omnium criticorum Callimacheorum' are
Pfeiffer's words[7] for A. Hecker, who published his *Commenta-
tiones Callimacheae* in 1842. Hecker found a key to identifying
many fragments of the *Hecale* which has proved its worth since
papyri began to emerge from the sands of Egypt nearly a century
ago. He started by observing of the Byzantine lexicon Suidas:

miratus sum nullum in eo exstare de deperdito Callimachi carmine
testimonium, quod ab aliis non sumserit et in suam farraginem retulerit,
ex una Hecale plura nobis servaverit fragmenta cum nemine communia,
vel, si apud alium quoque exstant, longe uberiora ... Hecales fragmenta
nomine et poetae et carminis addito in eius Lexico exstant tredecim, solo
Callimachi nomine a viris doctis ad Hecalen relata, viginti fere, multo
saepius tacite eius fragmenta laudantur.[8]

Ascription of the third group (mentioning neither the poem nor
the name of the author) is of course the most controversial. With
a leap of the imagination Hecker pronounced:

nullum in Suidae lexico legi versum heroicum alibi non inventum, qui
non in Hecale olim affuerit, adeo ut non nisi gravissimis argumentis aliis
poetis aliisve carminibus vindicari possint, i.e. si de eis certiores nos
fecerit disertum veteris scriptoris testimonium. talibus autem indiciis, si

---

[4] Pfeiffer, ii, pp. xliv–xlv.

[5] *Rh. Mus.* 2–5 (1833–7) = *Opuscula*, ii (1845). When referring to Naeke, I
quote page numbers from the *Opuscula*.

[6] pp. 53 ff.; cf. Schneider, ii, pp. 175 ff.

[7] ii, p. xlvi.

[8] Hecker, pp. 83, 87. I agree with Hecker's figure of 13 for Suidas citations
which mention the *Hecale* as well as Call. (if one includes frs. 69. 14–15 περὶ
Θησέως and 80. 1–5 περὶ Ἑκάλης θανούσης). My figure is 24 for those
mentioning only Call., and 157 for the anonymous citations which certainly or
probably refer to our poem (see below, Index Fontium).

adhuc inedita in lucem proferantur ... vix dubitamus nostras coniec-
turas firmatum iri.⁹

This bold conjecture by no means pleased everyone,[10] but was
taken up by R. Reitzenstein,[11] who added the important observa-
tion that some of Suidas' entries seem to come from a commen-
tary on the *Hecale* rather than the text itself; this may be the
commentary of Salustius mentioned by *Etymologicum Genuinum*
(see above, sect. VII). It is worth pausing here to illustrate the
different styles of citation in Suidas; I choose for the most part
examples which have been confirmed for our poem by papyri.
Suidas, s.v. ἱμαῖον ἆιϲμα,[12] quoting fr. 74. 25–6, gives author and
poem (Καλλ. Ἑκάληι). Another entry referring to the same
passage, s.v. ὑδατηγὸϲ ἀνήρ, is anonymous and was probably
taken from the commentary rather than from Callimachus' text,
as suggested by the inverse order of words.[13] Suidas mentions just
the poet e.g. s.v. ἐρωήϲαϲ (fr. 67). On two occasions no work or
poet is mentioned, but the context is stated, s.v. ϲτόρνηιϲι (fr. 69.
14–15) περὶ Θηϲέωϲ and s.v. ἐπαύλια (fr. 80) ... περὶ Ἑκάληϲ
θανούϲηϲ. An unharmonized chunk of Salustius' commentary
seems to have been transcribed in the note s.v. γεργέριμον (fr. 36.
4), ending with λέγει, of which the subject must be Callimachus
even though our poet has not been named by Suidas; similarly s.v.
Κωλιάδοϲ κεραμῆεϲ (fr. 92), λέγει οὖν (sc. Call.) ὅτι ... followed
by a paraphrase from which one might try to extract a few words
of the Callimachean original (see ad loc.).[14] A lemma may even
stand by itself, with no comment attached,[15] as s.v. κερκίδεϲ, on
the basis of which Pfeiffer gave to the *Hecale* an anonymous
snippet s.v. κερκίϲ in the *Etymologicum Magnum*; his conjecture has
now been confirmed by a papyrus (fr. 48. 7).

---

⁹ Hecker, p. 133.

[10] e.g. Schneider, ii, pp. 174.

[11] 'Inedita Poetarum Graecorum Fragmenta', *Index Lectionum in Acad. Rosto-
chiensi* (1890/1), 13 ff.

[12] Though ?Salustius may have been wrong in deducing the form of the
nominative (see ad loc.).

[13] Similarly s.v. γέγειαι βόεϲ (whence Reitzenstein supplied the first word of
fr. 102).

[14] The hazardous nature of the task may be illustrated from Suid, s.v. μή,
where the paraphrase ἵνα οὐ μετὰ δὴν καὶ ἐπὶ ϲοὶ θρηνήϲω ἀποθανόντι turns out to
conceal μὴ μετὰ δὴν ἵνα καὶ ϲοὶ ἐπιρρήξαιμι χιτῶνα (fr. 49. 3).

[15] See Pfeiffer on his fr. 271 (ἀλοίτηϲ).

An essential part of Hecker's theory was that the fragment should be 'alibi non inventum'. If he meant 'preserved anonymously by no other grammarian or lexicographer', some qualification is necessary, since a number of anonymous Suidas citations plausibly assigned to *Hecale* are shared, at least in part, with sources such as the *Etymologicum Genuinum*, which also drew on Salustius' commentary. Perhaps, however, he was stressing the need to make absolutely sure that the Suidas entry is not ascribable to any other known work. Certainly Suidas quotes anonymously from other hexameter poets. For example, the entry s.v. οὐρίαχος (ὄφρα κεν ἐξ ὑάλοιο πυρικμήτοιο ταθέντας | οὐριάχους δέξαιντο) was, in spite of its inappropriate subject-matter, taken to be a fragment of the *Hecale* by Ida Kapp in her 1915 edition (fr. 140), and by other scholars even later. But the author of these words was Paulus Silentiarius (*S. Sophia* 824–5).[16] Suidas s.v. οἶδμα (καὶ ἄγριον οἶδμα θαλάσσης) remains controversial; the phrase occurs twice in Gregory of Nazianzus, but it is still arguable that the citation may come from Callimachus rather than Gregory (see below on fr. 160 inc. auct.). There is also the problem of the so-called Μυθικά.[17] So the possibility of wrong attribution must always be borne in mind.

Hecker (p. 133, quoted above) was confident that any further discoveries would confirm his theory. Clearly he felt the peculiar fascination of our poem, and even cherished a wild hope that a complete copy might have survived somewhere:

quum igitur Suidae aetate Hecales exemplaria nondum omnia intercidissent, dulcem fovere licet spem, si aliquando Callimachi carmen aliquod hic illic in bibliothecis absconditum inveniatur, quod non fiet, sed si fiet, id Hecalen fore; eoque optime poetae famae et existimationi . . . consultum iri arbitramur.[18]

Some fifty years after Hecker wrote, Egyptian papyri (and the wooden Vienna Tablet) began to provide at least a partial check on his conjecture. The results have been remarkable. In Pfeiffer's edition you will find 25 anonymous quotations from Suidas which have been confirmed for the *Hecale* by papyri; and the success rate has continued with 9 more entries put in their place by

---

[16] Cf. Pfeiffer, ii, p. l.
[17] See below on fr. 119; Pfeiffer, i, p. 228.
[18] p. 134.

papyri published since Pfeiffer's time.[19] Particularly notable is the
way in which Hecker himself (pp. 105 ff.) arranged the anony-
mous citations of fr. 18 in an order now proved right by *P. Oxy*
2216—and he did not overlook fr. 19, which may, I think, find a
home in fr. 18. 11. According to Pfeiffer, 'ne unum quidem
frustulum a Suida allatum in multis et longis Aetiorum partibus
nunc nobis exstat, plurima in Hecalae paucis et parvis fragmentis
papyraceis' (i, p. 228). The latest discoveries have rendered the
matter more obscure, in that 2 individual words and perhaps a
phrase which were assigned to the *Hecale* on the basis of
anonymous quotation in Suidas (Hecker's Law), have now turned
up in the *Aetia*; these are Νωνακρίνη (*SH* 250. 9), ὑδέουϲιν (*SH*
257. 33), and ἐπικλινές ἐϲτι τάλαντον (more doubtfully restored in
SH 260A. 9). P. J. Parsons[20] rightly says that we must now keep a
careful eye on Hecker's Law, but that Callimachus may be
allowed to have used the same word or phrase more than once. I
have therefore retained these fragments for the *Hecale*.[21] The
importance of this whole question may be gathered from the fact
that Suidas contains nearly 200 entries (ascribed and anonymous)
which certainly, probably, or possibly refer to our poem.

The work of Otto Schneider, whose second volume, contain-
ing the fragments appeared in 1873, was very fairly assessed by
Pfeiffer:

Illius editionis vitia manifestiora sunt virtutibus ... Artis Callimacheae
elegantiam generisque dicendi tenuitatem non sensit, neque raro in re
metrica peccavit aut coniectandi libidine a vero longius aberravit.
Attamen negari nequit quin in universum sermonis Graeci peritus,
bonus grammaticus, multifaria eruditione instructus, exquisita diligentia
praeditus fuerit; eius modi virtutibus multa quae delituerant indagavit,
obscura explanavit, corrupta emendavit.[22]

In 1915 Ida Kapp produced an edition of the *Hecale* alone which,
in spite of its modest size, is sound and still useful: she had the
benefit of Wilamowitz' collaboration.

Perhaps this is the place to make explicit my enormous

[19] If I am right in suspecting that fr. 8 might be identified with fr. 6. 1, fr. 24
with fr. 23. 2, and fr. 19 placed in fr. 18. 11, these would be 3 more successes for
Hecker's Law.

[20] *ZPE* 25 (1977), 50. Cf. J. E. G. Zetzel, *CP* 82 (1987), 353–4.

[21] My frs. 140, 151, and 134 respectively.

[22] ii, p. xlvii.

admiration for Rudolf Pfeiffer's *Callimachus*, volume i (*Fragmenta*, 1949), which has been a constant companion for twenty-five years. Papyrologists tell me that his statements about how many letters a lacuna can (or cannot) contain occasionally overlook the fact that some letters are broader than others; he may also have missed a few references in Gregory of Nazianzus.[23] But Pfeiffer's learning, judgement, and taste were quite outstanding. By 1949[24] he was in complete harmony with the refinement of Callimachus' style and metre.[25] He approached the fragments in a cool and sceptical manner; when mentioning the imaginative constructions of other scholars, he will add 'plane incertum', 'at haec omnia incertissima esse moneo', *vel. sim.* My own edition is certainly not intended to supplant Pfeiffer on the *Hecale* (which would be a most arrogant ambition) but to supplement him and to be used in conjunction with his work; my hope (not entirely fulfilled) was to have something new to say on every fragment. In several areas (e.g. the interrelationship of ancient grammarians and lexicographers, and our debt to the older generations of modern scholars) I have skated lightly, or even passed in silence, over issues which Pfeiffer discussed in detail. But this book is big enough already, and I have preferred to give more space to problems of subject-matter and to parallels from other ancient poets. I am fortunate in being able to use Pfeiffer's foundation, and fortunate too that the post-Pfeiffer accretions have been brought together in another mighty work of scholarship, *Supplementum Hellenisticum*.[26] The present edition contains two fragments which are to be found neither in Pfeiffer nor in *SH*: fr. 6 (a few letters of text in which we may possibly recognize fr. 8, followed by remains of scholia) and fr. 85 (rereading of *P. Oxy.* 853 supports Wilamowitz' belief that the Thucydides scholiast quoted two full lines of the *Hecale*, not just the previously known part of the second line (= fr. 305 Pf.)). Note also the probable assignment of fr. 97 to Callimachus' text rather than (as in *SH* 291) to marginal scholia. Of these, only fr. 85 represents a significant addition to the text. Appendix V

[23] See on his frs. 319, 370.

[24] I say this because his 1923 edn. of *Callimachi Fragmenta nuper Reperta* does not show quite the same mastery.

[25] Contrast his remarks on Schneider quoted above. I particularly like Pfeiffer's restoration of *Aet.* fr. 178. 27–8, which he rightly confined to the apparatus criticus but is worthy of the Cyrenaean.

[26] Edd. H. Lloyd-Jones and P. J. Parsons (1983).

below tentatively ascribes to our poem ten further anonymous fragments from Suidas.

X. THE ARRANGEMENT OF FRAGMENTS

I have divided my material into Fragmenta Hecalae and Fragmenta Incerta.[1] The former group contains pieces which we can attribute to the *Hecale* with certainty or at least very high probability,[2] the latter those which in my opinion stand a good chance of belonging to our poem.[3] As between the two groups, there are borderline cases. I have elevated to the first section, without new evidence, just one piece (fr. 26 ἐλαχὺν δόμον) which Pfeiffer left among his Incerta, resisting the temptation to promote a few others;[4] the notorious fr. 160 inc. auct. καὶ ἄγριον οἶδμα θαλάccηc is relegated with regret. My system of numbering papyrus fragments differs from that of Pfeiffer (and *SH*) in that separate sides or columns of a papyrus are here counted as separate fragments. This allows fragments which clearly belong in a gap between sides or columns to be placed in their appropriate positions: fr. 41 can stand between the two sides of *PSI* 133 (frs. 40, 42), and fr. 71 between cols. ii and iii of the Vienna Tablet (frs. 70, 73).[5] But I have not inserted fragments into a measurable papyrus lacuna unless I felt confident that this is their correct place, to avoid distorting the calculation of how many lines are still missing in a particular lacuna. In admitting conjectural supplements, I have been a little less receptive than Pfeiffer, but a little more so than the editors of *SH*; mindful of their warning,[6] I hope that those supplements which I have put into the text are not substandard.

We know the narrative's main outline from the *Diegesis* in *P*.

---

[1] I have not followed Pfeiffer in having separate sections for frag. incert. sed. and incert. auct. but have noted prominently into which category each of the Fragmenta Incerta falls.

[2] Like Pfeiffer, I include here the anonymous entries in Suidas, according to Hecker's Law (see above, sect. IX).

[3] App. I below lists other fragments which are worth bearing in mind (though I do not feel strongly about any of them).

[4] e.g. frs. 165 and 166 (inc. auct.), 167 and 169 (inc. sed.).

[5] The placing of fr. 72 in the same lacuna, while less certain than that of fr. 71, seems to me highly probable.

[6] p. x.

Med. 18 (= pap. 1). But it must be stressed that this is only the outline.[7] For instance, the much-admired entertainment scene in Hecale's cottage, during which the old woman told her life-story at considerable length (frs. 41 ff.) is covered in two words, ἐνταῦθα ἐξενοδοκήθη (*Dieg.* x. 30–1), while the substantial episode of the talking birds (frs. 70 ff.) does not even rate a mention. Some deductions can be made from the text itself: fr. 40. 3 shows that the conversation in the cottage followed a natural course, with Hecale asking Theseus about his mission, and the young man, having satisfied this request, in turn questioning his hostess about her past life. In fr. 49. 14 Hecale speaks of the bandit Cercyon as still alive—but Theseus has already killed him. Presumably, therefore, Theseus himself later described to Hecale the killing of Cercyon (? and of other malefactors such as Sciron). Although the link of the talking birds to the main narrative is unclear, Gentili[8] guessed plausibly enough that it involved Hecale's death and a debate among the birds about whether to bring such bad news to Theseus. Doubts remain particularly over Theseus' upbringing in Troezen. Pfeiffer[9] thought that this topic was introduced retrospectively after the recognition of Theseus by his father (cf. *Dieg.* x. 22–3 ἅτ' αἰφνίδιον ἀνακομισθὲν ἐκ Τροιζῆνος μειράκιον αὐτῶι οὐ προςδοκήςαντι), and I have placed there a few fragments (12–15) which certainly or possibly refer to the young Theseus. Mystery also surrounds the hero's journey from Troezen to Athens. Could Theseus be the subject of frs. 96 and 98? If so, we might have found the context for a number of other Argive references (frs. 95 ff.). But the matter remains very uncertain; one would expect a learned Hellenistic poet to insert many brief allusions unconnected with his main narrative.

In Pfeiffer's edition frs. 230–64 are arranged 'ad ordinem narrationis', the rest (265–377) 'secundum fontium ordinem alphabeticum'.[10] Even his first part contained speculative el-

---

[7] One might expect the *Diegesis* to follow the text of the poem more closely at the beginning and the end than in the middle.

[8] *Gnomon*, 33 (1961), 342.

[9] i, p. 229. But his opinion about the context of fr. 238. 3 ff. Pf. has been proved wrong by discovery of the first half of l. 4 (my fr. 17. 4).

[10] He could not bring himself to arrange *all* the fragments according to alphabetical order of the sources (i, p. 229). Placing fr. 279 (my fr. 96) before fr. 280 (fr. 98) 'contra ordinem alphabeticum' was presumably his way of suggesting that the lines might originally have been consecutive—a possibility still worth bearing in mind, though the papyrus evidence is against it (see ad loc.).

ements; we now know that fr. 247 Pf. (my fr. 48. 5) does not after all describe Hecale washing Theseus' feet.[11] I have been freer than Pfeiffer in placing fragments 'ad ordinem narrationis', or at least 'secundum res narratas'; thus I have put frs. 65 and 66 (both probably describing Hecale) just before we lose contact with the old woman, and frs. 75–7 (all of which may concern birds) after the end of the Vienna Tablet. I fully realize that their position may turn out to be different and dispersed. By such expedients I have arranged frs. 1–83 roughly according to the narrative, and as far as possible grouped the remaining fragments by subject-matter[12] (e.g. frs. 84 ff., 'res Atticae') without at all meaning to suggest that every fragment in the group belongs to the same part of the poem. Only for those pieces where the subject-matter is not apparent do I follow Pfeiffer; an arrangement 'secundum fontium ordinem alphabeticum' is of course totally random as far as the subject-matter is concerned, and has only the rather negative virtue of not suggesting any connection which may prove to be false.[13]

XI. PAPYRI OF THE *HECALE*[1]

The numbers in brackets are those given by Pfeiffer[2] and Pack,[3] whose works give fuller descriptions and bibliography. All dates are AD. I have numbered the papyri according to the order in which they make their first contribution to the text.

1. **P. Med. 18** (8 Pf., 211 Pack[2]), first–second century. *Diegesis* to the *Hecale* and fr. 1 (also *Dieges* of *Aet.* 3–4, *Iambi, Lyrica,* and *Hymns* 1–2). Found at Tebtunis in 1934. The complete

---

[11] In my opinion fr. 245 Pf. (fr. 60) is not likely to, either.

[12] The same principles are followed with regard to the Fragmenta Incerta.

[13] And of making it easier to check all the references for e.g. Suidas (see below, Index Fontium).

[1] I have not attempted a fresh collation of the papyri (setting no value on my own opinion of such matters). But several experts have kindly re-examined and given their judgement on specific passages—particularly Mr P. J. Parsons, also Dr John Rea (on fr. 70. 5) and Dr Walter Cockle (through Mr W. S. Barrett, on fr. 85).

[2] ii, pp. ix ff.

[3] Roger A. Pack, *The Greek and Latin Literary Texts from Greco-Roman Egypt*[2] (1965).

text edited by A. Vogliano, *PRIMI* i (1937), 66 ff., with photographs of the whole (pls. ii–iii).

2. **P. Oxy. 2258** (37 Pf., 186 Pack²), sixth- or seventh-century codex. *Argumentum Hecalae*, frs. 5, 6, 96, 97. Edited by E. Lobel, *P. Oxy.* xx (1952), 69 ff., with photographs (pls. xiii–xvi). One cannot be absolutely certain that *Hecale* frs. 96–7, which Lobel published separately in *P. Oxy.* xxx (1964), 91–2, belong to the same papyrus, but, since the letter-sizes and line-spacing correspond satisfactorily (P. J. Parsons), the assumption is reasonable. A most remarkable manuscript, from which we also have fragments of every *Hymn* except no. 5, of *Aet.* 3,[4] *Coma Berenices*, and *Victoria Sosibii*. There are copious and learned notes[5] in the same 'Coptic' hand, but written in smaller letters; a few of these are placed between the lines of text, but most in the margin, above and below (thus frs. 5 and 6; probably not, however, fr. 97) as well as to right and left. Each page contained one column of text, and it seems that the normal complement of a column was 23 lines, but there was some irregularity (Lobel, *P. Oxy.* xx. 70, 81).[6]

3. **P. Oxy. 2216** (30 Pf., 226 Pack²), third-century codex. Fr. 17, fr. 18. 3–18, frs. 20–3. Edited by Lobel, *P. Oxy.* xix (1948), 41 ff., 145–6, with photographs (pls. iii, iv).

4. **P. Oxy. 2529** (too recent for Pfeiffer and Pack², but catalogued by F. Uebel in *APF* 22 (1973), 351, no. 1246), third- or fourth-century codex. Frs. 27, 36 (and probably 37). Edited by Lobel, *P. Oxy.* xxx (1964), 89 f., with photographs (pls. xiii, iii). Re-examined for *SH.*

5. **PSI 133** (part of 32 Pf., 201 Pack²), fourth- or fifth-century codex (see Lobel on *P. Oxy.* 2168), found at Oxyrhynchus. Frs. 40, 42 (and perhaps 43). Edited by G. Vitelli, *PSI* ii. (1913), 54 ff., with photograph (pl. i). Re-examined by V. Bartoletti, *SIFC* 31 (1959), 179, with enlarged photograph to

---

[4] Molorchus as well as Acontius and Cydippe.

[5] See above, sect. VII n. 11 for the possibility that they might be drawn from the commentator Salustius.

[6] Lobel (*P. Oxy.* xx. 70) mentions other fragments (relating to undetermined poems) which he collected but did not publish because he could make out too little continuously for it to be worth while (P. J. Parsons agrees). I have looked at these, in the Ashmolean Museum, Oxford; a few scraps contain letters of the text, which I could not identify with known pieces of Call.

clarify fr. 42. 1, and again for *SH*. One of the Berlin
fragments of the same papyrus (see Pfeiffer) reveals that the
column length was 37 or 38 lines; thus we can deduce that
there was a gap of some 32 lines between *Hec.* frs 40. 6 and 42.
1. Other papyri published separately but originally belonging
to the same codex (details in Pfeiffer) contain parts of *Aet.* 1
and 3, and *Lyrica.*

6. **P. Oxy. 2377** (230 Pack²), third- or fourth-century codex.
   Frs. 47 and 49. Edited by Lobel, *P. Oxy.* xxiii (1956), 92 ff.,
   with photographs (pls. i, vi). Re-examined for *SH*.

7. **P. Oxy. 2376** (229 Pack²), second century, from the bottom
   of two consecutive columns of a roll. Frs. 48 (end of lines) and
   49. 7–16 (beginning of lines). Edited by Lobel, *P. Oxy.* xxiii
   (1956), 89 ff., with photograph (pl. ii). Re-examined for *SH*.

8. **P. Rain. VI** (36 Pf., 227 Pack²), fourth–fifth century. Fr. 69.
   1–14, frs. 70, 73, 74. 14–28. The Vienna Tablet, found near
   Arsinoe in 1877–8 and first edited by T. Gomperz in 1893. A
   wooden board, of the sort used in schools. One side carries
   four columns of the *Hecale* (the second and third in much
   poorer state of preservation), the other, *E. Ph.* 1097–1107 and
   1126–37,[7] Thus we can determine approximately the original
   length of the columns of the *Hecale*. Collated afresh by J. R.
   Rea (*HSCP* 72 (1968), 125 ff., with photograph opposite p.
   136) with some remarkable results (particularly the new
   reading of fr. 69. 1).

9. **P. Oxy. 2398** (231 Pack²), first half of second century, 'on
   the back of a document in which figures and a mention of
   baked brick can be recognized' (Lobel). Fr. 74. 1–17 (begin-
   ning of lines). Edited by Lobel, *P. Oxy.* xxiv (1957), 97 ff.,
   with photograph (pl. xii). Re-examined for *SH*.

10. **P. Oxy. 2437** (232 Pack²), second century. Fr. 74. 1–6
    (middle of lines). Edited by Lobel, *P. Oxy.* xxv (1959),
    123 ff., with photograph (pl. ix). Re-examined for *SH*.

11. **P. Oxy. 2217** (33 Pf., 228 Pack²), fourth century. Fr. 74.
    3–17. Edited by Lobel, *P. Oxy.* xix (1948), 44 ff., with
    photograph (pl. viii). Re-examined for *SH*.

I have not included *P. Oxy.* 2823 (*SH* 280, the text given in my

---

[7] It will be noticed that both the Euripides and the Callimachus start in mid-
sentence.

note on fr. 4. 2) because the grounds for assigning this to the
Hecale seem hardly adequate, but draw attention here to *P. Oxy.*
853 (1536 Pack², the relevant part re-examined by W. E. H.
Cockle when he visited Cairo in 1985), a commentary on
Thucydides which almost certainly quoted two complete lines of
the *Hecale* (fr. 85), and also to *P. Oxy.* 3434, an unidentified prose
text which seems to mention Hecale (the mythical character or
the title of Callimachus' poem?) and perhaps other matters
connected with Theseus' Marathonian adventure and escape from
Medea's plot.

XII. OTHER MAIN SOURCES OF THE TEXT

Apart from papyri, the most important source of *Hecale* frag-
ments is the tenth-century lexicon known as the Suda or Suidas;
this we have already discussed at some length in connection with
the work of the Dutch scholar Hecker (above, pp. 41–4). But it is
desirable to say more about the various *Etymologica* which are
outstripped only by Suidas in the number of fragments which
they provide.

We no longer possess a full text of the ninth-century Byzantine
lexicon originally called τὸ Ἐτυμολογικόν, and later by Eustathius
τὸ μέγα Ἐτυμολογικόν. Since the time of R. Reitzenstein[1] this has
been generally known as *Etymologicum Genuinum*, and I retain the
familiar designation—Lasserre and Livadaras in their synoptic
edition[2] prefer 'Etymologicum Magnum Genuinum'.[3] Like Sui-
das, the compilers of *Et. Gen.* used the commentary on Callima-
chus' *Hecale* by Salustius, who is actually named three times (see
above, p. 37).

Two abbreviated and incomplete tenth-century copies of *Et.
Gen.* have survived, cod. A (Vaticanus gr. 1818) and cod. B (Laur.
S. Marci 304). Of these manuscripts Lasserre and Livadaras wrote:

A et B saepius inter se differunt, etsi ex eodem exemplari descripti sunt,
cum id librarii A veloci, ut videtur, labore innumerabilibusque mendis
integrum fere reddant, amanuenses B contra plerasque glossas decurta-

---

[1] *Geschichte der griechischen Etymologica* (1897).
[2] i (1976).
[3] And 'Etymologicum Magnum Auctum' in place of the usual *Etymologicum
Magnum*.

verint, multas praetermiserint, exempla auctorumque nomina saepe
neglexerint, haud raro glossas alienigenas in unam redegerint.[4]

We still await the full publication of codd. A and B (an enormous
and formidable undertaking) planned both by Lasserre–Livadaras
and by K. Alpers. Meanwhile various portions have appeared in
book form;[5] further entries have been described in periodicals or
mentioned incidentally elsewhere.[6]

E. Miller[7] gave copious information about *Et. Gen.* B; unfortu-
nately the method which he adopted did not always make the
reading clear (and sometimes led Pfeiffer astray). He was con-
cerned to mention all the entries, but 'lorsqu'ils ne contenaient
rien de nouveau ou d'important' (p. 9), Miller contented himself
with a reference to Gaisford's 1848 edition of the *Etymologicum
Magnum*. In such cases Pfeiffer deduced that the reading of *Et.
Gen.* B was identical with that of *Et. Mag.* (which may not have
been Miller's meaning)—e.g. that *Et. Gen.* B s.v. λύχνα has an
entry quoting *Hec.* fr. 260. 65 Pf. (my fr. 74. 24), and a substantial
note s.v. βιοπλανέc (fr. 489. 1 Pf. = my fr. 163. 1 inc. sed.). We
can now see from the publication of B's readings in Adler–Alpers
and Berger respectively[8] that these deductions were incorrect.
Miller was certainly at fault when he failed to record that in my
fr. 71. 1 (= fr. 261. 1 Pf.) *Et Gen.* B reads Ὑψιζώρου (as does *Et.
Gen.* A) rather than ὑψιζώνου (so *Et. Mag.* apart from cod. D); as a
result Pfeiffer was misled into adopting Bentley's unnecessary
conjecture ὑψίζωνοc.[9] Looking at a photocopy of *Et. Gen.* A
(available in Oxford), I found that in several cases[10] where Pfeiffer
relied on Miller for the reading of *Et. Gen.* B the Callimachean
quotation is missing from *Et. Gen.* A. This made me wonder

---

[4] Op. cit. i, p. xxii.

[5] See among the Editiones Fontium Praecipuorum below. C. Calame,
'Etymologicum Genuinum: *les citations de poètes lyriques*' (1970) contains little or
nothing relevant to the *Hecale*.

[6] Those given by R. Reitzenstein, *Index Lectionum in Acad. Rostochiensi* 1890/1
and 1891/2, utilized by Pfeiffer, are particularly important for the *Hecale*, but the
material in *Museum Criticum*, 15–17 (1980–2) and ibid. 18 (1983) happens to
include little for our purposes.

[7] *Mélanges de littérature grecque* (1868), pp. 1–318.

[8] See below, p. 61.

[9] See H. Lloyd-Jones and J. Rea, *HSCP* 72 (1968), 139. Pfeiffer was also
misled into believing that *Et. Gen.* B reads γραύιδι in my fr. 164 inc. sed.

[10] s.v. κερκίς (fr. 48. 7), ἐρωή (fr. 67), θάνατος (fr. 80. 1–2), διάκτορωι (fr. 167
inc. sed.), νηῖτης (fr. 173 inc. sed.). In all these cases, Professor Alpers tells me that
Et. Gen. B lacks the quotation from Call.

whether *Et. Gen.* B includes the quotations from Callimachus, or whether they appear only in *Et. Mag.*; in each case my suspicions about B have been confirmed by Professor Alpers.[11]

In the grammatical comment which surrounds the poetic quotations, the scribes of *Et. Gen.* A and B seem freely to alter, omit, and transpose; to catalogue every variation in the accompanying comment would make my apparatus criticus even longer, and so sometimes, when there is no significant point at issue, I have tacitly adopted the version appearing in *Et. Gen.* A. Nor did it seem necessary to record every trivial slip in the accompanying comment (as opposed to the citations of Callimachus). Thus on fr. 9. 1 I mention that *Et. Gen.* A has κολλουραίη in the quotation of line 1, but not that the scribe wrote πολλυραφῆ (for πολυρραφῆ) in the comment. A full publication of *Et. Gen.* would record such points as well, but they are hardly essential to an edition of the *Hecale*. One peculiarity of *Et. Gen.* A is that the letter *E* (though by no means every individual entry under *E*) appears twice—first abbreviated (A^{I}) and then more fully (A^{II}). Quotations from the *Hecale* occur, if at all, only in A^{II}; see app. crit. to frs. 15, 16, 26, 67, 109, 177 inc. sed.

The later *Etymologica* (*Et. Gudianum*, *Et. Magnum*, *Et. Symeonis*, and pseudo-Zonaras) contain information not to be found in *Et. Gen.* A or B; some of this they must have taken from the original *Etymologicum Genuinum* in its unabbreviated state, while other items have been incorporated from extraneous sources. Here is a diagram[12] showing the approximate dates and apparent interrelationships of the various *Etymologica*:

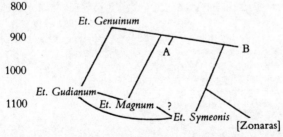

[11] I hope (but cannot be entirely certain) to have caught all the cases in which an incorrect or non-existent reading was assigned to *Et. Gen.* B through the mistaken inference from Miller that *Et. Gen.* B = *Et. Mag.* The photocopy of A has enabled me to give readings in the many instances where Pfeiffer wrote 'de A non constat'.

[12] Reproduced by kind permission of M. L. West from his *IEG* i, p. ix.

CALLIMACHI HECALA

TESTIMONIA

1 (37 Pf.), Schol. in Call. *H.* 2. 106 (ii, p. 53 Pf.) ἐγκαλεῖ διὰ
τούτων τοὺς cκώπτοντας αὐτὸν μὴ δύναcθαι ποιῆcαι μέγα ποίημα,
ὅθεν ἠναγκάcθη ποιῆcαι τὴν Ἑκάλην

2 Call. *Iamb.* fr. 194. 77 Pf. ἐν [δ' ἡ κολ]υμβὰς ἦν ἔπωγε χὠ
Θηcεύc (cf. *Hec.* fr. 36. 5, κολυμβάc = φθινοπωρίc)

3 Lucr. 6. 753–4 'usque adeo fugitant [sc. cornices] non iras
Palladis acris | pervigili causa, Graium ut cecinere poetae [cf. *Hec.*
frr. 70–3] | sed . . .'

4 (28 Pf.), Crin. *AP* 9. 545 = 11 G.–P. Καλλιμάχου τὸ τορευτὸν
ἔπος τόδε· δὴ γὰρ ἐπ' αὐτῶι | ὡνὴρ τοὺς Μουcέων πάντας ἔceιce
κάλωc· | ἀείδει δ' Ἑκάλης τε φιλοξείνοιο καλιήν (cf. *Hec.* fr. 80) |
καὶ Θηcεῖ Μαραθὼν οὓc ἐπέθηκε πόνουc. | τοῦ coὶ καὶ νεαρὸν χειρῶν
cθένος εἴη ἀρέcθαι, | Μάρκελλε, κλεινοῦ τ' αἶνον ἴcον βιότου

5 (29 Pf.), Ov. *Rem.* 747–8 'cur nemo est Hecalen, nulla est quae
ceperit Iron? | nempe quod alter egens, altera pauper erat'

6 (30 Pf.), *Priap.* 12. 3 sqq. 'quaedam . . . | aequalis tibi, quam
domum revertens | Theseus repperit in rogo iacentem' (cf. *Hec.* fr.
79)

7 (31 Pf.), Petr. 135. 8. 15 sqq.

> qualis in Actaea quondam fuit hospita terra [cf. *Hec.* frr. 1–2]
> digna sacris Hecale [cf. *Hec.* fr. 83], quam Musa †loquentibus annis
> †Baccineas veteres mirando† tradidit aevo

16 Hecale *Junius*: hecates codd.   17 Battiadae veteris *coni. vv. dd. saec.*
xvi   mirandam *Gronovius, alii*: miranti *Burman*

8 (32 Pf.), Stat. *Theb.* 12. 581–2 [uxor Capanei Theseo] 'si
patrium Marathona metu, si tecta levasti | Cresia, nec fudit vanos
anus hospita fletus' (cf. *Hec.* fr. 57)

9 Plut. *Thes.* 14 ἡ δὲ Ἑκάλη καὶ τὸ περὶ αὐτὴν μυθολόγημα (? sc. in Callimachi carmine) τοῦ ξενισμοῦ καὶ τῆς ὑποδοχῆς ἔοικε μὴ πάςης ἀμοιρεῖν ἀληθείας. ἔθυον γὰρ Ἑκαλῆςιν [ἐκαλήςιον codd., corr. Madvig] οἱ πέριξ δῆμοι cυνιόντες Ἑκαλείωι [Meursius: Ἑκάλωι codd.] Διὶ καὶ τὴν Ἑκάλην ἐτίμων Ἑκαλίνην ὑποκοριζόμενοι διὰ τὸ κἀκείνην νέον ὄντα κομιδῆι τὸν Θηςέα ξενίζουςαν ἀςπάςαςθαι πρεςβυτικῶς καὶ φιλοφρονεῖςθαι τοιούτοις ὑποκοριςμοῖς. ἐπεὶ δὲ εὔξατο μὲν ὑπὲρ αὐτοῦ τῶι Διὶ βαδίζοντος εἰς τὴν μάχην, εἰ cῶς παραγένοιτο, θύςειν, ἀπέθανε δὲ πρὶν ἐκεῖνον ἐπανελθεῖν, ἔςχε τὰς εἰρημένας ἀμοιβὰς τῆς φιλοξενίας τοῦ Θηςέως κελεύςαντος, ὡς Φιλόχορος (FGH 328 F 109) ἱςτόρηκεν

10 (33 Pf.), Apul. *Met.* 1. 23 'si contentus lare parvulo Thesei . . . virtutes aemulaveris, qui non est aspernatus Hecales anus hospitium tenue'

11 (34 Pf.), [Iul] *ep.* 186 Bidez–Cumont (= 41 Hertlein) πάντως οὐδὲ τῆς Ἑκάλης ὁ Θηςεὺς τοῦ δείπνου τὸ λιτὸν ἀπηξίωςεν, ἀλλ' ἤιδει καὶ μικροῖς ἐς τὸ ἀναγκαῖον ἀρκεῖςθαι

12 (24 Pf.), Suid. iii. 323. 28 Adler s.v. Μαριανός . . . πατρίκιος γεγονώς . . . κατὰ τὸν βαςιλέα Ἀναςτάςιον (491–518 p. Chr.). ἔγραψε βιβλία τοςαῦτα . . . Μετάφραςιν Καλλιμάχου Ἑκάλης, Ὕμνων καὶ τῶν Αἰτίων καὶ Ἐπιγραμμάτων ἐν ἰάμβοις ‚ϲωί (= 6810)

13 (23 Pf.), epigr. adesp. saec. vi p. Chr. vel fortasse posterioris (v. Pf.), 5–6 μέλπω δὲ γραὸς τῆς φιλοξένου τρόπους | καὶ τὴν τελευτήν, Θηςέως τε τὴν ἄγραν

14 (35 Pf.). Mich. Chon. *Theano* 337 sqq. (ii. 386 Lambros) εἰ δὲ γρηὶ πενιχρῆι, τὴν Ἑκάλην καλέεσκον, (? cf. *Hec.* fr. 81)| Θηςεὺς ὤφλε χάριν ξενίης ὀλίγης τε μιῆς τε (cf. *Hec.* fr. 82)| καί ἑ θανοῦςαν ἐνὶ μνήμηι θέτο οὐ θνηςκούςηι |—οὐ γὰρ ἔην νήκουςτα ἐτήςια δεῖπν' Ἑκάλεια—(cf. *Hec.* fr. 83) κτλ.

15 (cf. 36 Pf.), Mich. Chon. ed. Lambros:
(a) i. 157. 5 sqq. τὸν Θηςέα τοίνυν ἐκεῖνον βαδίζοντά ποτε Μαραθῶνάδε κατὰ ὑβριςτοῦ ταύρου, μυρία παρεχομένου τοῖς ἐκεῖ που Τετραπολίταις πράγματα (? cf. *Hec.* fr. 16), καταλῦςαί φαςι καὶ

ἐπιξενωθῆναι παρά τινι γυναικί ('Εκάλη τῆι γυναικὶ τὸ ὄνομα ἦν), γραῖ μὲν πεμπέλωι καὶ πενιχρᾶι, ξενοδόχωι δ' ἄλλως ἀγαθῆι καὶ τοῖς παροδεύουσιν ἄκλειστον ἀεὶ προβαλλομένηι τὸ οἴκημα (cf. *Hec.* fr. 2), καὶ οὕτω τι φιλοφρονηθῆναι ἥδιον ὡς ἀεὶ μεμνῆcθαι τῆς ὀλίγης τραπέζης ἐκείνης καὶ αὐχμηρᾶς, καὶ μὴ ἂν ἄλλην οὕτω ποτὲ τερπνοτέραν λογίcαcθαι (cf. *Hec.* fr. 82). Ibid. 159. 8 ὅτε καὶ Θηcεὺc ὡς ὁ λόγος ἀρχόμενος ἀνεβάλετο τὸ πτωχικὸν καὶ ⟨e.g. πρεσβυ-τικὸν suppl. Lambr.⟩ φιλοξένημα τῆς Ἑκάλης τῆς Ἀττικῆς ἥδι-cτον ἐλογίcατο (cf. *Hec.* fr. 82)

(b) ii. 345. 6 καὶ πού τις ταῦρος ... ὁποῖος καὶ τὴν ἐν Μαραθῶνι τετράπολιν ἀναστατῶν ἐcίνετο, ἕως ὁ Θηcεὺc οὐχ ἥττονα τοῦτον ἀνύcας ἄεθλον ἢ ὅτε Πιτυοκάμπταις ἢ Προκρούcταις cυνέπλεκτο κορύνηι θάτερον κεράτων ἠλόηcεν (cf. *Hec.* fr. 69. 1).

TESTIMONIA DUBIA

16 (Cf. *SH* 307), Phld. *Piet.* (*P. Herc.* 243, col. ii. 1–6; ed. A. Henrichs, *Cronache Ercolanesi*, 13 (1963), 33 sqq.)

    ] Καλλί˻μ˼[α-]
    χος] κ˻υφούς, Πάν-
    δρο]cον δὲ καὶ λί-
    θο]ν, διότι τὴν ἀ-
  5 δελ]φὴν {π} Ἕρσην
    οὐ] π˻ροήκατ' αὐτῶ[ι

2–5 fortasse ad Cecropidum historiam spectant (cf. *Hec.* frr. 70 sqq., fr. 179 inc. auct.). Pandrosus in lapidem vertitur, quod sororem Hersam Mercurio non proiecit. 2 κυφούς Henrichs: παγ]κύφους C. Robert, at sacra illa olea πάγκυφος sive ἀcτή una atque unica fuit (*SH*) 4 post]ν spatium in pap. 5 Perse nihil ad rem; {π} Ἕρcην G. Schmid 6 οὐ] π˻ροήκατ' αὐτῶι (scil. Pandrosus Hersam Mercurio) Henrichs

17 (38a Pf.). Mnaseas (?Patar.) ap. Zenob. iii in cod. Athen. 1083 (ed. S. Kougeas, *SB bay. Akad.* (Philos.-Philol. Kl.), 1914, 4, p. 18: cf. Crusius, ibid. pp. 82 sq.: Kapp, p. 14 n. 1) Βουλίας [βούνας cod.] γὰρ Ἀθηναῖος ἐγένετο, ὥς φησι [φαcὶ cod.] Μναcέας, Ἑκάλης [ἐκάλες cod.] υἱός

18 (38b Pf.), Ptolem. Chenn. Καινὴ Ἱcτ. iii. 3 ap. Phot. *Bibl.* 190, p. 148. 20 Bekker (ed. A. Chatzis, *Studien z. Geschichte d. Kultur d. Altert.*

vii. 2 (1914), p. 23. 18) περὶ Ἑκάλης καὶ πόϲαιϲ γέγονεν ἐπώνυμον τοὔνομα

19 Arethas (cf. ad *Hec.* fr. 91), *Scripta Minora*, 21 (ed. Westerink, i (1968), 205) ἔϲτιν ὧιτινι τούτων καὶ Ἰκαρίωι προϲχρήϲηι ὡϲ ὄνωι ϲοι ἐφιζάνοντι καὶ τὴν κατὰ ϲαυτὸν οἶμον ἐλαύνοντι. ναὶ μὴν καὶ Ἑκάβηι [Ἑκάληι coni. N. G. Wilson, post mentionem Icarii, qui Baccho hospes fuerat; sed locus omnino obscurus] τινὶ ἐγκαλλωπίϲηι τῶι γήραι πολλοῖϲ ϲοι παραπληϲίοιϲ τὴν ἀθεότητα τῶν εἰϲ αἰϲχρότητα ἀπορρήτων κεκοινωνηκυίαι κτλ.

EDITIONES ET CODICES FONTIUM PRAECIPUORUM

de Papyris ad Hecalam pertinentibus vide pp. 48–51.

Et. Gen.   *Etymologicum Genuinum* ('Etymologicum Magnum Genuinum' ap. Lasserre–Livadaras)

Et Sym.   *Etymologicum Symeonis*

Ediderunt has Etymologicorum partes:

α-ἀμωϲγέπωϲ   *Etymologicum Magnum Genuinum, Symeonis Etymologicum una cum Magna Grammatica, Etymologicum Magnum Auctum,* synoptice P. Lasserre et N. Livadaras (i, 1976)

β   *Etymologicum Genuinum et Etymologicum Symeonis* (β), G. Berger (1972)

λ   K. Alpers, *Bericht über Stand und Methode des Ausgabe des Etymologicum Genuinum, Etymologicum Genuinum quod vocatur,* Ada Adler[†] et Klaus Alpers, Littera Λ (1969)

λ   *Etymologicum Genuinum,* Littera Λ, A. Colonna (1967)

Quantum ad cetera, photographias *Et. Gen.* cod. A ipse inspexi; de cod. B notitias vulgavit E. Miller, *Mélanges de littérature grecque* (1868), 1–318 (quaedam mihi per litteras suppeditavit K. Alpers).

Et. Gud.   *Etymologicum Gudianum*

α-ζειαί   *Etymologicum Gudianum quod vocatur,* E. A. de Stefani (i, 1909; ii, 1920). haec et cetera ed. F. Sturz, *Etymologicum Graecae Linguae Gudianum* (1818)

Et. Mag.   *Etymologicum Magnum* ('Etymologicum Magnum Auctum' ap. Lasserre–Livadaras, v. supra) *Etymologicum Magnum,* ed. T. Gaisford (1848)

'Zonaras'   *Iohannis Zonarae Lexicon*, ed. Io. Tittmann (i–ii, 1808)

Codices Etymologicorum Saepius Laudati:

Et. Gen.:

A   Vaticanus gr. 1818, saec. x; littera *E* bis apparet, primum abbreviata (A^I), deinde plenius exscripta (A^{II})

B   Laurentianus S. Marci 304, saec. x

Et. Mag.:

D   Dorvillianus Bodl. xi. 1. 1. 2, saec. xv? (O ap. Lasserre–Livadaras)

M   Marcianus gr. 530, saec. xiii.

P   Parisinus gr. 2654, ann. 1273

R   Hauniensis reg. 414, saec. xv

Et. Sym.:

F   Vindobonensis phil. gr. 131, saec. xiii

V   Vossianus gr. 20, saec. xiii (tanquam *Et. Mag.* exemplar laudat Gaisford)

Suid.   *Suidae Lexicon*, ed. Ada Adler (i, 1928; ii, 1931; iii, 1933; iv, 1935; v 1938). Citamus volumen, paginam, lineam.

Codices Suidae Saepius Laudati

A   Parisini gr. 2625 et 2626 (quamquam non unius originis sunt), pars vetustior saec. xiii, pars recentior saec. xiv

F   Laur. 55. 1, ann. 1422

V   Vossianus, fol. 2, saec. xii

S   Vaticanus gr. 1296, ann. 1205

G   Parisinus gr. 2623, saec. xv

I   Angelicanus 75, saec. xv

T   Vaticanus gr. 881, ann. 1434

M   Marcianus gr. 448, saec. xiii

SIGLA

α̣β̣γ̣	litterae incertae
]...[	litterarum vestigia ambigua
[...]	litterarum quae perierunt numerus (aestimatus, non exactus)
⌊αβγ⌋	litterae, quae in papyro perierunt, ex alio fonte pro certo notae sunt
⟦αβγ⟧	litterae a librario deletae
⟨αβγ⟩	litterae ab editoribus additae
{αβγ}	litterae ab editoribus deletae
ηι, ῃ, ωι, ῳ	iota plerumque adscripsi; cum in papyro ipse librarius vel subscripsit vel omisit, tum (sed in textu et lemmatibus tantum) subscripsi
*	eadem versus sede

DIEGESIS HECALAE ET
ARGUMENTUM HECALAE

Diegesis Hecalae

Dieg. x. 18   Ἑκάλης
     Ἀκταίη τις ἔναιεν Ἐρεχθέος ἔν ποτε γουνῶι
 20   Θησεὺς φυγὼν τὴν ἐκ Μηδείης ἐπιβου-
     λὴν διὰ πάσης ἦν φυλακῆς τῶι πατρὶ Αἰγεῖ,
     ἅτ' αἰφνίδιον ἀνακομισθὲν ἐκ Τροιζῆνος
     μειράκιον αὐτῶι οὐ προσδοκήσαντι. βουλό-
     μενος δ' ἐπὶ τὸν λυμαινόμενον τὰ πε-
 25   ρὶ Μαραθῶνα ταῦρον ἐξελθεῖν ὅπως
     χειρώσαιτο, καὶ εἰργόμενος, κρύφα
     τῆς οἰκίας ἐξελθὼν περὶ ἑσπέραν ἀ-
     πῆρεν. αἰφνίδιον δὲ ὑετοῦ ῥαγέντος
     κατ' ἐσχατιὰν οἰκίδιον θεασάμενος
 30   Ἑκάλης τινὸς πρεσβύτιδος ἐνταῦθα
     ἐξενοδοκήθη. πρὸς δὲ τὴν ἔω ἀνα-
     στὰς ἐξήιει ἐπὶ τὴν χώραν, χειρωσάμε-
     νος δὲ τὸν ταῦρον ἐπανήιει ὡς τὴν Ἑκά-
Dieg. xi. 1   λην· αἰφνίδιον δὲ ταύτην εὑρὼν τεθνηκυῖ-
     αν ἐπιστε[νάξ]ας ὡς ἐψευσμένος τῆς προσδο-
     κίας, ὃ ἐφ[. . . .]εν μετὰ θάνατον εἰς ἀμοιβὴν
     τῆς ξενίας ταύτηι παρασχέσθαι, τοῦτο ἐπε-
 5   τέλεσεν δ[ῆ]μον συνστησάμενος ὃν ἀπ' αὐ-
     τῆς ὠνόμα[σ]εν, καὶ τέμενος ἱδρύσατο
     Ἑκαλείου Δι[ό]ς.

P. Med. 18 (= pap. 1), Dieg. x. 18–xi. 7

---

x. 27 εσσπεραν pap. 27–8 ἀπῆρεν Norsa et Vitelli: απηρετ pap. 29 καθε
pap. 32 εξηςι pap. xi. 2 suppl. N.–V. 3 ἐφ[ρόνης]εν ? Pf.: ἐφ[ή-
μις]εν N.–V. μετὰ θάνατον post l. 4 τοῦτο transp. Castiglioni, recte ut
opinor 4 ταυ pap., ut videtur: αὐτῆι N.–V. παρασχ pap.
5 suppl. Pf.

Argumentum Hecalae

<pre>
                .   .   .   .   .   .
              ]ην χωρ[   ]γα
              ]ενοςηνυ[
        . . .].πεφευ[.   .   .   .
          ]..ντ..λ[|]..[   ].[
   5   ]ν ἐκπέμπε[   ]ουκ[
          ]νης κρύβδ.[   ].ηεπ[
          ὑε]τοῦ κα[τ]αρραγέντος[.   .
          νυκτὸς ἐ]πιλαμβανούςης[
             ο]ἶκον Ἑκάλης· τ[
   10   ].[   ].[
                .   .   .   .   .   .
</pre>

P. *Oxy.* 2258 (= pap. 2) A fr. 9 a–d (quattuor frustula), pagina versa (in pagina recta, finis H. 6)

---

3 cf. *Dieg.* x. 20 de Medeae insidiis? (Pf.)   5 ἐκπέμπε[sc. contra taurum Marathonium?   6 κρύβδα cf. *Dieg.* x. 26   7 suppl. Lobel (vel ὄμβ]ρου)   8 sq suppl. Lobel

FRAGMENTA HECALAE

I (230 Pf.), initium carminis

> Ἀκταίη τις ἔναιεν Ἐρεχθέος ἔν ποτε γουνῶι

P. Med. 18 (= pap. 1), Dieg. x. 19 lemma Ἀκταίη—γουνῶι   Et. Gud. p. 230.
21 De Stefani Ἀττικὴ παρὰ τὴν ἀκτήν. καὶ γὰρ παραθαλασσία. καὶ Καλλ.
"Ἀκταίη—ἔναιεν" Eustat. p. 84. 5 τὴν ἅμαξαν κατὰ παραγωγὴν ἀμαξαίαν
φασὶ . . . καὶ τὴν ἀκτὴν ἀκταίην ὡς ἐπὶ Ἀττικῆς παρὰ Καλλ.; id. p. 475. 1   Suid.
ii. 275. 23 Adler ἔναιεν· ὤικει 'huc potius spectat quam ad E 543' (Pf.). Cf.
Hesychius s.v. ἔναιεν· ἔμενεν, ὤικει

2 (231 Pf.)

> τίον δέ ἑ πάντες ὁδῖται
> ἦρα φιλοξενίης· ἔχε γὰρ τέγος ἀκλήιστον

1–2 Schol. (ΕΓLh) Ar. Ach. 127a (p. 26 Wilson) τοὺς δὲ ξενίζειν οὐδέποτ' ἴσχει
γ' ἡ θύρα] ἐπὶ τῶν πολλοὺς ξένους ὑποδεχομένων· μέμνηται καὶ Εὔπολις (fr. 286
PCG) . . . καὶ Καλλ. ἐν Ἑκάληι "τίον—ἀκλήιστον" [καὶ—ἀκλήιστον om. Lh]
2 Cramer, AO ii. 436. 10 Eclogae et Et. Gud. p. 438. 22 de Stef. Ἑκάλη· ἡ πρὸς
ἑαυτὴν καλοῦσα· "ἔχε—ἀκλήιστον"   Suid. ii. 212. 23 Ἑκάλη· ὄνομα κύριον. ἡ
ἡρωὶς ἡ παρὰ Καλλ., ἡ πρὸς ἑαυτὴν καλοῦσα· "ἔχε—ἀκλήιστον"   Cf. Et. Gen.
cod. A, et Et. Mag. codd. DP, p. 319. 43 Gaisford Ἑκάλη ἡ ἡρωίς, εἰς ἣν καὶ
ποίημα ἔγραψεν Καλλ.· παρὰ τὸ εἰσκαλεῖν ἢ εἰς καλὴν [Reitzenstein, Ind. Lect.
Rost. 1890/1, p. 14: εἰσκάλλη ἢ εἰκαλλὴν codd.] πρὸς ἑαυτὴν προτρέπειν· φιλόξενος
γάρ· ὡς καὶ Καλήσιος (Z 18). Ἑκάλη οὖν ἡ πρὸς ἑαυτὴν πάντας καλοῦσα

---

1 τίον Pf. (cf. e.g. Ψ 705, Aet. fr. 59. 20 Pf.): τῖον schol. Aristoph.   2 ἔχε
γὰρ Suid., Et. Gud.: ἔσχε γὰρ AO: ἔσχ' ἐς γῆν schol. E: ἔσχε σιγῆς schol.
Γ τέγος] τέλος schol. E: τεῖχος Suid.

3 (364 Pf.)

> πολύθρονον

Suid. iv. 165. 1 πολύθρονον· πολυφάρμακον (sequitur explicatio vocabuli θρόνα
et X 441, tum:) τάττεται δὲ καὶ ἐπὶ τοῦ πανούργου
'Fort. schol. Call.' (A. Adler ad loc.); v. Wendel, Gnomon, 15 (1939), 43. 'Call.
in Hec. de Medea?' (Pf.)

4 (232 Pf.)

ἡ δ᾿ ἐκόησεν
τοὔνεκεν Αἰγέος ἔσκεν

1–2 Et. Gen. AB s.v. θυοσκόος· ὁ ἱερεύς, ὁ μάντις, ὁ ἀπὸ τῶν θυομένων κοῶν, ὃ
ἐστι νοῶν, τὸ μέλλον. Καλλ. "ἡ—ἔσκεν" [τὸ μέλλον—ἔσκεν deest in Et. Mag. p.
457. 41]   Et. Gen. AB s.v. κοάλεμος (cf. Et. Mag. p. 524. 21)· ὁ μωρός, . . . (Ar.
Eq. 198), παρὰ τὸ κοῶ ῥῆμα, δηλοῦν τὸ νοῶ, οἷον "ἡ—ἔσκεν" Καλλ. [Καλλ. om.
A]
   1 Hellad. Chrest. ap. Phot. Bibl. p. 531a11 Bekk. ὅτι τὸ μακκοᾶν ἀρχαϊκῶς ἐστι
τὸ μὴ ἀκούειν, ἢ τὸ μὴ κοεῖν ὅπερ τὸ νοεῖν ἐδήλου. Καλλ. δ᾿ ἐν Ἑκάληι [Scaliger:
-βηι codd.] "ἐκόησέν" φησιν ἀντὶ τοῦ ἐνόησεν.   Suid. ii. 224. 22 ἐκόησεν·
ἐνόησεν. Ἰακῶς παρὰ Καλλ. (cf. Hesych. ἐκόησεν· †ἀνέλαβεν)
   2 Ammon. de Diff. Verb. 473 (p. 123 Nickau) τοὔνεκα καὶ οὕνεκα διαφέρει. τὸ
μὲν γὰρ τοὔνεκά ἐστι τούτου ἔνεκα, τὸ δὲ οὕνεκα ἀντὶ τοῦ ὅτι. ἁμαρτάνει οὖν ὁ
Καλλίμαχος ἐν Ἑκάληι κατὰ δύο τρόπους, λέγων "τοὔνεκεν—ἔσκεν", ὅτι τε, δέον
εἰπεῖν "οὕνεκα", "τοὔνεκεν" εἶπε, καὶ ὅτι ἀντὶ τοῦ κα κεν εἶπεν (eadem fere in Et.
Gud. p. 533. 22 Sturz om. ἐν Ἑκάληι)   hunc versum dubitantissime in P. Oxy.
2823(= SH 280). 8, ubi]αιγεος[legitur, agnovit Lobel; v. commentarium

────────────

   1 ἐκβόησεν Et. Gen. B s.v. θυοσκόος   2 τοὔνεκεν Ammon. (Et. Gud.):
οὕνεκεν Et. Gen. (sed οὕνεκα B s.v. κοάλεμος) γένος Et. Gen. s.v. κοάλε-
μος ἔσχεν Ammon. codd. deter.: ἔκεν Et. Gud.
   ἡ, sc. Medea: sic primus Reitzenstein (Ind. Rost. 1891/2, p. 4), qui tamen
οὕνεκεν cum Et. Gen. scribere maluit

5 (i, p. 506 Pf.), scholia marginalia

               ] . φ . [.] . . [
               ]ωνεπανω[
               Cκί]ρου δὲ ὁ Αἰ[γεὺς
               Παν]δίονος [
           5   ἀκολ]ουθησα[
               ]νονμ [
               ]παρδα[

Scholia litteris minoribus scripta in margine inferiore P. Oxy. 2258 (= pap. 2),
A fr. 11, pagina 'versa' (pagina 'recta' = fr. 6; utra praecedat incertum). De
Hecala cogitaverunt Lobel, Pfeiffer, propter res narratas (Aegei genus, ut videtur,
et fortasse Medeae venenum)

────────────

   1 φ vel fort. ρ vel ψ   2 τ]ῶν ἐπάνω [προγόνων e.g. Pf.; fort. lemma
est τ]ῶν ἐπάνω[θεν (Pf.)   3 Cκί]ρου suppl. Pf. coll. Apollod.
3. 15. 5   Αἰ[γεὺς suppl. Lobel   4–5 suppl. Lobel   7]παρδα-
[λιαγχές e.g. Pf. coll. Nic. Alex. 38 c. schol.

6 (cf. i, p. 507 Pf.), textus cum scholiis marginalibus

].ọọ....[
]φοϲουκ[

]   [
].αιερε.[
]ωϲδ.[
]..[

1–2 Textus; tum scholia (litteris minoribus) in margine inferiore. *P. Oxy.*
2258 (= pap. 2) A fr. 11, pagina 'recta' (pagina 'versa' = fr. 5)

Textus 1]. hastae verticalis pars inferior. Altera post ọ littera, fortasse
litterae ε vel ϲ pes. Tum duarum hastarum verticalium partes inferiores. An]νόον
εἰλ[ήλουθαϲ = fr. 8 hic habemus (Hollis)? Teste Parsons, in νοọνẹι non male
quadrant vestigia; de λ dubitandum, sed fort. non omnino excluditur
Scholia 1]. fortasse κ .[hasta verticalis pede dextrorsum uncinato

7 (233 Pf.)

ἴϲχε τέκοϲ, μὴ πῖθι

Anon. *de Barbarismo et Soloecismo,* p. 291. 15 Nauck (pone *Lexic. Vindob.*
(1867) = Boissonade, *AG* iii. 239) ϲολοικιϲμὸϲ γίνεται ... περὶ τὰϲ ἐγκλίϲειϲ, ὡϲ
παρὰ Καλλ.· "ἴϲχε—πῖθι"· προϲτακτικὴ ἀντὶ τῆϲ ὑποτακτικῆϲ τῆϲ μὴ πίηιϲ
Epim. Hom. (Cramer, *AO* i. 207. 24) s.v. ἴϲτω ... (Call. fr. 561 Pf.) ... ἔϲθι ...
ὅπερ οἱ Ἀττικοὶ ἴϲθι κατὰ τροπήν, ὥϲπερ τὸ ἔϲχω ἴϲχε "ἴϲχε—πῖθι" Suid.
ii. 674. 20 ἴϲχε· κάτεχε. καὶ "ἴϲχε τέκοϲ" (Suid. s.v. πῖθι· ἀντὶ τοῦ πίε et s.v. τέκοϲ·
τέκνον potius e fonte lexic., v. adn. Adl.)
Propter Suidam, fragmentum Hecalae assignavit Hecker, p. 91: 'videntur
verba Aegei qui filium a potu veneni deterret'. Idem coniecit Reitzenstein, *Ind.
Rost.* 1891/2, 5

8 (234 Pf.)

παρὲκ νόον εἰλήλουθαϲ

Suid. iv. 49. 15 παρὲκ νόον· ἀντὶ τοῦ παρ' ἐλπίδα. "παρὲκ—εἰλήλουθαϲ"
Hecalae fragmentis inseruit Kapp (fr. 80 = fr. an. 53 Schn.), et coniecit Aegei
verba esse post ἀναγνωριϲμόν. fort. in fr. 6. 1 (v. ad loc.) agnosci potest
]νοọνẹι.[

9 (235 Pf.)

> ἐν γάρ μιν Τροιζῆνι κολουραίηι ὑπὸ πέτρηι
> θῆκε σὺν ἁρπίδεσσιν

1–2 *Et. Gen.* AB (cf. *Et. Mag.* p. 148. 36) s.v. ἁρπῖδες [-ίδες codd.]· τὰ
ὑποδήματα, ἃ δὴ καὶ κρηπῖδας καλοῦμεν. εἴρηται δὲ παρὰ τὸ ῥάπτω ῥαπὶς καὶ
ῥαπῖδες [-ίδες codd.], πολυρραφῆ γὰρ τὰ ὑποδήματα, καὶ κατὰ μετάθεσιν ἁρπῖδες
[-ίδες codd., desinit *Et. Gen.* B]· οὕτως Σαλούςτιος. μέμνηται δὲ τῆς λέξεως Καλλ.
οἷον "ἐν—ἁρπ."   Schol. (Tzetz., cod. s⁴) Lyc. 494 ἐκ κοίλης πέτρας] ὁ Αἰγεὺς
ὑπὸ κοίλην πέτραν ἔθετο ξίφος καὶ ὑποδήματα, ὥς φησι Πλούταρχος (*Thes.* 3), καὶ
Καλλ. λέγων "ἐν—ἁρπίδεσσι"; ibid. 1322 πάλιν δ' ὁ πέτρας] κολουραίαν δὲ αὐτὴν ὁ
Καλλ. καλεῖ λέγων "ἐν—ἁρπίδεσσιν"
1 Schol. (ss³) Lyc. 494 κοίλην οὖν πέτραν λέγει τὴν ἐν Τροιζῆνι. καὶ Καλλ.
"κολουραίαν" [κολλ. codd.] καλεῖσθαι λέγει   Suid. iii. 146. 23 κολουραία πέτρα·
κοίλη, κεκαμμένη ἢ στρογγύλη, παρὰ Καλλ. (e Salust. comment., non e Call.
textu)
2 Poll. 7. 85 κρηπῖδες· τὸ μὲν φόρημα στρατιωτικόν, ἔνιοι δ' αὐτὰς τῶν
ποιητῶν καὶ ἁρπῖδας [-ίδας codd.] ὠνόμασαν   Cf. Suid. i. 366. 15 ἄρπη ...
ἁρπὶς δὲ διὰ τοῦ ῑ τὸ ὑπόδημα, καὶ κλίνεται ἁρπῖδος; Hesych. s.v. ἁρπῖδες [ἁρπίδες
cod.]· κρηπῖδες ἢ ὑποδήματα. Λάκωνες

---

1 ἐν γάρ μιν *Et. Gen.* A, schol. Lyc. 1322: ἔργα δέ μιν schol. Lyc. 494 et cod.
Pal. 18 (γ2), schol. 1322   τρυζῆνι et κολλουραίη *Et. Gen.* A (Τροζῆνι scribendum suspicatur M. L. West; cf. Barrett ad E. *Hipp.* 12)   κολ. ὑπὸ π. om. *Et.
Mag.*   2 ἁρπ- scripsi cum P. Oxy. 2529 (= pap. 4) in fr. 27. 2 (ὑπ'), sicut
etiam Hesychii cod.: ἁρπ- cett.   ἁρπίδεσσιν schol. Lyc. 1322: -δεσσι schol. Lyc.
494: ἁρπήδεσι *Et. Gen.* A
Hoc fragmentum (? et fr. 10) ante fr. 7 locare possis

10 (236. 1–2 Pf.)

> εὖτ' ἂν ὁ παῖς ἀπὸ μὲν γυαλὸν λίθον ἀγκάσσασθαι
> ἄρκιος ἦι χείρεσσιν, ἑλὼν Αἰδήψιον ἄορ

1 Schol. (AT) E 99 (ii, p. 18 Erbse) θώρηκος γύαλον] ὅτι τὸ ὅλον κύτος τοῦ
θώρακος γύαλον διὰ τὴν κοιλότητα λέγει, οὐ μέρος ὡρισμένον τοῦ θώρακος. τὸ
γυαλὸν ὅταν ἐπίθετον ἦι ὀξύνεται· "εὖτ'—ἀγκάσασθαι". Eust. ad h.l. (p. 526. 42)
Ἀπίων ... καὶ Ἡρόδωρός φασι γύαλον μὲν θώρηκος προπαροξύνεσθαι, γυαλὸν δὲ
λίθον ὀξυτόνως λέγεσθαι, οἷον "γυαλὸν—ἀγκάσασθαι"   Suid. i. 27. 21 ἀγκάσασθαι· ταῖς ἀγκάλαις βαστάσαι
2 Steph. Byz. s.v. Αἴδηψος [Αἴγηψος RV], πόλις Εὐβοίας ... ἣν δὲ καὶ σιδηρᾶ
καὶ χαλκᾶ μέταλλα κατὰ Εὔβοιαν. Καλλ. (fr. 701 Pf.) ... Ἐπαφρόδιτος δὲ
μαρτυρεῖ ἐκεῖ χαλκὸν πρῶτον εὑρεθῆναι ... ὁ πολίτης Αἰδήψιος [Αἰγίψιος R,
αἰψηγήψιος V]. Καλλ. Ἑκάληι [ἐκ- vel ἐκ- codd.] "ἄρκιος—ἄορ".

---

1 ἀγκάσασθαι schol., Eust., Suid.: corr Hecker   2 ἦι Hecker, p. 130
(coll. Plut. *Thes.* 3): ἢ Steph. Byz.   ἑλὼν Steph.: ἐλεῖν dub. Hecker (sed *Philol.*

4 (1849), 479 χείρεccιν, ἐλὼν hunc versum cum v. 1 coniungens), Bergk: ἐλὼν δ'
Schneider: ἐλεῖν δ' Wilamowitz   Αἰγήψιον Steph. codd. RV
Versus coniunxit Hecker (*Philol.* 4 (1849), 479. Fragmentum sequenti coniun-
gere voluerunt Schneider, Pfeiffer (v. ad. loc.)

11 (236. 3 Pf.)

πέδιλα, τὰ μὴ πύcε νήχυτος εὑρώς

Suid. ii. 469. 22 εὑρώς· ὑγρότης cεcηπυῖα (cf. *Et. Mag.* p. 397. 52)· Καλλ.
"πέδιλα—εὑρώς". Id. iii. 465. 2 "νήχυτος εὑρώς" [ἔρως codd., corr. Ruhnken],
lemma sine explicatione
⟨καὶ τὰ⟩ πέδιλα suppl. Naeke, p. 87. Hoc fr. priori adiungere voluerunt
Schneider, p. 178 (ἐλὼν δ'...|⟨cπάccηι καὶ τὰ⟩ πέδιλα...|⟨ἐκκομίcηι⟩) et
Pfeiffer (e.g. ⟨ἔλθοι καὶ τὰ⟩ πέδιλα...)

12 (237 Pf.)

Schol. (MNAB) E. *Hipp.* 11 ἀγνοῦ Πιτθέως] ἦν δὲ ὁ Πιτθεὺς cοφὸς καὶ
χρηcμολόγος καὶ ἱερὸς [φίλὸς Wilamowitz, προcφιλὴς Ed. Schwartz] θεοῖς, ὃς καὶ
ἔλυcε τὸν χρηcμὸν τῶι Αἰγεῖ καὶ τὴν θυγατέρα ἔδωκεν, εἰδὼς τῆι cοφίαι οἷος ἔcται
ὁ τεχθηcόμενος. παρ' αὐτῶι δὲ ὁ Θηcεὺς ἐπαιδεύετο, ὡς Καλλ.
Hecalae trib. Blomfield (v. Naeke, pp. 69 sq.)

13 (345 Pf.)

τοιοῦτον γὰρ ὁ παῖς ὅδε λῆμα φαείνει

Suid. iii. 262. 24 λῆμα· ἀξία καὶ ἀνδρεία. φρόνημα, κέρδος. "τοιοῦτον—
φαείνει"
Fragmentum epicum aliunde non notum Call. *Hecalae* tribuit Maas, *SIFC* 14
(1937), 317: v. Adler, Suid, v, p. 38 Add.; Wendel, *Gnomon*, 15 (1939), 43 (qui
vix recte dactylum deesse inter ὅδε et λῆμα coniecit). De Theseo dictum esse
coniecit Maas; 'si recte, potius ad carminis partem "Troezeniam" pertinet' (Pf.)

14 (361 Pf.)

ἔτι πλοκάμοιο περίθριξ

Suid. iv. 99. 13 περίθριξ· ὁ ἀπὸ γενετῆς πλόκαμος, ὁ μηδέπω καρείς. "ἔτι—
περίθριξ"
Call. tribuit Toup (qui de *Coma Berenices* cogitaverat), *Hecalae* Naeke, pp. 160
sq.

15 (281 Pf.)

τὺ δ' ἐγκυτὶ τέκνον ἐκέρcω

Et. Gen. A^{II}B s.v. ἐγκυτί· ἐν χρῶι, ἐπίρρημα. Καλλίμαχος [καλλίουc codd.]· "cὺ
δ'—ἐκέρcω". εἴρηται δὲ παρὰ τὸ κύτος ὃ καὶ cκύτος καλεῖται, τὸ πρὸc αὐτῶι τῶι
δέρματι κεκάρθαι [Pf.: κέκαρcαι codd.]. Ἡρωδιανὸc δέ· ὀξυτόνωc τὸ ἐγκυτὶ
ἐπίρρημα γέγονε, κείμενον παρ' Ἀρχιλόχωι (fr. 217 West)· "χαίτην ἀπ' ὤμων
ἐγκυτὶ κεκαρμένοc". Cf. Hesych. ἐγκυτί· εἰc χρῶτα κεκάρθαι	*Et. Sym.* cod. V
(ap. Gaisford, *Et. Mag.* p. 311. 40) ἐγκυτί· ἐπίρρημα cημαῖνον τὸ ἐν χρῶι· οἷον
"οὐδ—ἐκέρcω" κτλ. [post κεκάρθαι desinit; *Et. Mag.* loc. cit. om. Call., laudat
Archilochum]	Iohann. Philop. Τονικὰ Παραγγέλματα (ex Herodian. prosod.
excerpt.), p. 37. 12 Dindorf τὸ δὲ ἀπαρτὶ παρ' Ἀθηναίοιc ὀξύνεται ⟨καὶ τὸ
ἐγκυτὶ⟩, [lacunam indicat et explet Lentz, Herodian. i. 506. 14]· "cὺ δ'—
ἐκέρcω". Ibid. p. 38. 21 (ὀξύνεται) ἐγκυτίc, ὃ χωρὶc τοῦ c̄ Καλλ. εἶπεν· "cὺ δ'—
ἐκέρcω" (Herodian. i. 511. 22 Lentz et ii. 1239 Addenda)	Suid. ii. 298. 1 ἐν
χρῶι· εἰc χρῶτα, πάνυ ἐγγύc . . . παρὰ δὲ Καλλ. ἐγκυτί, ἀντὶ τοῦ ἐγγύc, ἐν χρωτί,
πληcίον τοῦ χρωτόc· "τὺ δ'—ἐκέρcω"	Suid. ii. 198. 19 ἐγκυτί· ἀντὶ τοῦ ἐγγύc.
οὕτωc Καλλ.

τὺ Suid cod. A: τὸ rell. Suid. codd.: cὺ Herodian. in *Et.* et Philop. (οὐ *Et.*
Sym.): τί coni. Naeke, p. 159	ἐνκυτὶ et ἐνκέρcω Suid. cod. A: ἐγκύτιον rell.
Suid. codd.
Tonsuram Theseo propriam (Plut. *Thes.* 5) cont. Naeke, p. 159

16 (283 Pf.)

ἵν' ἔλλερα ἔργα τέλεcκεν

Et. Gen. A^{II}B s.v. ἔλλερα· τὰ βλέφαρα [??: βλαβερά coni. Küster. In *Et. Gen.* A^I
legimus ἐλ'έρα [sic]· τὰ βλέφαρα, ἐκ τοῦ ἔριν ἐλαύνειν, cf. 'Zonaras', p. 689 Tittm.
ἔλλερα· χαλεπά, κακά. cημαίνει καὶ τὰ βλέφαρα]· Καλλ. "ἵν'—τέλεcκεν". ὀλλύρα
τινὰ ὄντα· ὀλλύντα καὶ ἔρρειν ποιοῦντα (Call. testim. om. *Et. Mag.* p. 331. 31 s.v.
ἔλλερα).	Suid. ii. 244. 1 ἔλλερα ἔργα· φόνια, χαλεπά, κακά. Cf. Hesych. ἔλλερα·
ἐχθρά, πολέμια, ἄδικα

ἔργα Suid.: πολλὰ *Et. Gen.*: πολλὰ τέλεcκεν | ἔργα coni. Reitzenstein
Hoc fragmentum cum fr. 89 iungi posse coniecit Schneider, p. 608; si recte,
fort. ἐννοτίου Μαραθῶνος, ἵν' κτλ. (Pfeiffer). Vix in fr. 49. 20 (Barigazzi) restitui
potest

17 (versus 4 = *SH* 281; 238. 1–14 Pf.)

. . . . .

]. . . . .μεν . φ. . . [

]κέλευε δὲ μήποτ' ἐλέγξα[ι

]νε. η δ' ὑπὸ πάντας ἀέθλου[ς

⌊τῶι ⟨ῥα⟩, πάτερ, μεθίει με·⌋ cóον δέ κεν α⌊ῦ⌋θι δέχοιο

5   ]δ. . . . ′. εχ. . ά. . . [

]. αρὴν κεκύθεσθε κ. [

]. . . [.]. ′. . νε. [

]ε δ' ἦν τόδε χειραεcα[

]τας ἀκὴν ἔχε· τῆι δε. [

10   ]ν. ου αἰcυμνῆτιc[

†ῆ τ' ἄκρηcθ† ἵ⌊να Γλαυκώπιον ἵζε⌊ι

]εν ἀεὶ περὶ πότνια γα[

]c ὅτι πτολέμοιό μ' ἐπ. [

]. [   ]′[

. . . . .

1–14 *P. Oxy.* 2216 (= pap. 3), fr. 1, pagina recta (pagina versa = fr. 18. 3–18)
4 Ammon. *de Diff. Verb.* 89 (p. 23 Nickau) τὸ μὲν αὖθιc ἐcτὶ τὸ πάλιν ἢ μετὰ ταῦτα, τὸ δ' αὖθι ⟨τὸ⟩ αὐτόθι. κακῶc οὖν Καλλίμαχόc φηcι "αὖθι τὸ δ' ἐκδύοιμι" (*Aet.* fr. 1. 35 Pf.) ἀντὶ τοῦ μετὰ ταῦτα, ⟨καὶ ἐν τῆι βλῆ [lege τῆι Ἑκάληι] "τῶ πέρ μεθίει [μ]ε cῶον δέ κεν αὖθι δέχοιο", ἀντὶ τοῦ πάλιν add. 'Erenii' Philonis lexicon Parisinum ineditum⟩. Vide Nickau, *Philol.* 111 (1967), 126
10 Suid. ii. 183. 24 αἰcυμνῆτιc· ἡ δέcποινα
11 Schol. (BD) *E* 422 πάντ' οὖν [sc. ἐπίθετα] ἀπὸ τῶν παρεπομένων τοῖc θεοῖc. καὶ γὰρ ἡ γλαυκῶπιc οὐκ ἀπὸ τοῦ "ῆτ'—ἵζει" (Call fr. an. 332 Schn.), ἀλλ' ἀπὸ τῆc περὶ τὴν πρόcοψιν τῶν ὀφθαλμῶν καταπλήξεωc (inde *Et. Mag.* p. 547. 6 s.v. *Κύπριc*). Hexametrum corruptum Callimachi *Hecalae* adscripsit Naeke, p. 201. Schol. (MNAB) E. *Hipp.* 29–33 "πέτραν δὲ Παλλάδοc" φηcὶ τὸ ἐν τῆι Ἀττικῆι Γλαυκώπιον, οὗ Καλλ. ἐν Ἑκάληι [ἑκάβη codd.] μέμνηται (fr. 66f Schn. = 84 Kapp)

1]νιcπε vestigiis fort. convenit, post μεν fort αμ, post φ vix ι vel ο: ε]νιcπε μὲν ἀμφ. . . dub. Lobel (vel ἐνίcπε vel ἐνιcπέμεν) 2 οτ'ελεξ pap.; inter ε et ξ m¹ scr. litt. γ, quae a ceteris litt. γ differt: suppl. Lobel 3 inter ε et η hasta verticalis sine capite descendens infra lineam—ι potissimum, sed υ vel ρ non omnino excluduntur (Parsons) pro η, Barrett ν fort. legi posse arbitratur, sed η malit Parsons δ'ὺ pap. 4 ⟨ῥα⟩ suppl. Kassel: ⟨νυ⟩ Nickau cῶον 'Erenii' Philonis lexicon: cóονδέ pap. 5 litterae tertia et quarta hastae verticales, paulum infra lineam descendentes ante ε fort. υ (vel φ?), post χ (vel fort. λ?) partes inferiores hastarum, altera infra lineam post ά (sic pap.) littera altera, fort. ε 6]. finis superior lineae ascendentis a laeva ἀρηνκεκύθ pap. 7 fort.]ά 8 δ' pap., ut videtur post χειρ littera omnino deleta et α superscr. αεcα[corruptum? 'Expectes χειρώcα[cθαι sim., fin. spondaicum ut v. 10' (Pf.) 9]τ vel]γ. ακὴν et ·τη add. ι pap. fort. τ[10 post ν fort. ε, superscripta alia litt., fort γ. ῆτηc altera η del.

et ι sscr. pap.   11 ἦτ' ἄκρης θῖνα schol. D (sanum putat Naeke, p. 201, sed contra Call. artem metricam): ἄκρην τινὰ γλαυκῶπις schol. B: ἄκρης τινα et ἴξει codd. DM. *Et. Mag.* p. 547. 6 γλαυκῶπειον schol. Eur.   κώπ et ἴζ pap.   suppl. Lobel e fr. an. 332 (coll. 66f) Schn.   12 περιπότν pap.   γα[ίης suppl. Barigazzi   13 ὄθ et μ'επ pap.   post επ fort. ε[

In prioribus saltem huius fragmenti versibus Theseus patrem alloquitur, ut coniecerat Lobel et docet v. 4 pars prima, post Pf. reperta. Inter frr. 17 et 18 quot versus desint non constat.

18 (238. 15–32, ?319 Pf.)

⌊ὄφρα μὲν οὖν ἔνδιος ἔην ἔτι, θέρμετο δὲ χθών,
τόφρα δ' ἔην ὑάλοιο φαάντερος οὐρανὸς ἠνοψ⌋
οὐδέ⌋ ποθ⌊ι⌋ κν⌊ηκὶς ὑπεφαίνετο, πέπτατο δ' αἰθήρ
ἀγ[ν]έφελος· ς[
5   μητέρι δ' ὀππ[ότε
δειελὸν αἰτίζ⌊ουσιν, ἄγουσι δὲ χεῖρας ἀπ' ἔργου,
τῆμος ἄρ' ἐξ. [.] . . . [
πρῶτον ὑπὲρ Πά[ρνηθος,]⌊ἐπιπρὸ δὲ μᾶσσον ἐπ' ἄκρου
Αἰγαλέως θυμόε⌊ντος, ἄγων μέγαν ὑετόν, ἔστη·
10   τῶι δ' ἐπ[ὶ] διπλόον. [
τρηχέος Ὑμηττ[οῖο
ἀστεροπα[ὶ] σελάγι[ζον
οἶ[ο]ν ὅτε κλονέ. [
Αὐςόν[ι]ον κατὰ π[όντον
15   ἡ δ' ἀπὸ Μηρισοῖο θ⌊οὴ βορέαο κατάιξ
εἰςέπεσεν νεφέλ[ηισιν
. . . [. .]ν ὅθ[
]ερ. [
. . . .

1–2 Suid. ii. 273. 24 ἔνδιος· μεσημβρινός. "ὄφρα—ἠνοψ" (fr. an. 24 Schn. = 8. 1–2 Kapp), τουτέστιν ὁ λαμπρός

2 Suid. ii. 574. 23 ἠνοψ· ὁ λαμπρός. "οὐρανὸς ἠνοψ" (sequitur fr. 102. 2)

3–18 *P. Oxy.* 2216 (= pap. 3), fr. 1, pagina versa (pagina recta = fr. 17)

3 Suid. iii. 140. 1 κνηκίς· ἡ νεφελώδης ζώνη, τὸ μικρὸν νέφος. "οὐδέ—αἰθήρ" (fr. an. 36 Schn. = 8. 3 Kapp)

6 Schol. (V) ρ 599 cὺ δ' ἔρχεο δειελιήcαc] πρὸς τὴν δειλινὴν ὥραν παραγενόμενος, τουτέcτι τὴν μεcημβρίαν· ἢ τὴν ἑcπερινὴν διατρίψαc. ἔνιοι δὲ τὴν δειλινὴν τροφὴν αἰτῶν. καὶ Καλλ. φηcι· "δειελὸν—ἔργου" (fr. 190 Schn. = 32. 3 Kapp), τὴν πρὸς τῆι δειλινῆι τροφὴν αἰτοῦντεc Eust. p. 1832. 62 οἱ δὲ ἐπὶ τροφῆc δειλινῆc τὴν λέξιν νοοῦντεc προφέρουcι Καλλ. τὸ "δειελίην αἰτίζουcιν—ἔργου", τὴν πρὸς δείλην δηλαδὴ τροφὴν αἰτοῦντεc Suid. ii. 29. 2 δειελινόν· τὸ δειλινόν. καὶ "δείελον"· τὸ δειλινόν, 'altera gl. prob. ex h. l.' (Pf.)

8–9 Suid. iii. 334. 8 μᾶϲϲον· μεῖζον, μακρότερον· "ἐπιπρὸ—ἔϲτη" (fr. an. 46
Schn. = 10 Kapp)
9 Suid. ii. 157. 1 Αἰγαλέωϲ· ἐπὶ γενικῆϲ ἀντὶ τοῦ . . . [lacuna in codd. AFV post
τοῦ, prob. ⟨Αἰγάλεω⟩ supplendum] Suid. iv. 636. 21 ὑετόϲ· τὸ ῡ μακρόν·
"ἄγων—ἔϲτη"
12 Suid. iv. 336. 21 ϲελαγίζω· λάμπω [λάμπω om. AV, habent GFM] e Salusti
comment.
14 Suid. i. 417. 7 Αὐϲονίων . . . καὶ "Αὐϲόνιοϲ πόντοϲ"· ἡ Ϲικελικὴ θάλαϲϲα
15 Suid. iii. 45. 6 κατάϊξ· καταιγίϲ· "ἡ—κατάϊξ" (fr. an. 32 Schn. = 12
Kapp), ἤτοι ἀπὸ τῆϲ Θράικηϲ. Cf. Hesych. κατάϊξ· κατάϲειϲιϲ, ὁρμή
Omnia fragmenta anonyma a Suida allata eodem ordine quo nunc apud pap. 3
leguntur in versibus (1–2), 3, 8–9, 15, feliciter ad *Hecalam* revocaverat Hecker,
CC, pp. 105 sq. (addito fr. 19)

---

3 suppl. Lobel e fr. an. 36 Schn. = 8. 3 Kapp ποθ' ἡ Suid. cod. A: ποθι
cett. πέπατο Suid. cod. F 4 ἔφελοϲ· pap.: suppl. Lobel 5 τέριδ'
pap.: suppl. Lobel 6 suppl. Lobel e fr. 190 Schn. (= 32. 3 Kapp) διέλον
pap., addito ε post δ supra ι: δείελον Schol. *Od.* et Suid. (de accentu v. Pfeiffer):
δειελίην Eust. τίζ[pap. 7 τῇ pap. post ξ inferior pars dextera litt. ϱ? (ᾳ
excludi nequit); in ἐξαπίνηϲ vel ἐξ ὀλίγη– (ὀλίγο-) vestigia vix quadrant
(Lobel) 8–9 Πά[ρνηθοϲ suppl. Lobel, cetera e fr. an. 46 Schn. (= 10
Kapp) 8 ὑπερπά[pap. 9 αιγαλεωϲ pap. et Suid. s.v. Αἰγαλέωϲ:
Αἰγαλέω Suid. s.v. μᾶϲϲον: Αἰγάλεω edd. ante Pf. θῡμόε[pap. ἄγων Suid.
codd. praeter VM s.v. ὑετόϲ, ubi ἄγον 11 χέος pap. prob. ττ[pap.,
superscr. aliae litterae, duae vel tres: Ὑμηϲϲ[οῖο Lobel in hoc versu fr. 19 καὶ
ἠέροϲ ἀχλύϲαντοϲ fort. suppleri potest (Hollis) 12 αϲτέρόπ pap. άγι[
pap.: suppl. Lobel 13 [τ]οι pap. νέ.[pap. 14 όν[pap.: suppl.
Lobel 15 suppl. Lobel e fr. an. 32 Schn. (= 12 Kapp) ἠδ'ἀπομηρῑϲοῖο
pap.: litterae ϲ nil nisi punctum extat, ἴθοῖο legi potest: ἠδ' Suid. codd. (corr.
Toup): Μηριϲοῖο Suid. (Merithus Plin. *NH* 4. 80) 16 εἰϲέπ et φέλ[pap.:
suppl. Pf. 17 in init. laeva pars superior litt. rotundae, mox apex lineae
descendentis ad dexteram, at fort. non duae sed una littera, ut e.g. θ[ὄθ[
pap. 18 post ρ fort. γ, non ϲ (fr. 86 γαμβρὸϲ Ἐρεχθῆοϲ hic suppleri
nequit)

19 (319 Pf.)

καὶ ἠέροϲ ἀχλύϲαντοϲ

Suid. i. 440. 25 ἀχλύϲ· ϲκότοϲ, ὁμίχλη, ζόφοϲ, ἀμβλυωπία. "καὶ—ἀχλύϲαντοϲ"·
ἀντὶ τοῦ ϲκοτιϲθέντοϲ

'Particula καί ad verba poetae pertinere potest' Pf. (ii, p. 121), qui tamen in
textu ἠέροϲ ἀχλύϲαντοϲ tantum poetae dedit. fort. in fr. 18. 11 supplendum
(Hollis)
Descriptionem procellae in Call. *Hecala* trib. Hecker, pp. 105 sqq.

20 (238a Pf.)

> · · · · ·
>] .. [ ] . . . . . [
>]μεν ἐνιϛπ[
>] . [
> · · · ·

1–3 *P. Oxy.* 2216 (= pap. 3), fr. 2, pagina 'recta' (pagina 'versa' = fr. 21)
2 ἐνιϛ . [pap., π dispici nequit

21 (238b Pf.)

> · · · ·
>] . [
>]ἰω . [ ]βυ[
>]κ[.] . [. .] . πεθ . [
> · · · ·

1–3 *P. Oxy.* 2216 (= pap. 3), fr. 2, pagina 'versa' (pagina 'recta' = fr. 20),
litterae fere omnes satis incertae　　　3 vestigia atramenti supra εθ

22 (238c Pf.)

> · · · ·
>] . ϛον . . . [
>]δεν . [
> · · · ·

1–2 *P. Oxy.* 2216 (= pap. 3), fr. 3, pagina 'recta' (pagina 'versa' = fr.
23)　　　1] . , pars superior hastae verticalis, post υ fort. αλ vel αχ: ἐφύλα]ϛϛον
ἄλω[α = fr. 42. 1 vix legi potest (Pf.)　　　2 α[?

23 (238d Pf.)

> · · ·
>]γεγοιτο[
>]μοιαη[
> · · ·

1–2 *P. Oxy.* 2216 (= pap. 3), fr. 3, pagina 'versa' (pagina 'recta' = fr.
22)　　　2 an]μοι ἀή[ϛυρον, i.e. fr. 24, hic habemus (Hollis)?

24 (311 Pf.)

ἀήϲυρον ⟨–⟩ γόνυ κάμψοι

Suid. i. 64. 30 ἀήϲυρον· τὸ λεπτόν, τὸ μετέωρον καὶ κοῦφον, τὸ ἐλαφρόν, παρὰ τὸ ἀέρι ϲύρεϲθαι. ἐπὶ ὀρνέων. "ἀήϲυρον—κάμψοι". Cf. Hesych. ἀήϲυρον· κοῦφον, ἐλαφρόν   *Et. Mag.* p. 95 L.–L. (p. 23. 20 Gaisford); cf. *Et. Sym.*, *Et. Gen.* B, L.–L. pp. 98–9) ἀήϲυρον· ἀϲθενέϲ, κενόν, . . . ἔνιοι κοῦφον, ὑπ' αὔραϲ φερόμενον

Lacunam indicavit Meineke, *Anal. Alex.* p. 168, et ⟨ὄν⟩ suppl.: ⟨ὡϲ⟩ Bergk: ⟨ἐν⟩ M. L. West   κάμψαι? Pf., sed nil mutandum
Call. *Hecalae* fragmentum tribuit Hecker, p. 111; forsitan in fr. 23. 2 supplendum (Hollis)

25 (269 Pf.)

ὁππότε λύχνου
δαιομένου πυρόεντεϲ ἄδην ἐγένοντο μύκητεϲ

1–2 Exc. ex Herodian. π. Ὀνομ. ap. Cramer, *AO* iii. 230. 31 et ap. Choerob. in Theodos. (*Gr. Gr.* iv. i, p. 158. 1 Hilgard) μύκηϲ μύκου καὶ μύκητοϲ· τοῦτο . . . διάφορα ϲημαίνει· ϲημαίνει γὰρ καὶ [Choerob.: καὶ πόϲα ϲημαίνει; τέϲϲαρα *AO*] τὰ καρβώνια τὰ ἐπικείμενα τοῖϲ λύχνοιϲ, ὡϲ παρὰ Καλλ. ἐν τῆι Ἑκάληι [Ἑκάβηι *AO*] "ὁππότε—μύκητεϲ"   Schol. (*MΔKUAS*) Arat. *Phaen.* 976 (p. 469 Martin) ἢ λύχνοιο μύκητεϲ] τὸ πῦρ ὡμολόγηται ξηρᾶϲ οὐϲίαϲ, ὑγρὸϲ δὲ ἀὴρ πολλάκιϲ ἐν χειμῶϲιν ἐμπίπτων τῶι πυρὶ ἀποτελεῖ τούτουϲ τοὺϲ ϲπινθῆραϲ. δύο γὰρ οὐϲίαι ἐναντίαι ἀλλήλαιϲ ϲυνεμπίπτουϲι, καὶ μὴ φέρον τὸ πῦρ τὸ ὑγρὸν τοῦ ἀέροϲ τοῦ ἐμπεϲόντοϲ ἀφίηϲί τιναϲ ϲπινθῆραϲ. ὅπερ καὶ ὁ Καλλ. ὠφεληθεὶϲ [codd.: νοήϲαϲ Ald.] εἶπεν "εὖτ' ἂν ἀπὸ λύχνοιο δαιομένου—ἄδην ἐγένοντο μύκητεϲ"
2 Schol. (Lh Ald.) Ar. *Vesp.* 262b (p. 48 Koster) οὗτοὶ μύκητεϲ] . . . Ἄρατοϲ (*Phaen.* 976) . . . ὅθεν τεκμαίρονται τὸν ὑετόν, καὶ Καλλ. "ἄδην—μύκητεϲ"

1 ὁππότε Choerob.: ὡϲ ποτε *AO*: e schol. Arat. var. lect. εὖτ' ἀπὸ coni. E. Maass   1–2 λύχνοϲ | δαιόμενοϲ *AO*   2 πυρέοντοϲ Choerob. codd. NC: πυρέοντεϲ Choerob. cod. V   ἄδην Choerob. cod. P: ἄδδην Choerob. cod. V et schol. in Aristoph.: ἄρδην Choerob. codd. NC

26 (525 inc. sed. Pf.)

ἐλαχὺν δόμον

Et. Gen. AᴴB s.v. ἐλαχύϲ (cf. *Et. Mag.* p. 325. 30 s.v. ἐλάϲϲων, Hesych. s.v. ἐλαχύν· εὐτελῆ ἢ μικρόν)· ὁ μικρόϲ. Καλλ. "ἐλαχὺν δόμον", οἷον πενιχρόν· παρὰ τὸ ἑλῶ τὸ ἀφαιρῶ ἵν' ἦι ὁ ἀφαιρεθείϲ, καὶ ἐκ τούτου μειωθείϲ
His ipsis verbis utitur Greg. Naz. *Carm.* 1. 2. 2. 333 (*PG* xxxvii. 604), in quo carmine *Hecalae* saepe reminiscitur (v. Pfeiffer ad fr. 231). Itaque hoc fragmentum *Hecalae* tribuere (cum Schneider, fr. 349, Kapp, fr. 3) vix dubito

27 (*SH* 282; ?239 Pf.)

. . .

]πεκλινεν[
]ὑπ' ἁρπῖδα[
]άδα τὴν αγ[
]μο. φαε̣εc[

. . .

1–4 *P. Oxy.* 2529 (= pap. 4), pagina 'recta' (pagina 'versa' = fr. 36) 1 ἀ]π-, ἐ]π-, ὑ]π- 2 πῖδ pap. huic versui fr. 28 = 239 Pf. adiunxit T. B. L. Webster, ut fiat λύcαθ'] ὑπ' ἁρπῖδα[c, ⌊διερὴν δ' ἀπεceίcατο λαίφην 3]άδα pap. 4 μο̣ν,]μο̣ν,]μοιc,]μοια possis φαε̣εc[pap. De saxo (1 ἀ]πέκλινεν) et Aegei soleis (cf. frr. 10–11) cogitavit Lobel; melius autem Webster de Theseo Hecalae casam intrante (v. 2 adn.). Tum enim optime sequitur Thesei apud Hecalam cena in pagina 'versa' (fr. 36)

28 (239 Pf.)

διερὴν δ' ἀπεceίcατο λαίφην

Et. Gen. AB (= *Et. Mag.* p. 274. 1) s.v. διερόc· ὁ ὑγρόc. Καλλ. "διερὴν— λαίφην" Suid. iii. 241. 21 λαίφη· θηλυκῶc ἡ χλανίc [χλαμύc ed. pr.]. "διερὴν— λαίφην" Suid. ii. 86. 17 διερήν· δίυγρον (Suid. s.v. ἀπεceίcατο· ἀπέβαλεν fort. non ex *Hec.*, v. Pf.)

δ' om. Suid.
Hoc fragmentum optime fr. 27. 2 (v. ad loc.) adiunxit Webster. *Hecalae* trib. Schneider (fr. 245)

29 (240 Pf.)

τὸν μὲν ἐπ' ἀcκάντην κάθιcεν

Et Gen. AB (cf. *Et. Mag.* p. 154. 30) s.v. ἀcκάντηc· κλινίδιον εὐτελέc, ὃ καὶ ὑπὸ τῶν Ἀττικῶν cκίμπουc ὀνομάζεται. Καλλ. καὶ [καὶ fort. ante Καλλ. ponendum cum Schneider] "τὸν—κάθιcεν". καὶ Ἀριcτοφάνηc (*Nub.* 633) "ἕξει τὸν ἀcκάντην λαβών", καὶ Πλάτων ὁ φιλόcοφοc Πρωταγόραι (310c) "καὶ ἅμα ἐπιψηλαφήcαc τοῦ cκίμποδοc ἐκαθέζετο παρ' ἐμέ". ὁ δὲ κράβατοc οὐδὲ παρ' ἑνί [καὶ Ἀριcτ.—ἑνί om. B]. εἴρηται δὲ καὶ [om. B] ἀcκάντηc παρὰ τὴν κάννην· οὕτωc δὲ ἐκάλουν τὴν ψίαθον. ἀcκάντηc οὖν ἡ εὐτελὴc κλίνη μηδὲ κάννην ἔχουcα, ἀκάντηc καὶ ἀcκάντηc. οὕτωc Cαλούcτιοc εἰc τὴν Ἑκάλην Καλλιμάχου [οὕτωc—Καλλ. om. *Et. Mag.*, εἰc—Καλλ. om. *Et. Gen.* B] Suid. i. 381. 24 ἄcκαντοc· ἡ μικρὰ κλίνη, τὸ πτωχὸν κλινίδιον. ἢ ἀcκάντηc, κλίνη μὴ ἔχουcα κάνητα· κάνηc δὲ ἡ ψίαθοc (e

Salust. comment.). ἢ ὁ cκίμπους, ἢ δίφρου τι εἶδος, οἱ δὲ τὸν κράββατον (e schol.
Ar. *Nub.* 634)

ἀcκάντην E. Schwartz ap. Reitzenstein, *Ind. Rost.* 1890/1, 14: ἀcκάνταν *Et. Gen.*
A: ἀcκάντα *Et. Gen.* B, *Et. Mag.* (tamquam genetivam Doricam defenderunt
nonnulli)

30 (241 Pf.)

> αὐτόθεν ἐξ εὐνῆς ὀλίγον ῥάκος αἰθύξαca

Suid. ii. 167. 13 αἰθύξαca· κινήcαca. "αὐτόθεν—αἰθύξαca"
Call. *Hecalae* assignavit Hecker, p. 112

31 (242 Pf.)

> παλαίθετα κᾶλα καθήιρει

Etym. Graec. Par. (Cramer, *Anecd. Par.* iv. 53. 17) s.v. καλοcτρόφοι· cχοινοπ-
λόκοι· κάλωc γὰρ τὸ cχοινίον· ἴcωc ὅτι ἀπὸ φλοιοῦ ξύλου πρῶτον ἐπετηδεύθη.
κᾶλον (κάλον codd.) δὲ τὸ ξύλον εἴρηται, ἀφ' οὗ καὶ καλόπουc. Καλλ. Ἑκάληι·
"παλαίθετα—καθήιρει". Eadem fere *Et. Sym.* V (ap. *Et. Mag.* p. 486. 36); in *Et.
Gen.* AB = *Et. Mag.* p. 486. 6, nihil extat nisi s.v. καλόπουc· κυρίωc ὁ ξύλινος
πούc· κᾶλον γὰρ τὸ ξύλον   Suid. iii. 16. 16 κᾶλα παλαίθετα· ξηρὰ ξύλα, ἐκ
πολλοῦ ἀποτεθέντα χρόνου. κᾶλον γὰρ τὸ ξύλον. ἐξ οὗ καὶ καλόπουc, ὁ ξύλινος
πούc (nota ordinem verborum inversum; prob. e comment. Salust., non e textu
Call.)

κᾶλα Suid.: κάλα *Et. Sym.* V: καλὰ *Etym. Graec. Par.*

32 (243 Pf.)

> δανὰ ξύλα ... κεάcαι ...

Suid. ii. 5. 20 δανά· τὰ ξηρὰ ξύλα. τὸ δᾱ μακρόν· Καλλ. "δανὰ ξύλα κεάcαι".
τουτέcτι cχίcαι
    Non Callimachei, sed Homerici versus (ο 322 διά τε ξύλα δανὰ κεάccαι) partem
esse coni. Kuester ad Suid., alii. Sed, ut adnotat Kapp (fr. 17; cf. Naeke, p. 132),
vix casu factum esse credas quod apud Ovidium (*Met.* 8. 644–5) Baucis
'ramaliaque arida ...|... minuit'. Bentley in Call. δανὰ post ξύλα transposuit et
κεάccαι scripsit, ut apud Homerum est, fortasse recte. Dubitanter cum Schneider
(fr. 289), Kapp, et Pfeiffer lacunam indicavi

33 (244 Pf.)

αἶψα δὲ κυμαίνουσαν ἀπαίνυτο χυτρίδα κοίλην

Suid. iii. 211. 21 κυμαίνει· ταράccει. καὶ ἐπὶ τοῦ ζέειν. "αἶψα—κοίλην"
Callimachi *Hecalae* primus assignavit Ruhnken

34 (246 Pf.)

ἐκ δ' ἔχεεν κελέβην, μετὰ δ' αὖ κερὰc ἠφύcατ' ἄλλο

Suid. iii. 91. 20 κελέβη [cod. F: κελεύη rell.]· κόγχη, ἢ λεκάνη, ἢ τοιοῦτον
cκεῦοc, ἐν ὧι δυνατὸν νίψαcθαι πόδαc. "ἐκ—ἄλλο"   Suid. iii. 98. 6 κεράc·
ἐπίρρημα, ἀντὶ τοῦ κεραcτικῶc. "μετὰ—ἄλλο" ὁ δὲ νοῦc· ἀπὸ τοῦ κεράcματοc
[ἀπὸ τ. κ. codd.: κέραcμα coni. Bernhardy] ἄλλο ἤντληcεν ἀπὸ τοῦ ἄγγουc, ἐν ὧι
ἦν.

κελέβην Lobeck, *Paralipom.* p. 223 et Meineke, *Anal. Alex.* p. 168: κελεύη
Suid. codd.: κελέβη ed. pr.: κελέβηι Bernhardy: fort. ἐν—κελέβηι Schneider.
μετὰ κέραc unam esse vocem μετάκεραc coni. J. G. Schneider: μετά τ' αὖ κέραc
Meineke
Fragmentum Call. *Hecalae* tribuerunt et Meineke, *Anal. Alex.* p. 168, et
Hecker, pp. 112 sq.

35 (251 Pf.)

ἐκ δ' ἄρτουc cιπύηθεν ἅλιc κατέθηκεν ἑλοῦcα
οἵουc βωνίτηιcιν ἐνικρύπτουcι γυναῖκεc

1 *Et. Gen.* AB s.v. cιπύη (cf. 'Zonar.' p. 1645 Tittm.)· cημαίνει τὴν ἀρτοθήκην.
Καλλ. "ἐκ—ἑλοῦcα". εἴρηται οἰονεὶ cιτοὺνη τιc οὖcα, παρὰ τὸ ἐν αὐτῆι τὰ cιτία
ἐμβάλλεcθαι   Apollon. Dysc. *de Adv.* (*Gr. Gr.* i. 1., p. 191. 24 Schn.) βαρύνεται
τὸ Θήβηc ... Θήβηθεν ..., Ἀθήνηc Ἀθήνηθεν, cιπύηc cιπύηθεν· "ἐκ—cιπύηθεν"
2 *Et. Gen.* AB s.v. βωνίτηc (p. 165. 5–6 Berger = *Et. Mag.* p. 218. 22)·
cημαίνει τὸν βουκόλον. Καλλ. "οἵουc—γυναῖκεc", διὰ τοῦ ῑ ὡc πολίτηc   Cyrill.
lex. in Cod. Gr. Bodl. Misc. 211 (Cramer, *Anecd. Par.* iv. 180. 20) βωνίτηc· λέγει
αὐτῶι [οὕτω Wilamowitz ap. Kapp fr. 32. 2] Ἀλεξίων Αἰγύπτιοc διὸ διὰ τοῦ ῑ
γράφεται, ὡc καὶ Βούcιριc· ἄλλωc τε καὶ ὁ χαρακτὴρ τὸ ῑ αἰτεῖ, ὡc Μεμφίτηc ...
τοπίτηc. Καλλ. "βωνίτηιcιν—γυναῖκεc". cημαίνει δὲ ἡ λέξιc τοὺc βουκόλουc
Suid. i. 486. 26 βουνιτῆιcι [sic codd.]· τοῖc βουκόλοιc, τοῖc βοηλάταιc

1 παρέθηκεν Meineke   2 βωνίτηιcιν *Et. Gen.*, *Et. Mag.*, Cyrill.
(βωνήτιcιν Bodl.): βουνιτῆιcι Suid. (e Salust.?)
Duos versus coniunxit Naeke, p. 145

36 (SH 283; ?334, 248 Pf.)

```
                 . . . . . .
              ].νικ. .[ ].[
             ]ε φαῦλον ι.[
             ]ο. οἰϲεδελαι[
     γεργέριμον πίτυρίν τε καὶ⌋ ἦν ἀπεθήκ⌊ατο λευκήν
   5  εἰν ἁλὶ νήχεϲθαι φθινοπ⌋ωρ⌊ίδ⌋α [
                 . . . . . .
```

1–5 *P. Oxy.* 2529 (= pap. 4), pagina 'versa' (pagina 'recta' = fr. 27)
4 Athen. *Epit.* 2. 56c Φιλήμων (περὶ Ἀττικῶν Ὀνομάτων ἢ Γλωϲϲῶν, ibid.
11. 468e) φηϲίν· "πιτυρίδεϲ καλοῦνται αἱ φαῦλαι [φαύλιαι Kaibel coll. Hesych. s.v.
φαυλία] ἐλᾶαι, ϲτεμφυλίδεϲ δὲ αἱ μέλαιναι", Καλλ. δ' ἐν τῆι Ἑκάληι γένη ἐλαῶν
καταλέγει "γεργέριμον πίτυρίν τε"
4–5 (= fr. 248 Pf.) Suid. i. 518. 26 "γεργέριμον"· τὴν ἐν τῶι δένδρωι πεπαν-
θεῖϲαν ἐλαίαν. "πίτυρίν τε καὶ ἦν ἀπεθήκατο λευκήν", τουτέϲτι τὴν ϲυνθλαϲθεῖϲαν
καὶ οὕτωϲ ἀποτεθεῖϲαν ἐλάαν, "εἰν ἁλὶ" δὲ "νήχεϲθαι φθινοπωρίδα" τὴν κολυμ-
βάδα λέγει (Call. verba in Suid. disiecta coniunxit Bentley)

---

2 fort. = fr. 37 (334 Pf.), sed ι.[non dubie legitur (Lobel)   φαῦ
pap.   3 in pap. aliquid supra]ο. suprascr.   post]ο fort. ϲ (Lobel); tum
οἰϲε, fort. δελαι[.   fort. οἰϲε δ' ἐλαι[ῶν Lobel   4 θήκ[pap.   5]ωρ[ί'
pap.

37 (334 Pf.)

εἰκαίην, τῆϲ οὐδὲν ἀπέβραϲε φαῦλον ἀλετρίϲ

Suid. ii. 523. 19 εἰκαία· ὀλίγη [λιτή M. L. West], ὡϲ ἔτυχεν [ἔοικεν cod. V].
Καλλ. "εἰκαίην—ἀλετρίϲ", τουτέϲτιν ἧϲ τὰ ἀποβράϲματα, ἤγουν τὰ πίτυρα, οὐκ
ἀπέκρινεν οὐδὲ ἀπεκάθηρεν ἡ μυλωθρόϲ. ἀντὶ τοῦ ἄϲηϲτον [Portus: ἄϲειϲτον Suid.
codd.] τὸ ἄλευρον   Suid. i. 292. 11 ἀποβράϲματα· τὰ πίτυρα παρὰ Καλλ. "τῆϲ—
ἀλετρίϲ"   Suid. i. 106. 12 ἀλετρίβανοϲ ... καὶ "ἀλετρίϲ", ἡ μυλωθρὸϲ παρὰ
Καλλ.

ἀπέβραϲαϲ 'Zonaras', p. 250 Tittm. s.v. ἀποβράϲματα   ἀλεκτρίϲ codd. IS
Suid. s.v. ἀλετρίβανοϲ
Hoc fragmentum (fort. = fr. 36. 2, v. supra) Hecalae trib. Naeke, p. 142

38 (249 Pf.)

Plin. *NH* 26. 82 'eadem vis *crethmo* ab Hippocrate [*Nat. Mul.* 2] admodum
laudato; est autem inter eas quae eduntur silvestrium herbarum—*hanc certe apud
Call. adponit rustica illa Hecale*—speciesque elatinae [Urlichs: elatae codd.]

hortensiae' Schol. Nic. *Ther.* 909a (p. 311 Crugnola) πολλάκι κρῆθμον . . .
ἀμέργεο] ἤτοι λάχανόν ἐcτι. καὶ γὰρ μέμνηται αὐτοῦ καὶ Καλλ. ἐν τῆι Ἑκάληι
[ἑκάβηι ἢ ἑκάληι cod. A]

Quae forma vocabuli apud Call. fuerit (κρῆθμος, ὁ, ἡ, τό, κρῆθμον, τό)
nescimus; v. Naeke, pp. 136 sq.

39 (250 Pf.)

Plin. *NH* 22. 88 'estur et *soncos—ut quem Theseo apud Call.* adponat Hecale—
uterque, albus et niger; lactucae similes ambo'

Forte ad hanc cenam etiam nomina olerum in frr. 156–7 inc. sed. pertinent

40 (*SH* 285. 1–6; 253. 1–6 Pf.)

>] c Μαραθῶνα κατέρχομαι ὄφρα κ......
>] δε καθηγήτειρα κελεύθου
>]ηκας ἅ μ' εἴρεο καὶ cύ [γε] μαῖα
>]ι τι ποθὴ cέο τυτθὸν ἀκοῦcαι
> 5] χρηΰς ἐρημαίη ἔνι ναίειc
>].ι γενέθλη

1–6 *PSI* 133 (= pap. 5), pagina recta (pagina versa = fr. 42)

1]αc,]εc (ἐc) possis, vix]οc   ὄφρα κ......: primo loco prob. ε; secundo η,
π, τι?; tertio a, ε, θ, ο, c?; quarto ι, ρ?; quinto et sexto fort. η, ν, π, τι, deinde c vel
ω (sed etiam de tribus litteris agi possit): κ' ἀπάρω (Pf.) legi nequit (*SH*)   θῶνα
pap.   2 fort.]η, vix]c   δὲ, -δε   γήτ et λεύθ pap.   3 τὼc ἄρ' ἐμεῦ
μεμάθ]ηκαc suppl. e.g. Vitelli   cύ [γε] suppl. Pf. (cὺ [δὲ] Vitelli)   μ'εἴρεο et
μαῖα pap.   4 λέξον, ἐπεὶ καὶ ἐμο]ί suppl. e.g. Vitelli   ποθὴcέο pap., tum
ἀκούcαι in ἀκοῦcαι (vel vice versa) corr.   5 μάιη et νάι pap.   6 init.
e.g. χώρηι suppl. Pf.   ἐc]τι suppl. Vitelli   ].ι et ἐθ pap.

Inter frr. 40 et 42 stabant in pap. 5 fere 32 versus, quorum pro certo duos
(= fr. 41) aliunde habemus

41 (254 Pf.)

> οὐ γάρ μοι πενίη πατρώιος, οὐδ' ἀπὸ πάππων
> εἰμὶ λιπερνῆτιc· βάλε μοι, βάλε τὸ τρίτον εἴη

1–2 *Et. Gen.* AB (p. 41. 8 A.–A., p. 23. 115 Colonna) s.v. λιπερνήτηc
[λιπερήτηc A] καὶ λιπερνῆτιc θηλυκόν· cημαίνει ἡ λέξιc τὸν ἐνδεᾶ καὶ πτωχόν, οἷον
"οὐ—εἴη", παρὰ τὸ λείπεcθαι ἐρνέων, ὅ ἐcτι φυτῶν   *Et. Sym.* codd. FV (p. 41. 8
A.–A.; *Et. Mag.* p. 566. 50 Gaisf. s.v. λιπερνῆτιc om. Call. versus) . . . οἷον "οὐ—
λιπερνῆτιc"

2 Suid. iii. 275. 1 λιπερνῆτις· ἡ πτωχή. παρὰ τὸ λείπεςθαι ἐρνέων, ὅ ἐςτι
φυτῶν   Schol. Dionys. Thr. (*Gr. Gr.* iii, p. 60. 13 Hilg.) ἀβάλε· τὸ ἃ κατ᾽ ἰδίαν
ἐςτὶν εὐκτικὸν ἐπίρρημα, ὡς τὸ αἴθε, καὶ τὸ βάλε ὁμοίως κατ᾽ ἰδίαν ἐπίρρημα
εὐκτικόν. "βάλε—εἴη" Καλλ.   Suid. i. 451. 5 "βάλε—εἴη"· ἀντὶ τοῦ εἴθε μοι.
Cf. Hesych. βάλε . . . ἢ ὄφελον

___

1 οὐ γάρ *Et. Sym.*: οὐ γί *Et. Gen.* A: οὐ δέ *Et. Gen.* B   πενία et ππάπων *Et.*
Gen. A   2 λιπερνῆτις *Et. Gen.* A, Suid.: λιπερνήτης *Et. Gen.* B: λιπερνίτης
Et. Sym.   μοι om. Suid.
Huic fragmento fr. 158 inc. sed. adiunxit Hollis, ut sint prima verba Hecalae
respondentis τί δάκρυον εὗδον ἐγείρεις;| οὐ γάρ μοι πενίη πατρώιος κτλ.

___

42 (*SH* 285. 7–12; 253. 7 (= 255), 253. 8–12, ?293 Pf.)

δινομένην ὑπὸ βουςὶν ἐμὴν ⌊ἐφύλαccον ἅλωα·
τὸν δ᾽ ἀπ᾽ Ἀφιδνάων ἵπποι φ[έρον
εἴκελον, οἵ τ᾽ εἶεν Διὸς υἱέε[c
μέμνημαι καλὴν μὲν α[
5   ἄλ⌊λ⌋ικα χρυcείηιcιν ἐεργομ⌊ένην ἐνετῆιcιν,
ἔργον ἀ⌊ρα⌋χνάω⌊ν . .]. ´. . .[

1–6 *PSI* 133 (= pap. 5), pagina versa (pagina recta = fr. 40)
1 Choerob.[1] ap. Theodos. (*Gr. Gr.* iv. 1, p. 249. 32 Hilg) ἡ ἅλως τῆς ἅλω, ὅ
cημαίνει τὸ ἁλώνιον, γέγονε κατ᾽ ἐπέκταcιν Ἰωνικὴν τῆς ος cυλλαβῆς ἅλοος, ἐξ οὗ
καὶ ἡ αἰτιατικὴ ἅλωα, ὡς παρὰ Καλλ. ἐν τῆι Ἑκάληι [καλήι cod. V] "δινομένην—
ἅλωα"   Id.[2], p. 333. 17 ἡ ἅλως τῆς ἅλω· τὸ γὰρ ἅλοος πταῖcμα νεωτερικόν ἐcτι
. . . ὡς τὸ "δινομένην—ἅλωα" παρὰ τῶι Καλλ. ἐν τῆι Ἑκάληι [ἑλκάδι V]   Ex
Choerob., *Epimer. Alphab.*, Cramer, *AO* ii. 376. 3 ἅλωα, ὡς παρὰ Καλλ. ἐν τῆι
Ἑκάληι "διν.—ἅλ.", *Et. Gen.* AB s.v. ἅλωα . . . οὕτως ὁ Χοιροβοςκός (p. 352
L.–L., cf. *Et. Mag.*, *Et. Sym.*; ibid. pp. 351, 354; *Etym. Graec. Par.* (Cramer, *Anec.*
Par. iv. 7. 20))   Suid. ii. 33. 19 δεινουμένην· πατουμένην, "δεινουμένην—ἅλωα"
5 *Et. Gen.* AB p. 322 L.–L. s.v. ἄλλιξ (cf. *Et. Sym.*, *Et. Mag.*, ibid. pp. 322–3,
Etym. Graec. Par. s.v. ἄλληξ, Cramer, *Anecd. Par.* iv. 5. 23)· cημαίνει δὲ κατὰ
Θετταλοὺς τὴν χλαμύδα. Καλλ. "ἄλλικα—ἐνέτιcιν" (fr. 149 Schn.)   Suid.
i. 112. 12 ἄλλικα· χλαμύδα κατὰ Θετταλούς· "ἄλλικα—ἐνέτιcιν" (cf. Hesych.
s.v. ἄλλικα· χλαμύδα)   Suid. ii. 280. 4 ἐνέτηιcι· περόναιc. "χρυcείηιcιν—ἐνέτ-
ηιcιν"
6 Suid. i. 338. 20 ἀράχνη· θηλυκῶς τὸ ὕφαcμα . . . Καλλίμαχος "ἔργον ἀραχ-
νά⟨ων⟩" [ἀράχνα Suid., corr. Schneider (fr. 304), coll. Dion. Per. 757]

___

1 = fr. 255 Pf. primus pro certo in pap. 5 legit Bartoletti   δινομένην *Et.*
Gen. AB: δεινομένην pap., Choer.[1] cod. V, *Et. Sym.*: δινωμένην, δεινωμένην,
δεινουμένην, δεινομένης, δινομένη, δινόμενος testes alii   υπο pap., ὑπὸ Suid.:
περὶ Choerob. cum excerptoribus   ἐφύλαccον Suid., Choer., *AO, Et. Gen.*

(-ττ-): ἐφυλάσσατ' *Etym. Graec. Par.*: *Et. Mag.* codd. habent περὶ . . . ἐφύλα (   )
DPS, ἐφύλαττεν R, ἐφύλασεν LM, ἐφύλασσεν Vᵇ   2 δνάων pap. φ[έρον
suppl. Vitelli, tum·e.g. ἢ βασιλεύςιν Pfeiffer   3 ἵκελον, fort. οἷτ', deinde
διὸϲυΐέξ[pap.   e.g. ἢ θεῶι αὐτῶι suppl. Pfeiffer   4 μέμ et λὴν pap.
5 suppl. Vitelli e fr. 149 Schneider   χρυϲείηιϲιν *Et. Gen.* A, *Et. Mag.*, Suid.:
χρυϲείην *Et. Gen.* B: χρυϲείοιϲιν pap. ἐπεργομένην *Et. Gen.*
AB   6 suppl. Barber e fr. 304 Schn.   ἔργ et χνάω pap.   post haec fr. 43
(= 293 Pf.) inseruit H. Fincke, 'neque ϲτ]άδιϸ[vestigiis plane repugnat' (*SH*)

43 (293 Pf.)

ϲτάδιον δ' ὑφέεϲτο χιτῶνα

Schol. Ap. Rh. 3. 1226 Αἰήτης περὶ μὲν ϲτήθεϲϲιν ἕεϲτο | θώρηκα ϲτάδιον] ὅτι
οὐκ ἦν ἁλυϲιδωτός, ἀλλὰ ϲταδιαῖος· ἀπὸ τῆς ϲτάϲεως ἐϲχημάτιϲται. τινὲς δὲ
ϲτάδιον τὸν εὐπαγῆ, ὃν καὶ ὁ Καλλ. λέγει "ϲτάδιον—χιτῶνα"   Suid. iv. 422. 16
ϲτάδιον· . . . καὶ "ϲτάδιος χιτών", ὁ ποδήρης, ὁ τέλειος· παρὰ Καλλ. ἐν Ἑκάληι
(cf. Hesych. s.v. ϲτάδιος χιτών· ϲτατὸς θώραξ et ϲτάδιον· τέλειον ⟨sc. χιτῶνα⟩)

ὑφέεϲτο Laur. (e vulg. ὑφίεϲτο recte coniecerat Naeke, p. 85): ἠμφίεϲτο Par.
In fr. 42. 6 (v. ad loc.) inseruit H. Fincke

44 (376 Pf.)

ὅϲ τε φόβηιϲι
ξανθοτάταις ἐκόμα

1–2 Suid. iv. 747. 6 φόβη· κόμη, θρίξ. "ὅϲ—ἐκόμα."

1–2 ὅϲ τις et ἐκόμει cod. G
Call. trib. Ruhnken; *Hecalae* Hecker, p. 107 (at tauro, de quo cogitavit
Hecker, minime convenit)

45 (274 Pf.)

ἀρμοῖ που κἀκείνωι ἐπέτρεχεν ἁβρὸς ἴουλος
ἄνθει ἑλιχρύϲωι ἐναλίγκιος

1 *Et. Gen.* AB s.v. ἀρμοῖ (cf. *Et. Mag.* p. 144. 47 s.v. ἀρμῶι)· τὸ ἀρτίως ἢ τὸ
ἀρμοδίως. οἷον "ἀρμοῖ—ἴουλος". Καλλ. "ἀρμοῖ—†βουγενεϲέως" [fr. 383. 4
Pf. = *SH* 254. 4; B om. Καλλ.—βουγ.]· εἴρηται δὲ παρὰ τὸ ἀρῶ τὸ ἀρμόζω ἧρμαι
ἀρμοῖ. οὕτως Θέων ὁ τοῦ Ἀρτεμιδώρου (? in comment. ad *Aet.* 3). προϲτίθηϲι δέ,
ὅτι τὸ ἀρμοῖ ψιλούμενον μὲν τὸ ἀρτίως ϲημαίνει, δαϲυνόμενον δὲ τὸ ἀρμοδίως.

Μεθόδιος [Μεθόδιος om. B] Suid. i. 364. 23 ἁρμοῖ που· ἀρτίως, νεωςτί. οὕτω που Καλλ. ἐν Ἑκάληι· "ἁρμοῖ—ἴουλος". Cf. Hesych. ἁρμοῖ· ἀρτίως 2 Suid. ii. 248. 12 ἐλίχρυςος· τὸ τοῦ κιςςοῦ ἄνθος. "ἄνθει—ἐναλίγκιος"

1 ἁρμοῖ, sicut solus Theo praescribit = ἀρτίως, habet P. Oxy. 2173 in Call. fr. 383 (Aet. 3 = SH 254). 4 ἐπέτρεχεν ἁβρὸς Suid.: ἐπέτρεχε λεπτὸς Et. Gen. 2 ἐλιχρύςωι Suid. codd.: -ου Suid. ed. pr. et Call. editores plerique Versum secundum Call. trib. et priori adiunxit Hecker, p. 108

46 (304 Pf.)

ἀμφὶ δέ οἱ κεφαλῆι νέον Αἱμονίηθεν
μεμβλωκὸς πίλημα περίτροχον ἄλκαρ ἔκειτο
εἴδεος ἐνδίοιο

1-2 Schol. (Laur.) S. OC 314 κρατὶ δ᾽ ἡλιοςτερής | κυνῆ πρόςωπα Θεςςαλίς νιν ἀμπέχει] καὶ γὰρ περιςςοὶ ἦςαν οἱ Θεςςαλικοὶ πῖλοι, ὡς καὶ Καλλ. "εἴδεος ἀμφὶ— ἔκειτο" 2 Suid. iii. 359. 8 μέμβλωκε· παραμένει. καὶ "μεμβλωκός"· παραγενόμενον, μετ᾽ ἐπιμελείας καταςκευαςθέν Suid. iv. 131. 11 "πίλημα περίτροχον"· περιφερὲς ςκέπαςμα 3 Hesych. s.v. "εἴδεος ἐνδίοιο" [ἐν δήοιο cod., corr. Musurus]· καύματος μεςημβρινοῦ et s.v. ἴδεος· πνίγους Suid. ii. 609. 8 ἰδίειν· ἱδροῦν, κοπιᾶν. καὶ "ἴδεος"· καύματος, ἱδρῶτος

1 εἴδεος ad v. 3 removit Toup ἀμφὶ δέ οἱ RM, Lasc.: ἀμφιδέοι L 2 πίλημα πέτρου L (πέτρα l), corr. Toup ex Suid. 3 εἴδεος in init. v. 3 (e v. 1) posuit Toup: ἴδεος scr. Naeke, qui ex Hesychio add. ἐνδίοιο, Opusc. i. 63–9
Hecalae fragmentum esse primus vidit Valckenaer ad Theocr. 15 (p. 344)

47 (*SH* 286; 639, 327, 629 Pf.)

```
              ]λ. ων. [
              ].....λοκα[
              ]εν ὃc καὶ μο[
              ]. ιν Ὀρνείδαο κ[
    5         ]. λης ἐπὶ νηὸc ο. [
              ἵππουc_] καιτάεντοc ⌊ἀπ᾽ Εὐρώταο κομίccαι
              ].. κῦμα κ. [
              ]εια.. ν ὀθιδ[
              ].. αἰθυίης γὰρ ⌊ὑπὸ πτερύγεccιν ἔλυc-
    10    πείc⌋ματα τῆc μήτ᾽ αὐτ[
          μ]ήθ᾽ ὅτιc ἄμμι βεβουλ[
          ..]... ιηι κακονο. τ.. [
          .. ]. ν.[....]..[.].. [.].. [.].β[
          ἀν]θρώποιc ὅτε νῆα· τ[
    15    μ⌋έccον ἐπεὶ ναύταιc[
          .. ]. μεν ἐγὼ π[
          ...]κενανπ[
          ...]. χιδαc. [
          .....]ων ὀ. [
    20    ...]. οι βαcιλ[
```

1–20 P. Oxy. 2377 (= pap. 6), pagina ‘recta’ (pagina ‘versa’ = fr. 49; utra praecedat, incertum)

6 Schol. (HMQR) δ 1 κοίλην Λακεδαίμονα κητώεccαν (unde Eustath. 1478. 38)]... κητώεccαν δὲ ἢ μεγάλην ἀπὸ τοῦ κήτουc, ἢ μέγα κῆτοc ἔχουcαν. Ζηνόδοτοc δὲ γράφει καιτάεccαν [καιετάεccαν Eustath.] ἀντὶ τοῦ καλαμινθώδη, δοκεῖ δὲ καὶ Καλλίμαχοc ἐντετυχηκέναι τῆι γραφῆι, δι᾽ ὧν φηcιν "ἵππουc— κομίccαι" (fr. 639 Pf.)

9–10 Suid. ii. 167. 4 αἴθυια ... καὶ ἡ θαλαττία ὄρνιc. "αἰθυίηc—πείcματα †νηόc" (fr. 327 Pf.)

15 Schol. (bT) Ο 628 (iv, p. 131 Erbse) τυτθὸν γὰρ ὑπὲκ θανάτοιο φέρονται] τὸ τυχὸν γὰρ ἀπέχουcι τοῦ θανάτου. πρῶτοc δὲ εἶπε τοῦτο Ἀνάχαρcιc ὁ Cκύθηc [b: εἶπε τὸ Ἀναχάρcιδοc τοῦ Cκύθου Τ], ὅc ἐρόμενόc τινα τῶν ναυτῶν πόcον ἀπέχομεν τοῦ ὕδατοc καὶ μαθὼν ὡc τέccαραc δακτύλουc τοcοῦτόν φηcι καὶ τοῦ θανάτου. καὶ Ἄρατοc (*Phaen.* 299)· "ὀλίγον δὲ διὰ ξύλον" [desinit b], καὶ Καλλ. "†μέcον ἐπὶ ναύταιc†" (fr. 629 Pf.)

---

1 prob.]λ⟦λ⟧εων. [: ad fin. potissimum ρ   2 fort.
]. ε. λοκα[3 ὁc pap., quae et supra c aliquid (fort. ι) addidit μο[aut
fort. μω[; μο[ῦνο- Barigazzi   4]. ιν aut e.g.]ην   5 fort. ον[,

οπ[ὅπ[ως ... κομίσσαι? Lobel 6 ᵏαιτάεντ[[a͡]]c[pap., i.e. χαιτάεντας
in καιτάεντος corr. 7] κα̣ὶ fort. possis fr. 160 inc. auct. (= 370 dub.
Pf.) hic inseruerunt Barigazzi, Krafft, ut fiat κα̣ὶ κῦμα κα̣[ὶ ἄγριον οἶδμα θαλάσσης,
fort. recte, sed de auctore (Call.?, Greg. Naz.?) ambigitur 8]ειᾱ aut]ειὰ
pap.; Μαλ]ειάων dubitanter Lobel ad fin. ὅθι, ὅθ' ἴδ[9 αιθυης pap.:
αἰθύης Suid. codd. AGF: αἰθυίοις M: αἰθυίης cett. γὰρ om. Suid. ἔλυσαν
Suid.: ἔλυσε 'Zonaras' (test. Tittm., p. 79) 10 πείσματα νηός Suid. τη
pap., c suprascripsit manus secunda αὐτ[ός (de se poeta) Lobel, sed potius,
cum de se Hecala videatur loqui, αὐτ[ὴ ἐγὼ Barigazzi, Krafft 11 βέβου-
λ[ε(ν), ut vid. 12 fort. ἐμ]πορίηι κακὸν Lobel; deinde fort. ουτ-
. .[14 punctum in pap. non dubie legitur τ[aut fort.
π[15 μέcον ἐπὶ schol. O 628 (μέccον coniecerat Schneider)]εc̓ονεπει-
ναυταιc̓[pap. 16] . : γ, κ, ξ, c, τ? 18] . : fort. α (Cημ]α̣χίδας tempt.
Hollis) .[: ε, θ, ο, c, φ, ω? 19]ωνὸ̣ . [pap., fort. λ[in marg. inf.
fort. alterius versus vestigium (supra omissi, hic suppleti)

48 (SH 287. 1–10; 337, 366, 247, 284 Pf.)

τὼ μὲν ἐγὼ θαλέεσσιν ἀνέτρε ˩φον οὐδέ τις οὕτως
γε]νέθλην
ῥυδὸ ˩ν ἀφνύονται·
]ετονη. . c·
5 τινθαλέοισι κατικμήναι ˩ντο λοετροῖς
˩ανε παῖδε φερούσηι·
τώ μοι ἀναδραμέτην ἅτε κερ ˩κίδες, αἵτε χαράδρης
π]ουλὺ δὲ μήκει
]ον [ἠ]έξαντο
10] ἐπεμαίετο παισίν·

1–10 P. Oxy. 2376 (= pap. 7), col. i (col. ii = fr. 49. 7–16, initia versuum)
1 Suid. ii. 681. 5 θαλέεσσιν· τρυφαῖς [τροφαῖς V] θάλλειν ποιούσαις. "τὼ—
ἀνέτρεφον" (fr. 337 Pf.); cf. Hesych. s.v. θαλέεσσι· πιότητι, λιπαρίαις
3 Suid. iv. 305. 13 ῥύδην ... λέγεται καὶ ῥυδόν. "ῥυδὸν ἀφνύονται" (fr. 366
Pf.). ἀντὶ τοῦ ῥύδην καὶ ῥευστικῶς πλουτοῦσιν. ἢ κεχυμένως. ἀντὶ τοῦ πάνυ
5 Suid. iv. 560. 1 τινθαλέοισι· χλιαροῖς, θερμοῖς. "τινθαλέοισι—λοετροῖς" (fr.
247 Pf.). χλιαροῖς, θερμοῖς, καθυγρανθείησαν
7 Et. Mag. p. 506. 5 [om. Et. Gen. AB] s.v. κερκίς ... καὶ [pro καὶ novum
lemma in cod. D κερκίς·] εἶδος φυτοῦ· "τώ—κερκίδες" (fr. 284 Pf.). καὶ ἴσως ἐκ
τοῦ φυτοῦ ἐποίουν τὰς κερκίδας ταῖς γυναιξίν Suid. iii. 100. 1 "κερκίδες" (nil
nisi lemma; propter Suid. test. fragmentum *Hecalae* tribuerat Pfeiffer)

1 ἀνέστρεφον Suid. cod. F: ἐνέτρεφον Schneider 3 αφνυονται· pap.:

ἀφνύνονται Suid. cod. A (GVM): ἀφύνοντ F   4 η. . c· pap.   fort. -ετο
νηδύς, νηλής Lobel   6 φερουςηι· pap.   7]κιδες· pap.   9 ad
finem non interpungit pap.   10 παιcιν· pap.

49 (SH 287. 11–30; 350, 294, 368 Pf.)

<pre>
                         ]ερεcτερ. [
         ἠρνεόμην θανάτοιο πάλ⌋αι καλέοντ⌊ος ἀκοῦσαι
         μὴ μετὰ δὴν ἵνα καὶ coὶ ἐ⌋πιρρήξαιμι χ⌊ιτῶνα;
                         ]μαcεφιληc[
   5   ]. δ' ἀπο μέτρα[
                         ]άcκονταλε[
      πειο. [   ]. ελπιδεcη. [
      Κερκ[νον-   πα]λαίcμαcι πε[
      φθει. [   ]αcτεοc, ὅc ῥ' ἔ⌊φυγεν μέν
  10 Ἀρκ⌊αδίην, ἡμῖν δὲ κακὸc ⌋ παρενάccα⌊το γείτων
      μη. [   ]λαι χέρεc α. [
      τεκ[   ]. ιcεμονοικ[
      τουπ[   ]ρε. εμαπαν[
      αυτη[   ] ζώοντοc ἀναι⌋δέcι⌊ν⌋ ἐμπήξαι⌊μι
  15 cκώλου⌊c ὀφθαλμοῖcι καί⌋, εἰ θέμιc, ὠμὰ π⌊αcαίμην
      ειδουο[   ]ε[.]οc ἐcτινο. [
                         ]. ληεcε[
                         ]. ρcαντα[
                         ]. τοδα. . [
  20   ]. τελ. . [
</pre>

1–20 P. Oxy. 2377 (= pap. 6), pagina 'versa' (pagina 'recta' = fr. 47)
2–3 Suid. iii. 381. 26 μή· τὸ ἀπαγορευτικόν· ἀντὶ τοῦ οὐ κεῖται παρὰ Καλλ.
"ἠρνεόμην—δήν"· τουτέcτιν οὐκ ἀπέθανον πρὸ τούτου, ἵνα οὐ μετὰ δὴν καὶ ἐπὶ coὶ
θρηνήcω ἀποθανόντι [Portus, Bentley: ἀποθανόντοc codd.] = fr. 350 Pf.
7–16 (initia versuum) P. Oxy. 2376 (= pap. 7), col. ii (col. i = fr. 48)
9–10 Schol. Vet. Ar., Nub. 508a (p. 114 Holwerda) ἐc Τροφωνίου] οὕτωc ὁ
Χάραξ ἐν τῶι δ (FGH 103 F 5)· Ἀγαμήδηc ἄρχων Cτυμφήλου τῆc Ἀρκαδίαc ...
Τροφώνιοc δὲ ... ἅμα Κερκυόνι (filio Agamedis) φεύγει εἰc Ὀρχομενόν. Αὐγείου
δὲ ... ἐπιδιώκοντοc, καταφεύγουcιν ὁ μὲν Κερκυὼν εἰc Ἀθήναc· ὡc Καλλ., "ὅc—
γείτων" (fr. 294 Pf.)
10 Mich. Chon. ii. 353. 24 Lambros ἀποικία Cκυθική, ἢ τοῖc Ἀcιανοῖc "κακὴ
παρενάccατο γείτων"
14–15 Suid. iv. 387. 20 cκῶλοc· εἶδοc ἀκάνθηc ἢ cκάνδαλον· "τοῦ μὲν ἐγὼ
ζώοντοc—παcαίμην" (fr. 368 Pf.)

1 προγ]ερεcτερο[possis (Lobel)   3 e Suid. paraphrasi ἵνα—χιτῶνα resti-

tuit Lobel   4 fort. ἐφίλης[5].: η, ι, ν?   δ᾽ pap.   6]άϲ
pap.   7 πειο.[: fort. πειοτ[, i.e. πιοτερ-, πιοτατ- (Lobel)   ].: e.g. γ, τ?
aut melius ε, ϲ?   .[fort. λ   8]λαιϲμα[[τ]]ϲι (puncto supra λ) pap.
6   9 φθει.[: ο, ϲ, ω (non ρ)   ]αϲτεοϲόϲρε[(puncto supra τε) pap.
6   10 νάϲϲ pap. 6   11 .[: β, γ, η, ι, κ, ν, π, ρ   12 fort. τεκ[ν-
].: ᾱ potius quam ´]λ, i.e.]αιϲ vel]αιϲ᾽ ἐμὸν οἶκ[ον, vel οἶκ[ον ∪ − −? Si ´]λ
legi possit, de ἐκύ]λιϲε μονοικ[cog. Lobel   13–14 duorum versuum initia
in unum conflasse videtur Suid. (Lobel)   13 τοῦ π[οτε Lobel   ]ρε.:
prob. ϲ (vix ζ, ξ); si ita, -ρε̄ϲ ἐμὰ πάν[τα haud possis (SH)   14 αὐτὴ [ἐγὼ]
Lobel   ἀναιδέϲινοϲ Suid. cod. G   15 ὦμα pap. 6   16 ειδουο per-
obscurum (?corruptum)   17 fort. βαϲ]ιλῆεϲ   18]. γϲαντα potissi-
mum (Lobel—si ita, corruptum?); fort. et].λι possis   fr. 161 inc. sed. (= 591
Pf.) τεθναίην ὅτ᾽ ἐκεῖνον ἀποπνεύϲαντα πυθοίμην hic inseruit Barigazzi, 'optime,
quod ad sensum attinet; sed]ν̣ε̣υϲαντα aegerrime legas' (SH)   19].τ aut
fort.]π   20 fr. 16 ἵν᾽ ἔλλερα ἔργα τέλεϲκεν hic inseruit Barigazzi, 'sed in
pap. cum τελ.ϲ[possis, vix τελε̣ϲ[᾽ (SH)

Quot versus inter frr. 47, 48, et 49 desint, nescimus. Sed, in pap. 6, fr.
47 = pagina 'recta', fr. 49 = pagina 'versa'; in pap. 7, fr. 48 = col. i, fr.
49. 7–16 = col. ii. Neque ordo fragmentorum 47–9 certus est; fr. 47 post fr. 48
vel etiam post fr. 49 locare possis. Ordinem illum cui favent Bartoletti et SH
editores secutus sum

50 (367 Pf.)

τόδ᾽ ἔχω ϲέβαϲ

Suid. iv. 332. 1 ϲέβαϲ· τιμή, ἔκπληξιϲ. παρὰ δὲ Καλλ. τὸ θαῦμα. "τόδ᾽—ϲέβαϲ"
Hecalae trib. Naeke, p. 160. In fine hexametri Pfeiffer suppl. e.g. ⟨εἰϲορόωϲα⟩

51 (300 Pf.)

ἔκ με Κολωνάων τιϲ ὁμέϲτιον ἤγαγε δαίμων
τῶν ἑτέρων

1–2 Schol. (HQ) ξ 199 ἐκ μὲν Κρητάων] ἀπὸ τοῦ Κρῆται. καὶ τὰϲ Ἀθήναϲ γὰρ
ποτὲ ἑνικῶϲ, ποτὲ πληθυντικῶϲ ὀνομάζει. τοῦτο δὲ ζηλώϲαϲ [Mai: ζημιώϲαϲ
codd.] ὁ Καλλ. τὸν Κολωνὸν θηλυκῶϲ [H: ἑνικῶϲ Q] καὶ πληθυντικῶϲ εἶπεν·
"ἔκ—ἑτέρων"
1 Suid. iii. 147. 5 "Κολωνάων" καὶ "νηϲάων" (H. 4. 66, 275, Aet. fr. 67. 8 Pf.)
παραλόγωϲ ἐχρήϲατο Καλλ.· οὐ γὰρ παράγεται ἀπὸ Κολώνηϲ, ἀλλ᾽ ἀπὸ τοῦ
Κολωνοῦ   Suid. iii. 523. 26 ὁμέϲτιον· ὁμόοικον, ὁμωρόφιον γαμετήν utrum huc
pertineat, non liquet (cf. Hesych. ὁμέϲτιον· ϲύνοικον)

1 ἐκ μὲν HQ; corr. Porson et Buttmann   δαίμων coniecit Naeke, p. 127
(cum τῶν ἑτέρων, i.e. κακοποιῶν (Schneider) coniungit Maas): δήμου HQ
(glossam ad Κολωνάων esse suspicatur Maas)

52 (272 Pf.)

ἄνδρες †ἐλαιοὶ Δεκελειόθεν ἀμπρεύοντες

Et. Gen. AB s.v. ἀμπρόν (p. 419 L.–L.)· cχοινίον τι· καὶ ἀμπρεύειν δὲ τὸ ἕλκειν. Καλλ., "ἄνδρες—ἀμπρεύοντες" [Καλλ.—ἀμπρ. om. B], οἷον ἄμπερόν τι ὄν, τὸ δι' ἀμπερὲς ⟨ἐκ add. Reitzenstein⟩ τῶν ζυγῶν δεδεμένον. Μεθόδιος [v. ad fr. 274 Pfeiffer; Μεθ. om. B] Et. Gen. AB s.v. ἀμπρεύω (p. 418 L.–L. = Et. Mag. p. 421 L.–L.)· ὁ μὲν Καλλ. κυρίως ἐπὶ τοῦ ἕλκειν ἔλαβεν τὴν λέξιν· οἷον "ἄνδρες— ἀμπρεύοντες". ἀμπρὸν γὰρ κυρίως καλεῖται τὸ cχοινίον τὸ ἕλκον τοὺς βόας, ἢ τὸ ξύλον ⟨τὸ ἐπικείμενον e Schol. Lyc.⟩ τοῖς αὐχέcι τῶν ὑποζυγίων. ὁ δὲ Λυκόφρων ἐπὶ τοῦ κακοπαθεῖν ἔλαβε τὴν λέξιν, οἷον (Alex. 635)　　Steph. Byz. s.v. Δεκέλεια ... ἀπὸ Δεκέλου τοῦ ἡγησαμένου τοῖς Διοσκούροις εἰς Ἀφίδνας ... τὸ τοπικὸν Δεκελειᾶθεν ..., παρὰ δὲ Καλλ. "Δεκελειόθεν" (cf. Apollon. Dysc. de Adv. (Gr. Gr. i. 1, p. 188. 21 Schn.) περὶ τοῦ "Δεκελειόθεν", sine poetae nomine)　　Suid. i. 147. 9 "ἀμπρεύοντες"· παρακομίζοντες. ἀμπρὸν γὰρ cχοῖνός τις, μεθ' οὗ εἰώθασιν ἕλκειν ἤτοι παρακομίζειν μεγάλα φορτία. ἀμπρεύειν δὲ κυρίως τὸ μετὰ ἀμάξης πορεύεcθαι, καταχρηστικῶς δὲ καὶ ἐπὶ τῶν νωτοφόρων ζώιων λαμβάνεται

ἄνδρες Et. Gen. A s.v. ἀμπρόν (et B s.v. ἀμπρεύω): ἄνδρ' Et. Gen. A s.v. ἀμπρεύω, Et. Mag.　ἐλαιοί vel -οὶ codd.: ἄνδρες δ' ἤλαιοὶ Sylburg: ἄνδρες δ' Εἰλέcιοι Rutherford (Schol. Aristoph. ii, p. 175): ἐλαιόλογοι Diels ap. Kapp, fr. 85: δείλαιοι ('sed potius obiectum expectes') Pf.: ἐλαιηρούς ('secutum est e.g. κεράμουc') Barber　　Δεκελειόθεν Steph. Byz., Apollon. Dysc.: δ' ἐκλειόθεν, δ' ἐκ λειόθεν vel δ' ἐκ λίοθεν Et. Gen., Et. Mag. (emendaverat Bentley)
Hecalae assignavit Schneider (fr. 234)

---

53 (275 Pf.)

πάcχομεν ἄcτηνοι· τὰ μὲν οἴκοθε πάντα δέδαcται

Et. Gen. AB (cf. Et. Mag. p. 159. 11) s.v. ἄcτηνος· ὁ δυcτυχὴς καὶ πένης. Καλλ. "πάcχομεν—δέδαcται". εἴρηται παρὰ τὸ cτάcιν μὴ ἔχειν, μήτε οἴκηcιν. cύνεcτι δὲ τοῦτο πένητι [Καλλ.—εἴρηται deest in Et. Mag. et in Et. Gud. p. 218. 22 de Stef. s.v. ἄcτηνος· πένης παρὰ τὸ μὴ ἔχειν cτάcιν. Cελεύκου; cf. ibid. p. 384. 16 s.v. δύcτηνος . . . παρὰ τὸ cτένω . . . τὸ δ' αὐτὸ καὶ ἄcτηνος, τοῦ ᾱ ἐπίταcιν cημαίνοντος)　　Suid. i. 391. 3 "ἄcτηνοι"· οἱ δυcτυχεῖς, οἱ πένητες, οἱ cτάcιν καὶ οἴκηcιν μὴ ἔχοντες

οἴκοθε Pfeiffer (οἴκοθι Miller): οἴκοθεν Et. Gen. AB　　δέδαcται Schneider (fr. 476): λέλαcται B: λέλαcθαι A
Inter Hecalae fragmenta recepit Kapp (fr. 120) propter Suid. testimonium

54 (329 Pf.)

νυκτὶ δ' ὅληι βασιλῆας ἐλέγχομεν

Suid. ii. 241. 25 ἐλέγχομεν· ἀντὶ τοῦ κακολογοῦμεν. "νυκτὶ—ἐλέγχομεν"
Call. *Hecalae* trib. Hecker, p. 112. Fort. cum fr. 53 cohaeret (Hollis)

55 (290 Pf.)

γηφάγοι

Hesychius s.v. γηφάγοι· πένητες, ἄποροι ὡς τὰς ἐκ γῆς βοτάνας cιτιζόμενοι,
τροφῆς ἀμοιροῦντες [cιτίζεcθαι et ἀμοιροῦντας cod.: corr. Becker]. Καλλ. ἐν
Ἑκάληι [ἐνεκάλει cod.: corr. Musurus]. Cf. *Et. Mag.* p. 221. 50 γηφάγοι—
ἀμοιροῦντες

56 (365 Pf.)

ποιηφάγον

Suid. iv. 259. 6 ποίην· . . . καὶ "ποιηφάγον", τὴν cταχυολόγον (Hemsterhuys et
Toup: cταφυλολόγον codd.)· ἢ τὴν τοὺς ἀcτάχυας ὄπιcθεν τῶν θεριζόντων
cωρεύουcαν
'Fort. expl. in Call. Hec.' (Adler ad Suid. loc.; cf. Wendel, *Gnomon*, 15 (1939),
43)

57 (313 Pf.)

ἁλυκὸν δέ οἱ ἔκπεcε δάκρυ

Suid. i. 128. 24 ἁλυκόν· δριμύ. "ἁλυκὸν—δάκρυ". Cf. Hesych. ἁλυκόν· ἁλμυρόν
Stat. *Theb.* 12. 582 de Hecalae lacrimis contulerunt Naeke, p. 239, et Hecker,
p. 123

58 (310 Pf.)

ἀείπλανα χείλεα γρηόc

Suid. i. 62. 29 ἀείπλανα· πεπλανημένα, φλύαρα, πλήρη φλυαρίας. "ἀείπλανα—
γρηόc"
Call. *Hecalae* primus dedit Ruhnken (*Epist. ad Ernest.* p. 21 Tittm.; cf. Hecker,
p. 112)

59 (296 Pf.)

Schol. (NAB) E. *Hipp.* 979 ὁ Cκείρων ἦν ἐν Μεγάροιϲ τύραννοϲ ἄξενοϲ ὃν τῆι χελώνηι ἔρριψεν ὁ Θηϲεύϲ. Cκειρωνίδεϲ δὲ πέτραι καλοῦνται ἀπὸ Cκείρωνοϲ τοῦ τὴν χελώνην τρέφοντοϲ, οὗ μέμνηται Καλλ. *Et. Gen.* AB s.v. Cκείρων (cf. *Et. Sym.* V et *Et. Mag.* p. 716. 47)· ὄνομα ληιϲτοῦ, πολλῆϲ φθορᾶϲ ὦν αἴτιοϲ, καὶ γὰρ τοὺϲ παρερχομένουϲ ἔρριπτεν ἐπάνω τῆϲ χελώνηϲ· ἡ δὲ δεχομένη ἤϲθιεν αὐτούϲ. γράφεται δὲ διὰ τῆϲ εῑ διφθόγγου ἀπὸ ἱϲτορίαϲ [?: κατὰ ἀναλογίαν *Et. Mag.* p. 716. 48]. καὶ γὰρ Καλλιμάχου γεγραφότοϲ αὐτὸ διὰ τοῦ ῑ, Ἀριϲτοφάνηϲ ὁ γραμματικὸϲ προϲέθηκε τὸ εῑ

Hecalae trib. Naeke, p. 176

60 (245 Pf.)

> φράϲον δέ μοι, εἰϲ ὅ τι τεῦχοϲ
> χεύωμαι ποϲὶ χύτλα καὶ ὁππόθεν

1–2 Suid. iv. 835. 24 χύτλα· ὑδρέλαιον. καὶ χυτλάζειν τὸ μιγνύναι καὶ διαχεῖν. χύτλα λέγεται κυρίωϲ τὸ ὑγροῦ ἔτι ἀπὸ ὕδατοϲ ὄντοϲ τοῦ ϲώματοϲ ἀλείψαϲθαι (= Schol. V Ar. *Vesp.* 1213) "φράϲον—ὁππόθεν"

2 χεύωμαι codd. (nisi quod χεύε F): corr. H. Stephanus   ὁπόθεν AFC
Call. *Hecalae* trib. Schneider (fr. an. 66); de Theseo Scironem alloquente cogitavit Hollis (*CR*, NS 15 (1965), 259–60), coll. Euph. fr. 9. 7 Powell (v. etiam Kapp, p. 25)

61 (306 Pf.)

Steph. Byz. s.v. Ἰαπίϲ· χαράδρα Ἀττικὴ εἰϲ Μέγαρα ἀπάγουϲα, ὡϲ Καλλ. Ἑκάληι [ἑκάλει V: ἑκάλει R: ἑκάλη Ald.]
Post Scironem per Iapidem ad Cercyonem Theseum isse coni. Naeke, p. 182

62 (328 Pf.)

> ἧχι κονίϲτραι
> ἄξεινοι λύθρωι τε καὶ εἴαρι πεπλήθαϲι

1–2 Suid. ii. 188. 16 ἔαρ· ... ἔαρ λέγεται καὶ τὸ αἷμα διὰ τὸ ἐν τῶι ἔαρι πλεονάζειν. "ἧχι—πεπλήθαϲι" πλεοναϲμῶι τοῦ ῑ (inde Suid. s.v. ἄξεινοϲ "ἧχι—πεπλ." in mg. cod. A)
Eust. p. 1851. 45 ἰϲτέον δὲ καὶ ὅτι Ὀππιανὸϲ μὲν (Hal. 2. 618) καὶ τὸ αἷμα ἔαρ ἔφη, διὰ μόνου τοῦ εῑ ψιλοῦ. ἔτεροϲ δέ τιϲ (i.e. Suid.? (Pf.)) διὰ τῆϲ εῑ διφθόγγου

ὁμοίως τῶι αὐτῶι, ἔνθα περὶ ληιστηρίου [Παλαιστηρίου coni. Pf.] γράφει τὸ "ἦχι—πεπλ."

---

2 λύθρων Suid. cod. A s.v. ἄξεινος   εἴτι pro εἴαρι cod. V s.v. ἔαρ   πεπλήθωςι cod. A s.v. ἄξεινος et Eust.
Callimachi fragmentum esse primus coniecit Ruhnken (*Epist. ad Ernest.* p. 21 Tittm.); Naeke (p. 184) *Hecalae* tribuit et 'palaestram' Cercyonis describi vidit

63 (256 Pf.)

λέξομαι ἐν μυχάτωι· κλισίη δέ μοί ἐστιν ἑτοίμη

Suid. iii. 136. 10 κλισία· ἡ ςκηνή· λαμβάνεται δὲ καὶ ἐπὶ κλίνης. "λέξομαι—ἑτοίμη"

λέξομαι om. cod. V   μυχάτωι ed. Basil. 1543: μυχαιτάτωι AGM: μυχοτάτωι F: μυχωτάτωι V: μυχάντωι ed. pr.
Call. *Hecalae* trib. Hecker, pp. 94, 117; dominam casae de suo consueto cubili in angulo loqui credit Pfeiffer

64 (257 Pf.)

ὡς ἔμαθεν κἀκεῖνον ἀνιστάμενον

Suid. iii. 308. 24 μαθών· ἰδών . . . καὶ αὖθις· "ὡς—ἀνιστάμενον"

ἔμαθεν Schneider (fr. an. 44): ἔμαθε codd.   e.g. ⟨κλισίηθεν⟩ suppl. Pf.
Hexametri fragmentum esse et de Call. Hecala intellegi posse cognovit Schneider (fr. an. 44)

65 (292 Pf.)

ἔπρεπέ τοι προέχουσα κάρης εὐρεῖα καλύπτρη,
ποιμενικὸν πίλημα, καὶ ἐν χερὶ χαῖον †ἔχουσα

1–2 Schol. Ap. Rh. 4. 972 ἀργύρεον χαῖον] χαῖόν ἐςτι καμπύλη βακτηρία, ἧι οἱ ποιμένες χρῶνται· Ἀμερίας δὲ ψιλὴν ἀπέδωκε ῥάβδον. Καλλ. "ἔπρεπε—ἔχουσα" (Suid. iv. 793. 6 χαιός [lege χαῖον?, Pf.]· ἡ ῥάβδος, fort. e Salust. comment.)

---

1 κάρης LP: καρῆς Schneider   2 χερὶ LP: corr. rec. (Vind. et ed. Flor.)   †ἔχουσα corruptum crediderunt Barber et Maas (Pfeiffer, ii, p. 120): ἐχούςηι tempt. Maas
Hecalae fragmentum esse vidit Valckenaer ad Theocr. 15 (p. 344)

66 (355 Pf.)

γέντο δ᾽ ἐρείκης
ϲκηπάνιον ⟨   ⟩ ὃ δὴ πέλε γήραος ὀκχή

1–2 Suid. iii. 516. 10 ὀκχή· ϲτήριγμα, βάϲταγμα. "γέντο—ὀκχή" (Hesych. s.v. ϲκηπάνιον· βακτηρία et s.v. ὀκχή· ϲτήριγμα fort. ex *Hecala*)

———

2 ⟨πονόεντοϲ⟩ suppl. Toup: ⟨χείρεϲϲιν⟩ Naeke   πέλεν codd.: corr. ed. pr. Call. *Hecalae* fragmentum primus vindicavit Hemsterhuys in Ernesti Call. p. 439; v. Naeke, pp. 111 sq.

67 (258 Pf.)

θηρὸϲ ἐρωήϲαϲ ὀλοὸν κέραϲ

Et. Mag. p. 380. 49 (breviora *Et. Gen.* A¹, B, sine Call. verbis) s.v. ἐρωή· κυρίωϲ ἡ ὁρμὴ καὶ κατὰ μετάληψιν ἡ ἰϲχύϲ ... παρὰ τὸ ῥῶ ... ἢ ἀπὸ τῆϲ ἐράϲεωϲ· χύϲιϲ γάρ τιϲ καὶ ἀπόκλυϲιϲ [ἀπόκλιϲιϲ cod. D] ἐϲτιν ⟨ἢ ἀπὸ τοῦ ἔρα add. Naeke, p. 255⟩, ὡϲ Καλλ. "ἐρωήϲαϲ θηρὸϲ ὀλοὸν κέραϲ", τὸ ⟨κέραϲ add. Naeke⟩ εἰϲ τὴν ἔραν καταγαγών (cf. p. 369. 29 s.v. ἐρᾶν ... ἀφ᾽ οὗ ἔρα ἡ γῆ· καὶ ἐρωῆϲαι, τὸ ἀπ᾽ αὐτῆϲ ὑποχωρῆϲαι)   Suid. ii. 417. 6 ἐρωήϲαϲ· ἀντὶ τοῦ μειώϲαϲ, κατάξαϲ [Pf.: κατεάξαϲ codd.]. "ἐρωήϲαϲ—κέραϲ" Καλλ.

———

ἐρωήϲαϲ θηρὸϲ *Et. Mag.*: transp. Sylburg   ἀλοὸν Suid. cod. A
Ad taurum Marathonium rettulit P. Buttmann (cf. Naeke, pp. 254 sqq.)

68 (259 Pf.)

ὁ μὲν εἷλκεν, ὁ δ᾽ εἵπετο νωθρὸϲ ὁδίτηϲ

Schol. Ap. Rh. 1. 1162 ὁ τούϲγε ... ἐφέλκετο κάρτεϊ χειρῶν | Ἡρακλέηϲ] πρὸϲ τὴν πάντων αὐτῶν ἀργίαν καὶ τὴν τοῦ κύματοϲ ὑπερβολὴν τὸ "ἐφέλκετο" πρὸϲ πλείονα εἶπεν ἔμφαϲιν· ὅπερ καὶ Καλλ. ἐπὶ τοῦ ταύρου ἡττηθέντοϲ φηϲίν· "ὁ—ὁδίτηϲ"

———

ὁ μὲν εἷλκεν schol. Par.: om. L (perperam C. Wendel (*Hermes*, 72 (1937), 348) priorem partem in Par. coniecturam esse docti Byzantini censuit et pro εἵπετο scr. εἷλκετο)
Ad taurum Marathonium rettulerunt P. Buttmann et Naeke (v. ad fr. 67). Fr. 69. 1 adiunxerunt Barigazzi, Hollis, ut fiat ὁ μὲν εἷλκεν, ὁ δ᾽ εἵπετο νωθρὸϲ ὁδίτηϲ | οἰόκερωϲ κτλ.

69 (*SH* 288. 1–15; 260. 1–15 Pf.)

οἱόκερως· ἕτερον γὰρ ἀπηλοίῃςε κορύνῃ.
ὡς ἴδον, ὧ[ς] ἅμα πάντες ὑπέτρεςαν, οὐδέ τις ἔτλη
ἄνδρα μέγαν καὶ θῆρα πελώριον ἄντα ἰδέσθαι,
μέςφ ὅτε δὴ Θηςεύς φιν ἀπόπροθι μακρὸν ἄυςε·
5 "μίμνετε θαρςήεντες, ἐμῷ δέ τις Αἰγέϊ πατρί
νεύμενος ὅς τ᾽ ὤκιστος ἐς ἄστυρον ἀγγελιώτης
ὧδ᾽ ἐνέποι—πολέων κεν ἀναψύξειε μεριμνέων—
'Θηςεὺς οὐχ ἑκὰς οὗτος, ἀπ᾽ εὐύδρου Μαραθῶνος
ζωὸν ἄγων τὸν ταῦρον'." ὁ μὲν φάτο, τοὶ δ᾽ ἀϊόντες
10 πάντες ἰὴ παιῆον ἀνέκλαγον, αὖθι δὲ μίμνον.
οὐχὶ νότος τόςςην γε χύςιν κατεχεύατο φύλλων,
οὐ βορέης, οὐδ᾽ αὐτὸς ὅτ᾽ ἔπλετο φυλλοχόος μ⟨ε⟩ίς,
ὅςςα τότ᾽ ἀγρῶςται περί τ᾽ ἀμφί τε Θηςέϊ βάλλον,
οἵ μιν ἐκυκλώςα]ν̣τ̣ο περισταδόν, αἱ δὲ γυναῖκες
15 ⌊ςτόρνηισιν ἀνέςτεφον⌋

1–14 *P. Rain.* vi (Tabula Vindobonensis = pap. 8), col. i (col. ii = fr. 70)
4 Suid. iii. 368. 11 "μέςφ ὅτε"· ἕως οὗ, 'ad hunc locum [? vel ad fr. 70. 5], non
ad *hy.* 6. 111' (Pf.). Cf. Hesych. μέςφ ὅτε·μέχρις ὅτε
6 Suid. i. 394. 6 ἄστυρον· πόλιν, "ὅς τ᾽ ὤκιστος—ἀγγελιώτης" Καλλ. (fr. 288
Schn.). Cf. Hesych. ἄστυρον· πόλισμα
14–15 Suid. iv. 438. 4 ςτόρνηιςι· ζώναις. "αἱ δὲ γυναῖκες ςτόρνηιςιν ἀνέςτε-
φον". περὶ Θηςέως (fr. an. 59 Schn.). Cf. Hesych. ςτόρνη· ζώνη

1 fr. 68 adiunxerunt Barigazzi, Hollis   οἱόκερως M. L. West   ἀπηλοί-
ῃςε κορύνῃ (vel κορύνῃ, κορύνῃι) Lloyd-Jones   2 ὑπέτρεςαν Gomperz
οὐδέ τις ἔτλη Rea   3 αντα fort. ex ανδρα correctum   4 μεςφ, αϋςε
tab.; δη supra lineam insertum   5 διϲ tab.: corr. Gomperz   αιγει
tab.   6 ωϲτ᾽οκιϲτος tab.: corr. Gomperz e fr. 288 Schneider   7 ωϲ
tab.: corr. Pf.   8 ουχ᾽, deinde εκταϲ supra lineam insertum tab.: corr. Ellis,
alii   ευϋδ tab.   9 μεν e μετα (potius quam μεγα) correctum; τοιδ᾽
tab.   11 γε supra lineam insertum; χυ e χρυ correctum; χε supra lineam
insertum   12 ουδ᾽αυτοϲοτ᾽, μιϲ tab.   13 τοτ᾽, περιτ᾽, θηϲει
tab.   14 οἵ μιν ἐκυκλώςαν]το περισταδόν Gomperz, 'nec] .το vestigiis
pugnat' (*SH*); ante] .το apices tantum litterarum: περιϲτατον tab.
15 suppl. Gomperz e fr. an. 59 Schn.
Inter frr. 69 et 70 desunt versus fere 22

70   (*SH* 288. 16–29; 260. 16–29 Pf.)

καί ρ᾿ ὅτ᾿ ἐπ.. [.] . ιθυϲϲ......ε.......νεκ.. τοι
οὐρανίδαι..α. οιε.....π..ρ.....επαλλαϲ
τῆϲ μὲν ἐγὼ δην.......δρ............ι.

5   μέϲφ᾿ ὅτε Κεκροπίδ[η]ϲιν επ.....κατολ. αν
λάθριον ἄρρητον, γενεῇ δ᾿ ὅθεν οὔτε νιν ἔγνων
οὔτ᾿ ἐδάην φ.......ωγαγιουϲε...υται
οἰωνούϲ, ὡϲ δῆθεν ὑφ᾿ Ἡφαίϲτῳ τέκε Γαῖα.
τουτάκι δ᾿ ἡ μὲν ἑῆϲ ἔρυμα χθονὸϲ ὄφρα βάλοιτο,

10   τήν ῥα νέον ψήφῳ τε Διὸϲ δυοκαίδεκά τ᾿ ἄλλων
ἀθανάτων ὄφιόϲ τε κατέλλαβε μαρτυρίῃϲιν,
Πελλήνην ἐφίκανεν Ἀχαιΐδα· τόφρα δὲ κοῦραι
αἱ φυλακοὶ κακὸν ἔργον ἐπεφράϲϲαντο τελέϲϲαι
κ. ιϲτη....[.].....ακαδ.....ανειϲαι

1–14 *P. Rain.* vi (Tabula Vindobonensis = pap. 8), col. ii (col. i = fr. 69, col.
iii = fr. 73)
5 sqq. Schol. (AD) *B* 547 Ἐριχθονίου ... γεννηθέντοϲ δὲ ἐκ τοῦ Ἡφαίϲτου.
οὗτοϲ γὰρ ἐδίωκεν Ἀθηνᾶν ἐρῶν αὐτῆϲ ... ἀπεϲπέρμηνεν εἰϲ τὸ ϲκέλοϲ τῆϲ θεᾶϲ. ἡ
δὲ μυϲαχθεῖϲα ἐρίωι ἀπομάξαϲα τὸν γόνον ἔρριψεν εἰϲ γῆν· ὅθεν Ἐριχθόνιοϲ ὁ ἐκ
τῆϲ γῆϲ ἀναδοθεὶϲ παῖϲ ἐκλήθη, ἀπὸ τοῦ ἐρίου καὶ τῆϲ χθονόϲ· ἱϲτορεῖ Καλλ. (fr. 61
Schn.) ἐν Ἑκάληι [om. A]

───────

1 omnia evanida   2 καιρ᾿οτ᾿ tab.   ] . ιθυϲϲ: fort. -αιθυϲϲ- ad fin. ἐφ᾿
ὃν ἄν τιν᾿ ἕκαϲτοι Gomperz, quod vestigiis non omnino congruit   3 ἐπ᾿
ἄλλαϲ, -ε Παλλάϲ (cf. 9)   ἐπάγοιεν ἐμῷ πτ[ε]ρῷ, ἀλλά ἑ Παλλάϲ Gomperz,
pleraque contra vestigia   4 εγω vel ετω potius quam εϲω fort. δηναι
fin. δρ[ό]ϲον Ἡφαίϲτοιο Gomperz, contra vestigia   5 μεϲφ᾿ tab.   fin.
fort. τολμαν (Rea): θήκατο λᾶαν legerat Gomperz   6 γενεηδ᾿ tab.   ουδε
tab.: corr. Wilamowitz   7 ουτ᾿ tab.   φήμη δὲ κατ᾿ (spatio longius?)
ὠγαγίουϲ (lege -γυγίουϲ) Gomperz   ται: vel τη, ταϲ, τιϲ   8 οιωνουϲ·, υφ᾿
tab.   Γαῖα: γ ε ν (τέκεν Αἶα) correctum? 9 ταυτακιδ᾿ tab.   10 δε tab.:
corr. Gomperz   δυωκαιδεκατ᾿ tab.   12 αχαιιδα tab.   14 καιϲτηϲ
possis; de κειϲτηϲ (Gomperz) dubitandum   fin. prob. ἀνεῖϲαι: non excluditur
δεϲμά τ᾿ ἀνεῖϲαι (Gomperz)
Inter frr. 70 et 73 stabant in Tab. Vindob. (= pap. 8) versus fere 22, quorum
quinque (frr. 71 et prob. 72) aliunde habemus

71   (*SH* 289; 261 Pf.)

ἡ μὲν ἀερτάζουϲα μέγα τρύφοϲ Ὑψιζώρου
ἄϲτυρον εἰϲανέβαινεν, ἐγὼ δ᾿ ἤντηϲα Λυκείου
καλὸν ἀεὶ λιπόωντα κατὰ δρόμον Ἀπόλλωνοϲ

1–2 *Et. Gen.* AB (= *Et. Mag.* p. 160. 30) s.v. ἄςτυρον· τὸ ἄςτυ. Καλλ. "ἡ—
εἰςανέβαινεν". εἴρηται παρὰ τὸ ἄςτυ ὑποκοριςτικῶς ἄςτυρον. οὕτως Θέων (cf. ad
fr. 45. 1, et Pfeiffer ad *Aet.* fr. 42) ἐν ὑπομνήματι τοῦ β′ Αἰτίων [τῶν τοῦ β′ αἰτίου
codd.: corr. Sylburg]
2–3 Schol. (L) S. *OT* 919 πρός c′, ὦ Λύκει' Ἄπολλον] Λύκειον γυμνάςιόν ἐςτιν
Ἀθήνηςιν ἔνθα Ἀπόλλων τιμᾶται· καὶ Καλλ. "ἐγὼ—Ἀπόλλωνος"

1 Ὑψιζώρου *Et. Gen.* AB, *Et. Mag.* cod. D: ὑψιζώνου *Et. Mag.*, cett. (unde
ὑψίζωνος coniecit Bentley)
Duo fragmenta coniunxit et cornicis narrationi inserenda vidit Kapp (fr. 61)

72 (374 Pf.)

ἡ δὲ πελιδνωθεῖςα καὶ ὄμμαςι λοξὸν ὑποδράξ
ὀςςομένη

1–2 Suid. iv. 669. 20 ὑποδράξ· "ἡ—ὀςςομένη". τουτέςτιν ὠχριάςαςα καὶ ὑποβ-
λεψαμένη διὰ τὴν ὀργήν. Cf. Hesych. s.v. ὑποδράξ
1 Suid. iv. 82. 2 πελιδνόν· μέλαν. λέγεται καὶ "πελιτνόν" παρὰ Θουκυδίδηι
(2. 49. 5) καὶ "πελιδνωθεῖςα", ὠχριάςαςα
Call. trib. Ruhnken (*Epist. ad Ernest.* p. 20 Tittm.), *Hecalae* Hecker (p. 118). De
Minerva in cornicis narratione cogitavit Pfeiffer (qui pro ὄμμαςι fort. ὄθμαςι
scribendum adnotat)

73 (SH 288. 30–43A; 260. 30–43 Pf.)

5 . . . . ν. c
. . . . ουναι δὲ παραπ . . . . κορῶναι
δ . . . . . . ου γὰρ ἔγωγε τεόν ποτε πότνια θυμόν
. . . . πολλὰ παραίςια μήπο[τ]' ἐλαφροί
. . . . . . οἰωνοί, τότε δ' ὤφελον ε . . . .
10 υτω. [. .].τερην μὲ[ν] ἀπε. . εν . . . . . .
ἡμετερ[. .] ἐκλειν . ε. . . .λλ . ε. οι
μηδ[έ] ποτ' ἐκ θυμοῖο· βαρὺς χόλος αἰὲν Ἀθήνης.
αὐτὰρ ἐγὼ τυτθὸς παρέη[ν] γόνο[c .] δ[.] . . . γάρ
ἤδη μοι γενεὴ π. . .δε. .[. .]ευ. . . . . .
15]. . .ε.

1–15 *P. Rain.* vi. (Tabula Vindobonensis = pap. 8), col. iii (col. ii = fr. 70,
col. iv = fr. 74. 14–28)

1–4 omnia evanida   5 fort. νᾳς, νης (sed Ἀθήνης (Gomperz) confirmari
nequit)   6 fort. [μ]ουναι (Gomperz)   post παραπ fort. τυ, sed παραπτυό-

μεϲθα (Wessely) confirmari nequit (Rea)   7 δαίμοϲιν (Wessely) confirmari
nequit (Rea)   8 [τ]' tab.   9 e.g. .. ϛομεν Gomperz τοτεδ'
tab.   11 ἡμετέρην ἔκλεινε Barber ad fin. fort. ἀλλὰ πέϲοι[τε
12 ποτ' tab.   ἐκ θυμοῖο lect. dub.   interpunxit Barber   13 fin. vesti-
gia minima: [ὸ]γδ[ο]άτ[η] γάρ Gomperz   14 πέλ[εται] Gomperz, contra
vestigia: fort. potius πλο- vel παρ- (Rea)   fin. δεκάτη δὲ τοκεῦϲι Wessely,
contra vestigia
Inter frr. 73 et 74 desunt versus fere 11

74 (SH 288. 43B–69; 346, 260. 44–69, 351 Pf.)

```
    γαϲτέρι μ⌞οῦνον ἔ⌟χοιμι κ⌞ακῆϲ ἀλκτήρια λιμοῦ
    ]δουμεχ[......]έχειδο[
    ἀ]λλ' Ἑκάλ[η .].ε λιτὸν εδ.[
    ....ακ[......]νον παγ.[
5   καὶ κ⌞ρῖμν⌞ον⌟ κυκεῶνοϲ ἀπ⌞οϲτάξαντοϲ ἔραζε
    ..].μηϲ[....].  οὖτιϲ ἐπέϲϲεται[
    ...]θων[....]γ[ι] κακάγγελον· εἴθε γὰρ [εἴηϲ
    κεῖ]γ[ον ἔτι] ζώουϲα κατὰ χρόνον, ὄφρα τ[....]ηϲ
    ὡϲ Θρ⌞ιαὶ τὴν⌟ γρῆϋ⌞ν⌟ ἐπιπνείουϲι κορών⌞ην.
10  ναὶ μὰ τ⌞όν⌟—οὐ γάρ [π]ω πάντ' ἤματα—ναὶ ⌞μ⌟ὰ τὸ ῥικνόν
    ϲῦφαρ ἐμόν, ναὶ το⌞ῦτ⌟ο τὸ δένδ⌞ρ⌟εον αὖον ἐόν περ—
    οὐκ ἤδη ῥυμόν τε κ[α]ὶ ἄξονα καυάξαντεϲ
    ἠέλιοι δυ[ϲ]μέων εἴϲω πόδα πάντεϲ ἔχουϲι,
    δ]⟨ε⟩ίελοϲ ἀλλ' ἢ νὺξ ἢ ἔνδιοϲ ἢ ἔϲετ' ἠώϲ
15  εὖτε κόραξ, ὃϲ νῦν γε καὶ ἂν κύκνοιϲιν ἐρίζοι
    καὶ γάλακι χροιὴν καὶ κύματοϲ ἄκρωι ἀώτωι,
    κυάνεον φὴ πίϲϲαν ἐπὶ πτερὸν οὐλοὸν ἕξει,
    ἀγγελίηϲ ἐπίχειρα τά οἵ ποτε Φοῖβοϲ ὀπάϲϲει
    ὁππότε κεν Φλεγύαο Κορωνίδοϲ ἀμφὶ θυγατρόϲ
20  Ἰϲχυϊ πληξίππωι ϲπομένηϲ μιαρόν τι πύθηται."
    τὴν μὲν ἄρ' ὣϲ φαμένην ὕπνοϲ λάβε, τὴν δ' ἀΐουϲαν.
    καδδραθέτην δ' οὐ πολλὸν ἐπὶ χρόν[ο]ν, αἶψα γὰρ ἦλθεν
    ϲτιβήειϲ ἄγχαυροϲ, ὅτ' οὐκέτι χεῖρεϲ ἔπαγροι
    φιλητέων· ἤδη γὰρ ἑωθινὰ λύχνα φαείνει,
25  ἀείδει καί πού τιϲ ἀνὴρ ὑδατηγὸϲ ἱμαῖον,
    ἔγρει καί τιν' ἔχοντα παρὰ πλόον οἰκίον ἄξων
    τετριγὼϲ ὑπ' ἄμαξαν, ἀνιάζουϲι δὲ πυκνοί
    ....ωοι χαλκῆεϲ ἐναυόμενοι.........
```

1 Suid. iii. 272. 17 λιμόϲ· "γαϲτέρι—λιμοῦ" (fr. 346 Pf.)   Suid. i. 118. 8
"ἀλκτήρια λιμοῦ"· τὰ δυνάμενα ἀλαλκεῖν καὶ ἀπείργειν τὸν λιμόν

1–17 (initia versuum) *P. Oxy.* 2398 (= pap. 9)
1–6 (mediae partes versuum) *P. Oxy.* 2437 (= pap. 10)
3–17 *P. Oxy.* 2217 (= pap. 11)
5 Schol. Lyc. *Alex.* 607 (p. 206. 15 Scheer; cf. *Et. Gen.* AB s.v. κρίμνα, *Et. Mag.* p. 538. 16) κρίμνα] κρῖμνόν ἐcτι μὲν καὶ γένος κριθῆς, νῦν δὲ τὸ ἀπόσταγμα [*Et. Gen.*: ἀπόσπαςμα, ἀπόστομα vel ἀποστάλαγμα schol. Lyc.] τοῦ κυκεῶνος, ὡς καὶ Καλλ. "καὶ—ἔραζε" (fr. 205 Schn.)
9 Herodian. π. Κλίc. Ὀνομ. ed. Hilgard, *Herod. Exc.* (Progr. Heidelbg. 1887), p. 14. 5 (Cramer, *AO* iv. 337. 29 = Herodian. ii. 654. 32 Lentz) τὸ νηῦc ἢ γρηῦc διῃρημένον κατὰ τοὺς Ἴωνας οὐκ ἐκλίθη· τὴν δὲ αἰτιατικὴν καὶ κλητικὴν ἔχει· "θριαὶ—κορώνην" (Call. tribuerat Schneider, fr. an. 325)
10 Suid. iii. 443. 9 ναὶ μὰ τόν ... Καλλ. Ἑκάληι [Lloyd-Jones: καὶ Ἑκάλη codd.] εἶπε· "ναὶ μὰ τόν" (fr. 351 Pf.) καὶ οὐκέτι ἐπάγει τὸν θεόν. ῥυθμίζει δὲ ὁ λόγος πρὸς εὐσέβειαν   Suid. iii. 464. 4 "νὴ τὸν" καὶ "ναὶ μὰ τόν"· κατωμοτικὰ ταῦτα
10–11 Schol. Ap. Rh. 1. 669 ῥικνοῖcι] ῥυcοῖc. ἡ δὲ λέξις παρὰ Καλλ. "ναὶ μὰ τὸ—ἐμόν"   Suid. iii. 443. 5 ναὶ μὰ τόν· "ναὶ μὰ τὸ—ἐμόν", ὅ ἐcτι δέρμα. Καλλ. ἐν Ἑκάληι· "ναὶ τοῦτο—περ" (fr. 49 Schn.). οἱ ἀρχαῖοι οὐ προπετῶς κατὰ τῶν θεῶν ὤμνυον, ἀλλὰ κατὰ τῶν προcτυγχανόντων   Suid. iv. 482. 23 cύφαρ· τὸ δέρμα ... "ναὶ μὰ τὸ—περ" (Καλλ. ἐν Ἑκάληι etc. add. codd. MG)
14–28 (nisi quod et versuum 12–13 vestigia minima) *P. Rain.* vi (Tabula Vindobonensis = pap. 8), col. iv (col. iii = fr. 73)
16 Herodian., π. Κλίc. Ὀνομ. ed. Hilgard (cit. supra ad v. 9), p. 15. 10 τὸ γάλα, γάλακος, γάλακι [-ακτος, -ακτι cod., corr. Gomperz ad hunc versum], παρὰ Καλλ. (fr. 551 Schn.) ὡς ἀπὸ εἰς ξ ληγούςης εὐθείας   Suid. iii. 211. 14 κύματος ἄκρον ἄωτον· ὁ ἀφρός (e Salust. comment., non e textu Call.)
17 Schol. (A) ad Ξ 499 (iii, p. 675 Erbse) ὁ δὲ φῆ κώδειαν ἀναcχών] πρὸς δὲ τὸν Ζηνόδοτον ὑγιῶς ἀποφαίνεται (sc. Aristarchus) ἐκεῖνο, ὅτι ὁ ποιητὴς οὐδέποτε οἶδε τὸ φή ἀντὶ τοῦ ὡς, οἱ δὲ μετ' αὐτὸν ὥσπερ Ἀντίμαχος (fr. 121 Wyss) καὶ οἱ περὶ Καλλίμαχον ('fort. ad h. l. spectat' Pf.); v. etiam fr. 737 inc. auct. Pf.)
23 Suid. iv. 434. 6 στίβη· πηγυλίc, ἢ πάχνη. Ὅμηρος "στίβη ὑπηοίη", τουτέcτιν ὀρθρινή (ρ 25 c. Schol.). καὶ [? fort. Καλλ., Pf.] "στιβήεις", ἡ ὑπὸ τὴν ἔω γινομένη ψυχρότης τοῦ ἀέρος   Suid. i. 40. 17 "ἄγχαυρος"· ὁ παχνώδης ὄρθρος, παρὰ τὸ πλησίον ἔχειν τὴν αὔραν. Ὅμηρος (ε 469) "αὔρη δὲ ψυχρὴ πνέει ἠῶθι πρό" ('e Salust. comment. ad h. l.', Pf.)
24 Suid. iv. 723. 12 "φιλητέων" ληιστῶν. ἤτοι κατὰ ἀντίφρασιν ἢ κατὰ ὑφαίρεσιν τοῦ ῦ †πάνυ φιλητέων† [ὑφειλητέων sscr. cod. M], κλεπτῶν ('ad h. l.', Pf.)   *Et. Mag.* (cod. R; om. *Et. Gen.* AB, *Et. Sym.*, p. 46 A.–A.) p. 572. 22 λύχνα· ὡς παρὰ Καλλ. (fr. 255 Schn.) "λύχνα φανείη" (sic) κατὰ μεταπλασμόν· οὐδὲ γάρ ἐcτιν εὐθεῖα τὸ λύχνον
25 Schol. Ar. *Ran.* 1297 ἱμονιοστρόφου] ... ἱμονιὰ ... καλεῖται τὸ τῶν ἀντλημάτων σχοινίον καὶ τὸ δicμα ὃ ᾄδουσιν οἱ ἀντληταὶ ἱμαῖον (RV). Καλλ. (fr. 42 Schn.)· "ἀείδει—ἱμαῖον" (V)   Suid. iv. 634. 12 "ὑδατηγὸc ἀνήρ"· ὁ ἀντλῶν
25–6 Suid. ii. 633. 17 ἱμαῖον δicμα· τὸ ἐπὶ τῆι ἀντλήcει λεγόμενον· παρὰ τὸ ἱμᾶν ... "καί πού—ἔγρει". Καλλ. Ἑκάληι
26 Schol. Ap. Rh. 3. 1150 περιπλομένας] παριούσας, ἐπεὶ καὶ πλόος λέγεται ἡ ὁδός. Καλλ. (fr. 278 Schn.) "ἔγρει—περίπλοον".

1 καλῆς Suid. cod. F ἀλεκτήρια GVM 2]έχ pap. 10
3].ελει[pap. 11 (primo loco e.g. δ, κ, λ, μ, χ):]ειτονεδ.[pap. 10 (ultimo loco
fort. ο, ω, vix ε) 4]νονπ[pap. 11:]νονπαχ.[pap. 10 (ultimo loco
vestigium minimum cum suprascripta littera rotunda) 5 suppl. Lobel e
fr. 205 Schn.]. κεωνϱ[pap. 11:]ωνοcαπ[pap. 10 ἀποcτάξαντοc schol.
Lyc. cod. ss³ (-ζοντοc s⁶): -cτάξαντα *Et. Gen.* A: -cταξαντ (τ² supra ν) *Et. Gen.*
B 6].μηc pap. 9; primo loco potissimum μ (Lobel), fort. etiam α, λ,:
τό]λμηc [ᾰ χάρι]c tempt. Lloyd-Jones post Pf.].ρυτιcεπέccεται[pap. 11:
]ιϲεπ[pap. 10 7 [ι] poscit spatium in pap. 11 angustissimum]κακαγγε-
λον· pap. 11 [εἴηc suppl. Pf. 8 κεῖνον ἔτι coniecerat Pf.; teste Barrett
κει]ν in pap. 9 et κεῖνον ἔτι] ζώ- in pap. 11 spatiis satisfaciunt ὄφρα pap.
11 fin. τ[όδ' εἴδηc e.g. suppl. Pf., spatio longius (Lobel) nisi ιδ- scriptum
erat (tum τ[ότ' malit Barrett) 10 [π]ω suppl. Lloyd-Jones παντ'
pap. 11 11]ν·, δένδ[, ἀυονεόν pap. 11 12 όντεκ[, ἄξονα pap.
11 13].. λιοιδυ[.]. εω[pap. 9:].εωνειcωποδαπαντεcέχουcι· pap.
11 14 .] ελοc Tab. Vindob.:]ιελοc pap. 9 νυξ· pap. 11 εcετ' tab.,
pap. 11 17 πί]ϲϲα[pap. 11 20 ιcχυῖ, τε tab. 21 αρ'
tab. 22 τηνδ' tab. 23 ἄγχαυροc Pf., coll. Suid.: αγχουροcοτ' tab.
24 φανείη *Et. Mag.* cod. R 25 ὕδατ, ἵμαιον tab. 26 τιν' tab. παρ-
οπλοον tab.: περίπλοον Schol. Ap. Rh.: corr. Gomperz 27 ὗπ
tab. 28 init. fort. . δμ ὦοι (Gomperz) vel ... ζωοι χαλκηϵϲ vel fort.
-αϲ ἐναυόμενοι pro certo legit Rea, tum fort. πυροϲ

75 (267 Pf.)

γίνεό μοι τέκταινα βίου δαμάτειρά τε λιμοῦ

Choerob. ap. Theodos (*Gr. Gr.* iv. 1, p. 275. 36 Hilg.) ἰcτέον γάρ, ὅτι ταῦτα
κοινά εἰcι τῶι γένει, οἷον ὁ γείτων καὶ ἡ γείτων, ὁ τέκτων καὶ ἡ τέκτων· ἀλλ' οἱ
ποιηταὶ καὶ παρωνύμωc ποιοῦcιν αὐτὰ διὰ τοῦ αινα, οἷον γείταινα καὶ τέκταινα·
"γίνεο—λιμοῦ" Sophron. (*Gr. Gr.* iv. 2, p. 396. 20 Hilg.) καὶ γὰρ "γίνεο—
βίου" ὁ Καλλ. λέγει Suid. ii. 4. 12 "δαμάτειρα"· ἡ δαμάcτρια

γίναιο Choerob. cod. NC (om. V): γίνεο Sophron. cod. G: γείνεο H δαμά-
τειρα Choerob. NC: δεμάτειρα V λιμοῦ V: λιμοῖο NC
Hexametrum sine auctoris nomine a Choer. allatum Call. trib. Schneidewin
(ap. Schneider, fr. an. 290); quam coniecturam confirmat Sophronii testi-
monium. *Hecalae* vindicavit Pfeiffer, propter Suid. s.v. δαμάτειρα. Fort. cornix
loquitur?

76 (271 Pf.)

cὺν δ' ἡμῖν ὁ πελαργὸc ἀμορβεύεcκεν ἀλοίτηc

Et. Gen. AB (p. 416 L.–L.; cf. *Et. Sym.*, *Et. Mag.* pp. 416–17) s.v. ἀμορ-
μεύεcκεν· cυνωιδοιπόρει, οἷον· "cὺν—ἀλοίτηc". παρὰ τὸ ἀμορμεύειν. τοῦτο παρὰ
τὸ ἅμα ὁρμᾶν καὶ πορεύεcθαι Suid. i. 127. 25 "ἀλοίτηc" (nil nisi lemma)

ἡμῖν δ' Et. Gen. AB, Et. Mag. D πελαςγὸc Et. Gen. A ἀμορμεύεcκεν
codd. (sic etiam in lemm. et in fine ἀμορμεύειν)
Call. *Hecalae* trib. Blomfield; dubitavit Naeke, p. 230, at nota Suid. testimonium

77 (326 Pf.)

αἴθ' ὄφελεc θανέειν †ἢ πανύcτατον† ὀρχήcαcθαι

Suid. ii. 166. 8 "αἴθ'—ὀρχήcαcθαι"· ἐπειδὴ τὴν γλαῦκα [παρὰ [lege περὶ, Pf.]
τῆc γλαυκὸc τοῦτο· ἦν 'Zonar.' p. 97 Tittm.] ὅταν λάβωcι τὰ παιδία περιάγουcιν·
ἡ δὲ μὴ βλέπουcα δι' ἡμέραc ὥcπερ ὀρχεῖται [desinit 'Zonar.']. ἢ ὅταν πληγῆι
τελευτῶcα cτρέφεται ὥcπερ ὀρχουμένη. Καλλ. ἐν Ἑκάληι λέγει περὶ αὐτῆc

ὄφελοc Suid. cod. F   θανέειν 'Zonar.' codd. Tittm.: θανεῖν Suid. et 'Zonar.'
Par. 2669 (Cramer, *Anec. Par.* iv. 103. 26; correxerat Bentley)   πανύcτατον
Suid. codd., nisi quod πανύχιον cod. recens C (? e coni. Byzant., Pf.), unde ἢ
πάννυχον Naeke: ἢ ὕcτατον Bentley: θνήιcκουcα πανύcτατον Lloyd-Jones

78 (371 Pf.)

Αἴθρην τὴν εὔτεκνον ἐπ' ἀγρομένηιc ὑδέοιμι

Suid. iv. 634. 17 ὕδδειν ἔοικε. καὶ ὑδέοιμι, ἀντὶ τοῦ ὑμνοῖμι. "Αἴθρην—ὑδέοιμι"
Cf. Hesych. ὑδεῖν· ὑμνεῖν

ἐπ' αγρ. Suid. codd. (ἐπαγρομένηιc excludi nequit, Pf.): ἐν ἀγρ. Bernhardy,
Hecker, Wilamowitz
Call. *Hecalae* tribuerunt Toup (*Emend. in Suid.* ii, p. 291) et Ruhnken (*Epist. ad
Ernest.* p. 21 Tittm.); cf. Naeke, pp. 249 sq.

79 (262 Pf.)

τίνοc ἠρίον ἴcτατε τοῦτο;

Et. Gen. AB (cf. Et. Mag. p. 437. 11) s.v. ἠρία· διάφοροc τόνοc διάφορον ποιεῖ
cημαινόμενον. ἐὰν μὲν προπαροξυτόνωc, cημαίνει τὰ ἔρια κατὰ ἔκταcιν, ἐὰν δὲ
παροξυτόνωc ἠρία, cημαίνει τοὺc τάφουc παρὰ τὴν ἔραν τὴν γῆν ... ἢ παρὰ τὸν
ἀέρα, ἤγουν τὸν cκότον τὸν ἐπικείμενον τοῖc τεθνεῶcι. Θεόκριτοc ⟨... lacunam
indicavit Wilamowitz, qua Theocr. 2. 13 excidisset⟩ ... καὶ Καλλ. "τίνοc—τοῦ-
το" [Herodian.] π. Ἡμαρτημ. Λέξ. ap. G. Hermann, *de Emendenda Ratione
Graecae Grammaticae* p. 309, et ap. Cramer, *AO* iii. 253. 7 ἁμαρτάνουcιν οἱ
λέγοντεc ἐπὶ τῶν τάφων ἠρῶιον, δέον λέγειν ἠρίον, ὡc ὁ Καλλ. †παρὰ τίνοc ἠρίον
†τὰ γὰρ τούτων† [verba post ἠρίον, corrupta pro ἴcτατε τοῦτο, desunt in Cram.
codd.]

ἵςταται *Et. Gen.* AB, *Et. Mag.*: corr. Bentley   παρὰ ante τίνος [Herodian.]:
ὡς παρὰ Καλλ. Blomfield: alii παρὰ cum Callimachi verbis coniunxerunt et
corrigere temptaverunt: παραὶ τ. ἡ. ἔςτατε τ. Schneider (fr. 251), Kapp (fr. 69),
contra Call. artem metricam: πατέρες vel ἔταροι Naeke, p. 270: παῦρον Hecker,
p. 124: κατὰ γὰρ G. Dindorf ap. Naeke: παριών (sc. Theseus inquit) M. L. West
Hecalae dedit Naeke, p. 268

80 (263 Pf.)

ἴθι, πρηεῖα γυναικῶν,
τὴν ὁδόν, ἣν ἀνίαι θυμαλγέες οὐ περόωςι.
⟨   ⟩ πολλάκι ςεῖο,
μαῖα, ⟨   ⟩ φιλοξείνοιο καλιῆς
5   μνηςόμεθα· ξυνὸν γὰρ ἐπαύλιον ἔςκεν ἅπαςιν

1–5 Suid. ii. 333. 8 ἐπαύλια· ... ἐπαύλιον δὲ μονή. περὶ Ἑκάλης θανούςης·
"ἴθι—ἅπαςιν" [Καλλιμάχου in marg. add. codd. IM]
1–2 *Et. Mag.* p. 442. 30 (in *Et. Gen.* AB desunt Call. verba) θάνατος· ...
ἐτυμολογεῖται δὲ παρὰ τὸ ἄνευ ἄτης τὸν τεθνεῶτα εἶναι· θάνατος γὰρ ἀνδρὶ
ἀνάπαυςις. παρὰ τὴν ἄτην, τὴν βλάβην, ἄνατος καὶ θάνατος· ὁ ἄνευ βλάβης μένων
ἀποθανών. "ἴθι—περόωςι" Καλλ.   Orio, *Etym.* p. 72. 1 Sturz s.v. θάνατος ... ἢ
περιςςὸν τὸ θ ἄνατος· ἄνευ γὰρ ἄτης κτλ. "ἴςθι—περόωςιν" Melet. *de Nat.*
Hom. ap. Cramer, *AO* iii. 138. 1 adn. τὴν δὲ (sc. vitam futuram) ἀπαθῆ καὶ
ἀνώδυνον καὶ πολυχαρῆ, ὡς καὶ Καλλ. "ἴθι—περόωςιν" [verba Call. desunt in
codd. Oxon.]

---

1 ἴςθι πριεῖα Orio. *Etym.*   2 θυμαλγέες Suid.: θυμοφθόροι cett. (nisi
quod -φθόνοι Orio) περόωςι *Et. Mag.*: περόωςιν Orio, Melet. cod. Petr.:
ὑπερορώωςιν (om. οὐ) Melet. cod. Mon.: περέοςι Suid. cod. A: περῶςι Suid.
GIVM   3–4 sic in duos versus verba Suidae distribuit Maas (ap. Pf. i,
p. 507): in unum redigerunt alii, velut ςεῖό ⟨γε⟩ Pfeiffer (quem tamen posterius
paenituit, ii, p. 120), ςεῖο ⟨δὲ⟩ Mair, καὶ ςέο Toup, ςεῦ καὶ Schneider (fr. 131),
ςῆς ὦ Wilamowitz (ap. Kapp, fr. 70)   φιλοξένοιο Suid.: corr. Küster

81 (342 Pf.)

τοῦτο γὰρ αὐτήν
κωμῆται κάλεον περιηγέες

1–2 Suid. iii. 174. 7 κωμῆται· καὶ οἱ γείτονες· κώμη γὰρ ἡ γειτονία. Καλλ.
Ἑκάληι (ΑΜ: ἐκάλει GFV) "τοῦτο—περιηγέες"

---

1 αὐτήν Hemsterhuys, Ruhnken: αὐτῆς Suid. cod. A: αὐτῆι GVM: αὐτοί
F   2 περιηγέες Toup: περιαγέες codd.

82 (cf. *SH* 284, 252 Pf.)

(a) Suid. i. 424. 30 αὐχμηρὰ τράπεζα· ἡ ξηρὰ καὶ πενιχρά.
(b) Mich. Chon. i. 157. 11 sq. Lambros (= Test. 15a) καὶ οὕτω τι φιλοφ-
ρονηθῆναι ἥδιον (Theseum ab Hecala), ὡς ἀεὶ μεμνῆσθαι τῆς ὀλίγης
τραπέζης ἐκείνης καὶ αὐχμηρᾶς, καὶ μὴ ἂν ἄλλην οὕτω ποτὲ τερπνο-
τέραν λογίσασθαι
(c) Cf. Nonn. *Dion.* 17. 60 sqq. (Bacchus apud Brongum) ὀλίγης ἔψαυσε
τραπέζης | δαρδάπτων ἀκόρητος, ἀεὶ δ' ἐμνώετο κείνης | εἰλαπίνην ἐλάχειαν
ἀναιμάκτοιο τραπέζης

Suid. s.v. αὐχμηρὰ τράπεζα ad Hecalae mensam rettulit Hecker, p. 112 (e
Salusti commentario scilicet, non e textu Call.). Fort. respicitur oratio Thesei, in
qua Hecalae mensa et ὀλίγη et αὐχμηρή appellatur; cuius mensae heros se
nunquam obliturum, neque aliam iucundiorem habiturum esse promittit

83 (264 Pf.)

Mich. Chon. *Theano* 337 sqq. (ii, p. 386 Lambros = Test. 14) εἰ δὲ γρηὶ
πενιχρῇ, τὴν Ἑκάλην καλέεσκον, | Θησεὺς ὦφλε χάριν ξενίης ὀλίγης τε μιῆς
τε | καί ἑ θανοῦσαν ἐνὶ μνήμῃ θέτο οὐ θνῃσκούσῃ |—οὐ γὰρ ἔην νήκουστα
ἐτήσια δεῖπν' Ἑκάλεια κτλ.

Annuae dapes in memoriam Hecalae a Theseo institutae expressis verbis alibi
non commemorantur; Mich. Chon. igitur haec ex Call. ipso sumpsisse Reitzen-
stein coniecit (quae vocabula mutuatus sit, incertum). Hoc fragmentum fort.
cum fr. 82 arte cohaeret; possis etiam v. 337 τὴν Ἑκάλην καλέεσκον cum fr. 81
comparare

84 (266 Pf.)

πολυπτῶκές τε Μελαιναί

Choerob. ap. Theodos. (*Gr. Gr.* iv. 1, p. 187. 2 Hilg.) πᾶν γὰρ ὄνομα
μονοσύλλαβον ἐν τῆι συνθέσει ἀναβιβάζει τὸν τόνον, οἷον χθών αὐτόχθων ... χωρὶς
τοῦ πτώξ πολυπτώξ, "πολυπτῶκές τε Μελαιναί". τὸ δὲ Μελαιναὶ τόπος ... τῆς
Ἀττικῆς, πολυπτῶκες δὲ οἰονεὶ αἱ ἔχουσαι πολλοὺς λαγωούς· τοῦτο γὰρ τὴν ὀξεῖαν
τάσιν ἐφύλαξε τοῦ ἁπλοῦ   Et. Gud. p. 300. 1 Sturz s.v. Καρίς ... πᾶν γὰρ ὄνομα
μονοσύλλαβον ἐν τῆι συνθέσει βαρύνεται κτλ. (= Choerob.) ... πολυπτώξ, ὡς
παρὰ Καλλ. "πολ.—Μελ.". Μελαιναὶ δέ εἰσι τόπος τῶν Ἀττικῶν   Steph. Byz.
s.v. Μελαινεῖς, δῆμος τῆς Ἀντιοχίδος φυλῆς. Καλλ. δὲ Μελαινάς φησι τὸν δῆμον ἐν
Ἑκάληι [sic cod. P: ἐκεκάληι V: καὶ κεκάλη R: κεκλῆσθαι Π Ald.]

85 (*SH*–; + 305 Pf.)

οὐδὲ Διωνύ[cωι Μελαναίγ]ιδι, τόν [πο]τ᾽ Ἐλευθήρ
εἵ[cατο, ⌞Λιμναίωι δὲ χ⌟οροcτάδαc ἦγον ἑ⌞ορτάc

1–2 Schol. Thuc. 2. 15. 4 (= *P. Oxy.* 853, col. x. 7 sqq.)

                    τὸ ἐν Λ⌞ίμνα⌟ιc Διονύcο⌞υ·
                    μέν φηc[ιν] ευδε Διονυ[c
          ]. δι τον [. .] τ᾽ Ἐλευθηρ ει[
    10   δὲ χ⌟οροcτάδαc ἦγον ἑ⌞ορτάc
                    …]οc δὲ οὗτ[ωc] φηcιν[
                    δι]ὰ τὸ ἐκλελ[ι]μνάcθαι[
                    ἔc]τι δὲ καὶ ἐν τῆι Λακωνί[αι
                    ὅπ]ου Λιμνᾶτ[ί]c ἐcτιν Ἄρτ[εμιc.

De supplementis ad hoc scholium, v. comment.   7 τὸ ἐν Λίμναιc Διονύcου lemma esse videtur, quamquam, errore librarii, interstitium post Λίμναιc positum   9].: minimum atramenti vestigium   ]. δι possis, teste W. E. H. Cockle (]η legerant Grenfell et Hunt)

2 Schol. (RV) Ar. *Ran.* 216 ἐν Λίμναιcιν]… Λίμναι δὲ χωρίον τῆc Ἀττικῆc, ἐν ὧι Διονύcου ἱερόν. Καλλ. (fr. 66a Schn.) ἐν Ἑκάληι [-βηι V] "Λιμναίωι—ἑορτάc" Steph. Byz. s.v. Λίμναι… [add. cod. Vat. ap. Holsten] καὶ ἕτεροc τόποc τῆc Ἀττικῆc Λίμναι καλούμενοc, ἔνθα ὁ Διόνυcοc ἐτιμᾶτο. καὶ οἱ λιμναῖοι [Καλλίμαχοc Hemsterhuys, Λιμναίωι δὲ Meineke e schol. Aristoph.] "χορ.— ἑορτάc"

_____

1 οὐδὲ Barrett: ευδε Schol. Thuc.   Διωνύ[cωι Μελαναίγ]ιδι Barrett (Διώνυ[cον Μελαναίγιδ]⟨α⟩ iam Kapp, fr. 94): Διονυ[   ]. δι Schol. Thuc. (v. supra)   1–2 τόν [πο]τ᾽ Ἐλευθήρ | εἵ[cατο Wilamowitz

86 (321 Pf.)

                    γαμβρὸc Ἐρεχθῆοc

Suid. i. 507. 19 "γαμβρὸc Ἐρεχθῆοc"· ὁ Βορρᾶc. τὴν γὰρ Ὠρείθυιαν θυγατέρα αὐτοῦ ἔγημεν, ἐξ ἧc τίκτεται Ζήτηc καὶ Κάλαϊc
Call. *Hecalae* trib. Hecker, p. 111. In fr. 18. 18 restitui nequit

87 (338 Pf.)

                    Θείαc ἀμνάμων

Suid. ii. 713. 29 "Θείαc ἀμνάμων" [-άμμων codd., corr. ed. pr.]· ὁ Βορέαc ὁ ἄνεμοc. ἀμνάμων [-μμ– ut supra codd.] δὲ ⟨ὁ add. ed. pr.⟩ ἀπόγονοc. ὡc γὰρ Ἡcίοδοc λέγει (*Th.* 371 sqq., 378 sqq.), τῆc Θείαc ἀπόγονοι οἱ ἄνεμοι
Call. *Hecalae* fragmentum esse coniecit Pfeiffer. In *Coma Berenices* (fr. 110. 44 Pf.) Call. videtur ordine inverso sua ipse verba repetisse

88 (308 Pf.)

Steph. Byz. s.v. Τρινεμεῖς [Ald.: -εῖν R: -εῖ V] δῆμος τῆς Κεκροπίδος φυλῆς. Διόδωρος (*FGH* 372 F 24) καὶ Δίδυμος (p. 352 Schm.) Τρινεμεῖς ἀναγράφουσι τὸν δῆμον [Τρινεμεῖς prius—δῆμον confusum in RV cum ultima linea glossae praecedentis: textum rest. Xylander], Καλλ. Ἑκάληι [ἐκάλει RV: ἐκάλει ΠΡρ] Τρινέμειαν [Ald.: τρινέμει RV, V post -ει lacunam quattuor vel quinque litterarum indicans]

89 (349 Pf.)

Suid. iii. 322. 7 Μαραθών· τόπος Ἀθήνησιν· ἀπὸ Μαράθου, υἱοῦ Ἀπόλλωνος. τοῦτον Καλλ. ἐννότιον λέγει, τουτέστιν ἔνυδρον. καὶ "Μαραθώνιον ἔργον"

Propter rem narratum *Hecalae* iam vindicavit Brodaeus, *Epigr. Graec.* vii. 1549, p. 134 (v. Naeke, p. 60). Schneider (p. 608) cum fr. 16 coniungendum suspicatus est. Etiam verba "Μαραθώνιον ἔργον" ex *Hecala* deprompta et de tauro superato dicta esse coniecit Hecker, p. 107; quem secuti sunt Schneider (fr. an. 45a et p. 190), Kapp (fr. 91), at contradixit Pfeiffer

90 (288 Pf.)

Cκύλλα γυνὴ κατακᾶcα καὶ οὐ ψύθοc οὔνομ' ἔχουcα
πορφυρέην ἤμηcε κρέκα

1 *Et. Gud.* p. 574. 17 Sturz (cf. *Et. Mag.* p. 818. 56; deficit *Et. Gen.* A, in *Et. Gen.* B desunt Call. verba) s.v. ψιθυρίζειν τινὲς ὀνοματοποιεῖσθαί φασιν ὡς τὸ "κρίκε δὲ [κέκρικε τὸν *Et. Gen.* B] ζυγόν" (Π 470) καὶ τὸ "cίζει ὀφθαλμός [-ους *Et. Gen.* B, tum desinit]" (ι 394). ὅθεν κυρίως ἐπὶ τῶν ψευδομένων τὸ ψιθυρίζειν λαμβάνουσιν ἐγκειμένου τοῦ ψύθους. Καλλ. "Cκύλλα—ἔχουcα" *Et. Gud.* p. 304. 1 Sturz (et cod. Par. 2638 ap. Gaisf. *Et. Mag.* p. 494. 38) s.v. κατακᾶcα· ἡ κατωφερὴς καὶ πόρνη. Καλλ. "Cκύλλα—ἔχουcα" Suid. iii. 46. 17 "κατακᾶcα"· κατωφερής, ἡ ἀξία τοῦ κατακαυθῆναι (cf. *Et. Gen.* B = *Et. Mag.* p. 494. 38 s.v. κατακᾶcα et Hesych. s.v. κατακάcα) Suid. iv. 851. 1 ψύθος· ψευδές, ψεῦδος, "καὶ—ἔχουcα". ἀντὶ τοῦ ψευδές, παρὰ Καλλ. (cf. *Et. Gen.* B = *Et. Mag.* p. 819. 13 et Hesych. s.v. ψύθος)
2 Suid. iii. 184. 19 κρέκα· τὴν τρίχα. "πορφυρέην—κρέκα". ἀντὶ τοῦ ἔκοψε. Cf. Hesych. κρέξ· κορυφαία . . . τάσσεται δὲ καὶ ἐπί τριχός

---

1 ψυθές coni. Hemsterhuys   2 ἤμηcεν ⟨ἄπο⟩ coni. Naeke, pp. 61 sq., fort. recte
Duo fragmenta in unum coniunxit et *Hecalae* trib. Naeke, pp. 61 sq.

91 (297 Pf.)

Schol. Arethae ad Euseb. *Praep. Evang.* 4. 16. 2, p. 155b in marg. cod. Paris. 451 (ed. Dind. i, p. v; Gifford, iv, p. 147; v. S. Kougeas, *Arethas* (1913), p. 54. 3) ἐν δὲ τῆι νῦν Cαλαμῖνι, πρότερον δὲ Κορωνείαι ὀνομαζομένηι] οὐ τὴν πρὸc ταῖc Ἀθήναιc Cαλαμῖνα λέγει. αὕτη γὰρ Κούλουριc πάλαι ἐλέγετο, ὡc καὶ Καλλ. ὁ Κυρηναῖοc ἐν τῆι Ἑκάληι φηcίν, ἀλλὰ τὴν κατὰ Κύπρον Cαλαμῖνα λέγει

Forma Callimachea fort. Κόλουριc erat

92 (341 Pf.)

Κωλιάδοc κεραμῆεc

Suid. iii. 172. 1 "Κωλιάδοc κεραμῆεc". Κωλιάc, τόποc τῆc Ἀττικῆc, ἔνθα cκεύη πλάττονται. λέγει οὖν ὅτι ὅcοι (sc. κέραμοι vel πηλοί, 'terrae figulares'?) ἐπὶ τροχοὺc φέρονται (τροχὸν δὲ τὸν cκευοπλαcτικὸν λέγει), τουτέcτιν ὅcαι (sc. γαῖαι?) πρὸc cκευοπλαcίαν ἐπιτήδειαι παcῶν ἡ Κωλιάδοc κρείccων, ὥcτε καὶ βάπτεcθαι ὑπὸ τῆc μίλτου (sequitur excerptum e schol. Ar. *Lys.* 2) Suid. iii. 172. 7 Κωλιάc· ναόc ἐcτι τῆc Ἀφροδίτηc, οὕτω καλούμενοc, ἀπὸ τοῦ cυμβεβηκότοc τὴν προcηγορίαν λαβὼν κτλ. (= schol. V Ar. *Nub.* 52; duo aetia nominis referuntur) ... ὅθεν ὁ τόποc Κωλιάc ἐκλήθη. μέμνηται καὶ Καλλ. ἐν Ἑκάληι

'Sub explicatione λέγει οὖν κτλ. quam Suidas e Salusti commentario excerpsit, fort. pauca ipsius Callimachi vocabula latent, e.g. ἐπὶ τροχὸν οἵ τε φέρονται' (Pf.)

93 (268 Pf.)

ἔcτιν ὕδοc καὶ γαῖα καὶ ὀπτήτειρα κάμινοc

Choerob. ap. Theodos. (*Gr. Gr.* iv. 1, p. 352. 11 Hilg.) ὥcπερ γὰρ ἀπὸ τοῦ γῆραc γίνεται τὸ γῆροc ... οὕτω καὶ ἀπὸ τῆc ὕδαc εὐθείαc, ἐξ ἧc ἡ γενικὴ ὕδατοc, γίνεται ὕδοc, ὡc παρὰ Καλλ. "ἔcτιν—κάμινοc" Suid. iv. 634. 23 "ὕδοc"· τὸ ὕδωρ (cf. Hesych. s.v. ὕδοc· ὕδωρ). ἡ δοτικὴ "ὕδει" [sic A, om. F]

ὀπτήτειρα V: ὀπτῆρα C ap. Bekk. (emendaverat iam Naeke)
Hecalae trib. Hecker, p. 105)

94 (344 Pf.)

λάτριν ἄγειν παλίνορcον ἀεικέα τῶι κεραμῆι

Suid. iii. 237. 23 λάτρον· ὁ μιcθόc (v. fr. 107). λατρεία γὰρ δουλεία ἐπὶ μιcθῶι. λάτριc δὲ διὰ τοῦ ῑ "λάτριν—κεραμῆι"

Call. *Hecalae* trib. Hecker, p. 105

95 (307 Pf.)

Steph. Byz. s.v. *Λύρκειον· ὄρος Ἄργους. Καλλ. Ἑκάληι* [ἐκάλει RV]. *τὸ τοπικὸν* "*Λυρκήιον ὕδωρ*" [Λυρκειον sscr. η R: *Λύρκειον* V Ald.] *καὶ Λυρκήιος* [R: -ον V Ald.] *τὸ ἀρcενικόν, καὶ* [add. R] *Λύρκειος, ὡς Ῥοίτειος.* Cf. Hesych. *Λύρκειον· ὄρος τῆς Ἀργείας*

Fort. etiam *Λυρκήιον ὕδωρ* Callimachi verba sunt, qui non montis solum, sed etiam fluvii in *Hecala* mentionem fecisse potest (Pf.)

96 (*SH* 290; 279 Pf.)

$$\begin{aligned}
&\quad\quad\quad .\ .\ .\ .\ .\ .\\
&\quad\quad\quad\quad\quad\quad\quad\quad].\pi\underset{.}{\tau}[\\
&\quad\quad\quad\quad].\,.\ [\ \ ].\nu\mu\epsilon[\\
&\text{αὐτίκα Κενθίππην τε}\rfloor\ \text{πολύκριμν}\llcorner\text{όν τε Πρόcυμναν}\\
&\quad\quad\quad\quad\quad\quad\quad]c\tau\underset{.}{o}[\\
&\text{5}\quad\quad\quad\quad\quad\quad]oc\tau.\,[\\
&\quad\quad\quad .\ .\ .\ .\ .\ .
\end{aligned}$$

1–5 *P. Oxy.* 2258 (= pap. 2), novum fragmentum (*P. Oxy.* xxx. 91), pagina 'recta' (pagina 'versa' = fr. 97; nescimus utra praecedat) 3 *Et. Gen.* AB s.v. *Κενθίππη* (cf. *Et. Mag.* p. 503. 33, et *Et. Sym.* V ap. Gaisf.)· *τόπος Ἄργους. Καλλ.* "*αὐτίκα—Πρόcυμναν*" (fr. 279 Pf.). *εἴρηται δὲ* ⟨*ἀπὸ τοῦ* add. Pf. e cod. V⟩ *πρῶτον ἐκεῖ κεντῆcαι τὸν Πήγαcον ἵππον Βελλεροφόντην* Suid. iii. 94. 14 *Κενθίππη* (nil nisi lemma) *Et. Gen.* AB s.v. *πολύκρημνος* [ι supra η scr. in AB]· "*πολύκρημνόν τε Πρόcυμνον*". *ἐπίθετον τόπου Ἄργους ὃς καλεῖται Πρόcυμνα· γράφεται δὲ καὶ διὰ τοῦ ῆ καὶ διὰ τοῦ ῑ, καὶ ὅτε μὲν διὰ τοῦ ῆ, πολύκρημνος ἡ πολλοὺς κρημνοὺς ἔχουcα, ὅτε δὲ διὰ τοῦ ῑ, ἡ πολλὰς κριθὰς ἔχουcα, διὰ τὸ εὔκαρπον τοῦ τόπου* (cf. *Et. Mag.* p. 681. 36 et *Et. Sym.* V ap. Gaisf., sine Call. verbis) Suid. iii. 188. 24 *κρίμνον ... καὶ* "*πολύκριμνος*", *ἡ πολύκριθος* (Prosymna videlicet, e Salusti comment.)

---

3 *Κενθρίππης Et. Gen.* B (sed lemma *Κενθίππη*) *πολυκριμνον* pap., et v. l. *Et. Gen.* AB s.v. *πολύκρημνος: πολύκρημνον Et. Gen.* loc. cit. (et s.v. *Κενθίππη*) *Πρόcυμνον Et. Gen.* AB s.v. *πολύκρημνος* 4 fr. 98 *καὶ δόνακι πλήθοντα λιπὼν ῥόον Ἀ*]cτε[*ρίωνος* hic inseruit J. Blundell, 'ad sensum optime, sed ε[quoad dispicimus non legi potest' (*SH*) 5 fort. ρ[

97 (*SH* 291; – Pf.)

```
         · · ·
              ].[
        ] . . . . υ[
        ]ιφυλαττε[
        ]καιδ[
    5   ]ον. δ[
        ]μ εμ[
         · · ·
```

1–6 *P. Oxy.* 2258 (= pap. 2), novum fragmentum (*P. Oxy.* xxx. 91), pagina 'versa' (pagina 'recta' = fr. 96)

---

2 fort.]α̣ .̣ ε̣υ[3 φυλαττ- forma Attica; hoc fragmentum igitur scholiis marginalibus dederunt Lobel, *SH*. Sed haec litteris maioribus, scholia autem in pap. 2 minoribus scripta sunt. Porro in fr. 96. 3 pars media hexametri respondet. Itaque fragmentum videtur potius textui *Hecalae* esse tribuendum, φυλαττ- pro φυλασσ- librarii incuriae

98 (280 Pf.)

καὶ δόνακι πλήθοντα λιπὼν ῥόον Ἀστερίωνος

Et. Gen. AB s.v. δόναξ (= *Et. Mag.* p. 283. 2)· ὁ κάλαμος. Καλλ. "καὶ— Ἀστερίωνος", παρὰ τὸ δίνω τὸ στρέφω· καὶ ὡς λίθος λίθαξ, οὕτως δῖνος δίναξ. καὶ τροπῆι τοῦ ῑ εἰς ō δόναξ

πλήθοντα *Et. Gen.* A, *Et. Mag.*: πλήθουσιν *Et. Gen.* B
Hecalae trib. Naeke, p. 173. Versum in fr. 96. 4 restituere conatus est J. Blundell (sed v. ad loc.)

99 (278 Pf.)

τοὔνεκα καὶ νέκυες πορθμήιον οὔτι φέρονται
μούνηι ἐνὶ πτολίων, ὅ τε τέθμιον οἰσέμεν ἄλλους
δανοῖς ἐν στομάτεσσι †νεὼς Ἀχερουσίας ἐπίβαθρον δανάκηςϯ

1–3 *Et. Gen.* AB s.v. δανάκης (cf. *Et. Mag.* p. 247. 41) τοῦτο νομίσματός ἐστιν ὄνομα βαρβαρικοῦ, ⟨οὐ add. Barrett⟩ πλέον ὀβολοῦ, ὃ τοῖς νεκροῖς ἐν τοῖς cτόμαcιν ἐτίθεσαν (cf. Hesych. s.v. δανάκη). Καλλ. "τοὔνεκα—δανάκης" [τοὔ- νεκα—στομάτεσσι om. B]. Ἀχερουσία δέ ἐστι λίμνη ἐν Ἄιδου, ἣν διαπορθμεύονται οἱ τελευτῶντες τὸ προειρημένον νόμισμα διδόντες τῶι πορθμεῖ. εἴρηται δὲ δανάκης ὁ τοῖς δανοῖς [Sylburg: δαναοῖς AB] ἐπιβαλλόμενος· δανοὶ [Sylburg: δαναοὶ AB] γὰρ οἱ νεκροί, τουτέστι ξηροί· δανὰ γὰρ τὰ ξηρά. "διά τε ξύλα δανὰ κεάσσαι" (ο 322). Ἡρακλείδης ἐν τῶι β' τῶν Περcικῶν [FGH 689 F 3; Ἡρακλείδης κτλ. om. A]

    1 Suid. iv. 176. 5 πορθμήιον· ὁ μιcθὸc τοῦ ναύτου. Καλλ. "τοὔνεκα—φέρονται". ἐν Αἰγιαλῶι γὰρ καταβάcιόν ἐcτιν εἰc Ἅιδου, εἰc ὃ ἀπελθοῦcα ἡ Δημήτηρ ἔμαθε παρὰ τῶν περιοίκων περὶ τῆc Κόρηc καὶ ἐδωρήcατο αὐτοῖc, ὡc λέγει, ἄφεcιν τοῦ πορθμηίου 3 Suid. ii. 5. 30 δανάκη· τοῦτο νομίcματόc ἐcτιν ὄνομα, ὃ τοῖc νεκροῖc ἐδίδοcαν πάλαι cυγκηδεύοντεc "νεὼc Ἀχερουcίαc ἐπίβαθρον" (tum Ἀχερουcία—τῶι πορθμεῖ διδόντεc = Et. Gen.)

    1 νέκυος προcθμήιον Et. Gen. A   2–3 ἐπιπτολίοτε θυμιωνήccε μεν. ἀλλ' οὐ cάνοιc Et. Gen. A (πτολίων ὅτε θυμιονηcέμεν Et. Mag.): ἐνὶ—ἄλλουc corr. Casaubon (*Lect. Theocr.* c. 4, in J. Reiske (ed.), *Theocriti Reliquiae*, ii (1766), p. 75) qui v. 3 finxit ad verba *Et. Mag.* ἐν cτομάτεccι νεὼc (contra Call. artem metricam) Ἀχεροντείαc ἐπίβαθρον, arbitratus ανοιc compendium esse pro ἀνθρώποιc, additum a librario et mutandum in ἀνθρώπουc (unde initium v. 4 finxit Naeke ἀνθρώπουc δανάκην)   3 ⟨δ⟩ανοῖc Pf.   verba †νεὼc—δανάκηc† fort. Callimachi sunt potius quam soluta oratio; sanari posse despero. M. L. West autem versus Call. in *Et. Gen.* post ὁ τοῖc δανοῖc ἐπιβαλλόμενοc transponere vult, et ideo putat esse laudatos ut demonstrent nomen nummi δανάκηc a δανόc originem ducere; verba Ἡρακλείδης ἐν τῶι β' τῶν Περcικῶν ad "νεὼc Ἀχερουcίαc ἐπίβαθρον δανάκηc" referenda esse suspicatur   Si Suidae (s.v. πορθμήιον) et *Et. Gen.* credere possumus, nomen proprium loci Αἰγιαλόc antecessisse, et nomen nummi δανάκηc successisse veri simile est. At in hoc fragmento difficillimo fere omnia incerta

100 (285 Pf.)

Δηώ τε Κλυμένου τε πολυξείνοιο δάμαρτα

Et. Gen. AB s.v. Κλύμενοc (cf. *Et. Mag.* p. 521. 4, *Et. Sym.* V ap. Gaisf., sine Call. verbis)· ὄνομα ἥρωοc καὶ ἐπίθετον Ἅιδου. ἐπὶ μὲν τοῦ ἥρωοc ἀπὸ τοῦ κλύω τὸ δοξάζω, ἔνθεν καὶ κλυτὸc ὁ ἔνδοξοc· ἐπὶ δὲ τοῦ Ἅιδου ὁ πάνταc καλῶν πρὸc ἑαυτὸν ἢ ὁ ὑπὸ πάντων ἀκουόμενοc. Καλλ. "Δηώ—δάμαρτα" [πο ante Κλυμένου add. B: del. Dilthey]   Suid. iii. 138. 12 Κλύμενοc· οὕτω λέγεται ὁ Ἅιδηc· ἢ ὅτι πάνταc προcκαλεῖται εἰc ἑαυτόν, ἢ ὁ ὑπὸ πάντων ἀκουόμενοc, 'e comment. Salust., ut saepius, om. lemmate' (Pf.). Fort. cum fr.151 cohaeret?

101 (339 Pf.)

Κλεωναίοιο χάρωνος

Suid. iii. 129. 10 "Κλεωναίου χάρωνος"· τοῦ χαροποῦ λέοντος   Steph. Byz. s.v. Ἰώνη ... τὸ ἐθνικὸν Ἰωνίτηc ἢ Ἰωναῖοc, ὡc Κλεωναῖοc· "Κλεωναίοιο χάρωνοc"

Κλεωναίου Suid. codd.: Κλεωναῖοι ὁ χάρωνος Steph. codd. RV, -ναῖος Ald.:
corr. Bernhardy ad Suid. et Meineke, *Anal. Alex.* p. 85
De Call. cogitavit Schneider (fr. an. 310); propter Suid. testimonium *Hecalae*
trib. Pfeiffer

102 (277 Pf.)

βόες ἧχι γέγειαι
ἄνθεα μήκωνός τε καὶ ἤνοπα πυρὸν ἔδουσι

1–2 *Et. Gen.* A s.v. γέγειος (cf. *Et. Mag.* p. 223. 33; in *Et. Gen.* B desunt Call.
verba)· ὁ ἀρχαῖος. καὶ γέγειαι. εἴρηται παρ' Ἑκαταίωι (*FGH* 1 F 362) καὶ
Καλλιμάχωι . . . (fr. 510 Pf.) καὶ "ἧχι—ἔδουσι" [καὶ "ἧχι—ἔδουσι" om. *Et. Gen.*
B; "καὶ ἤνοπα—ἔδουσι" om. *Et. Mag.*]
    1 Suid. i. 511. 4 γέγειαι βόες· αἱ ἀρχαῖαι (e comment. Salusti)
    2 Suid. ii. 574. 23 ἤνοψ· ὁ λαμπρός . . . (fr. 18. 2) καὶ "ἤνοπα—ἔδουσι",
τουτέστι πυρρὸν cῖτον. καὶ ἡ δοτικὴ (ter apud Homerum) "ἤνοπι". Hesychius s.v.
"ἤνοπα"· λαμπρόν

    1 βόες e Suid. suppl. Reitzenstein   ἠχεῖ *Et. Gen.* A, *Et. Mag.*: corr. Sylburg
γέγειαι *Et. Gen.* A, Suid.: γέγεια *Et. Mag.*   2 ἠν ὁ πάπυρον *Et. Gen.* A
Fort. subsequitur fr. 177 inc. sed. (Hollis)

103 (302 Pf.)

οἵ νυ καὶ Ἀπόλλωνα παναρκέος Ἡελίοιο
χῶρι διατμήγουσι καὶ εὔποδα Δηωίνην
Ἀρτέμιδος

1–3 Schol. (BDPTU) P. *Nem.* 1. 3 Ὀρτυγία, δέμνιον Ἀρτέμιδος] ἔχοι δ' ἂν οὐ
φαύλως δέμνιον Ἀρτέμιδος λέγεσθαι τὴν Ὀρτυγίαν, οἷον ἐνδιαίτημα καὶ δια-
τριβήν· ἱερὰν γὰρ τὴν πᾶσαν νῆσον Φερσεφόνης εἶναι· ὅτι δὲ ἡ αὐτή ἐστι τῆι
Ἀρτέμιδι, Καλλ. ἐν Ἑκάληι· "οἵ—Ἀρτέμιδος"
    1 Suid. iv. 18. 17 "παναρκέος"· τοῦ μεγάλου καὶ δυνατοῦ. Ἡλίου δὲ παναρ-
κέος· τοῦ πανταχῆ λάμποντος
    2 Apollon. Dysc. *de Adv.* (*Gr. Gr.* i. 1, p. 138. 18 Schn.) τούτωι γὰρ τῶι λόγωι
καὶ τὸ χωρίς, ἀποβαλὸν τὸ ς, οὐκ ἐφύλαξε τὴν ἐπὶ τοῦ τέλους ὀξεῖαν, ἀνεβίβαζε δέ,
οὐχ ὑποπῖπτον τῆι ὀξύτητι τῶν εἰς ι ληγόντων ἐπιρρημάτων, ἐν τῶι "χῶρι
διατμήγουσι" Iohan. Philop. *Τονικὰ Παραγγ.* (ex Herodian. prosod.
excerpt.), p. 37. 7 Dindorf. τὸ δὲ "χῶρι διατμήγουσι" βαρύνεται

    2 χωρίον διατμ. cod. B: χωρὶ διατμ. cod. rec. U: correxerat iam Bentley, coll.
Et. Mag. p. 607. 23 χῶρι   3 δηιώνην codd.: corr. Valckenaer, *Epist. ad*
Ernest. pp. 49 sq. Tittm.

104 (273 Pf.)

Ἀπόλλωνος ἀπαυγή

Et. Gen. B (p. 24 L.–L. = *Et. Mag.* p. 25) s.v. ἀγαυγή (sic)· οἷον "Ἀπόλλωνος ἀγαυγή", παρὰ τὸ αὐγή   Suid. i. 266. 13 "ἀπαύγασμα", καὶ "ἀπαυγάζω" καὶ "ἀπαυγή". ἡ ἔκλαμψις

ἀγαυγή *Et. Gen.* B, *Et. Mag.*: corr. Hecker, p. 120
Call. *Hecalae* trib. Pfeiffer (propter Suidae testimonium)

105 (265 Pf.)

ὅθεν ἠληλούθειν

Choerob. ap. Theodos. (*Gr. Gr.* iv. 2, p. 114. 8 Hilg.) (τὰ Ἀττικὰ ἀπὸ βραχείας ἀρχόμενα κατὰ τὸν παρακείμενον ἐν τῶι ὑπερςυντελικῶι χρονικῶς μεγεθύνονται οἷον ἀλήλιφα ἠληλίφειν ... πλὴν τοῦ ἐλήλυθα· ἐληλύθειν γὰρ ὁ ὑπερςυντελικὸς διὰ τοῦ ε̄· ὅθεν ἀναλογώτερόν φασι παρὰ Καλλ. "ὅθεν ἠληλούθειν" Suid. ii. 527. 15 "εἰλήλουθα" καὶ "εἰληλούθειν" (nil nisi lemma)

ἠληλούθειν Choerob. codd. VO: ἐληλούθειν C: εἰληλούθειν Suid. (codd. AGITVM, -θει F), coniecerat Schneider (fr. 532)
Propter finem spondiacum, imitationem Homericam (cf. Δ 520), et Suidae testimonium *Hecalae* trib. Pfeiffer

106 (270 Pf.)

γέντο δ' ἀλυκρά

Et. Gen. AB (p. 336 L.–L.; cf. *Et. Mag.* p. 337, *Etym. Graec. Par.* ap. Cramer, *Anecd. Par.* iv. 6. 12) s.v. ἀλυκρόν· ἀντὶ τοῦ θαλυκρόν· οἷον ... (Call. fr. 736 inc. auct. Pf.)· εἶτα "γέντο δ' ἀλυκρά" ἔνδεια· καὶ διὰ τοῦ θ̄ καὶ χωρὶς τοῦ θ̄   Suid. i. 128. 25 ἀλυκρά· χλιαρά· "γέντο δ' ἀλυκρά"
De Call. cogitaverat Toup; *Hecalae* trib. Hecker, p. 113

107 (276 Pf.)

δέκα δ' ἄστριας αἴνυτο λάτρον

Et. Gen. AB (cf. *Et. Mag.* p. 159. 28) s.v. ἄστρις· Καλλ. οἷον "δέκα—λάτρον". εἴρηται δὲ ὑποκοριστικῶς. ὡς γὰρ ὁ Παρθένιος Πάρθις ... οὕτως ὁ ἀστράγαλος ἄστρις. Δίδυμος ἐν τῶι περὶ παθῶν   Suid. i. 392. 29 ἄστρια (sic)· οἱ ἀστράγαλοι. "δέκα—λάτρον" παρὰ Καλλ. Cf. Hesych. ἄστριες· ἀστράγαλοι Suid. iii. 237. 23 λάτρον· ὁ μισθός (v. ad fr. 94)

ἄcτριαc *Et. Gen.*: ἄcτρια Suid.   αὔνυτο codd.: 'prob. ἄρνυτο, ut μιcθὸν
ἄρνυcθαι passim' (Pf.)
Hecalae dedit Kapp (fr. 121)

108 (343 Pf.)

οὐδ' οἷcιν ἐπὶ κτενὸc ἔcκον ἔθειραι

Suid. iii. 198. 13 κτείc· τὸ ἐφήβαιον, καὶ τὸ τῶν τριχῶν κάλλυντρον. Καλλ.
"οὐδ'—ἔθειραι" *Et. Gen.* AB (cf. *Et. Mag.* p. 542. 18) s.v. κτείc· τὸ μόριον
ἤγουν τὸ αἰδοῖον, οἷον "οὐδ'—ἔθειραι" [οἷον—ἔθειραι om. *Et. Mag.*]. κλίνεται
κτενόc [om. A]· παρὰ τὸ ἐκτείνεcθαι ἐν ταῖc cυνουcίαιc   *Et. Gud.* p. 350. 19
Sturz κτεὶc cημαίνει τρία· τὸ μόριον ἤγουν τὸ αἰδοῖον οἷον "οὐδ'—ἔθειραι"
Choerob. ap. Theodos. (*Gr. Gr.* iv. 1, p. 203. 34 Hilg.) κτείc κτενόc . . . cημαίνει
πολλά . . . καὶ τὸ αἰδοῖον, ὡc παρὰ Καλλ. "ἐπὶ—ἔθειραι"   Schol. (T) *T* 382 (iv,
p. 641 Erbse) ἔθειραι δὲ αἱ τημεληθεῖcαι τρίχεc. κακῶc οὖν Καλλ. "ἐπὶ—ἔθειραι"

οἷcιν codd.: αἷcιν Hecker, p. 115: ᾗcιν Cobet, *Mnemosyne,* 10 (1861), 428,
Schneider (fr. 308)   ἐπεὶ Schol. T   ἔcκον Suid.: ἔκον *Et. Gen.* A: ἔcχον
Choerob., *Et Gen.* B, *Et. Gud.*   αἴθειραι Choer.
Hecalae dedit Kapp (fr. 136); de carmine nostro cogitaverat iam Hecker, p. 115

109 (282 Pf.)

ὀκκόcον ὀφθαλμοὶ γὰρ ἀπευθέεc, ὅccον ἀκουή
εἰδυλίc

1–2 *Et. Gud.* p. 409. 13 de Stef. s.v. εἰδυλίc (cf. *Et. Gen.* A'B, *Et. Mag.*
p. 295. 31, sine Call. verbis)· ἐπιcτήμων, εἰδυῖα· Καλλ. "ὀκκόcον—εἰδυλίc"· παρὰ
τὸ εἴδω, τὸ γινώcκω· εἴδω εἰδυλοc εἰδύλη, εἶτα παρωνύμωc εἰδυλίc
1 Suid. i. 277. 9 "ἀπευθέεc" ἄπειροι, ἀπαίδευτοι
2 Suid. ii. 522. 26 "εἰδυλίc" [εἰδηλίcα AV: εἰδυλίcα cett.: corr. Küster]· ἡ
ἐπιcτήμων

----

1 ὤκουcον cod. Vind.: ὀκοῦccον cod. Sorbon.: καὶ κόccον cod. Gud.: corr.
Naeke, *Opusc.* i. 71   ἀπευθέωc Sorb.: ἀπ' εὐθέωc Gud.
Hecalae trib. Naeke, *Opusc.* i. 71

110 (286 Pf.)

αὖτιc ἀπαιτίζουcαν ἑὴν εὐεργέα λάκτιν

Et. Gen. AB s.v. λάκτιν (p. 11. 21 Colonna, 30. 14 A.–A., = *Et. Mag.*
p. 555. 17)· cημαίνει ἡ λέξιc τὴν cκυτάλην [?: κώταλιν coni. Larcher et Ducange;
cf. Suid. infra], τορύνην. Καλλ. "αὖθιc—λάκτιν"   Suid. iii. 230. 23 λάκτιν· τὴν
λεγομένην κώταλιν, τορύνην, ὅ ἐcτι ζωμήρυcιν. "εὐεργέα λάκτιν"

αὖτις Naeke, p. 141 (v. ad fr. 197. 49 Pf.): αὖθις codd.   ἐὴν *Et. Gen.*,
Casaubon: ἔκνον *Et. Mag.* codd. DMR   εὐεργέτα *Et. Gen.* A: ἐναργέα Suid.
cod. F
Hecalae trib. Toup (cf. Naeke, pp. 140 sq.; Schneider, fr. 178)

111 (287 Pf.)

ἢ ἄφαρον φαρόωσι, μέλει δέ φιν ὄμπνιον ἔργον

Et. Gen. A s.v. φαρῶ (fere eadem in *Et. Gen.* B, cf. *Et. Mag.* p. 788. 24, *Et. Sym.*
V ap. Gaisf.)· τὸ ἀροτριῶ. Καλλ. "ἄφαρον—ἔργον". εἴρηται ἀπὸ τοῦ ἀρῶ
πλεονασμῶι τοῦ φ φαρῶ, παρ' ὃ καὶ ἄφαρον, τὴν λιπαρὰν γῆν, τὴν ⟨μήπω add.
Schneider ex Suid.⟩ πολλάκις ἀροτριωθεῖσαν. "ὄμπνιον" δὲ "ἔργον" τὸ
Δήμητρος   *Et. Gen.* A s.v. φάρυγξ (cf. Melet. *de Nat. Hom. ap.* Cramer, *AO*
iii. 84. 10 et adnot. Pf.)· παρὰ τὸ φέρω, δι' ἧς φέρεται τὸ πνεῦμα· ... καὶ
Λυκόφρων (sc. *Alex.* 154) ... Καλλ. "ἢ ἄφαρον φαρόωσι". ἄφαρον τὴν μηδὲν
φέρουσαν   *Et. Gen.* AB s.v. ἀφαυρός (cf. *Et. Mag.* p. 175. 42) ... ὀξύνεται δὲ τὸ
ἀφαρὸς [ἄφαρος B, φαρός *Et. Mag.*] πρὸς ἀντιδιαστολὴν τοῦ παρὰ Καλλ.
εἰρημένου, οἷον "ἢ ἄφαρον φαρόωσι". ἄφαρον δὲ τὴν ἀγεώργητον γῆν, παρὰ τὸ
φέρω [φαρῶ Schneider]   Suid. i. 426. 1 "ἄφαρον"· τὴν λιπαρὰν γῆν, τὴν πολλὰ
μήπω ἀροτριωθεῖσαν· "φαρόωσι" δὲ ἀντὶ τοῦ ἀροτριῶσιν. Cf. Hesych. ἄφαρον·
ἀνήροτον et φαροῦν· ἀροτριᾶν
ἢ *Et. Gen.* A s.v. φάρυγξ, B s.v. ἀφαυρός: ἡ codd. *Et. Mag.* teste Gaisf.
p. 175. 51 s.v. ἀφαυρός (qui tamen ἢ in adn. scribit)   ἀφαρόωσι vel ἀφαρώωσι
Suid. codd.   μέλλει *Et. Gen.* B, *Et. Sym.* V   cφιν *Et. Gen.* AB, *Et. Sym.* V, *Et.
Mag.* cod. D: cφίcιν cett.: corr. Bentley
Hecalae dedit Hecker, p. 90

112 (289 Pf.)

ἀλλὰ cὺ μὲν cιπαλός τε καὶ ὀφθαλμοῖcιν ἔφηλος

Et. Gen. AB s.v. cιπαλός (= *Et. Mag.* p. 714. 5)· ὁ εἰδεχθὴς καὶ ἄμορφος·
"ἀλλὰ—ἔφηλος"   Suid. iv. 365. 7 cίπαλος (de accentu, v. Pf.)· ὁ ἄμορφος
Propter Suid. test. Call. *Hecalae* trib. Pfeiffer

113 (291 Pf.)

ἡνίκα μὲν γὰρ †φαίνεται τοῖc ἀνθρώποιc ταῦτα†
αὐτοὶ μὲν φιλέουc', αὐτοὶ δέ τε πεφρίκαcιν,
ἑcπέριον φιλέουcιν, ἀτὰρ cτυγέουcιν ἐῷον

1–3 Olymp. in Arist. *Mete.* 1. 6. 343a20 (*Comment. in Aristot.* xii. 2, p. 53. 11
Stüve) αὕτη (sc. ἡ Ἀφροδίτη) γὰρ διὰ τὸ οἰκεῖον μέγεθος ἔcθ' ὅτε πλεῖον ἀπέχουσα
τοῦ ἡλίου κατὰ πλάτος ἐν μιᾶι ἡμέραι καὶ ἑῷα καὶ ἑcπέρια γίνεται. ὅθεν φησὶν ὁ
ἐξηγητὴς καὶ μόνον κατ' ἐξαίρετον ἑῷον καὶ ἑcπέριον λέγεσθαι τὸν τῆς Ἀφροδίτης
ἀστέρα διὰ τὸ δύνασθαι ἐν μιᾶι ἡμέραι καὶ ἑῷον καὶ ἑcπέριον φαίνεσθαι. ὅτι γὰρ
αὐτός ἐστι καὶ ἑῷος καὶ ἑcπέριος, δηλοῖ καὶ Καλλ. λέγων ἐν Ἑκάλῃ [Spanheim:
αἰκάλη codd.: αἰκάλλῃ Ald.] "ἡνίκα—ἑῷον"

3 Eust. p. 1271. 35 (ὁ ἀστήρ) ... τῆc Ἀφροδίτηc ... καὶ cτίλβων καλεῖται καὶ ἑωcφόροc δὲ κατὰ καιροῦ μεταβολήν, ὡc καὶ Καλλιμάχωι δοκεῖ, ἔνθα φηcὶν ὡc "ἑcπέριον—ἑῶιον" Ioann. Tzetzes, *Epist.* 43 (p. 63 Leone) οὐδὲ γὰρ κατὰ τὸν Κυρηναῖον Καλλ. "ἑcπέριον—ἑῶιον" (cf. id. *Chil.* viii. 834, p. 335 Leone)

1 ex Olymp. paraphrasi (ταῦτα codd.: ταῦτά Ald.), Hecker, p. 130 ἡνίκα μὲν γὰρ ταῦτὰ φαείνεται ἀνθρώποιcιν: alii alia. Fort. Olymp. paraphr. plus quam unum versum comprehendit (v. Naeke, p. 40 sqq.; Schneider ad fr. 52)   2 φιλέουcιν codd.: corr. Ald.   3 ἀτὰρ cτ. Olymp. codd., Eust., Tzetz.: ἀποcτ. Olymp. ed. Ald., e cod. ignoto: φιλέηιcιν et cτυγέηιcιν Tzetz. *Epist.*

114 (295 Pf.)

cὺν δ᾽ ἄμυδιc φορυτόν τε καὶ ἴπνια λύματ᾽ ἄειρεν

Suid. ii. 661. 12 ἴπνια· τὰ ἀποκαθάρματα τοῦ ἰπνοῦ, τοῦ λεγομένου φούρνου. ἢ τὰ πρὸc τὴν κάμινον ἐπιτήδεια καύcιμα. λέγει δὲ τὴν κόπρον τῶν ζῴων Καλλίμαχοc· "cὺν—ἄειρεν" [Καλλ.—ἄειρεν om. F]. Inde Schol. Ald. (om. V, pace Pfeiffer) Ar. *Vesp.* 837 (p. 132 Koster)   Suid. iv. 753. 6 φορυτόc· ... καὶ φορυτῶι, φρυγανώδει ἀκαθαρcίαι, cυρφετώδει, χορτώδει. "cὺν—ἀείραc" Suid. i. 63. 3 ἄειρεν· ἔβαλε. "καὶ—ἄειρεν"

ἄειρεν Suid. s.v. ἄειρεν et s.v. ἴπνια (schol. Ar. *Vesp.*): ἀείραc Suid. s.v. φορυτόc Hecalae trib. Meineke, *Call.* p. 146 (cf. Kapp, fr. 18)

115 (298 Pf.)

ἐπεὶ θεὸc οὐδὲ γελάccαι
ἀκλαυτὶ μερόπεccιν ὀιζυροῖcιν ἔδωκεν

1–2 Schol. an. in Greg. Naz. *Or.* 4. 113 (PG xxxvi. 1237) καὶ γέλωτα ἐν δακρύοιc ποιηταὶ γινώcκουcιν] Καλλίμαχειον τοιοῦτο φέρεται "ἐπεὶ—ἔδωκεν" Schol. (T) Z 484 (ii, p. 213 Erbse) δακρυόεν γελάcαcα] δυνατῶc ῥηθὲν ἀνερμήνευτόν ἐcτιν· οὐ γὰρ ἁπλοῦν τὸ πάθοc, ἀλλὰ cύνθετον ἐξ ἐναντίων παθῶν, ἡδονῆc καὶ λύπηc· εἰc γέλωτα μὲν γὰρ αὐτὴν προήγαγε τὸ βρέφοc, εἰc δάκρυον δὲ ἡ περὶ τοῦ Ἕκτοροc ἀγωνία. οὐκ ἐνόηcεν οὖν Καλλ. τὸν cτίχον εἰπών· "ἐπεὶ—ἀκλαυτί"· ὠιήθη γὰρ ὑπὸ τῆc διαχύcεωc τοῦ γέλωτοc τὰ δάκρυα γενέcθαι

1 γελᾶcαι Schol. Greg.: γέλαcεν Schol. Hom.   2 ἀκλαυτί Schol. Hom.: ἀκλαυcτί Schol. Greg.: ἀκλαυτεί Naeke Hecalae trib. Naeke, pp. 155 sq.; cf. Hecker, p. 124

116 (299 Pf.)

Αἴϲηπον ἔχειϲ, ἑλικώτατον ὕδωρ,
Νηπείηϲ ἤ τ᾽ ἄργοϲ, ἀοίδιμοϲ Ἀδρήϲτεια

1 Schol. (BCT) *A* 98 b¹ (i, p. 36 Erbse) ἑλικώπιδα] τὴν μελανόφθαλμον, ὡϲ *Καλλ.* Schol. (A) *A* 98 b² (i, p. 36 Erbse) ἑλικώπιδα] μελανόφθαλμον, ἀφ᾽ οὗ εὐπρεπῆ· ⟨lacunam indicat Pfeiffer; cf. Eust. infra⟩ ὡϲ "ὕδωρ μέλαν Αἰϲήποιο" (*B* 825) καὶ *Καλλ.* [Dindorf: *Καλλ.* post ὡϲ cod. A] "Αἴϲηπον—ὕδωρ" Eust. p. 57. 1 (ἑλικῶπιϲ) ἤ καὶ ἡ μελανόφθαλμοϲ καὶ οὕτωϲ εὐπρεπήϲ, διὰ τὸ ἑλικούϲ, ὅ ἐϲτι μέλαναϲ, ἔχειν τὰϲ ὦπαϲ. ὅτι δὲ τὸ μέλαν ἑλικὸν λέγεται, δηλοῖ καὶ ὁ εἰπὼν τὸν Αἴϲηπον ποταμὸν "ἑλικώτατον ὕδωρ" (cf. Eust. p. 354. 22; *Et. Gen.* B s.v. ἑλίκωπεϲ... ἑλικὸν γὰρ καλεῖται κατὰ γλῶϲϲαν τὸ μέλαν; *Et. Gud.* p. 457. 1 de Stef.) Schol. (BE³E⁴) *B* 825 (i, p. 341 Erbse) μέλαν] τοῦτο κοινὸν ὑδάτων ἐπίθετον, ὡϲ "κυανώπιδοϲ Ἀμφιτρίτηϲ" (μ 60) καὶ *Καλλ.* "Αἴϲηπον—ὕδωρ" Suid. ii. 247. 11 "ἑλικώτατον ὕδωρ"· τὸ ἑλικοειδῆ ἔχον τὴν ῥεύϲιν. ἤ διαυγέϲ 2 Schol. Ap. Rh. 1. 1116 καὶ πεδίον Νηπήιον] πεδίον Νηπείαϲ ἔϲτι περὶ Κύζικον. μνημονεύει δὲ αὐτοῦ καὶ *Καλλ.* ἐν Ἑκάληι· "Νηπείηϲ—Ἀδρήϲτεια". τὴν δὲ Νήπειαν Διονύϲιοϲ ὁ Μιλήϲιοϲ (*FGH* 32 F 9, sed v. comment.) πεδίον τῆϲ Μυϲίαϲ φηϲὶν εἶναι

---

1 Αἰϲήπου Hecker   2 ἤ τ᾽ schol. L: ἠδ᾽ schol. Par.: ἤιτ᾽ Bentley   ἄργοϲ schol. L: Ἄργον schol. Par.

Duo fragmenta coniunxit Naeke, p. 265 (cf. Hecker, p. 121 et *Philol.* 4. (1849), 479).

117 (301 Pf.)

βουϲόον ὅν τε μύωπα βοῶν καλέουϲιν ἀμορβοί

Schol. vulg. χ 299 sq. οἶϲτροϲ] (*a*) ὁ οἶϲτροϲ ἀπογεννᾶται ἐκ τῶν ἐν τοῖϲ ποταμοῖϲ πλατέων [Wellmann: πλαγίων Schol.] ζωιαρίων ... ὁ δὲ μύωψ ἐκ τῶν ξύλων ἀπογεννᾶται. καὶ *Καλλ.* περὶ τοῦ μύωποϲ "βουϲόον—ἀμορβοί". εἰϲὶ δὲ οὗτοι πολέμιοι τοῖϲ βουϲίν. (*b*) οἶϲτροϲ ὁ λεγόμενοϲ μύωψ. ἔϲτι δὲ ζῷον ὑπόχαλκον τὴν μορφήν, ὅπερ ἂν εἰϲέλθηι ἐϲ τὰ ὦτα τῶν βοῶν ἐξοιϲτρεῖν ἀναγκάζει τοὺϲ βόαϲ. καὶ *Καλλ.* "βουϲόον—ἀμορβοί" (cf. schol. Theocr. 6. 28 et schol. Ap. Rh. 1. 1265, unde *Et. Gen.* AB s.v. μύωψ) *Et. Gud.* p. 423. 38 Sturz s.v. οἶϲτροϲ = schol. χ 299(*b*) ... καὶ *Καλλ.* "βουϲόον—ἀμορβοί" Suid. iii. 426. 11 μύωψ [ὁ οἶϲτροϲ superscr. M]· μυῖά τιϲ ἐρεθίζουϲα τὰϲ βοῦϲ (= Hesych.)· λέγεται παρὰ *Καλλ.* ἐν Ἑκάληι "βουϲόοϲ [βοῦϲ ϲῶϲ codd.] μύωψ"· τοὺϲ [AF: τὰϲ M] βοῦϲ ϲοβῶν καὶ διώκων μύωψ

βουϲόον schol. (*a*) cod. Ox. et Ald.: βοῦϲ ϲόον schol. (*b*) cod. Ox. et *Et. Gud.* (cf. Suid.) ὅν τε Schol. (*a*) et (*b*) cod. Ox. et *Et. Gud.*: οὔτε Schol. ed. Ald. (correxerat iam Bentley) ἀμορβή cod. Gudian.

118 (303 Pf.)

κενεὸν πόνον ὀτλήσοντες

Schol. Laur.) S. *Tr.* 7 ὄκνον] εἰ δὲ γράφεται ὄτλον, τὴν ταλαιπωρίαν ἢ [῎Ομηρος del. Papageorg.] τὸ μεμορημένον καὶ πεπρωμένον· Καλλ. "κενεὸν— ὀτλήσαντες" Suid. iii. 572. 27 ὀτλήσοντες· ὑπομενοῦντες, κακοπαθήσοντες. ἐν Ἐπιγράμμασι (Paul. Sil. *AP* 5. 226. 7 sq.) "ἔνδικον ὀτλήσοντες ἀεὶ πόνον κτλ."

ὀτλήσοντες Suid.: -αντες schol. Soph.
Hecalae trib. Pfeiffer propter Suid. testimonium: 'multo veri similius est verba ὀτλήσοντες—κακοπαθήσοντες e Salusti comment. sumpta quam explicationem ad Paul. Sil. epigr. esse'

119 (309 dub. Pf.)

ποσσὶ δ' ἀνελθεῖν
ἄγκος ἐς ὑψικάρηνον ἐδίζετο· πᾶσα δ' ἀπορρὼξ
πέτρη ἔην ὑπένερθε καὶ ἄμβασις οὔ νύ τις ἦεν

1-2 Suid. i. 27. 26 ἄγκος· ὑψηλὸς τοῦ ὄρους τόπος. "ποσὶ—ἐδίζετο" ('Zonar.' p. 30 Tittm. s.v. ἄγκη καὶ ἄγκεα et 'Zonar.' cod. Par. 2669 ap. Cramer, *Anecd. Par.* iv. 90. 7 plura habet ex fonte etymologico adhuc ignoto)
2-3 Suid. i. 316. 29 ἀπορρῶγας· . . . καὶ ἀπορρώξ· ἀπόσπασμα ὄρους . . . "πᾶσα—ἦεν" . . . (interponuntur et sequuntur excerpta ex schol. Aristoph.)
3 Suid. i. 136. 11 ἄμβασις· ἀνάβασις. "καὶ—ἦεν."

1 ποσὶ δ' αὖ ἐλθεῖν codd. Suid. et 'Zonar.': corr. Toup et Valckenaer
3 ὑπένερθεν Suid. codd. GTSM
Fragmenta (nondum coniuncta) Call. *Hecalae* trib. Hecker, p. 122; coniunxit Bergk, *Anth.*[2] p. xx, et ad lupi et capreae fabulam in Μυθικοῖς rettulit (v. Babr. p. 219 Crusius). Pfeiffer de auctore dubitat

120 (312 Pf.)

ἄκμηνον δόρποιο

Suid. i. 84. 20 ἄκμηνος· ἄγευστος. "ἄκμηνον δόρποιο."

ἄκμηνον Suid. et 'Zonar.' cod. K, p. 100 Tittm.: ἄκμηνος 'Zonar.' codd. cett. Call. *Hecalae* trib. Hecker, p. 125. 'Neque error lexicographi est voc. δόρποιο (Toup, Bernhardy), neque v.l. ad *T* 163 ἄκμηνος σίτοιο (T. W. Allen ad loc.), sed Call. et imitatur locum Homericum et variat, ut saepius' (Pf.)

121 (314 Pf.)

ἀμιθρῆσαι

Suid. i. 141. 28 "ἀμιθρῆσαι"· μετρῆσαι, ἀριθμῆσαι παρὰ Καλλ. Cf. *Et. Gen.*
AB s.v. ἀμιθρῆσαι (p. 406 L.–L.; cf. *Et. Mag.* p. 407)· Cιμωνίδης τὸν ἀριθμὸν
ἄμιθρον εἶπεν καθ᾿ ὑπερβιβασμόν, οἶον "κυμάτων ἄμιθρον" [PMG, p. 314, Sim.
626; κυμάτων coni. Bergk: κύματα *Et. Gen.* A: κύματ᾿ B]. ἐκ δὲ τοῦ ἄμιθρος
ἀμιθρῶ καὶ ἀμιθρήcω ⟨καὶ ἀμιθρῆσαι add. Reitzenstein⟩ τὸ ἀριθμῆσαι. ἢ ἀπὸ τοῦ
ἀριθμῆσαι κατὰ μετάθεσιν τῶν cτοιχείων, ὡς πίτυλος τύπιλος. οὕτως Ἡρωδιανὸς
Περὶ Παθῶν (ii. 387. 1 Lentz) καὶ Μεθόδιος [οὕτως—Μεθ. deest in *Et. Gen.* B et
Et. Mag.; Methodius *Hecalam* affert, cf. ad fr. 45. 1 et fr. 52].

Plerique Suidae glossam ad *H.* 6. 86 ἀμιθρεῖ rettulerunt, at 'moneo Suidam ne
unam quidem glossam ex *Hymnis* sumpsisse, ut videtur . . . vix dubitandum quin
ἀμιθρῆσαι *Hecalae* tribuendum sit' (Pf.). Cf. Reitzenstein, *Gesch. Et.* p. 25; Kapp,
fr. 114

122 (315 Pf.)

ἀπούατος ἄγγελος ἔλθοι

Suid. i. 327. 7 "ἀπ᾿ οὔατος—ἔλθοι"· παρὰ Καλλ. τουτέστι δύσφημος, μὴ [del.
Bernhardy] ἄξιος τοῦ μὴ [τοῦ om. S: μὴ om. F] ἀκουσθῆναι

ἀπούατος Schneider (fr. 301), propter explicationem sequentem et coll. schol.
(D) C 272: ἀπ᾿ οὔατος Suid.

Hecalae trib. Hecker, p. 97

123 (316 Pf.)

Suid. i. 388. 7 ἀσπαστοί· ἄσμενοι, θεοειδεῖς· παρὰ δὲ Καλλ. "ἀσπαστύς",
ἀσπαστύος, τουτέστι προσηγορία φιλία

Fort. *Hecalae* fragmentum esse coni. Naeke, p. 154; propter Suid. test. *Hecalae*
trib. Pfeiffer, quamquam confitetur modum laudandi potius librum de rebus
grammaticis scriptum sapere quam Salusti commentarium

124 (317 Pf.)

ἀσταγὲς ὕδωρ

Suid. i. 389. 1 "ἀσταγὲς ὕδωρ"· τὸ πολυσταγές. Cf. Hesych. ἀσταγές· πολὺ καὶ
λάβρον

Call. *Hecalae* assignavit Hecker, p. 109. Fort. de tempestate?

125 (318 Pf.)

cχέτλιαι ἀνθρώπων ἀφραϲτύεϲ

Suid. i. 433. 28 ἀφραϲτύεϲ· ἀϲυνεϲίαι. "ϲχέτλιαι—ἀφραϲτύεϲ"
De Call. propter terminationem -τύϲ iam Ruhnken (*Ep. Crit.* ii. 132, *Epist. ad
Ernest.* p. 21 Tittm.) cogitavit, de *Hecala* dubitanter Naeke, p. 252; carmini
nostro propter Suid. test. assignavit Hecker, p. 124

126 (320 Pf.)

βέβυϲτο δὲ πᾶϲα χόλοιο

Suid. i. 466. 4 βέβυϲτο· ἐπεπλήρωτο. "βέβυϲτο—χόλοιο"
Call. *Hecalae* dedit Hecker, p. 118

127 (322 Pf.)

γέντα βοῶν μέλδοντεϲ

Suid. i. 516. 23 γέντα· τὰ μέλη· "γέντα—μέλδοντεϲ" Καλλ. Cf. Hesych. γέντα·
κρέα, ϲπλάγχνα.   Suid. iii. 351. 23 μέλδοντεϲ· τήκοντεϲ, ἕψοντεϲ. "γέντα—
μέλδοντεϲ"

βοῶν Suid. s.v. μέλδοντεϲ: βοὸϲ Suid. s.v. γέντα
Hecalae fragmentis inseruit Kapp (fr. 125)

128 (323 Pf.)

γοεροῖο γόοιο

Suid. i. 534. 7 γοερόν· θρηνῶδεϲ, λυπηρόν, κατανυκτικόν. καὶ "γοεροῖο γόοιο"

'Fort. "καὶ γ. γ." (Pf.: cf. ad fr. 19)   γοεροῖο γόοιο Suid. codd. GITVM:
γοεροῖϲ γόοιϲ AF: γοεροῖο γόνοιο dubitanter Schneider (fr. an. 14): 'expecto velut
γοεροῖο νόμοιο' Wilamowitz ap' fr. 126 Kapp: γοεροῖο γοοῖϲι dubitanter Pf.
Call. *Hecalae* trib. Kapp (fr. 126)

129 (324 Pf.)

οἰκίον εὖτε δέμοιμι

Suid. ii. 16. 18 δέδοιμι [sic]· οἰκοδομοίην. "οἰκίον—δέδοιμι" (inde s.v. οἰκία . . .
καὶ οἰκίον· τὸ μικρὸν οἴκημα. "οἰκίον—δέδοιμι" ἀντὶ τοῦ οἰκοδομοίην [om. AF]).

δέδοιμι semper Suid. (in alphab. inter δέδοικα et δέδυκα): corr. Stephanus,
Portus
Cal. *Hecalae* trib. Hecker, p. 119

130 (330 Pf.)

πότμον ἐλινύσειεν

Suid. ii. 247. 18 ἐλινύειν· στραγγεύειν [στρατεύειν vel στραγεύειν codd.] διατρίβοντας ἢ ἐγχρονίζοντας. καὶ "πότμον ἐλινύσειεν" ἀντὶ τοῦ τὴν δυστυχίαν παύσειεν

ἐλινύσειας F: ἐλινύσειε C. Dilthey (*De Call. Cydippa*, p. 85), fr. 131 subiungens
Call. *Hecalae* dedit Hecker, p. 108

131 (325 Pf.)

δύην ἀπόθεστον ἀλάλκοι

Suid. ii. 144. 21 δύη· ἡ κακοπάθεια, ἡ δυστυχία ... Καλλ. "δύην—ἀλάλκοι". ἦν οὐδεὶς ποθεῖ.

δύην ⟨δ'⟩ Dilthey (v. ad fr. 130)   ἀπόθ' ἐστ' Suid. cod. A: ἀπόθεστ' GIM:
ἀπόθεσθ' V: ἀπόθετ' F: corr. Porson   ἦν οὐδεὶς ποθ⟨έ⟩ει e Suid. add. Bentley,
ut initium versus alterius (sed a Salusti comment. potius verba sunt)
Hecalae trib. Naeke, p. 251

132 (331 Pf.)

ἐπήλυσιν ὄφρ' ἀλέοιτο
φώριον

1–2 Suid. ii. 346. 6 ἐπήλυσις· ἐπιδρομή. "ἐπήλυσιν—φώριον" τουτέστι ληιστρικήν   Suid. iv. 757. 4 φώρια· λαθραῖα, ληιστήρια· ἢ κλοπιμαῖα πράγματα.
"ἐπήλυσιν—φώριον" [ἐπήλυσιν κτλ. om. F]
Call. *Hecalae* trib. Hecker, p. 93

133 (332 Pf.)

ἐπιπρίσῃσιν ὀδόντας

Suid. ii. 350. 28 "ἐπιβρίσῃσιν ὀδόντας"· παρ' ὅσον οἱ θυμούμενοι τρίζουσι τοὺς ὀδόντας

ἐπιπρίσῃσιν Meineke (*Menand*. p. 278), Hecker (p. 108): ἐπιβρίσῃσιν Suid.:
ἐπιβρίσουσιν 'Zonaras' (teste Tittm., p. 836): ἐπιπρίουσιν J. Alberti, Toup:
ἐπιβρύκουσιν Küster
Call. *Hecalae* trib. Pfeiffer (fragmenti breviter mentionem fecerat Hecker,
p. 108)

134 (333 Pf.)

ἐπικλινές ἐcτι τάλαντον

Suid. ii. 361. 23 ἐπικλινές· ἐπιρρεπὲς εἰς κακόν. "ἐπικλινές—τάλαντον" Καλλ.

ἐcτι Suid. codd. AFVM: δὲ GI
Hecalae fragmentis inseruit Kapp (fr. 132). Etsi in *SH* 260A. 9 (*Aet.* 3) legi possit ἔτι μᾶλλον ἐπικλ{ε}ινές ἔ[cτι τάλαντον (v. edd. ad loc.), non tamen idcirco fragmentum *Hecalae* denegare debemus; nam isdem verbis poeta bis uti potuit

135 (335 Pf.)

ἠέρος ὄγμοι

Suid. ii. 555. 18 "ἠέρος ὄγμοι"· αἱ ὁδοί, οἱ τόποι
'Fort. Call. *Hec.*' (Adler ad loc.: cf. Wendel, *Gnomon,* 11 (1935), 237)

136 (336 Pf.)

ἑρπετὰ δ' ἰλυοῖcιν ἐνέκρυφεν

Suid. ii. 633. 1 ἰλυοῖcι· ταῖς καταδύcεcιν. "ἑρπετὰ—ἐνέκρυφεν" [post καταδύcεcιν add. τῶν ἑρπετῶν et om. ἑρπετὰ—ἐνέκρυφεν F]

ἐνέκρυφεν Suid. cod. V: ἐνέκρυφθεν rell. (metri causa excludi non potest, Pf.)
Call. *Hecalae* trib. Hecker, p. 109; descriptioni procellae W. Weinberger, *Philol.* 76 (1920), 72

137 (340 Pf.)

†ἀφ' ὑμέων† κοκύηιcι καθημένη ἀρχαίηιcι

Suid. iii. 144. 7 κοκκύαι· αἱ πρόγονοι. "ἀφ'—ἀρχαίης"   Cf. *Et. Gen.* AB s.v. κοκκύας (= *Et. Mag.* p. 524. 52; cf. *Et. Gud.* p. 333. 20 Sturz)· ὁ πρόγονος· ἐcτὶ δὲ Ἰακὴ ['Ιωνικὴ *Et. Mag.* codd. vulg.] ἡ λέξις, cημαίνει δὲ τοὺς ἤδη κεκοκυμένους [*Et. Gen.* AB, ?i.e. κεκωκυμένους Pf.: κεκομμένους *Et. Mag.*]; Hesych. s.v. κοκκύαι (cod.)· οἱ πάπποι καὶ οἱ πρόγονοι; 'Zonar.' p. 1228 κοκκύας· ὁ πρόγονος, πάππος

ἀμφ' ὑμέων Schneider (fr. an. 37): alii alia   κοκκύηιcι Suid.: corr. Portus ἀρχαίηιcι Suid. ed. pr.: ἀρχαίης codd.: ἀρχαίοιcι M. L. West, fort. recte
Call. fragmentum esse primus coniecit Toup (in Gaisf. Suid. s.v. κυμαίνει); de *Hecala* dubitanter cogitavit Naeke, p. 130; propter Suid. test. ei trib. Hecker, p. 122

138 (347 Pf.)

λίποιμι

Suid. iii. 275. 10 "λίποιμι"· καταλείψαιμι
'Glossa aliunde non nota ... fort. ex *Hecala*' (Pf.)

139 (348 Pf.)

τόδε μοι μαλκίcτατον ἦμαρ

Suid. iii. 314. 25 μαλκίcτατον· ψυχρότατον. "τὸ δέ—ἦμαρ"
Call. *Hecalae* tribuerunt Naeke, p. 239, et Hecker, p. 123. τόδε (potius quam
τὸ δέ) scripsit Naeke

140 (352 Pf.)

Νωνακρίνη

Suid. iii. 484. 25 "Νωνακρίνη" [Νώνα, κρίνη cod. F: Νώνα, κρήνη rell.: corr.
Portus]· λέγεται ἡ Καλλιcτώ
'Fort. schol. in Call. *Hec.*' (Adler); glossa aliunde non nota. In *SH* 250. 9–10
(*Aet.* 1) legimus Νωνακρίνη | Καλλιcτώ (cf. ad fr. 134)

141 (353 Pf.)

νωcάμενοc

Suid. iii. 485. 17 "νωcάμενοc"· νοήcαc, γνούc. παρὰ Καλλ. (cf. Hesych. s.v.
νωcάμενοc· κατανοήcαc; 'Zonar.' p. 1414 Tittm. νωcάμενοc· ἐνθυμηθείc)
Hecalae trib. Hecker, p. 91

142 (354 Pf.)

μέμβλετό μοι

Suid. iii. 359. 6 μεμβλώκατον ... καὶ "μέμβλετό μοι" ἀντὶ τοῦ μετ' ἐπιμελείαc
ἐγένετο
Fragmentum epicum cum explicatione, aliunde non notum, Call. *Hecalae* trib.
Pfeiffer

143 (356 Pf.)

ὀκχήcαcθαι

Suid. iii. 516. 10 ὀκχή· (v. fr. 66) ... καὶ "ὀκχήcαcθαι"· ἐπικαθεcθῆναι
Haec glossa cum explic. alibi exstare non videtur; Call. *Hecalae* trib. Pfeiffer

122 Callimachi Hecala

144 (357 Pf.)

ὄμπνιον ὕδωρ

Suid. iii. 535. 22 "ὄμπνιον ὕδωρ"· τὸ τρόφιμον, καὶ πολύ
De Call. Hecala cogitavit Hecker, p. 90

145 (358 Pf.)

εἰ δὲ Δίκη σε
πὰρ πόδα μὴ τιμωρὸς ἐτείσατο, δὶς τόσον αὖτις
ἔσσεται, ἐν πλεόνεσσι παλίντροπος,

1–3 Suid. iv. 63. 17 πὰρ πόδα [παρπόδας cod. G: παρπόδα rell.]· εὐθύς,
παραυτίκα. "εἰ—παλίντροπος" [εἰ—πλεόνεσσι om. F]
3 Suid. iv. 12. 9 παλίντροπος· ὀπισθόρμητος ('sequitur AP 9. 61. 1 παλίντροπον
ἐκ πολέμοιο, sed. gl. cum explic. aliunde non nota fort. ex Hecala', Pf.)

1 ἐς δὲ Suid. cod. V   δέ τε δίκη A: δέ σε δίκη GVM: transpos. Küster
2 πάρπηδα V   ἐτίσατο codd.   αὖτις Schneider: αὖθις codd.   3 'δὶς
τόσον (sc. τιμωρὸς) ἔσσεται, nisi δὶς τόσον τείσεται scribendum' (Pf.)
Call. Hecalae trib. Hecker, p. 122

146 (359 Pf.)

εἷλε δὲ πασσαγίην, τόδε δ' ἔννεπεν

Suid. iv. 64. 21 πασσαγίην· πανοπλίαν. "εἷλε—ἔννεπεν"
Call. trib. Ruhnken, Epist. ad Ernest. p. 21 Tittm.; Hecalae Naeke, p. 237

147 (360 Pf.)

οἷος ἐκεῖνος ἀεὶ περιδέξιος ἥρως

Suid. iv. 94. 1 περιδέξιος· ὁ καὶ τῆι ἀριστερᾶι ἐργαζόμενος ... περιδέξιος καὶ ὁ
σοφός. "οἷος—ἥρως" παρὰ Καλλ.

ἐκεῖνος ἀεὶ om. codd. FV: ἀεὶ om. A
Hecalae assignavit Hecker, p. 99 (contra Naeke, p. 95)

148 (362 Pf.)

περιπηχύναντες

Suid. iv. 105. 24 "περιπηχύναντες" [-ήναντες cod. V]· περιπλεξάμενοι παρὰ
Καλλ.
Hecalae trib. Naeke, p. 169

149 (363 Pf.)

καὶ ἀγλαὰ πίcεα γαίηc

βόcκεο

1–2 Suid. iv. 134. 22 πίcεα· οἱ κάθυγροι τόποι. "καὶ—βόcκεο"

___

2 βόcκετο coni. Hecker
Call. trib. Ruhnken, *Epist. ad Ernest.* p. 21 Tittm.; *Hecalae* Hecker, p. 108, de tauro Marathonio cogitans

150 (369 Pf.)

τέρπνιcτον

Suid. iv. 527. 26 "τέρπνιcτον"· ἐπιτερπέcτερον, προcφιλέcτερον [-τατον cod. G] 'Fort. Schol. in Call.' (Adler ad loc.); cf. Wendel, *Gnomon*, 15 (1939), 43

151 (372 Pf.)

ὑδέουcιν

Suid. iv. 634. 15 "ὑδέουcιν"· ἅιδουcι, λέγουcιν
Glossa cum explicatione alibi non invenitur; Call. *Hecalae* trib. Pfeiffer. In *SH* 257. 33 (*Aet.* 3) ὑδέουcιν legitur; cf. ad fr. 134. An cum fr. 100 cohaeret?

152 (373 Pf.)

ὑληωροί

Suid. iv. 639. 3 ὑληωροί [-οῖc cod. F]· οἷc τὰ [om. F] διὰ τῆc ὕληc ἔργα ἐν φροντίδι ἐcτί. λέγει δὲ τοὺc φύλακαc †τοῦ ὄρουc† [prob. ὤρουc δὲ λέγει τοὺc φύλακαc vel sim., Pf.]
'Fort. Schol. Call.' (Adler ad loc.); cf. Wendel, *Gnomon*, 15 (1939), 43

153 (375 Pf.)

θῆκε δὲ λᾶαν

cκληρὸν ὑπόκρηνον

1–2 Suid. iv. 672. 3 ὑπόκρηνον [-κρημνον cod. F]· ὑπὸ τὴν κεφαλήν. "θῆκε—ὑπόκρηνον"

___

2 ὑπόκρημνον F
Call. *Hecalae* dedit Hecker, p. 117

154 (377 Pf.)

ψιcθεῖεν

Suid. iv. 847. 23 ψίω ... καὶ "ψιcθεῖεν"· ψωμιcθεῖεν, τραφεῖεν διὰ ψιχῶν
'Fort. Schol. Call. *Hec.*' (Adler ad loc.); cf. Wendel, *Gnomon*, 15 (1939), 43. An
de infantibus quos Hecala nutriverat (Hollis, coll. fr. 48)?

155 (ad 245 Pf.)

χυτλώcαιντο

Suid. iv. 836. 1 "χυτλώcαιντο"· ἀλείψαιντο
'Nisi error codd. pro sing. = ζ 80, novum *Hecalae* fragmentum' (Pf.)

FRAGMENTA INCERTA

156 inc. sed. (495 Pf.)

Νικαίης ἀγλῖθες ἀπ' Ὀργάδος

Didym. ad Dem. 13. 32, *Pap. Berol.* 9780, col. xiv. 34 (Berl. Klass. Texte, i, p. 69 = Didym. *Comm. in Dem.* edd. Pearson et Stephens (1978), pp. 51–2) κ[αὶ] ἔστιν ὁ λόγος τὰ νῦν τῶι Δη[μ]οσθένε[ι π]ερ[ὶ] τῆς Μεγαρικῆς Ὀργάδ[ος], ἧς καὶ Καλλίμαχός που μνημονεύων φης[ί]· "Νικαίης—Ὀργάδος" (suppl. Diels)

νεικαιης pap.
Καλλίμαχός που, i.e. in *Hecala* coni. Wilamowitz in ed. pr.; fort. inter olera Theseo apposita (cf. frr. 36, 38–9, fort. 157)

157 inc. sed. (585 Pf.)

Plin. *NH* 25. 167 'erigeron a nostris vocatur senecio ... nomen hoc Graeci dederunt, quia vere canescit. caput eius numerosa [-ose v.l.] dividitur lanugine, qualis est spinae, inter divisuras exeunte, quare Callimachus eam *acanthida* appellavit, alii pappum. nec deinde Graecis de ea constat'
Inter olera Theseo ab Hecala apposita acanthida quoque fuisse coni. Naeke, p. 138

158 inc. sed. (682 Pf.)

τί δάκρυον εὗδον ἐγείρεις;

Schol. (L) S. *OC* 510 δεινὸν μὲν τὸ πάλαι κείμενον ἤδη κακόν, ὦ ξεῖν', ἐπεγείρειν] τῆς Ἰσμήνης ἀποστάσης ὁ χορὸς ἐρωτᾶι τὸν Οἰδίποδα καί φησι· τὸ ἐπεγείρειν μὲν καὶ ἀνακινεῖν τὰ πάλαι συμβάντα δυσχερές, ὅμως δὲ μαθεῖν ἐπιθυμῶ τὴν αἰτίαν τῆς πηρώσεως· καὶ ἔστι παθητικά· Καλλ. "τί—ἐγείρεις;"
Hecalae Theseo respondenti (cf. fr. 40. 3 sqq.) convenire vidit Naeke, p. 156 (cf. Schneider, p. 181). Fr. 41 adiunxit Hollis, ut fiat τί δάκρυον εὗδον ἐγείρεις; | οὐ γάρ μοι πενίη πατρώιος κτλ.

159 inc. sed. (619 Pf.)

ἀβάλε μηδ' ἀβόλησα

Schol.[1] Dionys. Thr. (*Gr. Gr.* iii, p. 100. 18 Hilg.) τὰ ... εὐχῆς σημαντικά] δι' αὐτῶν γὰρ εὐκτικὰς συντάξεις σημαίνομεν· "εἴθ'" ὡς ἡβώοιμι (*H* 157, al.)· τὸ γὰρ αἴθε εἴθε φησὶν ὁ ποιητής. καὶ Καλλ. "ἀβάλε—ἀβόλησα" Schol.² Dionys. Thr. (*Gr.* Gr. iii, p. 430. 29, 31 Hilg.) τὸ εἴθε καὶ τὸ ἀβάλε ἐκ παραλλήλου κεῖται ... τὸ ἀβάλε παρὰ Καλλ., ἔνθα φησίν· "ἀβάλε—ἀβόλησα", τουτέστιν εἴθε μηδὲ cυνέτυχον· τὸ γὰρ ἀβολῆcαι [ἀμβολῆcαι codd.] cυντυχεῖν ἐcτιν, ὡς καὶ παρ' Ὁμήρωι (Π 847) ... ἀντεβόλησαν ἀντὶ τοῦ cυνέτυχον

ἀβάλε schol.²: ἀβάλλε schol.¹ ἀβόλησα schol.¹: ἀμβόλησα schol.² bis: ἀβόλησαν e cod. quodam schol.¹ Ernesti, fort. per errorem 'In Suid. s.v. ἀβάλε· εἴθε· "ἀβάλε ⟨...⟩", fort. posterius ἀβάλε non per errorem repetitum et delendum, sed initium versus [*Hecalae*? an Agathiae, *AP* 7. 583. 1?] in exemplum allati' (Pf.)

160 inc. auct. (370 dub. Pf.)

καὶ ἄγριον οἶδμα θαλάσσης

Suid. iv. 616. 27 οἶδμα· κῦμα, ἢ πέλαγος. "καὶ—θαλάσσης" Call. *Hecalae* trib. Kapp (fr. 146, om. vocab. καὶ). Haec verba bis apud Greg. Naz. (*Carm.* 2. 1. 1. 21, 2. 2. 5. 203) invenies; qua de re certior factus, Pfeiffer (ii, p. 121) fragmentum deleri iussit. Sed in ambiguo manet unde sumpserit Suidas, nam Gregorius verba Callimachi (e.g. fr. 26) mutuari solet. In *Hec.* fr. 47. 7]καὶ κῦμα και̣ ἄγριον οἶδμα θαλάσσης reponere voluerunt Barigazzi et Krafft

161 inc. sed. (591 Pf.)

τεθναίην ὅτ' ἐκεῖνον ἀποπνεύσαντα πυθοίμην

Schol. (M) A. *Ch.* 438 ἔπειτ' ἐγὼ νοσφίσας ὀλοίμαν] ἐκ τούτου εἴρηται τὸ "τεθναίην—πυθοίμην" Καλλιμάχου

οὔτ' M: corr. P. Victorius *Hecalae* trib. Eldick (*Suspic. Spec.* c. 4, p. 23), tum Hecker, p. 120; contradixit Naeke, p. 248 sq. Hunc versum in fr. 49. 18 Barigazzi vult reponere, 'optime, quod ad sensum attinet; sed]ν̣ε̣ν̣cαντα] aegerrime legas' (*SH*)

162 inc. sed. (721 Pf.)

ἵν' ἀμαζόνες ἄνδρες ἔασιν

Theodos. π. Κλίc. τῶν εἰς ῶν Βαρυτόνων (*Excerpta ex Libris Herodiani*, ed. A. Hilgard, Heidelberg, 1886–7), p. 23. 2 et Theognost. *Can.* (*AO* ii, p. 38. 22) τὰ εἰς ῶν λήγοντα ὀξύτονα ἔχοντα πρὸ τοῦ ῶ ἕν τι τῶν διπλῶν ἢ τὸ c, ἐπίθετα ὄντα ἢ ἐθνικά, διὰ τοῦ ο κλίνονται [διὰ—κλίνονται Theod.: πρέπει τὸ ο ἐπὶ τῆς γενικῆς, οἷον Theogn.]. Αὐcών Αὐcόνος ... Ἀμαζών Ἀμαζόνος· λέγεται γὰρ καὶ ἀρcενικῶς, ὡς παρὰ Καλλιμάχωι [Theogn.: Κρατίνωι Theod.]· "ἵν'—ἔαcιν" Cf. *Et. Gud.*

p. 104. 21 de Stef. (inde *Et. Mag.* p. 75. 53) Ἀμαζών· ὄνομα ἔθνους ... καὶ ἀμαζόνες· οἱ πένητες, οἱ μᾶζαν μὴ ἔχοντες ἤτοι [v.l. ἤγουν] τροφήν

ἕαcιν Theodos.: ἑωcιν (sic) Theognost. cod. Barocc. (emendaverat Dindorf) Cf. fr. 55, ubi γηφάγοι simili modo explicatur; 'ludere possis ἵν' ἀμαζόνες ἄνδρες ἕαcιν | γηφάγοι (ex *Hecala*?)' (Pf.)

163 inc. sed. (489 Pf.)

οἱοί τε βιοπλανὲς ἀγρὸν ἀπ' ἀγροῦ
φοιτῶcιν

1–2 Choerob. ap. Theodos. (*Gr. Gr.* iv. 1, p. 401. 34 Hilg.) καὶ πάλιν ἐcτὶν ἐπιτηδέες καὶ κατὰ κρᾶcιν ἐπιτηδεῖc. καὶ βιοπλανέες καὶ κατὰ κρᾶcιν βιοπλανεῖc, καὶ λοιπὸν κατὰ ἀποβολὴν τοῦ ι γίνεται ἐπιτηδές καὶ βιοπλανές· ὡc παρὰ Καλλ. "οἵ τε—φοιτῶcιν" Iohann. Philop. Τονικὰ Παραγγέλματα (ex Herodian. prosod. excerpt.), p. 15. 25 Dind. αἱ μὲν οὖν εἰc εc λήγουcαι οὐδέποτε ὀξύνονται, Πάριδες, μῆνες, Αἴαντες· χωρὶς εἰ μὴ ἐκ πάθους εἶεν διὰ τὸ βιοπλανές: "οἷοι τε— ἀγροῦ" καὶ τὸ ἐπιτηδές (A 142) 1 *Et. Gen.* AB s.v. βιοπλανές (p. 67 Berger; cf. *Et. Mag.* p. 198. 11 Gaisf.)· τὸ ἐντελὲς βιοπλανέες, ὡc ἀκλεέες ἀκλεέc. οὕτως Ἡρωδιανόc (cf. ii. 428. 21 adn. Lentz) Apollon. Dysc. *de Pron.* (*Gr. Gr.* i. 1, p. 93. 8 Schn.) ἔνιοι τὸ "βιόπλανες" (βιοπλανεις cod.) βαρύνουcιν ἀπὸ τοῦ βιοπλανῆς καὶ ἐπίτηδες καὶ ἄκλεες

---

1 οἱοί τε Naeke: οἵ οἱ τε Iohann. Philop. codd.: οἵ τε Choerob.   βιόπλανες 'quidam' teste Ap. Dysc.   2 φητῶcιν Choerob. cod. C

Fr. 55 admovit P. Buttmann (*Lexilog. Hom.* p. 43) et alii, de mendicis Hecalae hospitalitatem expertis cogitantes (cf. Naeke, p. 109; Hecker, p. 115); 'id neque probari neque refutari potest' (Pf.)

164 inc. sed. (513 Pf.)

Et. Gen. AB s.v. γραίδιον (= *Et. Mag.* p. 240. 6) ... ἔcτι γραῦιc [γραύιc codd.] γραύιδοc [*Et. Gen.* AB: γραύιδι *Et. Mag.*, unde nonnulli dativum apud Call. fuisse collegerunt] παρὰ Καλλ.

De Hecala cogitavit Schneider (fr. 326; cf. p. 177)

165 inc. auct. (732 Pf.)

πολλὰ μάτην κεράεccιν ἐc ἠέρα θυμήναντα

Cic. *Att.* 8. 5. 1 'nam quod ad te non scripseram, postea audivi a tertio miliario tum eum isse πολλὰ—θυμήναντα' Catullum (64. 111, de Minotauro) hunc versum expressisse iam vidit J. Scaliger; 'erunt fort. qui eum Hecalae Callimacheae ei parti attribuant in qua sermo erat de tauro Marathonio' (M. Haupt, *Opusc.* ii. (1875), 81)

166 inc. auct. (756 Pf.)

μύρσον ἐc ὠτώεντα παλαιφαμένης ἄγνοιο

Et. Gen. AB s.v. μύρcοc (cf. *Et. Mag.* p. 595. 33, *Et. Sym.* V ap. Gaisf., 'Zonar.'
p. 1375 Tittm.)· "μύρcον—ἄγνοιο". μύρcοc πλεκτόν τί ἐcτιν ἀγγεῖον ἐξ ἄγνου
πλεκόμενον λύγων· παλαιφαμένης δέ, τῆς πάλαι τετμημένης ἄγνου [sic *Et. Gen.* A,
Et. Sym. V: παλαιφ. δέ om. *Et. Gen.* B]　　　Cf. Hesych. s.v. μύρcοc· κόφινος ὦτα
ἔχων

παλαιφαμένης τε *Et. Gen.* AB, *Et. Mag.*: τε del. Tittm., alii
De Call. *Hecala* primus cogitavit Meineke (*FCG* ii. 1, p. 6, *Anal. Alex.* p. 168),
tum Hecker, p. 117. Cornicis de Ericthonio narrationi trib. Pfeiffer, coll. Ov.
Met. 2. 554

167 inc. sed. (519 Pf.)

ἀλλὰ θεῆς ἥτις με διάκτορον ἔλλαχε Παλλάς

Et. Mag. p. 268. 10 διάκτορος (in *Et. Gen.* AB et *Et. Sym.* V s.v. διάκτορωι
desunt Call. verba)· ... ἢ ὁ διάγων τὰς ψυχάς· τοῦ γὰρ Ἑρμοῦ ἐπίθετον· παρὰ δὲ
τοῖς ἄλλοις ποιηταῖς ἁπλῶς ἐπὶ τοῦ διακόνου τίθεται. Καλλ. ἐπὶ γλαυκὸς τὸ
ἐπίθετον· "ἀλλὰ—Παλλάς"
Hecalae fragmentis adscripsit Meineke, *Call.* p. 145 (*Aetiis* Schneider, fr. 164)

168 inc. sed. (608 Pf.)

κάρτ᾽ ἀγαθὴ κικυμωίς

Schol. (VM Ald.) Ar. *Av.* 261 (p. 61 White) κικκαβαῦ] τὰς γλαύκας οὕτω
φωνεῖν λέγουcιν, ὅθεν κικαβᾶς [V: κικκαβὰς cett.: -άβας Dindorf in Thes. s.v.]
αὐτὰς λέγουcιν. ἔcτι δὲ ἱερὰ τῆς Ἀθηνᾶς. οἱ δὲ κικυμωῖδας [V: κικκυβοίδας M:
κικυμοίδας Ald.: κικυμίδας Bentley] ὡς Καλλ. "κάρτ᾽—κικυμωίς". Cf. Hesych.
κικυμῆϊς [lege -ωίς Pf.]· γλαῦξ

κικυμωίς V: κικκυβοίς M: κικυμίς Musurus in Ald.
Propter noctuae commemorationem *Hecalae* fragmentis incertis inseruit Kapp
(fr. 67)

169 inc. sed. (552 Pf.)

Βριληccοῦ λαγόνεccιν ὁμούριον ἐκτίccαντο

Galen. π. Προγν. Cφυγμ. 3. 16 (ix, p. 368 Kühn) ὁ μὲν τρόπος τῆς τοιαύτης
χρήσεως ὀνομάζεται μεταφορά ... καθ᾽ οἵαν ὁμοιότητα καὶ πόδες [πόδης Ἴδης
cod. Laud.] εἴρηνται καὶ κορυφαὶ καὶ λαγόνες ὄρους ... ἐὰν οὖν τις ἐπὶ ζώιου
ποιούμενος τὸν λόγον, εἶτα πόδας εἰπὼν ἢ λαγόνας ἀξιώσηι [-cει edd.] μήτε τῶν

ποδῶν ἀκούειν, ὡς ἅπαντες ἀκούουσιν, μήτε τῶν λαγόνων, ὡς σύνηθες, ἀλλ' οὕτως δεῖν φάσκηι [-σκει cod. Laud.] λαγόνων ἀκούειν, ὡς ἐπὶ τοῦ ὄρους τοῦ Βριλησσοῦ Καλλ. εἴρηκε, "Βριλησσοῦ—ἐκτίσσαντο", γελοιότατος ἂν εἴη, διττῆι τε καὶ παλινδρομούσηι χρώμενος ἀπὸ τῶν οὐ κυρίων ἐπὶ τὰ κύρια τῆι μεταφορᾶι

Βριλλήσου Galen cod. Laud. 57: corr. Bentley λαγόνεσσιν ὁμούριον ἐκτίσσαντο Bentley: λαγόνες εἰσὶ νόμου ὃν ἐκτήσαντο Galen. cod.
Propter Attici montis mentionem *Hecalae* dubitanter trib. Naeke, p. 225. Ad carminis finem refert Hollis, coll. *Dieg.* xi. 6–7 τέμενος ἱδρύσατο Ἑκαλείου Δι[ό]ς

170 inc. sed. (704 Pf.)

Steph. Byz. s.v. Ἁλιμοῦς (om. RV), δῆμος τῆς Λεοντίδος φυλῆς. Καλλ. δὲ πόλιν ἡγεῖται [-το R]
De *Hecala* cogitavit Hecker (*Com. Crit. de Anth. Gr.* (1843), p. 197)

171 inc. sed. (680 Pf.)

ὑπεὶρ ἅλα κεῖνος ἐνάσθη
Ἀλκαθόου τίς ἄπυστος

1–2 Schol. (L) S. OC 3 τίς τὸν πλανήτην Οἰδίπουν] ... δύναται ... καὶ τοῖς ἄνω συνάπτεσθαι τοῦ τίς μὴ πυςματικῶς κειμένου, ἀλλ' ἀντὶ τοῦ ἢ ἄρθρου, ὥστε τῶι "πόλιν" συντετάχθαι καὶ τὸν λόγον ἔχειν οὕτως· "τίνας χώρους ἀφίγμεθα ἢ τίνων ἀνδρῶν πόλιν, ἢ τὸν πλανήτην Οἰδίπουν δέξεται;" ὅτι δὲ τὸ [L: τῶι Brunck] τίς ἀντὶ ἄρθρου χρῶνται, Καλλ. φησιν οὕτως· "ὑπεὶρ—ἄπυστος"

2 ἀλκάθοου τις L, corr. l (Lobkovicianus): ἀλκάθοον Lascaris ἄπυστος L: corr. Bentley (ἄπυστ' Schneider, 'pentametrum' efficiens)
'Quis cuius Alcathoi ignarus sit non constat. ... Fort. fabula ignota de Alcathoo Megarensi. Res et Argolicae et Megarenses passim in *Hecala*; duo hexametri epici nulli carmini Callimacheo, quod sciamus, inseri possunt nisi *Hecalae* aut *Galateae*, fr. 378 (aut carmini de Arsinoes nuptiis, fr. 392?)' (Pf.)

172 inc. sed. (611 Pf.)

Καλλιχόρωι ἐπὶ φρητὶ καθέζεο παιδὸς ἄπυστος

Schol. (PM) Clem. Al. *Protr.* 2. 20. 1 (i, p. 303. 25 Stählin) ἀλωμένη γὰρ ἡ Δηὼ κατὰ ζήτησιν τῆς θυγατρὸς τῆς Κόρης περὶ τὸν Ἐλευσῖνα ... ἀποκάμνει καὶ φρέατι ἐπικαθίζει λυπουμένη.] τὸ φρέαρ Καλλίχορον οἱ παλαιοὶ ὀνομάζουσιν. Καλλ. φησιν· "Καλλιχόρωι—ἄπυστος"

ἄπυστος PM: corr. Naeke, p. 11
De *Aetiis* cogitavit Schneider, fr. 469 (probavit Pf.). Dubitantissime fr. 173 inc. sed. adiungit Hollis, coll. *H. Hom. Dem.* 98–101

173 inc. sed. (490 Pf.)

γρήϊον εἶδος ἔχουςα

[? Choerob.], π. Ποςότητος, exc. ex Herodian. orth. (Cramer, *AO* ii. 286. 9) τὰ εἰς ε̄ λήγοντα ὀνόματα μονοςύλλαβα περιςπώμενα διὰ τοῦ ειος παραγόμενα διὰ τῆς ει διφθόγγου γράφεται· οἷον βοῦς βόειος . . .· δεῖ δὲ προςθεῖναι μὴ ὄντα ἀπὸ τῶν εἰς αυς, ἐπειδὴ ταῦτα διὰ τοῦ ι γράφονται· οἷον γραῦς γράϊος καὶ γρήϊος παρὰ Καλλ.· "γρήϊον—ἔχουςα", τουτέςτι γραός   *Epim. Hom. Alph.* (*AO* i. 295. 25) νήϊον (Γ 62) διὰ τοῦ ι . . . ὁμοίως καὶ τὸ γραῦς γραὸς γράϊος καὶ γρήϊος καὶ "γρήϊον—ἔχουςα" (inde *Et. Gud.* p. 407. 41 Sturz et cod. Sorb. ap. Gaisf. ad *Et. Mag.* p. 603. 23)   *Et. Mag.* p. 603. 15 (cf. *Et. Sym.* ap. Gaisf.; om. *Et. Gen.* AB) s.v. νηΐτης· . . . "γρήιον—ἔχουςα"   Hesych. s.v. "γρήϊον"· παλαιόν (= *Et. Mag.* p. 241. 13)

γρηΐδιον cod. Sorb.
'Fort. *Hec.*' (Pf.; cf. Naeke, p. 116). Vide supra ad fr. 172 inc. sed.

174 inc. sed. (705 Pf.)

εἰς Ἀςίνην Ἁλυκόν τε καὶ ἃμ πόλιν Ἑρμιονήων

Steph. Byz. s.v. Ἁλυκος, πόλις Πελοποννήςου· "εἰς—Ἑρμιονήων", Καλλ.

πυλιν V   Ἑρμιονίων codd.: corr. Berkelius
Hecalae vindicare velit Naeke (p. 208), fabulae Thiodamantis in *Aet.* 1 Hecker (p. 78)

175 inc. sed. (684 Pf.)

Schol. Stat. *Theb.* 4. 46 sq. '(armat . . .) | quaeque pavet longa spumantem valle Charadron | Neris] "Neris" montis nomen Argivi, ut ait Callimachus'
Alia nomina Argiva ex *Hecala* in *Theb.* 4 Statius transtulit (v. comm. ad fr. 95); hic quoque de *Hecala* cogitavit Naeke (p. 174), etsi rem incertam esse ipse statuit

176 inc. sed. (687 Pf.)

δαίμων, τῆι κόλποιςιν ἐνιπτύουςι γυναῖκες

Schol. (K) Theocr. 6. 39 ἔπτυςα κόλπον] τὸ νεμεςητὸν ἐκτρεπόμενοι ποιοῦςι τοῦτο, καὶ μάλιςτα αἱ γυναῖκες. Καλλ.· "δαίμων—γυναῖκες"

δαῖμον Bentley   τῆι F. Jacobs (*Animadv. in Epigr. Anth. Gr.* ii. 3. 112): τι cod. K: τρίς Bentley   ἐνιπτύουςι Hecker (*Philol.* 4 (1849), 479): ἐπι- cod. K
Hoc fragmentum cum fr. 116 coniungere conati sunt Hecker (p. 121) et Schneider (fr. 235)

177 inc. sed. (527a Pf.)

ὅν τε μάλιστα βοῶν ποθέουϲιν ἐχῖνοι

Et. Gen. AᵘB s.v. ἐχῖνος (= *Et. Mag.* p. 404. 47, *Et. Sym.* V ap. Gaisf., *Et. Gud.* codd. interpolati, p. 574. 17 de Stef.)· χερϲαῖον ζῶιον ... ἐχῖνος δὲ καὶ ἡ γαϲτήρ, ὥϲ φηϲι Καλλ. [ὥϲ φηϲι om. *Et. Gen.* A: ὥϲ—Καλλ. om. *Et. Sym.* V et *Et. Gud.*] "ὅν τε—ἐχῖνοι" *Et. Gud.* p. 574. 8 Stef. Cελ(εύκου)· ἐχῖνος· τὸ ζῶιον ... κακῶς δὲ Καλλ. τῶν βοῶν τὰς κοιλίας εἶπεν

ὅν τε *Et. Gen.* B (teste Alpers), *Et. Mag.*: οὔτε *Et. Gen.* A: ὅτε *Et. Sym.* V: ὅτε vel ὅτι codd. *Et. Gud.*: ὅττι Schneider (fr. 250a)   ἐχῖνοι *Et. Gen.* AB, *Et. Sym.* V, *Et. Gud.*, *Et. Mag.* DM: ἐχῖνον *Et. Mag.* codd. cett.

De *Hecala* cogitaverat Schneider, p. 489. 'Ad lexeon librum, vix ad Salusti commentarium, redire videtur Suid. s.v. ἐχῖνος ... καὶ ἡ γαϲτὴρ τοῦ βοός; etsi hoc testimonium nihil valet, fr. fort. *Hecalae* fragmentis variis de bubus [v. ad fr. 301 Pf.] addendum est' (Pf.). Fort. fr. 102 admovendum (Hollis)?

178 inc. sed. (725 Pf.)

καὶ ὡς λύκος ὠρυοίμην

Zenod. Philet. tract. de vocibus animalium (G. Studemund, *Anec. Var. Graeca* (1886), p. 105. 1 e cod. Taurin. B VII. 20, ubi nomen auctoris deest; p. 289 e cod. Leid. Voss. IV. 76, quo iam Valckenaer (*Animadv. ad Ammon.* p. 229) usus est) ὠρυγὴ κυρίως λέγεται [λεγ. om. cod. Voss.] ἡ τῶν λύκων [Taur.: κυνῶν Voss.] φωνή, καὶ ὠρύεϲθαι· "καὶ—ὠρυοίμην" παρὰ Καλλ.· ὠρύεϲθαι γὰρ ἐπὶ λύκων εἶπεν

'Propter finem spondiacum et consecutionem vocalium ο—υ fort. potius de *Hecala* cogitandum est quam de *Aetiis*' (Pf.)

179 inc. auct. (741 Pf.)

Et. Gen. AB (cf. *Et. Mag.* p. 149. 13) s.v. ἀρρηφόροι καὶ ἀρρηφορία. ἑορτὴ ἐπιτελουμένη τῆι Ἀθηνᾶι ἐν Cκιροφοριῶνι μηνί· λέγεται δὲ καὶ διὰ τοῦ ε̄ ἐρρηφορία, παρὰ τὸ τὰ ἄρρητα ἢ [Eitrem: καὶ *Et.*] μυϲτήρια φέρειν, ἢ ἐὰν διὰ τοῦ ε̄, παρὰ τὴν Ἕρϲην τὴν Κέκροπος θυγατέρα ἐρϲηφορία· ταύτηι γὰρ ἦγον τὴν ἑορτήν. οὕτω Cαλούϲτιος

Salusti commentario in Call. *Hecalam* (quem affert *Et. Gen.* ad frr. 9 et 29) trib. Reitzenstein (*Ind. Rost.* 1890/1, p. 15)

COMMENTARY

COMMENTARY

THE *DIEGESIS* (AND *ARGUMENTUM HECALAE*)

The *Diegesis* in *P. Med.* 18 (= pap. 1) is of great value, since it includes the opening line of the poem complete, and also some details of the plot which were previously unknown. It seems to concentrate on the bare outline of the story, without much regard for the relative weight and proportion of the elements. For example, the centre-piece of the *Hecale*, much admired by later generations, was the entertainment of Theseus in Hecale's cottage (frs. 27 ff.) during which she told her life-story in a speech of hardly less than 100 lines, and perhaps appreciably more (frs. 41 ff.). The Diegetes passes over this whole episode in two words, ἐνταῦθα ἐξενοδοκήθη (x. 30–1). He is also not interested in digressions from the main theme, and so omits entirely the substantial interlude in which an old crow speaks for about 90 lines (frs. 70 ff.). In the notes below I give the numbers of the fragments which seem to correspond to phrases of the *Diegesis*, and also mention parallels in the much more fragmentary *Argumentum Hecalae* from *P. Oxy.* 2258 (= pap. 2).

x. 20–1 Θηςεὺς φυγὼν τὴν ἐκ Μηδείης ἐπιβουλήν: cf. frs. 3–7, and perhaps *Arg.* 3 πεφευ[.

22–3 ἅτ' αἰφνίδιον ἀνακομιϲθὲν ἐκ Τροιζῆνος μειράκιον: fr. 9. 1 mentions Troezen in connection with the sword hidden under a rock there (by means of which Aegeus recognized his son). Pfeiffer suggested (i, p. 229) that this recognition led the poet to digress retrospectively on the hero's upbringing in Troezen (fr. 12 and perhaps frs. 13–15).

23 οὐ προσδοκήσαντι: cf. fr. 8.

23–5 βουλόμενος ... ἐξελθεῖν: we now know that fr. 17 is part of a speech by Theseus attempting to persuade his father to let him go out against the bull.

24–5 ἐπὶ τὸν λυμαινόμενον τὰ περὶ Μαραθῶνα ταῦρον: ? cf. fr. 16.

25–6 ὅπωϲ χειρώϲαιτο: the verb is perhaps used in fr. 17. 8 (?corrupt).

26 καὶ εἰργόμενοϲ: ? cf. *Arg.* 5 ἐκπέμπε[. Presumably there was a speech of Aegeus expressing fears for Theseus' safety (cf. fr. 69. 7) and unwillingness to let him go to Marathon, but of this nothing seems to survive (?unless conceivably fr. 122).

26 κρύφα: cf. *Arg.* 6 κρύβδα.

27–8 Fr. 18 describes the transition from a brilliant midday to a thunderstorm at supper-time.

28 ὑετοῦ ῥαγέντοϲ: cf. *Arg.* 7 ὑε]τοῦ κα[τ]αρραγέντοϲ, fr. 18. 9 μέγαν ὑετόν.

29 κατ' ἐϲχατιάν: see LSJ for ἐϲχατιά = 'estate at the foot of a mountain'; the form ἐϲχατιή is Homeric, and may well have been used in the *Hecale*.

οἰκίδιον θεϲαϲάμενοϲ: ? fr. 26; cf. *Arg.* 9 ο]ἶκον Ἑκάληϲ.

30–1 ἐνταῦθα ἐξενοδοκήθη: frs. 27–63.

31–2 πρὸϲ δὲ τὴν ἕω ἀναϲτάϲ: fr. 64. Barrett also thinks of fr. 113 in this connection.

32–3 χειρωϲάμενοϲ δὲ τὸν ταῦρον: frs. 67–9.

x. 33–xi. 1 ἐπανήει ὡϲ τὴν Ἑκάλην: for Theseus' return to Hecale's cottage see below, App. IV.

xi. 1–2 αἰφνίδιον δὲ ταύτην εὑρὼν τεθνηκυῖαν: fr. 79.

2–3 ἐπιϲτε[νάξ]αιϲ ὡϲ ἐψευϲμένοϲ τῆϲ προϲδοκίαϲ: ? fr. 125.

μετὰ θάνατον: I am convinced by L. Castiglioni (*RIL* 70 (1937), 57) that these words should be transposed to follow τοῦτο (4), viz. τοῦτο ⟨μετὰ θάνατον⟩ ἐπετέλεϲεν, but have left the text unaltered so as to preserve the line-arrangement of the papyrus.

3–4 εἰϲ ἀμοιβὴν τῆϲ ξενίαϲ: cf. frs. 82–3.

6–7 τέμενοϲ ἱδρύϲατο Ἑκαλείου Δι[ό]ϲ: ? fr. 169 inc. sed.

FRS. 1–2

The poem opened with Hecale herself, who may have been named in the gap between frs. 1 and 2. In Petr. 135. 8. 15–16 (= above, Test. 7) 'qualis in Actaea quondam fuit hospita terra | digna sacris Hecale', the words 'in Actaea quondam fuit . . . terra' clearly allude to fr. 1, and 'hospita' perhaps to fr. 2. From the fact that the *Diegesis*, having quoted the first line, goes straight on to Theseus' escape from Medea's plot, one might infer that the introduction was quite brief.

Fr. 1 (230 Pf.)

Ἀκταίη τις ἔναιεν Ἐρεχθέος ἔν ποτε γουνῶι: the first line of the poem, as revealed by the *Diegesis*. Call.'s method of opening could hardly be more simple and straightforward: 'once upon a time there lived an Attic woman in the hill country of Erectheus'. Previously Ἀκταίη τις ἔναιεν was credited to Call. by *Et. Gud.*; Couat (*Alexandrian Poetry*, p. 387, wishing to read Ἀκταίην) and Weinberger (*Philol.* 76 (1920), 71) had already conjectured that these were the first words of the *Hecale*.

Ἀκταίη: Attica was also called Ἀκτή (Steph. Byz.; cf. Call. *Iamb.* fr. 194. 68 Pf.; Philoch. *FGH* 328 F 93; Paus. 1. 2. 6), an older name according to Euphorion (fr. 34. 1 Ἀκτῆς δὲ παροίτερα φωνηθείςης). The adjective Ἀκταῖος (but in Euph. fr. 16 Ἄκτιος Αἰγεύς) is not attested before Call.: its great popularity in subsequent Greek and Roman verse (e.g. Lyc. *Alex.* 504; Dion. Per. 1023; Maximus 494 (? this and Val. Flacc. glancing at Eratosthenes' *Erigone*); Nonn. *Dion.* 24. 95 Ἀκταίη ... Ἐρεχθέα; Virg. *Ecl.* 2. 24; Ov. *Met.* 2. 720 etc.; *Ciris* 102 'Actaeos ... colles'; Sen. *Phaed.* 900; Val. Flacc. 2. 68; Stat. *Theb.* 12. 464; Claud. *Rapt. Pros.* 3. 54) must be primarily due to this line of the *Hecale* (cf. Petr. 135. 8. 15, quoted above).

Ἐρεχθέος ἔν ποτε γουνῶι: a general description (modelled on Hes. *Th.* 54 γουνοῖςιν Ἐλευθῆρος) of the mountainous area surrounding Marathon. Hecale's cottage probably stood on the slopes of Brilessus (Pentelicus, cf. fr. 169 inc. sed.) whence Theseus must 'go down' to the Marathonian plain in fr. 40. 1 (for the location of the deme Hecale see above, Introd. sect. II with n. 10). Nonnus more than once (*Dion.* 38. 74, 39. 213) associates Erectheus with Marathon—but note that in Nonnus 'Marathon' may mean no more than 'Athens'—and, according to one school of thought, Erectheus' daughter Oreithyia ('gelidi coniunx Actaea tyranni' in Ov. *Met.* 6. 711, Μαραθωνίδος ... νύμφης in Nonn. *Dion.* 39. 113) was snatched by Boreas from Mt. Brilessus (see on frs. 86–7).

ἔν ποτε γουνῶι: γουνός is explained by *Et. Mag.* as ὑψηλὸς τόπος. Compare *Od.* 11. 323 ἐς γουνὸν Ἀθηνάων, [Hes.] fr. 43a. 67. For the word order (Lapp, *Tropis et Figuris*, p. 37) one can cite, at the beginning of a narrative, *Iamb.* fr. 194. 6 Pf. ἔν κοτε Τμώλωι, *H.* 5. 57 ἔν ποκα Θήβαις, and Theocr. 18. 1 ἔν ποκ' ἄρα Σπάρται (cf. Clausen, *HSCP* 90 (1986), 164–5).

Pfeiffer's description of the word-break after Ἀκταίη τις as metrically 'contra normam' (see above, Introd. sect. IV. 4a on Meyer's First Law) is not justified. Although τις is postpositive, clearly Call. did not regard Ἀκταίη τις as the equivalent of a single word; cf. *Aet.* fr. 20 Pf. ἐτμήγη δέ, ibid. fr. 75. 10 ἠῶιοι μέν, *H.* 2. 15, 3. 77, 126, 4. 144—note that in each case the first foot is spondaic, a point which perhaps tells against Callimachean authorship of fr. 787 Pf. inc. auct. See further E. G. O'Neill, *YCS* 8 (1942), 108–10, 111 n. 13.

Fr. 2 (281 Pf.)

Hecale's hospitality (also honoured by neighbours at her funeral, fr. 80) is perhaps the most important theme of the whole poem (see further below, App. III). She is like Axylus in *Il.* 6. 14–15 φίλος δ᾽ ἦν ἀνθρώποισι·| πάντας γὰρ φιλέεσκεν ὁδῶι ἔπι οἰκία ναίων, or Ovid's Hyrieus, who says 'hospitibus ianua nostra patet' (*Fast.* 5. 502). This fragment is paraphrased by Michael Choniates (see above, Introd. sect. VIII and below on fr. 69. 1), i. 157 Lambros (= above, Test. 15a) ξενοδόχωι ... ἀγαθῆι καὶ τοῖς παροδεύουσιν ἄκλειστον ἀεὶ προβαλλομένηι τὸ οἴκημα.

1 τίον δέ ἑ: as Pfeiffer notes, epic precedent (*Il.* 23. 705 τίον δέ ἑ; cf. *Od.* 19. 247, [Hes.] fr. 229. 12) and the practice of Call. (*Aet.* fr. 59. 20 Pf. = *SH* 265. 20 τίεν δέ ἑ) both indicate that, in this part of the line, we should write τίον rather than τῖον. Call. places ἑ almost always (exception: *H.* 3. 217), and οἱ usually (e.g. frs. 46. 1, 57, 74. 18), after a short final vowel, so that the original digamma comes into force to prevent hiatus (see Maas, *GM*, para. 133; Mineur, *HD*, p. 43).

2 ἔχε γὰρ τέγος ἀκλήιστον: the 'open door' of hospitality was proverbial: cf. P. *Nem.* 9. 2, Ar. *Ach.* 127 (where the scholiast quotes our fr.), Eup. fr. 265 K. = 286 *PCG*. Gregory of Nazianzus, in a poem much influenced by the *Hecale*, has τέγος ἀκλήιστον* (*Carm.* 1. 2. 2. 302 (*PG* xxxvii. 602)); cf. Nonn. *Dion.* 20. 282 εἰς δόμον ἀκλήιστον, Marian. *AP* 9. 668. 13–14.

It is conceivable that Hecale's hospitality may have been linked to a supposed etymology of her name. In Suid. s.v. Ἑκάλη we find ἡ πρὸς ἑαυτὴν καλοῦσα· 'ἔχε γὰρ τέγος ἀκλήιστον', while *Et. Gen.* offers παρὰ τὸ εἰσκαλεῖν ἢ εἰς καλιὴν πρὸς ἑαυτὴν προτρέπειν (adding that the generous Axylus has an attendant called Καλήσιος in *Il.* 6. 18). If that were so, fr. 81 τοῦτο γὰρ αὐτήν | κωμῆται κάλεον περιηγέες might belong in this vicinity. Etymologizing of names is certainly typical of the Hellenistic poets (e.g. Euph. frs. 57, 90, 96, 176 Powell, *SH* 418. 43–4); in fr. 90 Call. alludes to an etymology of Scylla (cf. also frs. 624 and 739 Pf.). But I am not wholly convinced that Call. is likely to have played with Hecale's name at this stage of the poem, and fr. 81 more probably, I think, relates to posthumous honours for Hecale near the poem's conclusion.

FRS. 3–7 MEDEA ATTEMPTS TO POISON HER STEPSON THESEUS

The *Diegesis* makes plain that Medea's plot against Theseus occurred immediately after the latter's arrival at Athens; it was frustrated when Aegeus recognized his son by means of the sword and sandals which he had left for the boy under a rock in Troezen (cf. frs. 9–11). Thereafter Theseus sets out on his own initiative to fight the Marathonian bull. All this suits what Pfeiffer calls the 'versio vulgata', found most fully in Plut. *Thes.* 12 and 14; at the end of 14, Plutarch cites the Atthidographer Philochorus (*FGH* 328 F 109 = above, Test. 9) who may have been an important source for Call. (see further above, Introd. sect. II, and below on frs. 81 and 169 inc. sed.). This common version is also reflected by the scholia on *Il.* 11. 741, Paus. 2. 3. 8, Dion. Per. 1023 ff., Diod. 4. 55. 6, Apollod. 1. 9. 28, and Tzetzes on Lyc., *Alex.* 175 (some of these references so brief that we can not be sure what further details are implied).

A striking variant occurs in Apollod. *Epit.* 1. 5–6 (cf. Mythogr. Vat. I, 48). There Medea persuades Aegeus to send his (unrecognized) son against the Marathonian bull, in the hope that this will prove fatal. Only after Theseus' triumphant return does she attempt to poison him; father recognizes son just in time, and Medea is banished. In Ovid too (*Met.* 7. 434) the recognition seems to follow the Marathonian triumph (though nothing suggests that Medea was responsible for sending Theseus against the bull). This variant version would make an excellent tragedy, and is commonly supposed to have been the plot of Euripides' *Aegeus* (e.g. T. B. L. Webster, *The Tragedies of Euripides* (1967), 77 ff.), particularly since vase-paintings of appropriate date can be taken to imply such a version (B. B. Shefton, *AJA* 60 (1956), 159–63; id., *Hesperia*, 31 (1962), 350 n. 86). If *P. Oxy.* 3530 comes from E. *Aegeus* (which Gregory Hutchinson doubts), it must be a messenger's speech describing Theseus' fight with the bull—an awkward point for the conventional reconstruction is that Theseus' double parentage is already recognized (ll. 10–11). Sophocles also wrote an *Aegeus*; Pfeiffer rejected as 'ne probabile quidem' the view of Pearson (*Fragments of Sophocles* (1917), i. 16) that Medea had a part in that play (but, for an elaborate construction based on the belief that she did, see Christiane Sourvinou-Inwood, 'Theseus as Son and Stepson' (*BICS*, Suppl. 40 (1979), 56–7)). Although Call. probably did not follow the plot of either tragedy, he would surely have known both, and may have borrowed a few small details from them (cf. on frs. 68, 69. 1, and 165 inc. auct.).

Finally, I draw attention to *P. Oxy.* 3434, a scrap of unidentified prose, which appears to include the bull, 'Hecale' (in Hutchinson's view (*Hellenistic Poetry* (1988), p. 61 n. 70) perhaps Call.'s poem rather than the mythical character), Theseus' arrival at Athens, and his encounter with his stepmother. Dosiadas (date uncertain, but his poem linked to Lycophron's *Alexandra* and the Theocritean *Syrinx*) has a curious detail: after the failure of her plot, Medea fled disguised in male clothing (*Ara* 1, as interpreted by schol.).

Fr. 3 (364 Pf.)

πολύθρονον: explained πολυφάρμακον by Suid.; θρόνα are flowers in *Il.* 22. 441, but, in Hellenistic verse, often φάρμακα (Theocr. 2. 59; Lyc. *Alex.* 674, 1313 (of Medea); Nic. *Ther.* 493, 936): according to schol. Theocr. 2. 59 the usage is Aetolian. I follow Pfeiffer's suggestion that Call. may refer to the poisoner Medea, κούρην Αἰήτεω πολυφάρμακον (Ap. Rh. 3. 27; cf. ibid. 4. 1677).

Elsewhere πολύθρονος occurs only as a variant in Nic. *Ther.* 875 (but Schneider and Gow–Scholfield prefer πολύχνοα); the medical poet Andromachus has πολυθρόνιος (62. 1 Heitsch). Other new compound adjectives with πολυ- in the *Hecale* are πολυπτώξ (fr.

84) and πολύκριμνος (v.l., in the papyrus of fr. 96. 3), the latter to be added to the lists of A. W. James (*Studies in the Language of Oppian of Cilicia* (1970), 169–70) and McLennan (*HZ*, on *H.* 1. 26).

Fr. 4 (232 Pf.)

1–2 ἡ δ' ἐκόηcεν| τοὖνεκεν Αἰγέος ἔcκεν: the subject is clearly Medea (as Reitzenstein first saw), who is quicker-witted than her husband in guessing Theseus' paternity (cf. Stephanie West on *Od.* 4. 141 ff.).

ἐκόηcεν: 'she realized' (ἐνόηcεν Suid.). κοέω is probably to be read in Epich. fr. 35. 14, and was conjectured by Bergk in Anacr. *PMG* 360(= *LGS* 304). 2. The same element is found in θυοcκόος (cf. Erbse, *Scholia Graeca in Homeri Iliadem*, v (1977), 557–8).

2 τοὖνεκεν: Pfeiffer explains this as a demonstrative used for a relative οὕνεκεν, as τόφρα probably stands for ὄφρα in *H.* 4. 39 (more examples in Pfeiffer, cf. Lapp, *Tropis et Figuris*, p. 132). Ancient grammarians vehemently debated such questions (see R. Schneider. *Grammatici Graeci*, i. 1. 238, 2. 241), and pseudo-Ammonius (*de Adfinium Vocabulorum Differentia*, 473) condemns Call. on two counts—because he wrote τοὖν- instead of οὖν-, and -κεν instead of -κα.

Αἰγέος: Lobel tentatively suggested that this word, and this fragment of Call., may be recognized in *P. Oxy.* 2823(= *SH* 280). 8, given below; the letters ΑΙΓΕΟC could be shared between more than one word, or else be αἴγεος (cf. *Od.* 9. 196 αἴγεον ἀσκόν), but Αἰγέος seems more likely. It is no great objection that the other 11 lines do not correspond with the earlier parts of any previously known lines from the *Hecale*, since this part of the poem is sparsely represented. According to Lobel, the *Hecale* 'may therefore be assumed, till disproof, to be the source of the passage'. I feel, however, that the onus of proof is the other way, and would not wish to incorporate this papyrus into a text of the *Hecale* unless some supporting evidence can be produced. In line 2 we apparently have]ν μ' ἄγε π[, or]ν μ' ἄγ' ἐπ[, the latter possibility being unattractive.

P. Oxy. 2823 (= SH 280)

```
 1              ]..αδα[
               ]νμαγεπ[
               ]αιηϲαπ[
               ]γαϲουκ[
 5             ]ηδυνο[
               ]..αγα.[
               ]εμονα[
               ]αιγεοϲ[
               ]αξενο.[
10             ].ποκα.[
               ].παλλαδ[
               ].επρωτ[
               . . . . . .
```

1 fort.]ρϲ   8 Αἰγέοϲ, αἴγεοϲ,]αι γ', al. Call. fr. 232. 2 Pf.
τοὔνεκεν Αἰγέοϲ ἔϲκεν (Αἰγέοϲ etiam Hdt. 1. 173. 3, sed cetera
discrepant)   10 fort.]ν   11 fort.]ν
de Hecala dubitantissime cog. Lobel, vide ad v. 8

FRS. 5-6

Two sides of P. Oxy. 2258A, fr. 11 (xx. 81). This scrap must have
been located near the bottom of a page. The 'front' has remains of
2 lines of text (in larger letters), and below them 3 lines of scholia
in the lower margin; on the 'back' there is no text, but 7 lines of
scholia. Thus the scholia on the 'back' start a good deal higher
than on the 'front', perhaps because the commentary on the 'back'
was more copious and demanded a greater portion of the page.

Ascription to the Hecale depends upon interpretation of the
scholia on the 'back'. There the names Scirus, Aegeus, and
Pandion can perhaps be restored; a discussion of Aegeus' parent-
age would of course suit the Hecale, and Pfeiffer suggests that line
7 may mention 'aconite', with which Medea tried to poison
Theseus. If the 'back' is Hecale, so presumably is the 'front'; P.
Oxy. 2258A fr. 9 has part of H. 6 on one side and the Argumentum

Hecalae on the other, but the two lines of text on fr. 11 'front' certainly do not belong to the Sixth Hymn.

I have placed the 'back' (fr. 5) before the 'front' (fr. 6) for two reasons, both quite speculative:

(*a*) *P. Oxy.* 2258 seems to have had a normal column length of 23 lines (Lobel, p. 70; but see ibid. p. 81 on 2258A, fr. 10). Clearly 2258A, fr. 11 comes from the foot of a column (above). If Pfeiffer was right in referring the 'back' to Medea's attempted poisoning, could this be the end of the first column in the poem? The *Diegesis*, having quoted the opening line, goes straight on to Medea's plot (Θησεὺς φυγὼν τὴν ἐκ Μηδείης ἐπιβουλήν κτλ.).

(*b*) There is a faint possibility of identifying line 1 of the 'front' with my fr. 8. If that were so, the 'front' would contain a speech by Aegeus to his son, delivered after the failure of Medea's plot.

Fr. 5 (i, p. 506 Pf.), marginal scholia

This piece (*P. Oxy.* 2258A, fr. 11 'back') comes from the bottom of a page. While the other side (fr. 6) has remains of two lines of text followed by scholia, here we have only scholia.

2 Pfeiffer suggested that τ]ῶν ἐπάνω[θεν might be a lemma, as in Theocr. 7. 5 and *epigr.* 22 Gow(= *AP* 9. 598 = 16 G.–P.). 3; cf. Call. *Aet.* fr. 75. 32 Pf. ἄνωθεν.

3–4 Perhaps Cκί]ρου δὲ ὁ Αἰ[γεύς and Παν]δίονος. For Scirus cf. Apollod. 3. 15. 5 ἔνιοι δὲ Αἰγέα Cκίρου [Cκυρίου codd.: corr. Robert, *Hermes*, 20 (1885), 354; cf. Philoch. *FGH* 328 F 111] εἶναι λέγουσιν. We cannot tell whether Call. alluded to the rarer version of Aegeus' parentage, or whether this is a piece of gratuitous learning from the commentator. In view of Pfeiffer's idea that this scholion may relate to Medea's attempted plot (see on l. 7), note that Dion. Per. (1023–4) calls Theseus 'offspring of the son of Pandion' in just this context, quite possibly with an eye on the *Hecale* (for Ἀκταίοιο cf. fr. 1):

> εὖτε γὰρ Ἀκταίοιο παρὰ ῥόον Ἰλισσοῖο
> φάρμακ' ἐμήσατο λυγρὰ γονῶι Πανδιονίδαο ...

7 Pfeiffer hazards]παρδα[λιαγχές, 'leopard's-choke', i.e. aconite (cf. Nic. *Alex.* 38), with which Medea tried to kill Theseus (Ov. *Met.* 7. 406 ff.).

Fr. 6 (cf. i, p. 507 Pf.)

From *P. Oxy* 2258A, fr. 11 'front'. Remains of two lines from the text (in larger letters) followed by scholia (smaller letters) in the bottom margin.

1   ].οο. . . . [: although only one letter can be read for certain, Lobel's description of the other traces made me wonder whether we might have]νοϱνειλ[, = fr. 8 παρὲκ⌋ νόον εἰλ⌊ἠλουθαc. P. J. Parsons comments:

]νοϱνει.[seems to be reconcilable with the traces and the spacing. Of these, ε is good; one sees the base. The difficulty comes after the putative ι, where possible traces are /˙ (more than Lobel saw, and certainly one or both may be a delusion); the first seemingly too straight for Λ, the second too far to the right to begin Λ (if the first trace is a delusion), and not far enough to belong to the RH side of Λ. All very dim—one can perhaps say just that the traces do *not* suggest Λ (or anything else obvious), but, since they are so much damaged, it is difficult to exclude it absolutely.

If by chance the identification proved correct, it would fit well with Pfeiffer's idea that the scholia on the other side of this papyrus (fr. 5) describe Medea's attempted poisoning of Theseus. Fr. 6 would then show Aegeus speaking to his son, some 23 lines later.

Fr. 7 (233 Pf.)

Aegeus appears to have been feeble and cowardly; he must at least suspect that the cup is poisoned, since Medea has persuaded him that this unknown young man threatens his throne (e.g. Plut. *Thes.* 12, schol. *Il.* 11. 741). Then, at the very moment when Theseus is about to drink the poison, Aegeus recognizes the ivory hilt of the sword, and dashes the cup from his son's lips. Thus e.g. Ov. *Met.* 7. 419–23:

> ea [sc. the aconite] coniugis astu
> ipse parens Aegeus nato porrexit ut hosti.
> sumpserat ignara Theseus data pocula dextra,
> cum pater in capulo gladii cognovit eburno
> signa sui generis, facinusque excussit ab ore.

ἴcχε, τέκοc, μὴ πῖθι: cf. Quint. Smyrn. 9. 313 ἴcχε, τέκοc, καὶ μή τι etc. For ἴϲχε μή + imperative, Pfeiffer quotes A. *Ch.* 1052 and S. *Ichneutae*, fr. 314. 101 Radt. Homer always has the middle ἴϲχεο.

μὴ πῖθι: for μή + aorist imperative (middle) cf. *Il.* 4. 410, 18. 134, *Od.* 24. 248; and, with an active aorist imperative, A. *Theoroe* (a satyr play), fr. 78c. 54 Radt and Soph. fr. 493 Radt μὴ ψεῦϲον (more examples in Pfeiffer). The form πῖθι belongs for the most part to satyr plays (Ion, *Omphale*, fr. 27 Snell *Tr. G. F.*; cf. E. *Cyc.* 570 ἔκπιθι), Comedy (Ar. *Vesp.* 1489; Crat. fr. 141 = 145 *PCG*; Amips. fr. 18; Antiph. fr. 163. 1; Diph. fr. 20. 2; Men. fr. 377; fr. adesp. 478 Koch), and mime (Herod. 1. 82). We shall constantly find Call. using comic language in the *Hecale*.

Fr. 8 (234 Pf.)

παρὲκ νόον εἰλήλουθαϲ: in Homer (*Il.* 10. 391*, 20. 133*) παρὲκ νόον means 'beyond good sense'; but here 'contrary to expectation', according to Suid. (παρ' ἐλπίδα). Apollonius Rhodius thrice (1. 130, 323, 4. 102) couples παρὲκ νόον with a genitive, 'without the knowledge and approval of'. εἰλήλουθαϲ ten times ends a hexameter in Homer (e.g. *Il.* 23. 94); for the pluperfect ἠληλούθειν see fr. 105. This fragment is probably reflected in *Dieg.* x. 23 οὐ προϲδοκήϲαντι, and might be identified with fr. 6. 1 (see ad loc.).

Fr. 9 (235 Pf.)

The reference is to the sword by which Aegeus recognized his son (cf. Ov. *Met.* 7. 422, quoted on fr. 7).

1 ἐν γάρ μιν Τροιζῆνι: for the insertion of a pronoun between the preposition and noun, cf. fr. 51. 1 ἔκ με Κολωνάων, and Lapp, *Tropis et Figuris*, p. 37. Here a conjunction too is interposed, as in *H.* 1. 10, 2. 74, 75. McLennan (*HZ*) on *H.* 1. 10 ἐν δέ ϲε Παρραϲίηι quotes examples from other poets (e.g. *Od.* 22. 217 ἐν δὲ ϲὺ τοῖϲιν) and even from prose (Hdt. 6. 69. 4 ἐν γάρ ϲε τῆι νυκτί). See also Barrett on E. *Hipp.* 10.

κολουραίηι ὑπὸ πέτρηι: κολουραῖοϲ is not found elsewhere (κόλουροϲ = 'dock-tailed'). Suidas, from the commentary of Salustius rather than the text of Call. (see above, Introd. sect. IX), explains κολουραία πέτρα as κοίλη, κεκαμμένη ἢ ϲτρογγύλη, of which Naeke (p. 73) preferred the second: 'saxum abruptum, incurvatum ac propendens in unam partem'. But one would expect the epithet to mean 'hollow' (κοίλη, Suid.); cf. Plut. *Thes.* 4 πέτραν μεγάλην, ἐντὸς ἔχουσαν κοιλότητα συμμέτρως ἐμπεριλαμβάνουσαν τὰ κείμενα, Lyc. *Alex.* 494 ἐκ κοίλης πέτρας, and γυαλὸν λίθον in fr. 10. 1 below.

2 θῆκε: sc. Aegeus.

cὺν ἁρπίδεccιν: 'with the sandals' (whether we should read -εccιν or -εccι remains an open question). The word is claimed by Hesychius as Laconian, and ascribed by Pollux 7. 85 s.v. κρηπίδες to ἔνιοι . . . τῶν ποιητῶν. Hitherto its one other known poetic occurrence is in fr. 27. 2, where]υπαρπίδα[of *P. Oxy.* 2529 implies a smooth breathing (paralleled only in the MS of Hesychius which, like almost all sources, accents ἁρπίδες as if the ι were short).

Fr. 10 (236. 1–2 Pf.)

This fragment appears to be direct speech by Aegeus to Aethra, Theseus' mother. The connection with fr. 9 could be 'for he placed it [the sword] in Troezen under a hollow rock together with the sandals [and on departing gave these instructions to Aethra:] "When the boy is strong enough . . . [let him come]" '. Pfeiffer quotes schol. Lyc. *Alex.* 494 κατέλιπε δὲ τὸ ξίφος αὐτοῦ καὶ τὰ ὑποδήματα τῆι Αἴθραι εἰπών· ἡνίκα ἐφαρμόςωςι τῶι παιδὶ τὰ ὑποδήματα καὶ τὸ ξίφος δυνηθῆι κομίςαι, τότε λαβὼν αὐτὰ ἐλθέτω εἰς Ἀθήνας. Christiane Sourvinou-Inwood (*JHS* 91 (1971), 94–109) discusses artistic representations of Theseus lifting the rock. She believes (p. 99) that this element of the myth appeared first in a late sixth-century *Theseid*. The purported rock of Theseus may have been a tourist attraction in Troezen (Paus. 2. 32. 7).

A story which resembles that of Theseus' birth (including the deposit of a γνώριςμα for the boy to use when he grows up) appears in Parth. *Narr.* 1.

1 ἀπὸ . . . ἀγκάccacθαι: in tmesis (unlike *Il.* 17. 722 ἀπὸ χθονὸς ἀγκάζοντο): Lapp (*Tropis et Figuris*, p. 48) gives examples of widely spaced tmesis in Call. Euph. *SH* 415. i. 9 has ἀγκάccοιτο*.

ἀπὸ μέν: Pfeiffer, postulating a close connection with fr. 11, believed that we have 'affirmative' μέν, following the preposition in tmesis, with no corresponding δέ. Barrett, however, doubts this, pointing out that *Il.* 10. 458 ff. and *Od.* 22. 475 ff., although having ἀπὸ μέν in tmesis, are inadequate parallels for the pattern which Pfeiffer seeks to establish. A corresponding δέ might be introduced in line 2 (ἐλεῖν δ' Wilamowitz: ἐλὼν δ' Schneider).

γυαλὸν λίθον: γύαλον is a hollow, in Homer always of the front or back plate of a metal corslet (θώρηκος γύαλον): used as an epithet only here.

2 ἐλών: so Pfeiffer with Stephanus Byzantius, envisaging the construction as 'taking the sword ... let him come ...'. Barrett remarks that it would be odd for Stephanus to quote a line consisting of two syntactically so incomplete halves. See further on line 1 above (ἀπὸ μέν) and on fr. 11 below.

Αἰδήψιον ἄορ: from Aedepsus in the north of Euboea, famous for iron and bronze work. Epaphroditus (?in his commentary on the *Aetia*; cf. frs. 52–3 Pf.) even claimed that bronze originated there. Stephanus Byzantius, who quotes this line, also gives another fragment of Call. concerning Euboean ironwork (701 inc. sed. Pf.), δέδαεν δὲ λαχαινέμεν ἔργα cιδήρου, which might belong to the *Hecale* (though any close connection with fr. 10 seems unlikely). Hyginus (*Astr.* 2. 6) cites the astronomical poet Hegesianax (*SH* 468) as giving Theseus an 'Ellopian' (i.e. Euboean) sword.

Fr. 11 (236. 3 Pf.)

Schneider (ii, pp. 178–9) first connected fr. 11 to fr. 10. 2, supplementing e.g. ἐλὼν ⟨δ'⟩ Αἰδήψιον ἄορ |⟨cπάccηι καὶ τὰ⟩ πέδιλα. Pfeiffer tried ἐλὼν Αἰδήψιον ἄορ |⟨ἔλθοι καὶ τὰ⟩ πέδιλα. I have not felt confident about so close a link, and prefer to print fr. 11 separately. M. L. West argues that the non-rotting of the sandals is more naturally mentioned at the point when they are found, rather than in anticipation.

τὰ μὴ πύcε: the ῠ in πύcε (*H. Hom.* 374 πῦcε) is surprising (but see Meineke, *Callimachi Cyrenensis Hymni et Epigrammata* (1861), 151, and Diels on fr. 73 Kapp); no less so the use of μή. Pfeiffer (joining to fr. 10) translates 'quae non putrefacta fuerint', but West doubts whether this is legitimate.

νήχυτος εὐρώc: 'the abundant moisture'. νήχυτος was probably coined by Philetas, and became very popular. Thus νήχυτον ὕδωρ

(Philetas fr. 21 Powell) = Ap. Rh. 3. 530 = Claud. *Gigant*. fr. 2. 25
Birt = Mus. *Her. et Lean*. 247 (see further Kost ad loc.). Nicander
has νήχυτον ἱδρῶ (*Alex*. 587). Some ancient scholars held that the
prefix νη- could have an intensifying rather than a negative force:
e.g. schol. *Od*. 1. 380 νήποινοι· πολύποινοι, and schol. *Od*. 19. 498
(Aristarchus understood νηλίτιδες as πολυαμάρτητοι).

εὐρώς: first in Theogn. 1. 452, but εὐρώεις is common in
Homer and Hesiod.

FRS. 12–15 THESEUS IN TROEZEN

Pfeiffer suggested (i, p. 229) that the recognition by means of the
tokens left behind in Troezen (frs. 9–11) could easily have led the
poet to a retrospective digression on Theseus' Troezenian child-
hood (it is worth remembering that Eurycleia's recognition of
Odysseus by his scar leads to a digression of 72 lines on the boar
hunt (*Od*. 19. 395–466), after which we return to the foot-
washing). This idea perhaps gains slight support from *Dieg*. x.
22–3, where, after the escape from Medea's plot, Aegeus keeps
watch over his son ἅτ᾽ αἰφνίδιον ἀνακομισθὲν ἐκ Τροιζῆνος
μειράκιον. But we know very little about this part of the poem,
and it is only a guess that frs. 13–14 may refer to Theseus; in case
they do, note the remarks of R. L. Hunter in *CQ*, NS 38 (1988),
449 and n. 60 on the passage of a boy to manhood.

Fr. 12 (237 Pf.)

The scholia on E. *Hipp*. 11 ἁγνοῦ Πιτθέως παιδεύματα tell us
that in Call. Theseus was brought up by Pittheus (his maternal
grandfather). This was first referred to the *Hecale* by Blomfield
(see Naeke, p. 69). Two other passages in the *Hippolytus* scholia
concern our poem: on 29–33 about the Γλαυκώπιον (Καλλ. ἐν
Ἑκάληι, see fr. 17. 11) and on 979 about Sciron (οὗ μέμνηται
Καλλ., see fr. 59). Pfeiffer wonders whether the mention of
Pittheus as a solver of oracles in the fifth *Iambus* (fr. 195. 33 Pf.)
could be an allusion to the *Hecale* (which is probably echoed
several times in the fourth *Iambus*, fr. 194 Pf.).

Fr. 13 (345 Pf.)

τοιοῦτον γὰρ ὁ παῖϲ ὅδε λῆμα φαείνει: an otherwise unknown
fragment in Suidas, assigned to the *Hecale* by Maas (*SIFC* 14
(1937), 317) with the remark that λῆμα is not an epic word. Maas
thought of Theseus as the subject (cf. fr. 10. 1 ὁ παῖϲ), and Pfeiffer
of the poem's 'Troezenian' section. I mention in passing what
Pausanias (1. 27. 8) calls 'the first of the Troezenian stories about
Theseus', involving a visit by Heracles to Pittheus (?cf. fr. 12) and
the skin of the Nemean lion (? cf. fr. 101), in which Theseus
'shows spirit' at the tender age of seven (?? cf. Ov. *Fast.* 2. 247 ff.
and Val. Flacc. 1. 263 on Achilles).

Fr. 14 (361 Pf.)

ἔτι πλοκάμοιο περίθριξ: certainly not to be restored in fr. 47.
2. If we can trust Suidas (? from the commentary of Salustius), the
unique περίθριξ is a noun, denoting the first growth of hair before
it is cut. There is a slight resemblance to Ap. Rh. 2. 707 (of the boy
Apollo) κοῦροϲ ἐὼν ἔτι γυμνόϲ, ἔτι πλοκάμοιϲι γεγηθώϲ. Pfeiffer
conjectured that this fragment might precede fr. 15 about
Theseus' tonsure.

Fr. 15 (281 Pf.)

τὺ δ' ἐγκυτὶ τέκνον ἐκέρϲω: an adaptation of Archil. fr. 217
West χαίτην ἀπ' ὤμων ἐγκυτὶ κεκαρμένοϲ. Scholars have followed
Naeke (p. 159) in linking these words to the special tonsure (with
only the fore part of the hair cut) adopted by Theseus when he
went from Troezen to dedicate his hair at Delphi, ἐκείρατο δὲ τῆϲ
κεφαλῆϲ τὰ πρόϲθεν μόνον, ὥϲπερ Ὅμηροϲ ἔφη τοὺϲ Ἄβαντας (*Il.*
2. 542)· καὶ τοῦτο τῆϲ κουρᾶϲ τὸ γένοϲ Θηϲηὶϲ ὠνομάϲθη δι' ἐκεῖνον
(Plut. *Thes.* 5; cf. Christiane Sourvinou-Inwood, *JHS* 91 (1971),
96–7 and John Boardman, 'Heroic Haircuts', *CQ*, NS 23 (1973),
196–7). The second person and vocative may, as so often in Call.,
represent the poet apostrophizing his character.

τύ: thus Pfeiffer with Suid. cod. A, 'propter "euphoniam"'.
For Doric pronouns in Call. cf. φιν (frs. 69. 4, 111), νιν (fr. 70. 6;
H. 1. 4 with McLennan's (*HZ*) note), τιν (*Aet.* fr. 24. 3 Pf.; *H.* 3.

90) with Giangrande, *Hermes*, 98 (1970), 273–4 = *Scripta Minora Alexandrina* i. 81–2 and Hopkinson, *HD*, pp. 47–8.

ἐγκυτί: 'close to the skin'. Call. has -τῐ (as e.g. *H.* 3. 25 ἀμογητί), Archilochus -τῐ (but Bergk conjectured ἐγκυτίς there). For Callimachean adverbs in -τῐ see on fr. 115. 2 ἀκλαυτί.

About Call.'s treatment of Theseus' journey from Troezen to Athens (Plut. *Thes.* 6–12) we know next to nothing. On the way he encountered and overcame a series of bandits and monsters: Periphetes, from whom he took his club (see fr. 69. 1; but Periphetes does not appear in Bacchylides 18. 19 ff., the earliest catalogue of these labours), Sinis, the Crommyonian sow, Sciron, Cercyon, and Procrustes. See R. Carden (*The Papyrus Fragments of Sophocles* (1974), 120–2) on *P. Oxy.* 2452 (perhaps S. *Theseus*) where in fr. 3. 16 ff. (= Soph. fr. 730c. 16 ff. Radt) the hero lists his own triumphs on the journey. How many of these were mentioned by Call., and whereabouts in the poem, is quite uncertain. We have good reason to think that the killing of Cercyon (see on frs. 49. 8 ff., 62) was reserved for the conversation of Theseus and Hecale (in fr. 49. 14 Hecale does not yet know that he is dead); Sciron (frs. 59–60) may perhaps have been linked to Cercyon. Beyond that, all is speculation. Naeke (p. 178; criticized by Wilamowitz on fr. 99 Kapp, cf. *Kl. Schr.* ii. 39 n. 3) believed that fr. 98 on the river Asterion (to which one might add fr. 96) describes Theseus on his travels, and brought in other Argive fragments too (frs. 95, 174 inc. sed.; cf. Webster, *Hellenistic Poetry and Art*, p. 113), but these would take Theseus surprisingly far westwards from his route to Athens. Fr. 153 θῆκε δὲ λᾶαν | cκληρὸν ὑπόκρηνον portrays someone sleeping in the open air.

Fr. 16 (283 Pf.)

Something must have been said about the Marathonian bull (τὸν λυμαινόμενον τὰ περὶ Μαραθῶνα ταῦρον (Dieg. x. 24–5)) before Theseus tried to persuade his father to send him out against it (fr. 17. 4). Schneider (p. 608) suspected a link with fr. 89; one might hazard ἐννοτίου Μαραθῶνος, ἵν' ἔλλερα ἔργα τέλεσκεν (Pf.). Fr. 149 καὶ ἀγλαὰ πίcεα γαίηc | βόcκεο has also been cited in this connection. But we cannot be certain that fr. 16 concerns the bull;

the subject might be a bandit such as Sciron (πολλῆc φθορᾶc ὢν αἴτιοc (*Et. Gen.*)). This fragment is probably not to be recognized in fr. 49. 20 (see ad loc.).

ἵν᾽ ἔλλερα ἔργα τέλεcκεν: ἔλλεροc is alleged to be the equivalent κατὰ διάλεκτον ('local' or 'colloquial' speech?—in either case, scepticism is justified) of κακόc (Eust. 635. 6 on *Il.* 6. 181; cf. the case of ἑλικόc in fr. 116. 2). But only here does it occur independently of the hero Bellerophon (Zenodotus read Ἐλλερο-φόντηc in *Il.* 6. 155 etc.). If the subject is the Marathonian bull, cf. Mich. Chon. i. 157 Lambros ταύρου μυρία παρεχομένου τοῖc . . . Τετραπολίταιc πράγματα and Plut. *Thes.* 14.

ἔλλερα ἔργα: Call.'s observance of the digamma (cf. on fr. 2. 1 δέ ἑ) is, as one might expect, variable—here ἔλλερα ἔργα, but in fr. 111 ὄμπνιον ἔργον (see further McLennan (*HZ*) on *H.* 1. 2). Pfeiffer rightly prefers the reading ἔλλερα ἔργα (Suid.) to the more commonplace ἔλλερα πολλά (*Et. Gen.*; cf. e.g. *Il.* 9. 540 on the Calydonian boar ὃc κακὰ πόλλ᾽ ἔρδεcκεν). He notes (cf. his Index Rerum Notabilium s.v. vocalium consecutio) the sequence of vowels ε–α–ε as typical of the *Hecale*; cf. e.g. fr. 46. 3 εἴδεοc ἐνδίοιο and fr. 118 κενεὸν πόνον ὀτλήcοντεc. See further Richardson on *H. Hom. Dem.* 289 f.

Fr. 17 (line 4 = *SH* 281; 238. 1–14 Pf.)

Pfeiffer believed that the early lines of this fragment concluded a conversation between Aegeus and Aethra. But discovery of the first half of line 4 (*SH* 281, published by K. Nickau in *Philol.* 111 (1967), 126–9) shows that Theseus is speaking (as Lobel had guessed, *P. Oxy.* xix. 43), in an attempt to persuade Aegeus to send him out against the bull. Lines 10–13 concern Athena (12–13 appear to be part of a prayer to the goddess). If ἀκὴν ἔχε (9) is imperative, 'keep quiet', the piece could be direct speech by Theseus throughout; if indicative, 'kept quiet', the direct speech would be interrupted briefly. This fragment was discussed by A. Barigazzi, *Hermes*, 82 (1954), 308–17 (before the publication of the first half of l. 4).

It is worth observing that the situation of Aegeus at this time is very similar to his position in Catul. 64 with respect to Theseus and the Minotaur; the sentiments which Catullus ascribes to him would be just as appropriate in the *Hecale*. Very soon after gaining his only son, he is asked to send him on a mission which may prove fatal (215–17):

> gnate, mihi longa iucundior unice vita,
> gnate, ego quem in dubios cogor dimittere casus,
> reddite in extrema nuper mihi fine senectae ...

But the protecting goddess of Athens may yet grant victory over the bull (228–30, perhaps also the theme of ll. 10–13 in our fragment):

> quod tibi si sancti concesserit incola Itoni
> quae nostrum genus ac sedes defendere Erecthei
> annuit, ut tauri respergas sanguine dextram ...

It seems likely that Catul. 64. 111 transfers to the Minotaur a motif used by Call. for the Marathonian bull (see on fr. 165 inc. auct.): Catullus' debt to the *Hecale* may be larger than just this one line (cf. L. Castiglioni, *RIL* 70 (1937), 56–7; Barigazzi, *Hermes*, 82 (1954), 316; Hollis, *CQ*, NS 32 (1982), 470). But there are no similar fragments of the *Hecale* which can be plausibly given to Aegeus—unless perchance fr. 122 expresses a fear that he might receive unwelcome news of Theseus' death.

1 Conceivably ἐ]ν̣ι̣cπεμεναμφ: more probably ἔνιcπε (or ἐνίcπε) μέν than ἐνιcπέμεν, as Lobel says.

2 κέλευε δὲ μήποτ᾽ ἐλέγξα[ι: we cannot know whether κέλευε is imperative, 'tell him never to ...' (? Theseus passing on to his father a message from some other person) or indicative, 'he [she] told [?me] never to ...'. See further on line 4. ἐλέγξαι can bear a variety of meanings in Call.: 'to speak ill of' (fr. 54 βαcιλῆαc ἐλέγχομεν), 'ask questions about' (*H.* 4. 88 τὸν αὐτίκα πότμον ἐλέγχειc, where, however, Mineur prefers 'test', 'bring to the proof'), 'put to the test' (*epigr.* 59 Pf. and G.–P. (= *AP* 11. 362), ll. 3–4 ἄτιc ἐλέγχει | τὸν φίλον), or 'overcome' (*Aet.* fr. 84 Pf. ἄνδραc ἐλέγξαc). Other shades of meaning not attested for Call. include 'put to shame', 'cross-examine', and 'refute'.

3 See *CQ*, NS 32 (1982), 470 and n. 2. The letter missing between *NE* and *H* is most likely to be iota; palaeographically *Y* or even *P* cannot be totally excluded (Parsons), but neither seems at all promising. In that case a word-break after *N* would be inevitable, and we would appear to have εἴη or εἴη. Barrett

wondered whether the *H* could be *N* (Parsons, while agreeing
that *H* and *N* can be very similar in this hand, still favours *H*); this
would open up further possibilities (e.g. μέ]νειν δ᾽ ὕπο, Hutchin-
son). The scribe has written ὕπο with a grave accent, which might
mean that we do not have ὕπο (inverse tmesis), but one can hardly
put much weight on that argument.

πάντας ἀέθλου[c: also Ap. Rh. 1. 1318* and epic. adesp. 8. 5
Powell* (both of Heracles).

4 ⌊τῶι <ῥα>, πάτερ, μεθίει με·⌋ cόον δέ κεν α⌊ῦ⌋θι δέχοιο:
in *CQ*, NS 32 (1982), 470 I argued that since Theseus says
'*Therefore*, father, let me go, and you would later receive me back
safe', he must in the preceding lines have given some reason *why*
he would return safely from Marathon. This might be a promise
of protection from Athena (see Parsons, *ZPE* 25 (1977), 41 for her
aid given to Heracles in the parallel Callimachean myth of
Molorchus, Heracles, and the Nemean lion (*SH* 254–69)). If that
were so, the subject of κέλευε (2) could be Athena ('she ordered
me . . .') and πάντας ἀέθλους (3) might even be the source of Stat.
Theb. 12. 583 (from a passage with other echoes of the *Hecale*) 'sic
tibi *non ullae* socia sine Pallade *pugnae*'. Hutchinson (*Hellenistic
Poetry*, p. 62 n. 71) tries a different approach, with the subject of
κέλευε (2) as Pittheus, who trained Theseus for future deeds of
heroism (2–3). In that case the emphasis of 'Therefore' (4) would
be on the necessity of responding to a heroic challenge (rather
than any promise of a safe return), with cόον δέ κεν αὖθι δέχοιο as a
piece of youthful self-confidence.

The first half of this line (which so fortunately reveals the
context of the fragment) comes from the unpublished 14th-cent.
'Erenii' Philonis lexicon in Paris (cod. gr. suppl. 1238). This
derives from the same source as [Ammonius], *de Adfinium Vocabu-
lorum Differentia*, and, although much briefer, occasionally has
additional examples. See Nickau's Teubner [Ammonius], pp.
xxxviii–xliv. In the present case [Ammon.] 89 (p. 23 Nickau)
objects to Call.'s use of αὖθι, which should, as he tells us, mean the
same as αὐτόθι, 'on the spot' (as indeed in *Hec.* fr. 69. 10 αὖθι δὲ
μίμνον), while for πάλιν or μετὰ ταῦτα one should write αὖθις.
Call. is then castigated for αὖθι τὸ δ᾽ ἐκδύοιμι (*Aet.* fr. 1. 35 Pf.),
and the 'Erenii' Philonis lexicon adds this example from the
Hecale (see Nickau, *Philol.* 111 (1967), 126–9).

τῶι <ῥα>: thus Kassel (cf. *H.* 3. 251*, 4. 59*); Nickau

proposed τῶι ⟨νυ⟩. For the question whether τῶι should be written with an iota or without see McLennan (*HZ*) on *H*. 1. 58.

μεθίει με: the son of Croesus, in very similar circumstances, says to his father μέθες με (Hdt. 1. 39. 2).

5 alpha with acute accent and long mark may be followed by epsilon (cf. another scribe's treatment of καιτάεντος in fr. 47. 6).

6 κεκύθεςθε: a reduplicated second aorist middle (whether indicative or imperative) which does not occur elsewhere. Pfeiffer suggests that the meaning may be 'try to conceal', 'keep quiet about'. The significance of the second person plural is not clear. After the final κ, the traces may represent two letters, e.g. ο followed by a dot level with the tops of the letters (Lobel).

8 Pfeiffer's articulation ε δ' ἦν is perhaps not quite certain. Thereafter it is hard to resist the feeling that the letters χειραεςα[contain a corruption (if ἐ were meant, one would, as Lobel says, expect some indication). Pf. contemplated e.g. χειρώςα[ςθαι with a spondaic fifth foot (cf. *Dieg*. x. 25–6 ὅπως χειρώςαιτο).

9 ἀκὴν ἔχε: indicative (as in Ap. Rh. 3. 521, Mosch. *Eur*. 18) or imperative (as in [Opp.] *Cyn*. 1. 32)? See introductory note to this fragment. At least from the time of Call. ἀκήν seems to have been regarded as the accusative of a noun ἀκή (though Lobel remarks that ἀκήν might be adverbial here, and ἔχε have another object). It is interesting that a papyrus contemporary with Call. (*P. Hibeh* 23) has ἀκὴν ἔχον in a line interpolated at *Od*. 20. 58–9. This suggests that Call. was not the first to use the phrase—perhaps he found it somewhere in his text of Homer (see Stephanie West, *The Ptolemaic Papyri of Homer* (1967), 276).

τῆι δε [: probably a reference to Athena.

10–13 Could Theseus be urging his father to have faith in the protection of Athena? Lines 12–13 appear to be part of a prayer to the goddess.

10 αἰςυμνῆτις: glossed δέςποινα by Suid. Not elsewhere applied to Athena, but, according to Pausanias (7. 21. 6), αἰςυμνήτης was an Achaean title of Dionysus. In *Od*. 8. 258 αἰςυμνῆται are umpires at games, while in *Il*. 24. 347 Hermes disguises himself as a prince, κούρωι αἰςυμνητῆρι [v.l. αἰςυητῆρι] ἐοικώς. Several Greek States had an elected ruler called an αἰςυμνήτης (*Aet*. fr. 102 Pf. adds the previously unknown example of Ephesus).

11 †ἧ τ' ἄκρηςθ† ἵνͺα Γλαυκῶπιον ἵζεͺι: the papyrus is supplemented by schol. BD on *Il*. 5. 522. Naeke (p. 201) believed that schol. D preserved the correct reading, ἥ τ᾽ ἄκρης θῖνα Γλαυκώπιον ἵζει, 'she who occupies the Glaucopian mound of the citadel'; Dindorf (see fr. an. 332 Schn.) added ⟨πόλιος⟩ after ἄκρης to complete the hexameter (cf. *Il.* 6. 257). As far as sense is concerned, Naeke's view has definite attractions. Hesychius' first gloss of θίς is ὄχθος, and for θῖνες he gives *inter alia* ὑψηλοὶ τόποι. But there is a serious metrical objection. Call. does not normally place a spondaic word after the masculine caesura unless there is also a bucolic diaeresis (see above, Introd. sect. IV. 3*b*). What might seem an exact parallel for θῖνα Γλαυκώπιον ἵζει in *H.* 6. 72 οὔτε ξυνδείπνια πέμπον turns out to be a special case because of Homeric reminiscence (e.g. *Od.* 3. 350) and repetition: οὔτε νιν εἰς ἐράνως οὔτε ξυνδείπνια πέμπον. Repetition also helps *H.* 6. 47 τέκνον ἐλίνυσον, τέκνον πολύθεστε τοκεῦσι (*pace* Maas, *GM*, p. 93, I see no good reason to suspect corruption in this line—cf. Hopkinson, *HD*, ad loc.). So we must probably conclude with regret that the true reading cannot be recovered. It remains quite possible (though the syntax of 10–11 is obscure) that Γλαυκώπιον is an 'accusative of the space occupied', as e.g. A. *Ag.* 982 and E. *Ion* 1314 βωμὸν οὐχ ἵζειν ἐχρῆν.

Γλαυκώπιον: the ancients quarrelled over the precise reference of the Γλαυκώπιον, making it variously (*a*) the name of an Attic mountain, otherwise Lycabettus (Seleucus in *Et. Gud.* p. 312. 5 de Stef.), (*b*) an old name for the Acropolis, (*c*) the temple of Athena on the Acropolis (the last two are alternatives in *Et. Gen.*). Here (*b*) seems appropriate (though Pfeiffer suspects that Call. had in mind a particular part of the Acropolis). See further Jacoby, *FGH* iiib, Suppl. ii. 491; Pfeiffer, *History*, i. 262; de Jan, *De Callimacho Homeri Interprete* (diss. 1893), pp. 67 ff., Euph. fr. 9. 4 κατὰ Γλαυκώπιον probably comes from Call. (see above, Introd. sect. VI).

12 ἀεὶ περὶ πότνια γα[: I suspect that πότνια is vocative (cf. fr. 73. 7 τεόν ποτε πότνια θυμόν). At the end of the line γα[ίης would be possible (Barigazzi, *Hermes*, 82 (1954), 312), in the sense of caring for the land. Bulloch (*FH*, p. 165 n. 2) suspects that περί may here be adverbial, expressing superiority (? Pallas loves the land of Attica more than any other).

13 ὅθι πτολέμοιό μ᾽ ἐπ. [: intriguing—some place where someone (possibly Athena, if she is still the subject) did something to the speaker (probably still Theseus) which concerned war (πτόλεμος could include combat against brigands or monsters, as e.g. in E. *HF* 1273). My mind returns to the idea mentioned on line 4, but of course there are many possibilities.

The lacuna between frs. 17 and 18 (i.e. between the recto and verso of *P. Oxy.* 2216, fr. 1) is of uncertain length. Fr. 18. 1–2 were previously known (fr. 8. 1–2 Kapp) and fit conveniently on to the beginning of the verso; otherwise there are no fragments which we can with any degree of conviction assign to this lacuna. It seems probable that Call. told how Aegeus rejected his son's plea to go out against the bull, and attempted to confine him (*Dieg.* x. 26 εἰργόμενος), but none the less Theseus slipped away unnoticed about evening (ibid. 26–8 κρύφα τῆς οἰκίας ἐξελθὼν περὶ ἑσπέραν ἀπῆρεν).

Fr. 18 (238. 15–32, ?319 Pf.)

We know that Theseus left Athens περὶ ἑσπέραν (above). Fr. 18 appears to give a general picture (not at this point connected with Theseus) of the Attic weather that day. A warm and brilliant afternoon (1–3) gave way to a violent storm about supper-time (5 ff.); this same storm will make Theseus seek refuge in Hecale's cottage. The whole description must have been vivid and vigorous, with an abundance of local colour. For the motif of refuge from a storm cf. Ov. *Met.* 5. 281 ff. (Pyreneus to the Muses) 'nec dubitate, precor, tecto grave sidus et imbrem' | (imber erat) 'vitare meo. subiere minores | saepe casas superi'; although Theseus is not a god, 'casas' suggests that Ovid may have the *Hecale* in mind.

1–7 ⌊ὄφρα μέν ...| τόφρα δ' ...|... ὁππότε ...| τῆμος:** a sequence very much in the Homeric manner, though not exactly paralleled by any passage of Homer. Perhaps closest would be *Il.* 11. 84 ff., which likewise uses a meal as an indication of time: ὄφρα μὲν ἠὼς ἦν καὶ ἀέξετο ἱερὸν ἦμαρ | τόφρα ...| ἦμος δὲ δρυτόμος περ ἀνὴρ ὡπλίσσατο δεῖπνον |... τῆμος ... Compare *Od.* 9. 56 ff. (a pattern including evening), *Il.* 8. 66 ff., 16. 777 ff.

1 ἔνδιος: 'midday'. This word provides a good example of Callimachean *variatio* (cf. Rüdiger Schmitt, *Die Nominalbildung in den Dichtungen des Kallimachos* (1970), p. 46 n. 2; de Jan, *De Callimacho*, pp. 77–8). In Homer we find the adjective ἔνδιος (*Il.* 11. 726, *Od.* 4. 450) which Call. uses in fr. 46. 3 (and fr. 522. 2 inc.

sed. Pf.), but our poet also has (*a*) a masculine substantive ἔνδῑος (here), (*b*) a masculine substantive ἔνδῐος (fr. 74. 14), and (*c*) a neuter substantive ἔνδῐον (*H.* 6. 38). Call.'s variation of quantity is paralleled in Ap. Rh. (ῑ at 1. 603, ῐ in 4. 1312). It is common for Hellenistic poets to convert Homeric adjectives into nouns (cf. McLennan (*HZ*) on *H.* 1. 14).

θέρμετο δὲ χθών: cf. *Il.* 18. 348 (*Od.* 8. 437) θέρμετο δ' ὕδωρ*, *Od.* 13. 352 εἴσατο δὲ χθών*.

2 ὑάλοιο φαάντερος: 'more brilliant than glass'. Amid so much Homeric colour, this striking comparison is new. It had great success with the Roman poets, and is almost certainly the source of Hor. *Carm.* 3. 13. 1 'o fons Bandusiae splendidior vitro' (cf. *Carm.* 1. 18. 16, Ov. *Met.* 13. 791, and Mary L. Trowbridge, *Philological Studies in Ancient Glass* (1930), p. 65 nn. 13, 14).

I would guess that Call. was thinking more of a brilliant glistening effect than of transparency. ὕαλος, a word of uncertain derivation, is attested first in Herodotus (3. 24, about Egypt), but, whatever it signifies there, it is not glass. Its earliest applications to glass are probably in Aristophanes (*Ach.* 74, *Nub.* 768 (though some think this refers to crystal)) and Plato (*Tim.* 61b). For Greek and Latin literary allusions to glass, including comparisons, see Mary Trowbridge's book (above); our line of Callimachus just creeps in anonymously (p. 28 n. 26). Although the fact that Call. lived and worked in Egypt has little influence upon his poetry (apart, of course, from his court pieces for the Ptolemies), the long predominance of Egyptian glass-making may not be irrelevant here.

φαάντερος ... ἦνοψ⌋: two points typical of Call., and of Hellenistic poetry in general: (*a*) Homer once has a superlative φαάντατος (*Od.* 13. 93), but the comparative first occurs here (it was much favoured by Call.'s admirer Gregory of Nazianzus, e.g. *Carm.* 1. 2. 1. 4 (*PG* xxxvii. 522) = 1. 2. 1. 528 (*PG* xxxvii. 562) χρυσοῦ τ' ἠλέκτρου τε φαάντερον; cf. Nonn. *Dion.* 40. 384, 45. 126); (*b*) although ἦνοπι χαλκῶι occurs three times in Homer (e.g. *Il.* 16. 408), you will search in vain for any case other than the dative. Call. also has an accusative in fr. 102. 2 ἦνοπα πυρόν.

3–4 οὐδέ⌋ ποθ⌊ι⌋ κν⌊ηκὶς ὑπεφαίνετο, πέπτατο δ' αἰθήρ | ἀγ[ν]έφελος: the atmosphere continues to be Homeric; cf. *Od.* 20. 114 οὐδέ ποθι νέφος ἐστί, *Il.* 17. 371–2 πέπτατο δ' αὐγή | ἠελίου ὀξεῖα, νέφος δ' οὐ φαίνετο, *Od.* 6. 44–5 ἀλλὰ μάλ' αἴθρη | πέπταται ἀνέφελος [v. l. ἀννέφελος]. We may suspect that in *Od*. 6. 44 Call. read αἰθήρ rather than αἴθρη, like his younger contemporary the scholar poet Rhianus (schol. ad loc.; cf. Pfeiffer, *History*, i. 122, 148–9) and also Lucretius (3. 21 'innubilus aether').

κνηκίς: a rare meteorological term, defined in an anonymous introduction to Aratus (Maass, *Commentariorum in Aratum Reliquiae* (1898), 126) as νεφέλη λεπτοτάτη κενὴ ὕδατος (cf. Plut. *Mor.* 581F, Cleom. 2. 1. 72); for κνηκίς in a different sense (μελανία τις τῶι cώματι) see *SH* 1084 (anon.).

4 Spacing indicates that the papyrus had ἀννέφελος, which Hainsworth on *Od*. 6. 45 describes as 'unetymological', rather than ἀνέφελος (with long α as in ἀθάνατος).

5–6 'Eo tempore quo puellae quae per diem stamina duxerunt matri pensum ferunt et cenam vespertinam petunt' (Pf.). See on fr. 74. 23 ff. for times of day described in terms of the accompanying human activity; a worker's meal serves as such an indication at *Il*. 11. 86 ff. (partially quoted on fr. 18. 1ff. above) and Ap. Rh. 1. 1173. The picture of women toiling long and hard over their wool, often by lamplight, is common in both Greek and Latin poetry (e.g. *Il*. 12. 433 ff.; Ap. Rh. 4. 1062 ff.; Virg. *G*. 1. 390, *A*. 8. 408 ff.). Maas compared Erinn. *SH* 401. 22 ff., but the text is too fragmentary for one to be sure of even the general sense.

6 δειελὸν αἰτίζ⌊ουcιν: 'ask for their evening meal'. The adjective δείελος (see fr. 74. 14 for its employment as a noun) does not elsewhere denote a meal, but Athenaeus (1. 11e) says that δειλινόν was so used. Compare *Od*. 17. 599 cὺ δ' ἔρχεο δειελιήcας (a controversial passage, as we can see from the scholia and Ath. 5. 193a; cf. de Jan, *De Callimacho*, pp. 41–2).

ἄγουcι δέ: *Il*. 1. 390*, Ap. Rh. 1. 1252*.

7 The missing part of this line must have contained a nominative noun meaning 'cloud', or perhaps 'storm'; if we are right to read ἄγων (with almost all the MSS of Suid.) rather than ἄγον in line 9, that noun was masculine.

8 ff. Lobel writes (on *P. Oxy*. 2216 (xix. 44)) 'I am not sure that a storm moving over Parnes and Aegaleos would much discommode a person travelling north-eastwards from Athens to Marathon.' But at this juncture we are not specially concerned with Theseus; Call. is describing a general storm over Attica, and at least two of the mountains mentioned (Parnes and Hymettus) were thought to be ὄρη cημαντικά, of particular importance for the weather. The pseudo-Theophrastean *de Signis Tempestatum* portrays in minute detail the predictive force of weather conditions over the Attic mountains, e.g. 3. 43 ἐὰν χειμῶνος ὄντος νεφέλη μακρά (? cf. Call. l. 10 διπλόον) ἐπὶ τὸν Ὑμηττον ᾖι, χειμῶνος ἐπίτασιν σημαίνει, 3. 47 τῆς Πάρνηθος ἐὰν τὰ πρὸς ζέφυρον ἄνεμον καὶ τὰ πρὸς Φύλης φράττηται νέφεσι βορείων ὄντων χειμέριον τὸ σημεῖον. Barigazzi discusses the storm further in *Hermes*, 82 (1954), 313 n. 1. The most famous poetic reference to clouds on a mountain top portending a storm was Archil. fr. 105. 2–3 West ἀμφὶ δ' ἄκρα Γυρέων ὀρθὸν ἵσταται νέφος,| σῆμα χειμῶνος (cf. *Il.* 5. 522 ff.).

8 Parnes was the highest mountain in Attica (1410 m.)—see Frazer on Paus. 1. 32. 1. From there the Clouds descend in Aristophanes' comedy (l. 323).

⌊**ἐπιπρὸ δὲ μᾶccον:** ἐπιπρό, 'onwards' (εἰς τὸ ἔμπροcθεν (schol. Ap. Rh. 1. 983)) does not occur before this passage, but Apollonius Rhodius uses it ten times (ἐπιπρὸ δέ* in 2. 133). μᾶccον comes once in Homer (*Od.* 8. 203) as an adverb, 'further'. If μᾶccον is an adverb here, the meaning could be 'further onwards', i.e. the cloud moves from Parnes to Aegaleos (the latter almost an extension of Parnes). Possibly, however, μᾶccον may be an adjective agreeing with a lost neuter noun (e.g. νέφος) in line 7. We should then read ἄγον rather than ἄγων in line 9; there would be a 'small' cloud over Parnes, a 'larger' one on Aegaleos—? and one 'twice as big' on Hymettus (10).

9 Αἰγαλέωc: a low chain of hills (at most 470 m.) beginning near the south-west foot of Parnes and stretching towards the strait of Salamis. The papyrus confirms Suidas' statement that Αἰγαλέωc is used as a genitive, as if from Αἰγαλεύc.

θυμόε⌊ντοc: 'thyme-bearing', *hapax legomenon*. LSJ's ascription of θυμόεις to Choerilus rests on the belief that this line was written by the poet of Samos (fr. 8 Kinkel, Xerxes watching the battle of Salamis!)—so it is not a case of *adding* the Callimachean occurrence (LSJ, Suppl. p. 72). See on fr. 74. 23 for Call.'s new adjectives in -ήεις and -όεις. According to C. Scherling (*Quibus Rebus*, p. 16) 'Nobilissima omnium herbarum thymus erat, quae ut in ceteris Atticae montibus, ita optima in Hymetto reperiebatur.'

ἄγων μέγαν ὑετόν: cf. *Il.* 4. 278 (νέφος) ἄγει δέ τε λαίλαπα πολλήν.

10 τῶι δ᾽ ἐπ[ί]: 'thereupon', cf. *Il.* 7. 163, 23. 290*.

11 τρηχέος Ὑμηττ[οῖο: cf. Nonn. *Dion.* 13. 183 γείτονος
Ὑμηττοῖο. Perhaps the scribe attempted correction to Ὑμηccοῖο
(cf. Hdt. 6. 137—in Nic. *Alex.* 446 the better MSS give
Ὑμηccίδος rather than -ττ-). Call. himself may have used the
form with -cc- in *Aet.* 1 (see Pfeiffer, ii, p. 104), and in fr. 169 inc.
sed. we find Βριληccοῦ. But Pfeiffer points out that there may be
an Attic place-name ending -ηττω in *Aet.* fr. 113. 8. Silius
combines Hymettus' reputation for predicting storms with its
even greater fame for honey, 'aut ubi Cecropius formidine nubis
aquosae | sparsa super flores examina tollit Hymettos' (2. 217–18).

This line might be completed with fr. 19 καὶ ἠέρος ἀχλύσαντος
(see ad loc.).

12 ἀcτεροπα[ὶ] cελάγι[ζον: the first known occurrence of
cελαγίζω (also *SH* 910, anon.; Page, *GLP*, no. 129. 16–17
ἀcτεροπαῖc . . .|. . . cελάγιζον), which was much patronized by
Nonnus, appearing more than 30 times in the *Dionysiaca* (note 41.
79 ἀcτεροπὴ cελάγιζε*) and thrice in the St John *Paraphrase* (1. 12
etc.); cf. Greg. Naz. *Carm.* 1.1.7.4 (*PG* xxxvii. 439) and Christo-
dorus, *AP* 2. 351.

13 Wind, clouds, and sea are favourite material for compari-
sons in the *Iliad*, usually to illustrate the conflict of warriors: see
W. C. Scott, *The Oral Nature of the Homeric Simile* (1974), 62 ff.
and Appendix. For example, in *Il.* 5. 522 ff. clouds stay motionless
on top of mountains until struck by the wind, and in 9. 305 ff. the
south and west winds attack the clouds. Here I would look for
some special point in the comparison (otherwise there seems little
purpose in likening one storm to another). Perhaps Call. concen-
trates on the lightning, and the point lies in the winds buffeting
the clouds (13 κλονέ. [, 16 εἰcέπεcεν νεφέλ[ηιcιν). A number of
Greek philosophers (see Bailey on Lucr. 6. 160–218) believed that
lightning is forced out from clashing clouds, and this doctrine
often appears in Latin poetry (e.g. Ov. *Met.* 6. 695–6, 11. 436).

Pfeiffer was confident that 15 ff. belong inside the simile (which
alternatively could have lasted only two lines, with 15 resuming
the main narrative). He also suspected that Zephyrus appeared in
the second half of line 13, supplementing e.g. οἷ[ο]ν ὅτε κλονέο[υcα
νέφη ζεφύροιο θύελλα. We would then have a Battle of the Winds
(cf. Nisbet and Hubbard on Hor. *Carm.* 1. 3. 13), one of the epic
set pieces which had so wearied Juvenal (1. 9 'quid agant venti').

venti'). By convention, winds blow simultaneously from two opposing quarters (e.g. *Il.* 16. 765 ὡς δ᾽ Εὖρός τε Νότος τ᾽ ἐριδαίνετον ἀλλήλοιιν), or even from every quarter (Bömer on Ov. *Met.* 11. 490–1 'omnique e parte feroces | bella gerunt venti' has many parallels).

13 κλονέ.[: cf. *Il.* 23. 213 (Boreas and Zephyrus together νεφέα κλονέοντε πάροιθεν—(note ibid. 230 Θρηΐκιον κατὰ πόντον) and Hes. *Op.* 553 (of Boreas νέφεα κλονέοντος).

14 Αὐςόν[ι]ον κατὰ π[όντον: an old name for the Sicilian sea, stretching from Sicily to Crete (Str. 2. 123); in the style of Hellenistic (and Roman) high poetry the sea must be particularized. The Αὔςονες, in Latin Aurunci (see Fordyce on *Aen.* 7. 39), were an Oscan-speaking people of central Italy, mentioned in the 5th century BC by Hecataeus (*FGH* 1 F 61) and Hellanicus (ibid. 4 F 79). Hellenistic poets take up Αὐςονία as a learned or romantic name (e.g. Ap. Rh. 4. 660); as well as Αὔςων, Lycophron has Αὐςόνειος, -ίης, and -ίτις. In the imperial age Greek poets often employ Αὐςόνιος etc. to refer to their Roman masters.

15 ἡ δ᾽ ἀπὸ Μηριςοῖο θ⌊ οὴ βορέαο κατάϊξ: Webster (*WS* 76 (1963), 78) saw here a 'clear case' for the priority of Apollonius Rhodius' *Argonautica* over the *Hecale*. Comparing Arat. *Phaen.* 423 ὑψόθεν ἐμπλήξῃι δεινὴ ἀνέμοιο θύελλα, Ap. Rh. 1. 1203 ὑψόθεν ἐμπλήξαςα θοὴ ἀνέμοιο κατάϊξ, and the present line, he found in Call. 'the last and most elegant development of the phrase'. But one could equally well argue that Apollonius Rhodius, writing third, wished to combine the unrelated lines of Aratus and Call., interweaving reminiscences of both (ὑψόθεν ἐμπλήξαςα ... ἀνέμοιο from Aratus, θοὴ ... κατάϊξ from Call.). βορέαο κατάϊξ* comes also in Call. *H.* 3. 114, and was restored by Livrea in his 1973 edition of the late epic poet Dionysius (fr. 72. 4).

ἀπὸ Μηριςοῖο: among Thracian mountains Pliny (*NH* 4. 50) lists Merithus (so cod. A, 'Meritus' cett.); it is conceivable that the papyrus had Μηριθοῖο here, but Suidas definitely gives Μηριςοῖο. Another little-known Thracian mountain (Hypsizorus) occurs in fr. 71. 1. Boreas is 'Thracian' from the time of Hesiod (*Op.* 553; see West ad loc.). In *H.* 3. 114 Call. links him to the more celebrated range of Haemus (cf. Val. Flacc. 2. 515, where surely one should read 'Haemi' rather than 'Hebri'), and there too Boreas has his ἑπτάμυχον ... ςπέος (*H.* 4. 65).

κατάϊξ: literally a 'downward-rushing' wind (cf. καταΐςςω).

The form was perhaps invented by Call. (cf. Ap. Rh. 1. 1203, 3. 1376 and ἄϊξ in 4. 820), and appears four times in the paraphrase of the Psalms by Call.'s admirer pseudo-Apollinarius (see M. Campbell, *Studies in the Third Book of Apollonius Rhodius'* Argonautica (1983), 126 n. 27). Democritus (fr. 14, D.–K.[6], ii, p. 144. 39) had spoken of καταιγίδες (cf. LSJ, s.v. αἰγίς II). In favour of accenting κατάϊξ (rather than καταῖξ with Herodian), M. L. West notes that the ι must be as long in the nominative singular as anywhere else.

16 εἰcέπεcεν: Pfeiffer, arguing that we are still in the simile which started at line 13, points out that the aorist is often used in Homeric similes after ὡc δ᾽ ὅτε (e.g. *Il.* 3. 33 ff.).

18]ερ.[: the third letter is probably Γ. In view of line 15 βορέαο and fr. 86 γαμβρὸc Ἐρεχθῆοc· ὁ Βορρᾶc, one should say that it can hardly be Ε. Even if it could, there is insufficient space for γαμβρόc at the beginning of the line (as Mr Parsons confirms).

Fr. 19 (319 Pf.)

καὶ ἠέροc ἀχλύcαντοc: it is unclear whether καί in Suidas belongs to the quotation from Call. (similarly in e.g. frs. 128, 130). Pfeiffer, like older editors, printed just ἠέροc ἀχλύcαντοc at the start of a line, but noted that we may have here the second half of a hexameter with spondaic fifth foot. It seems to me that the half-line might then fit very neatly in fr. 18. 11: καὶ ἠέροc ἀχλύcαντοc | ἀcτεροπαὶ cελάγιζον. Hecker, who placed several fragments relating to the storm in an order now confirmed by P. Oxy. 2216 (see my sources for fr. 18), did not overlook this piece. Compare Nonn. *Par.* 1.11–12 ἐν ἀχλυόεντι δὲ κόcμωι | οὐρανίαιc cελάγιζε βολαῖc γαιήοχοc αἴγλη. In *Dion.* 1. 303 the situation is paradoxical, ἀcτεροπὴ δ᾽ ἤχλυcε (with cελάγιζε in 304 and ἠέροc in 301).

ἀχλύcαντοc: cκοτιcθέντοc Suid. Compare *Od.* 12. 406 (= 14. 304) ἤχλυcε δὲ πόντοc ὑπ᾽ αὐτῆc (sc. νεφέληc). The verb is intransitive also in Ap. Rh. 3. 963 and Nonn. *Dion.* 1. 303 (above), but in late poetry more often transitive, e.g. Quint. Smyrn. 11. 248–9 ἤχλυcε δὲ πᾶcαν ὕπερθεν | ἠέρα (cf. ibid. 1. 598, Pancrat. fr. 2. 12 Heitsch, Greg. Naz. *Carm.* 1. 2. 14. 113 (*PG* xxxvii. 764, the reference which Pfeiffer could not find), Nonn. *Dion.* 4. 380).

After the smaller pieces of P. Oxy. 2216 (frs. 20–3, the last perhaps intersecting fr. 24), I have placed fr. 25, as possibly

connected with the storm. Kapp (her frs. 9, 11, 13) included in the
same area also my frs. 19 (? = fr. 18. 11), 85 γαμβρὸς Ἐρεχθῆος
(sc. Boreas, see on fr. 18. 18), and 139 τὸ δέ μοι μαλκίστατον ἦμαρ.
Pfeiffer adds my fr. 136 ἑρπετὰ δ᾽ ἰλυοῖϲιν ἐνέκρυφεν, and I would
think of fr. 124 ἀϲταγὲϲ ὕδωρ. We do not know exactly how, after
the apparently general account of a bright afternoon and stormy
evening (fr. 18), Call. returned to Theseus.

FRS. 20–3

Lobel remarks (*P. Oxy.* xix. 145–6) that frs. 20–1 (*P. Oxy.* 2216,
fr. 2 'recto' and 'verso') may well come from the immediate
neighbourhood of frs. 17–18 (*P. Oxy.* 2216, fr. 1), but that frs.
22–3 (*P. Oxy.* 2216, fr. 3 'recto' and 'verso') are stained a dark
colour, and have no special resemblance to frs. 1 and 2 of this
papyrus apart from the writing. Only about fr. 23 can one
perhaps say something positive (unless it were worth noting that
the letters]δενα[, if substantiated in fr. 22. 2, would be paralleled
in fr. 37).

Fr. 23 (238d Pf.)

2]μοι ἀη[: this word-division seems most probable (unless an
elided alpha has been written in *scriptio plena*), and words in ἀη-
are sufficiently rare to make me wonder whether we have part of
fr. 24 ἀήϲυρον ⟨–⟩ γόνυ κάμψοι. If that were so, it would be worth
pondering the letters]γενοιτο[in line 1 above. On the assumption
that they are correctly read, γένοιτο is not the only possible
articulation (*CQ*, NS 32 (1982), 471 n. 10), but seems the most
likely. Call.'s tight metrical technique (see above, Introd. sect. IV)
limits γένοιτο to three positions in the hexameter: (*a*) before the
feminine caesura, preceded by a trochaic word (as *H*. 3. 109
ὕϲτερον ὄφρα γένοιτο), (*b*) after the feminine caesura, followed by
a postpositive (e.g. δέ) to avoid the problem of Hermann's
Bridge, (*c*) at the line-ending. Of these placings, (*c*) is improbable
here on papyrological grounds (see Barrett's point in *CQ* 1982,
471 n. 10). Either (*a*) or (*b*) would be compatible with the position
of γένοιτο immediately above]μοι ἀή⌞ϲυρον.

164   *Commentary*

Fr. 24 (311 Pf.)

I have placed this fragment here to allow for the possibility that it may coincide with fr. 23. 2 from one of the small pieces of *P. Oxy.* 2216. Even if this proved correct, it would not necessarily follow that fr. 24 belonged near fr. 17 or 18 (see Lobel quoted above on frs. 20–3). But I suppose that the bird alighting could be linked to the animals seeking refuge in their holes (fr. 136) and both be associated with the storm. This fragment need not have anything to do with the talking birds whom we meet in the Vienna Tablet and perhaps elsewhere in the *Hecale* (see introductory note to frs. 75–7).

ἀήcυρον <–> γόνυ κάμψοι: for the missing syllable Meineke supplied ὄν, Bergk ὡc, M. L. West ἐν. Suidas' explanation, no doubt from Salustius' commentary, makes it probable that Call. describes a bird alighting for rest, as in A. *PV* 396 κάμψειεν γόνυ (*Il.* 7. 118 γόνυ κάμψειν refers to a human being).

ἀήcυρον: 'light': cf. A. *PV* 452 (of ants), Ap. Rh. 2. 1101 (a breeze), Maximus 424, Triph. 360 πόρτιc ἀήcυροc (Campbell (*Lexicon in Triphiodorum* (1985), p. 212) interprets 'restless, unsteady, volatile, flighty').

κάμψοι: *pace* Pfeiffer, not a future optative, but a mixed aorist: see Vian (ed. 1961) on Ap. Rh. 3. 644 cβέcοι (mentioning a variant ἀλύξοι at *Od.* 17. 547): Ap. Rh. 2. 471 μογήcοι: Campbell, *R. Ph.* 47 (1973), 76; Keydell, *Nonni Dionysiaca*, i, p. 47*. In Call. *H.* 1. 93 there is a variant ἀείcοι.

Fr. 25 (269 Pf.)

1–2 ὁππότε λύχνου | δαιομένου πυρόεντες ἄδην ἐγένοντο μύκητες: 'when, while the lamp was alight, fungus continually formed with sparks'. μύκητες = the snuff or fungus which forms on the wick of a lamp. This was a traditional portent of rain, and the sources which quote this fragment make it very probable that Call. used the motif in the same way. Compare Ar. *Vesp.* 262 ἔπεισι γοῦν τοῖσιν λύχνοιc οὑτοιὶ μύκητες; [Thphr.] *de Signis Tempestatum* (fr. 6 Wimmer) 2. 34 μύκητεc ἐπὶ λύχνου νότιον πνεῦμα ἢ ὕδωρ cημαίνουcιν and 42; Arat. *Phaen.* 976–7 (most likely to have been in Call.'s mind) ἢ λύχνοιο μύκητες ἀγείρωνται περὶ μύξαν | νύκτα κατὰ νοτίην; Verg. *G.* 1. 390–2 (perhaps owing something to this fragment and to fr. 18. 5–6) 'ne nocturna quidem carpentes pensa puellae | nescivere hiemem, testa cum ardente viderent | scintillare oleum et putris concrescere fungos'; Apul. *Met.* 2. 11. Wilamowitz (*GGN* 1893, 737 (= *Kl. Schr.* ii. 37) n. 2) conjectured that this sign of a storm was observed by Hecale in her cottage before Theseus' arrival.

2 πυρόεντεc: for adjectives in -ήειc and -όειc in Call. see on fr. 74. 23. πυρόειc does not certainly occur earlier (a rival for the honour would be Cleanth. fr. 1. 10 Powell); it became popular among later poets, above all Nonnus.

ἄδην: 'continually' (so Pfeiffer; cf. Hopkinson (*HD*) on *H.* 6. 55); schol. Ap. Rh. 2. 81 explains with cυνεχῶc.

Fr. 26 (525 inc. sed. Pf.)

ἐλαχὺν δόμον: this is the only case in which I have, without new evidence, judged worthy of the main section (rather than the Incerta) a fragment which Pfeiffer left among those 'incertae sedis'. Although the words are not ascribed to the *Hecale*, every indication points that way, so that there can be little doubt as to the origin (Kapp on her fr. 3). Gregory of Nazianzus in a poem much influenced by the *Hecale* (see on fr. 2. 2 τέγος ἀκλήιστον and on fr. 35) uses these same words in the context of hospitality (*Carm.* 1. 2. 2. 332–3 (*PG* xxxvii. 604)):

> μέτρα φιλοξενίηc ἀcπάζεο· εἴ τιc ἄριcτοc,
> οἵγε προφρονέωc ἐλαχὺν δόμον.

For Gregory's verbatim borrowings from Call. see also on fr. 160 inc. auct. (a controversial instance). ἐλαχὺν δόμον would of course admirably suit Hecale's cottage (cf. Ov. *Met.* 8. 630, the house of Baucis and Philemon, 'parva quidem'). I have placed the fragment here on the hypothesis that it may represent Theseus' first glimpse of Hecale's cottage (cf. *Dieg.* x. 28–30 αἰφνίδιον δὲ ὑετοῦ ῥαγέντος κατ' ἐcχατιὰν οἰκίδιον θεαcάμενος Ἑκάληc and *Arg. Hec.* 8–9). Other positions, e.g. near the beginning of the poem (Kapp. fr. 3) are equally possible.

ἐλαχύν: although ἐλαχύc is a perfectly correct positive of ἐλάccων, ἐλάχιcτοc, it seems that (apart from Gregory of Nazianzus) only Call. ventured the masculine (cf. *Aet.* fr. 1. 32 Pf.—

ἐλαχός in fr. 542 Pf. was wrongly confused with our fragment by Schneider, fr. 349). The feminine ἐλάχεια was a disputed v.l. in Homer (*Od.* 9. 116, where schol. ascribe it to Zenodotus; ibid. 10. 509; cf. *H. Hom. Ap.* 197), freely employed by later poets (e.g. Euph. fr. 11. 2, Nic. *Ther.* 324). Antipater of Sidon has a unique neuter ἐλαχύ (*AP* 7. 498(= 55 G.–P.) 1).

FRS. 27–39   THE ENTERTAINMENT

With fr. 27 (if Webster's guess was right—otherwise with fr. 28) we enter the most celebrated part of the poem, which described Theseus' reception in Hecale's cottage and the meal which she laid before him. The literary associations of this will be discussed fully below in Appendix III. For the moment I will merely say that the main model was the entertainment of Odysseus by Eumaeus (Pfeiffer notes on his fr. 241 how Call. makes special use of words prominent in *Od.* 13–15), and that, of later hospitality stories, much the closest to the *Hecale* is Ovid's *Baucis and Philemon* (*Met.* 8. 626 ff.; cf. I. Cazzaniga, *Parola del Passato*, 18 (1963), 23–35).

Fr. 27 (*SH* 282; ?239 Pf.)

The mention of sandals in line 2 persuaded Lobel that *P. Oxy.* 2529 'recto' related to the lifting of the γνωρίσματα from under the rock in Troezen (see frs. 9–11); in line 1 he wished to restore ἀ]πέκλινεν, of 'moving aside' the stone. But the other side of the same papyrus (my fr. 36) describes the meal which Hecale offered to Theseus; although Call.'s method of narration can be full of surprises, it seems scarcely credible that the Troezenian γνωρίσματα should be separated from the meal by a single page. T. B. L. Webster (*ap.* M. L. West, *CR*, NS 16 (1966), 24) made the much more attractive suggestion that in line 2 Theseus is removing his sandals after entering Hecale's cottage; very cleverly, Webster wished to supply fr. 28 in the second half of fr. 27. 2. The meal would then follow the reception at a decent interval.

1]πεκλινεν[: we can consider ἀ]π-, ἐ]π-, and ὑ]π-. Of these, ἐ]πέκλινεν is perhaps most promising. Barrett wonders whether it could be a case of leaning something against something else (e.g. Theseus disposing of his club: cf. *Od.* 1. 127–9).

2]ὑπ' ἁρπῖδα[: for ἁρπίς and its smooth breathing see on fr. 9. 2. Webster (*ap*. West, op. cit. 24) wished to insert here fr. 28, as follows:

> λύcαθ'] ὑπ' ἁρπῖδα[c, ⌊διερὴν δ' ἀπεcείcατο λαίφην⌋
>]άδα, τὴν ἀγ[

This is highly ingenious and plausible.]άδα could be part of a second adjective, describing the λαίφη. West considered διπλ]άδα, although the form is unattested; elsewhere δίπλαξ occurs as a substantive = 'a double-folded cloak' (*Il*. 3. 126, 22. 441; *Od*. 19. 241; Ap. Rh. 1. 326, 722), as an adjective in Theocr. 25. 254 δίπλακα λώπην. Thereafter τὴν ἀγ[might fall into place as a relative clause giving the cloak's origin or purpose, of a kind familiar from Homer (*Il*. 5. 338, 6. 290 ff., 16. 143 ff., 222 ff.; *Od*. 8. 372 ff.) and equally common in Hellenistic poetry (e.g. Philet. fr. 18; Call. *H*. 4. 31; Ap. Rh. 1. 325–6 καλὴν | δίπλακα, τήν οἱ ὄπαccε καcιγνήτη Πελόπεια, 1. 722–3, 2. 31 ff., 3. 1205 ff., 4. 424 ff.; Euph. frs. 42, 107. 2; Nonn. *Dion*. 18. 214–15).

4 φαέεc[: for the dative φαέεccι = eyes cf. *H*. 3. 211, Nic. *Alex*. 84*, [Mosch.] 4. 9; Greg. Naz. *Carm*. 1. 2. 2. 74 (*PG* 37. 584) etc.; (used of the moon's light in [Hes.] fr. 252. 4 and perhaps fr. 23a. 8). φάεα = 'eyes' first comes in a recurrent line, *Od*. 16. 15 = 17. 39 = 19. 417. See further Bulloch, *FH*, pp. 43, 203; as he himself recognizes, little if any weight can be put on his deduction that *H*. 5 may predate the *Hecale* (nor can we be certain of the meaning 'eyes' here).

Fr. 28 (239 Pf.)

διερὴν δ' ἀπεcείcατο λαίφην: on entering Hecale's cottage, Theseus 'shook off his wet cloak' (see above for the possibility of placing this fragment in fr. 27. 2). Pfeiffer believes that Call.'s model was *Od*. 14. 500 ἀπὸ δὲ χλαῖναν θέτο (though the context is not at all similar).

διερήν: in Homer (*Od*. 6. 201, 9. 43) διερός probably means 'living', 'active', though Apollonius Sophista (p. 58. 31 Bekker) glossed *Od*. 9. 43 διερῶι ποδί with διύγρωι. The meaning 'wet' (which Hainsworth on *Od*. 6. 501 seems to regard as the original sense) is certain in Hes. *Op*. 460 αὔην καὶ διερήν, and common thereafter; cf. Call. *H*. 1. 24, 2. 23 διερὸc λίθος of the transformed

Niobe (with Williams's full note (*HA*)), and Livrea's edition of
the late Greek epic poet Dionysius (1973), pp. 65–6. Eratosth.
Hermes, SH 397, col. ii. 1 perhaps maintains the alternative sense,
'living'.

λαίφην: only here for λαῖφος. The latter, when used of the
disguised Odysseus in *Od.* 13. 399, 20. 206, clearly has the
implication 'tattered garment', which is not suitable for Theseus
(unless he took an old cloak for concealment when he left
surreptitiously). According to Bacchylides (18. 53–4), Theseus on
his journey from Troezen to Athens wore οὔλιον | Θεσσαλὰν
χλαμύδ'.

Fr. 29 (240 Pf.)

τὸν μὲν ἐπ' ἀσκάντην κάθισεν: 'she made him sit down on the
couch'. From this point we start to have close imitations of Call.
in Ovid's tale of Baucis and Philemon: after Jupiter and Mercury
enter, 'membra senex posito iussit relevare sedili' (*Met.* 8. 639).
Eumaeus had received Odysseus similarly, κλισίηνδ' ἡγήσατο δῖος
ὑφορβός, | εἷσεν δ' εἰσαγαγών, ῥῶπας δ' ὑπέχευε δασείας, | ἐστόρεσεν
δ' ἔπι δέρμα ἰονθάδος ἀγρίου αἰγός, | αὐτοῦ ἐνεύναιον, μέγα καὶ δασύ
(*Od.* 14.48–51); cf. *Aen.* 8. 367–8 (Evander and Aeneas) 'stratisque
locavit | effultum foliis et pelle Libystidis ursae'.

ἀσκάντην: the conjecture of Ed. Schwartz. Cod. A of *Et. Gen.*
has ἀσκάνταν, cod. B (and *Et. Mag.*) ἀσκάντα, which was defended
by Naeke (p. 124), Schneider (fr. 237), and, most recently,
Giangrande (*Hermes*, 98 (1970), 272 = *SMA* i. 80) as a Doric
genitive. ἀσκάντης, defined by *Et. Gen.* as κλινίδιον εὐτελές (cf.
G. M. A. Richter, *The Furniture of the Greeks, Etruscans, and
Romans* (1966), p. 52) is one of the pieces of local colour which
Call. almost certainly drew from Attic Old Comedy, in this case
Ar. *Nub.* 633 ἕξει τὸν ἀσκάντην λαβών (found later in Antiphil. *AP*
7. 634(= 19 G.–P.). 6 of a bier, and in Luc. *Lex.* 6). The origin is
obscure, perhaps Eastern; similar words (ἀσγάνδης, ἀσκάνδης,
ἀστάνδης) are attested with the meaning 'messenger' (H. Happ,
Glotta, 40 (1962), 198–201).

Fr. 30 (241 Pf.)

αὐτόθεν ἐξ εὐνῆς ὀλίγον ῥάκος αἰθύξασα: if we may trust

Ovid (*Met.* 8. 640 'quo superiniecit textum rude sedula Baucis') the ὀλίγον ῥάκος ('textum rude') will be placed on the ἀσκάντης (fr. 29) to make it more comfortable for Theseus.

αὐτόθεν ἐξ εὐνῆς: 'from where it lay on the bed'; cf. e.g. *Il.* 19. 77 αὐτόθεν ἐξ ἕδρης, *Od.* 21. 420 αὐτόθεν ἐκ δίφροιο.

ῥάκος: this word, not to be found in the *Iliad*, is very common in the *Odyssey*, particularly applied to the rags of Odysseus when disguised as a beggar (13. 434, 14. 342, 512, etc.), also e.g. of distressed characters in Euripides (*Telephus*, fr. 697. 1 *TGF*² = 103 Austin, *Nova Fragmenta Euripidea in Papyris Reperta* (1968); cf. Ar. *Ach.* 432 Τηλέφου ῥακώματα).

αἰθύξασα: the essence of αἰθύσσω (first in Sapph. fr. 2. 7 L.–P. = *LGS* 192. 7 and Soph. fr. 542 Radt, Pearson; compounds in P. *Ol.* 10. 73, *Pyth.* 4. 83) is stirring up, setting in motion: Suidas here explains with κινήσασα. Hecale snatches up and shakes the ῥάκος. Call. perhaps uses this verb again in fr. 70. 2, and it is popular with other Hellenistic poets (e.g. Arat. *Phaen.* 1034 (intransitive); Ap. Rh. 2. 1253; Euph. *SH* 415. i. 23, 442. 8) with many instances in Nonnus (cf. also James, *Oppian of Cilicia*, pp. 224–5). See K. J. McKay, *CR* NS 24 (1974), 9.

Fr. 31 (242 Pf.)

παλαίθετα κᾶλα καθήιρει: the wood has been stored aloft to dry, as in Ov. *Met.* 8. 644–5 'ramaliaque arida tecto | detulit'. Fr. 114 might conceivably portray Hecale putting together material for her fire: cf. Eratosth. fr. 24 Powell (? Icarius lighting a fire for Dionysus in the *Erigone*—but Borthwick (*CQ*, NS 19 (1969), 310) interprets differently). The very detailed description is typical of Hellenistic poetry, and of Roman poetry inspired by the Hellenistic masters (e.g. [Virg.] *Mor.* 8 ff., Ov. *Fast.* 5. 505 ff.).

παλαίθετα: earlier only in Ion (a poet in whom Call. took some interest—see *Diegesis* to fr. 203 Pf.), *Omphale*, fr. 22. 1 *TGF*² (= *Tr. G. F.* 19 F 22 Snell).

Fr. 32 (243 Pf.)

δανὰ ξύλα . . . κεάσαι: hesitantly I follow Schneider, Kapp, and Pfeiffer, and print these words in the order given by Suidas, assuming a lacuna. Bentley wished to read ξύλα δανὰ κεάσσαι, exactly as in *Od.* 15. 322 (where there is a variant πολλά). This could be right. The _Hecale_ imitates Homer much more closely than do Call.'s other works; for example, frs. 48. 3 ῥυδὸν ἀφνύονται, 51. 1 (if Naeke's emendation δαίμων for δήμου is correct) ὁμέστιον ἤγαγε δαίμων, 57 ἁλυκὸν δέ οἱ ἔκπεσε δάκρυ. In fr. 74. 22 we find a substantial verbatim borrowing from Homer, καδδραθέτην δ' οὐ πολλὸν ἐπὶ χρόνον. Reitzenstein (_Hermes_, 26 (1891), 310 n. 1) believed that there has been a confusion in Suidas, whereby (?Salustius') use of _Od._ 15. 322 to illustrate δανός in connection with δανάκης (see on fr. 99) led to the false ascription of ξύλα δανὰ κεάσσαι to Call. But, as Kapp remarks (on her fr. 17), this would be a remarkable coincidence in view of Ov. _Met._ 8. 644–5 'ramaliaque arida . . . | . . . minuit' in a passage so full of Call. (cf. _Fast._ 5. 508). For δανός, 'dry', cf. also Ar. _Pax_ 1133–4 τῶν ξύλων . . . | δανότατα, and an anonymous epic fragment (_Pap. Berol._ 1969, _Berl. Klass. Texte_, v. 2, p. 145) ξ]ύλα δανὰ κελ[(concerning the last letter see Giangrande, _SMA_ i. 46 n. 52, though one might suspect that Λ was a scribal error for Α). The epithet was restored by Pfeiffer in fr. 99. 3 (see ad loc.).

Fr. 33 (244 Pf.)

αἶψα δὲ κυμαίνουcαν ἀπαίνυτο χυτρίδα κοίλην: we do not know what was boiling in the pot. Pfeiffer suggested that it might be no more than water for the foot-washing (see fr. 34). Otherwise one would think (with Naeke) of some vegetables; cf. Ov. _Fast._ 5. 509–10 (Hyrieus entertaining three gods unawares) 'stant calices; minor inde fabas, holus alter habebat; | et spumat testu pressus uterque suo'.

χυτρίδα: a rare word in literature (e.g. Hdt. 5. 88; Bato, fr. 3. 2 Kock and _PCG_) but also found on inscriptions (see _LSJ_).

Fr. 34 (246 Pf.)   _The Foot-washing_

In _Od._ 19. 386 ff. the old nurse Eurycleia washes Odysseus' feet (a famous episode, which leads to his recognition through an old scar). It is possible that there was a corresponding scene in the _Hecale_, but, of the three fragments (245–7) which Pfeiffer gave to it, only this one stands a good chance of being correctly assigned. Fr. 245 Pf. in my opinion more probably concerns Sciron (fr. 60), while a papyrus has shown the context of fr. 247 Pf. to be different (fr. 48. 5). The present fragment, however, is quoted by Suidas s.v. κελέβη, defined as τοιοῦτον cκεῦοc ἐν ὧι δυνατὸν νίψαcθαι πόδαc. Since the comment may derive from Salustius, there is reason to believe that this was also the context in Call.

One might wish to strengthen the case for a foot-washing episode in the *Hecale* by pointing to a parallel passage in Ovid's *Baucis and Philemon* (*Met.* 8. 652 ff.). Unfortunately the matter is complicated by doubts over the authenticity of those lines, but I myself believe, with the majority of scholars, that they may well be genuinely Ovidian (see my commentary, pp. 117–18).

ἐκ δ᾽ ἔχεεν κελέβην, μετὰ δ᾽ αὖ κερὰc ἠφύcατ᾽ ἄλλο: 'she poured out the basin, and drew another draught of warm water.' A faint echo of this line may be discerned in Euph. fr. 131 κελέβηι ἀποήφυcαc ὕδωρ. In *Od.* 19. 387 ff. Eurycleia ὕδωρ δ᾽ ἐνεχεύατο πουλύ,| ψυχρόν, ἔπειτα δὲ θερμὸν ἐπήφυcεν—then, after an accident when the tub is overturned (469–70), she has to fetch fresh water (504).

ἐκ δ᾽ ἔχεεν κελέβην: cf. *H.* 1. 32 ἐκ δ᾽ ἔχεεν*; but Pfeiffer notes the present construction as very rare, comparing Men. fr. 915 Kock = 670 Koerte τὸν χοᾶ | ἐκκέχυκαc. Although κελέβη was used in a variety of senses (see Athen. 11. 475c–f), it must here be quite a substantial vessel; one of Suidas' synonyms is λεκάνη (also, according to Poll. 10. 77, suitable for foot-washing).

μετὰ δ᾽ αὖ κερὰc ἠφύcατ᾽ ἄλλο: Suidas claims that κεράc is an adverb = κεραcτικῶc ('for mixing'), but Pfeiffer may be right in suspecting that this 'adverb' was invented (? by Salustius) in an attempt to explain our present line. He suggests more plausibly that μετά . . . κεράc is a tmesis of the noun μετάκεραc, often in the comic poets of warm rather than hot water (? cf. 'tepidis . . . aquis' in the Ovidian foot-washing, *Met.* 8. 654). Athenaeus (3. 123e) quotes (I take the following references from Kock's collection) Sophilus (fr. 1), Alexis (fr. 137), Philemon (fr. 40), and Amphis (fr. 7)—one can add Philyllius (fr. 32; cf. also Eratosthenes in Ath. 2. 41d). Tmesis of a noun is alleged in *Il.* 4. 235 οὐ γὰρ ἐπὶ ψευδέccι πατὴρ Ζεὺc ἔccετ᾽ ἀρωγόc, where schol. comments ἡ δὲ ἐπί πρὸc τὸ ἀρωγόc; Pfeiffer, however, approves Maas' ἐπιψευδέccι (*Kl. Schr.* 197). This expedient is of course necessary to accommodate μετάκεραc, but the tmesis of such a homely word has a deliberately incongruous effect, similar to that of the epic pleonasm inflicted upon another word from Comedy in fr. 35. 1 ἐκ ... cιπύηθεν.

Fr. 35 (251 Pf.)

'She set down in abundance loaves taken from a bread-bin, such as women hide under the ashes for herdsmen.' The two lines were linked by Naeke (p. 145), who unnecessarily supposed that a missing line separated them. Pfeiffer saw as Call.'s model Homeric passages such as *Od.* 3. 479–80 ἐν δὲ γυνὴ ... cῖτον ... ἔθηκεν | ὄψα τε, οἷα ἔδουcι διοτρεφέεc βαcιλῆεc. Both Gregory of Nazianzus (*Carm.* 1. 2. 2. 174 ff. (*PG* xxxvii. 592) ἐν πενιχρῆι cιπύηι ... φιλοξείνοιο γυναικόc) and Michael Choniates (ii. 386. 329 ff. Lambros Cιδονίηι δὲ γυναικί, λιμοῦ χθόνα βοcκομένοιο,| Ἡλίαc ὤπαcεν ἐγκρυφιάζεμεν ἀμφοτέροιcιν | ἀνθρακιῆι cποδοέccηι εὐρυτέραι μάκτραι τε | ἅλιc ἐπεί οἱ ἄλφιτ' ἄμυλα ῥέεν cιπύηθεν) adapt Hecale to the widow of Sidon (1 Kgs. 17: 8 ff.)—note that Michael's mingling of words from the two Callimachean lines supports their close association.

ἐκ δ' ἄρτουc cιπύηθεν: for the characteristic insertion between preposition and noun cf. frs. 1, 9. 1, 51. 1. ἐκ ... cιπύηθεν is an epic pleonasm, slightly humorous in this context (cf. on fr. 34), as e.g. *Il.* 8. 19 ἐξ οὐρανόθεν (to which grammarians objected, together with [Hes.] fr. 41 M.–W. ἐξ ἀγρόθεν). cιπύη (also in *Aetia* (*SH* 239. 9)), like μετάκεραc (fr. 34) is very much at home in Old Comedy (Eup. fr. 302 K. = 324 *PCG*; Pherecr. fr. 142 K.; Ar. *Eq.* 1296, *Plut.* 806, fr. 541 K. = 555 *PCG*); cf., in a context of poverty, Leon. *AP* 6. 302 (= 37 G.–P.). 2. See B. A. Sparkes, 'The Greek Kitchen', *JHS* 82 (1962), 124 n. 21 and pl. iv. 1.

2 οἷουc βωνίτηιcιν ἐνικρύπτουcι γυναῖκεc: ἐνικρύπτουcι alludes to the Athenian ἐγκρυφίαc ἄρτοc (Athen. 3. 110b ὁ παρ' Ἀττικοῖc ἐγκρυφίαc), baked in ashes. Athenaeus quotes Nicostr. fr. 14 Kock and Archestratus in his hexameter parody (*SH* 135. 15); note also Michael Choniates quoted above (without doubt taken from the *Hecale*). For other kinds of ash-baked bread see Athen. 3. 111e. The spirit of Call., if not the technical process, is reflected in the pseudo-Virgilian *Moretum* 49–50 'infert inde foco ...|... testisque tegit, super aggerat ignes'. See B. A. Sparkes, 'The Greek Kitchen', *JHS* 82 (1962), 128.

βωνίτηιcιν: a puzzling word—according to *Et. Gen.* βωνίτης cημαίνει τὸν βουκόλον. If so, perhaps it is a Doric form of βουνίτης (given by Suidas in our fragment): cf. βῶν at *Il.* 7. 238 and Call. *H.* 6. 108 (with Hopkinson's note); Giangrande, *Hermes*, 98 (1970), 271 = *SMA* i. 79. There may be no connection with Πὰν βουνῖτα, 'god of the hills' (βουνός) in Zon. *AP* 6. 106 (= 3 G.–P.). 5.

Fr. 36 (*SH* 283; ? 334, 248 Pf.)

From the 'verso' of *P. Oxy.* 2529; the 'recto', probably describing Theseus entering Hecale's cottage, = fr. 27.

2]ε φαῦλον ι [: almost certainly = fr. 37 εἰκαίην, τῆς οὐδὲν ἀπέβραcε φαῦλον ἀλετρίς, but I have not felt able to incorporate fr. 37 here because the scribe has undoubtedly written iota rather than the alpha which ἀλετρίς requires. The possibilities are: (*a*) the line is not to be identified with fr. 37: (*b*) we do have fr. 37 here, but the papyrus read a different word at the end of the line; (*c*) the scribe has simply made a mistake. Lobel wrote (*P. Oxy.* xxx. 90) 'I should not have thought that the removal of the "rubbish" from a grain was the function of the grinder, but of the thresher', perhaps an unnecessary doubt.

3 οἶcε: an unprecedented (later in Ael. fr. 123. 11 Hercher) mixed aorist indicative, 'she brought'. Homer has an imperative οἶcε (*Od.* 22. 106, 481) and infinitive οἰcέμεν (*Od.* 3. 429), both of which Call. took up (*H.* 6. 136 and *Hec.* fr. 99. 2 respectively), adding the plural imperative οἴcετε in *H.* 5. 17, 31, 48. See Bulloch (*FH*) on *H.* 5. 17; Catherine L. Prince, *Glotta*, 48 (1970), 155–63. As Giangrande says in *CQ*, NS 21 (1971), 146 n. 1, 'Hellenistic poets added their own forms to Homeric defective paradigms'. Similarly, where Homer has just the dative ἤνοπι, Call. produces a nominative ἤνοψ (fr. 18. 2) and accusative ἤνοπα (fr. 102. 2).

Lobel thought he could distinguish a grave accent over ἐλαί[. That would be compatible only with a genitive ἐλαι[ῶν.

4–5 Athenaeus quotes these lines (fr. 248 Pf.) in his chapter on olives (2. 56). Compare Ov. *Met.* 8. 664–5 'ponitur hic bicolor sincerae baca Minervae,| conditaque in liquida corna autumnalia faece'.

γεργέριμον: an over-ripe olive also known as δρυπεπής and ἰсχάс (Ath. 2. 56d). But the word is a strange one: some have sought a Hebrew origin (see B. Hemmerdinger, *Glotta*, 48 (1970), 41).

πίτυριν: the same as φαυλία, according to Philemon (Athen. 2. 56c, no doubt ἐν τοῖс Ἀττικοῖс Ὀνόμαсιν ἢ Γλώτταιс, cf. Athen. 11. 468 f); the latter is called μικρόκαρποс by Eustathius (1356. 64). Perhaps it got its name because the colour resembled bran (πίτυρον).

καὶ] ἦν ἀπεθήκ[ατο λευκήν | εἰν ἁλὶ νήχεсθαι φθινοπ]ω-ρ[ίδ]α: 'and the autumn kind which she set aside to swim in brine while still light green'; cf. Gaet. *AP* 6. 190(= 2 Page, *FGE*). 5 ἁλινήκτειραν ἐλαίην; Nonn. *Dion.* 17. 54 ff. χύδην δ' ἐπέβαλλε τραπέζηι | εἰν ἁλὶ νηχομένηс φθινοπωρίδοс ἄνθοс ἐλαίηс | Βρόγγος, ἔχων μίμημα φιλοсτόργοιο νομῆοс (sc. Molorchi). Nonnus' wording is clearly taken from the *Hecale*—we do not know how much similar material there was in Call.'s *Molorchus* (*SH* 254–69). The autumn olive (φθινοπωρίс) was also called ἁλμάс ('briny') or κολυμβάс ('swimmer') in accordance with its treatment; Call. uses the last name in the fourth *Iambus*, when making the most obvious of several references back to his own *Hecale*, ἐν δ' ἡ κολυμβὰс ἦν ἔπωνε χὠ Θηсεύс (fr. 194. 77 Pf.).

Fr. 37 (334 Pf.)

εἰκαιήν, τῆс οὐδὲν ἀπέβραсε φαῦλον ἀλετρίс: 'ordinary [?flour], from which the mill-woman did not shake out any of the waste'. This fragment is probably to be identified with fr. 36. 2 (see above); for the missing noun Naeke (p. 142) suggested κριθήν, Pfeiffer ἄλευρον (noting that *Et. Gud.* p. 85. 18 de Stef. recognizes a feminine ἄλευροс). The coarse flour would produce a darker bread, generally associated with the poor (L. A. Moritz, *Grain-mills and Flour in Classical Antiquity* (1958), 153). Pfeiffer well compares Pers. 3. 112 'populi cribro decussa farina'.

εἰκαιήν: 'ordinary', 'taken at random' (cf. Nic. *Ther.* 394–5 ἀπ' εἰκαίηс δὲ βοτεῖται | γαίηс); in earlier verse only at Soph. fr. 308 Radt, Pearson εἰκαία сχολή.

ἀπέβραсε: the one poetic occurrence of ἀποβράссω, a verb which suggests the use of a sieve (Moritz, op. cit. pp. 159–63). Without mentioning our fragment, Moritz (p. 160) draws attention to Aristoph. fr. 271 Kock = 282 *PCG*, where βράττω comes after πτίττω. The best flour-sieves were made of linen (Moritz, p. 166). Hesychius explains ἀποβράcαι (? in this line) with τὸ δι-αττῆcαι πυροὺc ἢ ἄλευρα ὀθόνηι.

φαῦλον: the 'worthless' part—apparently not a technical term (but see LSJ for φαύλιοc used of 'coarse' fruits).

FRS. 38–9

Two vegetables served by Hecale. We owe them both to the elder Pliny, who must have had a liking for this part of the poem: 26. 82 (crethmos) 'hanc certe apud Callimachum adponit rustica illa Hecale'; 22. 88 (soncus) 'ut quem Theseo apud Callimachum adponat Hecale'. He may also have read the corresponding scene in Eratosthenes' *Erigone* (22. 86 (scolymos) 'Eratostheni quoque laudata in paupere cena' (fr. 34 Powell inc. sed.)). Concerning the abundance of vegetables produced in Attica see Scherling, *Quibus Rebus*, pp. 17, 22, 31 (Euripides' mother).

Fr. 156 inc. sed. Νιcαίηc ἀγλῖθεc ἀπ' 'Οργάδοc and fr. 157 inc. sed. (from Pliny) could also belong to this part of the *Hecale*.

Fr. 38 (249 Pf.)

The vegetable is samphire, but we cannot be sure what form of the name Call. used. Pliny (*NH* 26. 82) has a feminine 'crethmos', but the neuter κρῆθμον has survived in medical writers and in Nic. *Ther.* 909 (with scholia). See further Naeke (pp. 136 ff.) and Pf.

Fr. 39 (250 Pf.)

cόγκοc (less commonly cόγχοc), 'sow-thistle', is mentioned e.g. by Matro, *SH* 536. 1; Antiph. fr. 226. 4 Kock; Nic. *Georg.* fr. 71. 3 G.–S. See Ath. 6. 250e for a dinner-table witticism provoked by this vegetable.

FRS. 40 FF. THE CONVERSATION OF HECALE AND THESEUS

Although the *Diegesis* says no more of Theseus' stay in Hecale's cottage than ἐνταῦθα ἐξενοδοκήθη (x. 30–1), after the meal the old woman would inevitably ask her young guest about himself and his mission. Fr. 40. 3 ἅ μ᾽ εἴρεο proves that this was so; it seems that fr. 40 contains the end of Theseus' reply (l. 6 γενέθλη may even have been his last word). In turn he enquires about her family, and why she should spend her old age in such a lonely place (fr. 40. 3–6). Theseus may have spoken briefly, but Hecale (in spite of fr. 40. 4 τυτθόν) clearly told her life-story at considerable length. By the start of fr. 42 she may have been talking for nearly 30 lines (some 32 lines separated fr. 40 from fr. 42), and is still dealing with her period of prosperity. Her downfall in frs. 47–9 spans 50 lines of text, plus immeasurable lacunae between frs. 47 and 48 and frs. 48 and 49—note however that frs. 47 and 49 are on opposite sides of the page in *P. Oxy.* 2377, while frs. 48 and 49. 7–16 stand in adjacent columns of *P. Oxy.* 2376.

Details of Hecale's life remain obscure, despite the publication since Pfeiffer of *P. Oxy.* 2376 and 2377, but we can discern references to three characters who played a part in her story. First there is the finely-dressed man whom she saw driving from Aphidnae (fr. 42. 2 ff.). Pfeiffer suggested, plausibly enough from the evidence then available, that this man might have been Theseus' father Aegeus; the new papyri make it perhaps more likely that he was Hecale's future husband—it being by no means a certain inference from Ov. *Rem.* 747–8 (= above, Test. 5) that she never married. In the latter case, perhaps it was he who drowned at sea when planning to bring back horses from Sparta (fr. 47. 6). Then there are two boys whom Hecale brought up (fr. 48), whether she was their nurse or (as now seems more probable) their mother. Both of these appear to have died young (fr. 49), one at the hands of Cercyon (fr. 49. 8 ff.). It is noteworthy that in fr. 49. 14 she speaks of the fearful revenge which she would like to take on Cercyon 'while he is alive'. But Cercyon has already been killed by Theseus on his way to Athens. Probably, therefore, Call. postponed the description of Cercyon's death (? and some of Theseus' other victories, e.g. over Sciron (see frs. 59–61)) until this point in the poem. So one might tentatively suggest the following structure for the conversation:

(a)   Hecale asks Theseus about himself and his mission (cf. fr. 40. 3 ἅ μ᾽ εἴρεο).

(b)   Theseus replies (? quite briefly), ending the account of himself at fr. 40.2, and in turn enquires about Hecale and her past (fr. 40. 3–6).

(c) A substantial speech by Hecale (not fewer than 100 lines, and perhaps appreciably longer). She reveals that she has not always been poor (fr. 41, perhaps immediately preceded by fr. 158 inc. sed.); she met (? and married) a rich and distinguished man (fr. 42. 2 ff.), and bore (? or merely looked after) two boys. But all three perished in turn (frs. 47–9), the last succumbing to Cercyon (fr. 49. 8 ff.), after which Hecale was left alone and destitute.

(d) ? Theseus reassures her that Cercyon at least (cf. fr. 62) has already paid for his misdeeds (? likewise Sciron; cf. frs. 59–61).

Other items belonging to this conversation may include the sufferings under which Hecale's people laboured (? frs. 52–6), a tearful appeal to Theseus that he should free them from the terror of the Marathonian bull (fr. 57; cf. Stat. *Theb.* 12. 581–2 = above, Test. 8), and the promise of a sacrifice to Zeus for Theseus' safe return (Plut. *Thes.* 14; see further on fr. 169 inc. sed.).

Fr. 40 (*SH* 285. 1–6; 253. 1–6 Pf.)

1 'I am going down to Marathon.' Hecale's cottage stands on high ground (fr. 1, see ad loc.), probably on the slopes of Mt. Brilessus (cf. fr. 169 inc. sed.). Before Μαραθῶνα,]ἐς is possible, but not certain. At the end of the line, ὄφρα κε or ὄφρα κ᾽ is likely, but Pfeiffer's ὄφρα κ᾽ ἀπάρω does not suit the traces (*SH*).

2 Although the *SH* editors see before δέ the traces of a letter hardly consistent with the sigma that Παλλάς (Vitelli) would require, it remains likely that Athena is the καθηγήτειρα κελεύθου (Pfeiffer compares e.g. *Od.* 2. 405 ἡγήσατο Παλλὰς Ἀθήνη). Concerning the help given to Theseus by Athena (in Paus. 1. 27. 10 he sacrifices the bull to her) see also on fr. 17. 4.

καθηγήτειρα: not attested before Call. (later in Orph. *H.* 76. 6; cf. ἡγήτειρα in *AP* 6. 43. 7 = Page, *FGE*, 'Plato' 21; Opp. *Hal.* 1. 665; Orph. *H.* 78. 6; Nonn. *Dion.* 28. 42). Note also Ap. Rh. 3. 1182 προηγήτειραν ὁδοῖο (the cow which leads the way to Thebes).

Call. likes words in -τειρα (a recent addition to the list is *SH* 303
μήτειρα(ν), which was a v.l. at *Il.* 14. 259; cf. Greg. Naz. *Carm.* 1.
2. 1. 117 (*PG* 37. 531) etc.); from the *Hecale* we have also fr. 75
δαμάτειρα and fr. 93 ὀπτήτειρα. So do other Hellenistic (e.g.
Euphorion with γενέτειρα, ἐμπελάτειρα, ὀλέτειρα) and late poets.
One can gather quite a harvest from the Oppians, the Orphic
Argonautica (e.g. 352 ἰθύντειρα Δίκη καὶ 'Ερινύες αἰνοδότειραι),
the Orphic *Hymns* (particularly 10, source of the most extrava-
gant coinages), the *Sibylline Oracles*, Paulus Silentiarius, and John
of Gaza. In Nonnus' *Dionysiaca* some 17 such forms occur some
68 times, the favourite being κυβερνήτειρα with 18 appearances.
See further Hopkinson (*HD*) on *H.* 6. 42 ἀράτειραν.

3 ff. It is amusing to note a remarkable piece of prescience
(mixed with other less plausible ideas) in Schneider's reconstruc-
tion (ii, p. 181): 'deinde quum Theseus quoque Hecalae talis viri
adventum miranti breviter narrasset quis esset et unde cur iret,
rursus ex Hecale quaesivit quo casu factum esset, ut in hac
solitudine habitaret'—all this before the discovery of the papyrus!

3–4 Vitelli's supplements τὼς ἄρ' ἐμεῦ μεμάθ]ηκας and λέξον,
ἐπεὶ καὶ ἐμο]ί give at least what seems likely to be the general
sense. At the end of 3 Vitelli restores καὶ cὺ [δέ], supported by
Barrett, who argues that since καὶ cύ means 'you also', we need
the δέ (cf. Nonn. *Par.* 21. 86–7 καὶ cὺ δὲ θυμῶι | οἶδας). Pfeiffer,
however, reasonably objects 'καὶ δέ voce interposita non seiungit
Call.'; in favour of cύ [γε] he cites *H.* 4. 162.

3 μαῖα: particularly recalling the way Eurycleia is addressed in
the *Odyssey* (e.g. 19. 482, 20. 129, 23. 11, 35). In fr. 80. 4 the
vocative μαῖα probably comes from Hecale's neighbours.

4 Pfeiffer compared *Aet.* fr. 178. 21–2 ὄccα δ' ἐμεῖο cέθεν πάρα
θυμὸς ἀκοῦcαι | ἰχαίνει, τάδε μοι λέξον ἀνειρομένωι.

τυτθόν: either 'for a little while', as in Ap. Rh. 2. 917 τυτθόν περ
... ἰδέcθαι, 3. 526 (more commonly of space, 'a little way'); or
else (Campbell) with τι, 'a little something'.

5 ἐρημαίη ἔνι ναίεις: for the hiatus see above, Introd. sect. IV.
6. One looks for a noun (e.g. χώρηι, Pf.) at the beginning of line
6; cf. Ap. Rh. 4. 1719–20 ἐρημαίηι ἔνι ῥέζειν | ἀκτῆι and
[Apollinar.] *Ps.* 105. 20 ἐρημαίηι ἄτε χώρηι. It seems less probable
that ἐρημαίηι is here a substantive (cf. Ap. Rh. 3. 1197 βῆ δ' ἐc
ἐρημαίην and Livrea on 4. 1263).

6 Conceivably ἐc]τι (Vitelli).

Fr. 41 (254 Pf.)

There can be little doubt that fr. 41 belongs in the gap of about
32 lines (see above, Introd. sect. XI on *PSI* 133, my pap. 5)
between frs. 40. 6 and 42. 1. In *CQ*, NS 32 (1982), 472 I suggested
that fr. 41 might immediately follow fr. 158 inc. sed. (see further
ad loc.) τί δάκρυον εὗδον ἐγείρεις; with the two fragments
together forming the start of Hecale's reply, separated by only a
few lines from 40. 6 (possibly the last words of Theseus):

> τί δάκρυον εὗδον ἐγείρεις;
> οὐ γάρ μοι πενίη πατρώιος, οὐδ' ἀπὸ πάππων
> εἰμὶ λιπερνῆτις· βάλε μοι, βάλε τὸ τρίτον εἴη

That Hecale's opening words were τί δάκρυον εὗδον ἐγείρεις; is by
no means a new idea (see Schneider, ii, p. 181; Kapp, p. 84;
Barigazzi, *Hermes*, 86 (1958), 470), but I do not think conjunction
with fr. 41 has been proposed before. In fr. 41. 1 γάρ would
follow well ('a sad story, for once I was prosperous') and οὐ γάρ
μοι πενίη πατρώιος covers both parts of Theseus' enquiry (fr. 40.
5–6)—her family, and why she spends her old age amid such
miserable surroundings. For direct speech starting in the middle
of a Callimachean hexameter see McLennan, *HZ*, pp. 147 ff. and
Mineur, *HD*, pp. 29–30; *H.* 4. 212 εἶπε δ' ἀλυσθενέουσα· τί μητέρα,
κοῦρε, βαρύνεις; provides a possible pattern.

1 οὐ γάρ μοι πενίη πατρώιος: cf. Dion. Per. 709 ff. (a synthesis
of this passage and *Aet.* fr. 178. 27 ff. Pf.) οὐ γάρ μοι βίος ἐστὶ
μελαινάων ἐπὶ νηῶν | οὐδέ μοι ἐμπορίη πατρώιος, οὐδ' ἐπὶ Γάγγην |
ἔρχομαι. It was something of a convention that the host in this
kind of episode (see below, App. III) should once have been
prosperous: Eumaeus was a king's son (*Od.* 15. 403 ff.), while the
farmer in Euripides' *Electra* (36 ff.) came of a good family too. For
a story starting 'I was once rich, but am now reduced to penury'
cf. also *Od.* 19. 75 ff.

This speech of Hecale was admired by an unknown poet
(Powell, *CA*, epic. adesp. 4. 17–18), who put into the mouth of an
old woman, previously rich and generous to others (16), but now
a beggar in the city (20–1) the words ἐπεὶ οὔτι λιπερνῆτις πάρος
ἦα, (cf. *Hec.* fr. 41. 2) and ἔσκε δέ μοι νειὸς βαθυλήιος, ἔσκεν ἀλωή
(cf. fr. 42. 1). Some indeed would actually ascribe the piece to the
Hecale, but that can hardly be so (see above, Introd. sect. VI).

Recollection of lost riches in Latin poetry may owe something to this tradition, e.g. *Pan. Mess.* 184 ff. 'cui fuerant flavi ditantes ordine sulci | horrea fecundas ad deficientia messes |...| nunc desiderium superest; nam cura novatur | cum memor ante actos semper dolor admonet annos'; Tib. 1. 1. 19 ff., 41–2; Prop. 4. 1. 129–30.

γάρ: *Et. Gen.* A has γί, which is not this scribe's normal abbreviation for γάρ, but may be a misunderstanding of another scribe's abbreviation (Alpers).

2 λιπερνῆτιϲ: λιπερνήϲ first occurs in Archilochus' much imitated (Cratin. fr. 198 Kock. = 211 *PCG*; Ar. *Pax* 603 ff.) address to his fellow citizens ὦ λιπερνῆτεϲ πολῖται κτλ. (fr. 109 West). In the sixth century AD both Macedonius the Consul (*AP* 9. 649. 5) and Paulus Silentiarius (*S. Soph.* 1010) start a hexameter with οὐδὲ λιπερνήτηϲ.

βάλε μοι, βάλε τὸ τρίτον εἴη: 'I wish, I wish I had a third part'. The repeated βάλε (cf. fr. 159 inc. sed. ἀβάλε) recalls Alcman's wish to escape from the miseries of old age, *PMG* 26. 2 βάλε δὴ βάλε κηρύλοϲ εἴην. Elsewhere in Call. (e.g. *Aet.* frs. 75. 18 and 178. 14 Pf., *H.* 3. 121) τὸ τρίτον means 'for the third time', and Barrett would consider so understanding the words here (with the sense to be made clear by what followed). But perhaps our poet has in mind *Od.* 4. 97 ff., where Menelaus would be content with a third of his former possessions, if only those who died at Troy were still alive ὧν ὄφελον τριτάτην περ ἔχων ἐν δώμαϲι μοῖραν | ναίειν κτλ.

Fr. 42 (*SH* 285. 7–12; 253. 7 (= 255), 253. 8–12, ?293 Pf.)

Following a gap since fr. 40. 6 of about 32 lines (in which we can confidently place fr. 41, and conceivably fr. 158 inc. sed.), the text resumes with Hecale still (as in fr. 41) talking of her prosperous days. She must recently have mentioned the man (picked up with τὸν δ' in fr. 42. 2) whom she saw driving from Aphidnae.

1 δινομένην ὑπὸ βουϲὶν ἐμὴν ⌞ἐφύλαϲϲον ἅλωα: credit for recognizing this line (= fr. 255 Pf.) belongs mainly to Bartoletti (*SIFC*, NS 31 (1959), 179–81). Only the lower parts of the letters remain; although Vitelli thought he could read ομ̣ε̣ν̣ην, Pfeiffer (on his fr. 255) denied that the line could be supplied here. Bartoletti's enlarged photograph shows that it can, and furthermore that the papyrus read ὑπό (with Suidas) rather than περί (Choeroboscus) which Pfeiffer doubtfully had preferred.

δινομένην: the oxen are yoked and driven round the threshing-floor in a circle until the grain is thoroughly trampled out of the husks (M. L. West on Hes. *Op.* 598 δινέμεν). Thus *Il.* 20. 495–7:

> ὡς δ᾽ ὅτε τις ζεύξῃ βόας ἄρσενας εὐρυμετώπους
> τριβέμεναι κρῖ λευκὸν ἐϋκτιμένῃ ἐν ἀλωῆι,
> ῥίμφα τε λέπτ᾽ ἐγένοντο βοῶν ὑπὸ πόσσ᾽ ἐριμύκων κτλ.

ἐφύλαccον: first person singular or third plural (with e.g. Hecale's servants as the subject)? The verb might imply no more than a supervisory visit, but Stephanie West is still surprised at a woman performing this task. Nor can we be entirely sure that ἐφύλαccον is the right reading (see app. crit.).

ἅλωα: this was the standard example of the form, which indeed does not seem to be attested elsewhere (ἅλων in a different sense at Nic. *Ther.* 166). According to Choeroboscus, the corresponding genitive ἅλωος, found in Nic. fr. 70. 1 and Adaeus, *AP* 6. 258 (= 2 G.–P.). 3, πταῖσμα νεωτερικόν ἐστι.

2 τὸν δ᾽ ἀπ᾽ Ἀφιδνάων ἵπποι φ[έρον: I have put Vitelli's φ[έρον into the text. It fits not only the sense, but also Call.'s metrical requirements (a spondaic word after the masculine caesura should be combined with a bucolic diaeresis: cf. above, Introd. sect IV. 4 (*e*)). Pfeiffer's conclusion of the line, e.g. ἢ βαcιλεῦcιν is also plausible in view of line 3 (note ἢ βαcιλ[η in *Aet.* fr. 1. 3 Pf.*) but perhaps tells against his own conjecture (see below) that this man was not merely 'like a king', but actually of royal blood.

Who is the man driving from Aphidnae? Pfeiffer suggested that he might have been Theseus' father Aegeus. This idea has in its favour the fact that, in a common pattern of epic poetry, when an older person meets a young prince, the former turns out also to have met the prince's father at a similar age, and is astonished by the likeness between the two. Thus e.g. *Od.* 4. 138 ff. (Helen and Telemachus); *Aen.* 8. 155 ff. (Evander and Aeneas); Sil. 16. 191 ff. (Syphax and Scipio); Quint. Smyrn. 7. 642 ff. (Phoenix and Neoptolemus). Kapp very plausibly conjectured that in fr. 45 (her fr. 42), Hecale compares Theseus to another young man whom she met in the past; Pfeiffer wished to include fr. 50 τόδ᾽ ἔχω cέβαc (see ad loc.) in the same pattern, with Hecale marvelling at the resemblance between Theseus and his father.

While this scheme retains certain attractions, we now know a little bit more about Hecale's background from the two papyri which cover frs. 47–9, and it seems on balance more likely that the man from Aphidnae had a far closer connection with Hecale, becoming her husband and the father of her two boys (fr. 48).

ἀπ' Ἀφιδνάων: Aphidnae (more commonly Aphidna, but cf. Str. 9. 397 λέγουcι δὲ καὶ πληθυντικῶc) was a deme of the tribe Aiantis, and is shown by Hdt. 9. 73 to have been not far from Decelea (mentioned in fr. 52); both demes (like Trinemea in fr. 88 and Semachidae, perhaps in fr. 47. 18) must have been near Hecale's home. For the identification of Aphidnae with the hill called Kotroni, which commands the valley bordered by the towns of Kalentzi, Kapandriti, and Kiourka see James R. Mc-Credie, *Hesperia*, Suppl. 11 (1966), 81–3.

3 As Pfeiffer says, the Διὸc υἱέεc seem more likely to be kings (*H.* 1. 79 = Hes. *Th.* 96 ἐκ δὲ Διὸc βαcιλῆεc) than demigods (Wilamowitz supplied ἡμιθέοιcιν at the end of the line). M. L. West notes the optative εἶεν as odd.

4 Hecale recalls vividly (cf. *Od.* 19. 221 ff.) the fine clothes of the visitor.

μέμνημαι: for the emphatic placing as an old person remembers events long past cf. *Il.* 9. 527 (Phoenix) μέμνημαι τόδε ἔργον κτλ. and *Aen.* 8. 157 (Evander) 'nam memini ...'. Here the construction is not clear. If fr. 43 were correctly supplied (H. Fincke, see below) in fr. 42. 6, then μέμνημαι could be paratactic, with another verb in the missing part of line 4: 'I remember, he [e.g. had cast round his shoulders] a fine cloak ... and wore underneath ...'. Otherwise καλήν ...| ἄλλικα might be direct object of μέμνημαι (as Trypanis takes it in the Loeb).

5 ἀλ‿λ‿ικα χρυcείηιcιν ἐεργομ‿ένην ἐνετῆιcιν: a line containing two very rare words. ἄλλιξ is stated by Suidas and the *Etymologica* to be a Thessalian term for a chlamys (cf. the Thessalian chlamys which the young Theseus wore in Bacchyl. 18. 53–4, quoted on fr. 28); Hesychius defines it as χιτὼν χειριδωτός (with sleeves) and ascribes the word to Euphorion (fr. 144 Powell, no doubt from Call.). The Homeric *hapax legomenon* ἐνετή (*Il.* 14. 180) occurs elsewhere only in an inscriptional elegy of the second century AD from Marathon (*BCH* 50 (1926), 527 ff.), line 23 δωρηθείc τ' ἐνετῆιcι κατωμαδὸν ἠλέκτροιο. Miss Lorimer (*Homer and the Monuments*, p. 379 and n. 2) concluded 'the round brooch is probably meant.'

6 ἔργον ἀ⌞ρα⌟χνάῳ⌞ν: the appositional phrase is to some extent based on Homer's ἔργα γυναικῶν, as in *Od.* 7. 96–7 πέπλοι | λεπτοὶ ἐΰννητοι βεβλήατο, ἔργα γυναικῶν (cf. *Il.* 6. 289). Comparisons of fine spinning with spiders' work stretch from Philox. *PMG* 836(e), 6 λεπτᾶς ἀράχνας ἐναλιγκί-|οιϲι πέπλοιϲ to John of Gaza (1. 343) λεπτὸν ἔχει μελέεϲϲιν ἀραχνιόωντα χιτῶνα. Particularly close to Call. is Dion. Per. 757 κείνοιϲ (sc. the εἵματα of the Seres) οὔτι κεν ἔργον ἀραχνάων ἐρίϲειεν.

In the second half of this line it may well be possible to restore fr. 43 ϲτάδιον δ' ὑφέεϲτο χιτῶνα, as suggested by H. Fincke *ap.* Bartoletti, *SIFC*, NS 31 (1959), 179 n. 3; 'neque ϲτ]άδ̣ι̣ο̣[vestigiis plane repugnat' (*SH*).

Fr. 43 (293 Pf.)

ϲτάδιον δ ὑφέεϲτο χιτῶνα: quoted by the scholiast on Ap. Rh. 3. 1225–6 Αἰήτης περὶ μὲν ϲτήθεϲϲιν ἔεϲτο | θώρηκα ϲτάδιον. According to LSJ the meaning is 'standing upright or straight' (they compare ὀρθοϲτάδιον and ϲτατός); ϲτάδιος would thus be applied to Aeetes' θώρηξ because it is made of stiff plates of metal. Schol. Ap. Rh. glosses our fragment with εὐπαγής. Pfeiffer, however, as far as the *Hecale* is concerned, prefers the explanation of Suid. (probably from Salustius) 'ϲτάδιος χιτών', ὁ ποδήρης, ὁ τέλειος. ὑφέεϲτο is unique—for ἔεϲτο cf. *Il.* 12. 464, *H. Hom. Aphr.* 86, Ap. Rh. (quoted above).

Pfeiffer thought of Theseus' arrival at Athens from Troezen, plausibly in view of Paus. 1. 19. 1 ἀγνὼς ἔτι τοῖς πᾶϲιν ἀφίκοιτο Θηϲεὺς ἐς τὴν πόλιν· οἷα δὲ χιτῶνα ἔχοντος αὐτοῦ ποδήρη κτλ. (he also quoted Bacchyl. 18. 52 ff.). But his own comment on ὑφέεϲτο, 'induerat chitona sub alia veste … cuius in priore hexametri parte mentio facta erat', shows how well the fragment would fit in fr. 42. 6 (see ad loc.). The man from Aphidnae would be wearing his ἄλλιξ, and under it a χιτών. In Homer men regularly wear χλαῖνάν τε χιτῶνά τε (e.g. *Od.* 17. 550).

FRS. 44–6

I have placed these fragments in what seems the most reasonable order, if they all refer to the same man. Should that man prove to be the driver from Aphidnae (fr. 42. 2), frs. 44 and 45 might stand before fr. 42, and fr. 46 after it. Since, however, the reference is quite uncertain, I have not ventured to intrude frs. 44–5 into the papyrus lacuna between frs. 40 and 42 (cf. above, Introd. sect. X).

Fr. 44 (376 Pf.)

The comparison of the beard with helichryse in fr. 45. 2 suggests that fr. 44 may refer to the same man. Pfeiffer (noting, however, Bacchyl. 18. 51 πυρcοχαίτου) points to frs. 14–15 as indications that this man is unlikely to be Theseus.

1–2 ὅc τε φόβηιcι | ξανθοτάταιc ἐκόμα: apparently an echo of the comic poet Pherecrates' ὦ ξανθοτάτοιc βοcτρύχοιcι κομῶν (fr. 189 Kock). φόβη, not in Homer, is common in lyric and Tragedy, e.g. Sapph. fr. 81b L.–P.(= *LGS* 213). 1; A. *Ch.* 188; S. *El.* 449; for other Hellenistic examples cf. Lyc. *Alex.* 976 and Euph. fr. 175. 1 dub. καλαὶ μέν ποτ' ἔcαν, καλαί, φόβαι Εὐτελίδαο. See on fr. 117 for 'epic τε'.

Fr. 45 (274 Pf.)

A young man from the past (κἀκείνωι) is being compared, perhaps to the one whom the speaker addresses. In our present state of knowledge it is natural to think (with Kapp, fr. 42) that the latter may be Theseus, the former the man from Aphidnae (or else possibly one of the boys mentioned in frs. 48–9), and Hecale the speaker.

1 ἁρμοῖ: 'recently', an old locative of ἁρμός. The form (said by *Et. Mag.* 144. 50 to be Syracusan) occurs in A., *PV* 615. Pind. fr. 10, more than once in Hippocrates—indicating, as Gow notes on Theocr. 4. 51, that it is not exclusively Doric—and in Lyc. *Alex.* 106. The grammarian Theon son of Artemidorus, who wrote commentaries on *Aet.* 1–2 and possibly other works of Call. (see Pfeiffer on his fr. 42) prescribed a smooth breathing for the sense 'recently', which is actually found in the papyrus of the *Victoria Berenices* (*SH* 254. 4 = fr. 383. 4 Pf.).

In Ap. Rh. 1. 972 (where Cyzicus is compared to Jason) the MSS read ἶcόν που κἀκείνωι ἐπιcταχύεcκον ἴουλοι, and schol. L records a variant ἁρμοῖ που κἀκείνωι ὑποcταχύεcκον ἴουλοι. Perhaps a commentator's quotation of the Callimachean parallel was at some stage mistaken for a variant, though Ardizzoni and Vian both print ἁρμοῖ in their text of Apollonius.

κἀκείνωι: cf. *Od.* 19. 370 οὕτω που καὶ κείνωι. For variation between καὶ κεῖνος and κἀκεῖνος in such a case see West on Hes. *Op.* 295. Call. uses both κεῖνος and ἐκεῖνος freely; we find κἀκεῖνον in fr. 64 (Lapp (*Tropis et Figuris*, pp. 137–8) discusses crasis in Call.).

ἐπέτρεχεν ἁβρὸς ἴουλος: with Kapp (fr. 42) I prefer ἐπέτρεχεν ἁβρός (Suidas) to ἐπέτρεχε λεπτός (*Et. Gen.*, accepted by Pf.). The alternatives may be very ancient, and there is little to choose between them (though Hecker (p. 87) pronounced ἁβρός 'much more elegant'). Possible imitations in later poets marginally favour ἁβρός: Orph. *Arg.* 228 ἐρύθηνε παρηίδας ἁβρὸς ἴουλος, Nonn. *Dion.* 10. 179 οὐδέ οἱ ἁβρὸς ἴουλος κτλ.; on the other side one can quote Asclep. *AP* 12. 36, 1–2 (see on Gow–Page 46 for doubts over the ascription) λεπτὸς ὑπὸ κροτάφοισιν ἴουλος | ἕρπει and Nonn. *Dion.* 3. 415 λεπτὸς ... κύκλος ἰούλων.

ἐπέτρεχεν: 'was spreading'; cf. also Xen. *Symp.* 4. 23 ἄρτι ἴουλος καθέρπει (Bulloch (*FH*, p. 183 n. 1) notes the poetic tone).

1–2 For the incipient beard cf. *Od.* 11. 319–20 πρίν σφῶϊν ὑπὸ κροτάφοισιν ἰούλους | ἀνθῆσαι and A. *Sept.* 534 στείχει δ' ἴουλος ἄρτι διὰ παρηίδων. Comparison of the first growth of golden down to a flower is conventional (see J. W. Fitton, *Glotta*, 53 (1975), 229).

2 ἄνθει ἑλιχρύσωι ἐναλίγκιος: cf. *Od.* 6. 231 κόμας ὑακινθίνωι ἄνθει ὁμοίας and *H. Hom. Dem.* 178. Theocr. 2. 78 τοῖς δ' ἧς ξανθοτέρα μὲν ἑλιχρύσοιο γενειάς strongly suggests that the point of comparison here too is the golden yellow colour of the young man's beard (? cf. fr. 44). If so, the plant would be *Helichrysum siculum*, common round the Mediterranean, which has upright stems crowned by yellow flower-clusters; it is also called χρυσανθές in Nicander's *Georgics* (fr. 74. 69 G.–S.). See Gow on Theocr. 1. 30, and Index I to Gow–Scholfield's Nicander. This interpretation, however, causes problems for Theocr. 1. 30 (see Gow and Dover ad loc.), and one must take seriously Suidas' explanation (no doubt from Salustius' commentary on the *Hecale*) ἑλίχρυσος· τὸ τοῦ κισσοῦ ἄνθος. Then Thphr. *HP* 1. 13. 1 τῶν ἀνθῶν τὰ μὲν ... χνοώδη, καθάπερ ... καὶ τοῦ κιττοῦ might indicate another point of comparison, the downy softness of the beard (particularly appropriate if one prefers to read ἁβρός in l. 1).

ἄνθει ἐλιχρύcωι: Pfeiffer was undoubtedly right to retain the reading of all Suidas' MSS, ἐλιχρύcωι (older editors amended to the more pedestrian ἐλιχρύcου; cf. Nic. *Ther*. 625 ἐλιχρύcοιο ... ἄνθην). This pattern is an elegant mannerism, like φηγῶι ὑπὸ πρέμνωι (*H*. 3. 239, see Bornmann), Πίνδον ἀν' εὐάγκειαν (6. 82, with εὐάγκειαν probably a substantive, as Hopkinson says). For some reason many of the examples are botanical (see also G. Daux, *REG* 54 (1941), 218–19). See further Pf. on fr. 788 inc. auct. βλητὶ λίθωι.

For the correptions in this fragment (κἀκείνωι and ἄνθεῖ) and the hiatus ἐλιχρύcῶι ἐναλίγκιος see above, Introd. sect. IV. 7. Hiatus at the masculine caesura (cf. Gow on Theocr. 2. 145) occurs also in *H*. 3. 238.

Fr. 46 (304 Pf.)

This fragment (minus ἐνδίοιο) is quoted to illustrate the outsize Thessalian petasos by schol. S. *OC* 314 (describing Ismene) κρατὶ δ' ἡλιοcτερής | κυνῆ πρόcωπα Θεccαλίc νιν ἀμπέχει. In fact the schol. makes two complete hexameters by transferring εἴδεος before ἀμφί. Toup removed εἴδεος to line 3, and Naeke added ἐνδίοιο from Hesychius.

If, as seems likely, fr. 65 describes Hecale with her hat and staff, we must look for someone else to fit fr. 46. Wilamowitz (on fr. 137 Kapp, cf. the editors on *SH* 287b. 1–10) tentatively suggested that he might be the man from Aphidnae (fr. 42. 2). This petasos is new, and seems to be something special, like the ἄλλιξ in fr. 42. 5; I would, however, hesitate to use the argument that the petasos comes from Thessaly and that ἄλλιξ is said to be a Thessalian word as a reason for connecting frs. 42 and 46. Pfeiffer inclined to think that these lines may portray Theseus (who is sometimes shown in art wearing the petasos, e.g. *CVA*, Great Britain, vii. 271. 3), whether journeying from Troezen to Athens (cf. Bacchyl. 18. 50–1 κηΰτυκτον κυνέαν Λάκαι-|ναν), or from Athens to Marathon.

1 Cf. *Il*. 18. 205 ἀμφὶ δέ οἱ κεφαλῆι, 10. 257 and 261 ἀμφὶ δέ οἱ κυνέην κεφαλῆφιν ἔθηκε.

1–2 νέον Αἱμονίηθεν | μεμβλωκός: 'newly come from Thessaly' (like Trypanis I take νέον as an adverb with μεμβλωκός). In

Thphr. *HP* 4. 8. 7, πετάcωι Θετταλικῆι is a probable restoration. A decorative phrase, giving the origin or purpose of the object (here both) is very much in Call.'s manner (e.g. frs. 65–6 on Hecale's hat and staff; cf. on fr. 27. 2).

Αἱμονίηθεν: perhaps also in Euph. *SH* 440. 8. 'Haemonia' is much favoured as a learned name for Thessaly (e.g. Rhian. fr. 25. 3).

2 πίληµα: (also fr. 65. 2, more frequently πῖλος) derives from πιλέω, to compress wool, fur, or hair into felt (cf. Theod. *AP* 6. 282 (= 1 G.–P. *HE*). 1–2 πιληθέντα . . .|. . . πέτασον; H. Blümner, *Technologie und Terminologie* [etc.], i². 222). Scherling (*Quibus Rebus*, p. 39) quotes the inscription *IG* ii. 2 Add. et Corr., no. 834b, col. 1. 70–1, mentioning πῖλοι τοῖc δηµοcίοιc παρὰ Θετ-τάλης.

περίτροχον: *hapax legomenon* in Homer (*Il.* 23. 455); cf. Ap. Rh. 3. 1229, Triph. 518.

2–3 ἄλκαρ . . .| εἴδεος ἐνδίοιο: ἄλκαρ + genitive, 'a defence against', is very common in all periods, e.g. γήραος ἄλκαρ, *H. Hom. Ap.* 193 = Emp. fr. 111. 1 = Quint. Smyrn. 3. 478; ἄλκαρ ἀνίης Quint. Smyrn. 3. 565 = Nonn. *Dion.* 7. 76. Cf. Ap. Rh. 2. 1074 ὑετοῦ . . . ἄλκαρ; Opp. *Hal.* 1. 46 πυρὸς ἄλκαρ ὀπωρινοῖο; Satyr. *AP* 10. 13(= 3 Page, *FGE*). 3–4 ἄλκαρ ὁδίταιc | δίψης καὶ καµάτου καὶ φλογὸς ἠελίου.

3 εἴδεος ἐνδίοιο: (Arat. *Phaen.* 954 ὕδατος ἐνδίοιο). Note the sequence of vowels (cf. on fr. 16). Some ancient grammarians (e.g. schol. Ambr. B on *Od.* 4. 450) wrongly believed that there was an etymological connection between ἔνδιος (for which see on fr. 18. 1) and εἶδος = 'heat' (first in [Hes.] *Sc.* 397—see West on Hes. *Op.* 415 for the spelling εἶδος rather than ἶδος).

FRS. 47–9

The 50 lines contained in these fragments are covered by the interlocking *P. Oxy.* 2376 and 2377. They pose some of the most intricate problems to face an editor of the *Hecale* in our present state of knowledge. We might seem to have four separate pieces of text: 10 lines each from the foot of two consecutive columns in *P. Oxy.* 2376 (col. i has the endings of lines, col. ii the beginnings) and 20 lines on each side of *P. Oxy.* 2377. Lobel, however, observed that *P. Oxy.* 2376, col. ii. 4 and 9 contain the beginnings of already attested lines, and that *P. Oxy.* 2377 'back', 10 and 15 give later parts of the selfsame lines. It follows that the whole of *P. Oxy.* 2376 col. ii must preserve the beginnings of those lines from which *P. Oxy.* 2377 'back', 7–16 give us later parts; as a result of this conjunction we have three pieces of text rather than four, and a total of 50 lines rather than 60. The subject-matter of these three pieces (for the moment I forbear to attach fragment numbers to them) appears to be as follows:

1. *P. Oxy.* 2376, col. i. 1–10. A woman tells how she reared two children with all possible care and devotion, and 'the pair of them sprang up like aspens'.

2. *P. Oxy.* 2377 'back', 1–20 (of which 7–16 = *P. Oxy.* 2376, col. ii. 1–10). A woman, who has apparently lost at least one dear person already, apostrophizes someone else whom she is in danger of losing; she goes on to curse the bandit Cercyon bitterly.

3. *P. Oxy.* 2377 'front', 1–20. The speaker tells how a man set out by ship to bring back horses from Laconia—but the omens were unfavourable, and it seems that the voyage ended in shipwreck.

While we can be certain that (1) comes before (2), the placing of (3) is entirely conjectural. One could put (3) either before (1), or after (2), or even between (1) and (2), i.e. in the missing top part of *P. Oxy.* 2376, col. ii). No papyrological argument enables us to solve this problem.

It seems plausible (cf. Maas quoted by Lobel on *P. Oxy.* 2377 'back', 2 ff.) to assign (1) and (2) to the same female speaker. Although Lobel (ibid. n. 1) toyed with the idea that she might be Medea, such a catalogue of disasters leading to utter desolation is much more what we expect from Hecale herself. The main obstacle to accepting Hecale as the speaker of these passages has been a seemingly firm statement in Ovid (*Rem.* 747–8 = above, Test. 5) that she never married:

> cur nemo est Hecalen, nulla est quae ceperat Iron?
> nempe quod alter egens, altera pauper erat.

A way of evading this difficulty (while assigning the lines in question to Hecale) would be to make her the nurse rather than the mother of the two boys—thus Webster (*Poetry and Art*, p.

116) who considers emending the corrupt fr. 527 Pf. inc. sed. so that it describes two illegitimate sons born to Aegeus. But perhaps *Rem.* 747–8 by no means proves that Hecale never married. Ovid merely says that nobody would have her *in her impoverished state*; it remains quite possible that in her earlier and more prosperous years she married and produced children (Barigazzi, *Hermes*, 86 (1958), 457). A very doubtful piece of evidence (above, Test. Dub. 17) even purports to name a son of Hecale—Bulias.

If we allow that the speaker of (1) and (2) may be Hecale, and the two boys in (1) her own sons, piece (2) could describe the death of both of them—first the elder (in *P. Oxy.* 2377 'back', 1 πρου]ϵνϵϲτϵρο[may be discerned) and then the younger, who perhaps succumbed to Cercyon. Furthermore the man in (3) who went to fetch horses from Laconia (? and drowned in the attempt) might have been Hecale's husband, conceivably identical with the man who drove from Aphidnae in fr. 42. 2. If all this proved correct, the most emotionally powerful ordering of the passages (following Bartoletti in *Miscellanea Rostagni* (1963), pp. 263–72) would be to place (3) before (1). First Hecale loses her husband, then her elder son, finally the younger son in whom all her remaining hopes reposed (? cf. *P. Oxy.* 2377 'back', 7, perhaps ἐλπίδεϲ).

The above pattern is commended, with all due reserve, by the editors of *SH*, and seems to me the most plausible in our present state of knowledge. But the evidence does not allow anything near certainty; many doubts remain, and at many points a different view could reasonably be taken (some of these alternatives are mentioned in the detailed notes below).

S. Medaglia (*Atti del XVII Congresso Internazionale di Papirologia*, ii (1984), pp. 297–304) tries to integrate *PSI* 133 (my frs. 40 and 42) with *P. Oxy.* 2376 and 2377. He produces a scheme, based on papyrological considerations, in which fr. 48 stands in the lacuna of about 32 lines between frs. 40 and 42. Fr. 42 (the man from Aphidnae) would follow fr. 48 (rearing of the children) after a gap of only 2 lines, and itself be followed, after the same interval, by fr. 47 (shipwreck); the whole sequence (from the beginning of fr. 40 to the end of fr. 49) occupies 96 lines. I confess that, from the point of view of subject-matter, this arrangement does not appeal to me.

Fr. 47 (*SH* 286; 639, 329, 629 Pf.)

With this placing of *P. Oxy.* 2377 'front' (= fr. 47) before the
'back' (= fr. 49), Hecale may be talking about her husband (see
above). If, however, this order were reversed, the subject of fr. 47
could be one of her sons (see Webster, *Poetry and Art*, pp. 115–16).

1–2 The editors of *SH* warn against attempting to supply frs.
101 and 14 respectively in these lines (the latter proposal made by
Barigazzi). Neither supplement fits the traces, and both would
violate Call.'s metrical conventions (the bridge of Hermann or
Naeke in line 1, and of Naeke in line 2).

3 ὃс καὶ μο[: perhaps referring to the man who was to set sail
for Laconia.

4 Ὀρνείδαο: almost certainly Peteos son of Orneus—patrony-
mics can of course sometimes be applied to grandchildren or
subsequent generations, but Orneus' grandson Menestheus would
be a contemporary of Theseus, and therefore too late for this
narrative of past times. Call. shows his taste for recondite learning
by introducing this very obscure figure; for the descent Orneus-
–Peteos–Menestheus see D. L. Page, *History and the Homeric Iliad*
(1959), pp. 173–5; M. L. West, *The Hesiodic Catalogue of Women*
(1985), p. 107. Among the scanty traditions about Peteos, it may
be significant that he was considered an enemy of Aegeus (Paus.
10. 35. 8), just as his son Menestheus became an enemy of Theseus
(Plut. *Thes.* 32). It seems possible that the man (? Hecale's
husband) who went to fetch horses from Laconia—and probably
perished on the voyage—did so at the behest of Peteos. If so,
Hecale might well cherish bitterness towards Peteos, which
would harmonize with the animosity between him and the father
of her young guest. In line 20 below we find βαcιλ[, and in fr. 49.
17 perhaps βαc]ιλῆες. Although the tone of these passages cannot
be determined, fr. 54 (see ad loc.) contains an attack (? by Hecale)
on βαcιλῆες—Pfeiffer naturally thought of Hesiod's unjust and
covetous kings.

It is possible that the latter part of this line included the genitive
Πετεῶο, which would be in the Hellenistic manner (e.g. Call. *SH*
254. 7 Εὐφητηϊάδαο . . . Ὀφέλτου. Euph. *SH* 415. i. 7 Ἰφικλείδαο
. . . Ἰολάου). But we do not know whether Peteos had been
mentioned before this line, and it would also be in the Hellenistic
manner to withhold the name, thus challenging readers to
recognize an obscure patronymic.

6 ἵππους⌋ καιτάεντος ⌊ἀπ' Εὐρώταο κομίσσαι: = fr. 639 Pf.
Compare *Il.* 11. 738 (Nestor taking spoils) κόμισσα δὲ μώνυχας
ἵππους. The precise nature of the present expedition is not clear.
In *Od.* 21. 22 Iphitus journeys to recover stolen horses, ἵππους
διζήμενος, αἵ οἱ ὄλοντο, and Glaucus visits Sparta for the same
purpose in schol. Ap. Rh. 1. 146 (from Eum. *Corinthiaca*, fr. 6
Kinkel). The editors of *SH* note that Peteos' son Menestheus
would become πλήξιππος (*Il.* 4. 327, cf. 2. 554).

καιτάεντος . . . Εὐρώταο: the Eurotas, that most poetic of
rivers, is by convention 'reedy': δονακόεις (E. *Hel.* 210–11),
δονακοτρόφος (*Theognidea* 785, E. *IA* 179), δονακόχλοος (E. *IT*
399–400: cf. *Hel.*, 349); and compare fr. 98 below of the Asterion
δόνακι πλήθοντα.

Homer twice (*Il.* 2. 581, *Od.* 4. 1) applies to Sparta the epithet
κητώεσσα 'which nobody in historical times understood . . .
presumably an inheritance from the remotest past' (Page, op. cit.
p. 160 n. 24; cf. Stephanie West on *Od.* 4. 1; Sarah Morris,
'Hollow Lakedaimon', *HSCP* 88 (1984), 1–11). The scholia on
Od. 4. 1, having attempted to explain κητώεσσαν, add Ζηνόδοτος δὲ
(Eust. 1478. 38 says 'Zenodotus among others') γράφει "και-
τάεσσαν" ἀντὶ τοῦ καλαμινθώδη. δοκεῖ δὲ καὶ Καλλίμαχος ἐντε-
τυχηκέναι τῆι γραφῆι, δι' ὧν φησιν "ἵππους—κομίσσαι". In fact
Eustathius gives the Zenodotean form as καιετάεσσαν, to which
most scholars (following Bentley) corrected the *Odyssey* scholion,
but *P. Oxy.* 2377 has καιτάεντος (Lobel thinks χαιτάεντας must
have been the scribe's first shot): although the line becomes more
spondaic than is customary in Call., one can cite enough parallels
(e.g. fr. 35. 2) for this not to be suspicious. The *Odyssey* scholiast at
least took Zenodotus' καιτάεσσαν to mean 'full of mint' (καλά-
μινθος, cf. Apoll. Soph. p. 99. 16 Bekker καιέτας . . . ἡ καλά-
μινθος, and Hesychius s.v. καιέτα· καλαμίνθη, Βοιωτοί), and seems
to believe that Call. used the word in the same sense, which is not
inappropriate to the river Eurotas (see above). That Call. used for
the Spartan river a variant, Doric in form, of the Homeric epithet
for Sparta can hardly be coincidence (Giangrande, *Hermes*, 98
(1970), 273 = *SMA* i. 81). On Zenodotus and Call. see further
above, Introd. sect. III, and below on fr. 74. 17.

A different interpretation, however, of the Homeric variant
καιτάεσσαν (καιετάεσσαν) was known to Strabo and may have
been current in Call.'s day (whether Zenodotus mentioned it is

not clear): 'full of cavities', with reference to the fissures (ῥωχμοί) caused by earthquakes: Str. 8. 5. 7 οἱ μὲν καλαμινθώδη δέχονται, οἱ δὲ ὅτι οἱ ἀπὸ τῶν ςεισμῶν ῥωχμοὶ καιετοὶ λέγονται (for ῥωχμοί in connection with a river cf. e.g. *Il.* 23. 420). At Sparta καιάδαc was the name for the underground pit or cavern into which criminals were thrown. A passage in Nicander (*Ther.* 59–60) may touch on this controversy in a tantalizing manner: τῆμος δὴ ποταμοῖο πολυρραγέος κατὰ δίνας | ὑδρηλὴν καλάμινθον ὀπάζεο χαιτήεσσαν (v.l. in the scholia καιτήεσσαν); as well as the mint, there is perhaps a hint of ῥωχμοί in πολυρραγέος (cf. Cazzaniga, *RFIC* 91 (1963), 461–9).

All in all, it seems most probable that Call. used καιτάεντος in the sense 'full of mint', but, as often, he may have been teasing his learned readers.

κομίccαι: we do not know whether this is optative (Lobel considered ὅπ[ως in l. 5) or infinitive.

7 After κῦμα, not impossible is κạ[ὶ (see Lobel's note). Both Barigazzi and Krafft consider placing here fr. 160 inc. auct. κạ⌞ὶ ἄγριον οἶδμα θαλάσσης. That may still be right, notwithstanding doubts about the authorship (see further ad loc.).

8 Lobel suggested Μαλ]ειάων (see his note for palaeographical objections which he judged not fatal), after which ὅθι would follow appropriately. Cape Malea would face all those who sailed from Attica to Laconia, and was proverbially (Str. 8. 6. 20) dangerous to sailors (e.g. *Od.* 4. 514 ff.). See further *RE*, s.v. Malea.

9–10 αἰθυίης γὰρ ⌞ὑπὸ πτερύγεσσιν ἕλυς-| πείς⌟ματα: giving the true form of a corrupt citation in Suid. s.v. αἴθυια (fr. 327 Pf.). It is still, however, unclear whether we should read ἕλυσαν (Suid.) or ἕλυσε (Zonaras); line 3 ὅς perhaps favours ἕλυσε, but the plural remains quite possible.

9 αἰθυίης . . . ⌞ὑπὸ πτερύγεσσιν: cf. *Aet.* fr. 43. 66 Pf. μέρμνου μοι πτερύγεσσι (a better omen for founding colonies than the ἅρπασος) and Hor. *Epod.* 10. 1 'mala soluta navis exit alite'. The αἴθυια (according to D'Arcy Thompson (*A Glossary of Greek Birds* (1936), p. 27) probably a shearwater) predicted storms (e.g. Arat. *Phaen.* 918–19; Arist. fr. 253. 8 Rose[2] νῆτται δὲ καὶ αἴθυιαι πτερυγίζουσαι πνεῦμα δηλοῦσιν ἰσχυρόν; Dionys. *Av.* 2. 6; Claud. *Bell. Gild.* 1. 493 'si revolant mergi'). In *SH* 429. 48 (? = Euph. fr.

130 Powell) the αἴθυια may also be a bad omen for seafaring, but the context is quite unclear.

9–10 ἔλυc-| πείcᴊματα: cf. *Aet.* fr. 18. 10 Pf. πείcματ'] ἔλυcαν. There is no close parallel in Homer (*Od.* 10. 127 has πείcματ' ἔκοψα νεὸc κυανοπρώιροιο) but many such phrases in Apollonius Rhodius (e.g. 1. 652 πείcματα νηὸc ἔλυcαν; see Campbell, *Echoes and Imitations of Early Epic in Apollonius Rhodius* (1981), ad loc.).

10 τῆc: 'understand ὑπὸ πτερύγεccι' (Lobel)—but one might think of other possibilities.

10–11 μήτ' αὐτ[. . .| μ]ήθ' ὅτιc ἄμμι βεβουλ[: in line 10, μήτ' αὐτ[ὴ ἐγώ (Barigazzi, Krafft) would be more plausible than αὐτ[όc (Lobel), since the speaker, if the same as in frs. 48–9, is a woman, quite probably Hecale herself.

We can recognize here a familiar pattern, in the fullest form of which the speaker (usually but not always the poet), having described an unpleasant fate or terrible danger, adds 'may not I, or any friend of mine, ever encounter such a thing'. The earliest example is *Od.* 15. 358 ff. (Eumaeus on the death of Laertes' wife):

> ἡ δ' ἄχεϊ οὗ παιδὸc ἀπέφθιτο κυδαλίμοιο
> λευγαλέωι θανάτωι, ὡc μὴ θάνοι ὅc τιc ἐμοί γε
> ἐνθάδε ναιετάων φίλοc εἴη καὶ φίλα ἔρδοι.

Closest to the present passage, and perhaps based upon it, would seem to be Dion. Per. 741–2 (the Massagetae):

> ἀνέρεc οἷc μήτ' αὐτὸc ἐγὼ μήθ' ὅcτιc ἑταῖροc
> ἐμπελάcαι . . .

A number of variations are found. Dionysius, *de Avibus* (prose summary of a lost poem) 2. 8 is more generous: 'neither I nor anyone else', κήυκοc δὲ φωνῆc μήτ' ἐγὼ μήτ' ἄλλοc ἀκούcαι τιc. Alternatively one might wish a bad experience on one's enemies, specifically exempting any friends (e.g. Prop. 2. 4. 17–18 'hostis si quis erit nobis, amet ille puellas;| gaudeat in puero, si quis amicus erit') or just on one's enemies (e.g. Nic. *Ther.* 186 (particularly venomous reptiles) ἐχθρῶν που τέρα κεῖνα καρήαcιν ἐμπελάcειε: Prop. 3. 8. 20 'hostibus eveniat lenta puella meis'; Ov. *Am.* 3. 11. 16); a poet may also express the hope that such a thing never happens to his readers (Nic. *Ther.* 305 μήποτέ τοι θήλει' αἱμορροῖc ἰὸν ἐνείη). Often too the poet, having mentioned a heinous crime, will add 'may the man who does such a thing never be a friend, neighbour, or partner of mine' (e.g. Call. *H*. 6. 116–17 with Hopkinson's (*HD*) full note, Jebb on S. *Ant*. 372 ff.). Call. likes such interpositions in his own person (*H*. 3. 136 ff., 175 ff.; and, in the Callimachean spirit, Catull. 63. 92–3). So Lobel not unnaturally wished to restore αὐτ[όϲ in line 10 here, but it seems more likely that the speaker is the same woman as in frs. 48–9. What continues to surprise me a little is that Hecale (if it is she) should employ the pattern 'may not I nor any associate of mine . . .' if (as appears quite likely) she is recounting the death of someone particularly close to her (? her husband). Campbell, however, finds it not so surprising, because we are dealing with a literary (and very probably sub-literary) stereotype.

11 μ]ήθ' ὅτιϲ ἄμμι βεβουλ[: 'neque alius quisquam qui nobis bene vult' (*SH*); 'nor a person who has undertaken a commission for me' (Lobel). The former is more what one expects (cf. *Od*. 15. 360 quoted above), but line 12 below may possibly contain a reference to trade. Did Hecale's husband set sail to Laconia on a commercial mission for Peteos (cf. on ll. 4 and 6 of this fragment)?

ἄμμι: an Aeolic form (cf. *Il*. 1. 384). We find ἄμμιν in Call. *H*. 3. 186, 4. 171.

βεβουλ[: apparently βέβουλ[ε(ν), a new form (cf. on fr. 36. 3 οἶϲε). The compound προβέβουλα occurs once in Homer (*Il*. 1. 113) = 'I have preferred' (προβούλομαι is not found), and often in late poetry, particularly Nonnus. See Livrea on Colluth. 200, where however (as in Nonn. *Dion*. 10. 118) προβέβουλε = 'he made plans', as if from προβουλεύω. In the only other instance known to me of the simple perfect (Eudocia, *S. Cypr*. 1. 228 οἶα βέβουλαϲ) 'made plans' seems appropriate—perhaps also in Call.?

12 Possibly ἐμ]πορίηι and then κακὸν οὐτ- (Lobel).

14 The papyrus clearly has a high point after νῆα, marking the end of a clause, though this is unexpected.

15 μ]έϲϲον ἐπεὶ ναύταιϲ: quoted in a corrupt form (fr. 629 Pf.) by a scholiast on *Il*. 15. 628 τυτθὸν γὰρ ὑπὲκ θανάτοιο φέρονται, who also cites Arat. *Phaen*. 299 ὀλίγον δὲ διὰ ξύλον Ἄϊδ' ἐρύκει. Lobel accordingly translated 'since there is for sailors between . . .' (cf. the use of μεταξύ in A. *Sept*. 761), completing the sentence with e.g. '. . . them and death a thin plank'. These passages of Homer and Aratus were very famous (compared in Longin. 10. 5. 6); the Homeric scholiast links to them a story told of Anacharsis the Scythian (more material in J. F. Kindstrandt, *Anacharsis* (1981), p. 146). Compare Ov. *Am.* 2. 11. 26 'et prope tam letum quam prope cernit aquam'. Death at sea caused special horror to the ancients (see R. Lattimore, *Themes in Greek and Latin Epitaphs* (1942), pp. 199 ff.).

18 Perhaps]αχιδαc. *SH* notes that ἡc]υχίδαc (cf. fr. 681. 2 Pf.) would in any case be too short for the space. Supposing that the reflections on the dangers of seafaring had by now finished, and that (?) Hecale were continuing with her life-story (cf. line 16]. μεν ἐγώ), it might be worth thinking of the small Attic deme Semachidae, not far from Hecale's home. Stephanus Byzantius writes s.v. Cημαχίδαι ... Φιλόχοροc δὲ (*FGH* 328 F 206) τῆc Ἐπακρίαc φηcὶ τὸν δῆμον. ὁ δημότηc Cημαχίδηc. This deme is usually placed at Kalenzi, on the east side of the modern Lake Marathon (cf. Traill, *Hesperia*, Suppl. 14 (1975), 54; E. Vanderpool, Ἀρχ. Δελτ. 25. 1 (1970), 215–16).

20 βαcιλ[: see on line 4.

In the lower margin of the papyrus are traces of what Lobel thinks might be a line omitted from the text above, possibly but not necessarily from the partially preserved portion (see his note on *P. Oxy.* 2377).

Fr. 48 (*SH* 287. 1–10; 337, 366, 247, 284 Pf.)

If fr. 48 is correctly placed after fr. 47 (see introductory note on frs. 47–9), perhaps Hecale is saying that even after the death of her husband, she continued to rear her two sons with all possible expense and devotion.

1 τὼ μὲν ἐγὼ θαλέεccιν ἀνέτρε⌋φον: = fr. 337 Pf. (Pfeiffer had already attributed to the same speaker his fr. 284 = l. 7 below). *SH* warns that there is no chance of identifying this line with fr. 47. 16, as Krafft (*Hermes*, 86 (1958), 476) had tried to do.

θαλέεccιν: 'with delicacies', τρυφαῖc θάλλειν ποιούcαιc (Suid.). The plural θάλεα comes once in Homer of the sleeping Astyanax θαλέων ἐμπληcάμενοc κῆρ (*Il.* 22. 504). Compare *Il.* 9. 143 (= 285) when Agamemnon says of his young son Orestes τρέφεται θαλίηι ἔνι πολλῆι.

οὐδέ τιc οὕτωc: the sense of 1–3 might have been something like 'neque erat alius quisquam genere tam amplo, ne inter illos quidem qui divitiis madent' (*SH*).

3 ῥυδὸ⅃ν ἀφνύονται: = fr. 366 Pf., where the MSS of Suidas offer ἀφνύνονται and ἀφυνοντ. Hesychius has ἀφνύει· ἀφνύνει· ὀλβίζει. The commoner form of the adverb is ῥύδην, 'abundantly'; ῥυδόν occurs just once in Homer, at the line-ending of *Od.* 15. 426 ῥυδὸν ἀφνειοῖο (from the speech of Eumaeus).

4 Conceivably -ετο νηδύς (Lobel, saying that νηλής would be equally possible). If so, the reference might be either to childbirth, or to the hunger of infants. E. Livrea (*Gnomon*, 57 (1985), 594) suggests ἐξάλλ]ετο νηδύς (cf. Hopkinson (*HD*) on *H.* 6. 88). Fr. 154 ψιcθεῖεν, from ψίζω (ψίω), to 'feed on pap' could belong in this area. One is reminded of A. *Ch.* 755 ff. and of Alcmena washing and suckling her two babies in Theocr. 24. 1 ff.

5 τινθαλέοιcι κατικμήναι⅃ντο λοετροῖc: = fr. 247 Pf. (there placed, following Hecker, in the belief that the words describe Hecale washing Theseus' feet). τινθαλέοc is not attested earlier, but Ar. *Vesp.* 328–9 κεραυνῶι | διατινθαλέωι makes one suspect that this is one of the many words which Call. borrowed from Old Comedy to give the *Hecale* an Attic flavour. The meaning is usually 'boiling hot', which may seem excessive if the young children themselves (? rather than their clothes) are being washed, but Suidas glosses χλιαροῖc (the word for the 'lukewarm' Laodiceans in Rev. 3: 16), θερμοῖc. It does appear probable that κατικμήναιντο is used in a passive sense (καθυγρανθείηcαν Suid.), as Hecker (p. 113) thought (contradicted by Schneider, fr. an. 60), but even this cannot be considered certain.

The line was much imitated, most closely by Nicander (*Alex.* 463 αἶψα δὲ τινθαλέοιcιν ἐπαιονάαcθε λοετροῖc), and more than once by Nonnus (*Dion.* 5. 606 καὶ χρόα λυcιπόνοιcι καθικμαίνουcα λοετροῖc; cf. 3. 89). Call. may be directly or indirectly responsible for later appearances of τινθαλέοc (also Nic. *Alex.* 445; Dionys. fr. 26 Heitsch.(= 81 verso Livrea). 4 (discussed in my edition of Ov. *Met.* 8, App. II); Nonn. *Dion.* 2. 501).

7 τώ μοι ἀναδραμέτην ἄτε κερ⅃κίδες: = fr. 284 Pf., 'the pair of them sprang up like aspens'. Compare Mich. Chon. ii. 380. 137 Lambros ἀλλὰ δύω μὲν πρέμνω ἀναδραμέτην ἀπὸ ῥίζης and, for the opening, *Il.* 10. 354 τὼ μὲν ἐπεδραμέτην. κερκίς, most often a weaver's shuttle, can also be εἶδος ... φυτοῦ εὐαυξοῦς (Suid.), probably the aspen *Populus tremula* (e.g. Thphr. *HP* 3. 14. 2).

The comparison is almost certainly suggested by *Il.* 18. 56, 437 ὁ δ᾽ ἀνέδραμεν ἔρνεϊ ἶϲοϲ (significantly, Thetis on her son who was destined to die young); in similar vein are *Od.* 14. 175 (on Telemachus). Theocr. 24. 103–4 Ἡρακλέηϲ δ᾽ ὑπὸ ματρὶ νεὸν φυτὸν ὣϲ ἐν ἀλωᾶι | ἐτρέφετ᾽, and Quint Smyrn. 7. 644–5 (Phoenix on Achilles) ὁ δ᾽ ἄρ᾽ ὦκα θεῶν ἐρικυδέϊ βουλῆι | ἔρνοϲ ὅπωϲ ἐριθηλὲϲ ἀέξετο (cf. ἠέξαντο in l. 9 below). Such sentiments are often found on inscribed epitaphs for those who die young (e.g. Peek, *GVI* i. 1555. 6 (two boys) ἄμφω πρωθήβαϲ ἔρνεϲιν εἰδομένουϲ, ibid. 1166. 10, 1238. 7; and, with the addition of a nearby stream (as probably in Call.) ibid. 575. 1 (a 7-year old) ὡϲ φυτὸν ἀρτιθαλὲϲ δροϲεροῖϲ παρὰ νάμαϲιν αὖξον, 1023. 2–3 οὗ (sc. the river Anthius) ποτὶ δείναιϲ | ἔρνοϲ ὅπωϲ ἀναβάϲ κτλ.).

αἶτε χαράδρηϲ: (probably an instance of 'epic τε'—see on fr. 117) 'increverunt tamquam populi in alveo fluminis ... multo proceriores ... facti sunt grandes' (*SH*). For the comparison, see above; in Chionid. fr. 2 Kock = 2 *PCG* οὐδὲν ἔτι γέ μοι δοκῶ | ἄγνου διαφέρειν ἐν χαράδραι πεφυκότοϲ the point is unknown.

8–9 We cannot tell how far the simile continued in these lines.

9 [ἠ]έξαντο: this aorist middle (cf. McLennan (*HZ*) on *H.* 1. 55) is not elsewhere attested. Possibly Ap. Rh. 4. 1325–6 μετὰ δ᾽ ἔρνεα τηλεθάοντα | πολλὸν ὑπὲρ γαίηϲ ὀρθοϲταδὸν ἠέξοντο has one eye on our passage; Barigazzi (*Hermes*, 86 (1958), 454) would even restore ὀρθοϲταδ]όν in Call.

10 ἐπεμαίετο παιϲίν: puzzling. ἐπεμαίετο 'aimed for', 'sought' is common enough (e.g. *Il.* 10. 401*, 17. 430*; Arat. *Phaen.* 127) but usually takes accusative or genitive. For a dative *SH* cites Orph. *Arg.* 932 φρουραῖϲ δ᾽ ἀδμήτοιϲ ἐπιμαίεται, and suggests that the meaning may be 'mors filiis inhiabat' (West adds that ἐπιμαίομαι + dative is a papyrus variant, *ante corr.*, in [Hes.] fr. 33a. 26). In Nic. *Ther.* 196–7 ὄλεθρον | μαίεται + dative = 'seeks destruction for'. Lobel was tempted to conjecture ἐπεμήδετο.

Fr. 49 (*SH* 287. 11–30; 350, 294, 368 Pf.)

Fr. 48 comes from the foot of *P. Oxy.* 2376, col. i and fr. 49. 7–16 from the corresponding position in *P. Oxy.* 2376, col. ii. As explained above (see introductory note on frs. 47–9), *P. Oxy.* 2376, col. ii preserves the beginnings of those lines from which *P. Oxy.* 2377 'back', 7–16 give later parts. Thus although we cannot determine the total number of lines missing between frs. 48 and 49, at least we can say that this total represents one complete column of *P. Oxy.* 2376 minus 6 lines.

It seems possible that in fr. 48 Hecale has been describing how she raised her two sons; if so, by the end of fr. 49 they are probably both dead. She speaks in fr. 49.3 of lamenting 'over you too': therefore at least one person has died already—this could be her husband (? cf. fr. 47), her elder son (perhaps mentioned in fr. 49. 1), or both. In that case 'you too' would presumably be her younger son, the last of the family to perish; the apostrophe of fr. 49. 2–3 would then transport us back to the time when she had still one child living.

Suppose, however, that we were wrong about the order of the two sides of *P. Oxy.* 2377, and that the 'front' (fr. 47) should be placed after the 'back' (fr. 49). Then fr. 47 would concern the last member of Hecale's family to survive (note l. 3, perhaps ὃς καὶ μο[ῦνο-); more probably, I think, her husband than her younger son. In a quite different interpretation, we might keep fr. 47 before fr. 49, but refer 'you too' (fr. 49. 3) to Theseus: Hecale, having lost her own family, is appalled to hear that her young guest plans to fight the Marathonian bull; she feels that he is certain to succumb (cf. Webster, *Poetry and Art*, p. 116). But both these alternatives seem to me less plausible than the scheme adopted.

1 The traces are consistent with προγ]ενεστερο[(cf. e.g. *Od.* 4. 205*, 7. 156*, 11. 343*; Ap. Rh. 1. 165).

2–3 ἠρνεόμην θανάτοιο πάλ‚αι καλέοντ‚ος ἀκοῦσαι | μὴ μετὰ δὴν ἵνα καὶ coὶ ἐ‚πιρρήξαιμι χ‚ιτῶνα: 'Did I refuse to listen to death calling from of old so that I should soon have to rend my cloak over you too?' There are two possible ways of understanding this:

(*a*) As a question expecting the answer Yes, with the ἵνα clause expressing not Hecale's own purpose but what R. G. Nisbet (*AJP* 44 (1923), 27–43) calls 'Voluntas Fati'. In such cases Fate is nearly always malicious, and here would be cruelly preserving Hecale so that she has to witness the death of her whole family. The lines need not necessarily be a question, but Maas, who suggested this interpretation (*ap.* Lobel), so understood them, and that is rhetorically most effective.

(*b*) As a question expecting the answer No, with the ἵνα clause expressing Hecale's true purpose (Barrett): she clung to life not in order to lament the death of her only remaining child (?), but rather to see him grow to adulthood and prosper. We could compare the situation of old Carme in the pseudo-Virgilian *Ciris* (cf. above, Introd. sect. VI and L. Lehnus, *RIL* 109 (1975), 358–9). She lost her daughter Britomartis (295 ff.), but refused to die, in the hope of seeing her nursling Scylla happily married (316–17): 'cum premeret Natura, mori me velle negavi, | ut tibi Corycio glomerarem flammea luto'.

Suidas quotes these lines (= fr. 350 Pf.) to illustrate (incorrectly) the use of μή for οὐ, but verbatim only down to δήν. Thereafter we get a paraphrase, ἵνα οὐ μετὰ δὴν καὶ ἐπὶ σοὶ θρηνήςω ἀποθανόντι. If Suidas (? Salustius) really took the meaning to be 'I lived as long as I could in order to lament your death as soon as possible' (Lobel), he must have misunderstood the passage very badly.

2 Compare [Apollinar.] *Ps.* 76. 5 ἠρνεόμην πραπίδεccι παρηγορέοντος ἀκοῦcαι, 105. 53 οὔαcιν ἠρνήcαντο θεοῦ καλέοντος ἀκοῦcαι (where καλέοντος is Stephanie West's emendation for λαλέοντος; cf. ibid. 119. 13).

θανάτοιο πάλ‚αι καλέοντˌος: the point is perhaps not (as with Carme in *Ciris* 316) that, because of Hecale's age, she should already have died in the natural course of events—she need not have been particularly old when her last child was killed—but rather that she should have died at an earlier stage of (or even before) the series of disasters which struck her family. Pfeiffer notes that death does not 'call' before E. *Alc.* 254–5 Χάρων | μ' ἤδη καλεῖ, but that in *Il.* 16. 693 and 22. 297 we find θεοὶ θάνατόνδε κάλεccαν. Lapp (*Tropis et Figuris*, p. 151, cf. pp. 83 ff.) comments on the abundance of personification in our poet.

3 ἵνα καὶ cοὶ ἐ‚πιρρήξαιμι χˌιτῶνα: for 'rending one's garments over' someone = mourning for them cf. Parth. *SH* 646(= fr. 29 Martini). 5–6 ταὶ δ' ἐπ' ἐκείνηι | βεύδεα παρθενικαὶ Μιληcίδες ἐρρήξαντο (A. *Pers.* 1030 has πέπλον δ' ἐπέρρηξ' ἐπὶ cυμφορᾶι κακοῦ). In fr. 133 below a similar figure may be applied to anger ('gnashing one's teeth over' something or someone).

4–7 Could the general sense be the disappointment of Hecale's hopes of seeing her boy grow to manhood?

4 Perhaps ἐφίλης[.

5 μέτρα: possibly 'vitae mensura decurtata est' (*SH*, noting phrases like ἥβης μέτρον ἱκέσθαι, e.g. *Od.* 4. 668).

6 e.g. γηρ]άσκοντα or γενει]άσκοντα (*SH*), of which the latter would appear the more promising (for the theme of youth cut off just when the beard begins to sprout cf. e.g. Peek, *GVI* i. 1555. 3).

7 At this point *P. Oxy.* 2376 col. ii starts supplying beginnings of the lines of which *P. Oxy.* 2377 'back' provides later parts.

ἐλπίδες: (if a single and complete word). Of course the frustrated hopes of parents is one of the commonest themes in epitaphs for those who die young. At the beginning of the line πειο- may have been written for πιο-, e.g. πιοτερ- or πιοτατ- (*SH*).

8 ff. It emerges that Hecale's sufferings are somehow connected with the notorious Cercyon, ὅστις διῆγε περὶ τὴν Ἐλευσῖνα καὶ τοὺς παρερχομένους ἠνάγκαζε παλαίειν αὐτῶι (Suid. s.v. Κερκυών). There were various traditions about an Eleusinian Cercyon, son either of Poseidon or of Hephaestus (see Roscher) and rarer traditions about an Arcadian Cercyon, son of Agamedes and grandson of Stymphalus (Paus. 8. 5. 3, 8. 45. 7). The idea that Cercyon fled from Arcadia and came to Attica may have been an attempt to unify two figures. A scholiast on Ar. *Nub.* 508 gives a detailed version of the flight of Trophonius and Cercyon, ascribed to Charax of Pergamum (*FGH* 103 F 5, a writer of uncertain date, but well into the Roman imperial age), and ends by quoting lines 9–10 (= fr. 294 Pf.) of our fragment. That the Cercyon killed by Theseus had come from Arcadia is stated also by Plut. *Thes.* 11. 1. See fr. 62 for more on Cercyon. Ov. *Met.* 7. 439 'Cercyonis letum vidit Cerealis Eleusin' (and *Ib.* 411–12) probably has Call. in mind.

8 πα]λαίσμασι: cf. Theocr. 24. 112* (metaphorical in Greg. Naz. *Carm.* 1. 1. 4. 54*, 1. 1. 8. 412* (*PG* xxxvii. 420, 455)). The plural may refer to Cercyon's habitual practice, rather than to one individual occurrence.

9 μέν: the only instance in Call. of μέν ending a hexameter— the same is true of γάρ in fr. 73. 13 (Maas, *GM*, 138).

10 ἡμῖν: perhaps generally 'to us inhabitants of Attica' rather than 'to me and my family'. We know nothing to connect Hecale with the vicinity of Eleusis at any stage of her life.

κακὸς Ὰπαρενάσσαᴌτο γείτων: cf. Mich. Chon. ii. 353. 24

Lambros ἀποικία Cκυθική, ἢ τοῖς Ἀσιανοῖς "κακὴ παρενάσσατο γείτων". The bad neighbour was a proverbial pest (Hes. *Op.* 346 πῆμα κακὸς γείτων with West's note: Call. *H.* 6. 117 ἐμοὶ κακογείτονες ἐχθροί).

11 χέρες: perhaps referring to Cercyon the wrestler.

12 Perhaps ἐμὸν οἶκ[ον, which might or might not be the line-ending. If]λις could be read (but]ᾱις seems more likely, according to *SH*) Lobel thought of ἐκύ]λισε (and the fate of Sciron), which would apparently leave some part of μόνοικος, elsewhere attested only as an epithet of Heracles, to complete the line.

13–15 Suid. s.v. ϲκῶλος gives τοῦ μὲν ἐγὼ ζώοντος ἀναιδέϲιν ἐμπήξαιμι | ϲκώλουϲ ὀφθαλμοῖϲι καί, εἰ θέμις, ὠμὰ παϲαίμην (= fr. 368 Pf.). But it appears from *P. Oxy.* 2376 that Suidas has compressed three lines into two. Line 13 perhaps started τοῦ π[οτε, and line 14 αὐτὴ [ἐγώ (Lobel). Curiously, τοῦ μὲν ἐγὼ ζώοντος starts a hexameter in Greg. Naz. *Carm.* 2. 1. 1. 169 (*PG* xxxvii. 983), which, before the discovery of the papyrus, might have been considered an echo of Call.

14–15 ἀναι⌊δέϲι⌊ν⌋ ...|... ὀφθαλμοῖϲι: shamelessness was held to reside particularly in the eyes (Longin. 4. 4 φαϲὶν οὐδενὶ οὕτωϲ ἐνϲημαίνεϲθαι τήν τινων ἀναίδειαν ὡϲ ἐν τοῖϲ ὀφθαλμοῖϲ, with Russell's note). Compare *Aet.* fr. 186. 29 Pf. ἀναιδέος ὄθματος, Ap. Rh. 2. 407 ἀναιδέα ... ὄϲϲε. The same applies to modesty in *Aet. SH* 239. 7 αἰδὼς ἷζεν ἐπὶ βλεφάροιϲ. See further Bulloch, *CQ,* NS 20 (1970), 270–1.

15 ϲκώλου⌊ϲ ὀφθαλμοῖϲι: perhaps thinking of Polyphemus' fate (Pf.)—in which case Stephanie West wonders whether ϲκῶλος is here a pointed stake (as in *Il.* 13. 564) rather than εἶδος ἀκάνθης (Suid.). In *Aet.* fr. 24. 1 Pf. ϲκῶλος is the thorn which has stuck in Hyllus' foot. Toup compared LXX Judg. 11: 35 εἰς ϲκῶλον ἐγένου ἐν ὀφθαλμοῖϲ μου, not the only point of contact between Call. and the Septuagint (see on fr. 112 and Fraser, *Ptolemaic Alexandria*, Gen. Index s.v. Septuagint).

καί⌋, εἰ θέμις, ὠμὰ π⌊αϲαίμην: (καί, εἰ θέμις, = Nonn., *Dion.* 46. 87*). Combination of such a ferocious sentiment with the cautionary εἰ θέμις (one might compare Tib. 2. 6. 15–16 'acer Amor, fractas utinam, tua tela, sagittas | *si licet*, exstinctas aspiciamque faces') is a nice piece of character-drawing. The same phrase occurs in a deliberately undignified context at Ar. *Nub.*

295, κεἰ θέμις ἐςτίν, νυνί γ' ἤδη, κεἰ μὴ θέμις ἐςτί, χεςείω. See also Hutchinson, *Hellenistic Poetry* (1988) pp. 58–9.

A threat to eat an enemy raw is common in Homer (e.g. *Il.* 22. 346–7 (Achilles to Hector) αἲ γάρ πως αὐτόν με μένος καὶ θυμὸς ἀνείη | ὤμ' ἀποταμνόμενον κρέα ἔδμεναι, οἷά μ' ἔοργας: ibid. 4. 35–6, 24. 212–13 (Hecuba on Achilles who has killed her son—Macleod ad. loc. comments that the figure seems to be based on popular speech) and in later prose and poetry (Xen. *An.* 4. 8. 14, *Hell.* 3. 3. 6; Men. *Dysc.* 468 καὶ κατέδομαί γε ζῶντα; Dionys. *Bassarica*, fr. 19. 46 verso Livrea). For the neuter plural ὠμά cf. *Il.* 23. 21 ὠμὰ δάςαςθαι. Pfeiffer notes on fr. 476. 1 that in Call. πατέομαι normally takes the accusative rather than the genitive which Homer for the most part prefers.

16 ειδουο: could be articulated, but there must be some suspicion of scribal error.

17 Possibly βας]ιλῆες. For complaints against kings in the *Hecale* see fr. 54 and on fr. 47. 4. Cercyon, coming from the Arcadian royal house, would count as a βαςιλεύς.

18 γςαντα: Barigazzi (*Hermes*, 86 (1958), 454) wished to supply here fr. 161 inc. sed. τεθναίην ὅτ' ἐκεῖνον ἀποπνεύςαντα πυθοίμην, 'optime, quod ad sensum attinet: sed]ν̣ε̣υ̣ςαντα̣ aegerrime legas' (*SH*). Although it is hard to see how γςαντα ∪−−| could be reconciled with Call.'s metrical conventions (cf. above, Introd. sect. IV. *4g* on Naeke's Law), the collocation of letters (which Lobel described as 'awkward but not impossible') might be accommodated at a slightly earlier point in the line, e.g. πολέω]ν̣ ς' ἀντά[ξιον −− (Barrett). The only chance for Barigazzi's otherwise desirable supplement would be if the doubtful first *N* (the *SH* editors wonder about ΔΙ instead) were correctly read, but a mistake by the scribe. Even then, the supplement appears rather short for the surviving letters' position on the papyrus (Barrett, who does not wish to press this argument).

20].τελ . [: Barigazzi (loc. cit.) would restore here fr. 16 ἵν' ἔλλερα ἔργα τέλεςκεν, 'sed in pap. cum τελ. ς[possis, vix τελε̣ς[' (*SH*).

Fr. 50 (367 Pf.)

τόδ' ἔχω cέβας: according to Suidas cέβας here means τὸ θαῦμα. Pfeiffer tentatively completed the line with εἰcορόωcα, recalling *Od.* 4. 142 cέβαc μ' ἔχει εἰcορόωcαν (Helen marvels at the resemblance of Telemachus to Odysseus; cf. *Od.* 3. 123). He conjectured that Hecale may be astonished by the similarity of Theseus to the man from Aphidnae (fr. 42. 2)—in Pfeiffer's opinion perhaps Aegeus. This could be on the right lines (see further on fr. 42. 2 for the pattern); fr. 45 quite possibly compares Theseus to another young man in Hecale's past. But it now seems more probable that the man from Aphidnae was Hecale's future husband. If so, perhaps Theseus reminds her of him, or else of one of her sons (cf. *SH*'s note at the foot of p. 127).

Fr. 51 (300 Pf.)

1–2 ἔκ με Κολωνάων τιc ὁμέcτιον ἤγαγε δαίμων | τῶν ἑτέρων: this tantalizing fragment perhaps gives us a glimpse of Hecale's earlier life, but text and interpretation are both open to doubt. I have adopted the emendation of Naeke (δαίμων for δήμου at the end of l. 1), and would translate 'Some spirit of the malevolent sort led me from Colonae to share the house of . . .'. Maas (in Pfeiffer, i, p. 508) suspected that a preceding dative (going with ὁμέcτιον) named the person whose house Hecale shared—perhaps her husband, since, as we have seen (introductory note to frs. 47–9), Ov. *Rem.* 747–8 (= above, Test. 5) does not prove that she never married.

First, however, we must consider the transmitted text with δήμου in line 1, and Suidas' comment that Call.'s Κολωνάων (together with νηcάων, *H.* 4. 66, 275, *Aet.* fr. 67. 8 Pf.) is an irregular form because it derives from Κολωνόc rather than Κολωνή. Accepting this criticism, Pfeiffer (following Schneidewin and Wilamowitz) coupled Κολωνάων with τῶν ἑτέρων, in the belief that there were two demes named Κολωνόc, viz. 'Hippios' and 'Agoraios'. He translates 'vir quidam e demo Colono altero me ad communem focum duxit'. D. M. Lewis, however, in an important article (*BSA* 50 (1955), 12–17) shows that 'Agoraios' was not a deme, leaving only one deme Κολωνόc (i.e. 'Hippios', a city-deme of the tribe Aigeis); furthermore that Κολωνῆθεν *should* derive from Κολωνή or Κολωναί, and that there were probably two demes called Κολωναί, one belonging to the tribe Leontis and the other to Antiochis. This is now generally accepted; B. D. Merritt (*Hesperia*, 36 (1967), 84–6) discusses an inscription mentioning a πύργος ἐγ Κολοναῖς, while Wesley E. Thompson (*Hesperia*, 39 (1970), 64–5; cf. Traill, *Hesperia*, Suppl. 14 (1975), 125) argues that the identification of two Colonae confirms the linking of Κολωνάων with τῶν ἑτέρων in our fragment. In Euph. *SH* 418. 23 Κολώνην (for variation between singular and plural cf. e.g. on fr. 42. 2, Aphidna/Aphidnae) may well be an Attic deme—note Aphidna, Acherdus, and Melaenae in the surrounding lines.

While one may be grateful for vindication of Call.'s Κολωνάων from grammatical criticism (to which νηςάων remains open—see Pfeiffer on fr. 786 and Mineur (*HD*) on *H*. 4. 66), I am not happy with the outcome for two reasons:

(*a*) What would Κολωνάων ...| τῶν ἑτέρων mean? Is it suggested that 'the Second Colonae' was a regular designation of this deme (e.g. because it was outstripped in distinction by its namesake)? I do not know a relevant parallel. Or perhaps the phrase could be explained by the particular context, e.g. if Hecale herself had come from one of the demes called Colonae, and went to live with someone from 'the other' Colonae? One *might* infer from fr. 42. 2 that her future husband belonged to Aphidnae.

(*b*) More seriously, ἐκ ... Κολωνάων ... δήμου | τῶν ἑτέρων does not sound to me like elegant Callimachean Greek, and I am not sure that it is Greek at all. Maas suspected that δήμου intruded as a gloss on Κολωνάων.

Therefore I have accepted Naeke's δαίμων for δήμου, to be coupled (as Schneider (fr. 428) and others have thought) with τῶν ἑτέρων, 'some spirit of the malevolent sort'. The genitive plural is elegant—as if there were a whole host of malicious spirits lying in wait, one of which attached itself to the speaker. This fragment may mark a step downwards in Hecale's progress from prosperity to desolation. See Barigazzi's good discussion in *Hermes*, 86 (1958), 458.

1 ἔκ με Κολωνάων: for the insertion see on fr. 9. 1.

ὁμέςτιον: glossed by Suidas with ὁμόοικον, ὁμωρόφιον γαμετήν (cf. Hesych. ὁμέςτιον· cύνοικον) which might give a hint of the context. Pfeiffer (partly, perhaps, because of his belief that Hecale never married) thought that this entry in Suidas does not come from Salustius' commentary, and that Hecale was taken on as a

nurse or housekeeper. Marriage is clearly implied in Nonn. *Dion.*
10. 3 ὁμέϲτιον εἶχε Θεμιϲτώ.

ἤγαγε δαίμων: cf. *Od.* 7. 248 ἀλλ' ἐμὲ τὸν δύϲτηνον ἐφέϲτιον
ἤγαγε δαίμων, ibid. 14. 386*; Call. *H.* 5. 81; Triph. 420 τίϲ ϲε . . .
δυϲώνυμοϲ ἤγαγε δαίμων.

1–2 δαίμων | τῶν ἑτέρων: cf. P. *Pyth.* 3. 34–5 δαίμων δ' ἕτεροϲ |
ἐϲ κακὸν τρέψαιϲ ἐδαμάϲϲατό νιν, where the scholiast explains ὁ
κακοποιόϲ, and quotes Call. *Iamb.* fr. 191. 63 Pf. οὐ πάντεϲ, ἀλλ'
οὓϲ εἶχεν οὕτεροϲ δαίμων (on which see Lloyd-Jones, *CR* 81
(1967), 125–7 and 88 (1974), 5; M. L. West, *CR* 85 (1971), 330–1).
For a similar phrase in Latin cf. e.g. Sil. 14. 495 'seu laevi traxere
dei'. Contrast *H.* 6. 31 ὁ δεξιὸϲ . . . δαίμων (with Hopkinson's
valuable note).

FRS. 52–6

I have grouped together five fragments concerning toil, injustice,
and poverty (note also fr. 94 λάτριν ἄγειν παλίνορϲον ἀεικέα τῶι
κεραμῆι, which, however, more probably belongs with two other
fragments about potters). Of these. fr. 54 νυκτὶ δ' ὅληι βαϲιλῆαϲ
ἐλέγχομεν can with fair plausibility be assigned to a speech by
Hecale, in view of likely references to βαϲιλῆεϲ in frs. 47. 20 and
49. 17 (see further on fr. 47. 4). Frs. 53 (πάϲχομεν) and 54
(ἐλέγχομεν) share the use of the first person plural; Hecale might
perhaps have described to Theseus the sufferings of her people. Fr.
53 looks as though it could introduce a catalogue of miseries.

Fr. 52 (272 Pf.)

ἄνδρεϲ †ἔλαιοι Δεκελειόθεν ἀμπρεύοντεϲ: 'men hauling . . .
from Decelea'. ἀμπρεύειν is one of the many Attic words which
give local colour to the *Hecale*. According to the grammarians
(see the sources quoted for this fragment) ἀμπρόν, which is found
on Attic inscriptions (e.g. Ἀρχ. Ἐφ. 1895, 73 (see now *IG* i³. 386.
24) and 1899, 179) is a rope attached to animals pulling heavy
loads on a cart; a minority view makes it the wooden yoke on the
animals' neck. Compare Soph. fr. 820 ὥϲπερ ἀμπρευτὴϲ ὄνοϲ
(with Pearson's note); E. *Protesilaus*, fr. 646a Snell ἕπου δὲ μοῦνον
ἀμπρεύοντί μοι, where Photius explains the verb with προηγεῖ-

cθαι; Ar. *Lys.* 289–90 χῶπως ποτ᾽ ἐξαμπρεύσομεν | τοῦτ᾽ ἄνευ κανθηλίου. Lycophron may derive his taste for the verb partly from this line of Call.: in addition to the orthodox meaning 'to drag' at *Alex.* 1298, we find a metaphorical sense of 'dragging out' a miserable life in *Alex.* 635, 975 (cf. the use of ἀμαξεύω in *AP* 9. 574. 1).

Pfeiffer thought that the men (? as a sign of extreme poverty and degradation) have taken over the work of animals ('tamquam boves funibus iugati') in pulling the heavily-laden carts with a rope. That is not quite clear to me. The corrupt ἐλαιοι is probably incurable: of the attempts to restore a nominative, Pfeiffer's δειλαίοι would be close to the MSS' reading; he himself added that one expects an accusative (though this could have come e.g. in the preceding line). E. A. Barber conjectured ἐλαιηρούς ('secutum est e.g. κεράμους', *CR* 69 (1955), 242) which Trypanis actually printed in the Loeb. Although unable to heal the textual corruption, I wonder whether the men are conveying timber. R. Meiggs (*Trees and Timber in the Ancient Mediterranean World* (1982), pp. 205–6) discusses [Demosthenes] 42. 7, where six asses are said to carry logs (ὑλαγωγοῦσι) all the year round from an estate in the region of Mt. Pentelicus to Athens, probably for firewood. I have even toyed with the idea of bringing in fr. 152 to produce ὑληωροί | ἄνδρες (ἀνήρ is often linked to the indication of a particular profession, as e.g. fr. 74. 25 ἀνὴρ ὑδατηγός).

Δεκελειόθεν: the form (argued over by the grammarians Tryphon (p. 53 Velsen) and Apollonius Dyscolos (*Gr. Gr.* i. 1, p. 188. 21 Schneider)) is irregular (cf. the remarks of D. M. Lewis in *BSA* 50 (1955), 13) but paralleled in the sober prose of Lysias (23. 2–3, twice); normal would be Δεκελειαθεν (Δεκελεῆθεν, Hdt. 9. 73). The deme of Decelea lay not far to the north-west of Hecale's home, and to the west of Aphidnae (mentioned in fr. 42. 2), in the vicinity of modern Tatoi. See Lilian Chandler, *JHS* 46 (1926), 16–17 and pl. 1; J. R. McCredie, *Hesperia*, Suppl. 11 (1966), 56; J. S. Traill, *Hesperia*, Suppl. 14 (1975), 52.

Fr. 53 (275 Pf.)

ἄστηνοι: perhaps a Callimachean coinage (elsewhere only in a 2nd-cent. BC verse inscription, *BCH* 29 (1905), 410); Hesychius offers also ἀστηνεῖ· ἀδυνατεῖ and ἀστῆνες· ταλαίπωροι· δυστυχεῖς.

Salustius in his commentary may have accepted from the grammarian Seleucus the explanation οἱ cτάcιν καὶ οἴκηcιν μὴ ἔχοντεc (see Pfeiffer). I suspect, however, that Call. meant ἄcτηνοc to be a surprise variant for the commonplace δύcτηνοc, with a- as an intensifying prefix (likewise probably fr. 124 ἀcταγὲc ὕδωρ). This view was also current in antiquity (*Et. Gud.* s.v. δύcτηνοc ... τὸ δ' αὐτὸ καὶ ἄcτηνοc, τοῦ ᾱ ἐπίταcιν cημαίνοντοc).

οἴκοθε: so Pfeiffer for *Et. Gen.*'s οἴκοθεν. One might have expected οἴκοθι (Miller), but οἴκοθεν is often used without any idea of motion, and Pfeiffer shows that τὰ οἴκοθεν *vel sim.* is a regular phrase.

πάντα δέδαcται: cf. *Od.* 15. 412 δίχα δέ cφιcι πάντα δέδαcται; Choeril. fr. 1. 3 Kinkel = *SH* 317 νῦν δ' ὅτε πάντα δέδαcται.

Fr. 54 (329 Pf.)

νυκτὶ δ' ὅληι βαcιλῆαc ἐλέγχομεν: Suidas glosses ἐλέγχομεν with κακολογοῦμεν. Pfeiffer naturally thought of Hesiod's βαcιλῆαc | δωροφάγουc (*Op.* 38–9; see West ad loc.). It now seems possible that there are two other (? uncomplimentary) references to βαcιλῆεc in a speech by Hecale (see on fr. 47. 4), which might suggest a context for this fragment; perhaps near fr. 53, e.g. νυκτὶ δ' ὅληι βαcιλῆαc ἐλέγχομεν, ⟨οἷα ∪ — —⟩ | πάcχομεν ἄcτηνοι · τὰ μὲν οἴκοθε πάντα δέδαcται.

FRS. 55–6

Slight support (apart from their subject-matter) for the association of these two fragments may come from Nic. *Ther.* 783–4, where ποηφάγοc and γαιοφάγοc appear in successive lines.

Fr. 55 (290 Pf.)

γηφάγοι: Numenius has γαιηφάγοι of earthworms (*SH* 584. 3), Nicander γαιοφάγοc of a scorpion (*Ther.* 784), while the work περὶ γεωφάγων ascribed to Plutarch (vii. p. 477 Bernadakis) may have been about primitive tribes who ate earth (Usener, *Kl. Schr.* i. 343). Call. apparently gave the word a more artificial sense, of those who have to eat what they can gather from the earth. Older scholars (e.g. Hecker, *CC*, pp. 114–15) thought of recipients of Hecale's hospitality; Pfeiffer speculated on a connection with fr. 162 inc. sed.

Fr. 56 (365 Pf.)

ποιηφάγον: according to Suidas of a woman who gathers the ears of corn behind the harvesters (cf. Ruth 2: 6 ff.). Compare the scholiast's explanation of Theocr. 3. 32 ποιολογοῦϲα as ϲταχυολογοῦϲα (with which Gow, however, disagrees).

Fr. 57 (313 Pf.)

ἁλυκὸν δέ οἱ ἔκπεϲε δάκρυ: this fragment and the next almost certainly refer to Hecale; the words are adapted from *Od.* 16. 16 of Eumaeus (= *Il.* 2. 266 of Thersites) θαλερὸν δέ οἱ ἔκπεϲε δάκρυ. ἁλυκόϲ, 'salty', appears in Hippocrates, and, in poetry, at Ar. *Lys.* 403 and fr. 93 *PCG*, Simias fr. 11. 2 Powell ἡ ἁλυκὴ ζάψ (cf. Dionys. Iamb. *SH* 389). More immediately relevant to Call. would be Knox's fine restoration in Herod. 2. 6 [τ]ὠλυκὸν γὰρ [ἂν] κλαύϲαι.

It is probable (as first suggested by Hecker, *CC* p. 123) that this fragment is alluded to by Statius (*Theb.* 12. 580–2 (= above, Test. 8), Euadne to Theseus—for other links between Statius and the *Hecale* see above, Introd. sect. VI, and below, Index of Allusions and Imitations):

> da terris unum caeloque Ereboque laborem,
> si patrium Marathona metu, si tecta levasti
> Cresia, *nec fudit vanos anus hospita fletus.*

Can we glean anything from Statius about the likely Callimachean context? The point in Statius appears to be that Hecale's tears were not ineffective, i.e. that they produced some result. This might suggest (as Kapp, p. 39, remarks) that she made a tearful appeal to Theseus; perhaps she described the sufferings inflicted on her neighbours by the Marathonian bull, and longed for her young guest to rid them of the monster. But such a deduction may rest more weight on the *Thebaid* passage than it can bear. Hecker (p. 123) placed the fragment at Hecale's final parting from Theseus.

Fr. 58 (310 Pf.)

ἀείπλανα χείλεα γρηόϲ: no doubt concerning the loquacity of Hecale (she might even be herself apologizing for it). Pfeiffer drew attention to his fr. 483 inc. sed. on a similar topic.

ἀείπλανα: 'ever-wandering', a unique form. Greg. Naz. has ἀειπλανήϲ (*Carm.* 2. 1. 43. 12 (*PG* xxxvii. 1347)); note also Nonn. *Par.* 3. 55 χείλεϲιν ἀπλανέεϲϲι.

FRS. 59–62

In fr. 49. 13 ff. Hecale cursed Cercyon as if he were still alive; one may reasonably infer that Theseus replied by telling her how he killed the bandit. It seems possible (one cannot say more) that this reply included the fight with Sciron, whom Theseus would have encountered immediately before Cercyon. Therefore I have placed these four fragments together; but Sciron could equally well have been dealt with near the beginning of the poem (a part of the *Hecale* about which we know very little).

FRS. 59–60

Sciron was the kind of character who became the subject of comedies and satyr-plays; he gave his name to works of the former type by Epicharmus (frs. 125–6 Kaibel, probably our earliest surviving literary reference) and Alexis (fr. 207 Kock), and of the latter by Euripides (*P. Oxy.* 2455 contains the hypothesis). He also had a place in conventional catalogues of Theseus' labours (e.g. Bacchyl. 18. 24–5; cf. R. Carden, *The Papyrus Fragments of Sophocles* (1974), pp. 118–19, giving *P. Oxy.* 2452, fr. 3 = Soph. fr. 730c Radt, 16 ff., perhaps from the *Theseus*; Mich. Chon. ii, 129. 21–2, 171. 4 Lambros). The depiction of Theseus and Sciron in art was discussed by Talfourd Ely, *JHS* 9 (1888), 272–81, and by Waser in Roscher s.v. Skiron.

Although so little remains of Call.'s treatment, we can be fairly confident that Euph. fr. 9. 6 ff. reflects Call. (see on fr. 60). [Virg.] *Ciris* 465–7 could also owe something to our poet: 'praeterit abruptas Scironis protinus arces,| infestumque suis dirae testudinis

exit | spelaeum, multoque cruentas hospite çautes'; cf. Ov. *Met.* 7.
443 ff. (from a passage generally indebted to Call.). Finally, faint
echoes of Call.'s Sciron may be recognized in Nonnus' Alpos
(*Dion.* 45. 173 ff.; see A. S. Hollis, *CQ*, NS 26 (1976), 143). Fr. 90
on Nisus, King of Megara, might have been linked to the story of
Sciron.

Fr. 59 (296 Pf.)

The scholiast on E. *Hipp.* 979 says that Call. made mention of
Sciron τοῦ τὴν χελώνην τρέφοντοϲ. This may leave us in doubt
whether the tortoise appeared in the *Hecale* together with Sciron,
but the evidence of Euphorion (see on fr. 60) indicates that it
probably did; Gow suggests that Nic. *Ther.* 703 βροτολοιγὸν . . .
χελύνην may allude to Sciron's tortoise (cf. also *Ciris* 466–7,
quoted above). From *Et. Gen.* we learn further that Call. wrote
Cκίρων (rather than Cκείρων), the old spelling given by vase-
inscriptions (P. Kretschmer, *Griechischen Vaseninschriften* (1894),
pp. 131 ff.) and e.g. in the papyrus of Bacchylides (see further R.
Carden, *The Papyrus Fragments of Sophocles* (1974), pp. 121–2).

Fr. 60 (245 Pf.)

**1–2 φράϲον δέ μοι, εἰϲ ὅ τι τεῦχοϲ | χεύωμαι ποϲὶ χύτλα καὶ
ὁππόθεν:** Pfeiffer, following Schneider (fr. an. 66) referred these
words to the foot-washing in Hecale's cottage (a disputed episode,
but fr. 34 may belong to it) with Theseus as the speaker. But it is
extremely odd for Theseus to ask Hecale such a question; one
would expect the old woman to pour out the water herself. A
much more plausible context is provided by Euph. fr. 9. 6 ff. (for
this fragment and the *Hecale* see above, Introd. sect. VI), as indeed
Kapp almost realized (p. 25 'nisi versus Euphorionis de Scironis
lavacro suspicionem moverent'):

> ἢ ὅϲϲον ὁδοιπόροι ἐρρήϲϲοντο
> Cκε]ίρων ἔνθα πόδεϲϲιν ἀεικέα μήδετο χύτλα
> οὐκ ἐπὶ δήν· Αἴθρηϲ γὰρ ἀλοιηθεὶϲ ὑπὸ παιδί
> νωϊτέρηϲ χέλυοϲ πύματοϲ ἐλιπήνατο λαιμόν.

in line 7 perhaps we might restore Cκ]ίρων, Call.'s form (fr. 59).
According to Apollod. *Epit.* 1. 2 οὗτοϲ ἐν τῆι Μεγαρικῆι κατέχων

τὰς ἀφ' ἑαυτοῦ κληθείςας πέτρας Cκειρωνίδας, ἠνάγκαζε τοὺς
παριόντας νίζειν αὐτοῦ τοὺς πόδας, καὶ νίζοντας εἰς τὸν βυθὸν
αὐτοὺς ἔρριπτε βορὰν ὑπερμεγέθει χελώνηι. Θηςεὺς δὲ ἁρπάςας
αὐτὸν τῶν ποδῶν ἔρριψεν ⟨εἰς τὴν θάλαccαν⟩; cf. Plut. *Thes.* 10. It
seems to me (*CR*, NS 15 (1965), 259–60) that fr. 60 would be
highly appropriate in the mouth of Theseus as a response to
Sciron's habitual command, προτείνοντα τῶ πόδε τοῖc ξένοιc καὶ
κελεύοντα νίπτειν (Plut. *Thes.* 10). Theseus would be playing for
time—Talfourd Ely (*JHS* 9 (1888), 277) distinguishes the prelimi-
nary parley between the pair as one of the scenes portrayed by
vase-painters. The words would have particular force (as Lloyd-
Jones remarked) if Theseus then used the foot-pan as a weapon
with which to strike Sciron. This is not the most common
version, and does not appear for certain in literature (note,
however, Epich. fr. 126 Kaibel πηλίνων λεκίc), but is attested in
art (Talfourd Ely, op. cit. p. 277). And the actual word used by
Euphorion (ἀλοιηθείc, fr. 9. 8) definitely suggests that, in the
Hecale, Sciron was stunned or killed by a violent blow, whether
from the foot-pan or Theseus' club (cf. fr. 69. 1 ἀπηλοίηcε of
breaking the bull's horn) before being thrown to the tortoise.

These lines of Euphorion may contain more echoes of the
Hecale. Pfeiffer (on fr. 296) writes of ἐλιπήνατο λαιμόν 'Callima-
chum sapit' (cf. Nonn. *Dion.* 45. 181 τυμβεύcατο λαιμῶι of
Alpos).

2 χύτλα: in this sense of 'water for washing' (rather than
'libations') used by Lycophron (*Alex.* 1099) as well as Call. and
Euphorion.

Fr. 61 (306 Pf.)

Apart from Stephanus Byzantius the only writer to mention
Iapis, a ravine on the borders of Attica and Megara, is pseudo-
Scylax (in *Peripl.* 56 and 57 Berkelius, on the evidence of
Stephanus Byzantius, twice emended Ἄπιδος to Ἰαπίδος). Naeke
(p. 182) conjectured that Iapis lay between the two mountains
called Κέρατα which separated Attic from Megarian territory
(Str. 9. 1. 11: cf. Plut. *Them.* 13; Lilian Chandler, *JHS* 46 (1926),
12) and that Theseus may have journeyed by this way from
Sciron to Cercyon.

Fr. 62 (328 Pf.)

1–2 ἧχι κονίϲτραι | ἄξεινοι λύθρωι τε καὶ εἴαρι πεπλήθαϲι: for Cercyon see on fr. 49. 8 ff.: like Sciron, he was the subject of a satyr-play (by Aeschylus: frs. 102–7 N² and *Tr. G. F.*). For his wrestling-floor see Bacchyl. 18. 26–7 τάν τε Κερκυόνος παλαίϲτραν | ἔϲχεν (sc. Theseus); Paus. 1. 39. 3 καὶ ὁ τόπος οὗτος 'παλαίϲτρα' καὶ ἐς ἐμὲ ἐκαλεῖτο 'Κερκυόνος'. Lyc. 866–7 (of Eryx) κακοξένους | πάλης κονίϲτρας provides perhaps the closest verbal link between the *Hecale* and *Alexandra*; cf. Nonn. *Dion.* 48. 96–7 λύθρωι | . . . ἐφοινίϲϲοντο παλαῖϲτραι, ibid. 103 κακοξείνοιο παλαίϲτρης (of Pallene; see A. S. Hollis, *CQ*, NS 26 (1976), 143).

1 ἧχι: also in fr. 102. 1; some preferred to write ἧιχι (see McLennan (*HZ*) on *H.* 1. 10. Erbse on schol. *Il.* 1. 607).

κονίϲτραι: literally, κονίϲτρα is a place covered with dust; κονίεϲθαι is used of wrestlers sprinkling themselves with dust as a preparation for combat.

2 εἴαρι: a regular Homeric coupling is αἵματι καὶ λύθρωι (e.g. *Il.* 6. 268). There was a famous v.l. εἰαροπῶτις for ἠεροφοῖτις (*Il.* 19. 87), and neoteric poets are fond of εἶαρ = blood (e.g. Nic. *Alex.* 314; cf. Pfeiffer's note on his fr. 177(= *SH* 259). 22, where ἔαρ denotes the oil in a lamp). Some saw a connection with ἔαρ = spring; in Euph. fr. 40. 3 there may even be a deliberate ambiguity, since εἴαρος could mean either 'from his blood' or 'in the spring'.

πεπλήθαϲι: cf. Maiist. *ap.* Powell, *CA*, p. 70. 25 πεπληθότα λύθρωι. The perfect πέπληθα occurs e.g. in Theocr. 22. 38 and Herod. 7. 84.

FRS. 63–4

Having finished with the fragments which can plausibly be assigned to the conversation of Hecale and Theseus, we find them going to bed (fr. 63) and rising early next morning (fr. 64).

Fr. 63 (256 Pf.)

λέξομαι ἐν μυχάτωι· κλισίη δέ μοί ἐστιν ἑτοίμη: various interpretations have been put on this line. Hecker (*CC*, pp. 94,

117) thought that Hecale was offering Theseus her own bed, having prepared another for herself in the innermost part of the cottage. Schneider (p. 187), on the other hand, attributed the words to Theseus declining the use of Hecale's bed. Pfeiffer believed, much more plausibly, that Hecale is talking about her own customary bed, in which she will sleep, having improvised a couch for Theseus elsewhere in the cottage. In Homer the host regularly sleeps μυχῶι δόμου (*Od.* 7. 346; cf. ibid. 3. 402, 4. 304); Eumaeus makes a bed for Odysseus near the hearth, τίθει δ' ἄρα οἱ πυρὸς ἐγγύς | εὐνήν, ἐν δ' ὀΐων τε καὶ αἰγῶν δέρματ' ἔβαλλεν.| ἔνθ' Ὀδυσεὺς κατέλεκτ' (*Od.* 14. 518–20).

μυχάτωι: this superlative does not seem to occur before Call.; Apollonius Rhodius has it 7 times (also the ? mid-3rd-cent. BC oracle in *Klio*, 15 (1918), 48; [Phoc.] *Sent.* 164).

Fr. 64 (257 Pf.)

Hecale sees Theseus getting up early in the morning. Compare *Dieg.* x. 31–2 πρὸς δὲ τὴν ἔω ἀναστάς. Pfeiffer considered restoring κλιςίηθεν at the end of the line.

κἀκεῖνον: see on fr. 45. 1.

FRS. 65–6

These two fragments seem to describe Hecale, but their position is unknown; the double mention of Hecale's staff might suggest that they belong to different contexts (in fr. 66 could the old woman be coming out to bid Theseus farewell?). I have, for convenience, placed them just before we lose contact with Hecale.

Fr. 65 (292 Pf.)

1 **ἔπρεπέ τοι:** we cannot be sure whether τοι = *tibi*, 'conveniebat tibi' (? the poet apostrophizing his character), or is the particle, 'conspicua quidem erat καλύπτρη' (Pf.), but the former seems more probable, since the particle occurs only at *H.* 4. 296 ἦ τοι (see Mineur (*HD*) ad loc.), while τοι = *tibi* is common in Call. (e.g. *Aet.* frs. 24. 4, 27. 1 Pf.). Compare Theocr. 15. 34–5 μάλα τοι τὸ καταπτυχὲς ἐμπερόναμα | τοῦτο πρέπει.

προέχουca κάρηc: 'projecting from your head'. Call. here and in *Aet.* fr. 110. 40 Pf. is apparently the first to treat κάρη as feminine (he also has κάρη neuter, e.g. in *Aet.* fr. 43. 12 Pf.). Later poets follow him (e.g. Nic. *Ther.* 131, 249; [Mosch.] 4. 74; Dion. Per. 562); see Pfeiffer in *Philol.* 87 (1932), 183 n. 13, with discussion of *Theognidea* 1024.

2 ποιμενικὸν πίλημα: see on fr. 46. 2 for another πίλημα. Pfeiffer compares John of Gaza 2. 302 κάρη δ' ἐκαλύπτετο πίλωι.

καὶ ἐν χερὶ χαῖον †ἔχουca: χαῖον is usually a throwing-stick (see Gow's detailed note on Theocr. 4. 49) carried by herdsmen and shepherds (e.g. Ap. Rh. 4. 972 ἀργύρεον χαῖον παλαμῆι ἔνι πηχύνουca), but here, it seems, a simple staff. At the end of the line Pfeiffer (ii, p. 120) came to agree with Barber and Maas (who conjectured respectively ἀρηρός and ἐχούcηι) that ἔχουca is corrupt.

Fr. 66 (355 Pf.)

1 γέντο: 'grasped'. Call. here and in *H.* 6. 43 follows the Homeric placing of γέντο = ἔλαβε after the bucolic diaeresis (e.g. *Il.* 18. 476 γέντο δὲ χειρί), while in *H.* 1. 50 he denies that position to γέντο = ἐγένετο (see Hopkinson (*HD*) and McLennan (*HZ*) ad locc.). If this was a rule for Call., it has implications for the place within the line of fr. 106 γέντο δ' ἀλυκρά.

2 cκηπάνιον: cf. *Il.* 13. 59 (where a scholiast says that the word is Cyrenaean) and 24. 247 (of the aged Priam). A possible supplement for the lacuna would be χείρεccιν (Naeke), as in fr. 10. 2.

γήραος ὀκχή: 'a support for old age'; ὀκχή (cf. fr. 143 ὀκχήcαcθαι) is a poetical form of ὀχή. For such conventional descriptions of an old person's staff, cf. e.g. Ap. Rh. 1. 670 βάκτρωι ἐρειδομένη; Maced. *AP* 6. 83. 6 cκηπανίωι τρομερὰς χεῖρας ἐρεισάμεθα; Ov. *Met.* 8. 693b (Baucis and Philemon) 'membra levant baculis'.

FRS. 67–9 THE CAPTURE OF THE MARATHONIAN BULL

We must now leave Hecale, destined to die the same day; we do not know the placing of her promised sacrifice to Zeus for Theseus' safe return, which is mentioned by Plutarch (*Thes.* 14) and, although absent from the *Diegesis*, may have been in Call. (see on fr. 83 and fr. 169 inc. sed.). An appropriate moment for this might be Hecale's parting from Theseus.

Of the struggle with the bull, only one certain fragment (67) and one probable (165 inc. auct.) survive. As a possible indication that Call. may not have gone into great detail, note that the breaking of the bull's horn by the hero's club is disposed of in parenthesis (fr. 69. 1). B. B. Shefton (*Hesperia*, 31 (1962), 347 ff.) discusses artistic representations of Theseus and the bull (see further on fr. 68).

Fr. 67 (258 Pf.)

θηρὸς ἐρωήϲαϲ ὀλοὸν κέραϲ: ἐρωέω in early epic usually means 'draw back from', with a genitive, but in *Il.* 13. 57 the verb is transitive, 'force back'. Compare Call. *H.* 4. 133 and Theocr. 22. 174 ('withhold'); somewhat different are Theocr. 13. 74 and 24. 101 (= 'quit' + accusative). Here the meaning seems to be 'forcing down'. *Et. Mag.* (though the implied etymology is absurd) explains εἰϲ τὴν ἔραν καταγαγών, while Suidas offers μειώϲαϲ (i.e. minorem fecit, 'demisit'? (Pfeiffer)), κατάξαϲ [so Pfeiffer: κατεάξαϲ codd., but, although Theseus did indeed break one of the bull's horns (fr. 69. 1), ἐρωέω could not mean 'break']. Forcing down the horn is regularly mentioned in poetic accounts of wrestling with a bull (e.g. Theocr. 25. 145 ff. ἐδράξατο χειρὶ παχείηι | ϲκαιοῦ ἄφαρ κέραοϲ, κατὰ δ' αὐχένα νέρθ' ἐπὶ γαίηϲ | κλάϲϲε βαρύν περ ἐόντα: Ov. *Met.* 9. 83–4 'depressaque dura | cornua figit humo' and ibid. 186; Sil. 13. 223 'trucis deducere cornua tauri'. One can make a more general comparison with other tauromachies, e.g. Ap. Rh. 3. 1306 ff., Val. Flacc. 7. 587 ff.

Particularly interesting is an anonymous epigram (*AP* 16. 105; cf. Shefton, *Hesperia*, 31 (1962), 351 n. 88) on a sculptured group of Theseus and the bull, wherein Theseus grasps the animal's nostrils with his left hand and horn with his right (l. 4 λαιῆι μυκτῆραϲ, δεξιτερῆι δὲ κέραϲ). As Gow remarks (on Theocr. 25. 145) a later sculptor could hardly disregard Call.'s poem. Perhaps in our fragment too Theseus has grasped a horn with one hand; the breaking of the horn with his club probably came later (in fr. 165 inc. auct., if from the *Hecale*, the bull still has both horns). Finally, note Cic. *Tusc.* 4. 50 'an etiam Theseus Marathonii tauri cornua comprehendit iratus?' This apparent sign of interest in the *Hecale* makes more likely the ascription to our poem of fr. 165 inc. auct., which we owe to Cicero.

FRS. 68–9

Theseus has captured and bound the bull; he drags it, maimed but still formidable, into view of the country people, who are terrified until he reassures them and asks for a messenger to go to his father in Athens.

One might possibly join the two fragments (Barigazzi, *RFIC* 99 (1971), 287–9; A. S. Hollis, *CR*, NS 22 (1972), 5) to produce:

> ὁ μὲν εἷλκεν, ὁ δ' εἵπετο νωθρὸς ὁδίτης
> οἰόκερως· ἕτερον γὰρ ἀπηλοίηςε κορύνη κτλ.

Compare *H.* 4. 77–8 ὁ δ' εἵπετο . . . | . . . βαρύγουνος. Campbell, however, suspects that something more violent preceded οἰόκερως, e.g. '. . . tried vainly to lash out at him | with his single horn . . . etc.'

Fr. 68 (259 Pf.)

The context is made certain by schol. Ap. Rh. 1. 1162 (ἐπὶ τοῦ ταύρου ἡττηθέντος). Soph. fr. 25 Radt, Pearson (from the *Aegeus*) describes Theseus binding the bull, κλωστῆρςι χειρῶν ὀργάςας κατήνυςε | ςειραῖα δεςμά. It is interesting to compare what Shefton (*Hesperia*, 31 (1962), 348) writes of the vase painters: 'With the early classical period, however, a new scheme appears. The bull no longer collapses forward at the feet of Theseus, but is on his way to Athens under leash. The moment chosen is when the animal (moving to the right) has become restive and requires chastening. Theseus (often wearing a distinctive hat, a petasos or pilos) comes up from behind, grasps one of the horns and is about to subdue the temper of the animal by a blow of his club.'

νωθρὸς ὁδίτης: 'a sluggish traveller' (the donkey beaten by boys in *Il.* 11. 559 is νωθής; cf. J. M. Jacques, *REA* 71 (1969), 46 ff.). The bull follows along slowly; not, I would guess, because its spirit has been broken—rather it fights every inch of the way against the pressure of the rope. This memorable phrase fascinated

Nonnus (see A. S. Hollis, *CQ*, NS 26 (1976), 142–3) who writes νωθρὸς ὁδίτης in *Dion.* 3. 101, 17. 27, 43. 381 (whence Nonnus' follower John of Gaza 2. 29), and other combinations with ὁδίτης in the *Paraphrase* (5. 30 κοῦφος ὁδίτης, 9. 48 τυφλὸς ὁδίτης) as well as the *Dionysiaca*. More generally, *Dion.* 15. 28 ταῦρον ἀπειλητῆρα μετήγαγε δέcμιον ἕλκων may recall this scene from the *Hecale* (see further Campbell, *Studies*, pp. 79–80). The adjective νωθρός is common in medical writings.

Fr. 69 (*SH* 288. 1–15; 260. 1–15 Pf.)

From this point up to the end of fr. 74 we are within the compass of our most valuable source for the *Hecale*. The 4th- or 5th-cent. Vienna Tablet, *P. Rain.* vi (my pap. 8; see above, Introd., sect. XI), a wooden board of the kind used in schools, contains on one side two columns of E. *Phoen.* (1097–1107, 1126–37) and on the other, in smaller writing, four columns of the *Hecale*. Although the bottom of the tablet is broken off, we can calculate from the Euripides approximately how many lines are missing at the foot of cols. i–iii of the Callimachus (and thus the extent of the lacunae after my frs. 69, 70, and 73). It will be noticed that col. i both of Euripides and Callimachus starts in mid-sentence. See on frs. 68–9 above for the possibility that fr. 68 might be joined to the first line of the Vienna Tablet.

1 **οἰόκερως· ἕτερον γὰρ ἀπηλοίηcε κορύνη**: 'single-horned, for the club crushed the other.' Rereading of the Vienna Tablet here produced the most spectacular improvement on what Pfeiffer had accepted from the first editor, Theodor Gomperz. οἰόκερως is due to M. L. West (after R. A. Coles had described the traces) and ἀπηλοίηcε κορύνη to Lloyd-Jones. Although the traces are not sufficient for certainty (Lloyd-Jones and Rea, *HSCP* 72 (1968), 128), various pieces of evidence confirm beyond reasonable doubt both the fact that Theseus broke one horn of the bull with his club, and the actual wording of the line:

(*a*) Michael Choniates, Archbishop of Athens at the time of the Frankish conquest in AD 1205, possessed perhaps the last complete copy of the *Hecale*, and took delight in alluding to it in his poems and letters (see further above, Introd. sect. VIII; Wilson, *Scholars*, pp. 204–6). According to Michael (ii. 345. 10–11

Lambros = above, Test. 15*b*), Theseus κορύνηι θάτερον κεράτων
ἠλόησεν. This piece of evidence was known to Ida Kapp (com-
menting on her fr. 56 = my fr. 67), but wrongly discounted;
Lloyd-Jones (*HSCP* 72 (1968), 134) applied it to the new reading
of the Vienna Tablet.

(*b*) Val. Flacc. 1. 36 'ambobus iam cornua fracta iuvencis'
(Pelias would like to send Jason to his doom, but all the more local
monsters have already been defeated). The two 'iuvenci' would
most appropriately be the Cretan and Marathonian bulls—among
other suggested candidates the Minotaur might be a starter, but
Achelous surely is not. For the breaking of the Cretan's horn by
Heracles cf. Nonn. *Dion.* 25. 228–9 τινάccων | τοccατίην κορύνην
ὀλίγην ἔτμηξε κεραίην. In Valerius Flaccus (cf. 7. 287 ff.), as in
Apollonius Rhodius (3. 997 ff.) and Catullus (64), the exploits of
Theseus antedate the Argo.

(*c*) Although the context is quite different, Nonn. *Dion.* 17.
210 ταυρείην . . . ἀπηλοίηcε κεραίην seems to echo the wording of
Call.'s line (A. S. Hollis, *CQ*, NS 26 (1976), 142, 146).

(*d*) The same Michael Choniates who tells us that Theseus
broke one of the bull's horns (above) also uses the extremely rare
compound οἰόκερωc in his own poetry (*Εἰc τὸν Μονόκερων* 6 (ii.
393 Lambros) οἰόκερωc θήρ). There must be a high probability
that he took it from Call. rather than from the only other writer
to use the word, pseudo-Oppian (*Cyn.* 2. 96—but note [Apolli-
nar.] *Ps.* 28. 14 οἰοκερῆοc, perhaps likewise from Call.).

οἰόκερωc: for -κερωc compounds as a whole see James, *Oppian
of Cilicia*, pp. 69–70.

ἕτερον γὰρ ἀπηλοίηcε κορύνη: with ἕτερον it is easy to
understand κέραc from the compound οἰόκερωc. Thus for ex-
ample in *Od.* 3. 304 ff. ἑπτάετεc δ' ἤναccε ... | ... τῶι δέ οἱ
ὀγδοάτωι we must supply ἔτει from ἑπτάετεc.

This parenthesis must surely have been the first mention of the
breaking of the bull's horn (see above, introductory note to frs.
67–9). Compare fr. 9, where, probably at the moment when
Aegeus recognizes his son, Call. inserts a retrospective parenthesis
explaining how the vital sword had been left under a rock in
Troezen (ἐν γάρ μιν Τροιζῆνι κτλ.). It is tempting to see in such
passages a germ of the parentheses in later epyllia, e.g. Virg. *G.* 4.
487 'pone sequens (namque hanc dederat Proserpina legem)' and
Ciris 187 (see Lyne ad loc. and his Introd. sect. V). Achelous'

account of how he lost his horn, 'cornua, dum potui! nunc pars caret altera telo | frontis' (Ov. *Met.* 8. 883–4) may owe something to Call. For parentheses in our poet see Lapp, *Tropis et Figuris*, pp. 52–3.

ἀπηλοίηϲε: a Homeric *hapax legomenon* (*Il.* 4. 522). It now seems unlikely that Sophocles used the verb in his *Aegeus* (fr. 20 Radt), as Pearson had thought (fr. 20; cf. Lloyd-Jones and Rea, *HSCP* 72 (1968), 134 n. 2). Later epic poets are fond of ἀπηλοίηϲε (cf. A. S. Hollis, *CQ*, NS 26 (1976), 142). Michael Choniates in his prose summary (above) writes ἠλόηϲεν.

κορύγη: the club which Theseus had taken from Periphetes (Plut. *Thes.* 8), who thus may have figured earlier in the poem. In Nonn. *Dion.* 47. 436 Theseus is κορυνηφόροϲ ἀϲτὸϲ Ἀθήνηϲ. If *P. Oxy.* 3530 belongs to E. *Aegeus* (see Parsons ad loc. and my introductory note to frs. 3–7), line 13 κο]ρύνηι δεξιὰν ὡ[πλιϲμένοϲ may describe Theseus attacking the bull with his club (for artistic representation see on fr. 68).

Lloyd-Jones (*HSCP* 72 (1968), 135) notes that one might read κορύνη⟨ι⟩, with Theseus as the subject, but that the nominative seems more in keeping with Call.'s style. If, as suggested above, this line immediately follows fr. 68, the nominative would be far superior (*pace* Barigazzi, *RFIC* 99 (1971), 289 n. 1).

2 ὡϲ ἴδον, ὥ[ϲ]: for this famous and much-discussed pattern (modelled on *Il.* 14. 294) see Gow on Theocr. 2. 82; Bühler on Mosch. *Eur.* 74 (and Exkurs IV); Livrea on Colluth. 255; Campbell on Quint. Smyrn. 12. 120 (with additional examples). The second ὥϲ is probably to be taken as demonstrative ('as they saw, so did they . . .') rather than exclamatory. This sequence is nearly always found in erotic contexts (for another non-erotic example, cf. [Apollinar.] *Ps.* 96. 8 ὡϲ δ' ἴδεν, ὡϲ δεδόνητο θεμείλια πάντοϲε γαίηϲ). Pfeiffer would restore ὡϲ δ' ἴδεϲ, ὡϲ in *H.* 4. 200.

ὥ[ϲ] ἅμα πάντεϲ ὑπέτρεϲαν: cf. Quint. Smyrn 1. 278 τοὶ δ' ἅμα πάντεϲ ὑπέτρεϲαν*, 3. 352; *Il.* 15. 636 αἱ δέ τε πᾶϲαι ὑπέτρεϲαν*.

οὐδέ τιϲ ἔτλη: 'The last four letters might be ἔτλη. Before that one must guess οὐδέ τιϲ, though the remains are too faint to support it' (Rea). This would be a welcome improvement over what Pfeiffer printed, ἠδ[ὲ φόβη]θεν. οὐδέ τιϲ ἔτλη ends a hexameter nine times in Homer. Lloyd-Jones notes particularly *Il.* 19. 14–15 Μυρμιδόναϲ δ' ἄρα πάνταϲ ἕλε τρόμοϲ, οὐδέ τιϲ ἔτλη | ἄντην εἰϲιδέειν, ἀλλ' ἔτρεϲαν. In fact the pattern 'nor did anyone/he dare to look at/approach him' is enormously common in Greek epic of all periods (e.g. *Od*. 11. 143–4; Ap. Rh. 2. 681–2; Quint. Smyrn. 4. 312–13, 482–3.

For the motif of the frightened onlookers it is interesting to compare Euph. fr. 51. 14–15 Powell (Heracles drags Cerberus to Eurystheus) καί μιν ἐνὶ τριόδοιϲι πολυκρίθοιο Μιδείηϲ | ταρβαλέαι ϲὺν παιϲὶν ἐθηήϲαντο γυναῖκεϲ. Campbell draws attention to Ap. Rh. 3. 1293 ἔδδειϲαν δ' ἥρωεϲ ὅπωϲ ἴδον (sc. Jason's bulls).

3 ἄνδρα μέγαν: in spite of Theseus' youth, victory has made him a fully-fledged hero, and, like the bull, he provides an awesome spectacle.

4 'until Theseus shouted to them from afar'.

μέϲφ' ὅτε: also (probably with an aorist verb) at fr. 70. 5. Campbell on Quint. Smyrn. 12. 296 observes that μέϲφ' ὅτε 'tries to fight its way into Homer's text' at *Od*. 19. 223 (see Allen's app. crit.) and 24. 310.

φιν: said to be a Laconian form, used by Empedocles (22. 3), elsewhere in the *Hecale* (fr. 111), and in *H*. 3. 125, 213 (cf. Nic. *Ther*. 725, *Alex*. 124, fr. 73. 2, and note on *SH* 1043, anon.). Call. may well have found φιν in a text of Homer (Giangrande, *Hermes*, 98 (1970), 273 = *SMA* i. 81 and n. 7); see e.g. Ludwich's apparatus at *Il*. 3. 302, 9. 95, *Od*. 11. 556, 15. 333. Ancient grammarians wrote treatises on such pronominal forms—we have περὶ Ἀντωνυμιῶν of Apollonius Dyscolus (*c*. 2nd cent. AD). Philip the epigrammatist (*AP* 11. 321 = 60 G.–P.; cf. Herodicus *ap*. Athen. 5. 222a (Page, *FGE*, p. 63)) attacks the Καλλιμάχου ϲτρατιῶται ... οἷϲ τὸ 'μίν' ἢ 'ϲφίν' | εὔαδε (both forms well patronized by Call.—see Pfeiffer's Index Verborum s.v. οὗ).

μακρὸν ἄυϲε from the Homeric τῶι δ' ἐπὶ μακρὸν ἄυϲε (*Il*. 5. 101 etc.), but deliberately placed at a different point in the line.

5 θαρϲήεντεϲ: see on fr. 74. 23 ϲτιβήειϲ for epithets in -ήειϲ. This one is a Callimachean coinage, not reappearing until the fifth century in the Empress Eudocia (*S. Cypr*. 1. 191) and Nonn. (*Dion*. 13. 562*, 26. 60, 30. 294, 48. 899 ἔλθετε θαρϲήεντεϲ*; *Par*. 12. 141 ϲτείχετε θαρϲήεντεϲ*). [Apollinarius] has περιθαρϲήειϲ (*Ps*. 24. 1, 70. 11) and ἐπιθαρϲήειϲ (ibid. 62. 9).

ἐμῷ ... Αἰγέϊ πατρί: the word order is worth noting (Gordon Williams compared Plaut. *Amph*. 1077 'tua Bromia ancilla'), even though it does not match the intricate appositional patterns of Latin poetry (e.g. Virg. *Ecl*. 1. 57 'raucae, tua cura, palumbes'; cf.

J. B. Solodow, *HSCP* 90 (1986), 132–53). I know only one Hellenistic specimen which exactly parallels the Latin practice: Hedyl. *AP* 5. 199(= 2 G.–P.). 5 μαλακαί, μαςτῶν ἐκδύματα, μίτραι. Hutchinson remarks that proper names are more liable than other words to be postponed or inserted in odd places, citing Theocr. 16. 104 ὦ Ἐτεόκλειοι Χάριτες θεαί.

5 ff. The sending of a message back to Aegeus may possibly be linked to fr. 122 ἀπούατος ἄγγελος ἔλθοι, if (see ad loc.) those words express Aegeus' fear that he might receive unwelcome tidings of his son's death. Theseus' consideration here for his father contrasts sharply with the forgetfulness which later caused the old man's suicide (e.g. Catull. 64. 207 ff., 231 ff.).

Jacoby (*FGH* iiib, Suppl. ii. 336) thought that this reference to the messenger may glance at one of the tragedies which covered the same part of the myth (see on frs. 3–7). Whether Call.'s first readers would be reminded of stories about a runner bringing back news of the Battle of Marathon, I do not know.

6 νεύμενος: 'going'; this form also in Antip. Thess. *AP* 9. 96(= 21 G.–P.). 2 (νεῦμαι at *Il.* 18. 136). Nonnus likes μετανεύμενος (*Dion.* 14. 89 etc., *Par.* 6. 66 etc.).

ἀγγελιώτης: cf. *H.* 1. 68* with McLennan's note (*HZ*, adding Eudocia, *S. Cypr.* 1. 200* to the late examples), *H. Hom. Herm.* 296*.

7 ἀναψύξειε: 'he would relieve him'; cf. E. *Hel.* 1094 δύ' οἰκτρὼ φῶτ' ἀνάψυξον πόνων. Aegeus had tried to prevent his son from leaving Athens to fight the Marathonian bull (cf. *Dieg.* x. 26 εἰργόμενος).

8 Θηςεὺς οὐχ ἑκὰς οὗτος: In *Od.* 2. 40 Telemachus says of himself οὐχ ἑκὰς οὗτος ἀνήρ*.

ἀπ' εὐύδρου Μαραθῶνος: (Nonn. *Par.* 4. 11 δι' εὐύδρου Cαμαρείης*). Somewhere else in the *Hecale* Call. called Marathon ἐννότιος (fr. 89). The plain of Marathon is marshy and 'subject to inundation from the two torrents which cross it' (Leake; cf. N. G. L. Hammond, *JHS* 88 (1968), 18–25). Frazer, in his edition of Pausanias (ii, p. 432), writes 'These pools, beside which cattle find green pasture in summer when the plains are scorched and brown with heat, are fed by powerful subterranean sources.' εὔυδρος is not Homeric, but found in Simonides and Pindar (cf. McLennan (*HZ*) on *H.* 1. 20).

9 ὁ μὲν φάτο, τοὶ δ' ἀΐοντες: neither Homeric, nor close to anything in Homer. 'Callimachus diverges openly and deliberately from previous (in epic, pretty rigid) specimens of speech-capping; cf. *H*. 4. 249 ἡ μὲν ἔφη, then Triphiodorus 417 and twice in Nonnus, *Dion*.' (Campbell, private communication). See further McLennan's *HZ*, App. II for the opening and closing of direct speech in Call.'s *Hymns*.

τοὶ δ' ἀϊόντες: cf. *Il*. 11. 532, *Od*. 10. 118*, Ap. Rh. 1. 519 'proecdosis'*, Opp. *Hal*. 4. 123–4 οἱ δ' ἀϊόντες | πάντες, Quint. Smyrn. 4. 145* (in every case, not immediately after direct speech); *Aet*. fr. 43. 78 Pf. φῆ θεός· οἱ δ' ἀϊόντες. I follow M. L. West in writing ἀϊόντες (aorist) rather than ἀΐοντες. See his note on Hes. *Op*. 9, referring to W. Schulze, *Kl. Schr*. pp. 344–8.

10 ἰὴ παιῆον: in his *Hymn to Apollo*, 97–104 (see Williams' commentary and L. Deubner, 'Paian' (*Kl. Schr*. pp. 204–25)) Call. traces back this cry to the infant god's killing of the Delphian serpent—remember that Theseus, like Apollo, has just overcome a monster. ἰὴ παιῆον can, however, be a shout of joy and triumph unconnected with Apollo (e.g. Ar. *Pax* 453; cf. *Il*. 22. 391, the Greek ἀείδοντες παιήονα at the death of Hector). Here Call. may have in mind Bacchyl. 17. 125 ff.: after Theseus returns safely from the deep, κοῦραι | ... ὠλόλυξαν ἔ-|κλαγεν δὲ πόντος· ἠΐθεοι δ' ἐγγύθεν | νέοι παιάνιξαν.

ἀνέκλαγον: for the form cf. E. *IA* 1062. This verb implies an emotional, even frenzied, cry—showing the magnitude of the peril from which they have been saved. Cf. Nonn. *Dion*. 4. 272 etc., *Paraphr*. 12. 58 (the Palm Sunday crowd).

αὖθι δὲ μίμνον: obeying the first part of Theseus' instruction μίμνετε θαρσήεντες (5). It was odd of Wilamowitz (rightly criticized by Kapp, p. 11 n. 29) to deduce from these words that nobody took the message back to Aegeus (see further below, App. IV).

11 ff. The φυλλοβολία was chiefly a way of congratulating athletic victors (e.g. P. *Pyth*. 9. 123–4), and is often portrayed on vases. The scholiast on E. *Hec*. 573 (objecting to 574 φύλλοις ἔβαλλον as anachronistic) quotes an account of φυλλοβολία from Eratosthenes (see on l. 15 below). Some believed (Suid. s.v. περιαγειρόμενοι) that the original φυλλοβολία had been performed in honour of Theseus, though on a different occasion (when he returned from killing the Minotaur). In another 3rd-cent. poem, Philicus' *Hymn to Demeter*—very much a learned *jeu d'esprit* which

may have other connections with the *Hecale* (see above, Introd. sect. VI)—the Attic women would like to pelt Demeter with leaves, but the land is barren, and so they must use whatever plants they can lay their hands on (*SH* 680. 52 ff.): πᾶc δὲ γυναικῶν ... π]έριξ θ' ἑcμὸc ἐθώπευcε πέδον μετώποιc | φυλλοβολῆcαι δ[ὲ] θεὰν [‐∪] ἀνέcχον τὰ μόνα ζώφυτα γῆc ἀκάρπου.

11–12 These lines were admired by Ap. Rh. (4. 216–17) ἢ ὅcα φύλλα χαμᾶζε περικλαδέοc πέcεν ὕληc | φυλλοχόωι ἐνὶ μηνί (cf. Nonn. *Dion.* 2. 641, 38. 278). In mentioning νότοc and βορέηc, Call. particularizes the celebrated *Il.* 6. 147 φύλλα τὰ μέν τ' ἄνεμοc χαμάδιc χέει.

11 οὐχὶ νότοc τόccην γε: the negative comparison is a rare Iliadic technique (14. 394 ff. οὔτε θαλάccηc κῦμα τόcον βοάαι κτλ. and 17. 20 ff., both multiple sequences), which I have not found in Apollonius Rhodius or Quintus Smyrnaeus; but cf. Triph. 369 (οὐχ οὕτω). Roman epic poets, with their greater love of hyperbole, employ negative comparisons (e.g. 'non sic') much more often; cf. Austin on *Aen.* 2. 496, and, for a series, e.g. Stat. *Theb.* 8. 407 ff.

χύcιν κατεχεύατο φύλλων: cf. *Od.* 5. 487 χύcιν δ' ἐπεχεύατο φύλλων*.

12 φυλλοχόοc μ⟨ε⟩ίc: adapted from [Hes.] fr. 333 φυλλοχόοc μήν* (where Rzach conjectured μείc). Hexameters ending with a monosyllabic noun occur already in Homer (e.g. οὐρανόθεν νύξ, χαλκοβατὲc δῶ), are much favoured by certain Hellenistic poets (see Maas, *GM*, para. 96), and are prominent in archaic Latin verse (Ennius, Cicero, *Aratea*, Lucretius). Call., however, uses them sparingly, and always linked to a bucolic diaeresis; from the *Hecale* cf. fr. 18. 1 θέρμετο δὲ χθών, and from the *Hymns* e.g. 2. 83, 100, 4. 259.

ἀγρῶcται: glossed by Hesychius with ἐργάται, θηρευταί (the latter probably referring to Ap. Rh. 4. 175). Manuscripts sometimes (e.g. at E. *Rh.* 266) vary between ἀγρώcτηc and ἀγρώτηc, but one need not doubt the legitimacy of either form (see Pearson on his Soph. fr. 94).

περί τ' ἀμφί τε: also *H.* 4. 300 περί τ' ἀμφί τε νῆcοι | κύκλον ἐποιήcαντο (see Schneider's note); *Il.* 17. 760; Hes. *Th.* 848; [Hes.] fr. 150. 28 περί τ' ἀμφί τε κυκλώcαντο; *H. Hom. Dem.* 276.

14 οἵ μιν ἐκυκλώcα]γτο: Gomperz' fine restoration seems to me sufficiently convincing to stand in the text, although the most

one can say about the Vienna Tablet is that] τọ is not inconsist-
ent with the traces. Possible imitations include Quint. Smyrn. 12.
362 μέccον ἐκυκλώcαντο περιcταδόν; [Apollinar.] Ps. 117. 19 ἀμφ'
ἐμὲ κυκλώcαντο (= Nonn. Dion. 47. 175) περιcταδόν; Nonn.
Dion. 22. 180 καί μιν ἐκυκλώcαντο (thrice in the Paraphr.
Χριcτὸν ἐκυκλώcαντο). Such expressions often describe hostile
encirclement, as also E. Andr. 1136–7 περιcταδόν | κύκλωι
κατεῖχον.

περιcταδόν (certain enough, in my opinion, though the Tablet
has περιcτατον) occurs once in Homer (Il. 13. 551*) and often in
later hexameters (see above and e.g. Ap. Rh. 2. 206; Theocr. 25.
103; Quint. Smyrn. 10. 158, 402, 464).

14–15 αἱ δὲ γυναῖκεc |... ⌊cτορνῆιcιν ἀνέcτεφον⌋: the first
column of the Vienna Tablet breaks off with the words αἱ δὲ
γυναῖκεc, but, thanks to an interrupted citation in Suid. s.v.
cτόρνηιcιν (fr. an. 59 Schn.) we have part of line 15. Conceivably,
as Schneider thought, cτόρνηιcιν should be the first word of line
15, followed by ∪∪–∪ ἀνέcτεφον.

15 ⌊cτόρνηιcιν⌋: 'with their girdles'. The only other occurrence
of cτόρνη is in Lyc. Alex. 1330, a context not unconnected with
Theseus (the girdle of Hippolyte). Garlanding with girdles is
mentioned by Eratosthenes (FGH 241 F 14) together with the
φυλλοβολία (see above on 11 ff.): καὶ νῦν ἐπὶ τοῖc ἐπιφανῶc
ἀγωνιζομένοιc προβάλλουcι ζώναc, πετάcουc, χιτωνίcκουc,
κρηπῖδαc. Compare Hedyl. AP 11. 123(= 11 G.–P.). 4 μίτραιc
βάλλετε καὶ cτεφάνοιc; Parth. Narr. 9 καὶ οἱ μέν τινεc αὐτὴν μίτραιc
ἀνέδουν, οἱ δὲ ζώναιc; Triph. 345–6.

Between frs. 69 and 70 (cols. i and ii of the Vienna Tablet) there is
a gap of some 22 lines. When the text resumes, the scene has
changed completely. No longer do we read of Theseus and
celebrations for the capture of the bull; instead it appears to be
night-time (cf. fr. 74, 22 ff.) and, perched on a tree (fr. 74. 11), an
old crow (fr. 74. 9 τὴν γρῆϋν ... κορώνην) is speaking to another
bird (fr. 74. 21) about the origin and discovery of the primeval
Attic king Ericthonius. She goes on to prophesy (fr. 74. 10 ff.)
how one day the raven will be changed from white to black as a
punishment for bringing bad news to Apollo. This speech by the
crow (of which the Diegesis contains no hint) spanned some 82

lines for which we can account, plus an indeterminable proportion of the *c.* 22 lines missing between frs. 69 and 70.

Many questions arise. Most obviously, what is the connection between the talking birds and the main narrative of Hecale, Theseus, and the bull? To this there is at least a plausible answer (B. Gentili, *Gnomon*, 33 (1961), 342; cf. T. B. L. Webster, *Poetry and Art*, 117). The moral to be drawn from the story of the crow, Ericthonius, and the daughters of Cecrops is that bringers of bad tidings are never welcome, and are more likely to be punished than rewarded; the same applies to the prophecy about Coronis and the raven, and, just before she launches into this prophecy, the crow may be trying to deter her hearer from carrying bad news in the present circumstances (fr. 74. 7 includes the word κακάγγελον). At the end of fr. 69 all has been triumph and rejoicing; so what disaster can have occurred in the mean time? One naturally thinks of Hecale's death. Perhaps therefore the crow dissuades the other bird from telling Theseus that his benefactor has died. If so, it would seem that her advice was accepted, since Theseus clearly had no inkling of Hecale's death when he returned to thank her, and found the neighbours preparing her funeral (fr. 79 τίνος ἠρίον ἴστατε τοῦτο;).

An even more knotty problem is the identity of the other bird (fr. 74. 21 τὴν δ' ἀίουcαν). The crow seems not ill disposed towards her hearer, if indeed she is warning her against a disastrous mistake (see above). Restoration of even the general sense in fr. 73. 10–12 is hazardous, but, if Lloyd-Jones's line of attack (*HSCP* 72 (1968) 140–2) proved correct, we should have reason to think that the second bird had profited from the crow's loss of Athena's favour. This could support Wilamowitz's suggestion (*Kl. Schr.* ii. 34 f.) that the addressee is an owl, who certainly played a part in the *Hecale* (fr. 77; cf. frs. 167–8 inc. sed.). The theory has definite attractions; could Ov. *Fast.* 2. 89–90 'et sine lite loquax cum Palladis alite cornix | sedit' distantly reflect the situation in Call.? But, as Lloyd-Jones fully recognized (op. cit., p. 141), it cannot be considered established, and there are difficulties. It is somewhat surprising that the crow should in any way wish to benefit the owl who supplanted her; enmity between the two birds was notorious (Thompson, *Greek Birds*, p. 170 s.v. κορώνη; cf. e.g. Ar. *HA* 9. 1. 609ᵃ8; Antig. *Mir.* 57; Ael. *HA* 3. 9, 5. 48), and is particularly marked in the episode of Ov. *Met.* 2 (564, 589 ff.) based upon this part of the *Hecale*. In fr. 77 someone curses an owl, while fr. 76 may describe attacks by storks and (?) crows on other, unidentified, birds.

In the *c.* 22 lines which separated fr. 69 from fr. 70 Call. must have concluded the celebrations of the country people and (though this can be disputed—see below, App. IV) sent Theseus on his way back to Athens (cf. fr. 69. 8 Θηϲεὺϲ οὐχ ἑκὰϲ οὗτοϲ). Although Plutarch (*Thes.* 14. 1) speaks of Theseus displaying the bull and driving it through the city to sacrifice (cf. Paus. 1. 27. 10), one may doubt whether Call. would linger over festivities at Athens after the similar rejoicings of the country people. Fr. 78, however, might come from a hymn of praise sung by the Athenian women (cf. Ov. *Met.* 7. 433 ff.). If Gentili (see above) was correct in his belief that the birds are debating whether or not to bring Theseus bad news about Hecale, it would follow that the lines between frs. 69 and 70 made some mention (not necessarily the first mention) of her death. Call. must also have introduced the two birds, and marked the coming of night (which by fr. 74. 23 gives way to dawn). Many have assumed that these lines described Hephaestus' unsuccessful wooing of Athena, and Ericthonius' birth. That may be so, but perhaps one should leave open the possibility that the crow related only Athena's nursing of Ericthonius, not the child's origin (see below). Pfeiffer wished to place here fr. 166 inc. auct. μύρϲον ἐϲ ὠτώεντα παλαιφαμένηϲ ἄγνοιο. Certainly a reference to Ericthonius being shut into his basket is highly plausible in view of Ov. *Met.* 2. 554, and this is the natural place for the line.

It will be seen that a great deal of material clamours for inclusion in the relatively brief lacuna (*c.* 22 lines). Call.'s narrative method is full of surprises, and may have been idiosyncratic in the present case.

The Birth of Ericthonius

Originally Ericthonius may have been identified with Erectheus (cf. W. Burkert, *Hermes*, 94 (1966), 24), the former name being more often used in connection with the birth-story. But it is of Erectheus that we read (*Il.* 2. 547–8):

ὄν ποτ᾽ Ἀθήνη
θρέψε, Διὸς θυγάτηρ, τέκε δὲ ζείδωρος ἄρουρα.

Nonnus, who owes so much to Call., always uses the name
Erectheus; but, although Ericthonius is not named in what
survives of the *Hecale*, Call. almost certainly regarded Erectheus,
mentioned in the opening line (fr. 1) and in fr. 86, as a distinct
individual. For more on the names see B. Powell, 'Ericthonius
and the Three Daughters of Cecrops', *Cornell Studies in Classical
Philology*, 17 (1906), 12 ff.; Robert Parker, 'Myths of Early
Athens', in J. Bremmer (ed.), *Interpretations of Greek Mythology*
(1987), 200 ff.

The legend became important for Athenian religion and
patriotism. Perhaps it was portrayed on the pedestals of the
images of Hephaestus and Athena in the Hephaesteum (H. A.
Thompson, *AJA* 66 (1962), 339); J. H. Oakley (*JHS* 102 (1982),
222) notes that a high percentage of the vases depicting Eric-
thonius derive from the Acropolis, perhaps because the cult of the
Arrephoria (cf. fr. 179 inc. auct. and the article by Burkert cited
above) was conducted there. Turning to literature, we find the
myth prominent in Euripides' patriotic play *Ion* (20 ff., 267 ff.,
1429; cf. Eur. fr. 925 *TGF*² from an unknown tragedy). The
story, as credited to Call.'s *Hecale* (fr. 61 Schn.) by the scholiast on
Il. 2. 547, appears on p. 96 above (as a source for fr. 70. 5 ff.).
Antigonus of Carystus (*Mir.* 12) quotes from the Atthidographer
'Amelesagoras' (*FGH* 330 F 1) a slightly less crude version
('bowdlerized', as Fraser puts it (*Ptolemaic Alexandria* ii. 906 n.
217)), in which Athena is given to Hephaestus, but vanishes
miraculously at the crucial moment. Almost certainly 'Amelesa-
goras' wrote before Call., who drew on him for the crow's
subsequent fall from grace.

It has been debated (Fraser, loc. cit.) whether Call. followed the
coarser or the bowdlerized version, or whether he himself could
have been responsible for the bowdlerization (in which case the
Iliad scholiast would be seriously astray). But when a scholiast
gives a myth at length, adding e.g. ἱστορεῖ Καλλ. ἐν Ἑκάληι, one
must be cautious about assuming that all the details mentioned
occurred in the poem. This applies particularly to Hellenistic
poets, who often prefer oblique allusion to straightforward
narrative; the scholiast may mean merely that the poet *referred* to

the myth, details of which the scholiast fills in from his own
knowledge. In the present case I find it hard to believe that the
crow gave a detailed account of Hephaestus' attempt on Athena
in the lines missing between frs. 69 and 70, and then said of
Ericthonius (fr. 70. 6–8) γενεῆι δ' ὅθεν οὔτε νιν ἔγνων | οὔτ' ἐδάην
(but a rumour reached the birds) ὡς δῆθεν ὑφ' Ἡφαίστωι τέκε
Γαῖα. Oblique allusion would also suit the character of the crow,
who once experienced the terrible wrath of Athena, and may
now prefer to be reticent about an episode so distasteful to the
goddess.

Although I doubt whether Call. described the circumstances of
Ericthonius' birth, there is one scene to which Nonnus returns
time and time again, and which may indeed have been found in
the *Hecale*—Athena nursing Ericthonius (Erectheus) by lamp-
light, e.g. *Dion.* 27. 113–15:

> Ἐρεχθέος, ὅν ποτε μαζῶι
> παρθενικὴ φυγόδεμνος ἀνέτρεφε Παλλὰς ἀμήτωρ,
> λάθριον ἀγρύπνωι πεφυλαγμένον αἴθοπι λύχνωι

or ibid. 317 ff. ('Marathon' probably stands for Athens):

> καὶ σύ, τελεσσιγόνου φιλοπάρθενε νυμφίε Γαίης
> ἠρεμέεις, Ἥφαιστε, καὶ οὐκ ἀλέγεις Μαραθῶνος
> ἧχι θεᾶς ἀγάμου γάμιον σέλας· οὔ σε διδάξω
> μυστιπόλους σπινθῆρας ἀειφανέος σέο λύχνου.
> λάρνακα παιδοκόμου μιμνήσκεο παρθενεῶνος
> ὧι ἔνι κοῦρος ἔην Γαιήιος, ὧι ἔνι κούρη
> σὸν σπόρον αὐτοτέλεστον ἀνέτρεφεν ἄρσενι μαζῶι.

Compare ibid. 13. 172 ff. The lamp may well be mentioned in a
passage of Euphorion (fr. 9. 3 Powell; cf. W. Burkert, *Hermes*, 94
(1966), 11) which owes much to Call. I wonder (cf. N. Robertson,
HSCP 87 (1983), 274 n. 90) whether this could be meant as an
aetion of the inextinguishable lamp in the shrine of Athena Polias
(e.g. Str. 9. 1. 16 ἐπὶ δὲ τῆι πέτραι τὸ τῆς Ἀθηνᾶς ἱερὸν ὅ τε ἀρχαῖος
νεὼς ὁ τῆς Πολιάδος ἐν ὧι ὁ ἄσβεστος λύχνος). For more on the
lamp see Pfeiffer, 'Die goldene Lampe der Athene', *SIFC* 27–8
(1956), 426–33 = *Ausgewählte Schriften*, pp. 1–7; he discounts,
however, any relevance to the *Hecale*. Athena's title of κουρο-
τρόφος, although of course shared with many other deities and
having basically nothing to do with Ericthonius, may sometimes

have been associated with the nursing of the child (Farnell, *Cults of the Greek States*, i. 344).

In the most primitive form of the legend Ericthonius was perhaps simply the child of Hephaestus and Athena—though this is a matter of dispute (B. Powell, op. cit. pp. 14–15). The only writers, as far as I know, who make the allegation in so many words can be considered hostile witnesses (Tert. *Spect.* 9; Lact. *Inst.* 1. 17; August. *Civ. Dei* 18. 12; Mich. Chon. i. 102. 18–19 Ἀθηνᾶ, παρ᾽ ἐκείνοις παρθενεύειν μυθευομένη, τίκτει τὸν Ἐριχθόνιον). The Athenian line on this is firm (E. *Ion* 269–70):

> Ιων ἦ καί cφ᾽ Ἀθάνα γῆθεν ἐξανείλετο;
> Κρ. ἐc παρθένουc γε χεῖραc, οὐ τεκοῦcά νιν.

But her raising of the child gave plenty of scope for innuendo (Ov. *Tr.* 2. 293–4):

> Pallade conspecta, natum de crimine virgo
> sustulerit quare quaeret Ericthonium.

Vedic parallels for the Ericthonius myth are discussed by Murray Fowler in *CP* 38 (1943), 28–32.

The Daughters of Cecrops

Cecrops had three daughters, Aglauros (this form supported by inscriptional evidence, but, if we can trust Antigonus of Carystus, 'Amelesagoras' called her Agraulos), Pandrosos, and Herse. All three names suggest an earth-goddess; the first two were also used as titles of Athena (Suid. s.v. Ἄγλαυροc and schol. Ar. *Lys.* 439). See Jane Harrison, 'Mythological Studies, I: The Three Daughters of Cecrops', *JHS* 12 (1891), 350–5. Fr. 179 inc. auct. may imply that Salustius, in his commentary on the *Hecale*, discussed an alleged link between the third sister, Herse, and the festival of the ἀρρηφορία, which perhaps derives from something in Call. (note the procession in Ov. *Met.* 2. 711 ff.).

To these Athena entrusted the infant Ericthonius (cf. S. Scheinberg, *HSCP* 83 (1979), 2 ff.). By good fortune Antigonus of Carystus (*Mir.* 12) preserves a paraphrase of 'Amelesagoras' (see above on the Birth of Ericthonius) who was probably the main source for Call.'s digression: Ἐριχθόνιον . . . τρέφειν τὴν Ἀθηνᾶν

καὶ εἰc κίcτην καθεῖρξαι (? cf. fr. 166 inc. auct.) καὶ παραθέcθαι ταῖc
Κέκροποc παιcίν, Ἀγραύλωι καὶ Πανδρόcωι καὶ Ἕρcηι καὶ ἐπιτά-
ξαι μὴ ἀνοίγειν τὴν κίcτην, ἕωc ἂν αὐτὴ ἔλθηι. ἀφικομένην δὲ εἰc
Πελλήνην φέρειν ὄροc, ἵνα ἔρυμα (cf. fr. 70. 9) πρὸ τῆc Ἀκροπόλεωc
ποιήcηι, τὰc δὲ Κέκροποc θυγατέραc τὰc δύο, Ἄγραυλον καὶ
Πάνδροcον, τὴν κίcτην ἀνοῖξαι καὶ ἰδεῖν δράκονταc δύο περὶ τὸν
Ἐριχθόνιον. τῆι δὲ Ἀθηνᾶι φερούcηι τὸ ὄροc ὃ νῦν καλεῖται
Λυκαβηττόc, κορώνην φηcὶν ἀπαντῆcαι (cf. fr. 71. 2) καὶ εἰπεῖν ὅτι
Ἐριχθόνιοc ἐν φανερῶι, τὴν δὲ ἀκούcαcαν ῥῖψαι τὸ ὄροc ὅπου νῦν
ἐcτιν· τῆι δὲ κορώνηι διὰ τὴν κακαγγελίαν εἰπεῖν ὡc εἰc Ἀκρόπολιν
οὐ θέμιc αὐτῆι ἔcται ἀφικέcθαι.

Bewilderingly different versions are given of the part played by
the individual sisters, and of their punishment. Before we plunge
into these, it is worth observing that fr. 70. 12–13 τόφρα δὲ κοῦραι
| αἱ φυλακοὶ κακὸν ἔργον ἐπεφράccαντο τελέccαι most naturally
imply that all three share the guilt equally. If so, Call. seems to
have varied from 'Amelesagoras', according to whom Aglauros
(Agraulos) and Pandrosos are guilty (and, presumably, Herse free
from blame). Euphorion, however, in a passage owing much to
the *Hecale*, singles out Herse as the sister who opened the basket
and was thereafter driven to suicide (fr. 9 Powell = 11 van
Groningen, quoted and discussed above, Introd. sect. VI). Other
variants (besides works already mentioned, see Jacoby, *FGH* iiib,
Suppl. ii. 490–2; W. Wimmel. 'Aglauros in Ovids *Metamorpho-
sen*', *Hermes*, 90 (1962), 326–33; R. Parker, 'Myths of Early
Athens', in J. Bremmer (ed.), *Interpretations of Greek Mythology*
(1987), 195 ff.):

(a) E. *Ion* 273–4: all three sisters are culpable. and all three jump
from the Acropolis to their death (in Hyg. *Fab.* 166 they jump
into the sea).

(b) Ov. *Met.* 2. 558 ff.: Aglauros leads her sisters astray, and is
eventually turned to stone, though not as a direct result of
opening the basket (see below).

(c) Paus. 1. 18. 2, 1. 27. 3 (cf. Apollod. 3. 14. 6): Pandrosos alone
of the sisters is blameless.

(d) There is also the doubtful evidence of Philodemus, *de pietate*
(my Test. Dub. 16—*SH* 307 gives an earlier draft of A. Henrichs'
text). If one follows Henrichs' later thoughts ('Die Kekropiden-

sage im *P. Herc.* 243: von Kallimachos zu Ovid', *Cronache
Ercolanesi*, 13 (1983), 33–43; cf. W. Luppe, ibid. 14 (1984), 109–24,
and, for a different try, N. Robertson, *HSCP* 87 (1983), 272–3),
Philodemus would be saying that according to Call. He Hermes
'made [unidentifiable male characters] bent, and also turned
Pandrosos to stone because she did not give up her sister Herse to
him'. The first part of this (? for people transformed into bent
statues cf. Hermesian. fr. 4 Powell and Ov. *Met.* 14. 751–61)
coheres with nothing which we know of the *Hecale*—if the text
were right, could it refer to some other poem by Call.? The
petrification of Pandrosos is rather more interesting. Philodemus
has previously (col. i) dealt with the thefts and perjuries of
Hermes; he will go on (col. iii) to the subject of gods making love
to mortal women. Bearing that in mind, we read in Ovid (*Met.* 2.
740 ff.) how *Aglauros* demanded money for furthering Mercury's
interest in Herse, and was turned to stone. It would be like Ovid
to borrow the story from Call., but to change the part played by
individual sisters (substituting Aglauros for Pandrosos). Thus
there might be room for an amorous Hermes in the (approxi-
mately) 17 lines still missing between frs. 70 and 73 (cols. ii and iii
of the Vienna Tablet). But we would not expect Athena, whose
ferocious wrath the crow repeatedly stresses, to leave the punish-
ment of even one guilty sister to another divinity.

The Crow and the Raven

That crows avoided the Athenian Acropolis was supposed to be
a matter of observation (e.g. Plin. *NH* 10. 30, with more evidence
quoted by Jacoby, *FGH* iiib, Suppl. i. 601; cf. D'Arcy Thompson,
Greek Birds, p. 170). Such interest in παράδοξα can be exemplified
from Call.'s own prose works (see Pfeiffer, *History*, i. 134–5;
Fraser, *Ptolemaic Alexandria*, i. 454 ff., 772 ff.); fr. 407. 163 ff. Pf.
gives a few 'marvels' involving birds. Elsewhere we hear of other
creatures not approaching the shrine of particular deities. It was
apparently 'Amelesagoras' who gave this zoological curiosity a
mythical explanation, perhaps modelled (as Jacoby suggested, op.
cit. p. 603) on the κακαγγελία through which the raven lost the
favour of Apollo (see fr. 74. 18 ff.). With this addition the story
becomes like others in which animals are prohibited from a shrine

because of some original offence—e.g. horses from the grove of
Diana at Aricia because of what they did to Hippolytus (*Aet.* fr.
190 Pf. = Serv. ad *Aen.* 7. 778).

This is also the domain of folk-tale. Stith Thompson, *Motif-
Index of Folk-Literature*, i. 271 ff. has a number of relevant
headings: A 2237 'Animal characteristics punishment for med-
dling'; A 2237. 1 'Animal reveals mistress' adultery; punished by
master' (cf. the raven, Coronis, and Apollo, fr. 74. 18 ff.); A 2281
'Enmity between animals from original quarrel' (? cf. the crow
and the owl, perhaps also fr. 76 on the 'avenging stork'). The
colour of birds is very often mentioned, and the raven attracts
special attention (p. 300; cf. e.g. p. 274, A 2234. 1. 1 'Raven does
not return to Ark in obedience to Noah; black colour is resulting
punishment').

Callimachus' Treatment and Future Influence

Enough remains of frs. 70–3 to show that Call. has enjoyed
viewing Attica from a rare chronological perspective (cf. pri-
meval Arcadia in *H.* 1), eight generations before Theseus, at a
time when Athena has only just won her realm in competition
with Poseidon, when a familiar geographical feature (Mt. Lyca-
bettus) is not yet in place, and when the land is populated by
strange creatures (Cecrops and Ericthonius) whose serpentine
form proclaims their earth-born origin. The device of the talking
birds set quite a fashion in later poetry; we see it in Call.'s own
fourth *Iambus* (frs. 194. 61–3 and 81–2 Pf.), in Apollonius Rhodius
(3. 930 ff.), Ovid (*Met.* 2. 547 ff.), and Nonnus (*Dion.* 3. 97 ff.).
This episode as a whole caught Lucretius' interest (6. 749 ff.) and
was ingeniously adapted by Ovid, whom we shall often have
cause to quote (in *Met.* 2 the crow, instead of predicting the
raven's downfall, actually tries to deter the raven from taking the
bad news to Apollo). As mentioned earlier, Nonnus often alludes
to the birth and rearing of Ericthonius (cf. also *Dion.* 29. 334–9,
41. 63–4, 48. 956).

This part of the *Hecale* could also have had a wider influence on
the digressions of later epyllia, in that it incorporates subject-
matter apparently quite remote from the main narrative, but
linked to it by an ingenious and unexpected transition—compare

e.g. Virg. G. 4 (Aristaeus/Orpheus and Eurydice) and several
episodes in Ovid's *Metamorphoses*.

Fr. 70 (*SH* 288. 16–29; 260. 16–29 Pf.)

2–3 Too little survives for any worthwhile attempt at restora-
tion, but Lloyd-Jones remarks that line 2 may have contained
some part of the verb αἰθύccω (see on fr. 30). In line 3 the
articulation ε Παλλάc is not certain, but probable (note οὐρανίδαι
at the start of the line), since the goddess is definitely referred to in
line 9 ἥ μέν, and quite possibly also in line 4 τῆc μέν.

4 Lloyd-Jones suggests that the sense could have been 'her did I
serve for a long while' (an alternative might be 'I long enjoyed
her favour'); if so, the crow must be talking as a representative of
her species, since this particular bird was apparently a fledgling in
the time of Cecrops (fr. 73. 13). In *Met.* 2. 588 the crow says of
herself 'data sum comes inculpata Minervae'. As well as δηναιὸν
ἐπὶ χρόνον (Ap. Rh. 4. 1547), δηναιόν by itself can mean 'for a long
time' (Ap. Rh. 3. 590). Could Suid. s.v. δηναιόν, ἐπὶ πολὺν χρόνον
belong here (cf. below, App. V(*a*))? The old reading at the end of
the line, δρ[ό]coν Ἡφαίcτοιο, at least provided a noun for λάθριον
ἄρρητον (6) to agree with, but suits neither traces nor sense—the
crow could hardly say what she says in lines 6–8 if she had already
called Ericthonius 'the offspring of Hephaestus' in line 4.

5 μέcφ' ὅτε: cf. fr. 69. 4. This much is clear. Thereafter the
scribe might have written Κεκροπίδ[η]cιν without iota adscript (as
almost always in the Vienna Tablet), or else Κεκροπίδ[ε]cιν for
Κεκροπίδεccιν (though this involves postulating a scribal error);
the letter following δ is totally destroyed. As Pfeiffer implies, one
rather expects Κεκροπίδεccιν (see below); 12–13 κοῦραι | αἱ
φυλακοί might suggest that the daughters of Cecrops have been
mentioned recently.

I am totally baffled by the rest of the line. In view of 6, it seems
that the second half of 5 should contain a verb, and a noun
denoting Ericthonius—to agree with λάθριον ἄρρητον (6, but see
ad. loc.) and to be picked up by νιν. This noun, if masculine, must
be in the accusative case (with a neuter, e.g. βρέφοc, the nomina-
tive would be possible). A natural sense might be 'until the time
when to the daughters of Cecrops she entrusted the child λάθριον

ἄρρητον etc.'; compare 'Amelesagoras' παραθέςθαι ταῖς Κέκροπος παιςίν and Ov. *Met.* 2. 555–6 'virginibusque tribus gemino de Cecrope natis |... dederat'. Turn now to the end of the line. Rea writes that τ̣ολμα̣ν, presumably τολμᾶν, is a possibility (an accusative τόλμαν might agree with λάθριον ἄρρητον, but would leave νιν stranded). But hardly enough letter-spaces remain to complete the line, even if one could think of an appropriate sense. It seems more promising to regard κατο̣ as the expected verb-ending. Thereafter, if λ.αν is correct, we would appear to have λᾶαν (for the form cf. fr. 153. 1), as originally read by Gomperz. He gave the whole line as μέςφ' ὅτε Κεκροπίδηιςιν ἐπ' ἀκτῆι θῆκατο λᾶαν (Ἀκτῆι Diels, but the word-break after a fourth-foot spondee in any case violates Call.'s metrical practice (see above, Introd. sect. IV. 4g)—Barber tried ἐπαλέα), which was commonly taken to be a parenthesis, and referred to the bringing of the rock which became Lycabettus (cf. l. 9 and fr. 71), 'until she set a rock in Acte for the sons of Cecrops' (A. W. Mair in his 1921 Loeb). Such a parenthesis clearly is unsatisfactory; can one produce any other explanation of λᾶαν? We do now have some doubtful evidence (my Test. Dub. 16) from Philodemus, *de Pietate*, discussed above) which *might* indicate that in the *Hecale* one of the daughters of Cecrops was turned to stone, but any such reference here seems wildly improbable, and impossible to accommodate without the most unwelcome hypothesis of a lacuna after line 5.

In favour of θῆκατο, Barrett notes that the only aorists ending in -κατο are θῆκατο, ἥκατο (restricted to compounds with προς- and προ-) and ἐνείκατο (impossible here because of Hermann's Bridge). He himself most ingeniously suggested ἐπωπέα θῆκατο λαῶν (with λαῶν as an emendation if necessary). ἐπωπεύς is not attested meaning 'king', but is the name of more than one king in mythology (e.g. a ruler of Sicyon). The exact sense of θῆκατο, however, would not be clear. John Rea writes: 'There are remains, probably, of all the letters in the line ... I think it quite likely that the right reading could be verified if we could find it. I cannot convince myself that I see ἐπωπέα θῆκατο in among the mess.'

6 λάθριον: of Ericthonius (Erectheus) also in Nonn. *Dion.* 27. 115* (quoted at p. 228 above). Hutchinson, however, suspects that here λάθριον ἄρρητον may be neuters in apposition to the sentence.

7–8 Although the traces in line 7 do not warrant hazarding a restoration (see Rea's detailed remarks, *HCSP* 72 (1968), 128–9), the general sense must have been 'but a story reached the birds'; ὡς δῆθεν adds a touch of scepticism, even incredulity (J. D. Denniston, *The Greek Particles*² (1954), p. 265). Call. may have in mind Arat. *Phaen.* 100–1 λόγος γε μὲν ἐντρέχει ἄλλος | ἀνθρώποις ὡς δῆθεν κτλ. (note also Ap. Rh. 2. 384 οἰωνοὺς οἳ δῆθεν*). This turn, while not of course confined to Hellenistic poets (cf. e.g. P. *Ol.* 1. 47 ff.; E. *Hel.* 17 ff. with Kannicht's commentary), is much favoured by them, especially to introduce a recondite myth, e.g. Nic. *Ther.* 343 ὡγύγιος δ᾽ ἄρα μῦθος ἐν αἰζηοῖσι φορεῖται; Nonn. *Dion.* 12. 293–4 ὑμνοπόλων δέ | ἄλλη πρεσβυτέρη πέλεται φάτις, 41. 155 ἀλλά τις ὁπλοτέρη πέλεται φάτις (cf. 18. 222 ff., 26. 354, 33. 283, 47. 256).

8 ὑφ᾽ Ἡφαίστῳ τέκε Γαῖα: (for the rhythm cf. e.g. *Il.* 8. 195 τὸν Ἥφαιστος κάμε τεύχων). Primeval kings are often strange children of the fire-god, as also Servius Tullius at Rome (Ogilvie on Liv. 1. 39. 1, 1. 39. 5) and Caeculus at Praeneste 'Volcano genitum pecora inter agrestia regem | inventumque focis omnis quem credidit aetas' (*Aen.* 7. 679–80) supposedly born from a spark and a virgin mother (see H. J. Rose, *Mnemosyne*, 53 (1925), 410 ff.). At the end of the line τέκε Γαῖα (Nonn. *Dion.* 41. 63* of Ericthonius, as emended by Lloyd-Jones (*HSCP* 72 (1968), 136); cf. νυμφίε Γαίης and κοῦρος . . . Γαιήιος in *Dion.* 27. 317, 322 quoted at p. 228 above) is welcome (rather than τέκεν αἶα)—as Lloyd-Jones says, the form αἶα seems not to be used when the Earth is personified.

9 ἔρυμα χθονός: (= Christodor. *AP* 2. 230*) an echo of ἔρυμα χροός (*Il.* 4. 137*, Hes. *Op.* 536*); for the phrase applied to a mountain cf. E. *Ba.* 55 Τμῶλον ἔρυμα Λυδίας. The word ἔρυμα is largely poetic, and its use by 'Amelesagoras' (quoted at p. 230 above) made Kapp (p. 45 n. 1) believe, but probably wrongly (see Jacoby, *FGH* iiib, Suppl. i. 602). that 'Amelesagoras' followed Call. rather than vice versa.

10 τήν ῥα νεόν: typical of the Hellenistic poets, who delight in the relative chronology of mythical times (cf. e.g. Nic. *Alex.* 103 Κηφῆος νέα δῶρα). A related turn is to say 'not yet' had such and such happened (e.g. *H.* 1. 18, 4. 49; Euph. fr. 84. 3; Pancrat. fr. 3. 4 Heitsch; Nonn. *Dion.* 13. 278 ff., 550 ff.; also in Latin, e.g. Tib. 2. 5. 23). Both techniques prove a fruitful source of transitions in

Ovid's *Metamorphoses* (e.g. 1. 450 'nondum laurus erat', 687–8 'namque reperta | fistula nuper erat'.

ψήφῳ τε Διός: Call. may allude to the fact that the place where judgement was given betweeen Athena and Poseidon for the possession of Attica was actually called Διὸς ψῆφος (Suid. s.v., quoting Cratin. fr. 7 Kock, *PCG*).

10–11 Cf. *Il.* 13. 524–5 Διὸς ... ἄλλοι | ἀθάνατοι; Ap. Rh. 3. 8–9 Διὸς ... καὶ ἄλλων | ἀθανάτων. Pallas herself portrayed the scene in her contest with Arachne: 'bis sex caelestes medio Iove sedibus altis | augusta gravitate sedent' (Ov. *Met*. 6. 72–3).

11 ὄφιός τε κατέλλαβε μαρτυρίῃcιν: Cecrops gave evidence that Athena had first produced the famous olive. He is a witness also in Apollod. 3. 14. 1, but in the *Iambi* (fr. 194. 66 ff. Pf.; cf. Nonn. *Dion*. 36. 26) a judge: Παλλάc, ἦμοc ἤριζε | τῶι φυκιοίκωι, κἠδίκαζεν ἀρχαίοιc | ἀνὴρ ὄφιc τὰ νέρθεν ἀμφὶ τῆc Ἀκτῆc. For Cecrops' double form (*Met*. 2. 555 'gemino ... Cecrope') cf. Ar. *Vesp*. 438; Eup. (fr. 156 Kock = 159 *PCG*) makes his lower parts piscine rather than serpentine.

12 Πελλήνην ἐφίκανεν 'Αχαιΐδα: see the splendid discussion of this line and fr. 71 (261 Pf.) by Lloyd-Jones in *HSCP* 72 (1968), 137–40, of which I present merely a summary. At first sight, one imagines that Athena must be going to Pellene in Achaea, particularly in view of Ap. Rh. 1. 176–8:

> Άcτέριοc δὲ καὶ Άμφίων, Ύπεραcίου υἶεc,
> Πελλήνηc ἀφίκανον Άχαιΐδοc, ἥν ποτε Πέλληc
> πατροπάτωρ ἐπόλιccεν ἐπ' ὀφρύcιν Αἰγιαλοῖο.

But, as Jacoby noticed (*FGH* iiib, Suppl. i. 602), if Athena was returning from the northern Peloponnese, she must have overshot her mark considerably before she dropped Mt. Lycabettus. Bergk (*Rh. M*. 9 (1854), 138 ff.) had earlier argued that Athena was coming from Pallene in Chalcidice (although that place is usually written with an alpha rather than epsilon, the two forms are almost interchangeable). This Pallene is close to one location of the Phlegraean Fields, where Athena had won a great triumph in the war against the Giants; her strong links with the area are shown by the fact that the Aeschylean Orestes conjectures she may hear him thence (*Eu*. 295–6 εἴτε Φλεγραίαν πλάκα | θραcὺc ταγοῦχοc ὡc ἀνὴρ ἐπιcκοπεῖ). Ovid, if nobody else, credits 'Hyperborea Pallene' with a 'Tritoniaca palus' (*Met*. 15. 356–8).

But what of Ἀχαιΐδα? Pallene in Chalcidice was founded by Ἀχαιοί from Pellene in the Peloponnese who were driven ashore on their way back from Troy (Thuc. 4. 120). Thus Ἀχαιΐδα, which one expects to mean 'in Achaea', could also mean 'of the Achaeans'. The question as to which place Call. intended is decisively settled in favour of Chalcidice by vindication of the reading Ὑψιζώρου in fr. 71. 1 (see ad loc.).

13 αἱ φυλακοί: φυλακός is found at *Il.* 24. 566, Ap. Rh. 1. 132, Theocr. 29. 38, but only here used as feminine.

14 Rea doubts whether Gomperz' κειϲτηϲ (for κίϲτηϲ) can be read, but κᾳιϲτηϲ is possible. κίϲτη would be an appropriate word for the basket in which Erictonius was kept (cf. 'Amelesagoras' quoted at p. 230 above; Euph. fr. 9. 5; Ov. *Met.* 2. 554; Nonn. *Dion.* 27. 116; note Hesych. κίϲτη· ἀγγεῖον πλεκτόν). This may also be described in fr. 166 inc. auct. μύρϲον ἐϲ ὠτώεντα παλαιφαμένηϲ ἄγνοιο. See J. H. Oakley, *JHS* 102 (1982), 221 and pls. ix–x for artistic representations. At the end of the line ἀνεῖϲαι is likely; before it, δεϲμά τ' (Gomperz) can neither be confirmed nor excluded.

Of the approximately 22 lines which stood between col. ii (fr. 70) and col. iii (fr. 73) of the Vienna Tablet, no one could doubt that 3 are preserved in fr. 71. Although it is less certain that the 2 lines of fr. 72 also belong here, the probability seems to me very high— increased still further by the new piece of Alcaeus which Pfeiffer was able to notice only in his Addenda to vol. ii (p. 125).

There would thus be some 17 lines still missing. These must have described the discovery of Ericthonius, which the crow witnessed—Lucretius (6. 754) speaks of her 'pervigilium' (cf. Ov. *Met.* 2. 557 'abdita fronde levi densa speculabar ab ulmo')—and the bird's resolve to carry the news to Athena. Their disastrous meeting (fr. 71) leads to the goddess's fury (fr. 72) and to the crow's banishment from the Acropolis. It also seems probable that somewhere in this lacuna we were told the fate of the daughters of Cecrops (see above, pp. 230–1).

Fr. 71 (*SH* 289; 261 Pf.)

Athena returns from Pallene in Chalcidice with an enormous chunk of Mt. Hypsizorus, destined to be the bulwark for Attica (cf. fr. 70. 9); the crow comes to bring the bad news of Ericthonius' discovery, meeting the goddess by the gymnasium of Lycean Apollo.

The two halves of this fragment were joined by Kapp (fr. 61). Note the two spondaic fifth feet in the space of three lines.

1–2 This picture of Athena as she enters the city carrying Mt. Lycabettus shows Call.'s imagination at its most extravagant.

1 ἀερτάζουσα: 'bearing aloft'; cf. fr. 597 Pf. (= *SH* 268c) θηρὸς ἀερτάζων δέρμα κατωμάδιον. In the fondness of Call. (also *Aet.* fr. 18. 6 Pf.) and Apollonius Rhodius (1. 738 (Zethus carrying huge rocks to build Thebes), 995, 4. 46) for this verb, we perhaps find a germ of Nonnus' penchant for verbs such as ἀερτάζω, ἐλαφρίζω, κουφίζω.

μέγα τρύφος Ὑψιζώρου: 'a great chunk of Hypsizorus'. This colourful phrase was perhaps remembered by Virgil when he wrote of a missile 'ingenti fragmine montis' (*Aen.* 9. 569, 10. 698; cf. 10. 128 'haud partem exiguam montis'); τρύφος (a part of a rock broken off by Poseidon at *Od.* 4. 508) is connected with θρύπτω, and so exactly paralleled by 'fragmen'.

Ὑψίζωρος is a good name for a Thracian mountain. The first part can be compared with the Odrysian tribe Hypsalti (Plin. *NH* 4. 40) or Ὑψηλῖται (Stephanus Byzantius), the second with a number of names in -ωρος, -ωρον, -ora (e.g. Γάζωρος). To a Greek the elements would suggest (whether truly or falsely) ὕψος, ὑψηλός, and perhaps ὦρος (ὄρος). See Lloyd-Jones and Rea, *HSCP* 72 (1968), 138–40; D. Detschew, *Die thrakischen Sprachreste* (1957), pp. 532, 535; I. Duridanov, *Živa Antika*, 18 (1968), 40–1. Pliny (*NH* 4. 36) lists Hypsizorus among mountains in the region of Pallene and Phlegra: 'oppida Pallene, Phlegra, qua in regione montes Hypsizorus etc.' ('Hypsizorus' is the reading of all manuscripts, save that the second hand of D has 'Hypsizonus'.) In our fragment both cod. A and cod. B of *Et. Gen.* (despite Pfeiffer's app. crit.) have Ὑψιζώρου, likewise cod. D of *Et. Mag.* The other MSS of *Et. Mag.* offer Ὑψιζώνου, whence Bentley conjectured ὑψίζωνος, 'high-girt'. But the manuscript evidence points strongly to Ὑψιζώρου. Lloyd-Jones further remarks (*HSCP* 72 (1968), 138), 'It would greatly surprise us to hear of any ancient work of art or literature in which Athene, however arduous the task which she might have in hand, felt obliged to adopt a fashion of dress congenial to her sister Artemis, but highly uncharacteristic of herself.' Carrying μέγα τρύφος Ὑψιζώρου would be but a small labour for the goddess who was supposed to have hurled the whole of Sicily on top of Enceladus (Quint. Smyrn. 14. 582–3 εὖτε πάρος μεγάλοιο κατ' Ἐγκελάδοιο δαΐφρων | Παλλὰς ἀειραμένη Cικελὴν ἐπικάββαλε νῆcον). Breaking off and hurling rocks in a Gigantomachia is discussed by Philip Hardie, *Virgil's Aeneid: Cosmos and Imperium* (1986), pp. 101–2.

2–3 Λυκείου | . . . κατὰ δρόμον Ἀπόλλωνος: 'Mirum sane Lyceum iam Thesei [he should have said 'Ericthonii'] temporibus esse institutum' (Pf.); the antiquarians merely argued whether it was founded in the time of Pisistratus or of Pericles (Suid. s.v. Λύκειον). This sportive anachronism was followed by Ovid, who makes Mercury look down upon 'culti . . . arbusta Lycei' (*Met.* 2. 710). It contrasts with the careful calculation that the crow, a fledgling in the days of Cecrops, would be eight generations old by the reign of Aegeus (if ὀγδοάτη γάρ can be restored in fr. 73. 13).

On the gymnasium of Lycean Apollo see Verrall and Harrison, *Mythology and Monuments of Ancient Athens* (1890), 219 ff.; Gow on Machon 47; and, for the cult title Λύκειος, Frazer on Paus. 1. 19. 3. Aristotle taught in this gymnasium, and it became the headquarters of the Peripatetics.

3 λιπόωντα: 'gleaming', because of the oil used by the wrestlers; cf. Cic. fr. 6. 73 Buechner 'nitidoque Lyceo' (for Cicero and the *Hecale*, see above, Introd. sect. VI). λιπάω (λιπόω) is a v.l. at *Od.* 19. 72: we find λιπόωντα* in Leon. *AP* 6. 324. 1 (Page, *FGE*, p. 516), Quint. Smyrn. 10. 274, and probably Dionys. fr. 71. 8 Livrea (see his p. 72).

δρόμον: cf. Suid. s.v. δρόμοιc· τοῖc γυμναcίοιc κατὰ Κρῆταc (Pfeiffer cites a Cretan inscription of 246 BC).

Fr. 72 (374 Pf.)

Although reference of this fragment to the meeting of Athena and the crow is not certain, it was always plausible (Pfeiffer ad loc.), and has become more so since the discovery of a piece of Alcaeus (see below). Fr. 72 would represent Athena's immediate reaction to the news ὅτι Ἐριχθόνιοc ἐν φανερῶι ('Amelesagoras') and would be followed by the sentence of banishment from the Acropolis.

1 ἡ δὲ πελιδνωθεῖca: 'turning livid'. A recently discovered fragment of Alcaeus describes Athena's wrath at the sacrilege of the lesser Ajax: ἀ δὲ δεῖνον ὑπ' ὄφρυcιν |... πελιδνώθειca (*SLG* S262, p. 81, but Page's reconstruction is more than doubtful—see L. Koenen, *ZPE* 44 (1981), 184; D. P. Fowler, *ZPE* 33 (1979), 17 ff.). Call.'s clear imitation of Alcaeus increases the likelihood that he too was writing of an angry Athena.

1–2 καὶ ὄμμαcι λοξὸν ὑποδράξ | ὀccομένη: 'and with her eyes looking grimly askance'. Athena's glance is fearful enough at the best of times (Bacchyl. 16. 20 κόραι τ' ὀβριμοδερκεῖ); there may be a faint echo of Call. in Ov. *Met.* 2. 752 'vertit ad hanc [sc. Aglauron] torvi dea bellica luminis orbem'. For the wording cf. *Iamb.* fr. 194. 101–2 Pf. ὑποδρὰξ ...|... ἔβλεψε; Nic. *Ther.* 457 καὶ λοξὸν ὑποδρὰξ ὄμμαcι λεύccων; [Theocr.] 20. 13 καὶ ὄμμαcι λοξὰ βλέποιca; Nonn. *Par.* 18. 78–9 ὄμματι λοξῶι | δερκομένη. In Homer we often find ὑπόδρα ἰδών (e.g. *Il.* 1. 148), and also κάκ' ὀccόμενος (*Il.* 1. 105, where schol. D explains δεινὸν καὶ ὀργίλον ὑποβλεπόμενος). The sidelong glance first comes in Sol. fr. 34. 5 West λοξὸν ὀφθαλμοῖc ὁρῶcι and Anacr. (*PMG* 417(Anacr. 72). 1 λοξὸν ὄμμαcι βλέπουca). ὑποδράξ is ascribed to οἱ νεώτεροι (which need mean no more than post-Homeric writers) by Apoll. Soph. p. 160. 9 Bekker, and not attested before Call. (also in Nic. *Ther.* 457, 765).

Perhaps we should read ὄθμαcι (see Pfeiffer on *Aet.* fr. 1. 37, Hopkinson (*HD*) on *H.* 6. 52), the Aeolic form which has turned up 5 times in papyri of the *Aetia* (most recently in *SH* 239b. 10). Call. writes ὄμμα at least in the Fifth and Sixth *Hymns*. The MSS of Nicander vary between ὄθμα and ὄμμα at *Alex.* 33 and 243, but, in the imitation of our fragment (*Ther.* 457), they agree on ὄμμαcι.

Fr. 73 (*SH* 288. 30–43A; 260. 30–43 Pf.)

1–4 'Much rubbed: no recognizable letters' (Rea).

5 At the end Gomperz' Ἀθήνης (? Ἀθήνας Weinberger) cannot be confirmed; -νας or νης is as much as can be read (Rea).

6 ff. By no means everything which we read in Pfeiffer can be confirmed; see the detailed comments of Rea, *HSCP* 72 (1968), 129–30.

6 μοῦναι (Gomperz) is plausible, although there is no trace of the μ, but Wessely's παραπτυόμεcθα less so, since one would expect the υ to be long in the present (Pfeiffer; cf. fr. 176 inc. sed.); after παραπ, τ is possible but by no means certain, then υ possible, no more (Rea). If μοῦναι were right, it would seem probable that the crow has come to the end of telling how Athena banished her; other birds may visit the Acropolis, 'but crows alone . . . (? 'fly past'; cf. 'Amelesagoras' οὐ . . . προcίπταcθαι; Lucr. 6. 751–2 'numquam pennis appellunt corpora raucae | cornices'). Concerning birds on the Acropolis, J. E. Harrison (*Primitive Athens as Described by Thucydides* (1906), p. 29) wrote: 'In days when on open-air altars sacrifice smoked [cf. Lucr. 6. 752], and there was an abundance of sacred cakes, birds were real and very frequent presences. To the heads of numbers of statues found on the Acropolis is fixed a sharp spike to prevent the birds perching.'

7–9 'Not even the general sense can be guessed at with any degree of probability' (Lloyd-Jones). If Gomperz' οὕτωc were correct at the start of 10, that line might be the summing-up of the story: 'Thus it was that . . .'. Before then, the crow apostrophizes Athena (πότνια 7—for the placing of the vocative cf., probably, fr. 17. 12), mentioning her anger (7), and utters a final expression of regret (τότε δ' ὤφελον, 9). Line 7 οὐ (if a complete word) γὰρ ἔγωγε τεόν ποτε, πότνια, θυμόν might conceivably be part of a resolve never to rekindle Athena's wrath by disregarding the prohibition (cf. Lucr. 6. 753, in shunning the Acropolis, crows 'fugitant . . . iras Palladis acris').

8 παραίcια: once in Homer (*Il.* 4. 381*, Zeus revealing signs of ill omen, παραίcια cήματα φαίνων).

8–9 ἐλαφροί|. . . οἰωνοί: Lloyd-Jones compares S. *Ant.* 342–3 κουφονόων . . . φῦλον ὀρνίθων; Th. 580; Ar. *Av.* 169.

10–12 Gomperz' οὕτωc at the start of 10 is possible (see on 7–9). Thereafter Lloyd-Jones suggests ὑμε]τέρην μέν in antithesis to ἡμετέρ[ην in 11, with an adversative such as ἀλλά later in 10. Taking up Barber's ἔκλεινε (*CQ*, NS 2 (1952), 92) in 11, he envisages a sense such as 'Your race she exalted, mine she depressed' (cf. S. *Aj.* 131 for κλίνει in a comparable antithesis), with possibly θ]ε[ὰ τόcον] to follow (rather than Barber's τόcον θεός, which does not suit the traces). If this proved correct, it would support the view of Wilamowitz and others that the bird

addressed is an owl, whose species had supplanted the crow in
Athena's favour. This theory has its attractions, but there are also
some difficulties (see above, p. 225).

11–12 Excellent sense would be provided by ἀλλὰ πέϲοι[τε |
μηδ[έ]ποτ᾽ ἐκ θυμοῖο, and this does not seem inconsistent with the
traces (except that Rea, *HSCP* 72 (1968), 129, was doubtful about
ἀλλά); positive support, however, in what can confidently be read
of the tablet, must be judged rather frail. Pfeiffer cited *Il.* 23. 595
ἐκ θυμοῦ πεϲέειν.

12 In any case, Barber's colon before βαρὺϲ χόλοϲ αἰὲν Ἀθήνηϲ
commends itself. Lucretius must have had this line (as well as fr.
72 and, possibly, fr. 73. 7) in mind when he wrote 'usque adeo
fugitant non *iras Palladis acris* | pervigili causa, Graium ut cecinere
poetae' (6. 753–4); cf. Ov. *Met.* 2. 568 (the crow speaks) 'quamvis
irata est, non hoc irata negabit'.

13 Crows traditionally lived nine generations of men (Aristo-
phanes (*Av.* 609) unusually allows them only five); cf. [Hes.] fr.
304. 1–2 ἐννέα τοι ζώει γενεὰϲ λακέρυζα κορώνη | ἀνδρῶν ἡβώντων
(v.l. γηράντων); Arat. *Phaen.* 1022 ἐννεάγηρα κορώνη; Ov. *Am.* 2.
6. 35–6 (with an eye on the *Hecale*) 'vivit et armiferae cornix
invisa Minervae,| illa quidem saeclis vix moritura novem'. Our
bird was a fledgling in the time of Cecrops, αὐτὰρ ἐγὼ τυτθὸϲ
παρέην γόνοϲ, and is now aged (fr. 74. 9). At the end of this line,
apart from a δ and γάρ, the traces are too slight to hazard anything
(Rea, *HSCP* 72 (1968), 130). But Gomperz' ὀγδοάτη γάρ would
have its attractions. Pfeiffer points out that, at least according to
the *Marmor Parium* (*FGH* 239) Aegeus is the eighth king of Attica
(the sequence is Cecrops, Cranaus, Amphictyon, Ericthonius,
Pandion, Erectheus, Pandion II, Aegeus); so it would be appropri-
ate enough for the crow born in the reign of Cecrops to be in her
eighth generation under Aegeus. Of course there were variant
king-lists (e.g. in Apollod. 3. 14 ff. Aegeus is the ninth king).

Hutchinson (cf. *Hellenistic Poetry* (1988) p. 60 n. 67) finds αὐτὰρ
ἐγὼ τυτθὸϲ παρέην γόνοϲ hard to reconcile with the notion that
the crow who speaks these words was the self-same bird who
brought bad news to Athena; he wonders whether our crow
could have been the offspring of the tale-bearer. But fr. 71
strongly suggests that only one crow is involved (likewise the
Ovidian imitation in *Met.* 2).

γάρ: the only instance in Call. of γάρ ending a hexameter (cf. on fr. 49. 9 μέν).

14 It is a relief that Rea rules out Wessely's δεκάτη δὲ τοκεῦcι at the end of the line, which Pfeiffer had described as 'vix credibile'.

15 This line (*SH* 288. 43A), the last of col. iii of the Vienna Tablet, is not mentioned by Pfeiffer—but only one letter can be read.

Between frs. 73 and 74 approximately 11 lines are missing. Col. iv of the Vienna Tablet begins with two lines (presumably = fr. 74. 12, 13) of which nothing can be read, so that the effective start of col. iv is at fr. 74. 14. Before that, however, we have contributions from three papyri: *P. Oxy.* 2398 (fr. 74. 1–17, beginnings of lines), *P. Oxy.* 2437 (fr. 74. 1–6, middle parts of lines), and *P. Oxy.* 2217 (fr. 74. 3–17).

Fr. 74 opens with the crow expressing her hopes of sustenance (perhaps also the context of fr. 75). It appears that these hopes are connected with Hecale, since line 3 begins ἀ]λλ' Ἑκάλ[η. Maybe the old woman used to feed her. The subject then switches to the bearing of bad tidings (κακάγγελον, 7); perhaps the crow is warning her hearer against carrying bad news in the present circumstances (? the death of Hecale). The thanklessness of such an errand has already been fully illustrated from the crow's own experience, and she reinforces the lesson by predicting (fr. 74. 14 ff.) how one day the raven will be turned from white to black as a punishment for bringing Apollo unwelcome news about Coronis' infidelity. By now the night is far advanced, and the two birds fall asleep briefly (22), until dawn arrives and the world comes to life.

Fr. 74 (*SH* 288. 43B–69; 346, 260. 44–69, 351 Pf.)

1 We knew this line already (fr. 346 Pf.). Crows were notorious both for greed and for begging (cf. l. 5 below, and perhaps fr. 75).

κ⌊ακῆc ἀλκτήρια λιμοῦ: cf. Quint. Smyrn. 9. 121, 11. 424 κακῆc ἀλκτήρια χάρμηc; Nic. *Ther.* 528 νόcων ἀλκτήρια, *Alex.* 350 (= Nonn. *Par.* 3. 74) ἀλκτήρια νούcων; Page, *GLP* (Loeb) 124 (anonymous 'Georgic', generally thought to be of Imperial date = Heitsch, lx, p. 203; cf. Fraser, *Ptolemaic Alexandria*, i. 624)11 ἀλκτῆρά τε λιμοῦ. For feminine λιμός see Richardson on *H. Hom. Dem.* 311.

2–4 'There is too little left to make it worth while to attempt supplements, as we have regretfully concluded after protracted efforts' (Lloyd-Jones, *HSCP* 72 (1968), 141). καί at the start of line 5 suggests that 4 contained some other kind of food for the crow.

3 ἀλλ' Ἑκάλ[η: almost, if not quite, certain. ἐκάλ[εσσε, considered by Lobel, would offend against Meyer's First Law (see above, Introd. sect. IV. 4*a*); ἐκάλ[ει is conceivable, but not found elsewhere in Call. It is curious that the only mention of our heroine's name in what survives of the poem should occur in the crow's speech. Webster (*Poetry and Art*, p. 117) tried to continue ἀλλ' Ἑκάλη λίπε λιτὸν ἕδος, but the π at least hardly suits the traces.

4 Lobel (*P. Oxy.* xxiv. 97–8 on no. 2398, not followed by *SH*) gave . . δ. ακ[, commenting:

Though I see traces of only four letters before *A*, it seems likely that there cannot have been fewer than five. The first is represented only by a short stroke, rising left to right, level with the tops of the letters, the next by parts of a cross-stroke and an upright descending from it, compatible with *T* and, I suppose, *Γ* and *Π* (of the second of which there is no, of the first no comparable, specimen); if *T* or *Γ*, there is room for a narrow letter between it and *Δ*. For *Δ* I cannot rule out *Λ*; between this and *A* there is an indeterminate trace at about mid-letter.

Peter Parsons agrees that the spacing suggests five letters. 'If the trace ⌐ is part of *T*, there would be space for another letter after it, before the delta/lambda; but if it is the beginning of *Γ* or *Π*, there would be space for a (narrow) letter before it.' He adds that the plate in *P. Oxy.* xxiv is unfortunately rather misleading: thus in line 7 the apparent upright trace before the initial theta is delusory.

5 καὶ κ⌋ρῖμν⌊ον⌋ κυκεῶνος ἀπ⌊οστάξαντος ἔραζε: 'and of a posset which dripped barley-groats on to the ground', if ἀποστάξαντος is transitive (Pfeiffer compared *H.* 2. 39, 3. 118) with κρῖμνον the object. This line is quoted complete by the scholiast on Lyc. 607 κρίμνα χειρῶν, where the context is slightly similar (Diomedes' companions, now transformed into birds, being fed by hand); κρῖμνον is explained as γένος κριθῆς, νῦν δὲ τὸ ἀπο-

cτάγμα τοῦ κυκεῶνος (compare Phoen. fr. 2. 1 Powell κορώνηι
χεῖρα πρόςδοτε κριθέων). κρίμνα and the κυκεών are also linked in
Eup. Δῆμοι, fr. 99. 81–2 CGF κυκεῶ πιών |. . . κρίμνων τὴν ὑπήνην
ἀνάπλεως.

κυκεῶνος: cf. *Il.* 11. 624 τεῦχε κυκειῶ and 638. 41, *Od.* 10. 316;
Hippon. fr. 39. 4; Nonn. *Dion.* 47. 88. The κυκεών was a mixture
of grain with liquid (water, wine, milk, honey, or oil); for its
importance in the Eleusinian cult of Demeter see A. Delatte, *Le
Cycéon* (1955) and *H. Hom. Dem.* 208 ff. with N. J. Richardson's
App. IV (cf. Nic. *Alex.* 128 ff.). Richardson shows that the κυκεών
came to be a symbol of frugality (e.g. Plut. *Garrul.* 17 = *Mor.*
511C) or of the rustic life (e.g. Ar. *Pax* 1169).

ἀπ⌊οcτάξαντος ἔραζε: cf. Ap. Rh. 3. 851 καταcτάξαντος
ἔραζε*; Herod. 6. 6 τὰ κρῖμν᾽ ἀμιθρεῖc, κἢν τοcοῦτ᾽ ἀποcτάξηι.

6 Pfeiffer aleady suggested (citing *Il.* 9. 316, *Od.* 22. 319) that
the subject of ἐπέccεται might be χάρις. Lloyd-Jones builds on this
τό]λμης [ἆ χάρις] οὗτις ἐπέccεται, 'ah, you will get no thanks for
your audacity' (cf. also Hes. *Op.* 190 οὐδέ τις εὐόρκου χάρις
ἔccεται). The interjection ἆ occurs e.g. in *Aet.* fr. 1. 33 Pf. and *H.*
3. 255. The restoration would of course suit the idea that the crow
may be dissuading her hearer from bringing bad news. One
should say that Lobel came to feel that the letter before μης in *P.
Oxy.* 2398 is more probably μ than λ, but it is impossible to be
dogmatic on this.

7 κακάγγελον: cf. Ant. Lib. 15. 4 (paraphrasing Boeus' *'Ορνι-
θογονία*) νυκτικόρακα κακάγγελον; A. *Ag.* 636–7 κακαγγέλωι |
γλώccηι: omitted from James's discussion of -άγγελος compounds
(*Oppian of Cilicia*, pp. 177–8). For the proverbially bad reception
cf. S. *Ant.* 277 cτέργει γὰρ οὐδεὶς ἄγγελον κακῶν ἐπῶν.

εἴθε γάρ: noted by Pfeiffer as not pre-Callimachean (also in the
anonymous *SH* 967. 7).

8 It would seem that the other bird has a fair chance of still
being alive, since Coronis' father Phlegyas is grandfather to
Theseus' friend Pirithous—hence the punishment of the raven
cannot be far distant.

κεῖ]γ[ον ἔτι: as conjectured by Pfeiffer before the publication of
P. Oxy. 2398. Lobel doubted whether there is room for κει before
γ, but Barrett (cf. *Gnomon*, 33 (1961), 690 n. 4), after a tracing,
believes that there is, and furthermore that κεῖνον ἔτι can quite
well be accommodated in *P. Oxy.* 2217, where the ζ of ζώουcα

stands approximately above the γ of γρῆϋν in line 9. At the end of
the line Pfeiffer suggested τ[όδ᾽ εἰδ]ῆιc, which seems too long for
the space, unless -ιδ were written for -ειδ (in which case Barrett
prefers τότ᾽). Lobel would have looked for ὄφρα δαείηc.

9 ff. From this point we enjoy the unparalleled luxury of 19
consecutive lines in an almost perfect state of preservation; they
provide a unique opportunity for appreciating the poem's qua-
lity. The whole passage (and particularly the picture of the world
coming to life in 23 ff.) has been much admired, e.g. by Fraser in
Ptolemaic Alexandria, i. 645: 'No passage shows better the curious
magic of the author.'

9 For the detached way in which the crow speaks of herself cf.
Nonn. *Dion.* 3. 119 ἐπαινήcειc δὲ κορώνην (A. S. Hollis, *CQ*, NS
26 (1976), 145); in Ovid (*Met.* 2. 550) the crow says 'ne sperne
meae praesagia linguae'. The notion of crows as prophetic birds
was widespread (*RE* xi. 1564, s.v. Krähe). Isidore (*Or.* 12. 7. 44)
defines cornix as 'annosa avis ... quam aiunt augures hominum
curas significationibus agere, insidiarum vias monstrare, futura
praedicere. magnum nefas haec credere, ut Deus consilia sua
cornicibus mandet' (compare with the last sentence Prudentius'
scornful allusion (*Apoth.* 298) to a 'sago clangore loquax et
stridula cornix' giving divine revelations).

Θριαί: cf. Philoch. *FGH* 328 F 195 (with Jacoby's commen-
tary) νύμφαι κατεῖχον τὸν Παρναccὸν τροφαὶ Ἀπόλλωνοc τρεῖc
καλούμεναι Θριαί. Hesych. s.v. Θριαί gives three explanations: αἱ
πρῶται μάντειc· καὶ νύμφαι καὶ αἱ μαντικαὶ ψῆφοι. See the full
note of F. Williams (*HA*) on *H.* 2. 45 (though he errs in believing
that Hecale is the speaker of the present passage). Hermann
wished to introduce the Θριαί by emendation at *H. Hom. Herm.*
552, but it seems that they are not to be identified with the Bee-
Maidens (see S. Scheinberg, *HSCP* 83 (1979), 8 ff.).

ἐπιπνείουcι κορών⌊ην: cf. Ap. Rh. 3. 937 ἐπιπνείουcιν
Ἔρωτεc* (likewise in the mouth of a talking crow); Nonn.
Dion. 3. 119 ff.

10 ff. *The time will assuredly come when the raven is turned from
brilliant white to darkest black as a punishment for bringing Apollo bad
news about Coronis' infidelity.*

10 ναὶ μὰ τ⌊όν⌋: we find ναὶ μά as far back as *Il.* 1. 234 ναὶ μὰ
τόδε cκῆπτρον. Here the expected name of the god is omitted. As
the scholiast on Ar. *Ran.* 1374 μὰ τόν explains, ἐλλειπτικῶc ὀμνύει

καὶ οὕτως ἔθος ἐστὶ τοῖς ἀρχαίοις ἐνίοτε μὴ προςτιθέναι τὸν θεὸν εὐλαβείας χάριν. This practice is called 'Attic' by Greg. Cor. p. 150 Schaef. and also occurs in Pl. *Grg.* 466e μὰ τόν (but see Dodds ad loc.). The oath here goes not with οὐ γάρ πω κτλ.—a point which has caused some trouble ('ναί cum negatione coniungi nequit', Pf.)—but with the positive assertion of 14 ff. δείελος ἀλλ' ἢ νύξ κτλ. (Barrett in *Gnomon*, 33 (1961), 691).

Great confusion has resulted from Suidas' apparent statement that ναὶ μὰ τόν was spoken by Hecale (καὶ Ἑκάλη εἶπε). This would be a unique way for Suid. to introduce a quotation (ascribing it not to the author or the poem, but to the mythical character who actually delivered the words), and there can be little doubt that καὶ Ἑκάλη is a corruption of Καλλ. Ἑκάληι (as e.g. in fr. 81, Suid. s.v. κωμῆται). For this kind of corruption, deriving from an abbreviation of the poet's name, see Pfeiffer on his frs. 30 and 800 and Lloyd-Jones, *Glotta*, 41 (1963), 68–70 (who sets out various examples). The same thing may have happened with Suid. s.v. cτίβη ... καὶ [? Καλλ. Pf.] "cτιβήεις"(see fr. 74. 23). Other points which might be made in an attempt to argue that Hecale is the speaker of these lines are rebutted by Lloyd-Jones (*HSCP* 72 (1968), 142–4); before the full context of lines 10–11 was known, they could reasonably have been put in the mouth of Hecale (with cῦφαρ as the old woman's hide, and δένδρεον her staff), but to maintain such a view in our present state of knowledge would be perverse.

πάντ' ἤματα: translated 'always' by Trypanis (Loeb), 'for ever' by Lobel (*P. Oxy.* xxiv. 98 on no. 2398) and Fraser (*Ptolemaic Alexandria*, i. 644). But it is much more natural to take the phrase as nominative (with Lloyd-Jones, *CR*, NS 9 (1959), 243–4), like ἠέλιοι ... πάντες (13): 'not yet have all the days'—we expect 'elapsed', but instead the crow changes tack with οὐκ ἤδη κτλ. (12). For aposiopesis in Call. see Lapp, *Tropis et Figuris*, p. 103; Lloyd-Jones, *Hermes*, 110 (1982), 119–20.

10–11 ναὶ μὰ τ⌊όν⌋ ... ναὶ ⌊μ⌋ά ...⌋... ναί: the multiple oath has a slightly comical vehemence. See Gomme–Sandbach on Men. *Sam.* 309–10, where we find a fourfold μά (also e.g. at Ar., *Av.* 194). After the 'elliptical' oath, the crow adds two more, swearing first by her own wrinkled skin—a nice touch because in the old days 'everyone swore by birds' (*Av.* 520; cf. Cratin. fr. 249 *PCG* = 231 Kock)—and then by the withered tree on which she perches. The latter oath recalls Pl. *Phdr.* 236d ὄμνυμι ... τὴν πλάτανον ταυτηνί (cf. Greg. Naz. *Carm.* 1. 2. 24. 306 ff. (*PG* xxxvii. 811)), and is quoted by Suidas to illustrate the ancient practice of swearing 'by whatever was at hand'.

10 ῥικνόν: 'shrivelled', first at *H. Hom. Ap.* 317 of Hephaestus ῥικνὸς πόδας (cf. Ap. Rh. 1. 669; epic. adesp. 2. 33 Powell; *SH* 1050, [Opp.] *Cyn.* 2. 346) and in medical writings.

11 cῦφαρ: 'hide', said by schol. Nic. *Alex.* 91 to be a Sicilian word (with reference to the 'skin' on milk), and applied by the Sicilian Sophron to an aged human being (fr. 55 Kaibel)— likewise of Odysseus in Lycophron's *Alexandra*, where the juxta-position of cῦφαρ (793) and κόραξ (794) could be due to subcon-scious recollection of our passage (cf. above, Introd. sect. VI). Lucian (*Herm.* 79) uses cῦφαρ of a snake's slough, and it quite appropriately here refers to the old bird's skin. See further Lloyd-Jones, *HSCP* 72 (1968), 143.

ναὶ τ⌊οῦ⌋το τὸ δένδ⌊ρ⌋εον αὖον ἐόν περ: the tree on which the crow is sitting; for the aspiration of αὖον cf. Hopkinson (*HD*) on *H.* 6. 6.

12–13 'Not all the suns, breaking their pole and axle, by now have set their foot in the West.' These colourful and somewhat oracular lines are usually taken to mean that 'Time has not yet come to an end', i.e. there is still time for the transformation to occur (cf. particularly Theocr. 16. 71 ff., quoted below). A slightly different interpretation would be 'the time has not yet come', in which case πάντ' ἤματα and ἠέλιοι ... πάντες would denote all the days which must elapse before the raven's transfor-mation (rather than all the days until the end of the world). The expression is clearly proverbial; we have four parallels, though it is not certain that the meaning is exactly the same in each—the presence of a dative ἄμμι in Theocr. 1. 102 and αὐτοῖς in Diodorus perhaps gives a different twist:

(*a*) Theocr. 1. 102 (Daphnis taunting Aphrodite) ἤδη γὰρ φράςδηι πάνθ' ἄλιον ἄμμι δεδύκειν; where the implication is 'I'm not yet beaten' (Dover).

(*b*) Theocr. 16. 71–3 οὔπω μῆνας ἄγων ἔκαμ' οὐρανὸς οὐδ' ἐνιαυτούς, | πολλοὶ κινήςουςιν ἔτι τροχὸν ἄρματος [ἄματος Wila-mowitz] ἵπποι.| ἔccεται οὗτος ἀνὴρ ὃς ἐμοῦ κεχρήςετ' ἀοιδοῦ. This would appear to be the closest parallel to Callimachus: there is still

time, before the end of the world, for the performance of heroic
deeds which will require a poet's services.

(*c*) Diod. 29. 16. The Thessalians, having won their freedom
through the Romans, abuse their former Macedonian masters,
οὐκ εἰδότες ὅτι οὔπω πᾶς αὐτοῖς (sc. the Macedonians) ὁ ἥλιος
δέδυκε. Barrett, while agreeing with Lobel (on *P. Oxy.* 2398) that
πᾶς ... ὁ ἥλιος must mean 'all the sun', finds the sentiment
incredible, and would delete the article to make the meaning
'every sun' (M. L. West, however, notes that Eust. 1266. 48
understands Theocr. 1. 102 πάνθ᾽ ἅλιον as πάντα τὸν ἥλιον).

(*d*) The same episode in Liv. 39. 26 'elatus deinde ira [sc. Philip
V of Macedon] adiecit nondum omnium dierum solem occidisse'.
Here the absence of a dative corresponding to Diodorus' αὐτοῖς
seems to bring the expression closer to that of Call.—time is not
yet at an end, and so the Macedonians may still regain their
power.

12 ἄξονα καυάξαντες: cf. Hes. *Op.* 693 ἄξονα καυάξαις. Call.
perhaps intended his readers to recall the old theory of Heraclitus
and Xenophanes, according to whom a new sun came into being
and was extinguished each day (see Bailey on Lucr. 5. 650–5; cf.
Man. 1. 184). In turn Ovid may draw on Call. for a more
frivolous mixture of mythology with scientific speculation in *Am.*
1. 13. 29–30 (to Aurora) 'optavi quotiens aut ventus *frangeret axem*
[compared with ἄξονα καυάξαντες by D. Little, *Hermes*, 99 (1971),
128] aut caderet spissa nube retentus equus'. The association of
Helios with a chariot (cf. *H.* 4. 169–70) is discussed by Richardson
on *H. Hom. Dem.* 63.

καυάξαντες: 'breaking', from κατάγνυμι. The form represents
καϝϝάξαντες for κατϝάξαντες. M. L. West (Hesiod, *Theogony*, p.
83) notes that diphthongization of the vowel + ϝ(ϝ) is typical of
Aeolic (e.g. αὔως, ναῦος), but also occurs in Arcadian.

14 δ]⟨ε⟩ίελος ἀλλ᾽ ἢ νὺξ ἢ ἔνδιος ἢ ἔσετ᾽ ἠώς: based upon
Achilles' prophecy of his own death in *Il.* 21. 111–12 ἔσσεται ἢ
ἠὼς ἢ δείλη ἢ μέσον ἦμαρ | ὁππότε κτλ. Mention of the four
alternative hours adds solemnity and mystery (as Mark 13: 35 on
the return of Christ ἢ ὀψὲ ἢ μεσονύκτιον ἢ ἀλεκτοροφωνίας ἢ
πρωΐ). For a similar touch applied to the seasons cf. the oracle in
Hdt. 7. 141. 4. 12 ἤ που σκιδναμένης Δημήτερος ἢ συνιούσης.
More generally, prophecies of the type 'the day will come

when . . .' (e.g. *Il.* 6. 448 ἔccεται ἦμαρ ὅτ' ἄν) are copiously exemplified by Headlam on Herod. 4. 50. I will add merely a fine but unexpected specimen in Cic. *Mil.* 69 'erit, erit illud profecto tempus [for the repetition cf. [Soph.] fr. 1128 Pearson = adesp. 620 Kannicht–Snell ἔcται γάρ, ἔcται κεῖνος αἰῶνος χρόνος and Sil. 15. 125] et inlucescet ille aliquando dies, cum tu . . .'. Prophecy is popular with Hellenistic poets (cf. Bulloch, *FH*, p. 218 n. 2 and e.g. in Lyc. *Alex. passim*; Alex. Aet. fr. 3 Powell.

δ]⟨ε⟩ίελος ἀλλ᾽ : postponement of ἀλλά to second position (as e.g. *H.* 1. 18, *Aet.* fr. 10 Pf.) is relatively mild. Elsewhere we may find ἀλλά as late as fifth word (*Aet.* fr. 110. 61 Pf.) and γάρ fourth word (*Aet.* frs. 67. 11, 75. 30 Pf.); Latin poets follow in their treatment of 'nam', 'namque', and 'sed' (e.g. Catull. 66. 65; Virg. *Ecl.* 1. 14; Val. Flacc. 2. 150, 277–8). δείελος as a substantive = 'evening' comes at *Il.* 21. 232, Ap. Rh. 1. 1160 (in fr. 18. 6 = the evening meal).

ἔνδιος: 'midday' (see on fr. 18. 1). For the double hiatus with ἤ, cf. above, Introd. sect. IV. 6 and below on fr. 77.

15 ff. This passage on the transformation of the raven is imitated and embroidered by Ovid (*Met.* 2. 534 ff.):

> quam tu nuper eras, cum candidus ante fuisses,
> corve loquax, subito *nigrantes* versus in *alas.*
> nam fuit haec quondam niveis argentea pennis
> ales, *ut aequaret* totas sine labe columbas,
> *nec* servaturis vigili Capitolia voce
> *cederet* anseribus nec amanti flumina *cycno.*

Thereafter a white raven became as portentous as a black swan; cf. Lucr. 2. 822–4; Claud. *Eutrop.* 1. 348–9 'veluti nigrantibus alis │ audiretur olor, corvo certante [? from Call.'s κόραξ . . . ἐρίζοι] ligustris'. For white ravens cf. also Luc. *AP* 11. 436. 1; Demon, *FGH* 327 F 7; anon. *FGH* 482 F 3. 2; Ergias, *FGH* 513 F 1.

16 γάλακι: (also perhaps in Pherecr. fr. 108. 18 Kock), as if from the nominative γάλαξ. The compound γαλακόχροες in [Opp.] *Cyn.* 3. 478 may be inspired by Call.

κύματος ἄκρωι ἀώτῳ: the foam on the crest of a wave; cf. *H.* 2. 112 (the purest spring-water) ὀλίγη λιβὰς ἄκρον ἄωτον (with Williams's note). In Homer ἄωτον (or ἄωτος—the nominative does not occur) denotes the finest sort of something, particularly of wool (*Il.* 13. 599, 716), once of linen, λίνοιό τε λεπτὸν ἄωτον (*Il.*

9. 661). Pindar is particularly fond of the word, e.g. *Isth.* 7. 18 coφίαc ἄωτον ἄκρον, whence probably Mich. Chon. ii. 40. 3 Lambros τὸ ἄκρον τῆc ἱερωcύνηc, ποιητὴc ἂν εἶπεν, ἄωτον (even though Pindar, like Theocritus, regards the noun as masculine, Call., Apollonius Rhodius, and [Oppian] as neuter). See further M. S. Silk, *Interaction in Poetic Imagery* (1974), App. XI; id., *CQ*, NS 33 (1983), 316 f.; R. A. Raman, *Glotta*, 53 (1975), 195–207.

ἄκρῶι ἀώτῳ: see above, Introd. sect. IV. 7 for the correction.

17 κυάνεον φὴ πίccαν: cf. *Il.* 4. 277 μελάντερον ἠΰτε πίccα, and perhaps Sil. 3. 682 of the dove which flew to Libya 'piceis . . . alis' (the text is uncertain). φή, 'as', was read by Zenodotus (rightly) at *Il.* 2. 144 and 14. 499, but cannot have been introduced by him; Antimachus of Colophon (fr. 121 Wyss φὴ γέρον οἶcον) must also have recognized φή in Homer, and it may occur in [Hes.] fr. 204. 138. So we cannot be sure that Call. took this specifically from Zenodotus (see further Pfeiffer on *Aet.* fr. 12. 6; id., *History*, i. 139–40). The scholiast on *Il.* 14. 499 ascribes the form to οἱ περὶ Καλλίμαχον, which may (but need not) imply that it was used by other Hellenistic poets (cf. Call. fr. 737 inc. auct. Pf., and conceivably the anonymous *SH* 924. 3).

ἐπὶ πτερὸν . . . ἕξει: very puzzling—what might seem to be a parallel in *H.* 4. 234 ἐπὶ πτερὸν ὕπνοc ἐρείcει does not help. ἐπί may perhaps be used adverbially, 'will have on him' (Lloyd-Jones), and πτερόν collectively, 'plumage' rather than 'wing'. Barrett has considered ἔτι for ἐπί, recognizing that this would be pleonastic: the crow might say either 'the time will come when the raven . . .' or else 'the raven will yet . . .' (as e.g. Theocr. 16. 72 (quoted above on 12–13) and A. *PV.* 907–8 ἦ μὴν ἔτι Ζεύc . . .| ἔcται ταπεινόc), but should not combine the two. Hutchinson tentatively suggests ἀνὰ . . . ἕξει. Gomperz tried ἐπὶ . . . ἕccει.

οὐλοόν: cf. Nonn. *Dion.* 15. 88 (of Sleep) ἑὸν πτερὸν οὖλον ἑλίξαc where again the sense is unclear. Call. studiously reproduces all the Homeric meanings of οὖλοc (cf. de Jan, *De Callimacho*, pp. 8–13 and Williams (*HA*) on *H.* 2. 76), none of which seems particularly appropriate here ('thick' might be possible). οὐλοόc is not attested before the Hellenistic period (Campbell, *Studies*, p. 127 n. 35). Bearing in mind that the raven is transformed as a punishment, one may wish to give the epithet an unpleasant sense (cf. *Aet.* fr. 78. 1 Pf. οὐλοὸν ἔγχοc; Nic. *Ther.* 565), even if Nonnus disagreed (see above).

18 ἀγγελίης ἐπίχειρα: cf. A. *PV* 318–19 τῆς ἄγαν ὑψηγόρου |
γλώccηc . . . τἀπίχειρα (ἐπίχειρα appears first in tragedy). While
the κακαγγελία of the crow cannot be traced before 'Amelesa-
goras' and Call., that of the raven who informed on Coronis is
found in [Hes.] fr. 60, quoted by the scholiast on P. *Pyth.* 3. 52
(Pindar himself omits the raven):

> τῆμος ἄρ' ἄγγελος ἦλθε κόραξ ἱερῆς ἀπὸ δαιτός
> Πυθὼ ἐς ἠγαθέην, καί ῥ' ἔφρασεν ἔργ' ἀΐδηλα
> Φοίβωι ἀκερσοκόμηι, ὅτι Ἴςχυς γῆμε Κόρωνιν
> Εἰλατίδης, Φλεγύαο διογνήτοιο θύγατρα.

If ἱερῆς ἀπὸ δαιτός refers to a wedding feast, perhaps Ischys is
marrying Coronis quite openly (no doubt unaware of her
condition), but in Pindar and later authors she conducts a
surreptitious affair; Ovid speaks of 'adulterium' (*Met.* 2. 545), and
Call.'s μιαρόν τι (20) tends to put her behaviour in the worst light.
In Boeus' *Ornithogonia* and/or Simias' *Apollo* (probably both 3rd
cent. BC) Coronis' lover was called Alcyoneus (Ant. Lib. 20. 7).
The fate of the two birds who bring bad tidings has the
common feature that just as the crow had been Athena's bird, so
the raven was particularly associated with Apollo (*Met.* 2. 544–5
'ales |. . . Phoebeius'; cf. Bömer on *Fast.* 2. 249). In *H.* 2. 66 Call.
tells how Apollo, in the form of a raven, led the Greek colonists to
Libya; also e.g. in Hdt. 4. 15 Aristeas takes the shape of a raven
when accompanying the god (cf. Ov. *Met.* 5. 329, Man. 1. 783).
Call.'s tendency to link parallel myths can be seen in other works
too (e.g. the Lindian sacrifice and Theiodamas in *Aet.* 1, frs. 22–5
Pf.; cf. A. S. Hollis, *CQ*, NS 32 (1982), 118).

19 Call. makes nothing special of the fact that the κορώνη
prophesies about Κορωνίς, but Jacoby (*FGH* iiib, Suppl. ii. 492 n.
12) believed that the resemblance could have facilitated the
transfer of motifs from one myth to the other (see above, p. 231).
Ovid may be indulging in free invention when he makes his crow
the transformed daughter of Coroneus (*Met.* 2. 569).

20 Ἴςχυϊ πληξίππωι: cf. *H. Hom. Ap.* 210 Ἴςχυϊ . . . εὐίππωι.
πλήξιππος is a conventional Homeric epithet (*Il.* 2. 104 etc.).

ςπομένης: for the form of the participle cf. P. *Pyth.* 4. 40
ςπομέναν—it is also found as a Homeric *varia lectio* (see Ardizzoni
on Ap. Rh. 1. 104), e.g. at *Il.* 13. 570. where ὁ δὲ ςπόμενος is v.l.
for ὁ δ' ἑςπόμενος. The employment of ἕπομαι as a sexual

euphemism, 'going with', may have been suggested by *Od.* 22.
324 coì δ' ἄλοχόν τε φίλην cπέcθαι καὶ τέκνα τεκέcθαι (though
cπέcθαι there need imply no more than accompanying her
husband to his home); cf. *Il.* 3. 447 ἅμα δ' εἵπετ' ἄκοιτιc and
Quint. Smyrn. 10. 396.

21 ὣc φαμένην: cf. Campbell on Quint. Smyrn. 12. 66.

τὴν δ' ἀΐουcαν: the only explicit reference in what survives to
the mysterious second bird (for the problem of her identity see
above, p. 225).

22 καδδραθέτην δ' οὐ πολλὸν ἐπὶ χρόγ⌊ο⌋γ, αἶψα γὰρ ἦλθεν:
another illustration (cf. above, Introd. sect. III and e.g. on fr. 32)
of how much closer the *Hecale* comes to Homer than do Call.'s
other poems. This line is composed of two pieces of Homer,
chiefly *Od.* 15. 493 ff. (Odysseus and Eumaeus):

> ὣc οἱ μὲν τοιαῦτα πρὸc ἀλλήλουc ἀγόρευον·
> καδδραθέτην δ' οὐ πολλὸν ἐπὶ χρόνον, ἀλλὰ μίνυνθα,
> αἶψα γὰρ 'Ηὼc ἦλθεν

with a contribution from *Od.* 12. 407 οὐ μάλα πολλὸν ἐπὶ
χρόνον· αἶψα γὰρ ἦλθε.

23 cτιβήειc ἄγχαυροc: 'the frosty pre-dawn' (in Ov. *Am.* 1. 6.
65 'pruinosus ... Lucifer' might be defended as an imitation of
Call., but see McKeown ad loc.), two words unattested before
Call. The unique cτιβήειc (from cτίβη, *Od.* 5. 467, 17. 25) shows
our poet's liking, paralleled in Nicander (whom James (*Oppian of
Cilicia*, p. 220) credits with 110 -όειc adjectives, 58 of them found
nowhere else; cf. A. Bartalucci, *Studi Classici e Orientali*, 12 (1963),
118–44) and, later, in Nonnus, for new formations in -ήειc and
-όειc (cf. C. D. Buck and W. Petersen, *Reverse Index of Greek
Nouns and Adjectives* (1944), pp. 460–3). The *Hecale* offers also
θαρcήειc (fr. 69. 5), θυμόειc fr. 18. 9) and πυρόειc (fr. 25. 2, not
certainly before Call.).

ἄγχαυροc [coni. M. Schmidt: ἀγχοῦροc cod. Hesychii] is said by
Hesychius to be a Cyprian word, and is used by Apollonius
Rhodius (4. 110–11 νύκτα | ἄγχαυρον) as an epithet (cf. McLennan
(*HZ*) on H. 1. 14). In fact the Vienna Tablet has ἄγχουροc rather
than ἄγχαυροc, and the former stood in pre-Pfeiffer editions
together with Gomperz' misreading ἵτ' for ὅτ', producing a
wonderful scene in which a third bird ('a frosty neighbour')
roused the other two, 'Come, no longer are the hands of thieves at

their prey etc.'. The 'vicinus pruinosus' enjoyed an undeservedly long career (Pfeiffer, *JHS* 75 (1955), 71 = *Ausgewählte Schriften*, pp. 152–3; id., 'Morgendämmerung', *Festschrift für Ida Kapp* (1954), 95–104 = Skiadas (ed.), *Kallimachos, Wege der Forschung* (1975), 160–6). Apollonius Rhodius splendidly describes the moment when night gives way to dawn also in 2. 669 ff.

ἔπαγροι: likewise very rare (previously only in Arist. *HA* 9. 18. 616ᵇ34, of herons).

23 ff. Descriptions of hours or seasons in terms of human or animal activity ('the time when . . .') are already well established in early Greek poetry (e.g. *Il.* 11. 86 ff. ἦμος δὲ δρυτόμος περ ἀνὴρ ὡπλίccατο δεῖπνον, *Od.* 12. 439 ff.; *H. Hom. Aphr.* 168 ff.; Hes. *Op.* 580–1 ἠώc, ἥ τε φανεῖcα πολέαc ἐπέβηcε κελεύθου | ἀνθρώπουc, πολλοῖcι δ' ἐπὶ ζυγὰ βουcὶ τίθηcιν. The present example is unusually elaborate (and, as Hutchinson remarks, sharply pointed, in that each clause gives a further reason why the thief must stop work); compare Apollonius Rhodius on the coming of night (3. 744 ff.), where we have a sequence of sailors, a traveller, a gatekeeper, a mother of dead children, and dogs who have ceased to bark. In *Hec.* fr. 18. 5 ff., evening is presented as 'the time when girls finish their work and ask for supper' (see ad loc.). Such pictures lie behind much of Ov. *Am.* 1. 13 (to Dawn): Sen. (*Ep.* 122. 11, *Lud. Mort.* 2) mocks the excessive use of these purple passages by his contemporaries. For an extended specimen in later Greek poetry cf. [Opp.] *Cyn.* 1. 129–46. See further W. Bühler, *Die Europa des Moschos*, Exkurs I, the main purpose of which is to illustrate the typical generalizing present tense—here φαείνει, ἀείδει, ἔγρει, ἀνιάζουcι, in fr. 18. 6 αἰτίζουcιν and ἄγουcι. Of course the whole description here is general, of dawn anywhere in the world, without special reference to the context in Call.'s poem (cf. Lloyd-Jones, *HSCP* 72 (1968), 145, a point reinforced by the 'impressionistic' που in l. 25).

23–4 The thief is a night-shift man (ἡμερόκοιτος ἀνήρ, Hes. *Op.* 605) who needs to knock off work before dawn (Catull. 62. 34–5 'nocte latent fures, quos idem saepe revertens,| Hespere, mutato comprendis nomine Eous'). Cf. E. *IT* 1026 κλεπτῶν γὰρ ἡ νύξ and Prudent. *H. Matut.* 17–20 'fur ante lucem squalido | impune peccat tempore,| sed lux dolis contraria | latere furtum non sinit'.

24 φιλητέων: 'robbers'; cf. Hes. *Op.* 375; *H. Hom. Herm.* 67,

446; Archil. fr. 49. 7; Hippon. frs. 79. 10, 102. 12 West. We often find alternative spellings of this word with φιλ- and φηλ- (cf. West on Hes. *Op.* 375); the former tends to have stronger manuscript support, but φηλ- was preferred by Ernst Fraenkel, *Geschichte der Griechischen Nomina Agentis*, i (1910), 122 n. 2 (cf. R. Carden, *BICS* 16 (1969), 36).

25 ἀνὴρ ὑδατηγός: unique; cf. *Il.* 21. 257 ἀνὴρ ὀχετηγός and Nic. *Alex.* 519 ἀνὴρ ἀλοπηγός*.

ἱμαῖον: according to schol. Ar. *Ran.* 1297 (who quotes the line complete), ἆιςμα ὃ ᾄδουςιν οἱ ἀντληταί, 'the well-song' (from ἱμάω). Robert Renehan ('Greek Lexicographical Notes', *Hypomnemata*, 45 (1975), 111–12) shows that the nominative should be not ἱμαῖον, τό (sc. μέλος or ἆιςμα) as LSJ state, but ἱμαῖος, ἡ (sc. ᾠδή), the adjective being of two terminations. He suggests that this line of Call., in which the word appears in the accusative, may have been the source of misunderstanding.

The *Hecale* draws much Attic vocabulary and local colour from Old Comedy (see above, Introd. sect. II), and it seems probable that Call. is here indebted to some commentator on Ar. *Ran.* 1297 ἱμονιοςτρόφου μέλη (cf. ἱμονιά), which may already have been a subject of dispute before our poet's time—though we can only trace the argument after Call. Not everyone agreed that the ἱμαῖος was a song for water-drawing; Aristophanes of Byzantium, *c.*257–180 BC, ἐν Ἀττικαῖς λέξεςιν (*ap.* Athen. 14. 619b) and Trypho Alexandrinus, first cent. BC (ibid. 618d) both made it a miller's song (cf. ἱμαλίς), and this view is repeated by later lexicographers. See J. J. Winkler, 'Callimachus Fr. 260. 66 Pf.', *CW* 72. 4 (1978–9), 237–8. If the controversy was already current in Call.'s day, we would see him making beautiful poetry out of a rather arid dispute. Another example of a controversial work-song which caught the interest of Hellenistic poets would be the ἴουλος (discussed by Gow on Theocr. 10. 41 and by schol. Ap. Rh. 1. 972, the latter quoting Eratosth. fr. 10 Powell—on which see J. W. Fitton in *Glotta*, 53 (1975), 223–6). See further M. L. West, *ZPE* 25 (1977), 105–6 for the early-morning songs of woolworkers in Erinna; Giangrande, *SMA* i. 179–80.

26 παρὰ πλόον: for πλόος of a path on land cf. Antim. fr. 106 Wyss (*SH* 76) τοῖςιν δ᾽ ὑλήεντα διὰ πλόον ἐρχομένοιςιν; Nic. *Ther.* 295. Hesychius recognizes a verb παραπλωΐζω, meaning to be situated or move along the highway.

26–7 ἄξων | τετριγὼc ὑπ' ἅμαξαν: an attractive touch, transferring to a peaceful context the motif of *Il.* 5. 838–9 (the chariot which bears Athena and Diomede) μέγα δ' ἔβραχε φήγινοc ἄξων | βριθοcύνηι (cf. Sil. 17. 490, the chariot of Mars, 'stridens sub pondere belliger axis'). Our passage was admired by Quint. Smyrn. 6. 108–9 ἀπήνην | ἄχθεϊ τετριγυῖαν ὑπ' ἄξονι δινήεντι. See further Hutchinson on A. *Sept.* 151–3; Virg. *G.* 3. 172–3 'sub pondere faginus axis | instrepat'.

27–8 With the break-up of the text in line 28 we run into severe problems. The last two examples (the water-drawer and the creaking waggon) involve sounds which intrude; one would rather expect ἀνιάζουcι to be transitive, and to denote a painful or irritating intrusion (cf. *Od.* 1. 133; Pl. *Grg.* 485b with ἀνιάω). In line 28 ἐναυόμενοι is certain (Rea); before that, either χαλκῆεc or χαλκῆαc. If the nominative, smiths are asking someone else for a light, which would be a little surprising (should they not keep their fire burning overnight?); if the accusative (favoured by West on Hes. *Op.* 493), χαλκῆαc is presumably the object of ἀνιάζουcι, and the smiths are merely being irritated by requests for a light. It would be somewhat easier to fit χαλκῆεc with . . . . ωρι at the start of 28. Lloyd-Jones suggested e.g. δύcζωοι (cf. *AP* 9. 574. 2 δύcζωον . . . βίοτον); West, wishing to read χαλκῆαc, wonders whether δύcζωοι could mean something like 'tramps'. At the end of 28 West contemplates πυρὸc αὐγήν (cf. *Od.* 6. 305*, Nic. *Alex.* 61*); Rea (*HSCP* 72 (1968), 130) pronounces πυρ óc and -ην to be possible, but the second letter after what might be πυρόc looks like α. In 27 πυκνοί, apparently certain, is customarily translated 'many a'; could it, however, be predicative, 'coming frequently', or even 'packed densely', 'in a queue'?

28 ἐναυόμενοι: 'asking for a light'. E. K. Borthwick (*CQ*, NS 19 (1969), 306–13), contends that the basic notion of αὔω is 'to draw with a scooping motion' (cf. 'haurio'), e.g. by inserting a shovel into the ashes of a fire. ἐναύεcθαι means 'to get a light for oneself', and may either be absolute (e.g. Luc. *Tim.* 6, Plut. *Num.* 9. 6) or take an accusative such as πῦρ. The transfer might be made by removing a single brand or a shovel-full of burning embers (cf. Borthwick, op. cit. p. 307) to start one's own fire. Giving a light to someone who asked was a sacred obligation among the ancients (e.g. Cic. *Off.* 1. 52 'pati ab igne ignem capere')—hence 'aquae et ignis interdictio'.

FRS. 75–7

It would be natural to assume that with the coming of dawn at the end of fr. 74 we should also have finished with the talking birds, and that their part in the poem was confined to the Vienna Tablet (i.e. between the lacuna which separates fr. 69 from fr. 70 and the end of fr. 74). But several other fragments definitely (frs. 76–7; cf. frs. 167–8 inc. sed.) or possibly (fr. 75) concern birds. Of these, frs. 75–7 might be spoken by the crow; fr. 167 inc. sed. certainly comes from the mouth of an owl, while fr. 168 inc. sed. commends the owl (? as a favourable omen). Might all these be accommodated within the Vienna Tablet? Fr. 75 (if I have guessed its reference correctly) may have stood between frs. 73 and 74 (less probably between frs. 69 and 70). Although the crow appears to speak uninterrupted from the start of fr. 70 until fr. 74. 20, the owl (if she is the second bird) could have had a say between frs. 69 and 70, thus conceivably accounting for fr. 167 inc. sed. Much more awkward are frs. 76–7. If we are right in thinking that the crow warns her hearer against a mistake (fr. 73. 10–12, see ad loc.), and if her hearer is an owl, it is hard to see how the same crow could curse the same owl with the virulent words of fr. 77. And fr. 76, perhaps describing past attacks by crows and storks on other (unidentified) birds, seems to imply a narrative of more than a few lines. This could not easily be fitted into the *c.* 11 lines missing between frs. 73 and 74 (which may have included fr. 75), nor into the *c.* 17 lines (the subject-matter of which seems fairly clear) missing between frs. 70 and 73; there would remain the gap of *c.* 22 lines between frs. 69 and 70, but other matters appear to have a stronger claim upon that space.

So perhaps one should leave open the possibility that the talking birds were not restricted to the Vienna Tablet, but also participated elsewhere in the poem, whether earlier or later. In face of these insoluble problems, I have gathered together the three fragments (75–7) which certainly belong to the *Hecale*, and placed them next after the Vienna Tablet, without, however, any great confidence that they all stood in this area.

Fr. 75 (267 Pf.)

γίνεό μοι τέκταινα βίου δαμάτειρά τε λιμοῦ: Pfeiffer thought of a prayer to a goddess, either Demeter (see his note for ancient suggestions of a link between Δημήτηρ and δαμάστρια) or Γαῖα (thus also Giangrande, *JHS* 86 (1966), 198). It is possible, however, to imagine a context which coheres with something we already know of the *Hecale*. P. Oxy. 2398 revealed that γαστέρι μοῦνον ἔχοιμι κακῆς ἀλκτήρια λιμοῦ (fr. 74. 1) was spoken by the crow; the next line but one began ἀλλ' Ἑκάλ[η. It seems that the crow's hopes of sustenance were in some way connected with Hecale (? endangered by her death). So this voracious bird may be the speaker here too, and the female person (τέκταινα and δαμάτειρα) could be Hecale. Webster (*Poetry and Art*, p. 114) makes the line an appeal by Theseus to Hecale, which is surely inappropriate.

Scholars appear to have taken for granted that γίνεο is imperative, as in line 4 of *epigr.* 26 Pf. = *AP* 7. 460 = 47 G.–P.; cf. Nonn. *Dion.* 27. 292, 33. 361 γίνεό μοι* (imperative γίνεο probable in ? Euph. *SH* 429. 17). That is likely enough—perhaps the crow recalls an earlier appeal. But an unparalleled indicative γίνεο, or maybe γείνεο (Sophron. cod. H) regarded as aorist (cf. Hopkinson (*HD*) on *H.* 6. 57), cannot altogether be ruled out (cf. the unprecedented indicative οἶσε in fr. 36. 3). Could the crow be apostrophizing Hecale, now dead, and remembering how she first attached herself to the old woman? If this line of thinking were correct, a plausible position for the fragment would be in the lacuna between frs. 73 and 74 (less probably in the lacuna between frs. 69 and 70).

τέκταινα βίου: as Pfeiffer says, 'provider of livelihood' rather than 'author of life'. In [Hes.] fr. 343. 14 Μῆτις is τέκταινα δικαίων.

δαμάτειρα: elsewhere only in *AP* 11. 403. 1 (Lucian or Lucillius) of gout, πλούτου δαμάτειρα, but δμήτειρα is found at *Il.* 14. 259 (v.l. μήτειρα) and Nonn. *Dion.* 35. 277, and πανδαμάτειρα is particularly common in the *Dionysiaca*. For nouns in -τειρα see further on fr. 40. 2 καθηγήτειρα.

Pfeiffer notes in this line a 'parallelism of limbs' (τέκταινα βίου—δαμάτειρα ... λιμοῦ) which he describes as very rare in Call. and traces back to the proem of the *Works and Days*. M. L. West (on *Op.* 1–10) speaks of 'a balancing of phrases which results in rhyme', particularly in 5–7 ῥέα μὲν γὰρ βριάει, ῥέα δὲ βριάοντα χαλέπτει,| ῥεῖα δ' ἀρίζηλον μινύθει καὶ ἄδηλον ἀέξει,| ῥεῖα δέ τ'

ἰθύνει cκολιὸν καὶ ἀγήνορα κάρφει. What we commonly meet in
Hellenistic poetry is balance and rhyme between pairs of lines,
e.g. *H*. 4. 84–5 νύμφαι μὲν χαίρουcιν ὅτε δρύαc ὄμβροc ἀέξει,|
νύμφαι δ᾿ αὖ κλαίουcιν ὅτε δρυcὶ μηκέτι φύλλα (more examples in
my note on Ov. *Met*. 8. 628–9).

Fr. 76 (271 Pf.)

cὺν δ᾿ ἡμῖν ὁ πελαργὸc ἀμορβεύεcκεν ἀλοίτηc: 'the avenging
stork used to travel with us'. Pfeiffer suspected that this line might
belong to a conversation of birds, and later (i. 507) adduced what
may be a vital clue to the context in St Basil, *Hom*. 8. 5 in
Hexaemeron (*PG* xxix. 176b). There we read of crows and storks
forming an alliance to fight against their enemies: δορυφοροῦcι δὲ
αὐτοὺc (sc. the storks) αἱ παρ᾿ ἡμῖν κορῶναι, καὶ παραπέμπουcιν,
ἐμοὶ δοκεῖν, καὶ cυμμαχίαν τινὰ παρεχόμεναι πρὸc ὄρνιθαc πολε-
μίουc. cημεῖον δὲ πρῶτον μὲν τὸ μὴ φαίνεcθαι ὑπὸ τὸν καιρὸν
ἐκεῖνον κορώνην παντάπαcιν, ἔπειθ᾿ ὅτι μετὰ τραυμάτων ἐπανερχό-
μεναι ἐναργῆ τοῦ cυναcπιcμοῦ καὶ τῆc ἐπιμαχίαc τὰ cημεῖα κομί-
ζουcι. On this rare piece of lore R. Arena (*RIL* 111 (1977), 295–6)
adds Isid. *Etym*. 12. 7. 16–17 'haе [sc. ciconiae] ... maria
transvolant et in Asiam collecto agmine pergunt. *cornices duces eas
praecedunt, et ipsae quasi exercitus prosequuntur*'. So it is tempting to
believe that the crow speaks this line. In Aristotle (*HA* 9. 1. 610ᵃ8)
and Aelian (*HA* 5. 48) crows are special friends to herons.

'The avenger' (ἀλοίτηc) may refer to storks' reputation for
justice (schol. Ar. *Av*. 1353 ff. πελαργοί ... δικαιοπραγεῖc ὄντεc),
and particularly for devotion to their father (*Av*. 1353). Dionysius
(*Av*. 1. 31) illustrates this bird's long memory for kindness and
injury by anecdotes, in one of which the stork makes an alliance
with another (unnamed) bird; see further D'Arcy Thompson,
Greek Birds, s.v. πελαργόc. Since the *Hecale* owes so much to
Comedy, it is worth mentioning Aristophanes' Πελαργοί. We
know very little about that play, but it can hardly be coincidence
that one of the few surviving fragments concerns failure to
support a father (fr. 445 *PCG* οὐ γὰρ cὺ παρέχειc ἀμφιέcαcθαι τῶι
πατρί); two more (frs. 447, 452 *PCG*) refer to the pursuit and
punishment of wrongdoers.

If crows and storks took part in regular punitive expeditions
(note the frequentative force in ἀμορβεύεcκεν), against whom

could their wrath be directed? The only plausible candidate in
our present (defective) state of knowledge is the owl, which
had supplanted the crow in Athena's favour; enmity between the
two species was notorious (see above, p. 225). In fr. 77 someone
curses the owl. According to Ov. *Met.* 2. 595 (from a passage
much influenced by the *Hecale*) the owl is driven away by all
other birds, 'a cunctis expellitur aethere toto' (cf. *Met.* 11. 24–5)
—the crime there attributed to the owl (592, 'patrium temerasse
cubile') might particularly incense a stork. but we have no
evidence whatever that Call. went into the owl's antecedents as
Ovid does.

Many have thought that the bird addressed in frs. 70–4 is an
owl; if so, the crow in fr. 73. 10–12 does not seem to show any
animosity towards her hearer. Nor is it easy to see where in the
Vienna Tablet this joint expedition, which surely must have
occupied quite a few lines, could be fitted (cf. my introductory
note to frs. 75–7). So this fragment still presents a number of
unsolved problems.

ἀμορβεύεσκεν: glossed ϲυνωιδοιπόρει by *Et. Gen.* (for the
iterative suffix see Bühler on Mosch. *Eur.* 86). Words in ἀμορβ-
(discussed by R. Arena, *RIL* 111 (1977), 285–302) are rare, and
(though Nauck conjectured ἀμορβοί for ἀμοιβοί at *Il.* 13. 793)
apparently confined to Antimachus, Call., Apollonius Rhodius,
Nicander, and pseudo-Oppian—Pfeiffer's inclusion of Euphorion
in this list depends on restoration of ἀμο[ρβοί in *SH* 415, col. ii.
15. The basic notion is of accompanying and attending (schol.
Nic. *Ther.* 349 explains ἀμορβεύειν with τὸ ἀκολουθεῖν καὶ
ὑπηρετεῖν). Antimachus seems to have been the originator (fr. 28.
1 ἐπίκουρος ἀμορβέων of a warrior's attendant). In later poets we
find such words applied to nymphs attending a goddess (Call. *H.*
3. 45, Ap. Rh. 3. 881) and, above all, to those who look after
animals, as elsewhere in the *Hecale* (fr. 117 βοῶν . . . ἀμορβοί) and
at Nic. *Ther.* 49, [Opp.] *Cyn.* 1. 132, 3. 295. For the active verb,
cf. Nic. fr. 90 βουκαῖοι ζεύγεϲϲιν ἀμορβεύουϲιν ὀρήων, while the
middle means 'they conveyed for carrying' in *Ther.* 349 (where
ἀμορβεύοντο λεπάργωι may be a curious echo of Call.'s
πελαργὸς ἀμορβεύεσκεν). Finally there is an adjective in Nic.
Ther. 489 ἀμορβαίους τε χαράδρας (also interpolated in *Ther.* 28),
explained by the schol. on *Ther.* 28 with βουκολικάς, ποιμενικάς,
or ϲκοτεινώδεις—the last, according to LSJ, connected with a

Homeric v.l. νυκτὸς ἀμορβῶι for ἀμολγῶι, the evidence for which is murky to say the least (cf. Arena, op. cit. pp. 297–8 with n. 41; *Et. Mag.* p. 85. 20 ἀμορβὴς καὶ ἀμορβές· cημαίνει τὸ μεcονύκτιον. παρὰ τὴν ὄρφνην ἀμορφνής).

ἀλοίτηc: used by Empedocles of Death the Avenger (θάνατον ... ἀλοίτην, (10)); cf. Euph. *SH* 418. 12 (ἀλοίτην*). Lycophron (*Alex.* 936) has Ἀλοῖτιc as a title of Athena.

Fr. 77 (326 Pf.)

αἶθ' ὄφελες θανέειν †ἦ πανύcτατον† ὀρχήcαcθαι: 'I wish that you had died, or danced [? for the last time]'. The comment of Suid. (no doubt from Salustius) shows that this curse is directed against an owl; 'dancing' refers to the dying bird's movements when, blinded by the daylight, it is tormented by children. The curse's 'tautology' (which Naeke (p. 240) ascribed to vehemence of wrath) perhaps glances at the Homeric ὡc ... ὄφελον θανέειν καὶ πότμον ἐπιcπεῖν (*Od.* 5. 308; cf. 14. 274 and *Il.* 3. 40 αἶθ' ὄφελες ... ἀπολέcθαι). We do not know any reason why a human being in the *Hecale* should express such venom against the owl—if she had brought Theseus news of Hecale's death (see above, p. 225), these words would be a possible rejoinder, but it appears from fr. 79 that Theseus does not know of his benefactor's death when he returns to thank her. Pfeiffer's conjecture that the crow speaks this line is in itself attractive, given the traditional hatred between crow and owl (see above, p. 225), but perhaps difficult to reconcile with fr. 73. 10–12 (see ad loc.) if the crow's addressee there is an owl. This fragment may conceivably be linked with fr. 76; for other birds mobbing the owl in daylight cf. also Ov. *Met.* 11. 24–5 'et coeunt ut aves, si quando luce vagantem | noctis avem cernunt'.

†ἦ πανύcτατον†: so the MSS of Suid., except that cod. Coll. Corp. Christi Oxon. 76 has ἦ πανύχιον, whence Naeke (p. 243) conjectured ἦ πάννυχον, followed by Schneider (fr. 43) and Kapp (fr. 65). But Suid.'s comment clearly refers to the owl 'dancing' in the daylight, and thus πάννυχον is inappropriate.

Bentley conjectured ἦ ὕcτατον, which may be right; the problem (discussed at length by Naeke, pp. 240–2) is whether the hiatus after ἦ (cf. West, *GM*, pp. 15, 156) can be justified. Pfeiffer first ruled out ἦ ὕcτατον on metrical grounds (treating examples such as fr. 73. 14 ἢ ἔνδιος as a special case because of the anaphora—see his note on fr. 287 = my fr. 111); but in vol. ii, p. 125 (on *H.* 5. 61) he retracted this argument. Bulloch (*FH*, p. 156 n. 4, on *H.* 5. 48) describes Bentley's conjecture as 'very dangerous'. I myself feel that it may be helped by Homeric reminiscence (*Il.* 1. 27 ἢ ὕστερον*, in anaphora) and would be prepared to accept it in this most Homeric of Call.'s poems. But one should add that, quite apart from the metrical question, ἢ ὕστατον has not pleased everybody; Hutchinson, for example, considers that the tautology is merely feeble. Lloyd-Jones, who objects to the disjunction rather than the tautology, would keep πανύστατον and try θνῄσκουσα before it. He suggests that the participle was corrupted to an infinitive through the proximity of ὄφελες, and then ἢ added in an (unsuccessful) attempt to heal the metre.

ὀρχήσασθαι: cf. the oracle in Hdt. 1. 66 (l. 6*), which Call. echoes also at *H.* 3. 36 διαμετρήσασθαι (= l. 7* of the oracle). ὁ]ρχήσα[σθαι can perhaps be restored in the *Aetia*, *SH* 259. 27*.

Fr. 78 (371 Pf.)

Αἴθρην τὴν εὔτεκνον ἐπ᾿ ἀγρομένῃς ὑδέοιμι: Suid. explains ὑδέοιμι as ὑμνοῖμι, and it is natural to think, with Kapp (p. 12) and Pfeiffer, that this may have been the beginning of a hymn in praise of Aethra and her son, sung by women (whether those who garland Theseus with their girdles in fr. 69. 14–15, or the women of Athens after his return to the city). Women praise a mother for the exploits of her son also in Theocr. 24. 76 ff. πολλαὶ Ἀχαιιάδων . . .|. . . ἀκρέσπερον ἀείδοισαι | Ἀλκμήναν ὀνομαστί. Ovid makes the Athenians sing to Theseus 'te, maxime Theseu,| mirata est Marathon Cretaei sanguine tauri' etc. (*Met.* 7. 433 ff.; cf. W. Weinberger, *Philol.* 76 (1920), 77).

τὴν εὔτεκνον: the adjective comes first in A. *Supp.* 275, and was favoured by Euripides; for the εὐτεκνία of Aethra cf. E. *Supp.* 66.

ἐπ᾿ ἀγρομένῃς: Pfeiffer translates 'coram mulieribus', comparing *Il.* 18. 501 ἐπὶ ἵστορι (which, however, may mean 'at the hands of' rather than 'in the presence of'); he adds that ἐπαγρομένῃς cannot be excluded, since ἐπαγείρεσθαι occurs in *Od.* 11. 632, and ὑδέοιμι might take a dative, as e.g. ἀείδω in *Od.* 22. 346. Campbell wonders whether ἐπ᾿ means 'in the wake of', the single singer *echoing* the praise of the assembled women at large (cf. Hopkinson

(*HD*) on *H*. 6. 1 ἐπιφθέγξαςθε). Several scholars (Bernhardy, Hecker, and Wilamowitz) have wished to emend ἐπ' to ἐν.

ὑδέοιμι: cf. fr. 151 ὑδέουςιν (which, in my opinion, need not be referred to *Aet*. *SH* 257. 33) and *H*. 1. 76 ὑδείομεν (with McLennan's note (*HZ*) on the various forms of the verb). Wilamowitz conjectured ὑδεῖν for ἰδεῖν in E. *Hyps*. *P*. *Oxy*. 852 fr. 1, col. iii. 15, but G. W. Bond in his 1963 edition (p. 27, commentary on pp. 72–3) retains ἰδεῖν. ὑδέω occurs before Call. in Aratus (*Phaen*. 257), later in Ap. Rh. 2. 528, 4. 264 and Nic. *Alex*. 47, 525.

FRS. 79–83   HECALE'S FUNERAL AND POSTHUMOUS HONOURS

Just these few fragments can at least plausibly be assigned to the conclusion of the poem (also fr. 169 inc. sed.). Theseus returns to Hecale's cottage (whether directly from Marathon or after taking the bull back to Athens—see below, App. IV), only to find the neighbours preparing her funeral (fr. 79). Having lamented for her (*Dieg*. xi. 2–3) he institutes honours in her memory: a deme named Ἑκάλη (*Dieg*. xi. 5–6), an annual banquet (fr. 83), and a τέμενος of Zeus Ἑκάλειος (*Dieg*. xi. 6–7, ? fr. 169 inc. sed.).

Fr. 79 (262 Pf.)

τίνος ἠρίον ἵςτατε τοῦτο;: cf. *Priap*. 12. 3–4 (= above, Test. 6) 'aequalis tibi quam domum revertens | Theseus repperit in rogo iacentem'. The questioner is obviously Theseus.

The citation of this fragment in pseudo-Herodian (whom Mrs. S. Argyle is about to edit, revealing his real name to be Cornelianus) runs ὡς ὁ Καλλ. †παρὰ τίνος ἠρίον †τὰ γὰρ τούτων†. The last three words are no doubt a corruption of ἵςτατε τοῦτο, but †παρὰ remains a mystery. Blomfield removed the problem with ὡς παρὰ Καλλ. Others believe that †παρὰ conceals something of Call.'s text (cf. Naeke, pp. 269–70). παραὶ τίνος ἠρίον ἔςτατε τοῦτο (Schneider, fr. 251, accepted by Kapp, fr. 69) fully satisfies neither sense (τοῦτο would be unwanted) nor metre (iambic word before masculine caesura; cf. above, Introd. sect. IV. 4*d*, Pf. on fr. 75. 23 and fr. 618 inc. sed.). τίνος ἠρίον ἵςτατε τοῦτο; reads well as a self-contained question (whether or not the opening words of direct speech).

ἠρίον: 'tomb' or 'mound', once in Homer (*Il.* 23. 126), very popular in Hellenistic verse (e.g. Alex. Aet. fr. 3. 33; Call. *Aet. SH* 254. 7; Anon. (early Hellenistic) *SH* 983. 1; Ap. Rh. 1. 1165; Theocr. 2. 13; Lyc. 444; Nic. fr. 108. 1); cf. κενήριον (Euph. fr. 91 (= Nonn. *Dion.* 13. 186), Lyc. 370) and ψευδήριον (Lyc. 1048, 1181).

Fr. 80 (263 Pf.)

Suid. s.v. ἐπαύλια quotes the whole fragment ἴθι—ἅπαϲιν (other sources give ἴθι—περόωϲι). It is possible to make four continuous lines by some small adjustment to the penultimate, e.g. πολλάκι ϲεῖό ⟨γε⟩, μαῖα, (Pf.). But, while wishing to retain ϲεῖο, Pfeiffer later (ii, p. 120) turned against ⟨γε⟩, which does indeed have the air of a 'remedium Heathianum'. At i. p. 507 he mentions Maas' idea that we have the remains of five lines rather than four, with πολλάκι ϲεῖο at the end of the third (cf. *H.* 4. 119*) and μαῖα at the beginning of the fourth, assuming a more extensive lacuna in Suid. I have followed Maas in setting out the fragment. As Wilamowitz saw (*Kl. Schr.* ii. 37 n. 1), these words would be more appropriate in the mouth of Hecale's neighbours than of Theseus, even though Theseus probably made a similar expression of gratitude and lasting memory (fr. 82).

Naeke (pp. 281–2) thought that these were the concluding lines of the poem—he could still be right, but one would expect the institution of posthumous honours for Hecale (frs. 81–3, ? fr. 169 inc. sed.) to come afterwards. There is a nice balance with the parallel sentiments of fr. 2, which must have stood very near the beginning of the poem.

1–2 ἴθι . . . τὴν ὁδόν: cf. Greg. Naz. *Carm.* 1. 2. 2. 48–9 (*PG* xxxvii. 582) ἀλλ' ἴθι πρόφρων | τὴν ὁδόν. For 'going along the road' as a euphemism for dying cf. Simm. *AP* 7. 203 (= 1 G.–P.). 4 ᾤχεο γὰρ πυμάταν εἰς Ἀχέροντος ὁδόν and Catull. 3. 11 'qui nunc it per iter tenebricosum'.

1 πρηεῖα γυναικῶν: modelled upon the Homeric δῖα γυναικῶν. Triphiodorus 659 has γυνὴ πρηεῖα Θεανώ in a context of hospitality (cf. Gerlaud's Budé edition, p. 168; Livrea, *RFIC* 104 (1976), 451 f.; and my App. III).

2 **τὴν ὁδόν ἦν** = *Il.* 6. 292*, Ap. Rh. 3. 473*.

ἀνίαι: for the rare ῐ cf. Giangrande, *SMA* i. 15.

θυμαλγέες: so Suidas (cf. e.g. *Il.* 4. 513, 9. 387), perhaps supported by the proximity of τρίβους περόωcιν and θυμαλγέα μῦθον in Greg. Naz. *Carm.* 1. 2. 1. 466, 475 (*PG* xxxvii. 557); other sources give θυμοφθόροι. To quote merely from Tragedy (perhaps most relevant here) for the sentiment that pain does not reach the dead, cf. e.g. Aesch. fr. 255. 3 *TGF²* (and *Tr. G. F.*) ἄλγος δ᾽ οὐδὲν ἅπτεται νεκροῦ (with Nauck ad loc.); S. *OC* 955; E. *Alc.* 937.

3 **cεῖο:** often used by Call. in place of the possessive pronoun (cf. *H.* 1. 8, 2. 80, 4. 119, 227). For this reason one may grant to Pfeiffer that whatever emendation or arrangement is adopted in this fragment (see above), it should not involve the obliteration of cεῖο.

4 **φιλοξείνοιο καλιῆc:** Crinagoras picked out these words to represent one of the two main themes of the poem, ἀείδει δ᾽ Ἑκάλης τε φιλοξείνοιο καλιήν (*AP* 9. 545(= 11 G.–P.—above, my Test. 4), l. 3). καλιή is a hut for habitation in Hes. *Op.* 503 (but in ibid. 301, 307, 374, and perhaps in Ap. Rh. 1. 170, 4. 1095, a barn or granary), later usually a bird's nest (in Call. *H.* 3. 96 the lair of a porcupine). The two words are associated in Greg. Naz. *Carm.* 2. 1. 16. 73 (*PG* xxxvii. 1259) φιλοξείνοιο φυτοῦ καθύπερθε καλιήν.

5 **ἐπαύλιον:** the first literary occurrence of this form, which would suggest 'steading', a place where animals took refuge for the night (cf. *Od.* 23. 358 ἐπαύλους and M. Campbell, *CQ*, NS 19 (1969), 273).

Fr. 81 (342 Pf.)

1–2 **τοῦτο γὰρ αὐτήν | κωμῆται κάλεον περιηγέες:** this fragment might belong near the start of the poem, in connection with some etymology of Hecale's name (thus Naeke, p. 103, Kapp, fr. 2)—see on fr. 2. 2. The alternative, which I have judged rather more probable, is that it concerned a 'pet name' (cf. Naeke, pp. 15 ff.) for Hecale, which was reflected in the posthumous honours granted to her: τὴν Ἑκάλην ἐτίμων Ἑκαλίνην ὑποκοριζό-μενοι διὰ τὸ κἀκείνην νέον ὄντα κομιδῆι τὸν Θηcέα ξενίζουcαν ἀcπάcαcθαι πρεcβυτικῶc καὶ φιλοφρονεῖcθαι τοιούτοιc ὑποκοριc-

μοῖc (Plut. *Thes.* 14 from Philoch. = above, Test. 9). Note also, in
the same context, Mich. Chon. ii. 386. 337 (= above, Test. 14)
τὴν Ἑκάλην καλέεcκον. The fragment might have stood near fr.
169 inc. sed. (see ad loc.).

τοῦτο ...|... κάλεον: cf. *Od.* 8. 550 εἴπ' ὄνομ' ὅττι cε κεῖθε
κάλεον μήτηρ τε πατήρ τε. Here too ο(ὔ)νομα might precede, but
this would not be necessary (Pfeiffer quotes A. *Ag.* 1232 τί νιν
καλοῦcα).

2 κωμῆται ... περιηγέεc: could these words reflect the later
participation of οἱ πέριξ δῆμοι (Plut. *Thes.* 14 = above, Test. 9) in
Hecale's cult? Gow and Page suggest that Antip. Thess. *AP* 7.
402(= 66 G.–P.). 3 κωμῆται ὁμώλακεc (of an old woman's
funeral) may deliberately echo Call. The motif of the name used
by the locals is in good aetiological style (Campbell compares e.g.
Ap. Rh. 1. 1221–2 ἣν καλέουcιν |... ἀγχίγυοι περιναιέται).
περιηγής (also *H.* 2. 59, 4. 198) comes first in Empedocles (27. 4),
then e.g. (all περιηγέεc*) Arat. *Phaen.* 401, Ap. Rh. 3. 138,
Eratosth. fr. 16. 3 v.l.

Fr. 82 (cf. *SH* 284, 252 Pf.)

Two related pieces of evidence (Suid. s.v. αὐχμηρὰ τράπεζα and
Mich. Chon. i. 157 Lambros = above, Test. 15*a*), together with a
probable imitation in Nonn. *Dion.* 17. 60 ff. (for the story of
Brongus see on fr. 36. 4–5 and below, App. III), enable us to
detect three words used by Call., and also some sentiments of
Theseus' gratitude for Hecale's hospitality, whether expressed (as
seems most likely) in a speech of Theseus, or in narrative by the
poet.

We may be confident that Call. described Hecale's τράπεζα as
both αὐχμηρή (cf. Mich. Chon. ii. 194. 7, in a context of simple
Attic fare, αὐχμηρὰν καὶ ἄνοψον ... τράπεζαν, ii. 339. 4 τὸ τῆc
τραπέζηc αὐχμηρόν) and ὀλίγη (the latter point made by F.
Bornmann, *Maia,* 25 (1973), 204). P. Bernardini Marzolla in
SIFC 25 (1951), 239–41 (an article of which Bornmann seems
unaware), stresses the importance of Nonn. *Dion.* 17. 60 ff., citing
also ibid. 47. 39 ὀλίγηι ξείνιccε τραπέζηι (sc. Icarius Dionysum)
and Mich. Chon. *Theano* 338 (ii. 386 Lambros) Θηcεὺc ὦφλε χάριν
ξενίηc ὀλίγηc τε μιῆc τε. Call. would not have used Suidas's
form αὐχμηρά, but, as often (see above, Introd. sect. IX), the entry

comes from the commentary of Salustius rather than the text of
Call., and so Schneider's intemperate criticism (ii, p. 192) of
Hecker's apparent slip (p. 112) does not end the matter. What
exactly Call. wrote cannot be determined; Pfeiffer proposed e.g.
αὐχμηρή τε τράπεζα (note also *Od.* 20. 259 ὀλίγην τε τράπεζαν).
The basic meaning of αὐχμηρός (which Suidas here explains with
ξηρὰ καὶ πενιχρά) is 'dry', 'parched', whence it graduates to
'squalid', 'rough' (often of hair) and to 'miserable' (e.g. Manetho
2. 169, 454, 3. 57).

Comparison of Mich. Chon. i. 157 L. ἀεὶ μεμνῆσθαι with
Nonn. *Dion.* 17. 61 ἀεὶ δ' ἐμνώετο suggests that in Call. Theseus
'always remembered' (or 'would always remember') Hecale's
hospitality. Perhaps Michael Choniates' καὶ μὴ ἂν ἄλλην οὕτω
ποτὲ τερπνοτέραν λογίσασθαι (cf. i. 159. 8 ff. Θησεύς ... τὸ
πτωχικὸν καὶ ⟨πρεσβυτικὸν⟩ φιλοξένημα τῆς Ἑκάλης τῆς Ἀττικῆς
ἥδιστον ἐλογίσατο) also goes back to Call.; one might postulate
a similar touch in the *Erigone* of Call.'s pupil Eratosthenes on the
basis of *Pan. Mess.* 9–11 'cunctis Baccho iucundior hospes | Icarus,
ut puro testantur sidera caelo | Erigoneque Canisque, neget ne
longior aetas' (see below for this combination of a guest's
gratitude with lasting honours for the host).

Pfeiffer placed his fr. 252 (Suid. s.v. αὐχμηρὰ τράπεζα) together
with fragments describing the meal, and that may well be right;
Theseus could have expressed his gratitude thus to Hecale in
person before he left her cottage. But it seems to me that such
sentiments would come even more appropriately at the end of the
poem after Hecale's death, in connection with Theseus' establish-
ment of honours which included an annual banquet. Several
sources mention Theseus' determination to make a worthy return
for Hecale's hospitality: *Dieg.* xi. 3–4 εἰς ἀμοιβὴν τῆς ξενίας; Plut.
Thes. 14 ἔσχε τὰς εἰρημένας ἀμοιβὰς τῆς φιλοξενίας τοῦ Θησέως
κελεύσαντος; Mich. Chon. ii. 386. 337 ff. (quoted fully on fr. 83).
Theseus 'will never forget' Hecale's hospitality, and so institutes a
'memorial' for her in the 'annual banquet' which commemorates
the 'small meal' she offered to him. Therefore I have placed this
fragment next to fr. 83 on the ἐτήσια δεῖπν' Ἑκάλεια. Before
leaving this area, we may observe the atmosphere of the *Hecale* in
Triph. 657 ff., where Menelaus saves the family of Antenor,
φιλοξείνοιο γέροντος | μειλιχίης προτέρης μεμνημένος ἠδὲ τρα-
πέζης | κείνης, ἧι μιν ἔδεκτο γυνὴ πρηεῖα Θεανώ (cf. on fr. 80. 1).

The material of fr. 82 would most naturally belong in the speech of Theseus implied by *Dieg.* xi. 2–5 ἐπιϲτε[νάξ]αϲ ὡϲ ἐψευϲμένοϲ τῆϲ προϲδοκίαϲ, ὃ ἐφ[. . .]εν μετὰ θάνατον εἰϲ ἀμοιβὴν τῆϲ ξενίαϲ ταύτηι παραϲχέϲθαι, τοῦτο ἐπετέλεϲεν κτλ.—for the missing word Pfeiffer suggested ἐφ[ρόνηϲ]εν. Castiglioni convincingly transposed μετὰ θάνατον after τοῦτο (*RIL* 70 (1937), 57).

Fr. 83 (264 Pf.)

This fragment may be closely linked to fr. 82. The *Diegesis* mentions two honours for Hecale (see below), but has omitted a third, the annual banquet, which is perhaps alluded to by Plut. *Thes.* 14 τὴν Ἑκάλην ἐτίμων Ἑκαλίνην ὑποκοριζόμενοι (see on fr. 81) and Petr. 135 (= above, Test. 7) 'digna sacris Hecale'. Michael Choniates is more explicit (*Theano* 337–40 = above, Test. 14), whence Reitzenstein claimed the banquet for the *Hecale*:

> εἰ δὲ γρηὶ πενιχρῆι, τὴν Ἑκάλην καλέεϲκον,
> Θηϲεὺϲ ὦφλε χάριν ξενίηϲ ὀλίγηϲ τε μιῆϲ τε,
> καί ἑ θανοῦϲαν ἐνὶ μνήμηι θέτο οὐ θνηϲκούϲηι·
> οὐ γὰρ ἔην νήκουϲτα ἐτήϲια δεῖπν' Ἑκάλεια.

As Pfeiffer says, lines 339–40 may contain echoes of Call.'s phraseology. ἐνὶ μνήμηι θέτο has a Callimachean ring (cf. *Aet.* fr. 7. 24 ἐνὶ μνήμηι κάτθεο and fr. 75. 55 Pf.), likewise ἐτήϲια δεῖπνα (cf. *Aet.* frs. 186. 3, 178. 3 Pf. ἐπέτειον ἀγιϲτῦν). Pfeiffer also quotes Ap. Rh. 1. 1075 ἔνθ' ἔτι νῦν εὖτ' ἄν ϲφιν ἐτήϲια χύτλα χέωνται and Nonn. *Par.* 10. 78 μνημοϲύνην τελεέϲκον ἐτήϲιον, 7.7 ἐτήϲιοϲ ἐγγὺϲ ἑορτή. Each year Hecale's demesmen would invite her to the banquet, as e.g. the citizens of Zancle invite their founders in *Aet.* fr. 43. 80 ff. Pf. For a yearly feast in quite a different context cf. Stat. *Theb.* 1. 666–7 'inde haec stata sacra quotannis | sollemnes recolunt epulae'.

Besides instituting the annual banquet, Theseus named a deme after Hecale (*Dieg.* xi. 5–6 δ[ῆ]μον ϲυνϲτηϲάμενοϲ ὃν ἀπ' αὐτῆϲ ὠνόμαϲεν—see, however, Jacoby, *FGH* iiib, Suppl. ii. 339). He also established a τέμενοϲ of Zeus Ἑκάλειοϲ. Although Plut. *Thes.* 14 does not make the matter wholly clear (Jacoby, op. cit. pp. 340–1), this cult, for which we have no evidence unconnected with Philochorus, Call., or Plutarch, is probably a return for

Hecale's intended sacrifice to Zeus on behalf of her young guest (see introductory note to frs. 67–9). I strongly suspect that fr. 169 inc. sed. Βριληccοῦ λαγόνεccιν ὁμούριον ἐκτίccαντο concerns the founding of the τέμενοc by the local people on Theseus' instructions (Plut. *Thes.* 14 τοῦ Θηcέωc κελεύcαντοc).

On the general topic of honours paid to the eponyms of Attic demes see Whitehead, *Demes of Attica*, ch. 7 (particularly pp. 208–11).

FRS. 84 FF.

Up to this point I have arranged the fragments (not without some speculation) according to what we can reasonably deduce about the order of the narrative. Henceforth this is no longer possible, but, before one resorts to a random arrangement as far as subject-matter is concerned—'secundum fontium ordinem alphabeticum' (Pfeiffer of his frs. 265–377)—it seems worth grouping together some fragments linked by their material, e.g. 'res Atticae' (frs. 84–92, with frs. 93–4 connected to fr. 92 by the theme of pottery) and 'res Argivae' (frs. 95–101). I do not intend to suggest thereby that all the fragments in each group came from the same part of the poem (though at least frs. 84 and 85 may have stood close to each other).

Fr. 84 (266 Pf.)

πολυπτῶκές τε Μελαιναί: being a learned poet, Call. probably has a special reason for crediting Melaenae with 'many hares'; if so, it eludes me. According to the 4th-cent. comic poet Nausicrates (fr. 3. 3 Kock) it was hard to find this delicacy in Attica (cf. Scherling, *Quibus Rebus*, p. 24). But Melaenae borders on Boeotia, whence the Theban brings hares, *inter alia*, in Ar. *Ach.* 878. πολυπτώξ is unique (see on fr. 3 πολύθρονον), based to some extent on *Il.* 2. 502 (cf. 582) πολυτρήρωνά τε Θίcβην, 'Thisbe of many doves'; note the similarity of the 'trembling' (τρήρων) and 'cowering' (πτώξ) creatures. Rhian. fr. 20 πολυδρύμους τε Μελαινάc (an Arcadian town; cf. Nonn. *Dion.* 26. 88 ἀχειμάντους τε Μελαινάc in a catalogue of Indians) may well be an echo of our fragment, which is also a possible source of Stat. *Theb.* 12. 619 'viridesque Melaenae'. A parallel for Call.'s epithet in a very different style would be Catull. 37. 18 'cuniculosae Celtiberiae'.

Melaenae was situated on the border of Attica and Boeotia, and closely connected with Eleutherae (for the shared cult of Dionysus Melanaegis see below and on fr. 85). See Wilamowitz, *Kl. Schr.* v. 1. 177 ff.; Lilian Chandler, *JHS* 46 (1926), 8–12; J. R. McCredie, *Hesperia*, Suppl. xi (1966), 83–4. Stephanus Byzantius claims that Melaenae was a deme of the tribe Antiochis, but, according to J. S. Traill (*Hesperia*, Suppl. xiv (1975), pp. 91. 118) this is misleading in that Melaenae did not technically become a deme until Roman imperial times, and incorrect in that it then belonged to Ptolemais (other scholars, e.g. D. M. Lewis in M. I. Finley (ed.), *Problèmes de la terre en Grèce ancienne* (1973), p. 193 n. 2, have thought of a transfer from Antiochis to Ptolemais).

We hear elsewhere how, when the Boeotians and Athenians fought over Melaenae in the reign of King Thymoetes (after the time of Theseus), an apparition of Dionysus wearing a black goatskin (Dionysus Μελάναιγις) settled the contest in favour of the Athenians. This incident is alluded to by Euph. *SH* 418. 25–6 ἀλλὰ Διωνύcου Ἀπατήνοροc, ὅc ῥα Μελαινάc | ὤπαcε Κεκροπίδαιc, ἱερῆc δείκηλα cιcύρνηc ('locum ubi monstrata est aegis sacra', *SH*); cf. Nonn. *Dion.* 27. 301–7 (discussed on fr. 85 below) and P. Vidal-Naquet, *The Black Hunter* (tr. A. Szegedy-Maszak, 1986), pp. 106–28.

Although fr. 84 looks as though it came from a catalogue of places, and fr. 85 has the air of a learned aside, Nonn. *Dion.* 27. 301–7 might suggest a link between the two.

Fr. 85 (*SH*–; + 305 Pf.)

A scholiast on Ar. *Ran.* 216 Διὸc Διώννυcον ἐν | Λίμναιcιν ἰαχήcαμεν ascribes to Call.'s *Hecale* the words Λιμναίωι δὲ χοροcτάδαc ἦγον ἑορτάc, which can also be recognized in P. Oxy. 853, col. x, 7 ff., a note on Thuc. 2. 15. 4 τὸ ἐν Λίμναιc Διονύcου (normally the copyist leaves a space between lemma and comment, but here he has left the space one word too soon, just as in col. xvii. 32 one word too late). The problem is whether our commentator on Thucydides limited his quotation to the words which we know from the Aristophanes scholiast, or whether, as

Wilamowitz (*ap.* Grenfell and Hunt on *P. Oxy.* 853) believed, he quoted two complete lines of the *Hecale*—later the same commentator gives us an otherwise unknown fragment of Call. (694 Pf.).

Grenfell and Hunt agreed with Wilamowitz on general grounds, but doubted whether space sufficed at the end of col. x. 9 for his εἴ[cατο Λιμναίωι. Pfeiffer was sceptical. In addition to worries about the space, he pointed out that a hexameter ending]η τόν [πο]τ᾽ Ἐλευθήρ would contravene Call.'s metrical practice (see above, Introd. sect. IV. 4*g* on Naeke's Law). So he inclined to the view of J. B. Bury (*ap.* Grenfell and Hunt ad loc.) that the words before the restored Λιμναίωι were prose, with ΕΛΕΥΘΗΡΕΙ a mistake for Ἐλευθερεῖ, dative of Dionysus' title Ἐλευθερεύς. But in that case how was the quotation from Call. introduced? What can one do with the letters ΕΥΔΕ after φηc[ιν]? It does not seem less troublesome to regard the words in question as prose.

Two papyrological difficulties have been raised:

(*a*) The right-hand margin in *P. Oxy.* 853, col. x. W. S. Barrett writes:

We know the position of line-end in 5 (supplement certain and measurable from same letters in next line) and in 15–17 (preserved). A straight line joining them (which will, if prolonged, fit necessary supplements lower in the column) gives for 7–12 lacunae of 8 average letters (*c.* 16 mm.), for line 13 of 7 [*sic*, not 6]. The supplements to be proposed in 7–10 [see below, p. 275] exceed this by *c.* 3 letters (*c.* 4–6 mm.). From this I infer not that the supplements are too long, but that the margin here was irregular; the copyist's margins elsewhere are not absolutely true (note especially xvi. 29–38 in relation to the preceding lines). These supplements on the other hand are either inescapable (7, 9) or desirable (8, 10); and they tally well enough with one another. If the supplements [given by Pfeiffer] in 11–13 are right, the margin will close in again at 11. But I am not convinced that they are right; in particular I expect a ποτε in the end of 12.

(*b*) The doubtful *H* which Grenfell and Hunt read before τόν in col. x. 9.   One must immediately grant to Pfeiffer that, if *H* is correct, the commentator cannot have quoted two full lines of the *Hecale*. Barrett first suggested (on the basis of an old photograph in the Ashmolean Museum, Oxford) that the supposed *H* might

be *I* preceded by the remains of *Δ*. Early in 1985 Dr Walter
Cockle kindly re-examined the relevant parts of *P. Oxy.* 853 in
the Egyptian Museum, Cairo. He reported: 'If you are to read
] . *ΔI, which I think you can* [my italics], the parallel must be
ΔIATHN in line 26 rather than *ΔION* in line 7. There is a fleck of
ink at the level of the tops of the letters before *Δ*, but nothing else
survives at the line beginning.' This 'fleck of ink' before *Δ* could
perhaps be the tip of an iota (Barrett), although no doubt it could
be many other things as well. Excellent new photographs (includ-
ing an enlargement of the crucial area) were taken by Dr Adam
Bülow-Jacobsen of Copenhagen, and now repose in the Univer-
sity College, London, archive. Incidentally, these show traces of
the *Δ* in χοροcτάδαc (line 10) and of the *T* in line 13 ἐν τῆι which
had in any case been restored by Grenfell and Hunt.

Before attempting to progress further, we should consider the
context in Thucydides. The historian, in discussing the physical
extent of Athens before Theseus' synoecism, says that it com-
prised the Acropolis and τὸ ὑπ' αὐτὴν πρὸς νότον μάλιcτα
τετραμμένον. He cites as evidence (2. 15. 4) that the (older)
temples are largely situated in this area, one of them being τὸ ἐν
Λίμναιc Διονύcου, ὧι τὰ ἀρχαιότερα [-ότατα *P. Oxy.* 853] Διονύcια
ποιεῖται ἐν μηνὶ Ἀνθεcτηριῶνι (i.e. the Anthesteria). The papyrus
comment on this consists of (*a*) our fragment of Call., and (*b*) an
explanation of ἐν Λίμναιc, 'the ground there was [?once] marshy',
followed by a reference to Artemis Λιμνᾶτιc in Laconia. One
might expect the fragment of Call. to be relevant to the greater
antiquity of the festivities honouring Dionysus in the Marshes, as
indeed Pfeiffer saw (on fr. 305: 'cultus Limnaeus opponi potest alii
nondum instituto illa aetate').

The most immediately convincing part of Wilamowitz' thesis
was τόν [πο]τ' Ἐλευθήρ | εἵ[cατο, with τόν referring to the deity,
as in *H.* 4. 308–9 ἥν ποτε Θηcεύc | εἵcατο (cf. *Iamb.* fr. 200 b. 1 Pf.
τὴν ὠγαμέμνων, ὡc ὁ μῦθοc, εἵcατο). Before that, as we have seen,
δι or perhaps even ιδι. The dative termination implies Διωνύ[cωι
(Barrett), which also harmonizes well with Λιμναίωι (correction
of Διον- to Διων- causes no worries; cf. e.g. Euph. *SH* 418. 25
with app. crit. at ibid. p. 861). We still need an epithet, ending in
-δι or -ιδι, to follow Διωνύ[cωι, and this is readily available, since
the cult established by Eleuther was that of Dionysus Μελάναιγιc,
already encountered in connection with fr. 84. Compare Suid.

s.v. μέλαν ... καὶ Μελαναίγιδα Διόνυcον ἱδρύcαντο ἐκ τοιαύτηc αἰτίαc. αἱ τοῦ Ἐλευθῆροc θυγατέρεc, θεαcάμεναι φάcμα τοῦ Διονύcου ἔχον μελάνην αἰγίδα, ἐμέμψαντο. ὁ δὲ ὀργιcθεὶc ἐξέμηνεν αὐτάc. μετὰ ταῦτα ὁ Ἐλευθὴρ ἔλαβε χρηcμὸν ἐπὶ παύcει τῆc μανίαc τιμῆcαι Μελαναίγιδα Διόνυcον. Kapp (fr. 94) had tried Διώνυcον Μελαναίγιδα in our fragment. The only remaining problem is ΕΥΔΕ (Dr Cockle confirms that the first *E* is certainly what the scribe wrote) before Διωνύ[cωι. One cannot rule out εὖ δέ (Kapp envisaged a pattern as in *Od.* 3. 188 ff. εὖ μὲν ... εὖ δὲ Φιλοκτήτην), but it would be odd to quote such a half-sentence which is not construable by itself (Barrett), and what could be the relevance to Thucydides? If emendation is required, εὖτε would be an easy change (note Dion. Per. 842 εὖτε Διωνύcοιο χορο-cταcίαc τελέοιεν), but I have not thought of an appropriate sense. Much more promising is Barrett's οὐδέ. Let us consider the results:

οὐδὲ Διωνύ[cωι Μελαναίγι]ιδι, τόν [πο]τ᾽ Ἐλευθήρ
εἴ[cατο, ⌊Λιμναίωι δὲ χ⌋οροcτάδαc ἦγον ἑ⌊ορτάc.

The cult instituted at Eleutherae (cf. on fr. 84) by the eponym Eleuther was transferred to Athens by one Pegasus (Paus. 1. 2. 5; schol. Ar. *Ach.* 243), probably in the reign of the third Attic king Amphictyon (a reasonable but not certain inference from Pausanias). Dionysus Ἐλευθερεύc ('of Eleutherae') was honoured at the 'City Dionysia' or 'Great Dionysia' (A. W. Pickard-Cambridge, *The Dramatic Festivals of Athens*[2], rev. J. Gould and D. M. Lewis (1968), ch. 2). So the point of these lines appears to be that the most primitive Athenians (before the time of Amphictyon) celebrated a festival with choral dances 'not to Dionysus of the Black Goatskin, whom Eleuther established, but to Dionysus of the Marshes': that is, before the institution of the City Dionysia, dramatic and dithyrambic contests (see further on χοροcτάδαc ... ἑορτάc below) took place at the Anthesteria. This would be intelligible, coherent, and not irrelevant to Thucydides. Several features are also very much in Call.'s manner: the learned suggestion that different cult titles in some way imply different deities (cf. *Iamb.* fr. 200a. 1–3 Pf. τὰc Ἀφροδίταc—ἡ θεὸc γὰρ οὐ μία—| ἡ Καcτνιῆτιc τῶι φρονεῖν ὑπερφέρει | πάcαc) and the interest in the comparative antiquity of two festivals (cf. e.g. *Aet.* fr. 59. 5 Pf. = *SH* 265. 5 ff. on the Isthmian and Nemean games) and in the

origins of Athenian drama (cf. Call.'s prose work. frs. 454–6 Pf.;
Pickard-Cambridge, *Dramatic Festivals*, p. 70).

Nonnus combines the (later) Athenian victory at Melaenae (see
on fr. 84) with an apparent echo of this fragment in a passage
worth quoting fully (*Dion*. 27. 301–7, Zeus asks Athena to help
Dionysus):

> αἰγίδα cεῖο τίναccε προαcπίζουcα Λυαίου
> cεῖο καcιγνήτου μελαναίγιδοc, ὃc cέο πάτρην
> ῥύcεται ἐξελάcαc Βοιώτιον ἡγεμονῆα,
> καὶ μέλοc ἀείcει ζωάγριον ἀcτὸc Ἐλευθοῦc
> πιcτὸν ἀνευάζων Ἀπατούριον υἷα Θυώνηc.
> οὐ μετὰ δὴν Φρύγα ῥυθμὸν ἀνακρούcουcιν Ἀθῆναι
> Λιμναῖον μετὰ Βάκχον Ἐλευθερίωι Διονύcωι.

In line 307 Ἐλευθερίωι, which Keydell prints in place of the MSS
Ἐλευcινίωι, is a conjecture made without reference to Call., and
long before the publication of *P. Oxy.* 853, by C. F. Hermann
(*Rh. M.* NF 6 (1848), 448–51). It suggests 'Dionysus of Eleuth-
erae', although of course the proper epithet is Ἐλευθερεύc, not
Ἐλευθέριοc (the latter is a common divine title, particularly of
Zeus, meaning 'deliverer'; I have been unable to confirm Her-
mann's statement (op. cit. p. 449) that it was 'notum usitatumque
Liberi patris cognomen'); the suggestion would be reinforced if,
as Hermann (p. 450) thought, ἀcτὸc Ἐλευθοῦc (304) = 'citizen of
Eleutherae'. The point of Λιμναῖον μετὰ Βάκχον (307) seems to
be, as in Call., that the cult of Dionysus Λιμναῖοc was of greater
antiquity in Athens than that of Dionysus Ἐλευθερεύc.

2 ⌊Λιμναίωι: the site of the Dionysion ἐν Λίμναιc is a much-
discussed puzzle. Thuc. 2. 15. 3 would make us look for it south of
the Acropolis, Is. 8. 35 ἐν ἄcτει, and its name on ground which
had once been marshy. Various proposals have been put forward,
none of them entirely free from objections (see Pickard-Cam-
bridge, *Dramatic Festivals*, pp. 19–25). The most recent discussion
is by N. W. Slater in *ZPE* 66 (1986), 259–63.

χ⌋οροcτάδαc . . . ἑ⌊ορτάc: in the fifth century BC dramatic and
dithyrambic contests were a prominent feature of the City
Dionysia honouring Dionysus Ἐλευθερεύc (Pickard-Cambridge,
Dramatic Festivals, pp. 74–9); Call. may be attributing these in the
earliest times to the Anthesteria, with which their connection is
much more tenuous (see ibid. pp. 15 ff. for controversial evi-
dence).

Although the noun χοροϲταϲία is not so rare (e.g. *H.* 5. 66 with Bulloch's (*FH*) note, often in Gregory of Nazianzus and Nonnus), χοροϲτάϲ occurs only here and in Nonnus' imitation, *Par.* 7. 140 ἀλλ᾽ ὅτε λοίϲθιον ἦλθε χοροϲτάδοϲ ἦμαρ ἑορτῆϲ. Incidentally, one argument for common authorship of the *Dionysiaca* and the St John paraphrase is the fact that the same pieces of learned poetry are echoed in both works (cf. *Dion.* 27. 307, quoted earlier).

I am greatly indebted to Mr Barrett for his work on this fragment, and end by giving the Thucydides scholion (*P. Oxy.* 853, col. x. 5 ff.) with his suggested supplements (continuing as far as ll. 15–17 where the right-hand margin is preserved). In lines 10–11 he restores the name of Apollodorus of Athens, following Pfeiffer's idea (cf. *History*, i. 253 ff.):

```
 5  ἢ ἁ[πάντων] ἤδη ξυντ[ελούντων
    ἐϲ αὑ[τήν· ϲυ]ντελούντω[ν . . .
    τὸ ἐν Λ[ίμνα]ιϲ Διονύϲο[υ· Καλλίμαχοϲ
    μέν φηϲ[ιν] "οὐδὲ Διωνύ[ϲωι μελαναί-
    γ]ι ᵨι, τόν [πο]τ᾽ Ἐλευθὴρ εἵ[ϲατο, ˪Λιμναίωι
10  δὲ χ˩οροϲτάδαϲ ἦγον ἑ˪ορτάϲ". [Ἀπολλό-
    δωρ]οϲ δὲ οὔτ[ωϲ] φηϲὶν [ἐπικαλεῖϲθαι
    δι]ὰ τὸ ἐκλελ[ι]μνάϲθαι [ποτὲ τὸ ἱερόν.
    ἔϲ]τι δὲ καὶ ἐν τῆι Λακων[ίαι λίμνη τιϲ
    ὅπ]ου Λιμνᾶτ[ί]ϲ ἐϲτιν Ἄρτ[εμιϲ.
15  ὧι τ]ὰ ἀρχαιότατα Διονύϲια τῆι ιβ' ποι-
    εῖται·] ἐπὶ τρεῖϲ μέ[ν] ἐϲ[τι]ν ἑορτὴ ἡμέ-
    ραϲ] ια' ιβ' ιγ', ἐπίϲ[ημόϲ ἐϲ]τι δὲ ἡ ιβ'.
```

FRS. 86–7

Two decorative periphrases (originally, I would guess, not too close to each other) for the north wind, Boreas. Call. repeated fr. 87 with words reversed in his *Lock of Berenice* (*Aet.* fr. 110. 44 Pf.); for the style, one could also compare *Com. Ber.* 52, where the west wind is 'brother of Ethiopian Memnon'. Kapp (fr. 11) placed fr. 86 in the description of the storm, where Boreas certainly occurred (fr. 18. 15), but Pfeiffer thinks that at least fr. 86 more probably concerns Boreas' rape of the nymph Orithyia. This was usually set by the Ilissus (e.g. Ap. Rh. 1. 215), but a rarer version

placed it on Mt. Brilessus (Simon. *PMG* 534 (= *LGS* 365) and
Choeril. fr. 5 Kinkel, Colace (see pp. 49–58 in the latter)). The
relevance to *Hecale* could be (Pfeiffer on his fr. 230) that the old
woman's cottage stood on the slopes of Mt. Brilessus.

Fr. 86 (321 Pf.)

γαμβρὸς Ἐρεχθῆος: before the battle of Artemisium the
Athenians received an oracle telling them τὸν γαμβρὸν ἐπίκουρον
καλέςαςθαι (Hdt. 7. 189); they understood him to be Boreas, who
had carried off Erectheus' daughter Orithyia. See Parker, 'Myths',
pp. 204–5. Nonnus often echoes our fragment (e.g. *Dion.* 37. 161,
640, 39. 113, 173–4 καὶ ἴαχε μῦθον Ἐρεχθεύς |"γαμβρὸς ἐμὸς
Βορέης"), which may lie behind Mich. Chon. ii. 212. 10 ff.
Lambros κηδεςτὴς Ἐρεχθέως· ἐκεῖθεν (sc. from Attica) γὰρ
Ὠρείθυιαν ἥρπαςεν, and also Euph. *SH* 418. 14–15 Ἐ]ρεχθέος, ὅς
μιν ἔμελλε |... ἄπο πενθερίοιο (where Lobel would restore
γαμβρός or γαμβρόν before Ἐρεχθέος, so that μιν might refer to
Orithyia). In Ov. *Met.* 6. 700–1 Boreas himself speaks of 'socer
...|... Erectheus'.

Fr. 87 (338 Pf.)

Θείας ἀμνάμων: 'descendant of Theia', once more Boreas—
Theia is mother of Eos who in turn bears the winds (Hes. *Th.*
371–2, 378–80). Pfeiffer wonders whether we should read Θείας
or Θείης (West on *Th.* 135 shows that Θεία is the only well-
attested early spelling). ἀμνάμων is described by Pollux (3. 19) as
even more poetical than ἶνις and κέλωρ. Slightly commoner is
ἄμναμος (a favourite of Lycophron) which some allege to be
Cyrenaean (e.g. *Et. Mag.* p. 84. 43).

In Catullus' translation of the *Lock of Berenice* we find 'pro-
genies Thiae' (66. 44), and Pfeiffer, having himself collated *PSI*
1092 (see i, p. 502: ii, p. ix) saw in the corresponding line (*Aet.* fr.
110. 44) traces not incompatible with ἀμνά]μῳ[ν Θείης (why he
there printed Θείης rather than Θείας, I do not know). He held
that in the *Lock* too Callimachus referred to Boreas (not to the
Sun, as Bentley had believed).

Fr. 88 (808 Pf.)

We learn from Stephanus Byzantius that Call. used the form
Τρινέμεια for the deme of the tribe Cecropis which other writers
called Τρινεμεῖc. Inscriptional evidence (see B. D. Meritt and J. S.
Traill, *The Athenian Agora*, xv (1974), p. 476) suggests that the
Callimachean form may have been commoner than Stephanus
Byzantius implies. Since the river Cephisus rose ἐκ Τρινεμέων
(Str. 9. 1. 24), this deme was apparently in the region of Mt.
Brilessus, near Hecale's home (cf. above, Introd. sect. II). For a
possible location at Kokkinaras see J. S. Traill, *Hesperia*, Suppl. 14
(1975), 51. Call. could have mentioned Theseus passing Trin-
emeia on his way to Marathon.

Fr. 89 (349 Pf.)

One can deduce no more than that Call. described Marathon as
ἐννότιοc, 'moist' (see on fr. 69. 8 ἀπ' εὐύδρου Μαραθῶνοc). The
epithet is unique, though it seems from the scholia that some may
have wished to read ἐννοτίωι as a single word in *Od.* 4. 785.
Schneider (on his fr. 434) postulated a connection with my fr. 16,
in which case one could write ἐννοτίου Μαραθῶνος, ἵν' ἔλλερα
ἔργα τέλεcκεν (Pf.). Several scholars, including Schneider (fr. an.
45a) and Kapp (fr. 91) have followed Hecker in thinking that
Suidas' continuation καὶ "Μαραθώνιον ἔργον" also comes from
the *Hecale*, but Pfeiffer argues that Μαραθώνιον ἔργον, a formula
applied to the Battle of Marathon, is not likely to have been
transferred by Call. to Theseus' struggle with the bull. None the
less we should bear in mind Μαραθώνιον ἔργον as another possible
fragment of the *Hecale*.

Fr. 90 (288 Pf.)

The past tense of ἤμηcε is surprising, in that Minos' war against
the Megarians, which led to the death of King Nisus at the hand
of his daughter Scylla, post-dates the main action of the *Hecale*.
But perhaps it was a case of καὶ τὰ μὲν ὡc ἤμελλε μετὰ χρόνον
ἐκτελέεcθαι (*Aet.* fr. 12. 6 Pf.). I doubt whether this was more than
a passing reference; the transformation of Scylla into a sea-bird
may have been recounted in the *Aetia* (fr. 113 Pf.). As to the

context, we can only guess—Pfeiffer gives a number of possibilities, e.g. a link with the Megarian bandit Sciron (frs. 59–60). Nisus was brother to Aegeus; concerning the division of Attica between the four sons of Pandion see Str. 9. 1. 6, Pearson on his Soph. fr. 24, and Lilian Chandler, *JHS* 46 (1926), 1–2.

1 Cκύλλα γυνὴ κατακᾶcα: in the oldest form of the legend Scylla betrays Megara to the invading Cretans out of covetousness, bribed with a golden necklace (A. *Ch.* 613 ff.). As often in stories of this type (cf. my commentary on Ov. *Met.* 8, pp. 32–5), the girl's motive later becomes love for the enemy commander; we meet this first in an unknown tragedy mentioned by Ovid (*Tr.* 2. 393–4 'impia nec tragicos tetigisset Scylla cothurnos | ni. patrium crinem desecuisset amor'). Love must have been the motive in Call., who calls Scylla a 'prostitute' because she offered herself to Minos. κατακᾶcα is a low word, cognate with e.g. κάccα, καcαλβάζω, καcωρεύω (the type patronized chiefly by Hipponax, the comic poets, and Lycophron). The origin is obscure, perhaps semitic (cf. above, Introd. sect. III); see further P. Chantraine, *La Formation des noms en grec ancien* (1933), p. 352; G. Frisk, *Griechisches Etymologisches Wörterbuch* s.v. καcαλβάc.

καὶ οὐ ψύθος οὔνομ' ἔχουcα: ψύθος is in apposition to οὔνομα (Pfeiffer compares *Il.* 9. 115). Call. suggests an etymology (cf. on fr. 2) of the name Scylla, probably from cκύλαξ (cf. *Od.* 12. 86–7 on the sea monster Scylla, φωνὴ μὲν ὅcη cκύλακος νεογιλῆc | γίγνεται, but there need be no suspicion that Call. has conflated the two heroines). Comparisons of a shameless woman to a bitch go back to Homer (*Il.* 6. 344, 356); cf. e.g. A. *Ch.* 621 κυνόφρων; M. Faust, *Glotta*, 48 (1970), 8–31.

2 Naeke (p. 62) may have been right in suggesting that we should read ἤμηcεν ⟨ἄπο⟩ κρέκα.

πορφυρέην ... κρέκα: the first occasion on which Nisus' lock is known to be purple (in A. *Ch.* 619 it is merely 'immortal'). Although this fragment looks like a passing allusion, it may have sufficed to establish the purple lock as a famous poetic theme (Tib. 1. 4. 63 'carmine purpurea est Nisi coma'; cf. Nemes. *Cyn.* 44); the Latin poets regularly make it purple (e.g. Virg. *G.* 1. 405; Prop. 3. 19. 22; Ov. *Met.* 8. 93; *Ciris* 52) as does Nonnus (25. 162).

ἤμηcε: literally 'reaped' (also Nonn. *Dion.* 25. 164 βόcτρυχον ἀμήcαcα πολιccούχοιο καρήνου) cf. Hes. *Th.* 181 ('according with the implement used', West). The exact Latin equivalent occurs in

Modestinus (Loeb *Minor Latin Poets*, p. 540, l. 6) 'crudelis "crinem" clamabat Scylla "metamus" '. Roman poets more often use *tondere*, to fit the sea-bird κεῖρις into which Scylla daughter of Nisus was transformed (e.g. Prop. 3. 19. 22, Ov. *Met.* 8. 151; ἀπεκείρατο in Nonn. *Dion.* 25. 162).

κρέκα: our only literary instance of κρέξ = 'lock of hair'.
Variation of our fragment may be recognized in Euph. *SH* 415, col. ii. 16–17 ἐκ δὲ τρίχα χρυσέην κόρσης ὤλοψε Κομαιθώ | πατρὸς ἑοῦ (a closely parallel myth—see further above, Introd. sect. VI).

Fr. 91 (297 Pf.)

The Byzantine scholar Arethas, born *c.*850 (see Wilson, *Scholars*, pp. 120–35 (but correct a slip on p. 131—this is the only allusion to the *Hecale*)) says that according to Call. in the *Hecale* the island of Salamis was previously called Κούλουρις. Not all scholars accepted this, because Κούλουρι(ς) or Κόλουρι(ς) was a well established name from medieval to near-modern times for the island/principal town (Salamis)/bay on the west coast (still called 'Bay of Koulouris' in the *Blue Guide* to Greece[4] (1981), p. 205), but we lacked evidence from antiquity. Wilamowitz (on fr. 72 Kapp) even thought that Arethas had confused Salamis with Troezen, and was referring to the epithet κολουραῖος (my fr. 9. 1)! Also Κουλ- does not sound like an ancient form. On the other hand, Call. might well have cause to mention Salamis in the *Hecale*, and he was certainly interested in the old names of islands—cf. the prose work, fr. 412 Pf., and Pfeiffer on fr. 601 (= *SH* 274. 4) ἐν Δίηι· τὸ γὰρ ἔσκε παλαίτερον οὔνομα Νάξωι.

Pfeiffer untypically overlooked an inscription found on Salamis (*IG* ii². ii. 2, *Addenda et Corrigenda*, p. 810, no. 1590a), from the first half of the fourth century BC, which includes the name Κόλουριν, and so goes a long way towards vindicating Arethas; as always seemed likely, the Callimachean form must have been Κόλουρις rather than Κούλουρις. See A. Chatzis, *Ἀρχ. Ἐφ.* 1930, 59–73, who also (pp. 64 ff.) follows in detail Κόλουρι(ς) or Κούλουρι(ς) from the middle ages to the nineteenth century, discussing the significance and original application of the name. The voluminous works of Philochorus included a Cαλαμῖνος Κτίcιc (*FGH* 328 T 1).

It is interesting that two other unsupported statements of

Arethas about Callimachus have been confirmed in recent times by papyri: his note on Paus. 6. 6. 4 by the *Diegesis* on *Aet.* fr. 98 Pf., and that on Paus. 8. 28. 6 by *SH* 276. Of course Arethas could merely have copied the information from some earlier commentator. But in an obscure piece of invective against Leo Choerosphactes (my Test. Dub. 19) he may even name Hecale (together with Icarius who entertained Bacchus), if Wilson (*Scholars*, p. 131 and in *Byzantine Books and Bookmen*, Dumbarton Oaks Colloquium, 1971 (1975), 14–15) was right in wishing to change Ἑκάβηι to Ἑκάληι, an emendation often necessary.

FRS. 92–4

I place together these three fragments concerning pottery, as did Kapp (frs. 87–9) following Hecker, p. 105. Pfeiffer suggested that fr. 93 (his fr. 268) might have to do with simple furnishing (? of Hecale's cottage) comparing Ovid's *Baucis and Philemon*, *Met.* 8. 668 'omnia fictilibus'. This is a possibility, but perhaps a remote one. Fr. 92 concerns high-class pottery (although the point could be that Hecale *did not have* Colian ware) and fr. 94 seems to stress the inadequate wages of the potter.

Fr. 92 (341 Pf.)

Κωλιάδος κεραμῆες: *Κωλιάς* is basically a title of Aphrodite (e.g. Ar. *Nub.* 52), whence the promontory of Attica on which her temple stood was called ἄκρα Κωλιάς, and the district also Κωλιάς. Ancient sources disagree about the site. Pausanias (1. 1. 5, see Frazer ad loc.) says 20 stades from Phalerum, and most of the other evidence can be squared with this; many modern scholars therefore have identified Colias either with the promontory called τρεῖς Πύργοι or with Cape Cosmas (cf. J. J. E. Hondius, *BSA* 24 (1919–21), 156–7, arguing for the latter). If Pausanias is right, Colias would (as Pfeiffer remarks) be in the deme Ἁλιμοῦς, which may also have been mentioned in the *Hecale* (fr. 170 inc. sed.). Strabo, however (9. 1. 21), puts Colias much further south, near Anaphlystos (Anávyso), and N. G. L. Hammond inclines to agree (*JHS* 76 (1956), 48 n. 65).

As Kapp saw (on her fr. 87), Suid. s.v. *Κωλιάδος κεραμῆες* has transcribed Salustius' commentary on the *Hecale*. The subject of λέγει is thus our poet, even though he has not been named by Suidas (similarly e.g. Suid. s.v. γεργέριμον (fr. 36. 4–5) ending λέγει). What follows must be a paraphrase of Call., who stated that the clay of Colias produced the best pots (cf. Eratosth. *ap.* Athen. 11. 482b; Plut. *Rat. Aud.* 42D; schol. Ar. *Lys.* 2). Kapp shrank from trying to restore any words of the original text, but Pfeiffer nicely suggests ἐπὶ τροχὸν οἵ τε φέρονται (or ἐπὶ τροχοῦ) for ὅcοι ἐπὶ τροχοὺς φέρονται.

Fr. 93 (268 Pf.)

The wheel (see on fr. 92 above), clay, and kiln are mentioned by Critias in an encomium of Attic pottery (2. 12–14 Diels, West τὸν δὲ τροχὸν γαίας τε καμίνου τ' ἔκγονον ηὗρεν | κλεινότατον κέραμον, χρήcιμον οἰκόνομον, | ἡ τὸ καλὸν Μαραθῶνι καταcτήcαcα τρόπαιον). For discussion of the technical processes see Gisela M. A. Richter, *The Craft of Athenian Pottery* (1923).

ὕδος: 'water', the nominative *hapax legomenon* (accusative ὕδος perhaps Orph. *Arg.* 1132), formed by analogy (possibly false, see West ad loc.) from the dative in Hes. *Op.* 61 γαῖαν ὕδει φύρειν.

ὀπτήτειρα κάμινος: 'a kiln for firing'. ὀπτήτειρα is unique (see on fr. 40. 2 for Call.'s nouns in -τειρα). Campbell notes the juxtaposition of high-sounding and mundane words.

Fr. 94 (344 Pf.)

I am not certain how Pfeiffer understands this line. He gives references for ἀεικής 'de personis'. But although λάτρις normally means 'a hired servant' (male or female), the meaning here is surely 'wage'; that is the implication of our source (Suid. s.v. λάτρον), and so Trypanis (Loeb) translates the word. λάτριν … ἀεικέα is a variation on Homer's ἀεικέα μιcθόν (*Il.* 12. 435). This 'meagre wage' recalls other fragments of the *Hecale* (52–6) which speak of toil, poverty, and injustice. Concerning the status of ancient potters, see Gisela M. A. Richter, *The Craft of Athenian Pottery* (1923), pp. 98 ff.

παλίνορcον: (Ap. Rh. 1. 416*), once in Homer (*Il.* 3. 33). Trypanis translates 'regular'—could it rather be used as an adverb = 'back', 'in return' (cf. *AP* 7. 608. 3)?

FRS. 95–101

It is noticeable that several *Hecale* fragments deal with matters Argive (from which Statius seems to have drawn some topographical allusions for his *Thebaid*). I have gathered them together (see also frs. 174–5 inc. sed.), without wishing to suggest that they all derive from the same part of the poem. Frs. 99–100 concern Demeter and Persephone (? cf. frs. 172–3 inc. sed.) and, probably, the Argive town of Hermione. Naeke (p. 173) thought that fr. 98 (to which fr. 96 may cohere) described Theseus on his way from Troezen to Athens; this remains possible, though flatly denied by Wilamowitz (*Kl. Schr.* ii. 39 n. 3; cf. on fr. 99 Kapp).

Fr. 95 (307 Pf.)

The mountain Λύρκειον (source of the river Inachus, between Argos and Arcadia) is known from Strabo (8. 6. 7) and schol. Ap. Rh. 1. 125. We also hear of a homonymous town (Hesych. s.v.; Str. 8. 6. 17) and river (Stat. *Theb.* 4. 117, 711). Since Statius probably drew on Call. for Argive geographical references (cf. on frs. 96. 3, 98, 175 inc. sed.), and since Stephanus Byzantius goes on to quote a poetic fragment Λυρκήιον ὕδωρ, it is possible that this too belongs to Call., who would then have mentioned the river as well as the mountain.

Fr. 96 (*SH* 290; 279 Pf.)

Line 3 of this extra piece of *P. Oxy.* 2258 (published by Lobel in *P. Oxy.* xxx (1964), p. 91) can be identified with fr. 279 Pf. It may be worth remarking that the other surviving fragments of *P. Oxy.* 2258 which relate to the *Hecale* (the *Argumentum Hecalae* and frs. 5–6) seem to belong at or near the beginning of the poem.

3 Κενθίππην: an otherwise unknown τόπος Ἄργους, explained by *Et. Gen.* with an unparalleled piece of mythological lore, ἀπὸ τοῦ πρῶτον ἐκεῖ κεντῆϲαι τὸν Πήγαϲον ἵππον Βελλεροφόντην.

πολύκριμγ‿όν τε Πρόϲυμναν: Pfeiffer printed πολύκρημνον, commenting 'epitheton sane mirum loci ascendentis et pensilis, non praecipitis'. Pausanias (2. 17. 2) describes Prosymna as 'the land beneath the [Argive] Heraeum'; for photographs see Carl W.

Blegen, *Prosymna* (1937), ii. 1–2. Our papyrus, however, definitely had πολύκριμνον 'rich in barley' (cf. the Homeric πολύπυρος and Euph. fr. 51. 14 Powell of another place in the Argolid πολυκρίθοιο Μιδείης). The latter epithet is unique; the former less common than one might expect (Bacchyl. 1. 121 and v.l. for πολύκνημον at *Il.* 2. 497). Suidas notices πολύκρημνον, but in this case, Pfeiffer thinks, probably not from the *Hecale*. Although I suspect that Call. wrote πολύκριμνον, *Et. Gen.* implies that πολύκρημνον stood in some ancient texts of the *Hecale* (Stat. *Theb.* 4. 44 'celsa Prosymna' (cf. 1. 383) may come from Call.).

4]cтο[: John Blundell wished to recognize here fr. 98 καὶ δόνακι πλήθοντα λιπὼν ῥόον Ἀ⌋cτε⌊ρίωνος: 'ad sensum optime, sed ε⌊ quoad dispicimus non legi potest' (*SH*). I do have doubts about the placing on the papyrus; one would expect the ρ of πολύκριμνον to coincide with an earlier letter of fr. 98 than the first c of Ἀcτερίωνος. None the less, this idea may be kept in mind (cf. Paus. 2. 17. 2, juxtaposing Prosymna and the Asterion). Pfeiffer was presumably hinting at the same possibility when he placed his fr. 279 before fr. 280 'contra ordinem alphabeticum'. A very long shot: if Blundell were right, Nonn. *Dion.* 47. 495 could make one think of β]όcτρ[υχ- in line 5.

Fr. 97 (*SH* 291)

From the additional piece of *P. Oxy.* 2258 which has fr. 96 on the other side. The Attic form φυλαττε[in line 3 was taken by both Lobel and the *SH* editors to indicate that we have here commentary rather than text (*P. Oxy.* 2258 is rich in explanatory material). Elsewhere, however, the marginal comments (but not the *Argumentum Hecalae*) are written in smaller letters; as P. J. Parsons confirms, the size of letters and spacing in fr. 9 agree closely with fr. 96 on the other side. Also the position of]ιφυλαττε[corresponds to that of]πολυκριμν[in fr. 96. 3. Therefore the fragment seems to come from mid-page rather than a left-hand or right-hand margin, and (although the notes in *P. Oxy.* 2258 are written above and below the text as well as to right and left) more probably from text than marginal commentary. φυλαττε[is perhaps just a scribal inadvertence for φυλαccε[. In *H.* 1. 81 φυλαccέμεν follows the feminine caesura.

Fr. 98 (280 Pf.)

Ascription to the *Hecale* is not certain, but extremely attractive
in view of fr. 96. 3 (even though the papyrus apparently does not
allow us to identify this line with fr. 96. 4). If Wilamowitz (*Kl.
Schr.* ii. 39 n. 3: cf. on fr. 99 Kapp) rightly rejected Naeke's notion
(p. 173) that the subject of λιπών is Theseus on his way to Athens
(cf. my note after fr. 15), we would have no idea to whom λιπών
ῥόον might refer.

δόνακι πλήθοντα: a conventional description of rivers (cf.
epithets for the Eurotas collected on fr. 47. 6).

λιπών ῥόον: cf. *Od.* 12. 1 λίπεν ῥόον*.

Ἀστερίωνος: cf. Paus. 2. 17. 2, immediately after mentioning
Prosymna (fr. 96. 3) ὁ δὲ Ἀστερίων οὗτος ῥέων ὑπὲρ τὸ Ἡραῖον ἐς
φάραγγα ἐσπίπτων ἀφανίζεται. Like many of Call.'s Argive
allusions from the *Hecale*, Asterion reappears in Statius (*Theb.* 4.
122, 714); cf. Nonn. *Dion.* 47. 493 (in connection with young men
dedicating locks of hair).

Fr. 99 (278 Pf.)

A fragment which positively bristles with difficulties of text
and interpretation, many of them scarcely soluble in our present
state of knowledge. First of all, what city is this, where alone the
corpses do not carry a coin to pay Charon's fee? And what earned
it such a privilege? Casaubon (*Lect. Theocrit.* ch. 4, in J. Reiske
(ed.), *Theocriti Reliquiae*, ii (1766), p. 75) first identified the city as
Hermione in the Argolid; according to Strabo (8. 6. 12) the
inhabitants' exemption from the fare was a hackneyed tale
(τεθρύληται). Interesting is Orph. *Arg.* 1136 ff. about an imagin-
ary city far from Greece, ἀμφὶ δέ οἱ χθαμαλή τε καὶ εὔβοτος
Ἑρμιόνεια | τείχεσιν ἠρήρεισται ἐυκτιμέναις ἐπ᾽ ἀγυιαῖς, | ἐν δὲ γένη
ζώουσι δικαιοτάτων ἀνθρώπων | οἷσιν ἀποφθιμένοις ἄνεσις ναύλοιο
[so Hermann for ἀποφθιμένοισιν ἅλις ναῦς ἴα] τέτυκται. This
fantasy might be based on Call. (see Naeke, pp. 208 ff.).

If we are to believe Strabo, the citizens of Hermione enjoyed
free passage because they had a short descent to Hades. Something
else which might be relevant appears in Apollodorus (1. 5. 1):
they told Demeter about Pluto's rape of her daughter (cf.
Richardson on *H. Hom. Dem.* 75 ff.). Demeter searching for her

daughter is the subject of fr. 172 inc. sed., and this is the explanation of our fragment offered by Suid. s.v. πορθμήιον— linked, however, not to Hermione, but to a certain Αἰγιαλός. It does not seem possible to connect Αἰγιαλός with Hermione, as Naeke (p. 211) wished; Barrett considered emending ἐν Αἰγιαλῶι to ἐν Αἰγαλέωι (see *CQ*, NS 32 (1982), 473 n. 23). But an old name for Sicyon was Αἰγιαλεῖς (Str. 8. 6. 25) or Αἰγιάλεια (Paus. 2. 5. 6), although no other source credits Sicyon with remission of Charon's fee; note also Steph. Byz. s.v. Αἰγιαλός: μεταξὺ Cικυῶνος καὶ τοῦ Βουπρασίου καλούμενος τόπος. Call. himself mentions an Αἰγιαλός together with Argos in *H.* 4. 73 (see Mineur (*HD*) ad loc.).

We ought to be able to rely on Suidas (from the commentary of Salustius); yet the case for Hermione remains strong—even stronger than in Naeke's day, since he did not know fr. 100 Δηώ τε Κλυμένου τε πολυξεινοῖο δάμαρτα, which very probably refers to Hermione. There is also fr. 174 inc. sed. εἰς Ἀcίνην Ἄλυκόν τε καὶ ἄμ πόλιν Ἑρμιονήων. Indeed if Hermione's exemption was as well known as Strabo (8. 6. 12) implies, it would be deliberately provocative for Call. to write μούνηι ἐνὶ πτολίων of any other city. So this problem must be left unresolved.

As to the text, Casaubon convincingly emended line 2, but the final words defy restoration. *Et. Gen.* A gives the whole fragment s.v. δανάκης (cf. Suid. s.v. δανάκη), which suggests that this name of a Persian coin occurred in Call.'s text—although there is apparently an attempt to derive δανάκης from the epithet δανός which Call. may have used in line 3. Another problem concerns the extent of the quotation from Call. in *Et. Gen.* A. Pfeiffer believed that it stretches only as far as cτομάτεccι, taking the subsequent words νεὼς Ἀχερουcίας ἐπίβαθρον δανάκης (cf. Suid. s.v. δανάκη including νεὼς Ἀχερουcίας ἐπίβαθρον) as prose. This view certainly avoids much awkwardness. But it is not only a desire to incorporate δανάκης in the text which lends colour to the suspicion that these words may be a part (irremediably corrupt) of the quotation from Call. After νεὼς—δανάκης, *Et. Gen.* continues Ἀχερουcία δέ ἐcτι λίμνη ἐν Ἅιδου, ἣν διαπορθμεύονται οἱ τελευτῶντες τὸ προειρημένον νόμιcμα διδόντες τῶι πορθμεῖ. On the assumption that νεὼς—δανάκης is prose, Ἀχερουcία δέ ἐcτι λίμνη κτλ. would, as Barrett remarks, have to be an explanation of an explanation, which is hard to credit.

Et. Gen. B omits τοὔνεκα—cτομάτεccι, continuing after ἐτίθετο
(rather than ἐτίθεcαν) with Καλλίμαχοc νεὼc Ἀχερουcίαc κτλ.
That is probably not significant, but M. L. West independently
suspected that the Call. quotation is misplaced in *Et. Gen.*, and
that it should read δανάκηc· τοῦτο—ἐτίθεcαν. "νεὼc Ἀχερουcίαc
ἐπίβαθρον δανάκηc" (anon.—perhaps Ἡρακλείδηc ἐν τῶι β' τῶν
Περcικῶν belongs with these words). Ἀχερουcία δέ—ὁ τοῖc δανοῖc
ἐπιβαλλόμενοc· Καλλ. "τοὔνεκα—⟨δ⟩ανοῖc ἐν cτομάτεccι". δανοὶ
γὰρ οἱ νεκροί κτλ. Then Call. is quoted simply to show that those
in whose mouth the coin is placed are δανοί, to support the
proposed etymology of δανάκηc. This would have the effect of
vindicating Pfeiffer's restoration ⟨δ⟩ανοῖc (see on l. 3), but it
seems far-fetched that anyone should have wished to quote these
lines of Call. to explain δανάκηc merely because δανόc was used as
an epithet of the corpses' mouths. On balance I am inclined to
believe, with the older commentators, that νεὼc—δανάκηc is
meant to be a quotation from Call.; to restore the original
wording seems a hopeless endeavour (see on l. 3). But there
remains a doubt in my mind whether Call. is likely to have
mentioned both a πορθμήιον and an ἐπίβαθρον in such close
proximity.

1 τοὔνεκα καί: in the aetiological manner (like μούνηι ἐνὶ
πτολίων, 2). Compare e.g. *Aet.* fr. 63. 9 Pf.; Arat. *Phaen.* 645; Ap.
Rh. 1. 1354, 4. 534; Euph. fr. 57. 2; Dion. Per. 90.

2 μούνηι ἐνὶ πτολίων: cf. *Aet.* fr. 43. 88 Pf. ἐν μούνοιcι
πολίcμαcι and fr. 51 Pf. μόνη πολίων. Correption (see above,
Introd. sect. IV. 7) in the first foot of a hexameter followed by a
preposition is a Callimachean mannerism (e.g. *H.* 1. 48, 2. 59, 3.
47).

ὅ τε τέθμιον: cf. *Aet.* fr. 43. 26 Pf.]. τε τέθμιον[.

οἰcέμεν: for this mixed aorist see on fr. 36. 3, and for -έμεν
infinitives in Call. McLennan's note (*HZ*) on *H.* 1. 81, pointing
out that Call. uses this form only when the metre requires it.

2–3 Charon's fee first appears in Ar. *Ran.* 140, 270 where (for
the sake of a contemporary political allusion) it is two obols. D.
C. Kurtz and J. Boardman (*Greek Burial Customs* (1971), p. 211
and Index s.v. 'Charon's Fee') summarize the archaeological
evidence.

3 δανοῖc ἐν cτομάτεccι: with some hesitation I print Pfeiffer's
⟨δ⟩ανοῖc. The fact that *Et. Gen.* tries to derive δανάκηc from δανόc

may support Pfeiffer (see above). Barrett objects that δανόc, probably connected with δαίω, means 'dry' in the sense of 'combustible'; if we leave aside this passage, in every other known instance it is applied to firewood (see on fr. 32). Casaubon had taken quite a different path, believing that ανοιc is an abbreviation (added in the margin and later misplaced) of ἀνθρώποιc—for such abbreviations see M. L. West, *Textual Criticism and Editorial Technique* (1973), pp. 27–8. This Casaubon emended to ἀνθρώπουc, and Naeke (p. 213), followed by Schneider (fr. 110) and Kapp (fr. 96), started a fourth line of the fragment with ἀνθρώπουc δανάκην.

†νεὼc 'Αχερουcίαc ἐπίβαθρον δανάκηc†: on the whole it seems more probable that these words are meant to be part of the quotation from Call. (see introductory note to this fragment). ἐπίβαθρον is mainly a poetical word: 'boarding fee' also in *Od.* 15. 449, Ap. Rh. 1. 421; 'landing fee' in Call. *H.* 4. 22 (plural); of uncertain meaning in *Iamb.* fr. 196. 23 Pf. For Ἀχερουcίαc we could try Ἀχερουcίδοc, Ἀχερουcιάδοc, or Ἀχεροντείαc. But it is not possible to arrange these words according to Call.'s metrical principles without assuming a considerable lacuna in the text. Casaubon's hexameter ἐν cτομάτεccι νεὼc Ἀχεροντείαc ἐπίβαθρον, though accepted by Naeke (p. 212), Schneider (fr. 110), and Kapp (fr. 96)—the last two preferring Ἀχερουcιάδοc—will not do; the rhythm of the second half would be unusual for Call., and that of the first half virtually impossible (see above, Introd. sect. IV. 4*a* on Meyer's First Law).

As argued above, δανάκηc (this form more plausible than Suidas' δανάκη) probably occurred somewhere in the text; for other eastern words used in the *Hecale* see above, Introd. sect. III. Numismatically, 'whether it was a denomination of the Imperial Persian currency may be doubted. But there are small coins, such as the $\frac{1}{16}$ shekel struck at Sidon ... and the Aradian "obol" ... which were fairly plentiful in Phoenicia and would fit the description' (G. F. Hill in *British Museum Catalogue, Arabia, Mesopotamia, Persia* (1922), p. cxxiv); Hesychius also recognizes ἡμιδανάκιον. For the disputed philological background see H. Frisk, *Griechisches Etymologisches Wörterbuch*, i. 347, iii. 68. Concerning Old Persian *dānaka-, Professor Anna Morpurgo-Davies writes: 'We have evidence from a number of different languages (including Elamite and Sanskrit) for a word which was widely borrowed, was Iranian, and must have existed in Old Persian, though it is not attested in the Old Persian texts we have.' The -ακη(ϲ) termination is typical of words borrowed by Greek from Iranian (cf. W. Belardi, 'Greko μανιάκηϲ tra celtico e iranico', in *Studia Classica et Orientalia Antonino Pagliaro Oblata*, i (1969), pp. 202–6).

Any hope of recovering Call.'s text is rendered even more remote by uncertainty about the scansion. If other Persian borrowings like ἀκινάκηϲ (Hor. *Carm*. 1. 27. 5, perhaps κῑνάκηϲ in Soph. fr. 1061 Radt) and καννάκηϲ (Ar. *Vesp*. 1137) are any guide, one would expect δανάκηϲ originally to have been a cretic. The quantity might have been altered in the borrowing process, or else by Call. himself through metrical exigency; whether he was more likely to make a molossus or an anapaest is a question over which it is impossible to be dogmatic. For general remarks about quantities in Greek borrowings from Persian see A. V. Cassio, *CQ*, NS 35 (1985), 40–1.

Fr. 100 (285 Pf.)

Δηώ τε Κλυμένου τε πολυξείνοιο δάμαρτα: fr. 99 may or may not concern Hermione, but this line is most plausibly connected with the Argive city. Schneider (fr. 478) first compared the *Hymn to Demeter* by Lasus of Hermione (*PMG* 702 = fr. 1 Privitera (1965), from Athen. 14. 624e) Δάματρα μέλπω Κόραν τε Κλυμέ-νοι' ἄλοχον, which Call. may well have in mind. Clymenus too is specially linked to Hermione. Some made him a son of Phoroneus (Paus. 2. 35. 4), but Pausanias himself (2. 35. 9) believes that Clymenus is a title for the king of the underworld. Hermione had a celebrated cult of Demeter Χθονία—cf. Farnell, *Cults*, iii. 320 and Michael Jameson, *Hesperia*, 22 (1953), 148 ff. (with further inscriptions). The three deities are also mentioned together in the opening of Philicus' choriambic *Hymn to Demeter* (*SH* 676 τῆι χθονίηι μυϲτικὰ Δήμητρί τε καὶ Φερϲεφόνηι καὶ Κλυμένωι τὰ δῶρα). Fr. 151 ὑδέουϲιν might precede this fragment (cf. fr. 78).

Κλυμένου ... πολυξείνοιο: πολύξενοϲ of Hades is found earlier only in Aeschylus (*Suppl.* 157, fr. 228 N² and *Tr. G. F.*), but Hades has other epithets as 'host of many', e.g. πολυδέκτηϲ, πολυδέγμων (see Richardson on *H. Hom. Dem*. 9).

Fr. 101 (339 Pf.)

We do not know in what context Call. mentioned the Nemean lion. But the labours of Theseus were often seen as rivals to those of Heracles (e.g. Diod. 4. 59 ζηλωτὴν ... τῶν Ἡρακλέους ἄθλων; Plut. *Thes.* 6. 6; Stat. *Theb.* 12. 584; cf. Homer A. Thompson, *AJA* 66 (1962), 346). Both heroes also enjoyed the help of Athena in their fight against the monstrous animal (cf. A. S. Hollis, *CQ*, NS 32 (1982), 470 n. 3). For a more far-fetched idea see on fr. 13.

Κλεωναίοιο χάρωνος: 'the Cleonaean bright-eyes'. Homer had written χαροποί τε λέοντες (*Od.* 11. 611) and Call. uses χάρων as a substantive, much as Ovid (*Met.* 8. 376) makes a noun 'saetiger' from Lucretius' 'saetigeris subus' (6. 974). Both Lycophron (*Alex.* 455) and Euphorion (fr. 84. 4) follow Call. with a substantival χάρων of the Nemean lion. This kind of expression is usually known as a 'kenning' (the term borrowed from Icelandic). For animal kennings, starting with Hesiod's ἀνόστεος = 'cuttlefish' and φερέοικος = 'snail' (*Op.* 524, 571), see Ingrid Wærn, *ΓΗΣ ΟΣΤΕΑ: The Kenning in Pre-Christian Greek Poetry* (1951), ch. 3. Hellenistic poets enjoy the decorative effect; e.g. in Nicander a donkey becomes 'the brayer' (βρωμήεις, *Alex.* 409, 486; βρωμήτωρ, *Ther.* 357; βρωμητής, fr. 74. 30) or 'the white-coat' (λέπαργος, *Ther.* 349) and a hare 'the nimble creature which sleeps with open eyes' (*Alex.* 67 σκίνακος δερκευνέος). Sometimes kennings are a kind of riddle, as in Lycophron or (the most extravagant example) Dosiad. *Ara* 14, where a snake turns into σύργαστρος ἐκδυγήρας. See my note on Ov. *Met.* 8. 376 for kennings in Latin poetry.

The lion is not Nemean but 'Cleonaean', from the nearby village of Cleonae, mentioned also in *Aet.* 3 (*SH* 259. 37, the story of Molorchus); in similar vein Panyasis had called it 'Bembinetan' (fr. 1 Kinkel, Matthews Βεμβινήταο λέοντος). Probably in imitation of Callimachus (whether *Aetia* or *Hecale*), Latin poets develop a great liking for the epithet, e.g. Luc. 4. 612 'Cleonaei ... leonis' (cf. Sil. 3. 34; Claud. *Ruf.* 1. 285; Aus. 7. 24. 1; more examples in *TLL*, Onomasticon, ii. 490).

Fr. 102 (277 Pf.)

These words may describe a sacred herd of cattle (cf. *H.* 3. 165 and W. Burkert, *Homo Necans* (tr. Peter Bing, 1983), p. 16 n. 21).

Wilamowitz (*Kl. Schr.* ii. 39 n. 2) thought of animals devoted to
Pallas, Pfeiffer of Argive Hera (cf. fr. 96. 3). It may be worth
remarking that the sacrifice of cattle was particularly important in
the rites of Demeter Χθονία at Hermione (see on fr. 100; cf. Paus.
2. 35. 5–7; Aristocl. *SH* 206; M. Jameson, *Hesperia*, 22 (1953),
151 ff.). Pfeiffer also drew attention to ἄνθεα μήκωνος (2) as
possibly suggesting a link with Demeter (cf. Hopkinson (*HD*) on
H. 6. 44)—but in ancient times the poppy was actually cultivated
for cattle-fodder (M. D. Merlin, *On the Trail of the Ancient Opium-
Poppy* (1984) contains all sorts of information).

One might speculate on a relationship with fr. 177 inc. sed.,
perhaps with only one foot in between: βόες ἧχι γέγειαι | ἄνθεα
μήκωνός τε καὶ ἤνοπα πυρὸν ἔδουσι |– ∪ ∪ ὄν τε μάλιστα βοῶν
ποθέουσιν ἐχῖνοι. If by chance this should be correct, ὄν τε could
refer either to πυρόν, or to some yet more desirable fodder
mentioned in the missing foot.

1 βόες ἧχι γέγειαι: (Maced. *AP* 11. 59. 5 ἧχι βόες). Before
Call. only Hecataeus (*FGH* 1 F 362) is known to have used
γέγειος, 'ancient'; our poet has also fr. 510 inc. sed. Pf. ἧ ῥ' ὅτι τὼς
ὁ γέγειος ἔχει λόγος and *Aet.* fr. 59 Pf.(= *SH* 265). 5 γεγειότερον.
The point here could be that the herd, rather than the individual
animals, is of great age (cf. Pfeiffer's 'antiquitus').

2 ἄνθεα μήκωνός τε καὶ ἤνοπα πυρὸν ἔδουσι: μήκων comes
once in Homer (*Il.* 8. 306); πυρὸν ἔδουσι = *Od.* 19. 536 (cf. *Il.* 10.
569 μελιηδέα πυρὸν ἔδοντες of Diomedes' horses). For ἤνοπα see
on fr. 18. 2 οὐρανὸς ἤνοψ (Homer uses only the dative). Reitzen-
stein commented on our fragment 'lepide ... descripsit flavam
segetem rubris papaveris floribus distinctam' (cf. de Jan, *de
Callimacho*, pp. 45–6).

Fr. 103 (302 Pf.)

This piece of mythological polemic ranks among the most
puzzling fragments of the *Hecale*. Naeke (pp. 46 ff.) and Schneider
(fr. 48) not unreasonably believed the target to be Call.'s fellow
poets or scholars, but we now know at least that the *Hecale*
contained no prologue in which such topics could perhaps most
conveniently be aired. The spirit seems akin to that of fr. 113. If it
reminds me of anything in another epyllion, that would be *Ciris*

303 ff. (spoken by the nurse Carme!) 'unde alii fugisse ferunt et nomen Aphaeae | virginis assignant; alii, quo notior esses,| Dictynnam dixere tuo de nomine Lunam', or the extended argument (*Ciris* 54 ff.) about whether or not Scylla daughter of Nisus should be identified with Scylla the sea monster.

The earliest certain literary identification of Apollo with Helios is in E. *Phaeth.* 225 Ἀπόλλων δ' ἐν βροτοῖc ὀρθῶc καλῆι—Diggle ad loc. argues that it is also implied in A. *Supp.* 212–14 (reading ἷνιν for ὄρνιν in 212). This idea may well have been more widespread (cf. Page, *PMG* 860; Jeffrey S. Rusten, *Dionysius Scytobrachion* (1982), p. 33 n. 18). F. Williams would see it behind Call. *H.* 2. 9 φαείνεται. But the people referred to here are not content with separating Apollo from Helios; neither will they allow that Persephone is the same as Artemis. While the first identification may have been commoner than we can now appreciate, the second was very much a minority opinion. Herodotus (2. 156; cf. Paus. 8. 37. 6) describes it as Egyptian, and attributes to Aeschylus (fr. 333 N² and *Tr. G. F.*) ἐποίηcε γὰρ Ἄρτεμιν εἶναι θυγατέρα Δήμητροc. Compare Servius on Virg. *Ecl.* 3. 26 'novimus eandem esse Proserpinam quam Dianam'. Some also made Hecate (often identified with Artemis) a daughter of Demeter; see Pf. on his fr. 466, which he inclines to ascribe to one of Call.'s prose works.

So the subject of this fragment appears to be those who, in general, distinguish gods whom others might conflate. Pfeiffer rightly says that one cannot deduce Call.'s own opinion either from the lines themselves or from the Pindar scholiast who quotes them. Although the tone most naturally suggests disapproval of the χωρίζοντεc, we do not know who is speaking—the fact that the *Ciris* poet puts mythological polemic into the mouth of an old nurse (303 ff.) should serve as a warning that few things can be ruled out in a learned *jeu d'esprit*. If these lines are not direct speech, Call. could either be criticizing others, or giving the views of critical opponents with whom he disagrees. Perhaps he is playing the favourite Hellenistic game of championing an unusual (unitarian) cause in order to be provocative.

1 παναρκέοc 'Ηελίοιο: τοῦ πανταχῆ λάμποντοc (Suid.). Call. may have read ἰὼ παναρκεῖc θεοί in A. *Sept.* 166 (Page (OCT) and Hutchinson prefer παναλκεῖc). Ael. fr. 101 (Suid. s.v. Ἀρίcταρχοc Τεγεάτηc) ἥλιόν τε ὁρᾶν καὶ τοῦ θεοῦ τοῦ τοcούτου τῆc παναρκοῦc ἀμιcθὶ μεταλαμβάνειν ἀκτῖνοc seems to come from our poet.

2 χῶρι: this form occurs on inscriptions from Thera, Cyrene, Crete and Cos (see F. Bechtel, *Die griechischen Dialekte*, ii. 762).

καὶ εὔποδα Δηωίνην: for the un–Homeric epithet cf. Sapph. 103. 5 L.–P. τὰν εὔποδα νύμφαν. Persephone is τανίσφυροc in *H. Hom. Dem.* 77. I accept Valckenaer's correction Δηωίνην for Δηιώνην (see Naeke, p. 43), even though Δηιώνηι was written in the papyrus of Anon. *SH* 927b. 7 (? influenced by Διώνη two lines above). From the time of Homer (*Il.* 5. 412 Ἀδρηcτίνη, 9. 557 Εὐηνίνηc) the feminine patronymic/matronymic in -ίνη provided a convenient ending for hexameters with a spondaic fifth foot. Call. seemingly used Νωνακρίνη* twice (fr. 140 and *Aet. SH* 250. 9). One can quote numerous examples (all*) from Hellenistic, late Greek, and Roman poetry; e.g. *SH* 962. 9 (anonymous elegiacs) Λητωίνη; Dion. Per. 490 Αἰητίνηc; Max. 191 Θειαντίνη; Catull. 64. 28 'Nereine' (cf. Opp. *Hal.* 1. 386, Quint. Smyrn. 3. 125 etc., and my App. V(*g*)).

Fr. 104 (273 Pf.)

Ἀπόλλωνοc ἀπαυγή: quoted anonymously by *Et. Gen.* B (*Et. Mag.*), and given to the *Hecale* by Pfeiffer on the basis of Suid. s.v. ἀπαύγαcμα. Homer often has ἠελίου τ' αὐγή *vel sim.* (e.g. *Od.* 12. 176; cf. Richardson's parallels for *H. Hom. Dem.* 35), and Apollo here may well be the sun (see on fr. 103 above). If so, could fr. 103 be a provocative justification of Ἀπόλλωνοc ἀπαυγή, pouring scorn on any potential objectors by claiming that Apollo and Helios are identical, and then, for good measure, throwing in an even more controversial proposition about Persephone and Artemis?

Fr. 105 (265 Pf.)

ὅθεν ἠληλούθειν: 'whence I had come'. This unique form of the pluperfect is, according to Choeroboscus, based upon analogy with ἠληλίφειν, ἠνηνόχειν. Thus it seems preferable to print ἠλ- rather than Suidas' εἰληλούθειν (a lemma without comment). εἰλ- would be the Homeric form (and ἐλ- the Attic); εἰληλούθει* appears six times in the *Iliad*, twice (4. 520, 5. 44) with a variant ἠλ-. See further W. Schulze. *Quaestiones Epicae* (1892), p. 259. In fr. 8 Call. uses the perfect εἰλήλουθαc.

Fr. 106 (270 Pf.)

γέντο δ' ἀλυκρά: ἀλυκρός = 'lukewarm' is found elsewhere only in Nic. *Alex.* 386 ἀλυκρότερον. A greater degree of heat is implied by θαλυκρός (fr. 736 inc. auct. Pf.; cf. Agath. *AP* 5. 219. 1). The position of these words in the line is of some interest. If Call. maintains the convention that γέντο = ἐγένετο (not Homeric, but in Hes. *Th.* 199, 283, 705) should not follow the bucolic diaeresis (see on fr. 66. 1), then, since the beginning of the line is ruled out by Meyer's First Law (above, Introd. sect. IV. 4*a*), there remains only the unobjectionable - ∪ ∪ γέντο δ' ἀλυκρά.

Fr. 107 (276 Pf.)

δέκα δ' ἄστριας αἴνυτο λάτρον: Pfeiffer (who suspected that we should read ἄρνυτο for αἴνυτο) remarks that ten knucklebones as a reward would hardly suit anyone but a child. Five ἀστράγαλοι usually made up a set (cf. the verb πεντελιθίζειν) as in fr. 676 inc. sed. Pf. (also the only parallel for the form ἄστρις) ζορκός τοι, φίλε κοῦρε, Λιβυστίδος αὐτίκα δώσω | πέντε νεοσμήκτους ἄστριας. In Asclep. *AP* 6. 308(= 27 G.–P.). 2 a boy receives 80 knucklebones (a number which puzzles G.–P.) as a prize for handwriting.

λάτρον: also A. *Suppl.* 1011 (cf. λάτριν in fr. 94).

Fr. 108 (343 Pf.)

οὐδ' οἶσιν ἐπὶ κτενὸς ἔσκον ἔθειραι: although κτείς can mean *pudenda muliebria* (e.g. Phld. *AP* 5. 132(= 12 G.–P.). 2), there is no need whatever to change οἶσιν to αἶσιν (Hecker). The reference of these words is quite unknown—conceivably the two boys about whom Hecale speaks in frs. 48–9? For ἔθειρα of human as opposed to animal hair cf. *H. Hom. Aphr.* 228; A. *Ch.* 175; E. *Hel.* 632. Fr. 543 inc. sed. Pf. ἀπότριχες . . . οἱ ἄνηβοι is on the same subject, but probably unconnected with this fragment.

Fr. 109 (282 Pf.)

A contribution to the long-standing debate about which of the senses carries most conviction. The majority view is expressed in Herodotus' ὦτα . . . ἀπιστότερα ὀφθαλμῶν (1. 8), which became proverbial (see A. Otto, *Sprichwörter der Römer* (1890), s.v. oculus 9 and Brink on Hor. *Ars* 181); Heraclitus had earlier said the same (fr. 101a D.-K.⁶). Empedocles is more cautious (fr. 4. 10 Diels, *Poetarum Philosophorum Fragmenta* (1901) = fr. 3. 10 D.-K.⁶) μήτε τιν' ὄψιν ἔχων πίϲτει πλέον ἢ κατ' ἀκουήν. A definite preference for the ears is stated by Strabo (2. 5. 11, perhaps from Call.). See further Fraenkel, *Horace* (1957), p. 393 n. 3 (suggesting that Call. may be influenced by Aristotle) and Brink on Hor. *Ep.* 2. 1. 187–8 'migravit ab aure voluptas | omnis ad incertos oculos et gaudia vana', where Porphyrion comments 'secundum Academicos, qui contenderunt oculos nostros in multis falli et ideo visibus non esse credendum, cum sit in pluribus rebus certius quod audiatur'. Call. stresses the importance of the ears also in the *Aetia*, frs. 43. 16 and 178. 30 Pf. Finally, one might argue that touch is more reliable than either sight or hearing (e.g. Lucr. 5. 100–3, partly at least from Emp. fr. 133 Diels and D.-K.⁶).

1 ὀκκόϲον . . . ὄϲϲον: ὄϲϲον is demonstrative, as probably in Theocr. 4. 39 (see Gow ad loc.) and in an anonymous hexameter from Plutarch as emended by Lobel (*CQ* 23 (1929), 118). See further Hopkinson (*HD*) on *H.* 6. 30 and S. Timpanaro, *Contributi di filologia e di storia della lingua latina* (1978), 263–5.

2 εἰδυλίϲ: 'knowing', an unparalleled feminine.

Fr. 110 (286 Pf.)

λάκτιν: normally a pestle, but 'ladle' here and in Nicander's imitation (*Ther.* 109 εὐεργῆ λάκτιν). Both Suidas and schol. *Ther.* 109 explain with τορύνη. See Naeke, p. 141.

Fr. 111 (287 Pf.)

This fragment might belong with others (particularly frs. 52–3) which describe toil and hardship. But if the sense of ἄφαρον is τὴν λιπαρὰν γῆν rather than τὴν μηδὲν φέρουϲαν (both explanations are given), the atmosphere seems redolent of fruitfulness and prosperity.

ἤ: (so at least *Et. Gen.* A s.v. φάρυγξ and B s.v. ἀφαυρόϲ— according to Gaisford the MSS of *Et. Mag.* s.v. ἀφαυρόϲ have ἤ) often followed by hiatus, particularly when there is anaphora of ἤ (at the start of a line in *H.* 5. 48, 6. 86, in the middle of a line at *Hec.* fr. 74. 14; cf. on fr. 77).

ἄφαρον φαρόωϲι: φάροϲ usually means a robe, but a marginal comment on Alcm. *PMG* 1. 61 runs Ϲωϲιφάνηϲ ἄροτρον. See Page's discussion (*Alcman, The Partheneion* (1951), pp. 78–9). For this sense Herodian adds Antim. fr. 119 Wyss (unfortunately the text is corrupt); and note Hesych. s.v. βούφαρον· τὴν εὐάροτον γῆν. φάροϲ γὰρ ἡ ἄροϲιϲ. The implication of ἄφαρον, 'unploughed' is more probably τὴν λιπαρὰν γῆν καὶ τὴν ⟨μήπω⟩ πολλάκιϲ ἀροτριωθεῖϲαν than τὴν μηδὲν φέρουϲαν (*Et. Gen.* offers both).

Call. is the only Hellenistic poet to pick up this rarity, unless Sosiphanes of the Alcman scholion was a tragedian (cf. Page, op. cit. p. 10). Snell (*Tr. G. F.* i) distinguishes two holders of this name (no. 92 who died in the second half of the fourth century and no. 103, born in 306/5 BC), but does not include the scholion under either. Although Ϲωϲιφάνηϲ ἄροτρον sounds more like a scholar than a poet, many Hellenistic men of letters combined both functions.

φιν: see on fr. 69. 4 (δέ φιν* also Nic. *Alex.* 124).

ὄμπνιον ἔργον: 'agricultural work' (compare App. V(i) ταλα-ϲήϊον ἔργον, 'wool-working'); the essence of the epithet seems to be 'nourishing' or 'well-nourished'. ὄμπνιοϲ is a rare Attic word, found in Soph. fr. 246 Radt, Pearson (cf. Moschion, fr. 6. 10 Snell and N²) ὀμπνίου νέφουϲ (glossed as μέγα, πολύ, ηὐξημένον, but Pearson wonders whether it could denote the rain-cloud's fertiliz-ing power), and restored as a title of Demeter in an Attic inscription of Roman imperial date. If we can trust schol. Ap. Rh. 4. 989, Philetas ἐν Ἀτάκτοιϲ Γλώϲϲαιϲ (fr. 44 Kuchenmüller) explained ὄμπνιον ϲτάχυν (? from an unknown tragedy, as in Lyc. *Alex.* 621) with τὸν εὔχυλον ('juicy') καὶ τρόφιμον. Conceivably Philetas used ὄμπνιοϲ also in his elegiac poem *Demeter* (see A. S. Hollis, 'Callimachus, *Aetia*, fr. 1. 9–12', *CQ* NS 28 (1978), 402 n. 3 on *Aet.* fr. 1. 10 Pf. ὄμπνια Θεϲμοφόροϲ). Thereafter the epithet became very popular (e.g. Eratosth. fr. 16. 17 Powell, ten times in Nonn. *Dion.*). Call. uses it again in the *Hecale* (fr. 144 ὄμπνιον ὕδωρ).

On Call.'s non-observance of the digamma here (contrast Max. 528 ὄμπνια ἔργα) see on fr. 16 ἕλλερα ἔργα.

Fr. 112 (289 Pf.)

The reference is unknown, but ϲιπαλόϲ has three terminations; thus the person described was apparently male. It is worth noting,

however, that Hesychius has a lemma ϲιπαλή, coupled, as Pfeiffer
says, with a comment more appropriate to ἔφηλοϲ.

ϲιπαλόϲ: ὁ ἄμορφοϲ (Suid.). Not found elsewhere outside
grammarians and lexica, but connected with ϲιφλόϲ.

ὀφθαλμοῖϲιν ἔφηλοϲ: having white specks in the eye; cf. Sext.
Emp. *adv. Math.* 7. 233 (ii, p. 55 Mutschmann) ἐφηλότηϲ λέγεται
λευκότηϲ ἐν ὀφθαλμῶι; Ael. *HA* 15. 18 on the victims of the
ϲηπεδών (from Nic. *Ther.* 320–33) τοὺϲ ὀφθαλμοὺϲ ἀχλὺϲ κατέχει
καὶ ἔφηλοι γίνονται: LXX Lev. 21. 20 ἢ ἔφηλοϲ ἢ πτίλοϲ τοὺϲ
ὀφθαλμούϲ (for Call. and the Septuagint see on fr. 49. 15).

Fr. 113 (291 Pf.)

On the identity of the morning star and the evening star. The
first poet to assert this was Ibycus (*PMG* 331) and the first
philosopher either Pythagoras or Parmenides (see on Call. fr. 442
Pf.). Olympiodorus, who quotes the fragment, holds that the
same star appears twice on the same day, i.e. is ἀμφιφανήϲ (in the
latitude of Greece, the planet Venus *can* be seen before sunrise and
after sunset on the same day), but does not credit Call. with such a
view.

Probably because of Call.'s influence, this subject became a
cliché among Roman neoteric poets: Catull. 62. 34–5 'nocte latent
fures, quos idem saepe revertens,| Hespere, mutato comprendis
nomine Eous' [*Schrader:* eosdem *codd.*]; Cinna, fr. 6. 1–2 Buechner
'... Eous |... Hesperus idem'; *Ciris* 351–2:

> quem pavidae alternis fugitant optantque puellae,
> Hesperium vitant, optant ardescere Eoum.

R. O. A. M. Lyne in his commentary argues, perhaps too
cautiously, for *indirect* imitation of Call. by the *Ciris* poet; he
suggests Cinna as a possible intermediary. But Cinna, fr. 6 does
not reproduce Call.'s structure in the same way as *Ciris* 352, and it
seems unlikely that Cinna would have used the motif twice in his
Zmyrna. Much more material is gathered by Ellis in his commen-
tary on Catullus—though he rejects Schrader's emendation as
'clever but weak'! See also A. Le Bœuffle, *REL* 40 (1962) 120–5;
D. A. Kidd, *Latomus*, 33 (1974), 22–33 (with scientific as well as
mythological lore).

Many scholars have approved the idea of Bentley that those

who love the evening star but hate the morning star are newly-
wed husbands. The *Ciris* poet would then be neatly reversing
Call. when he applies the pattern to timorous girls who dread the
evening but long for the morning (351–2, quoted above). We
may also compare Catull. 62, where the girls' 'Hespere, quis caelo
fertur crudelior ignis?' (20) is answered by the young men with
'Hespere, quis caelo lucet iucundior ignis?' (26). For Hesperus and
the Epithalamium see Lyne on *Ciris* loc. cit. and Q. Cataudella,
Museum Criticum 5–7 (1970–2), 155–63 (his restoration of Call.'s
first line should not win many friends). Bentley may well have
been right, though one can think of other people who have reason
to long for the evening and dread the morning, e.g. tired
workmen (Kapp on her fr. 103) or thieves (cf. fr. 74. 23–4 and
Catull. 62. 34–5 quoted above).

   Even if we could be quite sure to whom αὐτοί (2) refers, we
would still need to know for what purpose Call. used this conceit.
Perhaps simply as an indication of time (Pf.); poets like to
embroider allusions to the time of day (see on fr. 74. 23 ff.).
Barrett (his *exempli gratia* restoration given below in my note to l.
1) thinks of the dawn when Theseus rises to go out against the
Marathonian bull (*Dieg.* x. 31–2). John Tzetzes, however, states
quite explicitly that the reference is to inconstancy of friendship
(*Chil.* viii. 830 ff., p. 335 Leone; cf. *ep.* 43, p. 63 Leone:

> Ὁ ποιητὴς Καλλίμαχος οὗτος ὁ Κυρηναῖος
> περί τινος οὐ cῴζοντος cτάcιν ἐν τῆι φιλίαι
> ἀλλὰ μετολιcθαίνοντος καὶ μετατρεπομένου
> ταῦτα φηcὶ κατὰ ῥητὸν ἅπερ ἀκούων μάθε·
> "Ἑcπέριον φιλέουcιν, ἀτὰρ cτυγέουcιν ἑῶιον."

'Errat bonus vir' was Bentley's comment, and Tzetzes has
received short shrift from most modern scholars (e.g. Kapp:
'neglegi potest, quod Io. Tzetzes versum tertium de amico
inconstanti bis accepit, cum seiunctum eum legisse videatur').
That he (or indeed Eustathius) knew only the third line is,
however, no more than an assumption; supposing that he did,
Byzantinists whom I have consulted differ as to whether it would
be characteristic of Tzetzes simply to invent a context. N. G.
Wilson (*Scholars*, p. 196) grants that Tzetzes may have had access
to a complete Callimachus; recently, on his evidence alone, frs.
496 and 533 Pf. have been combined to form *SH* 295.

Although it seems most natural to interpret the fragment as a simple indication of time, one should at least mention Naeke's 'via media' (pp. 38–9) between Tzetzes and Bentley, using the morning and evening star as an analogy for human fickleness: 'quod in stellis accidat, ut eandem iidem, scil. sponsi, et ament et perhorrescant, ament vespertinam, matutinam odio habeant, idem cerni in hominibus, ut eundem iidem ament et perhorrescant, vespertinam ament, oderint matutinum'. Scholars who followed this path tended to think of literary animosities (cf. on fr. 103), e.g. Schneider on his fr. 52 ('apta autem erit sententia, si illis verbis virorum doctorum de aequalium operibus iudicium fluctuans et semper mutabile significari putaveris') or Legrand (*REG* 7 (1894), 281–3), who envisaged a polemical prologue (we now know that the *Hecale* did not open with a prologue). But mutability is not confined to men of letters—and in any case we have no idea who is speaking.

1 ἡνίκα μὲν γὰρ †φαίνεται τοῖc ἀνθρώποιc ταῦτα†: while ἡνίκα μὲν γάρ may be Callimachus (for the rhythm see above, Introd. sect. IV. 4*c*), the words between cruces represent Olympiodorus' paraphrase, from which the original text can hardly be recovered; perhaps, as Naeke (p. 40) and others have thought, the paraphrase spans more than one line. Of attempts at restoring a single line, most credence has been given to Hecker's ἡνίκα μὲν γὰρ ταὐτὰ φαείνεται ἀνθρώποιcιν. The ending gains some slight plausibility from Dion. Per. 36–7 αὐτὰρ ὅθι πρώτιcτα φαείνεται ἀνθρώποιcιν | ἠῶιον καλέουcι (cf. ibid. 451; Arat. *Phaen.* 135 ἔτι φαίνεται ἀνθρώποιcιν). But Naeke reasonably asked (p. 39) 'quorsum ταῦτά? Dicendum fuerat ὁ αὐτόc' (sc. the Ἀφροδίτηc ἀcτήρ). As a specimen of an extended restoration, Barrett produces (purely *exempli gratia*) ἡνίκα μὲν γὰρ νὺξ ἔτ᾽ ἔην, ἐπετέλλετο δ᾽ ἀcτήρ | πάντων ἀνθρώποιcι φαάντατοc, ὅν περ ἔριθοι | αὐτοὶ μὲν φιλέουc᾽ κτλ.

2–3 The repetition in successive lines with antithesis and variation is a particularly sharp instance of a characteristic Callimachean phenomenon (cf. e.g. Bulloch (*FH*) on *H.* 5. 70–84). In Homer we find patterns like *Il.* 22. 127–8 τῶι ὀαριζέμεναι, ἅ τε παρθένοc ἠΐθεόc τε,| παρθένοc ἠΐθεόc τ᾽ ὀαρίζετον ἀλλήλοιιν. See D. Fehling, *Die Wiederholungsfiguren und ihr Gebrauch bei den Griechen vor Gorgias* (1969), p. 185 and *passim*; Lapp, *Tropis et Figuris*, pp. 54–9. I would guess that these lines are the model for not only

Ciris 351–2 (above), but also Euphorion (who introduces a chiasmus of the verbs) on the dog-star which brings both bane and benefit (*SH* 443. 8–9) δὴ γάρ . [.]το [cί]νεται ἠδ᾽ ὀνίνηcιν· | εὖ φραcθ]εὶc ὀνίνη[cιν, ἐcίνα]το δ᾽ εὖτε λάθηιcι.

2 φιλέουc᾽: elision at the masculine caesura also occurs in *H.* 6. 65 and *epigr.* 42 Pf.(= *AP* 12. 118 = 8 G.–P.). 1, 3. Here, as often (cf. on fr. 17. 11), the prominent repetition of a word (αὐτοί) excuses a metrical rarity.

δέ τε: the only instance in Call. of the Homeric and Hesiodic δέ τε *metri gratia* (cf. J. D. Denniston, *Greek Particles²* (1954), pp. 530–1), though Pfeiffer wondered about δέ ce with an apostrophe (cf. Opp. *Hal.* 4. 31; [Opp.] *Cyn.* 2. 418). Probably δέ τε should be accepted as one small illustration of the fact that the *Hecale* is closer than Call.'s other poems to Homer.

πεφρίκαcιν: cf. *Il.* 24. 775 πάντεc δέ με πεφρίκαcιν*; Ap. Rh. 1. 689*, 4. 1341*; [Opp.] *Cyn.* 2. 459.

3 ἑcπέριον φιλέουcιν, ἀτὰρ cτυγέουcιν ἑῶιον: Lapp (*Tropis et Figuris*, pp. 40–2) collects examples of chiasmus in Call. This line was much imitated, e.g. *Ciris* 352 (quoted earlier); Greg. Naz. *Carm.* 2. 1. 1. 186 (*PG* xxxvii. 984) πρίν τι λαβεῖν τίουcιν, ἀτὰρ cτυγέουcι λαβόντεc; [Apollinar.] *Ps.* 118. 210 θεcμὸν còν φιλέεcκον, ἀτὰρ cτυγέεcκον ἀθέcμουc (more in Pfeiffer).

Fr. 114 (295 Pf.)

cὺν δ᾽ ἄμυδιc φορυτόν τε καὶ ἴπνια λύματ᾽ ἄειρεν: 'gathered together [if Suidas' ἄειρεν· ἔβαλε is correct—otherwise 'lifted up', 'removed'] the light rubbish and filth from the dunghill', a line redolent of Comedy, but with a suggestion of Homer in cὺν δ᾽ ἄμυδιc. We do not know who performs this menial task; conceivably Hecale, but I have judged the matter too obscure for the fragment to be placed with the others which more clearly concern our heroine. She could hardly be cleaning out her hearth (Meineke); Kapp (fr. 18), to whom Pfeiffer's note is not quite fair, wondered whether the old woman might be laying material for her fire (on the use of dried dung as a fuel, cf. E. G. Borthwick, *CQ*, NS 19 (1969), 307). This idea has some attractions, since in this kind of poetry it was a convention to describe the lighting of the fire in minutest detail (e.g. Ov. *Met.* 8. 641 ff., [Virg.] *Mor.* 8 ff. Could Call.'s φορυτόc (see below) even be represented by the 'foliis . . . et cortice sicco' with which Baucis gets her blaze going (*Met.* 8. 642)? But the context may be totally different (e.g. Pfeiffer followed Bentley and Schneider in thinking of Heracles cleaning the Augean stables). Note that there is a variant ἀείρας for ἄειρεν.

cὺν δ' ἄμυδιc: cf. *Od.* 5. 467 ἄμυδιc . . . τε . . . καί, 12. 412–13 cὺν δ' . . .|. . . ἄμυδιc (14. 305 Ζεὺc δ' ἄμυδιc*).

φορυτόν: literally 'what is carried on the wind'; any light rubbish, e.g. straw, carpenter's shavings, etc. (cf. Ar. *Ach.* 72, 927; com. adesp. 906 Kock).

ἵπνια λύματ': ἱπνός (frequent in Aristophanes and the title of a play by Pherecrates) is properly a furnace, but also a dunghill, κοπρών (e.g. Aristoph. fr. 353: cf. D. S. Robertson, *PCPS* 169 (1938), 10: Lloyd-Jones, *Gnomon*, 29 (1957), 425), whence the meaning of the adjective here, as Suidas explicitly states. λύματα (cf. *H.* 2. 109 λύματα γῆc, 6. 115 λύματα δαιτόc) appears twice in Homer (*Il.* 1. 314*, 14. 171).

Fr. 115 (298 Pf.)

The sentiment that grief follows hard upon happiness finds many parallels: e.g. Ap. Rh. 4. 1165 ff.; Lucr. 4. 1133–4; Ov. *Met.* 7. 453–4 (worth quoting because it follows the Athenians' hymn of praise to Theseus—? cf. fr. 78) 'usque adeo nulla est sincera voluptas | sollicitumque aliquid laetis intervenit'; Quint. Smyrn. 7. 635–6. This might suit e.g. the death of Hecale, which spoils the rejoicing over Theseus' victory (Hecker, p. 124). But the scholiast on *Il.* 6. 484 δακρυόεν γελάcαcα drew from Call. a rather different point—that laughter itself can cause tears, ὠιήθη γὰρ ὑπὸ τῆc διαχύcεωc τοῦ γέλωτοc τὰ δάκρυα γενέcθαι. And the complete fragment is given by a commentator on Greg. Naz. *Or.* 4. 113 (*PG* xxxvi. 1237) καὶ γέλωτα ἐν δακρύοιc ποιηταὶ γινώcκουcιν. We may wonder whether the *Iliad* scholiast has twisted Call. for his own purposes, but there is no adequate reason for rejecting his interpretation.

The anonymous *Scholia Alexandrina* on Gregory of Nazianzus, to which we owe the complete fragment, were written at the end of the sixth century, or during the first third of the seventh, but are drawn from earlier material; they appear in the margins of many manuscripts of Gregory's sermons. As yet there is no full critical edition of them. Among partial editions based on single MSS that by P. A. Bruckmayr, 'Untersuchungen über die Randscholien in der 28 Reden des hl. Gregorios von Nazianz im cod. theol. gr. 74 der Wiener Nationalbibliothek' (unpublished diss., Vienna, 1940) contains the fragment of Call. as note 23 on p. 106 (for this information I am most grateful to Dr Jennifer Nimmo Smith, who has written an Edinburgh University thesis on the Gregory of Nazianzus scholia).

2 ἀκλαυτί: ancient grammarians recommend that such adverbs should be written with -ῑ rather than -ει, and MSS of Homer offer ἀνωιστί, ἀνιδρωτί, ἀνουτητί (see Pfeiffer). Call. has νωνυμνί (*Aet.* fr. 43. 55 Pf.) and ἀφρικτί (*H.* 3. 65); only in *H.* 3. 267 do the manuscripts give ἀκλαυτεί (but most scholars prefer Blomfield's ἀκλαυτί). On the other hand, -ει has inscriptional support from the fifth century onwards (E. Schwyzer, *Griechische Grammatik*, i. (1939), 623).

μερόπεσσιν ὀιζυροῖσιν: = [Apollinar.] *Ps.* 95. 26*, Call.'s variation on the Homeric ὀιζυροῖσι βροτοῖσιν (*Il.* 13. 569, *Od.* 4. 197; cf. de Jan, *De Callimacho*, p. 43). In Homer μέροψ is an adjective (e.g. *Il.* 1. 250 μερόπων ἀνθρώπων)—a noun in A. *Ch.* 1018, E. *IT* 1264, Ap. Rh. 4. 536, and often thereafter.

Fr. 116 (299 Pf.)

The two lines of this fragment, preserved separately, were joined by Naeke (p. 265), whom Pfeiffer followed with some hesitation, 'nexus enim verborum satis incertus'. But the whole may be interpreted very convincingly (in my view) as an address to, or description of, the goddess Nemesis/Adrastea '<quae> Aesepum possides, quaeque campum Nepeum' (Pf.). The best Greek parallel for such a catalogue of a deity's abodes with repeated relative pronoun is perhaps Posidipp. *AP* 12. 131(= 8 G.–P.). 1 ἃ Κύπρον ἅ τε Κύθηρα καὶ ἃ Μίλητον ἐποιχνεῖς—in Latin cf. Catull. 64. 96 'quaeque regis Golgos, quaeque Idalium frondosum' (Catull. 36. 12 ff., a parody of this style, uses the relative no fewer than five times). See further E. Norden, *Agnostos Theos* (1913), 168 ff. It is not impossible that, as Hecker first suggested, fr. 176 inc. sed. δαίμων [δαῖμον Bentley] τῆι κόλποισιν ἐνιπτύουσι [Hecker for ἐπι-] γυναῖκες opened the address to (or description of) Nemesis; cf. L. Lehnus, *RIL* 109 (1975), 360–1.

Complications have been caused by the fact that Adrastea was, as well as a title of Nemesis, also the name of a town (*Il.* 2. 828, closely following the river Aesepus in l. 825), and in Strabo (13. 1. 13) of a plain as well. Bentley had conjectured ἦιτ' for ἤ τ' in line 2 (not yet joined to l. 1), and Naeke, accepting this, translated 'ubi campus Nepeae, nobilis Adrastea'. But the town is placed μεταξὺ Πριάπου καὶ Παρίου (Str. loc. cit.), far to the west of the river Aesepus, and Strabo himself remarks that there was no temple of Adrastea or Nemesis in that region; the temple of Nemesis stood near Cyzicus. For a map of the area and discussion of the worship of Adrastea (pp. 78–80) see W. Leaf, *Strabo on the Troad* (1923). Strabo goes on to quote Antim. fr. 53 Wyss, lines echoed down to the time of Nonnus (see Wyss's notes):

> ἔςτι δέ τις Νέμεςιϲ μεγάλη θεόϲ, ἣ τάδε πάντα
> πρὸϲ μακάρων ἔλαχεν· βωμὸν δέ οἱ εἴϲατο πρῶτοϲ
> Ἄδρηϲτοϲ ποταμοῖο παρὰ ρόον Αἰϲήποιο,
> ἔνθα τετίμηταί τε καὶ Ἀδρήϲτεια καλεῖται.

The plain of Nepea is mentioned by Ap. Rh. 1. 1116 ἄϲτυ τε καὶ πεδίον Νηπήιον Ἀδρηϲτείηϲ, where the scholiast comments πεδίον Νηπείαϲ ἔϲτι περὶ Κύζικον, and refers to Dionysius of Miletus (*FGH* 687, probably not identical with Dionysius Scytobrachion to whom Jacoby gave the fragment (*FGH* 32 F 9)—see J. S. Rusten's 1982 edition of the latter, p. 78). It seems that Call., in a prose work (fr. 464 Pf.), voiced the opinion Νέμεϲιν εἶναι τὴν τὸ πεδίον κατέχουϲαν.

1 ἑλικώτατον ὕδωρ: in apposition to Αἴϲηπον (as in *H.* 1. 40 παλαιότατον δέ μιν ὕδωρ). But the meaning of the epithet would probably be as obscure to most of Call.'s contemporaries as it is to us. We are offered (*a*) 'eddying', τὸ ἑλικοειδῆ ἔχον τὴν ρεῦϲιν (Suidas, from the commentary of Salustius), (*b*) 'black' (schol. on *Il.* 1. 98, explaining ἑλικώπιδα with μελανόφθαλμον; cf. the other sources quoted for our fragment). Modern authorities are split. D. L. Page (*History and the Homeric Iliad* (1959), 244–5) is prepared to accept ἑλίκωψ = 'black-eyed' in Homer, but J. N. O'Sullivan (in *Lexikon des frühgriechischen Epos* s.v. ἑλίκωπεϲ (1984)) believes this meaning to have been a misinterpretation of our line of Call. LSJ, Supplement (1968), changing the opinion of the ninth edition, give 'black' for ἑλικόϲ. I myself suspect that Call. did indeed mean 'black'. He would then, very characteristically, be alluding to *Il.* 2. 825 ὕδωρ μέλαν Αἰσήποιο, and, at the same time, expressing a view on the controversial Homeric epithet ἑλίκωψ. The same process almost certainly accounts for ἕλιξ = 'black' in Theocr. 25. 127. Whether ἑλικός had much independent existence, at least in historical times, may be doubted, though e.g. *Et. Gud.* s.v. ἑλικώπιδα writes ἑλικὸν δὲ τὸ μέλαν κατὰ διάλεκτον (cf. ἕλλεροc in fr. 16) and de Jan (*De Callimacho*, pp. 42–3) cites Hesych. ἑλίβοτρυc· ἄμπελόc τιc μέλαινα.

2 ἄργοc: 'plain', cf. Str. 8. 6. 9 ἄργοc δὲ καὶ τὸ πεδίον λέγεται παρὰ τοῖc νεωτέροιc . . . μάλιστα δ' οἴονται Μακεδονικὸν καὶ Θετταλικὸν εἶναι. Since this is presumably the origin of the place-name Ἄργοc (owned by more than one city) it is surprising that no certain instance exists before Call.; the later epic poet Dionysius wrote ἀνὰ Δώτιον ἄργοc (fr. 15b Heitsch = 29 Livrea; cf. Livrea, pp. 57–8). Some have been content with παλαιὸν ἄργοc in E. *El.* 1 (see Denniston ad loc.), but Diggle (OCT) obelizes.

ἀοίδιμοc: once in Homer, in a bad sense 'notorious' (*Il.* 6. 358). The nominative may here perhaps be used for the vocative, a common epic usage (cf. J. Wackernagel, *Vorlesungen über Syntax*, i (1920), 306 ff.).

Fr. 117 (301 Pf.)

βουcόον ὅν τε μύωπα βοῶν καλέουcιν ἀμορβοί: Call. seems to have in mind A. *Supp.* 307 ff. βοηλάτην μύωπα κινητήριον |. . .| οἶcτρον καλοῦcιν αὐτὸν οἱ Νείλου πέλαc. He was in turn imitated by Ap. Rh. 3. 276–7 οἶcτροc | τέλλεται ὅν τε μύωπα βοῶν κλείουcι νομῆεc. Very similar in structure to this line is fr. 177 inc. sed. ὅν τε μάλιcτα βοῶν ποθέουcιν ἐχῖνοι.

The context is unknown. Pfeiffer rejects the ascription of Naeke (p. 60) and Schneider (ii, p. 177) to the bull which Neptune sent against the Cretans (according to many, the same animal later ravaged Marathon). The bull or cow stung by a gadfly is often used as a simile (e.g. Ap. Rh. 1. 1265 ff., 3. 276–7; Triph. 360 ff.; Colluth. 41 ff. with Livrea's note).

βουcόον: the epithet, 'driving oxen wild', may agree with μύωπα, as in Cerc. fr. 8. 2 Powell βουcόω μύω[ποc and Nonn. *Dion.* 11. 191 μύωπα βοοccόον. It is equally possible that οἶcτρον stood in the previous line (Pfeiffer; cf. Ap. Rh. 3. 276–7 quoted above and R. F. Thomas, *HSCP* 86 (1982), 81–5).

ὄν τε: Denniston's remark (*Greek Particles*[2] (1954), 495) that τε has attracted considerable attention is all the more true since the publication of C. J. Ruijgh, *Autour de 'τε épique'* (1971), a book of 1,082 pages. The predominant view has been that of Wentzel (cf. Denniston, op. cit. p. 520) who saw in τε an expression of *habitual* action; this could explain why 'epic τε' is particularly common in similes. For criticism of Wentzel, see Ruijgh, op. cit., pp. 8–9. The latter (pp. 967–70) finds only 11 examples in the 1,083 lines of Call.'s *Hymns*, but does not go into details for the fragmentary poems. As to the *Hecale*, uncertainty of reading or context affects some cases, but the following (in addition to this one) seem at least plausible: frs. 42. 3, 44. 1, 48. 7, 69. 6, 99. 2, with frs. 163. 1 and 177 inc. sed. and conceivably fr. 17. 11 (corrupt). Perhaps, therefore, another instance of the *Hecale* standing closer than the *Hymns* to traditional epic.

ἀμορβοί: 'attendants' (see on fr. 76 ἀμορβεύεσκεν). The pattern 'which a particular group of people call such and such' is especially popular in Hellenistic poetry (add e.g. Nic. *Ther.* 103–4, 230, 554 τὴν ἤτοι μελίφυλλον ἐπικλείουσι βοτῆρες, 632 ff., *Alex.* 346). Campbell, *Studies*, p. 25 (cf. p. 102 n. 7) notes that many of the examples amount to 'called in the trade'.

Fr. 118 (303 Pf.)

κενεὸν πόνον ὀτλήσοντες: (Ap. Rh. 2. 1008 κάματον βαρὺν ὀτλεύουσιν). Given to the *Hecale* by Pfeiffer because of Suidas s.v. ὀτλήσοντες· ὑπομενοῦντες, κακοπαθήσοντες, which is more probably an extract from Salustius' commentary than an explanation of Paul. Sil. *AP* 5. 226. 7 (also quoted by Suidas) ἔνδικον ὀτλήσοντες ἀεὶ πόνον. Pfeiffer makes two further points: (*a*) the careful sequence of vowels, here ε and ο, seems most characteristic of our poem (cf. on fr. 16); (*b*) we have as yet no certain example in the *Aetia* (fr. 80. 8 Pf. is probable) of a hexameter combining masculine caesura with spondaic fifth foot, while such lines are not uncommon in the *Hecale* (e.g. fr. 2. 2; cf. above, Introd. sect. IV. 2*c*).

ὀτλήσοντες: the noun ὄτλος, 'suffering', is a rare tragic word (A. *Sept.* 18, S. *Tr.* 7 v.l.). ὀτλέω was probably first used by Aratus (*Phaen.* 428), thereafter also by Ap. Rh. (3. 769, 4. 381 with Livrea ad loc., 1227*) and Lycophron *Alex.* 819).

Fr. 119 (309 dub. Pf.)

Some suspicion has attached to this fragment. Bergk, who very convincingly joined the two parts, attributed it to the fable of the wolf and the goat in the μυθικά (cf. Babr. 199 Crusius). Some dactylic fragments given by Suidas have the title ἐν μυθικοῖς or ἐν μύθοις, and almost certainly Suidas quotes a few pieces from the same work without mentioning the source (see Pfeiffer, i, p. 228). But the section of Crusius' Babrius (ed. maior (1897), pp. 215–20) which contains this fragment (p. 219) is full of lines commonly given to the *Hecale* (one of them vindicated for our poem by a papyrus).

Turning to the content, I do not see anything unworthy of Call., although there is nothing markedly personal to him. Of the language Pfeiffer wrote 'singula vocabula omnia fere Homerica, sed usus et conexus differt', which could apply to much of the *Hecale*. According to Trypanis (Loeb) 'the style of line 3 is most unlike Callimachus', but to what does he object? If to the presence of ἔην and ἦεν in the same line, Pfeiffer points out that *Iamb.* fr. 193. 1 contains both ἦν and ἦα. The line has two instances of correption: κάί after the feminine caesura is enormously common in Call., but πέτρη ἔην rarer and more interesting. If we leave aside the monosyllable ἤ (a law unto itself), it seems that Call. restricts correption after -η in the *second* syllable of a dactyl to the first foot of a hexameter (see above, Introd. sect. IV. 7). This small point, if anything, favours Callimachean authorship. So ascription to the *Hecale* remains probable. Webster (*Poetry and Art*, p. 116) thought of the bull trying to escape from Theseus.

2 ἄγκος ἐς ὑψικάρηνον: for ἄγκος = 'mountain glen' cf. *Il.* 20. 490 etc. ὑψικάρηνος occurs once in Homer (*Il.* 12. 132, whence *H. Hom. Aphr.* 264)—Call. likes Homeric *hapax legomena*. It became a favourite word of Nonnus (? perhaps because of this passage), e.g. *Par.* 6. 7 εἰς ὄρος ὑψικάρηνον ἀνήιε.

2–3 ἀπορρώξ | πέτρη: cf. *H.* 5. 41–2 ἀπορρώγεσσιν ...| ἐν πέτραις. *Od.* 13. 98 has ἀκταὶ ἀπορρῶγες.

3 καὶ ἄμβασις οὔ νύ τις ἦεν: cf. *Od.* 12. 77 οὐδέ κεν ἀμβαίη βροτὸς ἀνήρ. For the run of the words it might be worth comparing *H.* 4. 164 καὶ εὔβοτος εἴ νύ τις ἄλλη.

Fr. 120 (312 Pf.)

ἄκμηνον δόρποιο: ἄκμηνος, 'unfed', occurs four times in *Il.* 19, but not elsewhere in Homer. Schol. on *Il.* 19. 163 says παρὰ τὴν ἀκμήν· οὕτω δὲ τὴν ἀcιτίαν Αἰολεῖc λέγουcι—for discussion see *Lexikon des frühgriechischen Epos.* Call. was probably responsible for reintroducing it, whence Ap. Rh. 4. 1295, Lyc. *Alex.* 672, Nic. *Ther.* 116. It seems unlikely that this item in Suidas could represent an error or variant for *Il.* 19. 163 ἄκμηνοc cίτοιο. Call., as usual, both imitates and alters Homer. δόρπον, sometimes generally meaning 'meal', 'food', is more often the evening meal eaten at sunset; these words might describe Theseus' condition when he arrived at Hecale's cottage.

Fr. 121 (314 Pf.)

ἀμιθρῆcαι: μετρῆcαι, ἀριθμῆcαι παρὰ Καλλ. (Suid.). There is no reason whatever to refer this gloss to *H.* 6. 86 where ἀμιθρεῖ is confirmed by *P. Oxy.* 2226. Simonides (*PMG* 626) has ἄμιθρον for ἀριθμόν, and the same metathesis (generally a feature of epic and Ionic, e.g. ἀτcρπόc for ἀτραπόc) occurs in Nicoch. fr. 5 Demiańczuk, Herod. 6. 6, and Phoen. fr. 1. 8 Powell.

Fr. 122 (315 Pf.)

ἀπούατοc ἄγγελοc ἔλθοι: (note *Od.* 1. 414 with ἀγγελίηι and ἔλθοι*) 'an unwelcome messenger might come'. The adjective ἀπούατοc (δύcφημοc, ἄξιοc τοῦ μὴ ἀκουcθῆναι, Suid.) is the most curious product of Homeric controversy to be found in the *Hecale* (cf. Pfeiffer, *History*, i. 140, where I presume that 'bringing the tidings' is a misprint for 'bringing bad tidings'). In *Il.* 18. 272 Polydamas says αἲ γὰρ δή μοι ἀπ' οὔατοc ὧδε γένοιτο, which perhaps means 'may [the word which I have spoken] be removed from my ear', i.e. let it be taken as unsaid, so far as the omen is concerned (Leaf); in *Il.* 22. 453–4, after ἐγγὺc δή τι κακὸν Πριάμοιο τέκεccιν, Andromache adds αἲ γὰρ ἀπ' οὔατοc εἴη ἐμεῦ ἔποc. But a scholiast on *Il.* 18. 272 reveals that some took ΑΠΟΥΑΤΟC there as a single word meaning κακόc (ἀντὶ τοῦ εἴθε γὰρ κακὸc ἐγένετο (sc. Achilles), τουτέcτι δειλόc). As an explanation of the Homeric line, that is absurd; but Call. obviously drew from the controversy his adjective ἀπούατος. Schneider (fr. 301) was the first to understand the fragment of Call. correctly (cf. de Jan, *De Callimacho*, pp. 90–1).

Pfeiffer refers to the κακαγγελία of the crow and the raven (see frs. 71–4). Another possible context might be Aegeus (or even Hecale) dreading a message that Theseus has succumbed to the Marathonian bull. Compare the words of other anxious parents in Quint Smyrn. 7. 269–70 (Deidamia to Neoptolemus) μὴ δή μοι Τροίηθε κακὴ φάτις οὔαθ᾽ ἵκηται | σεῖο καταφθιμένοιο and *Aen.* 8. 582–3 (Evander on Pallas) 'gravior neu nuntius auris | vulneret'. If Aegeus spoke these words, the dispatch of reassuring news back to Athens (fr. 69. 5 ff.) could be a response to his fear.

Fr. 123 (316 Pf.)

The unique ἀσπαστύς would be typically Callimachean (see on fr. 125 ἀφραστύες), and Naeke (p. 154) compared Plut. *Thes.* 14 ἀσπάσασθαι πρεσβυτικῶς (sc. Hecala Theseum). The only doubt concerns the form of citation, which is not a normal way for Suid. to excerpt Salustius' commentary, and might suggest one of Call.'s grammatical works (Pfeiffer).

Fr. 124 (317 Pf.)

ἀσταγὲς ὕδωρ: τὸ πολυσταγές (Suid.). A possible context might be the rainstorm which soaked Theseus. The force of ἀ- is more probably intensifying than privative ('not merely trickling, i.e. gushing', *LSJ*). Elsewhere ἀσταγής applies to tears (Ap. Rh. 3. 805), blood (Nic. *Ther.* 307, schol. πολυσταγές), and snow (Nonn. *Dion.* 1. 302, but there the ἀ- is privative). Compare Jebb on S. *OC* 1251 ἀστακτί. Although α ἐπιτατικόν (etymologically perhaps identical with α ἀθροιστικόν) is respectable enough (e.g. ἀτενής), many such formations in Hellenistic poetry seem artificial, possibly provoked by argument over *Il.* 11. 155 ἐν ἀξύλωι ... ὕληι (cf. schol. Ap. Rh. 3. 805): e.g. in Nicander, ἀνομβρήεις and ἀνυλήεις may be interpreted thus (Gow, *CQ*, NS 1 (1951), 98 n. 2); cf. *Alex.* 174 ἀχύνετον ... ὕδωρ (also Dionys. fr. 82 Livrea—see his p. 64). Another probable example in the *Hecale* is fr. 53 ἄστηνοι. Similar considerations apply to the even more artificial intensifying prefix νη- (cf. on fr. 11 νήχυτος εὐρώς).

Fr. 125 (318 Pf.)

cχέτλιαι ἀνθρώπων ἀφραcτύεc: a possible context (already in Hecker, p. 124) would be Theseus lamenting his inability to thank Hecale—cf. now *Dieg.* xi. 2–3 ἐπιcτε[νάξ]αc ὡc ἐψευcμένοc τῆc προcδοκίαc. N. J. Richardson on *H. Hom. Dem.* 256 νήιδεc ἄνθρωποι καὶ ἀφράδμονεc has a valuable collection of such derogatory addresses to mankind. They sometimes come from the mouth of a deity, prophet, or sage. As exclamations by the poet Richardson quotes *Aen.* 10. 501–2 'nescia mens hominum fati sortisque futurae,| et servare modum rebus sublata secundis' and Triph. 310–11 (no doubt based on Call.) cχέτλιον ἀφραδέων μερόπων γένοc.

ἀφραcτύεc: a scholiast on *Il.* 19. 233–4 says of ὀτρυντύc (by no means the only Homeric noun in -τύc) ἔcτι δὲ ἡ λέξιc Ἀντιμάχειοc, whence one can reasonably conclude that Antimachus used ὀτρυντύc (fr. 88 Wyss) as he did πωρητύc and ἀβολητύc (frs. 48, 161 W.). Although Call. may have had a low opinion (fr. 398 Pf.) of the *Lyde*, he certainly did not neglect Antimachus (see e.g. on fr. 116), and developed a great liking for nouns in -τύc (cf. fr. 123 ἀcπαcτύc, and below, App. V(e) ἐπητύι). In *Aet.* fr. 10 Pf. we find two in the same line μαcτύοc ἀλλ᾽ ὅτ᾽ ἔκαμνον ἀλητύι. See further R. Schmitt, *Die Nominalbildung in den Dichtungen des Kallimachos von Kyrene* (1970), pp. 72–3, 79; Williams (*HA*) on *H.* 2. 95 ἁρπακτύοc; C. D. Buck and W. Petersen, *Reverse Index of Greek Nouns and Adjectives* (1944), pp. 609–10. The Homeric scholiast (above) adds καὶ Ἐρατοcθένηc χαίρει ταῖc τοιαύταιc ἐκφοραῖc. Wyss (*Antimachus*, Praef. p. xxxii) suggests that Eratosthenes, a pupil of Call., may be making fun of Antimachus when he coins ἀντιμαχεcτύc or ἀντιμαχητύc (fr. 31 Powell). A recently published papyrus gives γραπτύc from the end of Eratosthenes' *Hermes* (*SH* 397).

Fr. 126 (320 Pf.)

βέβυcτο δὲ πᾶcα χόλοιο: 'she was stuffed full of anger', a vigorous phrase with a colloquial ring. I doubt whether these words would suit Athena's reaction to the crow's κακαγγελία, which is more probably conveyed by fr. 72. Perhaps the subject is Medea, after her unsuccessful plot against Theseus (frs. 3–7) has been detected—Pfeiffer suggested that the curse of fr. 145 might be aimed at Medea.

βέβυϲτο: cf. *Od.* 4. 134 (a basket) *νήματοϲ ἀϲκητοῖο βεβυϲμένον*; Hdt. 6. 125 *τό τε ϲτόμα ἐβέβυϲτο* (sc. *χρυϲοῦ*); Nonn. *Dion.* 9. 298. Sometimes the verb is coupled with a dative, as in Triph. 308, 450 *ἀφραδίηι τε βέβυϲτο* (of a city, with *πᾶϲα* in the next line).

Fr. 127 (322 Pf.)

γέντα βοῶν μέλδοντεϲ: 'softening the flesh of oxen' (by cooking). The verb is a Homeric *hapax legomenon* (*Il.* 21. 362–3 *λέβηϲ* ...| *κνίϲην μελδόμενοϲ ἀπαλοτρεφέοϲ ϲιάλοιο*; de Jan (*De Callimacho*, pp. 97–9) thought that Call.'s use of the verb reflects a Homeric controversy); cf. Nic. *Ther.* 108 *μελδόμεναι* (passive) and Man. 6. 464. We have no poetic precedent for *γέντα* (Thracian, according to Eustathius, variously glossed with *τὰ μέλη, κρέα,* and *ϲπλάγχνα*), and Call.'s only follower was Nic. *Alex.* 62–3 *καί τε βοὸϲ νέα γέντα περιφλίοντοϲ ἀλοιφῆι* | *τηξάμενοϲ κορέϲαιο* and 556a (as numbered by G.–S.).

Fr. 128 (323 Pf.)

γοεροῖο γόοιο: this collocation (Homer has *κρυεροῖο γόοιο** *Il.* 24. 524, *Od.* 4. 103) puts a strain on one's credulity, but cannot entirely be ruled out; Pfeiffer collects examples of pleonasms such as A. *PV* 1020 *μακρὸν μῆκοϲ* and Lucr. 3. 993 'anxius angor' (cf. D. Fehling, *Die Wiederholungsfiguren und ihr Gebrauch bei den Griechen vor Gorgias* (1969), pp. 159–60). The sequence of vowels is typical of the *Hecale*. Either word might be emended (e.g. for *γόοιο* Wilamowitz *ap.* fr. 126 Kapp thought of *νόμοιο*). Pfeiffer suggests that *γοεροῖο* might belong to another, preceding, substantive, as in e.g. *Od.* 17. 8 *κλαυθμοῦ τε ϲτυγεροῖο γόοιό τε δακρυόεντοϲ*. Conceivably something could have been lost between *γοεροῖο* and *γόοιο*, from an original pattern like e.g. *Il.* 23. 10 *ὀλοοῖο τεταρπώμεϲθα γόοιο*.

Fr. 129 (324 Pf.)

οἰκίον εὖτε δέμοιμι: *δέμον* occurs in *Od.* 23. 192. Of the isolated *Hecale* fragments with first person optative which Pfeiffer lists, his fr. 346 has since found a speaker in the crow (fr. 74. 1).

FRS. 130–1

Dilthey (*De Callimachi Cydippa* (1863), p. 85) wished to join these fragments. The idea has some slight plausibility. Kapp (on her fr. 128) points to a patched-up interpolation in Nicander (*Ther.* 920) ὄφρα δύην ὀλοοῦ καὶ πότμον θηρὸς [θηρὸς καὶ πότμον Bentley] ἀλύξηις, which could have such a model. Also *H.* 6. 47 contains both ἐλίνυσον and πολύθεστε. But to make a hexameter we would have to delete the final ν in ἐλινύσειεν, and add ⟨δ'⟩ after δύην. The result is a pleonastic verse which hardly repays the effort, but I have printed the fragments together in this order, so as to keep the possibility in mind.

Fr. 130 (330 Pf.)

πότμον ἐλινύσειεν: the verb ἐλινύω is Ionic (common in Herodotus and Hippocrates) and poetical; Call. uses it twice elsewhere (*H.* 6. 47, fr. 526 inc. sed. Pf.). Normally intransitive = 'rest', 'take a holiday'; only here transitive = 'bring to rest', 'halt'.

Fr. 131 (325 Pf.)

δύην ἀπόθεστον ἀλάλκοι: while δύη = 'wretchedness' (see below, App. V(b) for the adjective δυερός) occurs several times in the *Odyssey*, ἀπόθεστος (*Od.* 17. 296, of the dog Argos, where schol. H explains ἀπόθητος) is a Homeric *hapax legomenon*. Whether the adjective should be viewed as ἀ-πόθεστος (ἀ + ποθεῖν) or ἀπό-θεστος (connected with θέσσασθαι, 'to pray for') was, and remains, a matter of dispute. Hopkinson (*HD*), in an interesting note on *H.* 6. 47, argues that Call., by coining πολύθεστος, shows his preference for ἀπό + θέσσασθαι (in addition to the authorities quoted by Hopkinson see *Lexikon des frühgriechischen Epos* s.v. ἀπόθεστος). Possibly one can distinguish two senses: (a) ἀ-πόθεστος = 'despised', which suits Homer and perhaps Euphorion (*SH* 413. 15, where the text is fragmentary); (b) ἀπό-θεστος = 'which one prays not to encounter', seemingly more appropriate in Call., Lycophron (*Alex.* 540) and the anonymous *SH* 1066 (if ἀ⟨πό⟩θεστος Ἐρινύς is right).

Bentley's attempt to turn Suidas' explanation into the start of a second hexameter, ἦν οὐδεὶς ποθ⟨έ⟩ει, was a surprising lapse of judgement from so distinguished a scholar (de Jan (*De Callimacho*, pp. 79–81) hesitates).

Fr. 132 (331 Pf.)

1 ἐπήλυϲιν: 'onslaught' (cf. ἐπηλυϲίη in *H. Hom. Dem.* 228). This form is probably to be recognized in the Cologne Archilochus (Page, *SLG* S478. 50, cf. Merkelbach and West, *ZPE* 14 (1974), 101): later in Opp. *Hal.* 4. 228; Page, *GLP* (Loeb) no. 124(= Heitsch, *Die griechischen Dichterfragmente der römischen Kaiserzeit* (1961), p. 203 no. LX). 1; Paul. Sil. *AP* 5. 268. 3. James (*Oppian of Cilicia*, pp. 199–200) misses the Callimachean fragment.

ὄφρ' ἀλέοιτο: for the line-ending cf. Quint. Smyrn. 12. 378 θεῆϲ χόλον ὄφρ' ἀλέωνται. In *SH* 923. 11 (anon.—??Rhianus) West would like to restore ἐπηλυϲίην [ἀ]λέαιϲ[θε.

Fr. 133 (332 Pf.)

ἐπιπρίϲηιϲιν ὀδόντας: (so Meineke and Hecker for Suidas' ἐπιβρίϲηιϲιν); cf. Ar. *Ran.* 927 μὴ πρῖε τοὺϲ ὀδόντας. The compound verb recurs in Antip. Thess. *AP* 7. 531(= 23 G.–P.). 5 ἀφριόεν κοναβηδὸν ἐπιπρίουϲα γένειον. In Call. too the sense is probably to gnash the teeth *over* somebody or something (cf. Ap. Rh. 4. 1671 λευγαλέον δ' ἐπὶ οἷ πρῖεν χόλον and the similar figure applied to grief in *Hecale* fr. 49. 3). But the text is not certain, and perhaps (as Küster conjectured) we should look for a part of ἐπιβρύκω. [Apollinar.] *Ps.* 36. 24 ἐπιβρύξειεν ὀδόντας might be an imitation of our fragment; compare Tymn. *AP* 7. 433(= 6 G.–P.). 3–4 ὀδόντα |... ἐπιβρύκουϲ'.

Fr. 134 (333 Pf.)

ἐπικλινές ἐϲτι τάλαντον: cf. *Il.* 19. 223–4 ἐπὴν κλίνηιϲι τάλαντα Ζεύϲ. For ἐπικλῖνές Pfeiffer compares Leon. Tar. 79. 4 G.–P. ϲατακλῖνής and ἀποκλῖνής in Man. 6. 62.

This fragment gives rise to the most serious worry about Hecker's Law (cf. above, Introd. sect. IX; Pfeiffer, i, p. 228) whereby anonymous and otherwise unattested dactylic fragments in Suidas are given to Call.'s *Hecale*. In *SH* 260A. 9 (from *Aet.* 3) ἐπικλεινες.[was written, and, as far as we can judge, ἔτι μᾶλλον ἐπικλ{ε}ινές ἐcτι τάλαντον might make good sense. This would be more disturbing than other cases where single words assigned to the *Hecale* by Hecker's Law have turned up in other works of Call. (*SH* 250. 9 from *Aet.* 1 = *Hec.* fr. 140; *SH* 257. 33, *Aet.* 3 = *Hec.* fr. 151), since there is no difficulty in believing that Call. used an individual word more than once. None the less, Hecker's Law continues to claim successes in post-Pfeiffer papyri (see above, Introd. sect. IX). In *SH* 260A. 9 the restoration is by no means certain (the editors say that ἐπικλ{ε}ινεcθ[is possible); even if our fragment were correctly recognized there, Call. might have repeated the whole phrase. See P. J. Parsons, *ZPE* 25 (1977), 50. If Hecker's Law were not watertight, one would need a new theory explaining why these three anonymous entries in Suidas should turn up in Call. rather than some other poet.

Fr. 135 (335 Pf.)

ἤεροc ὄγμοι: perhaps Call.'s variation on the Homeric ἠερόεντα κέλευθα (*Od.* 20. 64). ὄγμοc is properly a furrow in ploughing (e.g. *Il.* 18. 546, *H. Hom. Dem.* 455), but also (cf. ὁλκόc and 'sulcus' in Latin) the path of a heavenly body (*H. Hom.* 32. 11; Arat. *Phaen.* 749) or the track of an animal (e.g. Nic. *Ther.* 571; Opp. *Hal.* 1. 625). Campbell compares Triph. 354 κύκλον ἐπογμεύουcιν, of cranes tracing a circle in the air.

Fr. 136 (336 Pf.)

ἑρπετὰ δ' ἰλυοῖcιν ἐνέκρυφεν: possibly a sign of changing weather or season, in the spirit of Aratus (though without parallel in the *Phaenomena*). W. Weinberger (*Philol.* 76 (1920), 72) thought of the storm in the *Hecale* (cf. frs. 18, 19, 25).

ἰλυοῖcιν: 'lairs' of reptiles (connected with εἰλύω); cf. *H.* 1. 25 ἰλυοὺc ἐβάλοντο κινώπετα (McLennan (*HZ*) ad loc. discusses the various spellings).

ἐνέκρυφεν: third person plural of the aorist passive (in Call. neuter plural nouns often take a plural verb, e.g. *H.* 1. 25, 64, 65). See Pfeiffer on *Aet.* fr. 26. 14 ἐκούφιcθεν and Hopkinson (*HD*) on *H.* 6. 93 ἔλειφθεν (which he prefers to ἐλείφθη of *P. Oxy.* 2226).

ἐνέκρυφεν seems more likely on metrical grounds than the variant ἐνέκρυφθεν (cf. E. *Hipp*. 1247 ἔκρυφθεν), but the latter can by no means be ruled out.

Fr. 137 (340 Pf.)

†ἀφ' ὑμέων† κοκύηισι καθημένη ἀρχαίηισι: perhaps the only emendation of the beginning which deserves a mention is Schneider's ἀμφ' ὑμέων (see on his fr. an. 37 for some other attempts). Call.'s κοκύαι = 'ancestors' found a single follower in Zonas of Sardis (*AP* 9. 312(= 7 G.–P.). 5). The word looks non-Greek (cf. above, Introd. sect. III); some connect it with Hesychius' γυγαί· πάπποι. This line might describe a bird (? as e.g. Claud. *Eutrop*. 2. 232 'veteri sedit . . . sepulcro'), but it is now clear that the loquacious crow sits on a tree (fr. 74. 11) rather than a tomb. The reference to this fragment in Webster (*Poetry and Art*, p. 117 n. 2) may be based on a misunderstanding of Pfeiffer's note.

Fr. 139 (348 Pf.)

τόδε μοι μαλκίστατον ἦμαρ: ψυχρότατον according to Suidas. Naeke (p. 239) would interpret 'crudelissima, mortifera dies', but that sense is not attested. The root appears first in Aesch. fr. 332 N² and *Tr. G. F.* μαλκίων ποδί (in Hes. *Op*. 530 μαλκιόωντες is merely a conjecture of Crates—see West), then in Arat. *Phaen*. 294 ναύτηι μαλκιόωντι. Nicander was very fond of such words (*Ther*. 382, 724; *Alex*. 540; frs. 22, 95). Schol. *Ther*. 382 tells us that τὴν μάλκην φησὶ Νίκανδρος ἐν Γλώccαιc (fr. 143 Schn.) ῥῖγος περὶ τοὺς πόδας καὶ χεῖρας, and quotes an anonymous line (*SH* 1167), adding, however, that Nicander uses μάλκη sometimes for 'cold', sometimes for 'numbness' (see fr. 22 G.–S.). A word from this root might be restored in Parth. *SH* 612a. 3, 626. 22. I. Cazzaniga discusses our fragment (*Parola del Passato*, 22 (1967), 365–6) without coming to any very definite conclusion.

For the form of the superlative (μάλκιστος is not attested) cf. *Aet*. fr. 93. 3 τερπνίστατα with Pfeiffer's note and Nic. *Ther*. 3 κυδίστατε, 344 πρεσβίστατον. We find other kinds of irregular comparatives and superlatives in pre-Hellenistic verse (e.g. *Od*. 2. 190 ἀνιηρέστερον (for metrical convenience); P. *Ol*. 3. 42 αἰδοιέcτατοc; Antim. fr. 87 Wyss ἀφνειέcτατοc.

If the anonymous entry in Suidas οὐ γὰρ ἔγωγε | ὧδ᾽ ἔ⟨α⟩ ῥιγηλή (see below, App. V(h)) belongs to the *Hecale*, a close relationship to the present fragment seems likely—it would be surprising if a speaker complained of the cold more than once in the poem. 'Most chilling' or 'most numbing' would be an appropriate sense for μαλκίστατον, and the sentiment might well fit the aged Hecale (? or even the old crow). See further below, App. V(h).

Fr. 140 (352 Pf.)

Νωνακρίνη | Καλλιστώ can now be read in *Aet.* 1 (*SH* 250. 9–10) but we need not for that reason delete Νωνακρίνη from the *Hecale* (see on fr. 134). Ovid, for example, has 'Nonacrinus' in the *Ars Amatoria* (2. 185), *Metamorphoses* (1. 690, 2. 409), and *Fasti* (2. 275). Suidas' entry might (but need not) suggest that in the *Hecale* Call. used Νωνακρίνη without an accompanying Καλλιστώ. See on fr. 103. 2 for the patronymic/matronymic in -ίνη. In Call. fr. 413 (from the prose work Περὶ Νυμφῶν) Νωνακρίνη is the name of a district in Arcadia—and in Buechner, *Frag. Poet. Lat. Incerta* 9. 2 (hexameters of a neoteric cast) of an Arcadian mountain.

Fr. 141 (353 Pf.)

νωcάμενοc: cf. *Theogn.* 1298 ἤπια νωcάμενοc and Theocr. 25. 262–3 τὸν μὲν ἐγὼν ὀδύνηιcι παραφρονέοντα βαρείαιc | νωcάμενοc. We find νώcατο in Ap. Rh. 4. 1409 and Greg. Naz. *Carm.* 1. 1. 4. 20 (*PG* xxxvii. 417), perhaps also in Euphorion, *SH* 447.7.

Fr. 142 (354 Pf.)

μέμβλετό μοι: 'was of concern to me': cf. *Il.* 21. 516 μέμβλετο γάρ οἱ τεῖχος, *Od.* 22. 12; Call. *Aet.* fr. 68 Pf. μέμβλετο δ᾽ εἰcπνήλαιc ὁππότε κοῦρος ἴοι | φωλεὸν ἠὲ λοετρόν.

Fr. 143 (356 Pf.)

ὀκχήcαcθαι: = 'to rest upon', 'take one's seat upon' (ἐπικα-θεcθῆναι, Suid.), no doubt the end of a hexameter with spondaic fifth foot (as e.g. fr. 77 ὀρχήcαcθαι); in fr. 66. 2 Call. uses the noun ὀκχή, 'support'. Forms with the κ (*metri gratia* for ὀχέω and ὀχή) appear earlier only in Pindar (*Ol.* 2. 74, 6. 24) and later in Euphorion (fr. 9. 13 ὀκχοίη). The MSS prefer ὀγχήϲει in Lyc. *Alex.* 64, 1049.

Fr. 144 (357 Pf.)

ὄμπνιον ὕδωρ: τὸ τρόφιμον, καὶ πολύ (Suidas). See on fr. 111 ὄμπνιον ἔργον.

Fr. 145 (358 Pf.)

'Si quidem ad personam nobis notam, ϲε fort. ad Medeam veneficam spectat' (Pfeiffer, citing E. *Med.* 1390)—although she was not supposed to have suffered ἐν πλεόνεϲϲι anything worse than marriage to Achilles. In that case the speaker would be Aegeus, or, less probably, Theseus; see frs. 3–7 for Medea's plot against her stepson. Already in the *Iliad* deferred punishment from the gods is heavier, εἴ περ γάρ τε καὶ αὐτίκ᾽ Ὀλύμπιος οὐκ ἐτέλεϲϲεν | ἔκ τε καὶ ὀψὲ τελεῖ, ϲύν τε μεγάλωι ἀπέτειϲαν (4. 160–1), and perjurers face vengeance in the underworld (3. 278–9, 19. 259–60); for a general judgement of the dead cf. P. *Ol.* 2. 57 ff.; A. *Supp.* 230–1, *Eu.* 269 ff. The futility of escaping detection in this life is expressed by e.g. Virg. *A.* 6. 568–9 'quae quis apud superos furto laetatus inani | distulit in seram commissa piacula mortem' (in Solon 13. 29 ff. West it is allowed that some wicked men may escape entirely, but the punishment will fall upon their guiltless descendants). After death the penalty may be much larger (Plut. *Mor.* 565), even tenfold (Pl. *R.* 10. 615b).

A double penalty after death occurs nowhere else (Prop. 3. 1. 22 hopes for a double reward, 'post obitum duplici faenore reddet Honos'), but for this world the idea is common (e.g. Hes. *Op.* 711 δὶϲ τόϲα τείνυϲθαι; *Theogn.* 1090; Herod. 2. 48, 54) particularly in cases of theft (Fraenkel on A. *Ag.* 537; Men. *Asp.* 367; A. R. W. Harrison, *The Law of Athens*, i. 207 n. 2; likewise in Rome, e.g. Cato, *Agr.* 1).

2 πὰρ πόδα: 'immediately'; cf. S. *Phil.* 838 and Pl. *Sph.* 242a παρὰ πόδα (in Plb. 1. 7. 5 etc. παρὰ πόδαϲ).

τιμωρόϲ: not Homeric but (like the uncontracted τιμάοροϲ) frequent in Tragedy (e.g. S. *El.* 14; E. *El.* 676, *Hec.* 843).

According to Pl. *L.* 4. 716a ἀεὶ cυνέπεται δίκη τῶν ἀπολειπομένων τοῦ θείου νόμου τιμωρός.

3 ἔccεται: sc. δὶc τόcον τιμωρός (unless, as Pfeiffer says, we should read τείcεται).

ἐν πλεόνεccι: 'among the majority', i.e. the dead. This euphemism (cf. Ar. *Eccl.* 1073) gives point to one of Call.'s most elegant epigrams (4 Pf. = *AP* 7. 317 = 51 G.–P. 2) wherein Timon the misanthrope finds death the harder to bear, ὑμέων γὰρ πλείονεc εἰν Ἀίδηι. It is equally at home in Latin, e.g. Lucil. 187–8 Warmington 'quando in eo numero mansi quo in maxima non est | pars hominum' (i.e. I have remained alive), Petr. 42. 5 'abiit ad plures'.

παλίντροπος: again, tragic (e.g. S. *Phil.* 1222, E. *HF* 1069), rather than epic.

Fr. 146 (359 Pf.)

εἶλε δὲ παccαγίην, τόδε δ' ἔννεπεν: a puzzling fragment. When Telemachus gets up in the home of Eumaeus, εἵλετο δ' ἄλκιμον ἔγχοc ... | καὶ ἐὸν προcέειπε cυβώτην (*Od.* 17. 4–5). Naeke (p. 237) sees here Theseus preparing to leave Hecale's cottage in the morning. But παccαγία (cf. cαγή, cάττω) = πανοπλία (thus explained also by schol. S. *Ant.* 107, the only other occurrence), i.e. a full set of armour with shield, helmet, breastplate, greaves, sword, and spear. This does not seem very appropriate for Theseus who, as far as we know, came to fight the Marathonian bull with only his club (fr. 69. 1)—perhaps also with the sword which served as one of the recognition tokens (frs. 9. 1, 10. 2). Pfeiffer wondered whether some irony could be involved, adducing Ar. *Plut.* 951–2 τὴν πανοπλίαν ... | ἔχων βαδίζειc. Webster (*Poetry and Art*, p. 115) thought of Aegeus in Troezen. Parallels for direct speech starting after the bucolic diaeresis (if it did) would be *H.* 4. 150, 162.

Fr. 147 (360 Pf.)

οἷος ἐκεῖνος ἀεὶ περιδέξιος ἥρως: strictly περιδέξιος = 'ambidextrous', as in *Il.* 21. 163 (which Call. has in mind) ἥρωc Ἀcτεροπαῖοc, ἐπεὶ περιδέξιος ἦεν and Nonn. *Dion.* 38. 86 ἀμφοτέρηι παλάμηι περιδέξιος. For οἷος ἐκεῖνος cf. *Il.* 11. 653 (οἷος κεῖνος *Od.* 2. 272, 14. 491). I doubt whether the ἥρως of this fragment can be Theseus (as Schneider thought), but conceivably Theseus is being compared to some other hero.

Fr. 148 (362 Pf.)

περιπηχύναντες: 'embracing', the only occurrence of this compound (see McLennan (*HZ*) on *H.* 1. 46 for the simple verb). Probably the conclusion of a spondaic hexameter, as *H.* 1. 46 προσεπηχύναντο.

Fr. 149 (363 Pf.)

1–2 καὶ ἀγλαὰ πίσεα γαίης | βόσκεο: cf. [Apollinar.] *Ps.* 82. 28 (of fire) βοσκομένωι κατὰ πίσεα (according to Campbell, the only imperial occurrence of the noun). The subject may be, as Hecker and others have thought, the Marathonian bull, but the style seems to me surprisingly 'lush' for such a ferocious creature. βόσκεο no doubt represents Call.'s favourite technique of apostrophe (particularly common in the *Aetia*).

1 πίσεα: 'meadows': cf. *Il.* 20. 9 = *Od.* 6. 124 πίσεα ποιήεντα— some condemn the latter as an interpolation, in which case this would be another Homeric *hapax legomenon*—Ap. Rh. 1. 1266, 3. 1218. Vian in the Budé Apollonius (i, p. lxxvi) prefers the spelling πείσεα.

2 βόσκεο: with an accusative, as e.g. *H. Hom. Herm.* 72 βοσκόμεναι λειμῶνας and Nic. *Ther.* 27 βόσκεται ὕλην.

Fr. 150 (369 Pf.)

τέρπνιστον: for τερπνότατον (*Theogn.* 256). Call. seems to have introduced this form of the superlative; cf. fr. 536 inc. sed. Pf. τέρπνιστοι, [Apollinar.] *Ps.* 132. 1 τέρπνιστον. In *Aet.* fr. 93. 3 Pf. we find the more extravagant τερπνίστατα (see on fr. 139 μαλκίστατον).

Fr. 151 (372 Pf.)

ὑδέουσιν: now in *SH* 257. 33 (*Aet.* 3), but not for that reason to be denied to the *Hecale* (cf. on frs. 134, 140). Nicander follows Call. with ὑδέουσι (*Alex.* 525); see further on fr. 78 ὑδέοιμι. Note the first gloss ἀίδουσι (cf. fr. 78); could fr. 100 follow?

Fr. 152 (375 Pf.)

ὑληωροί: 'wardens of the wood'. Also Ap. Rh. 1. 1227 (nymphs), Leon. *AP* 9. 337 = 29 G.–P. 3 (of Pan). It seems from Suidas that the reference in Call. was to woodmen. See on fr. 52.

Fr. 153 (375 Pf.)

1–2 θῆκε δὲ λᾶαν | cκληρὸν ὑπόκρηνον: surely not Hecale making a hard couch for herself (Hecker). The words suggest something strenuous, even heroic (? Theseus spending a night on his way from Troezen to Athens).

λᾶαν: the Homeric accusative (in *Aet.* fr. 11. 4 Pf. Call. writes λᾶα).

2 ὑπόκρηνον: 'under the head', unique.

Fr. 154 (377 Pf.)

ψιcθεῖεν: from ψίζω (ψίω), to feed on pap. Conceivably from the section in which Hecale recalls rearing two children (cf. on fr. 48. 4). In other Hellenistic poets we find ψίcεται (Lyc. *Alex.* 639), ἔψιcα (Euph. fr. 92. 5), and ἐψιcμένον (Antip. Thess. *AP* 9. 302 = 69 G.–P. 3).

Fr. 155 (see on 245 Pf.)

χυτλώcαιντο: ἀλείψαιντο Suid. Pfeiffer notes (on his fr. 245) 'nisi error codd. pro sing. = ζ 80, novum Hecalae fragmentum', but does not include it in his text. There is no reason why this should be a slip for *Od.* 6. 80. Call. apparently uses the verb in the Homeric sense of anointing rather than washing with water; see McLennan (*HZ*) on *H.* 1. 17 χυτλώcαιτο.

FRAGMENTA INCERTA (156–79)

I have included in this section fragments which, in my view, stand at least a fair chance of belonging to the *Hecale*. They are arranged, as far as practicable, in the same order as the Fragmenta Hecalae; thus (if correctly assigned) frs. 156–69 would represent the meal, the conversation of Theseus and Hecale, the capture of the bull, Ericthonius, the talking birds, and posthumous honours for Hecale.

Fr. 156 inc. sed. (495 Pf.)

Νιcαίηc ἀγλῖθεc ἀπ' 'Οργάδοc: from the commentary on Demosthenes (*Berl. Klass. Texte*, i. 69) by Didymus, who says ἧc καὶ Καλλίμαχός που μνημονεύων φηcί. Wilamowitz assigned the fragment to the *Hecale*, and it would fit well enough with the other vegetables served by Hecale to Theseus (cf. frs. 36, 38–9, and perhaps 157 below).

Νιcαίηc . . . ἀπ' 'Οργάδοc: for the epithet cf. *Aet.* fr. 43. 52 Pf. Νιcαῖοι Μεγαρῆεc (= Ap. Rh. 2. 747 = Theocr. 12. 27); Nisaea was the port of Megara. ὀργάc (on which Didymus spends much time) means a rich tract of land sacred to the gods; the Athenians gave the name 'Οργάc (ἱερά ὀργάc in an inscription, *BCH* 13 (1889), 434. 7 etc.) to land between Attica and the Megarid, sacred to Demeter and Persephone. On the prohibition against cultivating such territory and the disputes which it caused see P. Foucart, *BCH* 13 (1889), 436–7 and Lilian Chandler, *JHS* 46 (1926), 12. ἀπ' ὀργάδοc* comes also in Nonn. *Dion.* 4. 424.

ἀγλῖθεc: (e.g. Ar. *Ach.* 763, *Vesp.* 680), technically αἱ κεφαλαὶ τῶν cκορόδων. A scholiast on Ar. *Pax* 246 writes ἡ Μεγαρικὴ γῆ cκοροδοφόροc—all the more pitiable therefore is the Megarian who offers his daughter for a bunch of garlic in *Ach.* 813. The proverbial ancient equivalent to 'crocodile tears' was Μεγαρικὰ δάκρυα.

Fr. 157 inc. sed. (585 Pf.)

Pliny (*NH* 25. 167) says that Call. used the name 'acanthis' for the vegetable erigeron. It will be remembered that we owe to Pliny two other vegetables which Hecale set before Theseus (frs. 38–9), but in those instances—unlike the present one—the context is clearly stated. Theophrastus (*HP* 7. 7. 1) classes ἠριγέρων among vegetables 'of the type of chicory'. The sense which Call. gives to ἄκανθιc may be paralleled in K. Preisendanz (ed.), *Pap. Mag. Graec.* ii (1931), p. 84. 424.

Fr. 158 inc. sed. (682 Pf.)

τί δάκρυον εὖδον ἐγείρεις: perhaps the first words of Hecale's reply to Theseus' request (fr. 40. 3 ff.) for details of her past life, and possibly (A. S. Hollis, *CQ*, NS 32 (1982), 472) to be joined to fr. 41 (see further ad loc.), thus producing τί δάκρυον εὖδον ἐγείρεις;| οὐ γάρ μοι πενίη πατρώιος κτλ. If this were correct, fr. 158 may be separated from fr. 40. 6 by only a few lines.

The protest against renewing old griefs comes well as an immediate response to a request for information about the past, as e.g. *Od*. 7. 241–2 ἀργαλέον, βασίλεια, διηνεκέως ἀγορεῦσαι | κήδε', 17. 46–7 μῆτερ ἐμή, μή μοι γόον ὄρνυθι, μηδέ μοι ἦτορ | ἐν cτήθεccιν ὄρινε, 19. 116–18 (though not the first words of direct speech) μηδ' ἐμὸν ἐξερέεινε γένος καὶ πατρίδα γαῖαν,| μή μοι μᾶλλον θυμὸν ἐνιπλήcηιc ὀδυνάων | μνηcαμένωι; Virg. *A*. 2. 3 'infandum, regina, iubes renovare dolorem'; Ov. *Met*. 9. 4 'triste petis munus'; Stat. *Theb*. 5. 29–30 'immania vulnera, rector,| integrare iubes'. For the image of the sleeping ill cf. Sol. 4. 19 πόλεμόν θ' εὖδοντ' ἐπεγείρει; Simon. *PMG* 543. 22 εὐδέτω δ' ἄμετρον κακόν; E. *Supp*. 1146, *El*. 41–2 εὖδοντ' ἂν ἐξήγειρε τὸν Ἀγαμέμνονος | φόνον. Nonn. *Dion*. 22. 394–5 παύεο νύμφαιc | δάκρυα Νηιάδεccιν ἀδακρύτοιcιν ἐγείρων may glance at Call.

Fr. 159 inc. sed. (619 Pf.)

ἀβάλε μηδ' ἀβόληcα: if this fragment belongs to the *Hecale* (note the characteristic alliteration), one can think of several encounters which someone might wish not to have occurred, e.g. the crow with Athena (see frs. 71–2), Aegeus with Medea, Hecale with anyone responsible for her catastrophe—and probably others of which we know nothing. A good fit might be Aegeus on Medea: 'I wish I had not even met her [let alone made her my wife]'; cf. Ov. *Met*. 7. 403 'nec satis hospitium est; thalami quoque foedere iungit'.

ἀβάλε: cf. Alcm. *PMG* 111 ἀβάλε καὶ νοέοντα (and possibly *PMG* 3. 77). In fr. 41. 2 we find βάλε, which also had a precedent in Alcman. From Call. came Agath. *AP* 7. 583. 1 ἀβάλε μηδ' ἐγένοντο and anon. *AP* 7. 699. 3. The interjection was usually taken to be composed of ἆ and βάλε (see Pfeiffer).

ἀβόληcα: ἀβολέω, a later form of the Homeric ἀντιβολέω,

occurs also in *Aet.* fr. 24. 5 Pf.; Ap. Rh. 2. 770, 3. 1145. Antimachus used ἀβολήτωρ (fr. 76 Wyss) and probably ἀβολητύς (fr. 161).

Fr. 160 inc. auct. (370 dub. Pf.)

καὶ ἄγριον οἶδμα θαλάccηc: a notorious fragment. Pfeiffer included it 'valde dubitanter', but withdrew his support (ii, p. 121) after Wyss (*Mus. Helv.* 6 (1949), 193 n. 43) observed that these words occur twice in Gregory of Nazianzus (*Carm.* 2. 1. 1. 21, 2. 2. 5. 203 (*PG* xxxvii. 971, 1536)). But the question of authorship remains entirely open; several arguments can be deployed on either side. The words were given to the *Hecale* by Hecker's Law (see above, Introd. sect. IX). On the other hand, there are anonymous quotations from poems other than Call.'s *Hecale* in Suidas (above, Introd. sect. IX), and some of these have been mistaken for *Hecale* fragments in the past. Does Suidas elsewhere cite the verse of Gregory of Nazianzus anonymously? To judge from Ada Adler's Index Auctorum (v, p. 71, col. 2), there is just one certain instance in the whole Lexicon (s.v. cφαδάζοντεc, giving Greg. Naz. *Carm.* 2. 1. 11. 848–9 (*PG* xxxvii. 1088, iambic))—N. G. Wilson points to a citation in Hesych. ii, p. 807 Latte (*E* 1203) which went unrecognized for a long time and led scholars astray. A complicating factor is that Gregory liked to quote Callimachus verbatim (see e.g. on frs. 2. 2 τέγοc ἀκλήιcτον and 26 ἐλαχὺν δόμον).

It hardly seems possible to decide whether Suidas took the fragment from Call. or from Gregory of Nazianzus. Kost (on Musae. 203) is still prepared to allow that this may be a piece of the *Hecale*, and I sympathize, though, in view of the uncertain authorship, it must for the present languish among the Incerta. Both Barigazzi and Krafft consider restoring]καὶ κῦμα κα⌊ὶ ἄγριον οἶδμα θαλάccηc in fr. 47. 7 (see ad loc.) where, as far as we can judge, the context would be appropriate.

οἶδμα θαλάccηc does not occur in Homer, but must have been a familiar phrase in archaic epic (*H. Hom. Dem.* 14, *Cert. Hom. et Hes.* 131 Allen; cf. Ar. *Av.* 250 πόντιον οἶδμα θαλάccηc). In later poetry οἶδμα θαλάccηc becomes enormously popular, e.g. Dion. Per. 83. 540; [Opp.] *Cyn.* 2. 147; five times in [Apollinar.] *Ps.* (68. 72 etc.).

Fr. 161 inc. sed. (591 Pf.)

τεθναίην ὅτ' ἐκεῖνον ἀποπνεύσαντα πυθοίμην: for the faint possibility (Barigazzi) of restoring this line in fr. 49. 18 see ad loc. The traces of the papyrus are against it, although the sense would be excellent. Hecale has just (ll. 13–15) spoken of the terrible vengeance which she would like to inflict on Cercyon 'while he is still alive'—not knowing that Theseus has already killed him. She might well feel that she could die happy on hearing of Cercyon's death, about which Theseus presumably told her in his reply. And of course Hecale *will* die very soon after her meeting with Theseus.

The motif 'may I die when such and such has happened' occurs most often in the context of love fulfilled; see Naeke, p. 248; and Kost on Musae. 79 αὐτίκα τεθναίην λεχέων ἐπιβήμενος Ἡροῦς (the earliest example is *H. Hom. Aphr.* 153–4). In a grimmer sense, Orestes prays to die when he has killed his mother (A. *Ch.* 438, where schol. quote our fragment; cf. E. *El.* 281). The closest parallel might be E. *El.* 663, where an old man says of Clytemnestra's death εἰ γὰρ θάνοιμι τοῦτ' ἰδὼν ἐγώ ποτε.

Frs. 162 and 163 could correspond to frs. 51–6, on the subject of toil, poverty, and injustice.

Fr. 162 inc. sed. (721 Pf.)

ἵν' ἀμαζόνες ἄνδρες ἔασιν: in itself the phrase ἀμαζόνες ἄνδρες is sportive. The whimsical humour is increased by the fact that Call. is playing with an absurd etymology; he means poor men, οἱ μᾶζαν μὴ ἔχοντες (*Et. Gud.*). Pfeiffer suggested a link with fr. 55 γηφάγοι, which is also used in an artificial sense.

Fr. 163 inc. sed. (489 Pf.)

1–2 οἷοί τε βιοπλανὲς ἀγρὸν ἀπ' ἀγροῦ | φοιτῶσιν: possibly to be connected with the preceding fragment and/or fr. 55 (cf. Naeke, pp. 107–8), but, as Pfeiffer says, one can think of many different contexts (e.g., perhaps in a simile, with reference to nomadic tribes who change their habitation).

1 βιοπλανές: not before Call.; later in Nonn. *Par.* 13. 123

πτωχοῖcι βιοπλανέεccιν (cf. 15. 73, 20. 99). Some ancient grammarians held that in Homer ἐπιτηδέc, ἀκλεέc, and παλιμπετέc (the last two in Call. *H.* 4. 294–5) could be nominative (or accusative) plural rather than neuter accusative used adverbially. H. L. Ahrens (*De Graecae Linguae Dialectis* (1843), ii. 174) compared ἱαρέc (sometimes nominative, sometimes accusative) for ἱερεῖc on inscriptions from Cyrene, and believed that Call. was using the Doric dialect of his homeland. This view was rejected by most later scholars (including Pfeiffer), but see Giangrande, *Hermes*, 98 (1970), 272–3 = *SMA* i. 80–1.

Fr. 164 inc. sed. (513 Pf.)

From the fact that *Et. Mag.* has γραῦιc γραύιδι παρὰ Καλλ., some conclude that Call. used the dative; that may be so, but in *Et. Gen.* AB (B checked by Professor Alpers) we find γραῦιc γραύιδοc π. Κ. The unique form may be compared with οἶιδα in Theocr. 1. 9.

Fr. 165 inc. auct. (732 Pf.)

πολλὰ μάτην κεράεccιν ἐc ἠέρα θυμήναντα: quoted by Cicero (*Att.* 8. 5. 1) without indication of author or work, but in such a way as to suggest that the line was well enough known to be recognized easily by Atticus. This impression is strengthened by Catullus' apparent imitation of the same line when writing of Theseus' struggle with the Minotaur 'sic domito saevum prostravit corpore Theseus | nequiquam vanis iactantem cornua ventis' (64. 110-11; see further above, Introd. sect. VI for links between the *Hecale* and Catull. 64). M. Haupt (*Opuscula*, ii (1875), 81) first assigned Cicero's hexameter to the combat between Theseus and the Marathonian bull in the *Hecale*; most (but not all) later scholars have approved. Cicero gives other evidence of familiarity with this part of our poem: *Tusc.* 4. 50 'an etiam Theseus Marathonii tauri cornua comprehendit iratus?' may glance at fr. 67 θηρὸc ἐρωήcαc ὀλοὸν κέραc. As Pfeiffer says, this cπονδειάζων is worthy of Call., and the subject-matter seems entirely apt. If correctly assigned, it must refer to a stage of the combat before Theseus breaks off one of the bull's horns with his club (see fr. 69. 1). More remote echoes of the line may be found in later Roman

poetry (Ov. *Met.* 7. 786 'vanos exercet in aera morsus' of
Cephalus' dog; Man. 5. 601–2 'saevit in auras | morsibus' of
Andromeda's monster).

P. J. Parsons on *P. Oxy.* 3530 (I, p. 27) has a nice note on the
conventional behaviour of enraged bulls in poetry (see also
Campbell, *Studies*, pp. 79–80, noting 3. 1326 θυμαίνεςκον*). In
that Euripides papyrus, line 6 has κυρτὸν ἐς κ[έρας θυμούμενον (for
the supplement cf. E. *Ba.* 743 and Virg. *G.* 3. 232 'irasci in
cornua'); if the play were *Aegeus* (which is open to doubt), the
reference would be to the Marathonian bull, and this might be
Call.'s model.

Fr. 166 inc. auct. (756 Pf.)

μύρςον ἐς ὠτώεντα παλαιφαμένης ἄγνοιο: although not even
the authorship of this fragment is stated, Pfeiffer very convinc-
ingly referred it to the enclosure of Ericthonius in a wicker basket
for safe keeping by the daughters of Cecrops. Thus Ovid (*Met.* 2.
553 ff.):

> Pallas Ericthonium, prolem sine matre creatam
> *clauserat Actaeo texta de vimine cista,*
> virginibusque tribus gemino de Cecrope natis
> et legem dederat, sua ne secreta viderent.

Compare the Atthidographer 'Amelesagoras' quoted at pp.
229–30 above: Ἐριχθόνιον ... τρέφειν τὴν Ἀθηνᾶν καὶ εἰς κίστην
κατεῖρξαι. The line therefore would come from the speech of the
crow, and belong in the lacuna between frs. 69 and 70.

μύρςον: 'a basket', elsewhere only in lexicographers. Accord-
ing to *Et. Gen.*, μύρςος πλεκτόν ἐστιν ἀγγεῖον ἐξ ἄγνου. In fr. 70. 14
(as in 'Amelesagoras', Euphorion, Ovid, and Nonnus) the same
receptacle may be called a κίστη, for which Hesychius gives an
almost identical explanation (ἀγγεῖον πλεκτόν). See John H.
Oakley, *JHS* 102 (1982), 221 and pl. ix–x for vase-painters'
rendering of this wickerwork basket and, on basket-weaving in
Attica, Scherling, *Quibus Rebus*, p. 35.

ὠτώεντα: having 'ears' or handles, the Homeric form of the
epithet (applied to tripods in *Il.* 23. 264, 513; cf. Hes. *Op.* 657). In
Aet. fr. 1. 31 Pf. Call. uses οὐατόεις of a donkey.

παλαιφαμένης ἄγνοιο: (Nic. *Ther.* 591 παλαιςταγέος οἴνοιο*).

Only one other Callimachean cπονδειάζων ends with a trisyllabic word: *H.* 1. 41 (*Λυκαονίηc ἄρκτοιο*). The unique *παλαιφάμενοc* perhaps owes its existence to controversy over *Od.* 19. 163 δρυὸc

... *παλαιφάτου*, where the normal meaning ('spoken of old', 'legendary') seemed inappropriate to many (whence the variants *παλαιφάγου, παλαιφύτου*). An alternative explanation for the second element is suggested by schol. *Od.* 2. 355 *μυληφάτου*] τοῦ ἐν τῶι μύλωι πεφαμένου, ὅ ἐcτι κεκομμένου (cf. Hesych. s.v. *φατοί· τεθνεῶτεc* and *φαμένων· τετελευτηκότων*, also various compounds in -*φατοc* discussed by James, *Oppian of Cilicia*, pp. 53–5). Call. here means 'cut a long time ago'. Pfeiffer points out that Columella (11. 2. 92) prescribes different treatment for willow according to whether it is 'decisa pridie', 'ante quindecim dies', or 'iam pridem caesa'. *ἄγνοc* is the 'chaste tree' (*Vitex agnus castus*); cf. *H. Hom. Herm.* 410, Nic. *Ther.* 71, etc.

Fr. 167 inc. sed. (519 Pf.)

ἀλλὰ θεῆc ἥτιc με διάκτορον ἔλλαχε Παλλάc: first given to the *Hecale* by Meineke, whose conjecture we can take up with fair confidence now that cols. ii–iv of the Vienna Tablet (frs. 69, 72–3) have revealed more about the talking birds. The speaker (as *Et. Mag.* states) is an owl; if she was the silent listener of fr. 74. 21 *τὴν δ᾽ ἀΐουcαν* (see discussion at p. 225 above), this fragment shows that the owl too had something to say for herself.

θεῆc ἥτιc ... Παλλάc: the noun attracted into the case of the preceding relative (for the commoner attraction into the case of a *following* relative cf. Jebb on S. *OT* 449 and Austin on *Aen.* 1. 573 'urbem quam statuo vestra est'). Dislocation of the natural word order is a marked feature of Call.'s style; Pfeiffer on *Aet.* fr. 6 gives examples of the antecedent noun placed within a relative clause, e.g. *H.* 4. 156 *ἥτιc Κέρκυρα φιλοξεινωτάτη ἄλλων* and fr. 550 Pf. ὅ πρὸ μιῆc ὥρηc θηρίον οὐ λέγεται.

θεῆc: see McLennan (*HZ*) on *H.* 1. 30 and Campbell on Quint. Smyrn. 12. 112 for variation between *θεά* and *θεή*.

διάκτορον: this mysterious Homeric epithet of Hermes (cf. R. Janko, *Glotta*, 56 (1978), 192–5) was generally taken by later poets to mean either 'servant, assistant' or 'messenger' (both senses can be discerned in Nonnus). Antip. Sid. *AP* 7. 161(= 20 G.–P.). 1

ὄρνι Διὸς Κρονίδαο διάκτορε (to an eagle) probably comes from Call.

ἔλλαχε: for λαγχάνειν = 'to become the tutelary deity of' see Williams (*HA*) on *H*. 2. 43. Schneider compared schol. A *Il*. 8. 247 ἐν τῆι διανεμήσει τῶν πτηνῶν Ζεὺς τὸν ἀετὸν εἵλετο (cf. Pfeiffer on his fr. 119); but, in the *Hecale* at least, the owl was not Athene's original bird—the crow lost this privileged position because of her κακαγγελία (see frs. 70–4).

Fr. 168 inc. sed. (608 Pf.)

κάρτ' ἀγαθὴ κικυμωίς: ascribable to the *Hecale* with less confidence than fr. 167. κικυμωίς is one of many similar onomatopoeic names for an owl (D'Arcy Thompson, *Greek Birds*, s.v. κικκάβη; cf. Ar. *Av*. 261 κικκαβαῦ, *Lys*. 761 κακκαβιζουςῶν). Sometimes the owl brings bad omens, sometimes good (particularly for battle, see D'Arcy Thompson, op. cit. p. 78 s.v. γλαῦξ). If this fragment really belongs to the *Hecale*, one might wonder whether *Theb*. 3. 507–8 'flavaeque sonans avis unca Minervae | . . . auguriis melior' should be added to the Statian echoes of our poem.

Fr. 169 inc. sed. (552 Pf.)

Βριληccοῦ λαγόνεccιν ὁμούριον ἐκτίccαντο: proposed for the *Hecale* by Naeke (p. 225), who added 'nullum excogito idoneum locum'. Since the discovery of the *Diegesis* in 1934 a very appropriate context has become available. It seems likely that Hecale's cottage stood on the slopes of Mt. Brilessus (Pentelicus), and this would be the general area of the new deme which Theseus called after her (*Dieg*. xi. 5–6; see above, Introd. sect. II). Theseus at the same time τέμενος ἱδρύσατο Ἑκαλείου Διός (*Dieg*. xi. 6–7) and I suggest that the object of ἐκτίccαντο, agreeing with ὁμούριον, may be (if not the deme itself) the τέμενος, and the subject, as in fr., 81, Hecale's new demesmen, who are following the instructions of Theseus (cf. Plut. *Thes*. 14, from Philochorus, τοῦ Θηcέωc κελεύcαντοc). If so, this might be among the last lines of the poem.

Βριληccοῦ: note the form (as in Thuc. 2. 23, Plin. *NH* 4. 24); in fr. 18. 11 the papyrus has Ὑμηττοῖο (which the scribe may have tried to change to Ὑμηccοῖο). The pseudo-Theophrastean *de Signis Tempestatum* used -ττ- for both mountains; Strabo (9. 1. 23) writes Ὑμηττόc but Βριληccόc, and that was probably conventional.

λαγόνεccιν: 'flanks', perhaps the first example of this metaphorical use (e.g. κνημόc and ὀφρῦc had previously been applied to mountains). Later parallels include probably *SH* 940. 8 (anon.) λ]αγόνεccι*, Dion. Hal. *Ant. Rom.* 3. 24 παρὰ τὴν λαγόνα τοῦ ὄρουc, and the curious Alciphr. 2. 20. 3 αἱ Βριλήccιαι λαγόνεc (in a very poetical context—could there be a common source in Comedy?). Often λαγών is the side of a tomb (Peek, *GVI* i. 1903. 12 λαγόνεccιν*, 1937. 3, 1984. 2).

ὁμούριον: cf. Ap. Rh. 3. 1095 Καδμείοιcιν ὁμούριον ἄcτυ πολίccαι (the adjective is common in Dionysius Periegetes and Nonnus). τέμενοc is a perfectly good poetical word; otherwise I might wonder whether the noun agreeing with ὁμούριον was the more exquisite ἔδεθλον (see below, App. V(c)). One could amuse oneself by bringing in fr. 81: τοῦτο γὰρ αὐτήν | κωμῆται κάλεον περιηγέεc, ⟨οἳ τότ'⟩ ἔδεθλον | Βριληccοῦ λαγόνεccιν ὁμούριον ἐκτίccαντο (a fantasy, of course, but not, I think, un-Callimachean),

ἐκτίccαντο: (Nic. *Alex.* 448*); cf. *Aet.* fr. 11. 5 Pf. ἄcτυρον ἐκτίccαντο, fr. 12. 4 Pf.; ἔκτιcε Κερκυραῖον ἐδέθλιον. Pindar applies the verb to an altar (*Ol.* 7. 42).

FRS. 170–9

Up to this point the Fragmenta Incerta (like the Fragmenta Hecalae as far as fr. 83) have been arranged according to my tentative reconstruction of the narrative. Although this is no longer possible for the remaining Fragmenta Incerta, I have grouped together a small number (170–5 (cf. 179), corresponding to 84–101 in the main section) which definitely or possibly relate to Attic and Argive matters.

Fr. 170 inc. sed. (704 Pf.)

The deme Ἁλιμοῦc was considered by Call. to be a πόλιc (Stephanus Byzantius); Pfeiffer compared *Aet.* fr. 31, whence we

learn that Call. also described as a πόλιc the Megarian village
Τριποδίcκη. Halimous (see J. J. E. Hondius, *BSA* 24 (1919–21),
151–60; D. M. Lewis, *Historia*, 12 (1963), 32–3; Wesley E.
Thompson, *Hesperia*, 39 (1970), 65) was situated on the south
coast of Attica; it included Colias (perhaps the modern Cape
Cosmas) which Call. mentions in fr. 92. In Philicus' *Hymn to
Demeter* (*SH* 680. 54; cf. above, Introd. sect. VI and Richardson,
H. Hom. Dem. p. 214) Iambe comes from Halimous.

It is not clear whether Call.'s use of πόλιc has any special
significance. Could it reflect the status of Halimous as 'an area of
old settlement with a very primitive Demeter cult' (D. M.
Lewis)? Could it be a humorous touch when applied to a place
which in 346 BC boasted only some 80 demesmen (Hondius, op.
cit. p. 156)—or perhaps Call. is suggesting that in mythical times
Halimous was more populous?

Fr. 171 inc. sed. (680 Pf.)

1–2 ὑπεὶρ ἅλα κεῖνοc ἐνάcθη | Ἀλκαθόου τίc ἄπυcτοc: ? 'the
man who has not heard of Alcathous must live overseas' (M. L.
West). The fact that hexameter follows hexameter (Pfeiffer
rightly rejected Schneider's ἄπυcτ' with elision at the diaeresis of a
pentameter) creates a certain presupposition in favour of the
Hecale—the only other lost or fragmentary poem which we *know*
to have been in hexameters is the *Galatea* (frs. 378–9 Pf.). I have
not allowed the same argument to earn for fr. 655 Pf. (the subject-
matter of which seems alien to the *Hecale*) a more honourable
place than in Appendix I. Alcathous here might be the founder of
Megara (e.g. Theognis 773–4, *Ciris* 105–6: see Roscher for other
mythical characters called Alcathous), and the *Hecale* contains
many references to Megara. But the matter remains very obscure.

1 ἐνάcθη: 'habitare factus est' according to Pfeiffer, who
compares *Il.* 14. 119–20 πατὴρ δ' ἐμὸc Ἄργεϊ νάcθη | πλαγχθείc—
in fr. 744 Pf. inc. auct. ἐνάcθη* perhaps = 'habitata est' or 'condita
est' of a town.

2 τίc: relative (according to schol. Soph.). as in *Iamb.* fr. 191. 67
Pf., *epigr.* 28 Pf. = *AP* 12. 43(= 2 G.–P.). 1–2 οὐδὲ κελεύθωι |
χαίρω τίc πολλοὺc ὧδε καὶ ὧδε φέρει.

ἄπυcτοc: going against the convention inherited from Homer
(which Call. observes in fr. 172 inc. sed.) whereby ἄπυcτοc at the

end of a hexameter means 'not hearing', but in this position 'not heard of'. See Hopkinson (*HD*) on *H*. 6. 9.

Fr. 172 inc. sed. (611 Pf.)

Καλλιχόρωι ἐπὶ φρητὶ καθέζεο παιδὸς ἄπυςτος: the subject is of course Demeter searching for Persephone. This line bears a close resemblance to *H*. 6. 15 *τρὶς δ' ἐπὶ Καλλιχόρωι χαμάδις ἐκαθίςςαο φρητί* (and note ibid. 9 *ἄπυςτα*); we cannot know which was written first. Pfeiffer inclines to the *Aetia*. I include this line among Fragmenta Incerta of the *Hecale* on the off chance (*CQ*, NS 32 (1982), 473) that it might be joined with fr. 173 inc. sed. to produce two consecutive hexameters: *Καλλιχόρωι ἐπὶ φρητὶ καθέζεο παιδὸς ἄπυςτος | γρήϊον εἶδος ἔχουςα*. In *H*. *Hom*. *Dem*. 98 ff. the goddess *ἕζετο . . . | Παρθενίωι φρέατι . . . | γρηΐ παλαιγενέϊ ἐναλίγκιος*. It would be like Call. to recall the earlier passage while changing the name of the well. If this idea did prove right, we could point to at least two contexts in the *Hecale* which might prompt a brief allusion to Demeter's search for Persephone: fr. 99 may refer to the same search (fr. 100 mentions the two goddesses together), or, if Eleusis were the connecting link, that was where Theseus killed Cercyon (cf. fr. 49. 8 ff. and fr. 62; Ov. *Met*. 7. 439 'Cercyonis letum vidit Cerealis Eleusin').

Καλλιχόρωι ἐπὶ φρητί: cf. Nic. *Ther*. 486 *Καλλίχορον παρὰ φρεῖαρ*. Richardson (*H*. *Hom*. *Dem*. App. I) discusses the archaeological evidence, and concludes that Parthenion and Callichoron were probably two names for the same well at Eleusis. The contracted form *φρητί* (cf. Hopkinson (*HD*) on *H*. 6. 15) does not occur earlier. See above, Introd. sect. IV.6 for the hiatus *Καλλιχόρωι ἐπί*.

ἄπυςτος: see on fr. 171. 2 above.

Fr. 173 inc. sed. (490 Pf.)

γρήϊον εἶδος ἔχουςα: Pfeiffer notes 'fort. Hec.?'. Whether or not this fragment could be joined to fr. 172 (above), I feel confident that these words do not describe an old woman—rather someone (almost certainly a goddess) pretending to be an old woman; compare e.g. Nonn. *Dion*. 2. 207 (Nike) *Λητοῦς εἶδος ἔχουςα*, 3. 85 (Peitho) *θνητῆς εἶδος ἔχουςα*, 40. 8 (Athena) *Μορρέος* εἶδος ἔχουςα. Instances of goddesses disguising themselves as an old woman are collected by Richardson on *H. Hom. Dem.* 101 (cf. Hopkinson (*HD*) on *H.* 6. 42).

Fr. 174 inc. sed. (705 Pf.)

εἰς Ἀσίνην Ἄλυκόν τε καὶ ἂμ πόλιν Ἑρμιονήων: this hexameter, with its three Peloponnesian cities, could well belong to the *Aetia*. In book 1, frs. 24–5 Pf., Call. told of the war between Heracles and the Dryopes, which ended with the latter being transported to the Peloponnese, and established as Ἀσινεῖς (i.e. citizens of Asine and also 'harmless'; cf. fr. 25 Pf.). According to Diodorus (4. 37. 2) the Dryopes τρεῖς πόλεις ὤικιςαν ἐν Πελοποννήςωι, Ἀσίνην καὶ Ἑρμιόνην, ἔτι δὲ Ἡιόνα. The third city of our fragment, Alycus, is so called elsewhere only in schol. Ar. *Lys.* 403, but may be the same as Pausanias' Ἁλίκη (2. 36. 1); see W. Dittenberger, *Hermes* 42 (1907), 3 ff. for other forms of the name. It can hardly be identical with Eion in Diodorus (above).

Although one can make quite a good case for the *Aetia*, the *Hecale* too has many Argive references (frs. 95–101 and fr. 175 inc. sed.); Hermione in particular is very probably connected with fr. 100, and perhaps with fr. 99 too. So, following Naeke (p. 208) and Kapp (fr. 149), I have, hesitantly, included this among my Fragmenta Incerta.

εἰς Ἀσίνην Ἄλυκόν τε: cf. *Il.* 2. 560(= [Hes.] fr. 204. 49 M.–W.) Ἑρμιόνην Ἀσίνην τε.

ἂμ πόλιν: = Ap. Rh. 1. 166*, 2. 996*.

Fr. 175 inc. sed. (684 Pf.)

A scholiast on Stat. *Theb.* 4. 46–7 'quaeque pavet longa spumantem valle Charadron | Neris' writes 'Neris montis nomen Argivi, ut ait Callimachus' (though Statius surely is speaking of a town). Naeke (p. 174) thought of the *Hecale*, reasonably enough in view of the other Argive references which Statius seems to have drawn from our poem (cf. above, Introd. sect. II n. 19 and on fr. 95). Euphorion apparently had Neris as a river, puzzling a commentator who remarked Νῆριν δ[ὲ ποτα]μὸν μὲν οὐκ οἶδα (*SH* 430. 31–2; see ibid. p. 219 for an attempt to recover the text on which this is based). Pausanias (2. 38. 6) speaks of a κώμη Neris.

We may compare the case of Λύρκειον (fr. 45), which is variously described as a mountain, river, and town (of course there need be no incompatibility).

Fr. 176 inc. sed. (687 Pf.)

δαίμων, τῆι κόλποιϲιν ἐνιπτύουϲι γυναῖκεϲ: without doubt the deity is Nemesis; as Hecker and Schneider thought, this line may somehow be connected with fr. 116 Αἴϲηπον ἔχειϲ, ἑλικώτατον ὕδωρ | Νηπείηϲ ἤ τ᾽ ἄργοϲ, ἀοίδιμοϲ Ἀδρήϲτεια. Spitting into the bosom aims to avoid punishment for arrogance or extravagant ambition (cf. Frank W. Nicolson, *HSCP* 8 (1897), 35–9; Gow on Theocr. 6. 39); it is most often done by women (e.g. Theocr. 7. 127, 20. 11; *Ciris* 372; Petr. 74. 13), but by no means confined to the female sex. Nemesis is specifically mentioned in e.g. Men. *Sam.* 503, Strat. *AP* 12. 229. 2. and anon. *AP* 16. 251. 5.

δαίμων: possible is Bentley's δαῖμον (as e.g. Euph. fr. 10 δαῖμον ὃϲ Ἀμφιλύϲοιο ῥόον), but the nominative could be used for the vocative, or else this might be a description of, rather than address to, the goddess; for the style see on fr. 116.

ἐνιπτύουϲι: like Schneider (fr. 235), I accept Hecker's correction for ἐπιπτύουϲι.

Fr. 177 inc. sed. (527a Pf.)

ὅν τε μάλιϲτα βοῶν ποθέουϲιν ἐχῖνοι: the structure of this fragment closely resembles that of fr. 117 ὅν τε μύωπα βοῶν καλέουϲιν ἀμορβοί (see ad loc. for 'epic τε'), and thus a place in the *Hecale* is at least possible. We do not know the nature of this most desirable food. I have suggested a link with fr. 102 (see ad loc.) where two different kinds of cattle fodder are mentioned; in the present fragment, however, the relative clause could be purely decorative, as e.g. in Nic. *Alex.* 412–13 φυλλάδα τ᾽ ἰϲχνήν | πηγάνου, ἥν τ᾽ ὤκιϲτα βορῆι ἐπεϲίνατο κάμπη.

ἐχῖνοι: Aristotle often used ἐχῖνοϲ for the stomach of ruminating animals (why the grammarian Seleucus should reprehend Call. for this is unclear). Compare Nic. *Ther.* 579 ἤ ἐλάφου νηδύν, τὸ μὲν ἄρ καλέουϲιν ἐχῖνον, where schol. comments ἐχῖνοϲ κυρίωϲ μὲν ἡ κοιλία τοῦ βοόϲ.

Fr. 178 inc. sed. (725 Pf.)

καὶ ὡc λύκοc ὠρυοίμην: Pfeiffer notes the spondaic ending
(with this verb also in Arat. *Phaen.* 1124; Theocr. 1. 71, 2. 35;
Opp. *Hal.* 1. 399; Quint. Smyrn. 12. 518; Triph. 611) and the
sequence of vowels as somewhat favouring the *Hecale*. ὠρύομαι is
the *vox propria* for wolves (and dogs), occasionally applied also to
jackals, lions, and beavers.

Fr. 179 inc. auct. (741 Pf.)

According to *Et. Gen.* the ἀρρηφορία or ἐρρηφορία, a festival in
honour of Athena, was also called ἐρcηφορία, from Herse
daughter of Cecrops, ταύτηι γὰρ ἦγον τὴν ἑορτήν. οὕτω Cαλού-
cτιοc. Although no individual work of Salustius is specified, this
may derive from his commentary on Call.'s *Hecale*, to the use of
which by Suidas and *Et. Gen.* we owe so many otherwise
unknown fragments of the poem. Salustius is also named by *Et.
Gen.* s.v. ἁρπῖδεc (see the sources quoted for fr. 9. 1–2), while his
commentary on the *Hecale* is specified s.v. ἀcκάντηc (fr. 29): οὕτωc
Cαλούcτιοc εἰc τὴν Ἑκάλην Καλλιμάχου (cf. above, Introd. sect.
VII). On the daughters of Cecrops in the *Hecale* (including the
doubtful evidence of Phld. *Piet.* (*SH* 307 = above, Test. Dub. 16,
which may refer to Herse's part), see above, p. 231). The supposed
link between Herse and Hersephoria is discussed by Jane E.
Harrison (*JHS* 12 (1891), 350–5), and the whole significance of
the festival by W. Burkert (*Hermes*, 94 (1966), 1–25).

    The close similarity between *Et. Gen.*'s extract and schol. Ar.
Lys. 642 (where this lore is attributed to Istros (*FGH*, 334 F 27)
may be due to the use of the same lexicon by Salustius and the
Aristophanes scholiast.

APPENDIX I
Some Other Fragments

To discuss every fragment incertae sedis (let alone incerti auctoris) which some scholar at some time may have wished to ascribe to the *Hecale* would be a thankless task. But here is a sample of such fragments, together with a few notes mainly confined to the problem of attribution; see Pfeiffer (or *SH*) for sources, apparatus criticus, and fuller commentary. While believing that my Fragmenta Incerta stand at least a fair chance of belonging to our poem, I hold no special brief for those below. Undoubtedly there are further pieces of the *Hecale* in Pfeiffer which are not to be found in my book at all—fragments which (unless I have overlooked something) contain nothing to link them with the *Hecale* rather than some other poem. Whenever new evidence about the *Hecale* comes to light, all the unplaced material (including those of Schneider's anonymous fragments which Pfeiffer omitted) should be looked at afresh.

Fr. 476 inc. sed. Pf. μύθου δὲ πασαίμην | ἥδιον. Naeke (p. 164) gave these words to Hecale, but the *Aetia* is an equally possible home (cf. frs. 43. 16 ff. and 178. 30 Pf.).

Fr. 483 inc. sed. Pf. μή με τὸν ἐν Δωδῶνι λέγοι μόνον οὕνεκα χαλκόν | ἤγειρον. Older scholars (e.g. Naeke, p. 49, Schneider, fr. 306) thought of literary polemic, perhaps in a prologue (? *Aetia*). Although we now know that the *Hecale* did not start with a prologue, Pfeiffer favours our poem because of the sequence of vowels ε–ο (cf. fr. 118) and consonants μ–ν (he also refers to fr. 58, perhaps on Hecale's loquacity). For the gong of Dodona see Gomme and Sandbach on Men. fr. 60. 3 ff.

Fr. 516 inc. sed. Pf. (also in *Et. Gen.* cod. A) τῶν ἔτι σοι δεκάφυια φάτο ζωάγρια τίσειν (better τείσειν, as in Pfeiffer's Index Vocabulorum). 'Similia vota Molorchi . . . et Hecalae [Plut. *Thes.* 14]; at neutri pretium decemplex convenire videtur' (Pfeiffer).

Fr. 520 inc. sed. Pf. (also in *Et. Gen.* A) εἰ δέ ποτε προφέροιντο διάσματα, φάρεος ἀρχήν (cf. Nonn. *Dion.* 6. 152). Pfeiffer approves the suggestion of Schneider (fr. 244) that the robe is Athena's (cf. Suid. s.v. χαλκεῖα). Salustius in his *Hecale* commentary may have talked about the origin of the ἀρρηφορία (see fr. 179 inc. auct.).

Fr. 530 inc. sed. Pf. χολῆι δ' ἴcα γέντα πάcαιο. If this fragment comes from the *Hecale*—and the ferocious curse is not alien to our poem—could Athena be banishing the crow (cf. fr. 72 and perhaps fr. 73. 6), who will henceforth be denied any more succulent offerings from the Acropolis (cf. Lucr. 6. 752)? But E. A. Barber thought rather plausibly of the Lindian Sacrifice in *Aet.* 1 (frs. 22–3 Pf.).

Fr. 536 inc. sed. Pf. τέρπνιϲτοι δὲ τοκεῦϲι τόθ᾽ υἱέεϲ. A father–son relationship is important in the *Hecale*, but that would be a flimsy reason for ascription to our poem.

Fr. 543 inc. sed. Pf. ἀπότριχεϲ παρὰ Καλλ. οἱ ἄνηβοι (Eustathius, the same gloss anonymously in *Et. Gen.* A). Compare fr. 108.

Fr. 546 inc. sed. Pf. κρήνη | λευκὸν ὕδωρ ἀνέβαλλεν. If κρήνη stood at the end of the preceding line, we would have successive hexameters, and thus probably the *Hecale*. But, as Pfeiffer says, Eustathius is capable of omitting, or changing the position of, words.

Fr. 563 inc. sed. Pf. ἄοζοι. Given to Call. by Hesychius. Suid. also has ἄοζοι · πολύοζοι, πολλὰ ξύλα καίοντεϲ · ἤγουν οἱ μάγειροι, which might go back to Salustius.

Fr. 566 inc. sed. Pf. καταρήϲτην (?) ... παρὰ Καλλ. τὴν χάλαζαν (Hesych.). Schneider (fr. 357) thought of the storm in the *Hecale*.

Fr. 567 inc. sed. Pf. See below on fr. 638 inc. sed. Pf.

Fr. 575 inc. sed. Pf. †τοί δ᾽† ὥϲτ ἐξ ὀχεῆϲ ὄφιϲ αἰόλοϲ αὐχέν᾽ †ἀναύχην. At the end of the line Ruhnken's αὐχέν᾽ ἀναϲχών might be supported by Greg. Naz. *Carm.* 1. 1. 9. 94* (*PG* xxxvii. 464). Naeke (p. 179) thought of a simile for Sciron (see on frs. 59–60) darting out from behind the rocks to attack Theseus or another traveller, Pfeiffer of the snake (sometimes there are two) which lay beside the infant Ericthonius (cf. Ov. *Met.* 2. 561). For a metrical objection to Pfeiffer see Bulloch, *CQ*, NS 20 (1970), 259 n. 3.

Fr. 628 inc. sed. Pf. ἄνωγε δὲ πορθμέα νεκρῶν. Pfeiffer suggests the *Hecale*. ἄνωγε might point to one of the people, like Heracles, whom Charon conveyed unwillingly (cf. *Aen.* 6. 392 ff.).

Fr. 631 inc. sed. Pf. †ῆϲεν ἐκδοὺϲ ϲάμβαλον αὐλείου. *SH* 297 contains the remnants of a commentary on these words. From what we can read in the papyrus, W. Luppe (following A. H. Griffiths) in *ZPE* 32 (1978), 12–13 tentatively restores the text as ἧϲ ἔνεκ᾽ ἐκδούϲ (?ἐκδύϲ) | ϲάμβαλον αὐλείου ... οὐδοῦ, and, because of the consecutive hexameters, mentions the *Hecale*.

Fr. 636 inc. sed. Pf. μὴ ὀφέλετ᾽ ἀλλήλοιϲιν ἐπὶ πλέον ὄμματα δῦναι. Compare above, fr. 159 inc. sed.

Fr. 638 inc. sed. Pf. ἱλαθί μοι φαλαρῖτι, πυλαιμάχε. A prayer to Athena would suit the *Hecale* (cf. fr. 17. 9 ff.). *H.* 5. 43–4 might then suggest an association with fr. 567 inc. sed. Pf.: ἱλαθί μοι φαλαρῖτι, πυλαιμάχε, ⟨e.g. χρυϲεοπήληξ⟩, | ἡδομένη νεκάδεϲϲιν †ἐπιϲκυρῶν† πολέμοιο (in place of ἐπικυρῶν, Barber (*CR*, NS 9 (1959), 101–2) conjectured ἐπὶ cκύρωι). But Naeke (p. 274) saw in fr. 638 Pf. a prayer by the poet at the end of an aetion.

Fr. 655 inc. sed. Pf. καὶ τριτάτη Περcῆοc ἐπώνυμοc, ἧc ὀρόδαμνον | Αἰγύπτωι κατέπηξεν. Consecutive hexameters; although the subject-matter seems alien to *Hecale*, note Suid. s.v. ὀρόδαμνοc · παραφυάc, which might or might not come from Salustius' commentary.

Fr. 694 inc. sed. Pf. (= fr. 154 inc. Kapp) ἀεὶ δ᾽ ἔχον ἔντομα cηκοί. The sole (and very fragile) reason for giving to the *Hecale* is that the Thucydides commentary which quotes this previously unknown snippet also quotes, without attributing to a particular poem, fr. 85.

Fr. 701 inc. sed. Pf. δέδαεν δὲ λαχαινέμεν ἔργα cιδήρου. Steph. Byz. s.v. Αἴδηψοc later gives fr. 10.2 with Αἰδήψιον ἄορ. As Pfeiffer says, fr. 701 may have been abbreviated; one expects Aedepsus or Euboea to appear in the text. Perhaps from the *Hecale*, but Stephanus Byzantius explicitly assigns fr. 10. 2 to our poem, while remaining silent about the present fragment.

Fr. 709 inc. sed. Pf. Call. called Attica Μοψοπία. Naeke (p. 226) referred to the *Hecale*, but the *Aetia* too contained many Attic stories.

Fr. 718 inc. sed. Pf. (= fr. 115 Kapp) ἀπεcτώ · ... παρὰ Καλλ. ἡ ἀποδημία (Suid.); but the style suggests some grammatical source rather than Salustius (Pf.).

Fr. 719 inc. sed. Pf. (= fr. 59 Kapp) θεῶι τ᾽ ἀλάλαγμα νόμαιον | δοῦναι; but Suidas' citation clearly comes from scholia (more detailed than those which we have) on Ar. *Av.* 364.

Fr. 730 inc. auct. Pf. ἀδρανίη †τοδεπολλον†. Suidas has ἀδρανία · ἡ ἀδυναμία, ἀcθένεια; 'de Hecala igitur cogitare licet' (Pf.). The obelized letters may represent τὸ δὲ πολλόν (Hecker; cf. *H.* 1. 27).

Fr. 738 inc. auct. Pf. ἀμίcαλλοί τε γέροντεc. 'Fortasse ex sermone Hecales. Etsi Hecale ipsa quam minime ἀμίcαλλοc fuit' (Naeke, p. 154).

Fr. 745 inc. auct. Pf. Βύνηc καταλέκτριαι αὐδηέccηc. Pfeiffer (on his fr. 303) notes that as yet there is no certain example in the *Aetia* of spondaic fifth foot combined with masculine caesura, but several examples in the *Hecale*. In vol. i p. 510 Pfeiffer argues that we should read καταδέκτριαι.

Fr. 752 inc. auct. Pf. ὡc δ᾽ ἐνὶ κορcωτῆροc ὑπὸ τρίχα καλλύνονται (cf. Pfeiffer, i, p. 510). Pfeiffer endorses Hecker's ascription to our poem, and certainly this line sounds like the *Hecale*. But the subject-matter (beautification in a barber's shop) seems remote; 'comparatio, in carmine epico satis festiva' (Pf.).

Fr. 763 inc. auct. Pf. πολιὴ δ᾽ ἀνεκήκιεν ἅλμη. The MSS of Herodian have πολλή—if that is correct, the fragment cannot be by Call. (who allows a spondaic word after the masculine caesura only when there is also a bucolic diaeresis, as e.g. my fr. 74. 13, 21). But Pfeiffer's πολιή is plausible (cf. Nonn. *Dion.* 39. 248); to his parallels add now Euph. *SH* 442. 6 νοτερὴ δ᾽ ἀνεκήκιεν ἅλμη.

Fr. 766 inc. auct. ἑcπέριον ξένον might suit Theseus visiting Hecale (or Heracles Molorchus). See below, App. III.

Fr. 768 inc. auct. Pf. ἠκαλέον γελόωcα 'Call. (Hecal.) tribuit Meineke, *Call.* p. 145, recte opinor' (Pf.).

Fr. 771 inc. auct. Pf. κλεψίρρυτον ὕδωρ. 'De partibus arcis Athenarum in Hecala passim' (Pf.).

Fr. 785 inc. auct. Pf. (cf. fr. 23 Kapp) †δίκρανον ἤρυγε φιτρὸc ἐπαιρόμενον ⟨φιτρὸν ἐπαιρόμενοc Hecker⟩. In *Aet.* fr. 177. 2 Pf., claimed for the Molorchus episode (= *SH* 259. 2) by Livrea (*ZPE* 34 (1979), 37 ff.), we find a pentameter ending δίκρον φιτρὸν ἀειραμένη. This corrupt anonymous citation by schol. Ar. *Pax* 637 (p. 101 Holwerda) is almost certainly a different line. Many scholars have wished to recognize a parallel in the *Hecale* to Ov. *Met.* 8. 647–8 'furca levat ille [sc. Philemon—some prefer 'illa', sc. Baucis] bicorni | sordida terga suis'. But this is at best a very remote possibility.

Fr. 803 inc. auct. Pf. Πειρήτιδοc ἱερὸc ὄρνιc. 'Omnia, et deae nomen et loci . . . et avis, nimis incerta' (Pf.).

Fr. 805 inc. auct. Pf. ἐc ὀλίζοναc ἀcτέραc ἄρκτου. Pfeiffer suggests ὀλίζονοc and the *Hecale* in view of Suid. s.v. ὀλίζονοc · μικρᾶc (? from Salustius).

Fr. 813 inc. auct. Pf. αὐτόν με πρώτιcτα cυνοικιcτῆρα †γαίαc | ἔcδεξαι τεμενοῦχον. Probably consecutive hexameters. Maas' suggestion of the *Hecale* is taken up by K. Nickau, *Rh. M.* 132 (1989), 298–307.

SH 1003. γρηὸc ὀδυρομένηc. Maas (*Kl. Schr.* p. 129) thought of Call.

SH 1046. ἦμοc δ᾽ ἠπεροπῆαc ἀνεπτοίηcεν ὀνείρουc | ἠέλιοc ⟨   ⟩ ἀναcχών. Schneider (fr. an. 93), seeing an imitation of the fragment in Ap. Rh. 3. 617–18, would ascribe to Call. these (probably) consecutive hexameters.

SH 1103. ῥάκε᾽ ἄζει · ἱμάτια ξηραίνει (Hesych.). Schneider (fr. an. 229, cf. ii, p. 181) pointed to the *Hecale*.

APPENDIX II
The Length of the *Hecale*

The scholiast on *H.* 2. 106 (= above, Test. 1) implies that *Hecale* was a
μέγα ποίημα. An attempt to estimate the original length is of some
interest for its own sake, and also for our view of the whole literary
category known as Hellenistic epyllion, in which our poem may have
occupied an honoured and influential place. First, however, let us
consider how much has actually survived. The firmest figure that can be
given is for complete lines (among which I have included fr. 49. 14 and
fr. 74. 8 as virtually complete). I count 125 in the text of this edition; one
might add 8 from the Fragmenta Incerta (which have at least a fair
chance of belonging to the *Hecale*). The computation of partially
preserved lines is less precise. If we reckon one partially preserved line
for each fragment such as 12, 38, or 59, it could be said that we have 254
partially preserved lines (of which at least 11 would have to be
discounted because no letters, or hardly any, are legible) and 18 in the
Fragmenta Incerta. But it is possible, even likely, that some of the 254
represent different parts of the same line—e.g. that fr. 19 should be
combined with fr. 18. 11, fr. 43 with fr. 42. 6, and so on (including cases
which cannot at present be suspected). A very few of the partially
preserved lines may belong to a complete line which we already know;
fr. 36. 2 probably does duplicate fr. 37, even though the papyrus has iota
rather than alpha after φαῦλον. Thus, simply to add the total of partially
preserved to that of complete lines would rather overstate the number
represented.

Something might be said also about certain of the lacunae between
sides or columns of a papyrus (and columns of the Vienna Tablet):

Between frs. 17 and 18 the lacuna is of uncertain length (one side of *P.
Oxy.* 2216 minus 2 lines).

Between frs. 27 and 36 the lacuna is of uncertain length (one side of *P.
Oxy.* 2529; frs. 29–35, some 8 lines, probably stood in this gap).

Between frs. 40 and 42 stood *c.* 32 lines, of which we have 2 (fr. 41).

Between frs. 69 and 70 stood *c.* 22 lines (fr. 76 might be one, and
fr. 166 inc. auct. another).

Between frs. 70 and 73 stood *c.* 22 lines (fr. 71 = 3 lines and fr. 72 = 2
lines very probably belong here).

Between frs. 73 and 74 stood *c.* 11 lines.

(For the very complex interrelationships of frs. 47–9 see my final note to the app. crit. of fr. 49 and also Commentary, pp. 187–8). It would be astonishing, however, if these lacunae did not contain other already preserved fragments, even though at present we may be unable to identify them.

The conventional estimate of *Hecale*'s length is about 1,000 lines. Various different approaches might be tried to test this, even though none can be anywhere near conclusive. Perhaps the most ingenious is that of Gregory Hutchinson, based upon the frequency with which ancient sources quote those passages of the *Hecale* which happen to have survived on papyrus. I am most grateful to Dr Hutchinson for allowing me to reproduce verbatim his thoughts (communicated to me privately); references to Pfeiffer and *SH* can be converted to my numeration by means of the tables on pp. 396–401 below.

Dr Hutchinson writes:

The papyri of the *Hecale* accommodate a striking number of quotations. Quotations from the poem are generally made for scholarly purposes rather than literary, and presumably derive from a tradition of thoroughgoing exegesis. Hence it is unlikely that quotations will come mostly from famous passages. Call.'s mode of writing makes it unlikely that there were extended passages which would need no explanation. It would seem plausible a priori that the proportion of quotations to original lines should be reasonably constant—save that the exegesis (or the appropriation of it) might in the course of the poem become rather less full. Such a diminution would be wholly typical. The papyri seem to support these notions remarkably well. In the list that follows I have excluded those quotations one would not have supposed to come from the *Hecale*. This is done to promote parity when extrapolating from the quotations not represented in papyri. In fact remarkably few are excluded in this way. On the other hand, I have not counted lines in the papyri of which there are preserved no more than three letters; quotations would have a slender chance of being recognized there. Fragments are listed in the accompanying table according to their order in the poem, save for *SH* 290–1, the place of which is unknown.

Fragment	No. of lines quoted	No. of lines preserved on papyrus
238 Pf.	10	32
(including a–d) with *SH* 281		
SH 282–3	2	8
SH 285	3	12
SH 286–7	12	46
SH 288 (with Pf.)	13	69
SH 290–1	1	3

The figures do seem coherent enough to offer some kind of indication about the whole poem. There is a decline in the proportion of quotations as the poem proceeds: from just under 1 in 3 (31%) with fr. 238 Pf. to just under 1 in 5 (19%) with *SH* 288, quite near the end of the poem (one naturally excludes *SH* 290–1 for this purpose, since its position in the poem is not known, and it does not even 'preserve' 5 lines). This would seem to suggest a diminution in exegesis of the kind we envisaged. Accordingly, if one estimated the proportion of all quotations to original lines at 1 : 5, one would probably overshoot the size of the poem. Even if one rejected the idea of diminution, and stressed the accidents of preservation, it would still be implausible to suppose that the proportion exceeded 1 : 5. The average proportion with the papyri (excluding *SH* 290–1) is roughly 1 : 4 (26%). Suppose that we apply the proportion 1 : 5 to the quotations assigned to the *Hecale* by Pfeiffer, but not represented on papyri (172). We would postulate that no quotations came from the same line or in fact belonged to a line preserved, but scantily, on papyrus. We should then add the number of lines preserved by the papyri. This yields 1,030. If we add the 18 fragments Pfeiffer thinks might come from the *Hecale*, we obtain 1,120. The proportion 1 : 4 would actually seem rather closer to the probable figure. If one follows the same procedure, and includes the 18 doubtfuls, one arrives at the total 930.

So Dr Hutchinson's method produces a result agreeing well with the traditional estimate of 1,000 lines for the *Hecale*. Let us now try a different approach, based upon Pfeiffer's hypothesis about the original contents of *P. Oxy.* 1011 (pap. 35 in Pfeiffer, ii, p. xxii), a late 4th-cent. codex (published by A. S. Hunt in *P. Oxy.* vii (1910), pp. 15 ff.) in which the epilogue to *Aet.* 4 (fr. 112 Pf.) ended near the top of p. 185. The number of lines per page, where we can check, varies from not more than 37 up to 43; if one guessed at an average of 39 lines, the codex would have contained up to that point nearly 7,200 lines. Pfeiffer argues, plausibly enough (ii, pp. xxii–xxiii; cf. Bulloch, *FH*, p. 80); 'codex, in cuius pagina 185 Aetiorum epilogus legitur, non ab Aetiorum prologo incipere potuit; ne magnum quidem Aetiorum opus plus quam 7,000 versuum fuisse credibile est; alia igitur carmina (Hymni scilicet et Hecala) ante Aetiorum lib. I collocata fuisse veri simillimum est.' We do not know the length of *Aet.* 1 and 2, but can get a fairly good idea about 3–4 (P. J. Parsons, *ZPE* 25 (1977), 48):

(a) A stichometric kappa ('line 1,000') stands in the right margin of fr. 80. 7 Pf. (*P. Oxy.* 2213); therefore line 1,000 occurred in the next column. Fr. 80 belongs to Phrygius and Pieria, the penultimate or antepenultimate poem of *Aet.* 3.

(b) The pagination of *P. Oxy.* 1011 shows that the latter part of *Aet.* 3 (from the end of Acontius and Cydippe, fr. 75. 77 Pf.) and the whole of *Aet.* 4 comprised about 1,400 verses (see Pfeiffer, ii, p. xxii).

Suppose that we allow a combined total of 2,200 lines for *Aet.* 3 and 4,

and a total of 7,200 lines for the original contents of *P. Oxy.* 1011 up to
the end of the *Aetia* (see above). What now of Pfeiffer's suggestion that
in *P. Oxy.* 1011 the *Hymns* and *Hecale* preceded the *Aetia*? The *Hymns*
amount to 1,084 lines in Pfeiffer's text (there may be a few lacunae, but
probably not substantial ones). So nearly 4,000 lines would remain for
the *Hecale* and *Aet.* 1–2; a *Hecale* of 1,000 lines (the common estimate)
would then leave nearly 3,000 lines for *Aet.* 1–2, an uncomfortably large
number, unless one were to use it as an argument for divorcing the
composition of *Aet.* 1–2 from that of 3–4. If Pfeiffer were right about the
original contents and order of poems in *P. Oxy.* 1011, we could suspect
either that *Aet.* 1–2 were substantially longer than 3–4, *or* that Call.'s
μέγα ποίημα, the *Hecale*, contained appreciably more than 1,000 lines.
Possibly, however, *P. Oxy.* 1011 included other poems (besides *Hymns*
and *Hecale*) before the *Aetia*; if the principle were 'hexameters before
elegiacs' (which apparently became established from about the fourth
century, cf. Pfeiffer, ii, p. xxxviii), at least the *Galatea* (frs. 378–9 Pf.)
comes into consideration.

   Marianus of Eleutheropolis, who lived in the time of the emperor
Anastasius, made a paraphrase of Call.'s *Hecale*, *Hymns*, *Aetia*, and
Epigrams in 6,810 iambics (see above, Test. 12). A. S. Hunt (*P. Oxy.* vii
(1910), 19) opined that Marianus 'is hardly likely to have affected a
considerable reduction in the number of lines; the tendency would be
rather in the opposite direction'. But, for our purpose, the uncertainties
are so many that this particular hare seems not worth pursuing. On the
other hand, there may be some value in considering the length of other
Hellenistic poems perhaps comparable to the *Hecale*. No help is forth-
coming from the 'epyllia' in the Theocritean corpus—the longest,
'Heracles and Lion-slayer' (*Id.* 25) amounts to 281 lines—nor from
Moschus' *Europa* (166 lines). The four books of Apollonius' *Argonautica*
contain 1,362, 1,285, 1,407, and 1,781 lines; these might provide a
parallel for a longer *Hecale*. And a precious piece of recent evidence (*SH*
397; cf. Parsons on *P. Oxy.* 3000) may indicate that the hexameter
Hermes by Call.'s pupil Eratosthenes had between 1,540 and 1,670 lines.
So while the usual estimate of 1,000 lines for the *Hecale* perhaps has most
to be said for it, there are other indications compatible with a longer
poem. I myself feel some sympathy for the words of Naeke (p. 7),
written at a time when far less was known about Call.'s epyllion: 'Ego
pro imagine Hecales, quae meo animo obversatur, versus mille et
ducentos, vel mille et quingentos fuisse statuo; vel si cui ita placeat, mille
et octingentos, ad quem numerum proxime accedit Apollonii liber qui
longissimus, quartus.'

APPENDIX III
The Hospitality Theme

The theme of a god/hero/holy man who receives hospitable entertainment on his travels is by no means confined to the Greco-Roman world,[1] but can be called a universal story pattern. We shall have cause to mention examples from both the Old and the New Testament; Stith Thompson, *Motif-Index*, vol. v, Q. 1. 1 collects parallels from many different cultures. Before we plunge into detailed literary history, it is worth giving some general characteristics of the type, even though they are not all relevant to Callimachus' *Hecale*. The wandering god or hero is almost always unrecognized at first (we cannot be sure at what point Hecale realizes Theseus' identity). Perhaps he has deliberately disguised himself, so that those whom he visits believe him to be an ordinary traveller and will be rewarded or punished according to how they respond.[2] He often arrives in the evening;[3] Pfeiffer notes that his fr. 766

---

[1] The subject is a very large one; the following bibliography (and citation of examples) makes no claim to completeness. The fullest treatment of classical material (though hardly concerned with the niceties of poetic style and tradition) is Daniela Flückiger-Guggenheim, *Göttliche Gäste: die Einkehr von Göttern und Heroen in der griechischen Mythologie* (1984). Among other works I will mention J. Fontenrose, 'Philemon, Lot, and Lycaon', *Univ. of Cal. Publ. in Class. Phil.* 13 (1945), 93–120; G. d'Ippolito, *Studi nonniani* (1964), 150–63; Anne P. Burnett, *CP* 65 (1970), notes on pp. 24–5 (a useful collection). For Old Testament examples (particularly Gen. 18, 19) together with parallels from the ancient Near East, see Dorothy Irvin, *Mytharion* (1978).

[2] This most naturally applies to gods (e.g. *Od.* 17. 485–7, quoted below). But the motif of putting a host to the test also occurs in connection with lesser visitors. Eumaeus in the *Odyssey* at first (14. 55 ff.) has no reason to think that his disguised master is more than an ordinary beggar. The widow of Zarephath receives a blessing only when she has fulfilled Elijah's apparently unreasonable request that she should feed him before herself and her starving son (1 Kgs 17: 8 ff.). Abraham's wife Sarah fails a test when she laughs scornfully at the prediction that she will have a son (Gen. 18: 12). Compare the parable of the Sheep and the Goats (Matt. 25: 35 ff.): 'As you did it [not] to one of the least of these my brethren, you did it [not] to me.'

[3] e.g. Theseus at Hecale's cottage νυκτὸς ἐ]πιλαμβανούϲηϲ (*Arg. Hec.* 8); the three gods who visit Hyrieus 'tempus erat quo versa iugo referuntur aratra | et pronus saturae lac bibit agnus ovis' (Ov. *Fast.* 5. 497–8); Zeus at Lycaon's house 'traherent cum sera crepuscula noctem' (Ov. *Met.* 1. 219 in a grim reversal of the conventional hospitality story); the angels coming to Lot (Gen. 19: 1); Christ at Emmaus (Luke 24: 29).

inc. auct. ἑϲπέριον ξένον might suit either Theseus in the *Hecale* or Heracles in the episode of 'Molorchus (*Aet.* 3). The host or hostess is usually poor[4] (though perhaps of good family and once prosperous[5]) and more often than not old as well.[6] The eating of a meal forms a central part of the story; Hellenistic poets and their Roman admirers tend to linger lovingly over every detail.[7] If the guest is divine, he may reveal his true nature in the course of the meal by some miracle.[8] Then the hospitable will be rewarded—in Hecale's case only after her death[9]—and perhaps the inhospitable punished.[10]

In Homer Diomedes kills a Trojan, Axylus, who is in some ways a type of Hecale (*Il.* 6. 14–15):

$$\text{φίλος δ' ἦν ἀνθρώποιϲι·}$$
$$\text{πάντας γὰρ φιλέεϲκεν ὁδῶι ἔπι οἰκία ναίων.}^{11}$$

And when the arrogant Antinous mistreats Odysseus (disguised as a beggar), the other suitors reprove him as follows (*Od.* 17. 485–7):

$$\text{καί τε θεοὶ ξείνοιϲιν ἐοικότες ἀλλοδαποῖϲι}$$
$$\text{παντοῖοι τελέθοντες ἐπιϲτρωφῶϲι πόληας}$$
$$\text{ἀνθρώπων ὕβριν τε καὶ εὐνομίην ἐφορῶντες.}$$

[4] This point noted by Stith Thompson, *Motif-Index*, v. 185.

[5] Eumaeus was born a prince (*Od.* 15. 403 ff.); the farmer in Euripides' *Electra* (to be discussed later) came from a distinguished family (35 ff.); for Hecale's previous good fortune see fr. 41. Compare the impoverished old woman in Powell, *CA*, epic. adesp. 4 (though this does not appear to be a hospitality story, it owes much to Call.'s *Hecale*).

[6] e.g. Hecale, Molorchus, Hyrieus, Baucis and Philemon, Abraham and Sarah.

[7] e.g. in Call.'s *Hecale*, frs. 35 ff.—we cannot be sure whether there was an equally detailed account in the *Molorchus* aetion (see P. J. Parsons, *ZPE* 25 (1977), 43–4); perhaps in Eratosthenes' *Erigone* (? cf. fr. 34 Powell); Ovid's *Baucis and Philemon* (and *Hyrieus*); Silius Italicus' *Falernus* (*Pun.* 7. 166–211); Nonnus' *Brongus* (*Dion.* 17. 37 ff., referring to Molorchus, ibid. 52–4).

[8] e.g. in Ovid's *Baucis and Philemon* and Silius' *Falernus*. On the basis of *Pun.* 7. 187 ff. one might postulate a similar miracle in Eratosthenes' *Erigone* (cf. G. Procacci, *RFIC* 42 (1914), 441–8 and R. Merkelbach in *Miscellanea di studi alessandrini in memoria di Augusto Rostagni* (1963), 493–4).

[9] *Dieg.* xi. 3–7; cf. frs. 81–3 (the same applied to Icarius and Erigone in Eratosthenes). Abraham and Hyrieus are promised a son, Icarius and Falernus are given the vine (the former is also catasterized), and Baucis and Philemon become priests.

[10] e.g. Lycaon (Ov. *Met.* 1. 230 ff.) and Baucis and Philemon's inhospitable neighbours (*Met.* 8. 689–90).

[11] *Hec.* fr. 2 may owe something to these lines. The *Etymologicum Genuinum* tries to connect Hecale's name with that of Axylus' attendant Καλήϲιος (*Il.* 6. 18)—see above, sources for fr. 2.

But more important by far is the long episode in which the swineherd Eumaeus entertains his master unawares (*Od.* 14. 1 ff.). This became the prototype for tales of hospitality in later classical poets.[12] The guest, even if unrecognized, is more distinguished than his host. He enters the poor man's house, and is seated with elaborate courtesy (*Od.* 14. 48–51):[13]

ὡς εἰπὼν κλισίηνδ' ἡγήσατο δῖος ὑφορβός,
εἶσεν δ' εἰσαγαγών, ῥῶπας δ' ὑπέχευε δασείας,
ἐστόρεσεν δ' ἐπὶ δέρμα ἰονθάδος ἀγρίου αἰγός
αὐτοῦ ἐνεύναιον, μέγα καὶ δασύ.

Food and drink are provided (*Od.* 14. 72 ff.).[14] After the meal will come an opportunity for either participant to reminisce, ὄφρα καὶ αὐτός | cίτου καὶ οἴνοιο κορεσσάμενος κατὰ θυμόν | εἴπηις ὁππόθεν ἐσσὶ καὶ ὁππόσα κήδε' ἀνέτλης (*Od.* 14. 45–7),[15] until the night is well advanced and special provision has to be made for the guest to sleep (ibid. 518 ff.):[16]

τίθει δ' ἄρα οἱ πυρὸς ἐγγύς
εὐνήν, ἐν δ' ὀίων τε καὶ αἰγῶν δέρματ' ἔβαλλεν
ἔνθ' Ὀδυσεὺς κατέλεκτ'.

It is typical of the Hellenistic poets that they should have taken the model for a favourite scene from the intimate *Odyssey* rather than the more heroic *Iliad*.

Before leaving the archaic period, note that in the *Homeric Hymn to Demeter* the goddess disguises herself as an old woman and visits the house of Celeus and Metaneira. But that theoxeny ends unhappily, and bears only a slight resemblance to the kind of story which concerns us here. Let us move on to Euripides' *Electra*, and the remarkable character of the farmer (αὐτουργός) who is married, in name alone, to the princess; he can perhaps be counted among those features of Euripides which look forward to the Alexandrians. His family was once prosperous, but has now fallen on evil days (35 ff.);[17] though poor, he possesses that nobility

---

[12] Pfeiffer notes on his fr. 239 (= my fr. 28) how, in recounting Theseus' stay with Hecale, Call. used language designed to recall the corresponding passages in the *Odyssey*. Observe also how the scene in which Eumaeus' dogs bark at Odyssesus (14. 29 ff.) is reflected in Theocr. 25. 68 ff. (Heracles and the countryman) and also, it seems, in *CA*, epic. adesp. 2. 38 ff. where Powell (p. 75) comments 'Pheidon alter Eumaeus est, velut humiles curas depingere amant Alexandrini' (cf. Gow on Theocr. 25. 57, 68).

[13] Cf. *Hec.* frs. 27–30; *Aen.* 8. 366–8 (Evander and Aeneas); Ov. *Met.* 8. 637 ff.

[14] See note 7 above for the increased attention given to this part of the proceedings in Hellenistic and Roman poets.

[15] Eumaeus tells his life-story at 15. 403 ff. For the conversation between Theseus and Hecale (about which we still know relatively little) see frs. 40 ff.

[16] Cf. *Hec.* fr. 63.   [17] Cf. above, n. 5.

of spirit which characterizes the host in stories of our type. The farmer's cottage is situated in the Argive hill-country (210, 489),[18] and, when distinguished guests arrive in the persons of Orestes and Pylades, he prepares to entertain them to the best of his ability (357 ff.), πενιχρῶν μὲν ἀλλὰ [φι]λοτίμων ξενίων μεθέξοντας.[19]

P. J. Parsons has shown in a masterly article[20] that Call.'s story of Molorchus, who entertained Heracles before that hero went out against the Nemean lion and founded the Nemean Games (*Aet.* frs. 54–9 Pf.), was joined to a celebration of Queen Berenice's chariot victory at Nemea (previously fr. 383 Pf.), and that the whole, a substantial poem perhaps 200 lines long, stood at the head of book 3 in the final version of the *Aetia*. Probably, therefore, the *Hecale* antedates *Molorchus*.[21] A further important advance was made by E. Livrea,[22] who perceived, on grounds of subject-matter as well as papyrology, that the old man who sets two mousetraps in fr. 177 Pf. is none other than Molorchus. The close similarities between the two stories are obvious. A great hero, about to confront a monster, is received (? at evening[23]) by an aged host in a country cottage. Both poems probably described the meal in detail.[24] Each host has tragically lost one or more close relatives,[25] and promises a sacrifice for the safety and success of the hero;[26] each hero wishes to reward his host, and the entertainment is commemorated in a continuing cult.[27] Both the old people give their name to a place or

---

[18] As Hecale probably lived on the slopes of Mt. Brilessus (cf. on frs. 1, 40. 1, and 169 inc. sed.) and Baucis and Philemon 'collibus . . . Phrygiis' (*Met.* 8. 621; cf. 692 ff.).

[19] I quote from the hypothesis in *P. Oxy.* 420 (3rd-cent. AD) with Barrett's restoration [φι]λοτίμων.

[20] *ZPE* 25 (1977), 1–50.

[21] Unfortunately we have little evidence about the *Hecale*'s date of composition (see above, in Introd. sect. I). Among past scholars there are some who have taken it to be a very early, others a very late work.

[22] *ZPE* 34 (1979), 37 ff.

[23] Cf. p. 341 and n. 3 above on Call. fr. 766 Pf. inc. auct. ἑσπέριον ξενόν.

[24] Parsons (*ZPE* 25 (1977), 43–4) queries whether this was true of *Molorchus*. But to my mind Nonn. *Dion.* 17. 52–4 makes it probable; the fact that *Dion.* 17. 55 seems to echo *Hec.* fr. 36.5 may merely indicate that the two models were very close to each other (cf. R. F. Thomas, *CQ*, NS 33 (1983), 104 n. 68).

[25] Molorchus' son was killed by the lion (schol. Stat. *Theb.* 4, 160; cf. P. J. Parsons, *ZPE* 25 (1977), 3, 43). For the death of the two children who may have been Hecale's sons see frs. 48–9.

[26] Molorchus: 'Probus' on Virg. *G.* 3. 19 (Parsons, *ZPE* 25 (1977), 1 = *SH* 266). Hecale: Plut. *Thes.* 14 (it is not clear where, if anywhere, this fits in Call.— perhaps on the morning of the combat with the bull, when Hecale and Theseus part at dawn (fr. 64 and *Dieg.* x. 31–2; cf. on fr. 83)).

[27] Molorchus: *SH* 265 (= fr. 59 Pf.). 20–1 (but the precise reference is obscure, and the *SH* editors throw some doubt on the reading of l. 21). Hecale: *Dieg.* xi. 3–7; cf. frs. 81–3.

district.[28] There are also some differences (apart from the metre). Hecale lives a solitary life (fr. 40. 5); Molorchus apparently has female company.[29] Theseus captures the Marathonian bull in a single day, while Heracles seems not to return for a month.[30] Hecale dies almost immediately after the entertainment, but Molorchus lives on to receive Heracles for a second night and to enjoy his lasting esteem (*SH* 265. 18–20). Of the two poems, *Hecale* without doubt became the more celebrated and influential, but there are many references to Molorchus too, which in principle should go back to Call., since his was the only full-scale treatment of the legend.[31] It is interesting to find a motif from *Molorchus* which is not in the *Hecale*—the host's refusal of an offered sacrifice (*SH* 266)—recurring in Ovid's *Baucis and Philemon* (*Met.* 8. 684 ff.) and Nonnus' *Brongus* (*Dion.* 17. 46–8).

Something of Call.'s wit, elegance, and poetic ability seems to have passed in the next generation to his fellow Cyrenaean Eratosthenes. It is sad that we possess so little of the latter's elegiac *Erigone*,[32] διὰ πάντων γὰρ ἀμώμητον τὸ ποιημάτιον ([Longin.] 33. 5). But we know the outlines of the plot[33] from a number of sources, chiefly Hyginus (*Astr.* 2. 4) who even quotes a line of the original, Ἰκαριοῖ, τόθι πρῶτα περὶ τράγον

---

[28] Molorchus: Μολορκία (Stephanus Byzantius; cf. P. J. Parsons, *ZPE* 25 (1977), 3–4)—could this be referred to in *SH* 265 (= fr. 59 Pf.). 15 c]ὴν κατ' ἐπω[νυμίην? Hecale: the deme named after her.

[29] The woman in *SH* 259 (= fr. 177 Pf.). 2–4 is mysterious. Could she be Molorchus' wife or servant (cf. Livrea, *ZPE* 34 (1979), 38 and in R. Pintaudi (ed.), *Miscellanea Papyrologica* (1980), 137–8)? If the former, *Molorchus* might be a more important source for Ovid's *Baucis and Philemon* than was previously realized (though a parallel has long been drawn between fr. 177. 2 Pf. and *Met.* 8. 647).

[30] *SH* 266; cf. Apollod. 2. 5. 1 (P. J. Parsons, *ZPE* 25 (1977), 1–3).

[31] See P. J. Parsons, *ZPE* 25 (1977), pp. 1–4, 43–4.

[32] Powell (*CA*) includes under the *Erigone* frs. 22–7, of which frs. 24, 25, and 27 are not ascribed to a specific poem in the sources. Fr. 25 is certainly very appropriate; likewise, in my opinion, fr. 36, a charming 4-line encomium of wine. Fr. 34 (and conceivably fr. 32) might belong to a description of the meal which Icarius sets before the god.

[33] See Flückiger-Guggenheim, *Göttliche Gäste*, pp. 108–12; E. Maass, *Analecta Eratosthenica* (1883), pp. 59–138 with a large collection of ancient testimonia (he could not know the brief but interesting reference to Erigone in Call. *Aet.* fr. 178. 3–4 Pf., and to the catasterized dog Maera in *Aet.* fr. 75. 35); F. Solmsen, *TAPA* 78 (1947), 252–75 (particularly interested in Eratosthenes' Platonic connections—for the entertainment see pp. 262–4, 269). Fraser (*Ptolemaic Alexandria*, ii. 903 n. 202) criticizes the contention of R. Merkelbach (see above, n. 8) that the *Erigone* was meant to be interpreted in terms of Egyptian as well as Greek religion. None the less there is much else of interest and value in Merkelbach's article.

ὠρχήϲαντο (fr. 22 Powell).[34] We hear of Bacchus visiting the old man Icarius[35] and his daughter Erigone, and giving him the vine, previously unknown in Attica. But Icarius' fellow countrymen, having drunk the unfamiliar liquid, believed themselves poisoned, and set about their benefactor with such violence that he died. His daughter Erigone, led by the family dog Maera, found her way to the corpse, and there hanged herself; as a punishment Dionysus visited upon the Athenian women an epidemic of suicide by hanging, which later generations expiated when the women instead hung little images on trees at the Αἰώρα or 'Swinging Festival' (part of the Anthesteria). In the end Icarius' family (including the dog) was catasterized, the old man becoming Boötes and his daughter Virgo.[36] Within this framework there were probably learned digressions. For example, Icarius killed an importunate goat which gnawed his vines, and tethered its bladder; he then made his companions dance round it, thus unwittingly inventing Attic tragedy ('goatsong'; cf. fr. 22 quoted above).[37]

Like Call., Eratosthenes may have drawn his little-known legend from some Atthidographer.[38] Both Hecale and Icarius are eponyms of Attic demes (which incidentally stood very close to each other); the two poets share an interest in regional geography[39] and festivals.[40] Whether Eratosthenes described the entertainment in as much detail as Call. is open to question, but, in my view, probable enough. This feature is not particularly prominent in Nonnus' account of Icarius (*Dion.* 47. 34–264), which presumably drew on Eratosthenes; note, however, *Dion.* 47. 39 ὀλίγηι ξείνιϲϲε τραπέζηι (perhaps a phrase found in the *Hecale*[41]); ibid. 40 ff., where Erigone is about to mix goat's milk for Bacchus, until restrained; and ibid. 56 φιλοξείνωι δὲ γεραιῶι. Among the surviving

---

[34] Hiller was surely right to discern here a locative Ἰκαριοῖ (cf. Steph. Byz. s.v. Ἰκαρία) rather than Ἰκάριοι. The clausula echoes Eratosthenes' master Callimachus (*H.* 1. 52 περὶ πρύλιν ὠρχήϲαντο).

[35] Probably Eratosthenes' form (cf. Call. *Aet.* fr. 178. 3 Pf.), though he is sometimes called Icarus.

[36] For the doubtful possibility that the Nemean lion was catasterized in Call.'s *Molorchus*, see P. J. Parsons, *ZPE* 25 (1977), 2, 43.

[37] Cf. Virg. *G.* 2. 380 ff. I suspect that all this was not entirely serious, and so need not be discussed in too grave a tone. F. Solmsen (*TAPA* 78 (1947), 271) points out that (as Eratosthenes' learned readers would appreciate) Thespis came from Icaria.

[38] Cf. Fraser, *Ptolemaic Alexandria*, ii. 905.

[39] Eratosth. fr. 23 mentions another deme, Thoricus. For Attic demes in the *Hecale* see above, Introd. sect. II and associated notes; also fr. 84 (Melaenae, even if not technically a deme) and perhaps fr. 170 inc. sed. (Halimous).

[40] Cf. *Hec.* fr. 85 on different forms of the Anthesteria.

[41] See on fr. 82.

fragments given to the *Erigone* by Powell, fr. 24 μέcον δ' ἐξαύcατο βαυνόν might describe Icarius lighting his fire.[42] Fr. 34 (inc. sed. in Powell) on the cκόλυμοc, 'Eratostheni quoque laudata in paupere cena' (Plin. *NH* 22. 86) could well belong to the *Erigone* in view of Pliny's similar references to vegetables in the *Hecale* (frs. 38–9 and perhaps fr. 157 inc. sed.). In my commentary on *Hec.* fr. 82 I have suggested (on the basis of *Pan. Mess.* 9–11 'cunctis Baccho iucundior hospes | Icarus, ut puro testantur sidera caelo | Erigoneque Canisque, neget ne longior aetas') that the two poems may have contained similar expressions of the visitor's gratitude, coupled with lasting honours for the host.

It may be worth making a detailed comparison of Silius' *Falernus* episode (7. 166–211) with Nonnus' *Icarius* (*Dion.* 47. 34–264), since Silius' story, as far as it goes, is almost a doublet of the *Erigone* with names changed, and thus it seems possible that Eratosthenes was a common source for Silius and Nonnus. One of our few *Erigone* fragments, περιπλέγδην κρεμόνεccι (27 Powell) might even be set alongside *Pun.* 7. 198 '*Nysaeo redimivit palmite mensas*'. *Pun.* 7. 192–4;

> 'en cape', Bacchus ait, 'nondum tibi nota, sed olim
> viticolae nomen pervulgatura Falerni
> munera'

closely resemble *Dion.* 47. 45 ff.:

> δέξο, γέρον, τόδε δῶρον, ὃ μὴ δεδάαcιν Ἀθῆναι.
> ὦ γέρον, ὀλβίζω cε· cὲ γὰρ μέλψουcι πολῖται κτλ.

and *Pun.* 7. 200–3:

> postquam iterata tibi sunt pocula, iam pede risum
> iam lingua titubante moves, patrique Lyaeo
> tempora quassatus grates et praemia digna
> vix intellectis conaris reddere verbis

are hardly less close to *Dion.* 47. 62–5:

> ἀλλ' ὅτε δὴ κόρον εὗρε κυπελλοδόκοιο τραπέζης,
> δόχμιος ἀμφιέλικτος ἐριcφαλὲς ἴχνος ἑλίccων
> ποccὶν ἀμοιβαίοιcιν ἀνεcκίρτηcεν ἀλωεύc,
> Ζαγρέος Εὔιον ὕμνον ἀνακρούων Διονύcωι . . .[43]

One would, however, expect Eratosthenes' style to be more chaste and restrained than Nonnus'! If, as seems likely, the goat which gnawed

---

[42] E. K. Borthwick, however, would emend Eratosth. fr. 24 and interpret rather differently (*CQ*, NS 19 (1969), 310–11).

[43] Note also Sil. 189 'pauperis hospitii pretium' and Nonn. 67 φιλεύια δῶρα τραπέζης.

Icarius' vine-shoots was the first of its kind to be killed for food,[44] Eratosthenes could have made a point of the old man's previous vegetarianism, as in Sil. 182–3 'nulloque cruore | polluta castus mensa'.[45] Finally, in Ovid's *Baucis and Philemon* (*Met.* 8. 679 ff.) Zeus and Hermes reveal their divinity by a miracle involving the mixing bowl, much as in Sil. 187 ff. While Silius may simply have borrowed the idea from Ovid, it is particularly appropriate for a wine-god to announce himself in such a way, and so perhaps both Ovid and Silius took the motif from the *Erigone*.[46] Although the evidence may not be sufficient to prove the case, I would not be surprised if Eratosthenes' *Erigone* contained an entertainment scene similar in spirit to that of the *Hecale*, with the differences mainly due to the divine status of the guest.

No doubt there were other hospitality stories in Hellenistic poetry. For example, Hyrieus[47] (familiar from Ov. *Fast.* 5. 493 ff.), appeared in Euphorion (fr. 101 Powell; cf. Nonn. *Dion.* 13. 96–103). The problem is that we have no idea whether this was a full-length treatment, or just a passing allusion (as so often in learned poets). Call. refers briefly (*Aet.* fr. 75. 67–9 Pf.) and Nicander at unknown length (fr. 116 Schn.) to Macelo and Dexithea who received Zeus,[48] while the very fragmentary *SH* 418. 16 ff. (Euphorion) perhaps concern the entertainment of Heracles before he fought the Cithaeronian lion.[49]

In addition to accounts of mythical hospitality, it is worth considering that type of invitation poem in which the writer asks a friend (usually a patron) to dinner. The fact that the first surviving example in Greek (Phld. *AP* 11. 44 = 23 G.–P.) is more or less contemporary with Catullus' invitation to his friend Fabullus (13) is not particularly significant; there must have been earlier epigrams of the same type, now lost. Philodemus' poem to his patron Piso indicates that this genre shares many conventions with the mythical tales which we have been discussing:

---

[44] Cf. Porph. *Abst.* 2. 10.1 αἶγα δ' ἐν Ἰκαρίωι τῆς Ἀττικῆς ἐχειρώσαντο πρῶτον, ὅτι ἄμπελον ἀπέθρισεν.

[45] A similar phrase in Nonnus' *Brongus*, *Dion.* 17. 62 ἀναιμάκτοιο τραπέζης.

[46] The obscure Ov. *Met.* 6.125 'Liber ut Erigonen falsa deceperit uva' (quoted by Merkelbach, *Miscellanea Rostagni*, p. 494) might also conceivably refer to such a miracle, but the context suggests something discreditable, perhaps erotic, which is hard to fit with what we know of the *Erigone*.

[47] Flückiger-Guggenheim, *Göttliche Gäste*, pp. 45–50.

[48] Ibid. pp. 42–4. An even briefer allusion to the same myth may be detected in Euph. *SH* 443. 10–11 (cf. Nonn. *Dion.* 18. 35 ff.).

[49] Flückiger-Guggenheim, *Göttliche Gäste*, pp. 72–3; Apollod. 2. 4. 9–10.

αὔριον εἰς λιτήν ϲε καλιάδα, φίλτατε Πείϲων,
ἐξ ἐνάτηϲ ἕλκει μουϲοφιλὴϲ ἕταροϲ
εἰκάδα δειπνίζων ἐνιαύϲιον · εἰ δ᾽ ἀπολείψειϲ
οὔθατα καὶ Βρομίου Χιογενῆ πρόποϲιν,
ἀλλ᾽ ἑτάρουϲ ὄψει παναληθέαϲ, ἀλλ᾽ ἐπακούϲηι
Φαιήκων γαίηϲ πουλὺ μελιχρότερα.
ἢν δέ ποτε ϲτρέψηιϲ καὶ ἐϲ ἡμέαϲ ὄμματα, Πείϲων,
ἄξομεν ἐκ λιτῆϲ εἰκάδα πιοτέρην.

The guest is regularly of higher social standing; often the poet will deliberately undervalue his own status and resources.[50] Consequently the food and drink are not what the great man is used to,[51] and the furniture and dishes may also be of inferior quality (Hor. *Ep.* 1. 5. 1–3):

> si potes Archiacis conviva recumbere lectis
> nec modica cenare times holus omne patella,
> supremo te sole domi, Torquate, manebo.

But, to compensate, the fellowship and conversation will be superb.[52] Even when the gods and heroes of Greek mythology give way to Roman businessmen and politicians relaxing from the stresses of their work, the familiar pattern is still very recognizable (Hor. *Carm.* 3. 29. 13–16):

> plerumque gratae divitibus vices
> mundaeque parvo sub lare pauperum
> cenae sine aulaeis et ostro
> sollicitam explicuere frontem.

Many features of the Greek hospitality myth would have attracted Roman writers. For example, the typical host (Molorchus, Icarius, Hyrieus) must have seemed like the hardy peasants (usually Sabine) whom Romans loved to recall from their own past, such as Sp. Ligustinus who says of himself in 171 BC: 'pater mihi iugerum agri reliquit, et parvum tugurium in quo natus educatusque sum; hodieque ibi habito' (Liv. 42. 34). The cottage of Hecale might remind them of the thatched 'casa Romuli' on the Palatine, carefully preserved by later generations,[53] and its simple furnishings of the earthenware dishes ('fictilia') from which even great men used to dine.[54] All these elements

---

[50] Cf. Gow–Page on καλιάδα (l. 1).

[51] As in Phld. ll. 3–4 (above) and Hor. *Carm.* 1. 20.

[52] Phld. ll. 5–6; Hor. *Ep.* 1. 5. 11, 24.

[53] See Ov. *Fast.* 1. 199 with Frazer's note. Reflections prompted by the 'casa Romuli' include Prop. 2. 16. 19–20, Val. Max. 4. 4. 11, and Sen. *Cons. ad Helv.* 9. 3.

[54] e.g. Catus Aelius who dines off earthenware, but cannot be bribed with silver dishes (Plin. *NH* 33. 142).

can be seen in the most famous of Roman hospitality stories, Ovid's
Baucis and Philemon (Ov. *Met.* 8. 626–724) even though it is set 'in the
Phrygian hills' (621). This is also much the closest to Call.'s *Hecale*, with
several of the verbal echoes approaching a translation.[55] Ovid, however,
has adapted some details of Call.'s Attic meal to suit Italy, e.g.
introducing pork (648), and substituting the Italian cornel (665; cf. Col.
12. 10. 3) for one of the olives in *Hec.* fr. 36. 4–5. He has also idealized the
whole. We find none of Hecale's fierce regret for the loss of her property
(fr. 41), nor the vivid description of toil and injustice (frs. 52 ff.). Instead
(*Met.* 8. 633–4):

> paupertatemque fatendo
> effecere levem nec iniqua mente ferendo

—a perfect paradigm of Horace's advice to Roman youth 'angustam
amice pauperiem pati' (*Carm.* 3. 2. 1).

In *Met.* 5. 281 ff. Ovid combines a hint of the hospitality theme with
the motif of seeking refuge from a rainstorm (surely from the *Hecale*; cf.
frs. 18–19 and *Dieg.* x. 28–31) when Pyreneus says to the Muses:

> 'nec dubitate, precor, tecto grave sidus et imbrem'—
> imber erat—'vitare meo. subiere minores
> saepe casas superi'.

We have already mentioned the episode of Hyrieus (*Fast.* 5. 493 ff.), in
many ways a doublet of *Baucis and Philemon*.

Latin hexameter poets also turn the hospitality theme to a use which
we cannot find in surviving Alexandrian epic (though it does occur in
late Greek epic poetry). That is to employ an episode of rural entertain-
ment as an idyllic interlude in a martial epic. The originator is Virgil
when he takes Aeneas to the home of Evander in *Aen.* 8. No particular
echoes of the *Hecale* can be noted, but the whole has an unmistakable
Hellenistic air.[56] The lines in which Evander leads Aeneas into his cottage
(8. 364–8) are fully in our tradition:

> 'aude, hospes, contemnere opes et te quoque dignum
> finge deo, rebusque veni non asper egenis.'
> dixit, et angusti subter fastigia tecti
> ingentem Aenean duxit, stratisque locavit
> effultum foliis et pelle Libystidis ursae.

---

[55] See on *Hec.* frs. 29 ff. and, from the other side, my commentary (1970) on
Ov. *Met.* 8, 639 ff. An interesting question is whether there should be a foot-
washing scene in either poem or both (see on *Hec.* fr. 34 and *Met.* 8. 651 ff.).

[56] e.g. the list of μετονομασίαι in *Aen.* 8. 328–32 (cf. Rhian. fr. 25 Powell) and
the contrast between the past and present site of Rome in *Aen.* 8. 347 ff. (cf. Call.
H. 1. 18 ff. on Arcadia).

We have already discussed Silius Italicus' *Falernus* (*Pun.* 7, 166–211) in some detail because of a possible link with Eratosthenes' *Erigone*; the immediate model, however, is clearly Ovid's *Baucis and Philemon*. This pleasant interlude shows Silius at his best.

Lucan is by no means a conventional epic poet; he has a way of writing so that the more familiar episodes are adumbrated and just recognizable, but twisted, often in a sinister and alarming fashion. At *BC* 5. 516–17. Julius Caesar knocks at night-time on the door of a poor fisherman whose hut at first sounds like the cottage of Baucis and Philemon:

> domus non ullo robore fulta
> sed sterili iunco cannaque intexta palustri.[57]

His host is 'pauper Amyclas' (539) and there are commonplace reflections on poverty ('o vitae tuta facultas | pauperis angustique lares', 527–8), which lead, however, to the disturbing thought that this is the only door on which Caesar can knock without causing panic (529–31).[58]

In Appendix II of my edition of Ov. *Met.* 8 I discussed a fragment of the late Greek epic poet Dionysius (26 Heitsch = 81ᵛ Livrea (1973)). Only the first half of each line is preserved, but the subject-matter is clearly domestic, with mention of undistinguished food (beans, pulse, and grain), a boiling cauldron, and dry sticks. The language shows the influence of learned Hellenistic poetry in the use of rare words and forms.[59] If this were a hospitality scene (which of course is quite unprovable) I suggested that it might come from Dionysius' *Bassarica* (rather than *Gigantias*), and be a precursor of Nonnus' *Brongus* (*Dion.* 17. 37 ff.). Should the piece belong to the *Gigantias*,[60] then the discrepancy of the subject-matter from what one expects in such a work would be even more striking. We now know from papyrological evidence[61] that the epic poet Triphiodorus was not a successor of Nonnus, but preceded

---

[57] Cf. *Met.* 8. 630 (also [Theocr.] 21. 6 ff.).

[58] M. P. O. Morford (*The Poet Lucan* (1967), pp. 37 ff.) doubts the historicity of the episode, since it is not in Caesar himself (*BC* 3. 18–30): but Valerius Maximus has it (9. 8. 2), perhaps from Livy. My former pupil Dr Simon Swain draws my attention to Plut. *Mar.* 37. 5 where, in the marshes of Minturnae, the great man ἐπιτυγχάνει καλύβηι λιμνουργοῦ γέροντος.

[59] For more on the language of the fragment see Livrea's edn., pp. 51, 59, 70.

[60] To which Livrea (fr. 81; cf. p. 18), like Heitsch, gives it. But, granted that this papyrus preserves fragments of both *Bassarica* and *Gigantias*, I can see no reason to ascribe our fragment to the latter rather than the former.

[61] *P. Oxy.* 2946 (3rd–4th cent., ed. J. R. Rea, *P. Oxy.* xli (1972)). For Triphiodorus and the *Hecale* see E. Livrea, *RFIC* 104 (1976), 451–2. In Triph. 659 I deliberately prefer κείνης to κοινῆς (see Livrea, op. cit. p. 451 n. 2).

him by at least a century. In lines 657 ff. of the Ἰλίου ἅλωcιc, Menelaus
saves the household of Antenor:

φιλοξείνοιο γέροντος
μειλιχίης προτέρης μεμνημένος ἠδὲ τραπέζης
κείνης, ἧι μιν ἔδεκτο γυνὴ πρηεῖα Θεανώ.

Here Antenor sounds like a Molorchus-figure, and the description of his
wife Theano, γυνὴ πρηεῖα, undoubtedly is meant to recall *Hec.* fr. 80. 1
πρηεῖα γυναικῶν (probably spoken by neighbours at the old woman's
funeral). See also on *Hec.* frs. 82–3 for the guest's characteristic desire to
repay his host for hospitality received. Finally, Nonnus states (*Dion.* 17.
52–4) that his *Brongus* episode is based on the Molorchus legend, and the
motif of the sacrifice declined (ll. 46–8) no doubt came from Call.;[62] yet
at the same time line 55 seems to echo *Hec.* fr. 36. 5.[63]

Perhaps the secret of the hospitality story's lasting appeal was that it
contained something for everyone. Poets could enjoy—as Call. clearly
did in the *Hecale*—contrasting the characters of host and guest, and
describing in minutest detail the food and the interior of the cottage (e.g.
Baucis and Philemon's three-legged table which required the insertion
of a potsherd to stop it wobbling[64]). Those of a more philosophical or
moralistic bent could admire the virtue, independence, and simple life-
style of the host, as in the Seventh or Euboean Dialogue of Dio
Chrysostom;[65] this appealed particularly to Romans, and the subject of
primitive cottages moves Seneca to epigrams such as 'culmus liberos
texit, sub marmore atque auro servitus habitat'.[66] Then again, the theme
could be given a deeper spiritual significance. We have mentioned Old
Testament examples of the hospitality story. There is also much material
in the New Testament, e.g. Christ's visit to Emmaus (Luke 24: 13 ff.).
The idea of testing men by their hospitality towards an unrecognized
guest occurs in one of the most striking parables: 'I was a stranger and
you welcomed me [did not welcome me] ... Lord, when did we see
thee a stranger and welcome [did not welcome] thee? ... As you did it
[not] to one of the least of these my brethren, you did it [not] to me'
(Matt. 25: 35 ff.). Sometimes the hospitality becomes symbolic, as in
Rev. 3: 20 'Behold I stand at the door and knock; if any one hears my

---

[62] See above, p. 345.

[63] See above, n. 24.

[64] *Met.* 8. 661–3; cf. Architrenius (quoted in Burman's 1727 Variorum edition
of the *Metamorphoses*): 'o terque quaterque | Baucida felicem, sociumque
Philemona lecti | pauperis et mensae, cuius pes tertius impar | aequa sub inducta
tenuit mensalia testa'.

[65] Particularly paras. 65–6, 75–6, 83 ff. (with reflections on Odysseus and
Eumaeus).

[66] *Ep.* 90. 10 (cf. above, n. 53 on the 'casa Romuli').

voice and opens the door, I will come in to him and eat with him, and he with me', which no doubt lies behind Prud. *Psych*. Intr. 62 (of Christ) 'parvam pudici cordis intrabit casam'.

When talking about Biblical hospitality stories Christian poets cast them in the classical mould, e.g. Prud. *Psych*., Introd. 45–6 on Abraham who entertained angels unawares (Gen. 18: 1 ff.; cf. Heb. 13: 2):

> mox et triformis angelorum trinitas[67]
> senis revisit hospitis mapalia.

'Mapalia', as well as creating an eastern atmosphere, perhaps conveys a note of disparagement which is typical of the genre (see above, n. 50 on καλιάδα in Philodemus) even if not very appropriate to the wealthy Abraham. And Greek Christian poets show themselves specifically aware of Call.'s *Hecale*, as can be seen from references to the widow of Sidon (1 Kgs. 17: 8 ff.) in Gregory of Nazianzus (*Carm*. 1. 2. 2. 174–6 (*PG* xxxvii. 592)):

> οὔ ποτέ γ' ἐν πενιχρῆι cιπύηι λήγοντος ἀλεύρου
> καὶ κεράμοιο βρύοντος ἀεὶ τόcον ὑγρὸν ἔλαιον,
> ὅccον ἀφύccετο χερcὶ φιλοξείνοιο γυναικόc

and in Michael Choniates[68] (writing *c*. AD 1200, when people's idea of the hexameter would not have pleased Call.) ii, p. 386 Lambros, lines 329 ff.:

> Cιδονίηι δὲ γυναικί, λιμοῦ χθόνα βοcκομένοιο,
> Ἠλίας ὤπαcεν ἐγκρυφιάζεμεν ἀμφοτέροιcιν
> ἀνθρακιῆι cποδοέccηι εὐρυτέραι μάκτραι τε
> ἅλιc ἐπεί οἱ ἄλφιτ' ἄμυλα ῥέεν cιπύηθεν

The words with spaced letters recall *Hecale*, some of them in particular fr. 35 ἐκ δ' ἄρτουc cιπύηθεν ἅλιc κατέθηκεν ἑλοῦcα, | οἵουc βωνίτηιcιν ἐνικρύπτουcι γυναῖκεc.

Let us end in the Byzantine world with Nicetas' life of St Philaretus of Amnia in Paphlagonia[69] (AD 702–92). I. Cazzaniga[70] has even argued that this is influenced by Call.'s *Hecale*. I do not see any compelling reason to believe that, but the Life certainly illustrates the continuing popularity of the hospitality theme. Here is a brief extract,[71] which shows the saint welcoming imperial envoys:

---

[67] 'Triformis ... trinitas' no doubt reflects a Christian interpretation that Abraham's three guests were in fact the three Persons of the Trinity.

[68] Perhaps the last person to possess a complete copy of the *Hecale* (see above, Introd. sect. VIII).

[69] Text from M.-H. Fourmy and M. Leroy, *Byzantion*, 9 (1934), 85–170.

[70] *Parola del Passato*, 23 (1968), 224–7.

[71] *Byzantion*, 9 (1934), 137.

ὁ δὲ φιλόξενος ἀνὴρ ἀληθῶς καὶ φιλόθεος λαβὼν τὴν βακτηρίαν αὐτοῦ ὑπήντησε τοὺς βασιλικοὺς ἔξωθεν τοῦ οἴκου αὐτοῦ, μετὰ χαρᾶς πολλῆς προσπτυσσόμενος αὐτοὺς καὶ λέγων "καλῶς Θεὸς ἤνεγκε τοὺς ἐμοὺς δεσπότας εἰς τὰ δουλικὰ αὐτῶν . τί ἐμοί τοῦτο, ὅτι κατηξιώσατε εἰς πτωχοῦ καλύβην εἰσελθεῖν;"

APPENDIX IV
Theseus' Return from Marathon

In Fr. 69. 5 ff. Theseus says to the country people of Marathon:

"μίμνετε θαρςήεντες, ἐμῶι δέ τις Αἰγέϊ πατρί
νεύμενος ὅς τ᾽ ὤκιστος ἐς ἄστυρον ἀγγελιώτης
ὧδ᾽ ἐνέποι—πολέων κεν ἀναψύξειε μεριμνέων—
'Θηςεὺς οὐχ ἑκὰς οὗτος, ἀπ᾽ εὐΰδρου Μαραθῶνος
ζωὸν ἄγων τὸν ταῦρον'." ὁ μὲν φάτο, τοὶ δ᾽ ἀϊόντες
πάντες ἰὴ παιῆον ἀνέκλαγον, αὖθι δὲ μίμνον.

Wilamowitz (*Kl. Schr.* ii. 36) made two points about the hero's return:

1. From the words αὖθι δὲ μίμνον (10) he inferred that nobody took Theseus' message to his father in Athens. A poetic purpose behind this was discerned, in that a messenger would have stopped at Hecale's cottage, and relieved her of anxiety about Theseus (anxiety which, as Wilamowitz thought, caused her death).

2. Because of the distance between Marathon and Athens, he considered it likely that Theseus did not return to Athens the same day, but stayed the night somewhere near Marathon (thus also Webster, *Poetry and Art*, p. 117).

Point 1 seems to me (as to Kapp, p. 11 n. 29) unconvincing. αὖθι δὲ μίμνον implies merely that they obeyed the first part of Theseus' command (μίμνετε θαρςήεντες) and did not run away in panic; there is no implication whatever that the second part (ἐμῶι δέ τις Αἰγέϊ πατρί κτλ.) was neglected.

Point 2 raises more difficult questions. In any case one would expect Theseus not to drag the captive bull by the arduous path over Mt. Brilessus, but to choose an easier route, starting over the Marathonian plain and passing to the south of Brilessus (cf. Frazer's *Pausanias*, ii, p. 441). Furthermore, if Gentili (*Gnomon*, 33 (1961), 342) was right in believing that the nocturnal birds (cf. fr. 74. 22) are debating whether or not to bring Theseus the bad news (cf. fr. 74. 7) of Hecale's death, it would follow that a night must have intervened before Theseus went back to Hecale's cottage. Bearing these factors in mind, we could construct alternative sequences of events:

(*a*) Following Wilamowitz: Theseus disposes of the bull for the night, and stays somewhere near Marathon. Next morning he goes to thank

Hecale, but finds her dead; he attends her funeral (instituting honours in her memory), and only then retrieves the bull for conveyance to Athens.

(b) Theseus captures the bull and takes it back to the city the same day. On the morrow he journeys a second time out to Hecale's cottage, where he finds the neighbours preparing her funeral. He institutes honours in her memory (a new deme called Ἑκάλη, a τέμενος of Zeus Ἑκάλειος, and an annual banquet), thus bringing the poem to an aetiological conclusion.

Dieg. x. 32–3 χειρωσάμενος δὲ τὸν ταῦρον ἐπανήιει ὡς τὴν Ἑκάλην hardly enables us to decide between these alternatives, since it is unclear whether or not χειρωσάμενος includes taking the bull back to Athens. One testimonium (my no. 6, *Priap.* 12. 3 ff.) definitely favours scheme (a):

> aequalis tibi, quam *domum revertens*
> Theseus repperit in rogo iacentem.

It seems to me, however, that this argument in favour of (a) may be outweighed by a number of contrary ones:

i. The force of the message Θησεὺς οὐχ ἑκὰς οὗτος, ἀπ' εὐύδρου Μαραθῶνος | ζωὸν ἄγων τὸν ταῦρον (fr. 69. 8–9) would be greatly diminished if Theseus does not arrive in Athens for at least another 24 hours; the natural implication of οὐχ ἑκάς is that he will reach the city not so long after the 'speediest messenger' (l. 6).

ii. A second night's stay near Marathon would be sad anticlimax after the hospitality of Hecale.

iii. It might not be so easy to dispose of the ferocious bull for a night (although artistic representations show it as hobbled, and Heracles has apparently found temporary accommodation for Cerberus in E. *HF* 1386–7). I hope this is not too prosaic an objection.

iv. The *Diegesis* suggests that the poem had an aetiological conclusion, with the establishment of honours for Hecale—and of course this would be very much in Call.'s manner. Since it seems improbable that Call. could have omitted altogether Theseus' reunion with his father (unless by chance the sending of a messenger was meant to be a substitute for the reunion), it would be more convenient for Theseus to have returned to Athens before he attended Hecale's funeral.

On balance I feel that scheme (b) has more to commend it; but Call.'s method of narration can be full of surprises, and in this case may not have followed a straightforward path. Finally, it is worth considering Wilamowitz' implied suggestion that the distance between Marathon and Athens (some 22 miles through the hills, 25 miles by the modern road) would make it hard for Theseus to return to Athens the same day.

Similar doubts have been felt as to whether the Athenian army, after fighting the battle of Marathon, could have marched back to the city the selfsame day (as stated by Plut. *Arist.* 5. 4). N. G. L. Hammond (*JHS* 88 (1968), 13 ff.) believes that they could (pp. 28 and 54), citing (pp. 36–7) his own personal experience of walking from Athens to the Marathonian mound and back on the same day, by the most difficult route over Mt. Pentelicus (Brilessus), in a total of 13 hours. Call. may never have been to Attica; the vivid local colour which pervades the *Hecale* could derive from the working of his imagination on his scholarly reading. But one would expect him to read thoroughly, and to make the resulting narrative plausible. On the outward journey (of course unencumbered by a captive bull) Theseus made quick time: he left the city περὶ ἑσπέραν (*Dieg.* x. 27) and reached Hecale's cottage, probably on the slopes of Brilessus, νυκτὸς ἐ]πιλαμβανούϲηϲ (*Arg. Hec.* 8). Next morning he gets up at dawn to leave Hecale (*Dieg.* x. 31–2). We simply do not know how long he took to capture the bull, but I doubt whether the distance between Marathon and Athens need exclude the possibility that Theseus returned to the city with his captive the same day.

APPENDIX V
Ten Poetic Citations in Suidas

In the Introduction (sect. IX) I have already discussed 'Hecker's Law', which assigns to Call.'s *Hecale* anonymous verse citations in the Byzantine lexicon known as Suidas (or 'the Suda'). At a late stage in my present work I started to read through Suidas, in case there were entries relating to the newer papyrus fragments which had not yet been picked up; in this I had only slight success (e.g. s.v. κρίμνον, clearly a note on πολύκριμνος in fr. 96. 3). At the same time, however, I came across several more entries of a Hellenistic or even specifically Callimachean colour which, as far as I could see, had as good a claim on the *Hecale* as some of the fragments accepted by Pfeiffer. This surprised me greatly, since other scholars have been on the same quest, and I thought that the mine was exhausted. Both Adler and Pfeiffer added new fragments, many of them single-word citations. But, in spite of a suspicion that Pfeiffer must have deliberately rejected at least some of my candidates, I give below ten glosses which seem to me to deserve serious consideration. The list could be lengthened (e.g. to include unparalleled forms like δμηκότες· δαμάσαντες, or κεκότητο· ὤργιστο which suggest learned poetry); I think there is still room for a further painstaking investigation.

A word about the transmission of these fragments. Most bear the symbol Δ in the margin of Ada Adler's Suidas, which means that the same, or a similar, entry appears in the unpublished *Lexicon Ambrosianum* (see Adler, *Suidae Lexicon*, i (1928), pp. xvii–xviii). Adler's hope that the *Lexicon Ambrosianum* would be edited by her collaborator K. Barr was not fulfilled, and we are no further advanced now than when Pfeiffer wrote in 1949 (i, p. 228) 'de Lexico Ambrosiano adhuc inedito nondum iudicare licet'. I did not give references to the *Lexicon* in my apparatus, but it will be seen from Pfeiffer's edition that appearance in that lexicon does not tell against ascription to the *Hecale*. The case of entries bearing the symbol Σ (= Συναγωγή, see Adler, op. cit. i, p. xvii) seems to be different. Pfeiffer believed that items from the Συναγωγή cannot be taken to derive from the *Hecale*; none of the fragments given below comes to Suidas via that route.

I am particularly grateful to Mr W. S. Barrett for comments on this Appendix.

(*a*) Suid. ii. 49. 27 ... καὶ δηναιόν, ἐπὶ πολὺν χρόνον ('cf. Ambr. 442',

Adler), a sense paralleled in Ap. Rh. 1. 334, 3. 590, Lyc. 1139. I have
toyed with the idea that this entry might refer to *Hec.* fr. 70. 4, where
δηναι- can perhaps be read.

(*b*) ii. 144. 18 δυερόν · βλαβερόν, ἐπιβλαβές (no source given by Adler).
The noun δύη was common enough in Homer (once in Call.—*Hec.*
fr. 131). δυερὸς βροτός is known as a variant for διερὸς βροτός in *Od.* 6.
201 (see above, Introd. sect. III for Call.'s interest in Homeric *hapax
legomena* and disputed variants). Recently δυερῆι . . . ἀξυλίηι has turned
up in *Aet.* 3 (*SH* 257. 24 = fr. 176. 4 Pf.); otherwise the adjective appears
only in Call.'s admirer the astrological poet Maximus (65, 182) and on a
(?2nd-cent. AD) verse inscription, *IG* iii. 2. 1337 (= Peek, *GVI* 1029). 2.

(*c*) ii. 202. 27 ἔδεθλον· ἕδρασμα (no source given). In fact Adler herself
ad loc. considered attribution to our poem ('fort. gl. in Call. Hec.').
Pfeiffer's silence is puzzling; although Diehl (*Hypomnema*, p. 398 n. 16)
referred the gloss to *H.* 2. 72, Pf. believed (on his fr. 314) 'Suidam ne
unam quidem glossam ex hymnis sumpsisse'. While Pfeiffer was right
not to follow all of Adler's suggestions for the *Hecale*, this one seems to
me quite as plausible as others which he accepted from her. Conjectured
by Auratus in A. *Ag.* 776, ἔδεθλον (like ἐδέθλιον) is a favourite word of
learned Hellenistic poets (see Livrea on Ap. Rh. 4. 331); first in Antim.
fr. 35 Wyss, then Call. *H.* 2. 72, and restored by Lobel in *Aet.* fr. 162. 1
Pf. The meaning is 'seat' or 'abode', whether of gods or men. When
applied to a god, ἔδεθλον may refer either to his ἱερόν, or to the city in
which he is established.

(*d*) ii. 267. 27 ἐνναέται· οἰκήτορες ('cf. Ambr. 892') followed by a
quotation from *AP* containing the accusative singular. This noun is not
attested before the Hellenistic period (Barrett holds strongly that the
anonymous epigram Page, *FGE*, pp. 374–5 was a later forgery written
for insertion into the pseudo-Demosthenes speech); the nominative
plural occurs five times in Ap. Rh. Several Callimachean examples have
come to light fairly recently: ἐνναέτης (*Aet. SH* 259. 36 = fr. 177. 36 Pf.),
ἐνναέτα[ς (*Aet.* fr. 186. 24 Pf.), ἐνναέταις perhaps in *Aet. SH* 238.13 and
253. 10 (the latter more speculative).

(*e*) ii. 348. 18 ἐπητῦϊ· τῆι ςυνέςει ('cf. Ambr. 1465'). The genitive
ἐπητύος was *hapax legomenon* (better still, a disputed h.l. of obscure
meaning and etymology) in *Od.* 21. 306, there explained by a scholiast
with μεταιτήςεως, 'request for a share'; ἐπήτης (*Od.* 13. 332, 18. 128) is
most commonly glossed with λόγιος or ςυνετός, less often πρᾶος or
εὐγνώμων. Ap. Rh. has ἐπητέες (fem.) in 2. 987 (schol. λόγιαι), and
ἐπητείηισι (schol. ἐπιστήμαις, φρονήςεςιν) in 3. 1007. Lobel restored
ἐπ]ητέα μῦθον in the late epic poet Dionysius (fr. 35. 1 Livrea). To my
mind ἐπητῦϊ strongly suggests a learned poet, and Call. had a special
liking for nouns in -τύς (cf. *Hec.* frs. 123, 125). For discussion of Homeric

ἐπητής/ἐπητύς, see Annette T. Dale, *Glotta*, 60 (1983), 205–14; she favours one of the ancient connections, that with ἔπος (which, however, Barrett numbered among 'fabrications from childish etymologies').

(*f*) ii. 596. 26 ηὐδάξαντο· ἐφήμισαν ('= Ambr. 616'). ηὐδάξαντο ends a cπονδειάζων in Euph. fr. 48 Powell = *SH* 427.3 (before the feminine caesura in Euthyd. *SH* 455. 2 γναθμὸν ⟨ὃν⟩ ηὐδάξαντο δυcείμονες ἰχθυβοληêc). Call. has ηὐδάcατο in *Aet*. fr. 75. 21 Pf., where, as in Euphorion, the verb refers to oracular utterance; in Euthydemus the meaning is simply 'they called'.

(*g*) iii. 462. 19 Νηρηῖνη· θυγάτηρ τοῦ Νηρέωc (so cod. M; the explanation is lacking in other MSS. Adler gives *Δ*, i.e. *Lexicon Ambrosianum*, in the margin, but no reference below). For this form and other patronymics in -ίνη see on fr. 103. 2 Δηωίνην. It would be welcome to have a Greek example of Νηρηῖνη earlier than Catull. 64. 28.

(*h*) iv. 294.4 ῥιγηλή · ἡ ταχέωc ῥιγῶcα. οὐ γὰρ ἔγωγε ὧδε ῥιγηλή (no note of origin in Adler). A particularly intriguing entry; the only sign of scholarly interest which I have found is in LSJ, who note the application to a person, 'susceptible to cold'. Although words from the same root are common enough in Homer, ῥιγηλόc itself first appears in pseudo-Hesiod (*Sc.* 131) and is predominantly Hellenistic (e.g. Nic. *Alex.* 220); the Homeric καταριγηλόc may occur in Euphorion (*SH* 442.10). McLennan (*HZ*) on *Hymn* 1. 63 discusses the suffix -ηλοc in Hellenistic poetry. ῥιγηλόc can be seen to have three terminations also in Antipater of Thessalonica, *AP* 7. 640 (= 57 Gow-Page). 1.

It seems natural to take οὐ γὰρ ἔγωγε as the ending of a hexameter (as e.g. *H*. 4. 122 and six times in Homer). Lengthening of a short final vowel in 'thesis' before ρ (*ὧδε ῥιγηλή*) would be unparalleled, and to my mind very unlikely, in Call. (Homer has *Il*. 24. 755 πολλὰ ῥυστάζεcκεν and *Od*. 13. 438 = 17. 198 = 18. 109 πυκνὰ ῥωγαλέην). I suggest the addition of one letter, ὧδ᾽ ἔ⟨α⟩ ῥιγηλή (for ἔα = *eram* see Pfeiffer on fr. 384. 32 τῶιδ᾽ ἔα λιτότεροc). The sentiment 'for I was not so susceptible to cold' might be appropriate to the aged Hecale conversing with Theseus or to the old crow touched by the frosty dawn of fr. 74.23. There is even a chance of linking this to fr. 139 τόδε μοι μαλκίcτατον ἦμαρ (where Suidas explains with ψυχρότατον). Metre and sense do not rule out οὐ γὰρ ἔγωγε | ὧδ᾽ ἔα ῥιγηλή · τόδε μοι μαλκίcτατον ἦμαρ . . . Barrett, however, thinks of a pattern with the reverse order, offering (purely *exempli gratia*) τόδε μοι μαλκίcτατον ἦμαρ | ⟨πάντων ὅccα πάροιθέ μ᾽ ἀνίαcαν·⟩ οὐ γὰρ ἔγωγε | ὧδ᾽ ἔα ῥιγηλὴ ⟨πρὶν χείματι τῶιδ᾽ ἐπικύρcαι⟩.

(*i*) iv. 498. 25 ταλαcήιον ἔργον· ἡ ἐριουργία (*Δ* in margin, but no reference below). Again I am surprised by the apparent lack of interest.

Adler appends 'cf. Ap. Rh. 3. 292', where we find ταλασήϊα ἔργα. This *could* be a misquotation of Apollonius Rhodius, but such an attitude, if adopted more widely, would rob us of several *Hecale* fragments. For example, frs. 247 and 366 Pf., both now confirmed for our poem by papyri (my frs. 48. 3 and 48. 5), were considered by some to be misquotations or variants of Nicander and Homer respectively (cf. app. crit. to fr. 120 = 312 Pf.). It seems to me more probable that ταλασήϊον ἔργον derives from another poet, closely related to Apollonius Rhodius—and (even without Hecker's law) Call. comes first to mind. The expression (including its disregard of digamma) would be paralleled in *Hecale* fr. 111 ὄμπνιον ἔργον, 'agricultural labour'.

(*j*) iv. 515. 21 τέθμια· νόμιμα (the same gloss in Hesychius). τεθμός, τέθμιον (e.g. *Hec.* fr. 99. 2) and τέθμια (e.g. *H.* 6. 18 with Hopkinson's *HD* note) are favourite Callimachean forms.

SELECT BIBLIOGRAPHY

I. EDITIONS AND DISCUSSIONS OF THE *HECALE* FRAGMENTS

Graevius   *Callimachi Hymni, Epigrammata et Fragmenta, ex recensione Theodori J. G. F. Graevii cum eiusdem animadversionibus. Accedunt N. Frischlini, H. Stephani, B. Vulcanii, P. Voetii, A. T. F. Daceriae, R. Bentleii commentarius, et annotationes viri illustrissimi Ezechielis Spanhemii*, 1697 [2 vols: the fragments, of which Bentley's collection was much the most significant, are at i. 234–429].

Ernesti   *Callimachi Hymni, Epigrammata et Fragmenta, ex recensione Jo. Augusti Ernesti*, tom. I, 1761 [largely repeats Graevius, but includes an Auctarium Fragmentorum, pp. 569–80].

Ruhnken   *David. Ruhnkenii, Lud. Casp. Valckenaerii et aliorum ad Io. Aug. Ernesti Epistolae. Accedunt Dav. Ruhnkenii observationes in Callimachum* [etc.]. Ed. *Ioh. Aug. Henr. Tittmann*, 1812.

Blomfield   *Callimachi quae supersunt, recensuit et cum notarum delectu edidit C. J. Blomfield*, 1815 [adding a Spicilegium Fragmentorum, pp. 314–20].

Naeke   *Augusti Ferdinandi Naekii Opuscula Philologica. Volumen II, Callimachi Hecale. Fragmenta collegit et disposuit Augustus Ferdinandus Naeke*, 1845 [posthumously edited by F. T. Welcker. Almost all of Naeke's *Hecale* had already appeared in *Rheinisches Museum* (2 (1833–4), 509–88; 3 (1835), 509–68; 5 (1836–7), 1–100). Thus it predates Hecker's *Commentationes Callimacheae*].

Hecker   *Commentationum Callimachearum Capita duo ... publico omnium examini offert Alphonsus Hecker*, 1842 [Caput II, pp. 79–148, = 'Callimachi Hecale'].

Schneider   *Callimachea, edidit Otto Schneider. Vol. II: Fragmenta a Bentleiio collecta et explicata ab aliis aucta. Accedunt Commentationes et Indices tres*, 1873.

Kapp   *Callimachi Hecalae Fragmenta. Dissertatio Inauguralis ... scripsit Ida Kapp*, 1915.

Mair   *Callimachus and Lycophron, with an English translation by A. W. Mair* (Loeb Classical Library), 1921 [including a collection of fragments (pp. 183–355) which was dropped from the 1955 reprint because of the imminent publication of Trypanis' new edition (see below)].

Pfeiffer   *Callimachus, edidit Rudolfus Pfeiffer, Volumen I: Fragmenta,* 1949 [superseding his own *Callimachi fragmenta nuper reperta* (1923). Pfeiffer's vol. ii, *Hymni et Epigrammata* (1953) contains Prolegomena to the fragments, Addenda et Corrigenda, and Indices].

Trypanis   *Callimachus, Aetia, Iambi, Lyric Poems, Hecale* [etc.] Text [based upon that of Pfeiffer, but incorporates some additional papyri, and new ideas due particularly to Barber and Maas], *English translation and notes by C. A. Trypanis* (Loeb Classical Library), 1958.

SH   *Supplementum Hellenisticum, ediderunt Hugh Lloyd-Jones, Peter Parsons,* 1983 [the new *Hecale* pieces are nos. 280–91, pp. 122–35; no. 307, pp. 142–3, may also refer to our poem].

For editions of Lexicons etc. which regularly quote fragments of the *Hecale* see above, Introd. sect. XII and Editiones et Codices Fontium Praecipuorum.

II. RECENT EDITIONS WITH COMMENTARY OF CALLIMACHUS' *HYMNS*

McLENNAN, G. R., *Callimachus*, Hymn to Zeus: *introduction and commentary* (1977).

WILLIAMS, F., *Callimachus*, Hymn to Apollo: *A Commentary* (1978).

BORNMANN, F., *Callimachi Hymnus in Dianam: Introduzione, Testo critico e Commento* (1978).

MINEUR, W. H., *Callimachus*, Hymn to Delos: *Introduction and Commentary* (1984).

BULLOCH, A. W., *Callimachus*, The Fifth Hymn: *Edited with Introduction and Commentary* (1985).

HOPKINSON, N., *Callimachus*, Hymn to Demeter: *Edited with an Introduction and Commentary* (1984).

III. OTHER BOOKS AND ARTICLES

ARENA, R., Ἀμορβός, ἀμορβεῖν, *RIL* 111 (1977), 285–302.

BARBER, E. A., 'Callimachus, Hecala (fr. 260 Pfeiffer)', *CQ*, NS 2 (1952), 92.

—— 'Callimachea Varia', *CR*, NS 5 (1955), 241–2.

—— 'Callimachus, fr. 567 Pfeiffer', *CR*, NS 9 (1959), 101–2.

BARIGAZZI, A., 'Sull' *Ecale* di Callimaco', *Hermes*, 82 (1954), 308–30.

—— 'Il dolore materno di Ecale (*P. Oxy.* 2376 e 2377)', *Hermes*, 86 (1958), 453–71.

—— 'Sul fr. 259 Pf. dell'*Ecale* di Callimaco', *RFIC* 99 (1971), 287–9.

BARTOLETTI, V., 'Un verso di Callimaco', *SIFC*, NS 31 (1959), 179–81.

—— 'Sui frammenti dell'*Ecale* di Callimaco nei *P. Oxy.* 2376 e 2377', in *Miscellanea di Studi Alessandrini* [see below, s.v. Ferrero], 263–72.

BERGK, R., 'Zu Kallimachus', *Rh. M.* 9 (1854), 138–41.

BERNARDINI MARZOLLA, P., 'Callimaco, fr. 252 Pf.', *SIFC* 25 (1951), 239–41.

BORNMANN, F., 'Un nuovo frammento dell'*Ecale*?', *Maia*, NS 25 (1973), 204–6.

BORTHWICK, E. K., 'The Verb *AYΩ* and its Compounds', *CQ*, NS 19 (1969), 306–13.

BROWN, R. D., 'Lucretius and Callimachus', *Illinois Classical Studies*, 7 (1982), 77–97.

BULLOCH, A., 'A Callimachean Refinement to the Hexameter', *CQ*, NS 20 (1970), 258–68.

—— 'Hellenistic Poetry' in *Cambridge History of Classical Literature*, i (1985), 541–621.

BURKERT, W., 'Kekropidensage und Arrhephoria', *Hermes*, 94 (1966), 1–25.

CAMPBELL, M., *Studies in the Third Book of Apollonius Rhodius' Argonautica* (1983).

CAZZANIGA, I., 'Il *Deipnon Adeipnon* della Baucis Ovidiana', *Parola del Passato*, 18 (1963), 23–35.

—— 'Nicandro, *Theriaca* v. 60', *RFIC* 91 (1963), 461–9.

—— 'Osservazioni a tre frammenti d'Antimaco e a Callimaco fr. 348 Pf.', *Parola del Passato*, 22 (1967), 363–6.

—— 'Uno spunto dell'*Hecale* Callimachea in un passo della *Vita di S. Filareto* di Niceta d'Amnia?', *Parola del Passato*, 23 (1968), 224–7.

CHANDLER, LILIAN, 'The North-west Frontier of Attica', *JHS* 46 (1926), 1–21.

CHATZIS, A., ' Ἐπιγραφὴ ἐκ Σαλαμῖνος', Ἀρχ. Ἐφ. 1930, 59–60, and Τὰ ἀρχαῖα ὀνόματα τῆς νήσου Σαλαμῖνος, ibid. 60–73.

CLAPP, E. B., 'On Correption in Hiatus', *CP* 1 (1906), 239–52.

COUAT, A., *Alexandrian Poetry under the First Three Ptolemies, With a Supplementary Chapter by E. Cahen* (ET by James Loeb, 1931).

DIEHL, E., *Hypomnema. De Callimachi Librorum Fatis Capita Selecta* (1937).

ELY, TALFOURD, 'Theseus and Skiron', *JHS* 9 (1888), 272–81.

FARNELL, L. R., *Cults of the Greek States* (5 vols., 1896–1909).

FERGUSON, J., *Callimachus* (1980).

FERRERO, L. *et al.* (eds.), *Miscellanea di studi alessandrini in memoria di Augusto Rostagni* (1963).

FLÜCKIGER-GUGGENHEIM, DANIELA, *Göttliche Gäste: die Einkehr von Göttern und Heroen in der griechischen Mythologie* (1984).

FRASER, P. M., *Ptolemaic Alexandria* (3 vols., 1972).

GIANGRANDE, G., 'Der stilistische Gebrauch der Dorismen im Epos', *Hermes*, 98 (1970), 255–77.

—— *Scripta Minora Alexandrina* (2 vols., 1980–1).

GUTZWILLER, K. J., *Studies in the Hellenistic Epyllion* (1981).

HAMMOND, N. G. L., 'The Campaign and the Battle of Marathon', *JHS* 88 (1968), 13–57.

HARRISON, JANE E., 'Mythological Studies, I: The Three Daughters of Cecrops', *JHS* 12 (1891), 350–5.

HENRICHS, A., 'Die Kekropidensage im *P. Herc.* 243: von Kallimachos zu Ovid', *Cronache Ercolanesi*, 13 (1983), 33–43.

HERMANN, C. F., 'Parergorum Fascic. III, part. 2', *Rh. M.* NF 6 (1848), 445–60.

HERTER, H., 'Kallimachos', *RE*, Suppl. 13 (1973), 184–266.

HOLLIS, A. S., 'Some Fragments of Callimachus' *Hecale*', *CR*, NS 15 (1965), 259–60.

—— 'Two Notes on Callimachus', *CR*, NS 22 (1972), 5.

—— 'Some Allusion to Earlier Hellenistic Poetry in Nonnus', *CQ*, NS 26 (1976), 142–51.

—— 'Notes on Callimachus' *Hecale*', *CQ*, NS 32 (1982), 469–73.

HOROWSKI, J., *Folklor w Twórczości Kallimacha z Cyreny* (1967).

HUTCHINSON, G., *Hellenistic Poetry* (1988).

JACOBY, F., *Die Fragmente der griechischen Historiker* (14 vols., 1923–58).

JAMES, A. W., *Studies in the Language of Oppian of Cilicia* (1970).

JAN, F. DE, *De Callimacho Homeri Interprete* (diss. 1893).

KLEIN, T. M., 'Callimachus, Apollonius Rhodius, and the Concept of the "Big Book"', *Eranos*, 73 (1975), 16–25.

KRAFFT, F., 'Die neuen Funde zur *Hekale* des Kallimachos', *Hermes*, 86 (1958), 471–80.

LAPP, F., *De Callimachi Cyrenaei Tropis et Figuris* (diss. 1965).

LEFKOWITZ, Mary, *The Lives of the Greek Poets* (1981).

LEHNUS, L., 'Una scena della *Ciris*: Carme e l'*Ecale* di Callimaco', *RIL* 109 (1975), 353–61.

—— *Bibliografia Callimachea 1489–1988* (1989, too late for me to use)

LITTLE, D., 'Ovid, *Amores* I. 13. 29–30 and the *Hecale* of Callimachus', *Hermes*, 99 (1971), 128.

LIVREA, E., 'Per una nuova edizione di Trifiodoro', *RFIC* 104 (1976), 443–52.

LLOYD-JONES, H., 'A Hellenistic Medley', *SIFC* 77 (1984), 52–72.

—— and Rea, J., 'Callimachus, Fragments 260–261', *HSCP* 72 (1968), 125–45.

LUPPE, W., 'Zum Kallimachos-Commentar P. Ticinensis 1', *ZPE* 32 (1978), 11–13.

—— 'Epikureische Mythenkritik bei Philodem', *Cronache Ercolanesi*, 14 (1984), 109–24.

MAAS, P., *Greek Metre* (ET with additions by H. Lloyd-Jones, 1962).

—— *Kleine Schriften* (1973).

MEDAGLIA, S., 'Su alcuni papiri dell'*Ecale*', *Atti del XVII Congresso Internazionale di Papirologia*, ii (1984), 297–304.

MERKELBACH, R.; 'Die *Erigone* des Eratosthenes', in *Miscellanea di studi alessandrini* [*see* above, s.v. Ferrero], 469–526.

MORRIS, SARAH P., 'Hollow Lakedaimon', *HSCP* 88 (1984), 1–11.

NEWMAN, J. K., 'Callimachus and the Epic', in J. L. Heller (ed.), *Serta Turyniana* (1974), 342–60.

NICKAU, K., 'Zu Kallimachos' *Hecale* (fr. 238. 4)', *Philol.* 111 (1967), 126–9.

OAKLEY, JOHN H., 'A Louvre Fragment Reconsidered: Perseus Becomes Erichthonios', *JHS* 102 (1982), 220–2.

O'NEILL, E. G., 'The Localization of Metrical Word-Types in the Greek Hexameter: Homer, Hesiod, and the Alexandrians', *YCS* 8 (1942), 105–78.

PACK, ROGER A., *The Greek and Latin Literary Texts from Greco-Roman Egypt*² (1965).

PARKER, R., 'Myths of Early Athens', in J. Bremner (ed.), *Interpretations of Greek Mythology* (1987), 187–214.

PARSONS, P. J., 'Callimachus: *Victoria Berenices*', *ZPE* 25 (1977), 1–50.

PFEIFFER, R., 'Morgendämmerung', in *Festschrift für Ida Kapp* (1954), 95–104 = *Kallimachos* [*see* below; s.v. Skiadas], 160–6.

—— 'The Future of Studies in the Field of Hellenistic Poetry', *JHS* 75 (1955), 69–73 = *Ausgewählte Schriften*, 148–58.

—— *Ausgewählte Schriften* (1968).

—— *History of Classical Scholarship*. i: From the Beginnings to the End of the Hellenistic Age (1968); ii: From 1300 to 1850 (1976).

PICKARD-CAMBRIDGE, A. W., *The Dramatic Festivals of Athens*² (rev. J. Gould and D. M. Lewis, 1968).

PONTANI, F. M., 'In margine alla fortuna dell'*Ecale*', *Giornale Italiano di Filologia*, 24 (1972), 85–95 [on the modern Greek *Hecale* by Spyros Theodoropoulos (1876–1961) who, as far as he was able, took note of new discoveries, and sometimes reflects the wording of his Callimachean model].

POWELL, J. U., *Collectanea Alexandrina: Reliquiae Minores Poetarum Graecorum Aetatis Ptolemaicae, 323–146 A.C.* (1925).

PREVITALI, C., 'Filico di Corcira e Callimaco', *SIFC*, NS 41 (1969), 13–18.

REA, J., *see* Lloyd-Jones.

REINSCH-WERNER, H., *Callimachus Hesiodicus* (1976).

REITZENSTEIN, R., 'Inedita Poetarum Graecorum Fragmenta', *Index Lectionum in Acad. Rostochiensi* 1890/1, 1–18.

—— *Geschichte der griechischen Etymologika* (1897).

ROBERTSON, N., 'The Riddle of the Arrephoria at Athens', *HSCP* 87 (1983), 241–88.

SCHERLING, C., *Quibus Rebus Singulorum Atticae Pagorum Incolae Operam Dederint* (diss. 1897).

SCHMITT, RÜDIGER, *Die Nominalbildung in den Dichtungen des Kallimachos* (1970).

SHEFTON, B. B., 'Herakles and Theseus on a Red-Figured Louterion', *Hesperia*, 31 (1962), 330–68.

SKIADAS, A. D. (ed.), *Kallimachos* (Wege der Forschung, Band CCXCVI, 1975) [includes 'Literaturübersicht', pp. 401–18].

SOLMSEN, F., 'Eratosthenes' *Erigone*: a Reconstruction', *TAPA* 78 (1947), 252–75.

SOURVINOU-INWOOD, C., 'Theseus Lifting the Rock and a Cup near the Pithos Painter', *JHS* 91 (1971), 94–109.

—— 'Theseus as Son and Stepson', *BICS*, Suppl. 40 (1979).

THOMPSON, D'ARCY, W., *A Glossary of Greek Birds* (new edn., 1936).

THOMPSON, STITH, *Motif-Index of Folk-Literature* (6 vols., 1955).

THOMPSON, WESLEY E., 'Notes on Attic Demes', *Hesperia*, 39 (1970), 64–7.

TRAILL, J. S., 'The Political Organization of Attica', *Hesperia*, Suppl. 14 (1975).

WEBSTER, T. B. L., 'Chronological Problems in Early Alexandrian Poetry', *WS* 76 (1963), 68–78.

—— *Hellenistic Poetry and Art* (1964).

WEINBERGER, W., 'Zur *Hekale* des Kallimachos', *Philologus*, 76 (1920), 68–91.

WEST, M. L., *Textual Criticism and Editorial Technique* (1973).

—— *Greek Metre* (1982).

WHITEHEAD, D., *The Demes of Attica 508/7–c.250 BC* (1986).

WIFSTRAND, A., *Von Kallimachos zu Nonnos* (1933).

WILAMOWITZ-MOELLENDORFF, U. VON, *Hellenistische Dichtung in der Zeit des Kallimachos* (2 vols., 1924).

—— *Kleine Schriften* (6 vols., 1935–72) ['Über die *Hekale* des Kallimachos' (1893) is at ii. 30–47].

—— *History of Classical Scholarship* (ET by Alan Harris, edited with introduction and notes by Hugh Lloyd-Jones, 1982).

WILSON, N. G., *Scholars of Byzantium* (1983).

WIMMEL, W., 'Aglauros in Ovids *Metamorphosen*', *Hermes*, 90 (1962), 326–33.

WINKLER, JOHN J., 'Callimachus Fr. 260. 66 Pf.', *CW* 72 (1978–9), 237–8.

WYSS, B., 'Gregor von Nazianz', *Mus. Helv.* 6 (1949), 177–210.

ZANKER, G., 'Callimachus' Hecale: a New Kind of Epic Hero?', *Antichthon*, 11 (1977), 68–77.

—— *Realism in Alexandrian Poetry* (1987).

INDEX VERBORUM

In this and the following Indexes I have not added 'inc. sed.' or 'inc. auct.' to the Fragmenta Incerta (nos. 156–79). A double asterisk (which might have been used more widely) indicates that the reading is uncertain. I have included the fragments proposed for the *Hecale* in Appendix V, but not those mentioned in Appendix I. References are to fragment and line.

I. COMPLETE WORDS

ἄςτυρον 69. 6; 71. 2

ἀτάρ 113. 3

ἄτε 48. 7

αὖ 34

(αὐδάζομαι) ηὐδάξαντο App. V(ƒ)

αὖθι 17. 4; 69. 10

αὖον 74. 11

Αὐςόνιον 18. 14

αὐτάρ 73. 13

αὐτίκα 96. 3

αὖτις 110; 145. 2

αὐτόθεν 30

αὐτός 69. 12; αὐτοί 113. 2 (bis); -ή 47.
    10**; 49. 14; -ήν 81. 1

αὐχμηρά 82**

(αὔω = clamo) ἄϋςε 69.4

ἄφαρον 111

Ἀφιδνάων 42. 2

ἀφνύονται 48. 3

ἀφραςτύες 125

(ἀφύςςω) ἤφύςατ' 34

Ἀχαιίδα 70. 12

†Ἀχερουςίας 99. 3

ἀχλύςαντος 19

ἀώτωι 74. 16

βάλε (adv.) 41. 2 (bis)

(βάλλω) βάλλον 69. 13; βάλοιτο 70. 9

βαρύς 73. 12

(βαςιλεύς) βαςιλ[47. 20; βας]ιλῆες
    49. 17; βαςιλῆας 54

βιοπλανές 163. 1

βίου 75

(βλώςκω) μεμβλωκός 46. 2

βορέης 69. 12; -έαο 18. 15

βόςκεο 149. 2

(βούλομαι) βέβουλ[ε(ν) 47. 11

(βοῦς) βόες 102. 1; βοῶν 117; 127; 177;
    βουςίν 42. 1

βουςόον 117

Βριληςςοῦ 169

(βύω) βέβυςτο 126

βωνίτηιςιν 35. 2 (v.l. βουν-)

Γαῖα 70. 8

γαῖα 93; γαίης 149. 1

γάλακι 74. 16

γαμβρός 86

γάρ 2. 2; 9. 1; 13; 41. 1; 47. 9; 69. 1;
    73. 7, 13; 74. 7, 10, 22, 24; 80. 5; 81.
    1; 109. 1; 113. 1; App. V(h)

γαςτέρι 74. 1

γε 40. 3**; 69. 11; 74. 15

γέγειαι 102. 1

γείτων 49. 10

(γελάω) γελάςςαι 115. 1

γενεή 73. 14; -ῆι 70. 6

γενέθλη 40. 6; γε]νέθλην 48. 2

γέντα 127

γέντο (= ἔλαβε) 66. 1

γεργέριμον 36. 4

γήραος 66. 2

γηφάγοι 55

(γίγνομαι) γίνεο (vel γείνεο) 75; γέντο
    106; ἐγένοντο 25. 2; γένοιτο 23. 1**

(γιγνώςκω) ἔγνων 70. 6

Γλαυκώπιον 17. 11

γοεροῖο 128

γόνος 73. 13

γόνυ 24

γόοιο 128

γουνῶι 1

γραῦις 164

γρηΐον 173

γρηῦς 40. 5; γρηός 58; γρῆϋν 74. 9

γυαλόν 10. 1

γυνή 90. 1; γυναῖκες 35. 2; 69. 14; 176;
    -κῶν 80. 1

δαίμων 51. 1** (δήμου codd.); 176

(δαίω = accendo) δαιομένου 25. 2

(δαίω = divido) δέδαςται 53

δάκρυ 57

δάκρυον 158

δάμαρτα 100

δαμάτειρα 75

†δανάκης 99. 3

(δανός) δανά 32; δανοῖς 99. 3**

(*δάω) ἐδάην 70. 7

δ(έ) 2. 1; 4. 1; 15; 17. 2, 3, 4, 8, 9**; 18.
    1, 2, 3, 5, 6, 8, 10, 15; 28; 33; 34
    (bis); 35. 1; 36. 3; 40. 2**; 42. 2; 43;
    46. 1; 48. 8; 49. 5, 10, 16**; 54; 57;
    60. 1; 63; 66. 1; 68; 69. 5, 9, 10, 14;
    70. 6, 9, 12; 71. 2; 72. 1; 73. 6, 9; 74.
    21, 22; 76; 85. 2; 106; 107; 111; 113.

(ὀτλέω) ὀτλήϲοντεϲ 118
οὐ (οὐκ, οὐχ, οὐχί) 6. 2**; 41. 1; 69. 8,
  11, 12; 73. 7**; 74. 10, 12, 22; 80. 2;
  119. 3; App. V(h)
(οὗ, pron. pers.) οἱ 46. 1; 57. 1; 74. 18; ἑ
  2. 1; μιν 9. 1; 69. 14**; νιν 70. 6; φιν
  69. 4; 111
οὐδ(έ) 18. 3; 41. 1; 48. 1; 69. 2, 12;
  85. 1**; 108; 115. 1
οὐδέν 37
οὐκέτι 74. 23
οὐλοόν 74. 17
οὖν 18. 1
οὔνομ(α) 90. 1
οὐρανίδαι 70. 2
οὐρανόϲ 18. 2
οὔτ(ε) 70. 6, 7
οὗτοϲ 69. 8; τοῦτο 74. 11; 79; 81. 1;
  †ταῦτα 113. 1
οὕτωϲ 48. 1; 73. 10**
(ὀφείλω) ὤφελον 73. 9; ὄφελεϲ 77
(ὀφθαλμόϲ) -μοί 109. 1; -μοῖϲι(ν) 49.
  15; 112
ὄφιοϲ 70. 11
ὄφρ(α) 18. 1; 40. 1; 70. 9; 74. 8; 132. 1

παιῆον 69. 10
παῖϲ 10. 1; 13; παιδόϲ 172; παῖδε
  (dual.) 48. 6; παιϲίν 48. 10
πάλαι 49. 2
παλαίθετα 31
πα]λαίϲμαϲι 49. 8
παλαιφαμένηϲ 166
παλίνορϲον 94
παλίντροποϲ 145. 3
Παλλάϲ 70. 2**; 167
παναρκέοϲ 103. 1
Παν]δίονοϲ 5. 4 (schol. marg.)**
†πανύϲτατον 77
πάππων 41. 1
παρά 74. 26; 145. 2 (πάρ)
παραίϲια 73.8
(παραναίω) παρενάϲϲατο 49. 10
παρδα[λιαγχέϲ fort. lemma in 5. 7
  (schol. marg.)**
(πάρειμι) παρέην 73. 13
παρέκ 8
(Πάρνηϲ) Πάρνηθοϲ 18. 8

(πᾶϲ) πάντεϲ 2. 1; 69. 2, 10; 74. 13;
  πάντας 17. 3; πᾶϲα 119. 2; 126;
  πάντα 49. 13**; 53; 74. 10
παϲϲαγίην 146
(πάϲχω) πάϲχομεν 53
(πατέομαι) παϲαίμην 49. 15
(πατήρ) πατρί 69. 5; πάτερ 17. 4
πατρώιοϲ 41. 1
πέδιλα 11
πειοτ[? i.e. πιοτερ— vel πιοτατ- 49. 7
πείϲματα 47. 10
πελαργόϲ 76
πελιδνωθεῖϲα 72. 1
Πελλήνην 70. 12
(πέλω) πέλε 66. 2; ἔπλετο 69. 12
πελώριον 69. 3
πενίη 41. 1
περ 74. 11
(περάω) περόωϲι 80. 2
περί 17. 12; 69. 13
περιδέξιοϲ 147
περιηγέεϲ 81. 2
περίθριξ 14
περιπηχύναντεϲ 148
περιϲταδόν 69. 14
περίτροχον 46. 2
(πετάννυμι) πέπτατο 18. 3
πέτρη 119. 3; -ηι 9. 1
πίλημα 46. 2; 65. 2
(πίνω) πῖθι 7
(πίπτω) πέϲοιτε 73. 11**
πίϲεα 149. 1
πίϲϲαν 74. 17
Πιτθεύϲ 12
πίτυριν 36. 4
(πλήθω) πλήθοντα 98; πεπλήθαϲι 62. 2
πληξίπποι 74. 20
πλοκάμοιο 14
πλόον 74. 26
ποθέουϲιν 177
ποθή 40. 4
ποθί 18. 3
ποιηφάγον 56
ποιμενικόν 65. 2
(πόλεμοϲ) πτολέμοιο 17. 13
πόλιϲ v. ad 170; πόλιν 174; πτολίων 99.
  2
πολλάκι 80.3

τοιοῦτον 13
τό]λμης 74. 6**
(τόςος) τόςςην 69. 11; τόςον 145. 2
τότ(ε) 69. 13; 73. 9; 74. 8**
τοὔνεκα, τοὔνεκεν v. ἔνεκα
τουτάκι 70. 9
τόφρα 18. 2; 70. 12
τράπεζα v. ad 82
(τραχύς) τρηχέος 18. 11
(τρίζω) τετριγώς 74. 27
Τρινέμεια 88
τρίτον 41. 2
Τροιζῆνι 9. 1
τροχόν v. ad 92**
τρύφος 71. 1
τυτθός 73. 13; -όν 40. 4

ὑάλοιο 18. 2
ὑδατηγός 74. 25
(ὑδέω) ὑδέουςιν 151; ὑδέοιμι 78
ὕδος 93
ὕδωρ v. ad 95**; 116. 1; 124; 144
ὑετόν 18. 9
(υἱός) υἱέες 42. 3
ὑληωροί 152
Ὑμηττ[οῖο 18. 11
ὑπένερθε 119. 3
ὑπέρ 18. 8; 171. 1 (ὑπείρ)
ὕπνος 74. 21
ὑπό (ὑπ᾿, ὑφ᾿) 9. 1; 17. 3; 27. 2; 42. 1;
    47. 9; 70. 8; 74. 27
ὑποδράξ 72.1
(ὑποέννυμι) ὑφέεστο 43
ὑπόκρηνον 153. 2
(ὑποτρέω) ὑπέτρεςαν 69. 2
(ὑποφαίνω) ὑπεφαίνετο 18. 3
Ὑψιζώρου 71. 1
ὑψικάρηνον 119. 2

φαάντερος 18. 2
φαέες[27. 4
φαείνω (φαίνω) φαείνει 13; 74. 24;
    †φαίνεται 113. 1
(φαράω) φαρόωςι 111
φαῦλον 36. 2 (prob. = 37); 37
(φέρω) φερούςηι 48. 6; φ[έρον 42. 2;
    οἷςε 36. 3; οἰςέμεν 99. 2; φέρονται
    99. 1; v. ad 92**

(φεύγω) ἔφυγεν 49. 9
φή 74. 17
(φημί) φάτο 69. 9; φαμένην 74. 21
φθινοπωρίδα 36. 5
(φιλέω) φιλέους(ιν) 113. 2, 3; ἐφίλης[
    49. 4**
φιλητέων 74. 24
φιλοξείνοιο 80. 4
φιλοξενίης 2. 2
Φλεγύαο 74. 19
φόβηςι 44. 1
Φοῖβος 74. 18
(φοιτάω) φοιτῶςιν 163. 2
φορυτόν 114
(φράζω) φράςον 60. 1
(φρέαρ) φρητί 172
(φρίςςω) περφρίκαςιν 113. 2
φυλακοί 70. 13
(φυλάςςω) ἐφύλαςςον 42. 1**;
    φυλαττε[97. 3**
φυλλοχόος 69. 12
φύλλων 69. 11
φώριον 132. 2

χαῖον 65. 2
χαλκῆες 74. 28
χαράδρης 48. 7
χάρωνος 101
χείλεα 58
(χείρ) χερί 65. 2; χεῖρες 74. 23; χέρες
    49. 11; χείρεςςιν 10. 2; χεῖρας 18. 6
†χειραεςα[17. 8
(χέω) χεύωμαι 60. 2
χθών 18. 1; χθονός 70. 9
χιτῶνα 43; 49. 3
χόλος 73. 12; χόλοιο 126
χοροςτάδας 85. 2
χροιήν 74. 16
χρόνον 74. 8, 22
χρυςείηιςιν 42. 5
χύςιν 69. 11
χύτλα 60. 2
(χυτλόω) χυτλώςαιντο 155
χυτρίδα 33
χῶρι 103. 2

ψήφωι 70. 10
(ψίω) ψιςθεῖεν 154

ψύθος 90. 1

ὠγυγίους 70. 7**
ᾦδ(ε) 69. 7; App. V(h)
(ὠκύς) ὤκιστος 69. 6

ὠμά 49. 15
ὠρυοίμην 178
ὡς 64; 69. 2 (bis); 70. 8; 74. 9; 178
ὥς 74. 21
ὠτώεντα 166

2. INCOMPLETE WORDS
from papyri and the Vienna Tablet

A few have already appeared in the preceding section. I have placed a square bracket immediately before the first (or after the last) letter for which a reading is here offered. Sometimes, particularly in the Vienna Tablet, there may be doubtful traces of earlier (or later) letters; uncertainties abound.

(a) *Beginnings of words*

α[42. 4; 49. 11
αγ[27. 3
αη[23. 2
απε[73. 10
γα[17. 12
δ[47. 8
δην[70. 4
δο[74. 2
ε[49. 17; 73. 9
εδ[74. 3
ει[85. 2
εξ[18. 7
επ[70. 1, 5
επε[17. 13
ηλ[49. 7
ι[36. 2
κ[17. 6; 47. 4, 7
λε[49. 6
με[96. 2
μεχ[74. 2**
μη[49. 11
μο[47. 3
νη . . c 48. 4
ο[47. 5, 19
οικ[49. 12
οπ[47. 5
ο . τ[47. 12
π[47. 16; 73. 14
παγ[74. 4
παραπ[73. 6

πε[49. 8
πειοτ[49. 7
ς[18. 4
τ[47. 14**; 74. 8
φ[70. 7
φθει[49.9

(b) *Endings of words*

]άδα 27. 3
]ανε 48. 6
]αρὴν 17. 6
]άσκοντα 49. 6
]αχιδας 47. 18
]δε 40. 2
]δι 85. 1
]δου 74. 2**
]ε 17. 8; 36. 2; 74. 3
]εια . . ν 47. 8
]εν 17. 12**; 47. 3
]ετο 48. 4
]ι 40. 4, 6; 97. 3
]ιηι 47. 12
]ιν 47. 4
]κατο 70. 5**
]λης 47. 5
]μας 49. 4
]μεν 20. 2
]μο 27. 4
]μοι 23. 2

INDEX FONTIUM

This index does not include papyri of the *Hecale* (for which see above, Introd. sect. XI). References are given in brief form; more details (e.g. manuscripts and editions of scholia, page numbers of *Et. Mag.* and Suidas) may often be found in the list of sources printed below the text. I have not recorded here every entry in the *Etymologica* which may derive from the *Hecale* if, in its present form, it does not contain a quotation from the poem; omitted entries are usually marked by 'cf.' in the list of sources. In the case of Suidas I have been more receptive in the interests of Hecker's Law (see above, Introd. sect. IX and App. V).

14. 199: 51. 1–2
17. 599: 18. 6
22. 299 sq.: 117
Lyc. *Alex.* 494: 9. 1–2
607: 74. 5
Nic. *Ther.* 909: 38
P. *Nem.* 1. 3: 103. 1–3
S. *OC* 3: 171. 1–2
314: 46. 1–2
510: 158
OT 919: 71. 2–3
Tr. 7: 118
Stat. *Theb.* 4. 46 sq.: 175
Theocr. 6. 39: 176
Thuc. 2. 15. 4 (*P. Oxy.* 853): 85. 1–2
Sophronius
Gr. Gr. iv. 2, p. 396. 20 Hilg.: 75
Stephanus Byzantius
s.v. Αἴδηψος: 10. 2
Ἁλιμοῦς: 170
Ἄλυκος: 174
Δεκέλεια: 52
Ἰαπίς: 61
Λίμναι: 85. 2
Λύρκειον: 95
Μελαινεῖς: 84
Τρινεμεῖς: 88
Suidas
s.v. ἀβάλε: v. ad 159
ἀγκάσασθαι: 10. 1
ἄγκος: 119. 1–2
ἄγχαυρος: 74. 23
ἀείπλανα: 58
ἄειρεν: 114
ἀήσυρον: 24
Αἰγαλέως: 18. 9
αἴθ'—ὀρχήσασθαι: 77
αἴθυια: 47. 9–10
αἰθύξασα: 30
αἰσυμνῆτις: 17. 10
ἄκμηνος: 120
ἀλετρίβανος: 37
ἀλκτήρια λιμοῦ: 74. 1
ἄλλικα: 42. 5
ἀλοίτης: 76
ἀλυκόν: 57
ἀλυκρά: 106
ἄμβασις: 119. 3
ἀμπρεύοντες: 52

ἄοζοι: v. App. I ad fr. 563 Pf.
ἀπαύγασμα: 104
ἀπεστώ: v. App. I ad fr. 718 Pf.
ἀπευθέες: 109
ἀποβράσματα: 37
ἀπορρῶγας: 119. 2–3
ἀπ' οὔατος—ἔλθοι: 122
ἀράχνη: 42. 6
ἀρμοῖ που: 45. 1
ἄρπη: 9. 2
ἄσκαντος: 29
ἀπαστοί: 123
ἀσταγὲς ὕδωρ: 124
ἄστηνοι: 53
ἄστρια: 107
ἄστυρον: 69. 6
Αὐσονίων: 18. 14
αὐχμηρὰ τράπεζα: 82
ἄφαρον: 111
ἀφραστύες: 125
ἀχλύς: 19
βάλε: 41. 2
βέβυστο: 126
βουνιτῆισι: 35. 2
γαμβρὸς Ἐρεχθῆος: 86
γέγειαι βόες: 102. 1
γέντα: 127
γεργέριμον: 36. 4–5
γοερόν: 128
δαμάτειρα: 75
δανάκη: 99. 3
δανά: 32
δέδοιμι: 129
δειελινόν: 18. 6
δεινουμένην: 42. 1
δηναιόν: App. V(*a*) (?? = fr. 70.
4)
διερήν: 28
δυερόν: App. V(*b*)
δύην: 131
ἔαρ: 62. 1–2
ἐγκυτί: 15
ἔδεθλον: App. V(*c*)
εἰδυλίς: 109. 2
εἰκαία: 37
εἰλήλουθα: 105
Ἑκάλη: 2. 2
ἐκόησεν: 4. 1
ἐλέγχομεν: 54

INDEX OF ALLUSIONS AND IMITATIONS

※

This index contains passages (not all, but, in my view, the most significant) which are arguably derived from the *Hecale*. Where possible, I have linked imitations to particular lines of the *Hecale*; if, however, the influence is of a more general nature, I may refer to a page number.

GENERAL INDEX

References are to page numbers

Numbering of Fragments: Comparative Tables

I. PFEIFFER–HOLLIS

230 = 1	261 = 71	302 = 103
231 = 2	262 = 79	303 = 118
232 = 4	263 = 80	304 = 46
233 = 7	264 = 83	305 = 85. 2
234 = 8	265 = 105	306 = 61
235 = 9	266 = 84	307 = 95
236. 1–2 = 10	267 = 75	308 = 88
236. 3 = 11	268 = 93	309 dub. = 119
237 = 12	269 = 25	310 = 58
238. 1–14 = 17	270 = 106	311 = 24
238. 15–32 = 18	271 = 76	312 = 120
238a = 20	272 = 52	313 = 57
238b = 21	273 = 104	314 = 121
238c = 22	274 = 45	315 = 122
238d = 23	275 = 53	316 = 123
239 = 28	276 = 107	317 = 124
240 = 29	277 = 102	318 = 125
241 = 30	278 = 99	319 = 19
242 = 31	279 = 96. 3	320 = 126
243 = 32	280 = 98	321 = 86
244 = 33	281 = 15	322 = 127
245 = 60	282 = 109	323 = 128
246 = 34	283 = 16	324 = 129
247 = 48. 5	284 = 48. 7	325 = 131
248 = 36. 4–5	285 = 100	326 = 77
249 = 38	286 = 110	327 = 47. 9–10
250 = 39	287 = 111	328 = 62
251 = 35	288 = 90	329 = 54
252 = 82	289 = 112	330 = 130
253. 1–6 = 40	290 = 55	331 = 132
253. 7–12 = 42	291 = 113	332 = 133
254 = 41	292 = 65	333 = 134
255 = 42. 1	293 = 43	334 = 37
256 = 63	294 = 49. 9–10	335 = 135
257 = 64	295 = 114	336 = 136
258 = 67	296 = 59	337 = 48. 1
259 = 68	297 = 91	338 = 87
260. 1–15 = 69	298 = 115	339 = 101
260. 16–29 = 70	299 = 116	340 = 137
260. 30–43 = 73. 1–14	300 = 51	341 = 92
260. 44–69 = 74. 3–28	301 = 117	342 = 81

343 = 108
344 = 94
345 = 13
346 = 74. 1
347 = 138
348 = 139
349 = 89
350 = 49. 2–3
351 = 74. 10
352 = 140
353 = 141
354 = 142
355 = 66
356 = 143
357 = 144
358 = 145
359 = 146
360 = 147
361 = 14
362 = 148
363 = 149

364 = 3
365 = 56
366 = 48. 3
367 = 50
368 = 49. 14(13)–15
369 = 150
370 dub. = 160 inc. auct.
371 = 78
372 = 151
373 = 152
374 = 72
375 = 153
376 = 44
377 = 154
489 = 163 inc. sed.
490 = 173 inc. sed.
495 = 156 inc. sed.
513 = 164 inc. sed.
519 = 167 inc. sed.
525 = 26
527a = 177 inc. sed.

552 = 169 inc. sed.
585 = 157 inc. sed.
591 = 161 inc. sed.
608 = 168 inc. sed.
611 = 172 inc. sed.
619 = 159 inc. sed.
629 = 47. 15
639 = 47. 6
680 = 171 inc. sed.
682 = 158 inc. sed.
684 = 175 inc. sed.
687 = 176 inc. sed.
704 = 170 inc. sed.
705 = 174 inc. sed.
721 = 162 inc. sed.
725 = 178 inc. sed.
732 = 165 inc. auct.
741 = 179 inc. auct.
756 = 166 inc. auct.

II. *SUPPLEMENTUM HELLENISTICUM*—HOLLIS

280	v. comment. ad fr. 4. 2
281	17. 4
282	27
283	36
284	cf. 82
285. 1–6	40
285. 7–12	42
286	47
287. 1–10	48
287. 11–30	49
288. 1–15	69
288. 16–29	70
288. 30–43A	73
288. 43B–69	74
289	71
290	96
291	97

III. HOLLIS—PFEIFFER—*SUPPLEMENTUM HELLENISTICUM*

1	230	
2	231	
3	364	
4	232	(v. 2 vix = 280. 8)
5 (scholia)	p. 506	
6 (? v. 1 = fr. 8)	(p. 507)	
7	233	
8 (? = 6. 1)	234	
9	235	
10	236. 1–2	
11	236. 3	
12	237	
13	345	
14	361	
15	281	
16	283	
17	238. 1–14	v. 4 = 281
18	238. 15–32; ?319	
19 (? = 18. 11)	319	
20	238a	
21	238b	
22	238c	
23	238d	
24 (? = 23. 2)	311 (? = 238d. 2)	
25	269	
26	525 (inc. sed.)	
27	(?239)	282
28 (? = 27. 2)	239	(?282. 2)
29	240	
30	241	
31	242	
32	243	
33	244	
34	246	
35	251	
36	?334; 248	283
37 (? = 36. 2)	334	(? = 283. 2)
38	249	
39	250	
40	253. 1–6	285. 1–6
41	254	
42	253. 7 (= 255); 253. 8–12; (?293)	285. 7–12
43 (? = 42. 6)	293 (? = 253. 12)	(? = 285. 12)
44	376	

45	274	
46	304	
47	639; 327; 629	286
48	337; 366; 247; 284	287. 1–10
49	350; 294; 368	287. 11–30
50	367	
51	300	
52	272	
53	275	
54	329	
55	290	
56	365	
57	313	
58	310	
59	296	
60	245	
61	306	
62	328	
63	256	
64	257	
65	292	
66	355	
67	258	
68	259	
69	260. 1–15	288. 1–15
70	260. 16–29	288. 16–29
71	261	289
72	374	
73	260. 30–43	288. 30–43A
74	346; 260. 44–69; 351	288. 43B–69
75	267	
76	271	
77	326	
78	371	
79	262	
80	263	
81	342	
82	cf. 252	cf. 284
83	264	
84	266	
85	+305	
86	321	
87	338	
88	308	
89	349	
90	288	
91	297	
92	341	

93	268	
94	344	
95	307	
96	279	290
97	–	291
98 (vix = 96. 4)	280	(vix = 290. 4)
99	278	
100	285	
101	339	
102	277	
103	302	
104	273	
105	265	
106	270	
107	276	
108	343	
109	282	
110	286	
111	287	
112	289	
113	291	
114	295	
115	298	
116	299	
117	301	
118	303	
119	309	
120	312	
121	314	
122	315	
123	316	
124	317	
125	318	
126	320	
127	322	
128	323	
129	324	
130	330	
131	325	
132	331	
133	332	
134	333	
135	335	
136	336	
137	340	
138	347	
139	348	
140	352	

141	353	
142	354	
143	356	
144	357	
145	358	
146	359	
147	360	
148	362	
149	363	
150	369	
151	372	
152	373	
153	375	
154	377	
155	ad 245	
156 inc. sed.	495	
157 inc. sed.	585	
158 inc. sed.	682	
159 inc. sed.	619	
160 inc. auct.	370	(?? = 286. 7)
(?? = 47. 7)		
161 inc. sed.	591	(vix = 287. 28)
(vix = 49. 18)		
162 inc. sed.	721	
163 inc. sed.	489	
164 inc. sed.	513	
165 inc. auct.	732	
166 inc. auct.	756	
167 inc. sed.	519	
168 inc. sed.	608	
169 inc. sed.	552	
170 inc. sed.	704	
171 inc. sed.	680	
172 inc. sed.	611	
173 inc. sed.	490	
174 inc. sed.	705	
175 inc. sed.	684	
176 inc. sed.	687	
177 inc. sed.	527a	
178 inc. sed.	725	
179 inc. sed.	741